Preventing Genocide

Practical Steps Toward Early Detection and Effective Action

Revised and Updated

David A. Hamburg, M.D.

foreword by Elie Wiesel

Paradigm Publishers

Boulder • London

Copyright © 2010 Paradigm Publishers

Published in the United States by Paradigm Publishers, 3360 Mitchell Lane, Suite E, Boulder, CO 80301 USA.

Paradigm Publishers is the trade name of Birkenkamp & Company, LLC,
Dean Birkenkamp, President and Publisher.

Library of Congress Cataloging-in-Publication Data

Hamburg, David A., 1925–
    Preventing genocide : practical steps toward early detection and effective action /David A. Hamburg, revised and updated.
        p. cm.
    Includes bibliographical references and index.
    ISBN 978-1-59451-558-3 (pbk.)
    1. Genocide.   2. Genocide—Prevention.   I. Title.
    HV6322.7.H36 2008
    363.34—dc22

                                                                                    2007052290

Printed and bound in the United States of America on acid-free paper that meets the standards of the American National Standard for Permanence of Paper for Printed Library Materials.

Designed and typeset by Straight Creek Bookmakers

14 13 12 11 10   1 2 3 4 5

With deep respect to a set of people whose insightful, dedicated commitment to prevention of genocide inspired and sustained the whole enterprise:

Alexander George
Elie Wiesel
Kofi Annan
Javier Solana
Desmond Tutu
Noel Lateef
Gareth Evans
Jimmy Carter
Sadako Ogata
Cyrus Vance
Herant Katchadourian
Jack Barchas
Betty Hamburg

Contents

Foreword

by Elie Wiesel

The unprecedented horrors of the Second World War introduced for all time into our political and ethical lexicon a new word: *genocide*. It terrifies us by its magnitude. Dictionaries offer a concise definition: "systematic destruction of an ethnic group by the extermination of its members." Passing years have made the word *ethnic* seem too restricted, too limited. It became recognized almost everywhere that the word's meaning had to be extended to include religion as well as nationality. To put it differently, destruction of a human group, because of its religious belief or nationality, also constitutes genocide.

And yet, can we conceive of a comparable undertaking that was not planned beforehand? In other words, is planning a genocide or taking the first steps toward genocide part of genocide?

These are important questions when we recall the recent past. In Cambodia under the horrendous and cruel Pol Pot, was it already genocide when, making use of a depraved and perverse ideology, the political leaders professed that they wanted the elimination of only a part of the population?

Similarly for Rwanda. And for Bosnia too, where "ethnic cleansing" provoked rapes, tortures, and mass murders on a scale that defies classification.

One of the most troubling, if not disconcerting, aspects of the debate on genocide is that in almost every case, it could have been prevented. The examples of Rwanda and Srebenica are proofs of this. In both places, it is undeniable that a well-planned international intervention could have stopped the deaths and saved the numberless victims already condemned. It was not done, and more than one political leader bears responsibility for this.

But in general—since it is necessary to foresee in order to act—how and by what means, following what analyses, is it possible to locate and identify in advance that monstrous crime against humanity, the attempt to commit genocide?

Those questions, and many others, all weighty and pertinent, are found in this remarkable work, whose importance and urgency cannot be overemphasized.

Its author, Professor David Hamburg, is admirably qualified to address those questions. A thinker of great renown worldwide, he has devoted years to this project, which has almost become his obsession. It is he, more than anyone else, who has succeeded in engaging the highest levels of the United Nations in these problems. For him, it is purely and simply a matter of sounding the alarm to prevent disasters and catastrophes, all works of men who are playing with the danger of genocide in order to attain abominable goals. Anyone who knows Professor Hamburg's life and work will say in a resounding voice, "No one is better qualified to show, as he does in this lucid and well-documented book, what to do, what non-violent pressures to use, in order to stop a menace whose deadly shadow already broods over the newborn 21st century."

Teachers and students, diplomats and scholars, the young and the not-so-young, will all find here reasons to discover for themselves the unshakeable courage to hope.

Introduction

In the short time since this book was published in April 2008, many advances have occurred in terms of preventing genocide and related mass violence. While bearing in mind that the ultimate fulfillment of aspirations in this regard will take decades or generations, there is nevertheless clear evidence of an intellectual and moral ferment in the field. Numerous individuals, groups, governments, and intergovernmental organizations have either undertaken new initiatives or strengthened rudimentary activities in prevention.

One prominent example is provided by President Barack Obama. As a senator and as a presidential candidate, he expressed a strong interest in the problem of genocide. During his 2008 campaign for the White House, Obama repeatedly pledged to "respond forcefully to all genocides," including the one currently raging in Darfur.[1] In April 2009, he gave a moving speech on remembrance of the Holocaust. He has yet to translate his words into preventive action, but it is noteworthy that in his formulation of health care reform, he has embraced preventive medicine and public health in the way that these concepts are utilized in this book for the prevention of mass violence.

The basic concepts of prevention are now more widely understood, and they have led to a variety of innovations. In the new concluding chapter to this updated edition, I have discussed a few of these advances to convey the flavor of what is going on. These examples reflect several approaches, regions, and conceptual formulations. Taken together, they cover a good deal, though by no means all, of the prevention field. Some of them show how much can be done in a short time with the proper understanding, initiative, dedication, and courage. Others exemplify building blocks on which step-by-step progress can be envisioned in the next few years. So even though this is a long-term commitment of necessity, the feasibility of useful near-term action is becoming clear. Whatever the distance that has to be traversed, these are signs pointing in the right direction.

The global economic crisis that emerged so vividly in the fall of 2008 will probably slow progress in this as in virtually every other field. Moreover, the severe stress of economic conditions may well exacerbate some intergroup tensions and offer new opportunities for genocidal tyrants—much as we saw so vividly in the Great Depression of the 1920s and early 1930s the fall of the democratic Weimar Republic in Germany and the rise of Adolf Hitler.

Yet the economic crisis has also stimulated extraordinary efforts to mobilize international cooperation to improve economic conditions and indeed the world's financial system. By the same token, it reminds us that today's global dangers, not least of all genocide, require exceptional international cooperation for resolution and even for human survival. There are profound lessons that humanity can learn from these harsh conditions. The prevention of genocide and other looming dangers of the twenty-first century, such as drastic climate change, depends fundamentally on human learning capacities. Throughout history, these capacities have often been applied in cooperative efforts for solving difficult problems and ameliorating widespread suffering. These capacities must now be applied to the exceedingly dangerous problems of the current century. Yet at the same time, science-based, internationally cooperative efforts present a great opportunity that might well exceed any previous accomplishments.

What is distinctive about the approach of this book?

1. It emphasizes proactive help to countries in trouble—if possible, prior to any killing. Since danger signals are typically evident years before the carnage begins, there is ample warning time to act before blood flows.
2. It recommends the formulation and dissemination of specific response options and contingency plans to deal with early warning signals.
3. It draws together many tools, strategies, and practices to prevent mass violence.
4. It clarifies which international organizations can use those tools, strategies, and practices most effectively, and it emphasizes the role of the established democracies.
5. It recommends ways to achieve a comprehensive program of preventing mass violence through cooperation among organizations that share mechanisms for ongoing conflict resolution below the threshold of mass violence, and it suggests models for assisting democratic socioeconomic development that meets basic human needs.
6. It lays out a plan for establishing two cooperating international centers for the prevention of genocide, each with a base in a strong international institution and links to other organizations that offer complementary strengths and cooperative opportunities.
7. It recommends expanding those links in the next decade to create a worldwide network of cooperating entities for preventing mass violence.
8. It outlines a strategy for encouraging increased political will in leaders by molding a constituency for prevention through comprehensive public education on the necessity and feasibility of prevention.

In one new chapter to the updated edition, I cover some of the most promising developments that have occurred in preventing mass violence since this book was originally published. These are addressed in the sections titled:

1. Preventive Diplomacy: Kofi Annan's Inspiring Example in Kenya, 2008
2. Training and Support in Preventive Diplomacy
3. Building Violence Prevention into Development
4. The Genocide Prevention Task Force in the United States
5. EU-Related Activities in Genocide Prevention: New Developments
6. Nongovernmental Organizations Strengthening Their Efforts in Prevention: The Carter Center
7. Commonwealth: A Significant International Organization Clarifies Civil Paths to Peace
8. Greatly Diminishing the Nuclear Danger

In the new concluding chapter, I preview an innovative film documentary and oral history archive project that is an extension of the work of this book. "Pioneers in the Prevention of Mass Violence" is a set of interviews with key world figures who speak from their experiences in order to educate and inspire the general public.

Acknowledgments

There is a strong cumulative effect of the stimulation, encouragement, and kindness that occur in every phase of personal and professional development, so I want to recognize those who have made contributions to the information, ideas, and writing of this volume. It germinated over many years.

I start with Alexander George, a great behavioral scientist and great person, who was originally to be coauthor of this volume. To my deep regret, serious illness intervened, and then his death occurred while the book was in preparation. Nevertheless, he read chapters while he could and made valuable suggestions. He made so many significant contributions to human understanding in his career that it would take a whole chapter to spell them out, but let me mention a few.

I first met him when we were Fellows at the Center for Advanced Study in the Behavioral Sciences in 1957, and we worked together in various ways in most of the intervening years. From 1945 to 1948, he had served in the occupation of post–World War II Germany. It was his first test of efforts to convert totalitarian, genocidal states into vibrant democracies. What a task! We have more to say about that in this book, but suffice it here to say that people like Alex George made a real difference in helping to bring Germany from its degraded position to the deserved respect it now enjoys.

Then, working at RAND, he did important research on propaganda analysis and also on leadership decisionmaking. He began a career-long pattern of scholarship on building for the social sciences case studies that were accurate, highly pertinent to the issue at hand, and useful for students as well as advanced scholars. Appropriately, his final book, published in 2006, is the culmination of this line of inquiry.

Just as he was concerned with basic methodology in the social sciences, so too he was concerned with the uses of in-depth social science for the formulation of policy, especially in the arena of war and peace. Throughout his career, he sought to bridge the gap between research and policy.

In the early 1960s, at the time of the Cuban missile crisis, both he and I became alarmed about the possibility that such crises could occur again and very likely lead to nuclear catastrophe. He pursued this interest in his scholarly work by studying several crises and formulating principles of crisis management. In the course of this, he asked my help in studying decisionmaking processes in the face of terrible risks, such as those of nuclear confrontation. This led to our formulation of the crisis prevention approach that is described in the first chapter of this book. It is important to say that early collaborators in this work were Graham Allison and Sam Nunn. Bill Perry, Ashton Carter, Jim Watkins,

Dick Lugar, John Warner, Joseph Nye, and Albert Carnesale were exceedingly helpful. So, a crisis prevention enterprise grew in both universities and the government.

We then linked the crisis prevention approach to Soviet counterparts, and perhaps this had a beneficial effect on both superpowers. In any event, Alex George was a major intellectual leader in this field and patiently worked with others to enlist their good ideas and operational help. Moreover, he published several seminal books on ways of reducing the nuclear danger through a mutual learning process between the United States and the Soviet Union.

In the 1990s, he served as an exceedingly valuable member of the Carnegie Commission on Preventing Deadly Conflict that I had the privilege to cochair with the late Cyrus Vance. Among other contributions, Alex joined with me and Jane Holl Lute, executive director of the commission, to set in motion a number of studies that could enrich the commission's own report and begin to get around the contours of this large, complex subject. I vividly recall a touching moment during a commission meeting when Cyrus Vance leaned over to me and whispered, "What a remarkable person." Indeed!

During the five-year life of the commission, we ultimately published twenty-some books and fifty other papers and monographs. So, it came to constitute a unique resource on prevention of deadly conflict. Alex never took credit for any of this. In his typical, low-key, highly professional, deeply responsible approach to others, he simply made good things happen.

A few years ago he received an award that meant more to him than any other: the National Academy of Sciences Award for Contributions of Behavioral and Social Sciences to Avoid Nuclear War.

When I began to consider seriously the possibility of an innovative book on preventing genocide, difficult though that topic certainly is, he gave me great encouragement and offered to help in every way he could, health permitting.

One other point: he was legendary for his patience and generosity with his students and other young scholars, helping them at every level of development in their work and so leaving a real legacy in the cause of peace.

I also pay tribute to his splendid wife and collaborator, Julie.

On the specific subject of *preventing genocide*, I have had particular inspiration from Elie Wiesel, Desmond Tutu, Jane Holl Lute, Kofi Annan, Javier Solana, Graham Allison, Bruce Alberts, Noel Lateef, Jimmy Carter, John Hardman, William Perry, Sidney Drell, Gareth Evans, Jack Barchas, Enrique Mora, Raymond Georis, Francis Deng, Betty Hamburg, and several leaders of the Swedish efforts on prevention of violent conflict: Jan Eliasson, Ragnar Ängeby, Anders Bjurner, and Monica Andersson.

Among those who also encouraged and helped me, some of whom read parts of the book and gave valuable suggestions, were Melanie Greenberg, Larry Diamond, Herant Katchadourian, Melanne Verveer, John Stremlau, Joshua Lederberg, Elena Nightingale, Sadako Ogata, Bruce Jentleson, Ellen Futter, and Andrea Bartoli. Additional friends who gave me great encouragement include Ann Pusey, Barbara Smuts, Carrie Hunter, Steve Smith, Lewis MacFarlane, Beverly Carter, Michelle Trudeau, Emilie Riss, Shirley Williams, Gro Brundtland, Arno Motulsky, Huda Akil, Stanley Watson, Joel Dimsdale, William Bunney, Robert Hinde, John Bowlby, Ralph Tyler, Sherwood Washburn, Jane Goodall, Charles Townes, Al Solnit, Eli Evans, Abdul Msangi, Theodosius Dobshansky, Zoë Baird,

Judith Rodin, William Bowen, Franklin Thomas, Susan Berresford, Pat McPherson, and Frank Ferrari. To all of them, my deep gratitude!

In the background of my work, certain continuing associations have always been helpful, and these old friends have given me meaningful encouragement for the work on prevention of genocide. They cluster in certain institutions where I have had the privilege of working.

At Indiana University, in the state where I grew up, I was inspired by one of the great pioneers of modern genetics, Tracy Sonneborn. He turned me on to science and changed my life altogether. Others who were very helpful include J. O. Ritchey, David Boyd, John Mason, George Lukmeyer, Herman Auerbach, Charles Buck, Robert Oswald, William Breneman, Ralph Collins, and Herman Wells.

At Stanford University: Joshua Lederberg, Donald Kennedy, Larry Diamond, Sidney Drell, Bill Dement, Keith Brodie, Albert Bandura, Eleanor Maccoby, Scott Sagan, David Holloway, Coit Blacker, Kenneth Arrow, Warren Christopher, John Gardner, Irwin Yalom, Wolfgang Panofsky, Sanford Dornbusch, Bob and Nancy Hofstadter, Helene Kramer, Alan Shatzberg, Avram Goldstein, Mary Kiely, Craig Heller, Dick Atkinson, Ernest Hilgard, Arthur Kornberg, Paul Berg, Lowell Rantz, James and Jewelle Gibbs, Rudy Moos, Gabriel Almond, Condoleezza Rice, Peter Bing, Bob Alway, Dick Lyman, Wally Sterling, Robert Glaser, James Mark, Robert Chase, Peter Rosenbaum, George Gulevich, Bert Kopell, Frank Ochberg, David Daniels, Erich Lindemann, Alberta Siegel, Gerhart Casper, and John Hennessy.

At Harvard University: Martha Minow, Derek Bok, Sissela Bok, Abram and Toni Chayes, Julius Richmond, Richard Wrangham, John Dunlop, Arthur Kleinman, David Ellwood, Barry Bloom, Daniel Tosteson, Samantha Power, Leon Eisenberg, David Blumenthal, Alexander Leaf, Irving London, Neal Rudenstine, Linda Wilson, and Daniel Federman.

At Rockefeller University: Joshua Lederberg, David Rockefeller, William Baker, Torsten Wiesel, Paul Greengard, Eric Kandel, Joseph Goldstein, Rodney Nichols, Fred Bohen, Paul Nurse, Jules Hirsch, Marnie Imhoff, and Marguerite Lederberg.

At the Carnegie Corporation of New York: During my fifteen years as president and a decade since then, my intellectual contacts, friendships, encouragement, and help of every kind could constitute a chapter. But I restrict myself now to those who were most directly involved in the work on genocide. David Speedie not only provided much information and many good ideas over fifteen years, he made excellent contributions in the writing of the book, especially in his deep knowledge of the subject matter and his superb editing. In our grant-making on avoiding nuclear war, Fritz Moser and Jane Wales served with distinction. Carnegie's work on South Africa made a deep impact, thanks especially to Francis Wilson, Mamphela Ramphele, Stuart Saunders, and, of course, Desmond Tutu. In New York, Avery Russell and Alan Pifer were helpful on South Africa. Vartan Gregorian was encouraging and supportive at all times. So too were the board chairmen who served during my presidency: John Taylor, Helene Kaplan, Warren Christopher, Newton Minow, and Thomas Kean. Over those years, I had unfailing practical help, encouragement, and kindness from Susan Smith Santini. So too, Jeanne D'Onofrio, Natasha Davids, Irene Germain, Mary Lou Sandwick, Pat England, Judy Smith, Annette Dyer, Trisha Lester, Lorraine Lahuta, and Dee Holder. Patricia Rosenfield, Geraldine Manion, Vivien

Stewart, Shirley Malcom, Michael Levine, Anthony Jackson, Roy Marshall, Bob Rubin, John Whitehead, Dick Beattie, Billie Tisch, Henry Muller, Sheila Widnall, and Deanna Arsenian were also very helpful. Michael and Anne Mandelbaum have been stimulating over the years, and so too has been Bob Legvold. David Robinson and Barbara Finberg were pillars of strength.

At the National Academy of Sciences, I am especially indebted to Bruce Alberts, Walter Rosenblith, Phil Handler, Frank Press, Harvey Fineberg, Fred Robbins, Ralph Cicerone, John Boright, Michael Clegg, David Challoner, Karl Yordy, Lee Schorr, Sarah Brown, and Elena Nightingale.

At the American Association for the Advancement of Science: Bill Carey, Bill Golden, Shirley Malcom, Jim Rutherford, Dan Koshland, Phil Abelson, Floyd Bloom, and, once again, Don Kennedy.

At the Mount Sinai Medical Center, I am deeply indebted to John Rowe, William Golden, Kenneth Davis, Frederick Klingenstein, Lawrence Smith, David Thomas, Kurt Hirschhorn, Valentin Fuster, and Arthur Rubenstein.

At the Council on Foreign Relations, I have drawn special benefit from the Center on Preventive Action involving particularly General John Vessey, General William Nash, Leslie Gelb, Barnett Rubin, Richard Haass, Fred Tipson, Lee Feinstein, and Peter Tarnoff.

At the International Center for Transitional Justice, I am particularly indebted to Priscilla Hayner, Vincent Mai, Juan Méndez, Paul van Zyl, and Alex Boraine.

At the Project on Ethnic Relations, I learned a great deal from Allan Kassof and Livia Plaks.

Very special gratitude is due to Noel Lateef, president of the Foreign Policy Association, and to its board. From an early point, they have taken a great interest in our work on preventing deadly conflict and have been out front in thinking of ways to achieve broad public understanding of the unexpected possibilities for prevention of genocide. Lateef has achieved extraordinary insight into the whole prevention approach and made it a major theme of the Foreign Policy Association. All of us who care about the risks of war and genocide should be indebted to him.

The Carnegie Commission on Preventing Deadly Conflict (1994–1999) has been a rich source of information, ideas, and innovative practices for me and for people all over the world. It was an incomparable opportunity of enduring value. Among those who had the strongest effect on me with respect to this book were Cyrus Vance, Jane Holl Lute, Alexander George, Gareth Evans, Brian Urquhart, Gro Brundtland, Olara Ottunnu, Graham Allison, Flora McDonald, David Owen, Mikhail Gorbachev, Jimmy Carter, Desmond Tutu, Bruce Jentleson, John Stremlau, Tom Leney, Anna Cutter Patel, Esther Brimmer, William Zartman, Connie Peck, John Steinbrunner, Herbert Okun, Roald Sagdeev, John Whitehead, Murray Gell-Mann, Jonas Salk, Jerome Wiesner, and Adele Simmons. Gorbachev was inspiring in other ways, as I met him early in his term of office and worked with him to seek ways of winding down the Cold War.

At the United Nations, I had the privilege of working closely for a decade on building a culture of prevention with Kofi Annan. Others who were very helpful include Boutros Boutros-Ghali, Nita Yawanarajah, Tapio Kanninen, Danilo Türk, Angela Kane, Edward Mortimer, Robert Orr, John Ruggie, Lakhtar Brahimi, Michael Doyle, Gillian Sorensen, Elizabeth Lindenmeyer, Shashi Tharoor, James Wolfensohn, Gus Speth, Mark Malloch-

Brown, Maurice Strong, Sadako Ogata, Gareth Evans, Desmond Tutu, Roméo Dallaire, Louise Arbour, Ekkehard Strauss, Louise Frechette, Carol Bellamy, and, once again, Jane Holl Lute. Most recently Ban Ki-moon, Vijay Nambiar, and Kim Won-soo have taken a very constructive interest in prevention of genocide and are strengthening the UN's role, especially in fostering the unit led by Francis Deng. Among the prevention-oriented UN ambassadors, particularly strong encouragement came from Hisashi Owada and Peter Maurer. From the World Health Organization, several were helpful: David Alderslade, Khadija Rejto, Halfdan Mahler, Sune Bergstrom, V. Ramalingaswami, John Evans, Ade Lucas, Norman Sartorius, and Gro Brundtland.

In the work for the European Union, I am deeply indebted to Javier Solana, Enrique Mora, Raymond Georis, Marie Vincent, Ragnar Ängeby, and John Stremlau.

Five presidents of the United States were, in various ways, stimulating and at times inspiring: Gerald Ford, Jimmy Carter, Ronald Reagan, George H. W. Bush, and Bill Clinton.

In the Congress of the United States, I can name some of those who made an enduring impact on me: Lee Hamilton, Dick Clark, John Kerry, Sam Nunn, Dick Lugar, Hillary Rodham Clinton, John Warner, Jeff Bingaman, Doug Beureuter, Connie Morella, Nancy Pelosi, Paul Sarbanes, Tim Wirth, Ted Kennedy, Paul Rogers, Henry Waxman, Alan Cranston, Nancy Kassebaum, Daniel Inouye, Alan Simpson, John Chafee, Carl Levin, Al Gore, and John Heinz.

I was also influenced over many years by two great historians, Fritz Stern and Gordon Craig, and by my three main mentors in psychiatry, Fritz Redlich, Roy Grinker, and Gerhart Piers. In the formative Chicago years, I also was helped greatly by Therese Benedek, Joan Fleming, Thomas French, John Spiegel, and Rachmiel Levine.

Among serious media professionals, I have been consistently encouraged by Richard Heffner, Charlie Rose, Judy Woodruff, Henry Muller, Doyle McManus, Phillip Taubman, Ted Koppel, and Daniel Schorr.

So I express my heartfelt appreciation to many remarkable people and fine institutions that have given me the stimulation and encouragement and friendship over the years to pursue this difficult and vitally important subject.

I pay tribute to a wonderful group of immediate staff and immediate family who helped me virtually every day in every way to do this book. At the very beginning, my research associate, Rosalind Rosenberg, offered great help in launching the project.

After she left, her successor, Linda Newman, has been absolutely essential—a highly intelligent, well informed, dedicated, reliable, and collegial person as well as a fine editor. The book could not have been written without her creative help and deep knowledge.

My executive secretary, Elva Murphy, who for so many years was Cyrus Vance's right-hand person, effectively managed the activities of my office with knowledge and skill during a hectic period. She was succeeded by the exceedingly capable and farsighted Emily Benedetto.

My son, Eric, and his son, David; my daughter, Peggy, her husband, Peter, and their children, Rachel and Evan, have been loving, generous, thoughtful, and creative. So too the Los Angeles branch of the Hamburg family: Shirley and Leonard, Debbie, Nancy, and Richard—always helpful.

Finally, Betty, my wife and collaborator—personally and professionally—of fifty-six years, has contributed so much in so many ways that she is one of the wonderful people to whom this book is dedicated.

The context that made the book possible was provided by my dear friend and collaborator over half a century—at Stanford, the Institute of Medicine, and Cornell—Jack Barchas, professor and chairman of the Department of Psychiatry at Cornell and one of the world's leaders in his field. Beyond that, his intellectual stimulation, personal kindness, and institutional support have surpassed any reasonable expectation. Several colleagues at the Weill Cornell Medical College were also helpful: Rosemary Stevens, Antonio Gotto, Herbert Pardes, Theodore Shapiro, and Mary Ferguson.

Finally, it has been a blessing to work again with Jennifer Knerr, whose superb editing did so much for the books of the Carnegie Commission on Preventing Deadly Conflict, those of Alex George, and my book, *No More Killing Fields*. Her editing skills, knowledge of human conflict, and creative judgment all make this book better than it otherwise would have been.

David A. Hamburg

Credits

PART I

NATURE AND SEVERITY OF THE PROBLEM

CHAPTER 1

Prevention of Genocide

Overview

Many consider genocide a modern invention. Far from it. Genocides have been recorded throughout history, often with approval by those chronicling a "victory" of their particular tribe or nation. The number of victims might have been smaller in earlier times and the technology used against them cruder, but there is no question that intensive efforts to obliterate ethnic or religious groups and their cultures have occurred repeatedly—that is, genocide.

Given this dreadful history, it would be plausible to suppose that modern ingenuity, with all its scientific strengths, would have sought and found ways to prevent genocide in the twenty-first century. Not so. Today the mass murders in Darfur drag on, with more than 200,000 dead from attacks, an equal number dead from conditions the attacks created, and more than 2.5 million internally displaced persons and refugees.

These figures do not convey the reality of the situation: strafed and burned villages; wells stuffed with the collected parts of mutilated corpses; brutal, premeditated rapes accompanied by racial insults; and then—if and when the victims (mostly women and children) can reach some place of uncertain refuge—overcrowding, malnutrition, disease, and threat of further attacks and rapes. In a land where seasonal variations put agriculture on a tight time schedule and where changing climate has shrunk the amount of productive soil and grazing land available to a growing population, fields have been left unsown and unprepared for future sowing. Atrocities and war, fed by cynically calculated government incitement to "racial" hatred, make most commerce, education, and medical care impossible. Militia service has become an attractive career for young men, especially when peaceful opportunities are lacking. Revenge is satisfying, looting means instant wealth, and fear of retaliation (strengthened by hardening attitudes on all sides) makes both rebels and government-backed forces reluctant to lay down easily available arms—often supplied by great powers, especially China. All this creates a self-perpetuating cycle of conflict that has spread in a growing bloody pool of abuse throughout the region.

The Darfur rebellion that began in 2003 and the massacres that followed (now almost universally acknowledged as genocide) could not have surprised international observers.

They are essentially a replay in the west of the twenty-year rebellion of "African" groups in Sudan's largely Christian south against the repressive monopoly of political and economic power by the Muslim central government in Khartoum. This central government, a legacy of colonial rule, has identified itself as "Arab" and has flirted with both Arab nationalism and Islamic terrorism to consolidate its power. Sudanese president Omar Hassan al-Bashir responded to the southern rebellion with the same tactics he would later use in Darfur—incitement to ethnic (and, in southern Sudan, religious) hatred, use of brutal unofficial militias to carry out a scorched-earth policy of ethnic cleansing, repopulation with favored ethnic groups, as well as divide-and-rule tactics and many unkept promises directed at both rebels and concerned observers outside his borders. As is the case with Darfur today, international concern was high about the southern rebellion. In the United States alone, beginning as early as 1989, ex-president Jimmy Carter used his good offices in a number of efforts to facilitate peace between the government of Sudan and the southern rebels. (His Carter Center also provided humanitarian assistance.) As they did later in Darfur, Christian evangelical groups made vigorous efforts to rescue and relieve victims of the struggle and brought pressure on Congress and the president to take action. Their success was evident in President George W. Bush's appointment of Senator John Danforth as U.S. mediator for peace in Sudan. But before long he was gone from the Bush administration.

When southern rebel victories, growing dissatisfaction in other regions of Sudan, the desire to capitalize on recently found oil reserves, and strong if uncoordinated international pressure finally forced Khartoum to negotiate an agreement with the south, al-Bashir exploited the differences and jealousies that divided both his international and internal opponents to ensure that the final accord did not include sharing power with marginalized and disgruntled "African" groups in Sudan's west (i.e., Darfur) and north. The Comprehensive Peace Agreement (CPA), signed in January 2005, explicitly stated that it could not be reopened. Like the later peace settlement for Darfur, it was an agreement between only two parties, the ruling National Congress Party (NCP) and the rebel Sudan People's Liberation Movement/Army (SPLM/A), but it locked in allocations of power sharing that affected the whole country. This left other regions of Sudan disaffected, and many decided that the only way of asserting their own rights was the way the SPLM/A had chosen—armed rebellion. So more rebel groups emerged. For its part, Khartoum intended to implement only those CPA provisions it could not defer or avoid, unless implementation suited its own purposes. By playing on their divisions, the NCP immobilized the international community just as it would do later in Darfur and carried out only selected elements of the CPA but blocked any fundamental change in the way it ruled Sudan. At the same time it encouraged conditions that created chaos among the southern ex-rebels. Sudan has reportedly backed incursions against the SPLA by the vicious Ugandan Lord's Resistance Army (LRA), and the Darfur Peace Agreement, signed on May 5, 2006, itself created a situation that weakened the CPA.

The unscrupulous Sudanese president has evidently learned more from experience than his opponents have. Analysts have pointed out that al-Bashir is consistent in responding only to pressure that is resolute, concerted, and costly to him and to his party. Yet the Darfur rebels continue to fragment, only to end up isolated, co-opted, and/or marginalized by Khartoum. The African Union (AU) has seen its individual members bullied and cajoled almost to the point of allowing Sudan to take its chairmanship. The rest of the international community has been distracted and divided by its other interests.

The United States, with its attention and resources focused on Iraq, perceives Sudan as too useful an ally in getting intelligence on terrorists to be alienated completely. It is also nervous about joining too closely with the Europeans, who are enthusiastic about endorsing the use of the International Criminal Court (ICC), which is anathema to Bush foreign policy. One can only hope that this will change with leadership changes in the UK, in France, and later in the United States.

China's characteristically amoral foreign policy is manifested in its tender solicitude for Sudan's oil and trade. It also wants to gain influence throughout the developing world by promoting its image as an indulgent uncle who will not ask unwelcome questions about human rights abuses committed by the governments with which it conducts business. And most nations, even those that nominally accept a nation's "responsibility to protect" its own citizens, tend to become very cautious when that principle is actually used to trump the venerated principle of "national sovereignty." Khartoum has skillfully used this disunity to resist effective international monitoring and peacekeeping in Sudan, despite thoughtful efforts by the dedicated and high-caliber diplomats Jan Eliasson (for the UN) and Salim Salim (for the AU) and by the gifted UN Secretaries-General Kofi Annan and Ban Ki-moon. It will be a terribly difficult job to build international unity and resolve to stop the bloodshed and heal the wounds of Darfur; if and when that can be achieved, the costs will be very high, far higher than if early preventive action had been applied. The near impossibility of stopping an ongoing genocide is vividly and grotesquely illustrated by the Darfur experience. It should provide all democratic societies and, indeed, the international community with a powerful stimulus to turn toward prevention.

Sudan has long held the spotlight of international attention, but several other countries—notably Burma and Zimbabwe—stand precariously on the brink of mass murder. Both are catastrophes foreshadowed by severe governmental repression, flagrant and growing abuse of human rights, and hate speech—especially incitement by despotic leaders against vulnerable groups blamed for the country's troubles. So atrocities in various forms that lead to mass violence, even genocide, have not gone away, and given the worldwide spread of highly lethal weapons, as well as today's enhanced capacity for destructive communication, we can expect to see more genocides.

Until now very little work has been done on the *prevention* of genocide, especially when prevention means stopping a problem before it becomes murderous. The time has come to draw together the world's knowledge pertinent to this subject and to stimulate worldwide reflection, discussion, research, and education on prevention of genocide.

The complaint that no one can predict genocide, or even identify it until it is at least halfway through its bloody course, is both an unsubstantiated shibboleth and a convenient way to sidestep responsibility. In fact, time after time—as in the case of Darfur—the approach of genocide has been discernible decades before its arrival. These years must not be wasted. They must be used for prevention—before massive bloodshed occurs, not after. But how?

Worldwide concern to avoid the recurrence of an eminently preventable and highly contagious disaster cries out for establishment of strong focal units within major international institutions that will assemble from around the world the knowledge and skill of many professions, disciplines, and nations. They will develop and make public ways to recognize emerging intergroup tensions that are likely to lead to violent abuses. Action must not wait until it can be determined whether a particular threat of impending violence will lead to genocide or to some other atrocity—any hint of mass violence. Action must be taken to prevent a lesser atrocity than genocide, not only because it *is* an atrocity (and that in itself is a sufficient reason) but also because unresolved hatred and emerging violence in a society can grow into recurrent massacres, even war or genocide, destruction on a vast and hideous scale. Thus it is necessary for strong democracies and humane organizations to reach out *proactively* to nations in trouble and help them to avoid descent down the slippery slope to mass violence. The international community needs to have information ready at hand about practical measures for prevention that follows the public health model—an approach that uses empirical research to identify high-risk factors and apply a wide array of strategies, tools, and practices for preventing violent outbreaks of all kinds.

Such prevention involves identifying an ailing nation's specific problem(s) and employing evidence-based responses toward resolving them. Some measures, such as early, skillful, and respectful preventive diplomacy, can quickly show beneficial results, just as expert care of a sprained ankle results in rapid healing and prevents an injury from getting worse. Longer-term measures, especially helping a troubled nation build a democratic, equitable, socioeconomic infrastructure, take longer to apply and even longer to show results, but the effects are likely to be lasting and pervasive, just as promoting a healthy lifestyle and environment can achieve much better health for a society that is accustomed to health-damaging habits such as cigarette smoking. This book considers such measures and recommends that they could best be developed, analyzed, disseminated, and applied through the help of two centers in large international organizations for the prevention of genocide. These centers are now coming into existence, bringing the promise of a critical mass of knowledge, skill, and best practices for prevention in focal points of high leverage for accomplishment.

The first third of the book deals with how genocides come about and considers some recurring twists and turns in the paths to genocide throughout the nineteenth, twentieth, and twenty-first centuries. The second part deals with pillars of prevention: elements of human societies that have strong preventive potential for mass violence of all kinds. These pillars, if adequately built, can greatly reduce the risk of genocide, war, and atrocity behavior. The third part of the book deals with who can do what to build and maintain such pillars: organizations and institutions that are already doing good work in this area and could do much more. Since international cooperation is essential for genocide prevention, I describe four institutions that have already shown considerable promise and try to look ahead toward fulfillment of their potential in the future, including their stimulating effect on international institutions all over the world.

As its subject demands, this book is highly interdisciplinary and international in scope, and its conclusions rely on strong links between research and policy. These conclusions have already stimulated highly significant changes in two of the world's great international institutions, the United Nations and the European Union (EU). I had the privilege of chairing for each of them a committee reporting at the highest level: to Kofi Annan, then Secretary-General of the United Nations, now to his successor Ban Ki-moon; and to Javier Solana for the European Union. There has been an ongoing interplay between these activities and the preparation of the book. I think this interplay was helpful to all concerned; it was certainly stimulating in my work on the book.

The special qualities of the book include

- examination of different categories of prevention to show how they put out small fires before they become conflagrations and, beyond that, help in resolving the root causes of conflict before they reach the level of recurrent and expanding violence. This is far more effective than reacting to crises after much blood has been shed, many lives lost, revenge motives aroused, and reconciliation made very difficult;
- use of case histories of actual genocides that occurred in different cultures, times, and localities to illustrate how preventive measures at an early stage might have averted the genocide, and, in the genocide's later phases, how opportunities were missed for effective action to contain and cut short a deadly situation;
- identification of warning signals of impending violent conflict—signals that are invariably evident years, even decades, before actual mass violence begins—and their importance to national and international bodies in developing, institutionalizing, and sharing an armamentarium of responses to which these signals can be firmly linked and employed as appropriate;
- analysis of the particular assets and limitations of specific international and regional organizations—both government and civil society—in carrying out the work of prevention;
- recommendation to establish collaborative centers for the prevention of genocide in appropriate regional and international bodies, with key functions of these centers dedicated to the service of effective prevention.

The Case for Prevention

Recent research has documented that all the genocides of the twentieth century were clearly visible years in advance, but largely dismissed, even denied, by the international community until mass killing was well under way. The paths of genocide-prone behavior are clear; we are learning how to provide help and apply pressure at strategic points along those paths to prevent it. Yet international leaders, confronted with impending genocide, still fail to devise policy alternatives to large-scale military action. Military action is extremely difficult, expensive, distasteful, politically unpopular, and costly of human life. So, genocide-prone behavior continues to be condoned, even as it is verbally deplored.

Yet unchecked genocide is catastrophic for all concerned. Once in progress, Hitler's Final Solution was ended only after years of global carnage that devastated much of Europe and brought down upon Germany pervasive destruction far beyond anything it had suffered before. More recently, a similar pattern held in the former Yugoslavia and in Rwanda: first, evident and serious danger signals were ignored; then clear-cut genocide was met with equivocation and semantic dispute over the definition of genocide. Efforts to prevent mass violence encounter this central problem: countries, regions, or groups in trouble are in need of international help. The trouble, which may combine political, social, psychological, and economic ills, can exacerbate intergroup or international tensions that are then readily exploited by ambitious, aggressive, ruthless leaders who gain support and consolidate power through incitement to violence against vulnerable scapegoats.

Today the capacity for mass destruction is at an all-time high; so too is the capacity for incitement to violence. In the interest of adversarial parties, their neighbors, and ultimately all humanity, therefore, the international community must join in a common effort to learn to live together, diminish tension and the causes of tension between in-groups and out-groups, and engage in early, ongoing conflict resolution. Prompt, sustained efforts to prevent genocide and other mass violence are likely to have multiple benefits—usually achieved without military action. Paths to ongoing conflict resolution and lasting peaceful relations are mapped out best through early, strongly preventive diplomacy and world-wide education for learning to live together in a framework of democratic socioeconomic development. These approaches are fundamental to preventing all forms of mass kill-ing, whether interstate war, civil war, or genocide. So too the precursors of mass killing: egregious, systematic violation of human rights such as torture and "ethnic cleansing." The path to prevention of mass violence and establishment of decent human relations is usually long and difficult but increasingly feasible. I will identify these promising paths and, where needed, suggest new ways to broaden them to help the international com-munity succeed in ending the most egregious mass violence.

I conclude, firmly supported by recent research, that there is ample warning time to act, since danger signals are typically clear—and even vivid—years in advance of the carnage. A crucial need is specific response options and contingency plans to deal with these danger signals—i.e., how to cope with foreseeable likely genocide. Neither genocide literature nor policy circles have thus far provided much insight on such preparation, and leadership is diminished by this weakness. Leaders in effect say, "Even though I recognize the danger, what can I do?"

I use recent studies and analyses that examine appropriate tools, strategies, and practices to prevent violent conflict, such as the work of the Carnegie Commission on Preventing Deadly Conflict, and many follow-up studies as well as multiple preventive initiatives and explorations. Thus it is possible to survey the world's experience, for better and worse, and seek to extract the most promising actions. Examples of successful prevention provide an authentic basis for hope. These can prevent mass violence, using mechanisms for ongoing conflict resolution below the threshold of mass violence, building capacity for solving intergroup problems, and providing models for assisting democratic socioeconomic development that meets basic human needs.

I propose a plan for establishing two International Centers for the Prevention of Genocide, each with a base in a strong international institution and links to other institu-tions/organizations that offer complementary strengths and cooperative opportunities. Thus a visible, dynamic reservoir of knowledge and skills for prevention can become available to the entire world in due course. I recommend expanding links over the years to create a worldwide network of cooperating entities for preventing mass violence and a strategy for creating a strong basis for this enterprise by helping leaders, in the spirit of our common humanity, to increase political will and mold a constituency for prevention through comprehensive public education on the necessity and feasibility of preventing mass violence.

The Crisis Prevention Approach: A Trusted Precursor to Genocide Prevention

The urgent global issues raised by the Cold War alerted me to the critical importance of a crisis prevention approach. In 1978, in collaboration with Professors Alexander George and Graham Allison, I chaired a Pugwash conference that assembled strong international talent from relevant disciplines to clarify the immense difficulty of nuclear crisis management (e.g., the Cuban missile crisis of 1962) and the advantage of a crisis prevention approach. In 1979 the Soviet invasion of Afghanistan and the intense U.S. response it provoked placed the world in great danger.

Beginning in 1982, the Carnegie Corporation under my presidency inaugurated a series of grants to leading universities and scientific organizations to pursue these issues with wide-ranging analyses—first, of the paths that would lead to nuclear war and then of preventive interventions for avoiding the slippery slope toward catastrophe for humanity. The studies, which examined critical "hot spots" from the standpoint of crisis prevention, became influential in the United States, Europe, and the Soviet Union, especially in confronting the leaders of those countries with the horrible potential effects of nuclear war and by demonstrating the feasibility of prevention.

Much has been learned from the Cold War, the most dangerous conflict in all of history. The likelihood of irreversible disaster soars in the highly stressful setting of a nuclear confrontation, which demands instant decisions and fine-tuned control of far-flung military operations. The superpowers were faced with this harsh fact and were urged to recognize that it was in their national interests to retreat a respectful distance from the brink of a shared final calamity. This demanded a regimen for crisis prevention, not crisis management. In the context of the Cold War, such a regimen would emphasize finding ways to decrease the likelihood of use of nuclear weapons. It would not assume a warmer relationship between the United States and the USSR or a mutual rapid reduction of their nuclear hoards—desirable as these changes might be. It would simply assume their recognition that confrontations on the level of the Cuban missile crisis could not be managed safely time after time.

The main points of the crisis prevention approach can be stated concisely and are still useful in hostile international or intergroup situations:

1. *Avoid nasty, unpleasant surprises.* For example, upgrade the hotline between Washington and Moscow for rapid use to clarify an unsettling event.
2. *Agree in advance on "rules of the road."* Such rules deal with sensitive and potentially explosive situations. The "incidents-at-sea" agreement, for example, is a model for highly professional military-to-military contacts to diminish the risk of accidental firing or even inadvertent nuclear war.
3. *Clarify vital interests in touchy situations.* To this end, a policy of holding regular regional consultations covering different areas of the world gradually evolved and proved useful.
4. *Create new and strengthen existing institutional mechanisms.* These might include such things as nuclear risk reduction centers that provide professional exchange of information and ideas on a regular basis regarding issues that could readily become highly dangerous, such as unanticipated missile tests.

The crisis prevention approach has applicability to post–Cold War conflicts and has led to broad international interest in confidence-building measures. They can now be applied to every region of the world. This is one of the valuable lessons we have learned from the dangers of the Cold War. More generally, it has turned our attention to the ultimate mission of preventing mass violence altogether in view of the vast destructive capacity of states and terrorist groups in the twenty-first century.

Leaders of the Cold War superpowers were urged to accept and observe rules of mutual accommodation: avoid direct nuclear confrontation, do not make nuclear threats, do not expound grandiose interests, respect the common humanity and vital interests of the adversary, avoid dehumanization or humiliation of the adversary, and take advantage of all opportunities to widen contacts across adversarial boundaries. Over years, mutual rules of prudence evolved. These remain useful guidelines for preventing deadly conflicts in the twenty-first century.

In due course, from many influences and from personal character, both Mikhail Gorbachev and Ronald Reagan adopted a preventive orientation and the Cold War ended, almost without violence. As we note time and again in this book, leadership matters. If global catastrophe that could have destroyed humanity was successfully avoided in this case, the hope of devising feasible ways to prevent genocide does not seem far-fetched.

Toward International Cooperation for Prevention of Genocide

A strong impetus to genocide prevention came from the January 2004 Stockholm International Forum on Genocide, sponsored by the Swedish government, long a committed leader in combating this problem. On January 26, 2004, in the opening address to the Stockholm Forum, UN Secretary-General Kofi Annan affirmed, "There can be no more important issue, and no more binding obligation, than the prevention of genocide. Indeed, this may be considered one of the original purposes of the United Nations."[1]

Two days later, Javier Solana, European Union high representative for the common foreign and security policy, concluded the forum with these words:

> In the European Union, we ... are [prepared] to assume greater responsibility for security.... Second, prevention ... is at the heart of our approach to security.... A culture of prevention requires the imagination to see ahead to the consequences of our inaction. And it demands the political will and courage to take preventive action where this is costly, dangerous or unpopular and where the benefits may never be seen.... Third, effective multilateralism.... The establishment of the International Criminal Court has shown that the multilateral system can be adapted and strengthened to meet new challenges. We have a responsibility now to ensure that it can do its job.... We have a responsibility also to ensure that the UN can do its job.... Kofi Annan ... has made concrete proposals on how the UN might be better equipped to identify and prevent potential genocides. In the European Union we too will adopt a practical approach to supporting him.[2]

Prevention of genocide is highly desirable. But is it feasible? I assert here that prevention is indeed within human capacity and recommend ways to achieve this vital aim. The final two chapters of this book outline the fulfillment of these 2004 statements.

New Research on Genocide: Clues to Future Prevention

Recent in-depth, comparative studies have enriched our understanding of genocides and "ethnic cleansing" before and after the Holocaust. These studies have implications for future prevention of genocide. German archives have been valuable. So, too, the archives of the former Soviet Union illuminate the scope of the mass murders committed by the Soviets from the 1930s into the post–World War II era and enhance our comprehension of genocide.[3] In the 1960s and 1970s, genocide occurred in Indonesia, East Timor, and Cambodia. Africa also witnessed mass murders in Burundi in 1972, in Ethiopia in 1974, and in Rwanda in 1994. Similar slaughter took place in Bosnia in 1991–1995 and now in Darfur. These diverse twentieth-century tragedies have some common ideological themes. Throughout this bloody era, the intense nationalism that fueled the potential for genocide was deliberately manipulated by leaders for this purpose.

What makes one group condone the extermination of another? Examples have been especially common under the stress of war, imperial conquest, religious fervor, social upheaval, economic freefall, state failure, or revolution. Recent studies show that clear warning signals appear typically not weeks, not even months, but *years* before a genocide.

The genocidal regimes of Nazi Germany, the Soviet Union, the Cambodian Khmer Rouge, and former Yugoslavia shared several elements that are spelled out in Chapter 2. All four genocides sprang from organized state policies that required the cooperation of many people over a period of years and thus offered opportunities for preventive actions, but these were missed.

Every modern case of genocide has been preceded by a propaganda campaign directed through the mass media by political leaders, who applied to human destruction the latest technological and organizational capabilities available to them. The world observed the inflammatory use of radio, film, and print media as well as the roundups, deportations, and killings that followed. Ethnic cleansing—and genocide even more so—relies upon widespread broadcast media to spread propaganda that glorifies the state, then justifies deportation and extreme harm to the putative enemy. Incitement works only when prejudice already exists and the listener is receptive to it. The progression of events toward genocide is gradual. Small but frequent and consistent harmful acts become familiar and therefore more acceptable, especially if they meet no rapid and vigorous response from inside or outside the country. The larger harmful actions then begin, along with more elaborate justifications for them. But the years from the initial threat to full genocide offer an interval for the international community to take preventive actions. All too often, members of society not directly affected are passive in the face of danger to others, and the tacit acquiescence of outside groups—including nearby nations and powerful democracies (not to mention dictatorships)—allows the damage to expand. Active opposition by internal groups or by outside nations—preferably both—can raise internal concerns about retaliation or stir up the moral values latent in the offending society.

Political leaders make genocide possible by kindling hatred, but they do not act alone. They are supported by machinery of the state, the dominant political party, the police forces, paramilitary and military forces, and professionals such as lawyers, professors, doctors, and engineers. We emphasize that the time required to build the machinery of genocide can be used for prevention. The deadly warning signs are especially manifested in the expression of virulent, persistent, and flagrant prejudice.

Anti-Semitism: The Prototypical Prejudice

In recent years, the United Nations broke its long silence on anti-Semitism in a June 21, 2004, meeting featuring UN Secretary-General Kofi Annan as well as the great leader of Holocaust remembrance, Elie Wiesel. I quote now from their memorable remarks, included in their short volume, *Confronting Anti-Semitism.*[4]

Kofi Annan:

Sixty years ago, in adopting the Charter of the United Nations, the world's peoples asserted their determination "to practice tolerance and live together in peace with one another as good neighbors." Clearly, our success in this struggle depends on the effort we make to educate ourselves and our children. Intolerance can be unlearnt. Tolerance and mutual respect have to be learnt.

Yet throughout history, anti-Semitism has been a unique manifestation of hatred, intolerance, and persecution. Anti-Semitism has flourished even in communities where Jews have never lived, and it has been a harbinger of discrimination against others. The rise of anti-Semitism anywhere is a threat to people everywhere. Thus, in fighting anti-Semitism we fight for the future of all humanity. ...

Worldwide revulsion at this terrible genocide was the driving force behind the Universal Declaration of Human Rights. As the Preamble to the Declaration says, "disregard and contempt for human rights have resulted in barbarous acts which have outraged the conscience of mankind." And it was no coincidence that, on this day before it adopted the declaration in 1948, the General Assembly had adopted the Convention on the Prevention and Punishment of the Crime of Genocide.

It is hard to believe that, 60 years after the tragedy of the Holocaust, anti-Semitism is once again rearing its head. But it is clear that we are witnessing an alarming resurgence of this phenomenon in new forms and manifestations. This time the world must not, cannot, be silent.[5]

Elie Wiesel:

There is divine beauty in learning, just as there is human beauty in tolerance. To learn means to accept the postulate that life did not begin at my birth. Others have been here before me, and I walk in their footsteps. The books I have read were composed by generations of fathers and sons, mothers and daughters, teachers and disciples. I am the sum total of their experiences, their quests. And so are you.

Other people, other traditions, other religious communities and cultures have been persecuted for a variety of reasons; anti-Semitism combines them all. The anti-Semite doesn't know me—but he hates me. Actually, he hated me even before I was born. He even hates the dead—otherwise why such sacrilege in so many profaned cemeteries? ... [6]

I have devoted most of my adult life to combating many evils of society: intolerance, bigotry, racism, fanaticism, and indifference to other people's suffering and fears. But I never thought I would have to fight anti-Semitism. Naively I was convinced that it died in Auschwitz. Now I realize my mistake: it didn't. Only the Jews perished there. Anti-Semitism is alive and well in too many lands. Doesn't the organized world and its moral and intellectual leadership remember the consequences of anti-Semitism?[7]

So, we have learned valuable lessons from the hideous anti-Semitism and other similar prejudices against other groups, before and after the Holocaust. I will sketch some lessons from the Nazi regime in Chapter 4 on the Holocaust. Then, in the course of the book, I add lessons from the earlier Armenian genocide and several later ones. Altogether, we now have multiple, informed perspectives on the human proclivity for atrocity behavior of various sorts, all prone to genocide sooner or later unless we build firewalls.

Improving Warning and Response to Prevent Possible Genocide

An integrated warning response system dedicated to genocide, ethnic cleansing, and massive human rights violations must be created and housed in a suitable strategic position, preferably in one or more strong international bodies, and coordinated with similarly focused agencies in multilateral and international organizations that can strengthen capability for the tasks of prevention. The net effect will be a critical mass of knowledge and skill for preventing mass violence, plus moral commitment and public education to support effective actions.

What must be emphasized is the need to plan a number of specific and appropriate responses to likely developments before they occur and to associate particular response options with foreseeable cues. If measures are taken in other spheres—political, economic, social, and psychological—intervention in problematic situations need not be military. Still, military capability is essential for certain purposes—not to fight a war, but to separate the adversaries (as might well have been done in Rwanda)—and thereby allow space for mediation, negotiation, and, in due course, democratic socioeconomic development.

A Sketch of Important Ways to Prevent Mass Violence

Preventive Diplomacy

The international community cannot afford to wait for a crisis. Governments, intergovernmental organizations, and nongovernmental organizations must establish permanent mechanisms for settling conflicts peacefully before they become explosive and must collaborate in offering ongoing programs of international help that build the capacity of groups to resolve grievances without violence. Fortunately, momentum has grown toward using techniques of active, nonviolent problem solving and sharing of experience across national boundaries, to profit from the world's experience in different local conflicts. Tackling serious grievances as early as possible denies political demagogues and hateful fanatics the long-rankling discontent that makes incitement to violence easier. Important recent studies converge on key points of preventive diplomacy.[8] They are spelled out in Chapter 7.

Changing International Norms of Hatred and Violence Through Education

Just as potential episodes of conflict must be recognized and addressed early, so must the potential underlying causes of those conflicts. Throughout history, much of human aggressive behavior has been exerted in the service of personal bonds of attachment.[9] For millennia, a human individual's survival and success depended on loyal membership in a group, which provided the strength to defend oneself against other groups or to wrest valued resources from them. Aggression toward other people has always and everywhere been facilitated by a pervasive human tendency to draw invidious distinctions between a positively valued "us" and a negatively valued "them." Warlords, demagogues, and tyrants have traditionally encouraged this tendency for their own purposes, a practice that shows little sign of abating, as we have seen recently in Yugoslavia, central Africa, and Afghanistan under Taliban rule. Ridding mankind of the ancient habits of blaming, dehumanizing, and attacking will be very difficult, but not impossible. The human need to be part of a group has also fostered in our species positive tendencies of cooperation that make us highly interdependent and capable of positive intergroup as well as intragroup relations.

We must find ways to raise our children to welcome constructive, tolerant, and prosocial human relations rather than hatred and violence. It is a central challenge of our time to provide the foundation for a humane, democratic, and safe course of child and adolescent development, ultimately aiming to protect humanity. Directing attitudes and beliefs along a positive path involves a life-span perspective, from infancy through adulthood. It involves an institutional perspective that starts in the family, then continues from preschool through elementary, secondary education, college or university, with constructive roles for media, the Internet, religious institutions, and community organizations as well. At the adult level, education of political leaders in the prevention of war and genocide would make a valuable contribution to global security. Educational innovations in the past two decades—based on independent scholarship—directly involved political and military leaders of the United States, Europe, Russia, and Africa. Experts from various fields brought to bear knowledge and skill in preventing war and genocide. The dynamic interplay of these experts with distinguished governmental leaders has set a valuable precedent. We can see in scholarship and practice how research-based knowledge of human conflict and the paths to mutual accommodation can become a universal part of education, conveying both the facts of human diversity and our common humanity.[10]

International Cooperation for Preventing Mass Violence

The formidable tasks of preventive diplomacy in near-crisis situations and of long-term socioeconomic development to promote peaceful societies are demanding and require sometimes expensive, often dangerous, and always sustained efforts. They call for cooperation across national boundaries and among various institutions and organizations. So far, individual states, groups of states, the United Nations, regional organizations, nongovernmental organizations, and eminent individuals have approached prevention in a groping, uncoordinated way. These good intentions are useful but not sufficient—more widely accepted and regularized arrangements are necessary and are beginning to emerge.

UN Secretary-General Kofi Annan led a major effort for a decade (1996–2006) to strengthen the UN's capability to foster international cooperation for these purposes. Even though serious problems remain within the United Nations, there simply must be a worldwide forum in which all kinds of information can be shared, ideas tried out, views exchanged, and positive relationships formed. Yet the organization is so large, so multifaceted, so disparate in its composition and outlook of its members, so emotionally charged from its past history and from current difficulties in the world, that it will take a long time to fulfill its potential. Nevertheless, if the UN did not exist, something very much like it would have to be invented. Moreover, it has agencies that are making vital contributions: WHO (the World Health Organization), UNICEF (the United Nations Children's Fund), UNDP (United Nations Development Programme), the World Bank for economic development, and the UN High Commission for Refugees, among others. Preventive diplomacy is gaining via the Secretary-General and his Secretariat, especially the Department of Political Affairs, and by means of analytical units such as UNITAR (United Nations Institute for Training and Research) and UNRISD (United Nations Research Institute for Social Development).

Role of Established Democracies in Prevention of Genocide

A particularly attractive option, indeed a unique resource, is that of closer cooperation among established democracies—an enlarging group of nations that share humane values, effective mechanisms for coping with conflict, and formidable resources for preventing mass violence. This group of states can act in different groupings for a variety of purposes all over the world and within the spirit of the UN Charter in instances where the UN is unable to act effectively. This could provide a flexible system of action for peace and justice. It would amount to an extensive coalition of states sharing basic common values, arranged in different configurations depending on the requirements and opportunities of a particular conflict. The European Union is the closest approximation we now have of such a strong and cohesive democratic grouping, led in the genocide problem with vision and courage by Javier Solana.

By and large, the established democracies have the moral, technological, economic, and political strength to formulate norms that will be widely accepted, even if tyrannical regimes are offended. The democracies have it within sight to upgrade and regularize cooperation in preventing mass violence.

There are three areas in which this indispensable role of the established democracies may be employed with singular value. They are explored below in "Democratic Development: Political Aspects," "Democratic Development: Economic Aspects," and "International Centers for the Prevention of Genocide."

Democratic Development: Political Aspects

Aggression is most likely to occur when authoritarian leaders can lie to, inflame, and coerce an unresisting public. On the other hand, democratic traditions evolve in ways that encourage and maintain ongoing mechanisms for coping with conflicts.[11] To endure, democracies must search out ways to deal fairly with disputes, differences, and grievances and to resolve them below the threshold of mass violence. Of course, this is a difficult process, and failures occur even in democracies. But on the whole, democratic habits and institutions offer the best means for dealing justly and peacefully with the ubiquitous tensions of humanity.

The attitudes, beliefs, and procedures that sustain democratic societies are useful in intergroup conflict not only within but also beyond state borders. In democratic governments and civil society, processes of negotiation and mediation are common. Citizens are educated to understand the perspectives of other people and to learn mutual accommodation—starting in childhood. Most people get used to a pluralistic society. They learn to compromise in order to gain something satisfactory for all elements of the society.

To be sure, the transition from a closed authoritarian society to a fully viable, open democratic society can be stormy—and requires the kind of international help the fragile Weimar Republic did not get. The social contexts of democracy are highly variable. No one size fits all. Still, there are effective means for promoting democracy internationally. International cooperation can provide valuable help in strengthening the political and civic infrastructure of new, emerging, and fragile democracies.

For this purpose, the democratic community is establishing special funds to strengthen emerging democracies through technical assistance, financial aid, and social exchanges to build the requisite processes and institutions, including widespread education of citizens about the actual workings of democracy. Such funds may be administered through nongovernmental organizations as well as through government agencies and international multilateral organizations. International support of the complicated processes of democracy building must be sustained over many years. There is much more to it than one successful election. Despite the many obstacles, much can be accomplished—especially if multilateral cooperation is empathetic, flexible, and determined. The establishment of new democracies requires decades or even generations, so we must be persistent and resourceful in working with democratic reformers all over the world.

Democratic Development: Economic Aspects

Economic development is a vital partner of democratic political development.[12] We have learned important lessons from successes and failures of socioeconomic development in Asia, Africa, and Latin America during the past half century. Yet there are still widely prevalent threats to survival even though modern science and technology have made such powerful contributions to human well-being. Much of the world's population still cannot rely upon access to sources of food, water, shelter, and other necessities of life. What can we do to diminish the kind of vulnerability that leads to desperation—often to violence? Many nations in the global south have been late in getting access to the unprecedented opportunities now available for economic and social development. They are seeking ways to modernize in keeping with their own cultural traditions and distinctive settings. They need help in finding ways to adapt useful tools others have used for their own development—not a cookie-cutter approach. It is surely in the interest of wealthy countries everywhere to facilitate the development of knowledge, skill, health, and freedom in these countries so they can become contributing, responsible members of the international community rather than breeding grounds for social pathology, serious infectious disease, terrorist violence, or genocide. An avoidable excess of human suffering tends to recruit alienated youth into genocidal or terrorist movements.

To foster economic development, it is essential to promote inclusive political participation, basic education and health care, and respect for human rights. All of these contribute powerfully not only to individual well-being but also to the economic progress of the society.

The education of girls and women—badly neglected in many poor countries—is a valuable investment for developing countries. It enhances women's skills and choices and improves their health and nutrition—as well as their children's. The more educated the mothers, the less likely that their children will die, regardless of differences in family income. Education also helps delay marriage for women, partly by increasing their chances for employment, and makes them more likely to know about and to use contraceptives—thus moderating unsustainable population growth. And with only modest borrowing opportunities, educated women can contribute significantly to economic growth. Overall, the nearly worldwide discrimination against women must be ended and their opportunities increased for the benefit of all.

The judicious use of science and technology is a key element in development; yet it is curiously neglected in many countries, as if it were a luxury reserved for rich countries. On the contrary, participation in the world economy now requires a modicum of technical competence everywhere. This must be fostered by the international cooperation of scientists and educators.

On the whole, the essential ingredients for development center around knowledge, skill, and freedom. Knowledge is mainly produced by research and development; skills are mainly achieved by education and training; freedom is mainly a function of democratic institutions. Making all of these available to the developing world requires sustained international cooperation.

We can learn from the steps taken after World War II that laid the groundwork for today's flourishing European cooperation. Leaders such as Franklin and Eleanor Roosevelt, George Marshall, Harry Truman, Robert Schuman, and Jean Monnet looked beyond the wartime devastation and the hateful fanaticism that had caused it and envisioned a Europe in which regional cooperation would transcend adversarial boundaries and traditional rivalries. They foresaw that large-scale, sustained economic cooperation would facilitate not only postwar recovery but also the long-term democratic prosperity that has given Europe peace and security—in dramatic contrast with its bloody and degraded experience in the first half of the twentieth century.[13]

International Centers for Prevention of Genocide

An essential part of this task would be to establish two International Centers for the Prevention of Genocide: one in the UN and one in the EU. Their design would include the capacity for simulating both operational and structural means of prevention. This means a strong, ongoing, proactive version of preventive diplomacy, linked to democratic socioeconomic development. Both are essential to long-term success.

The centers would perform a number of valuable activities that are spelled out in the final chapter of this book. Overall, the centers should elicit cooperation to pool strengths; share burdens, knowledge, and skill; divide labor; and provide a moral compass. In so doing, they would keep the world's focus on this dreadful problem and provide hope for effective action.

The European Union's dedication to a vigorous, proactive, and coherent program to prevent deadly conflict makes it an excellent candidate to sponsor a center for the prevention of conflict's ugliest subspecies, genocide. The International Center for the Prevention of Genocide would be an outstanding example of the Göteborg Programme's recommendation, "EU action guided by principles of value-added and comparative advantage."[14]

There is a powerful logic in concentrating the initial major, pathbreaking effort in the European Union, in explicit collaboration with the UN, which is making similar progress toward prevention of mass violence. As soon as possible, ties to other regional organizations around the world, such as the African Union, would be valuable.

Pillars of Prevention

This book draws on a great deal of research, field observations, and careful descriptions of the paths to genocide. It relates this most poignant body of information to the growing research literature on prevention of mass violence by building *pillars of prevention*. These pillars of prevention are mostly long-term measures that are useful for prevention of all sorts of mass violence: war, genocide, and crimes against humanity. They depend largely on international organizations but also on excellent nongovernmental organizations. The pillars can become strong in crucial ways.

1. *A continuous flow of accurate information on emerging conflicts,* especially violent outbursts of extensive hate speech, and early warnings of serious trouble between groups or between nations
2. *The proactive use of preventive diplomacy,* with respectful engagement in an *assistance* approach to countries in trouble
3. *Building good governance* leading toward democracy and equitable socioeconomic development
4. *Education for conflict resolution,* mutual accommodation, learning to live together
5. *Serious restraints on weaponry,* arms control regimes
6. *International justice in preventing human rights abuses*

These pillars are multipurpose in preventing human suffering related to hatred and violence. War and genocide have important shared properties—often virulent prejudice predisposes to civil war, revolution, or interstate war. Under those conditions, the door is opened to genocide as the norms and institutions that restrain genocidal behavior are badly eroded. Killing becomes the order of the day, and established targets become exceedingly vulnerable. So it is highly desirable and increasingly feasible for the international community—especially the established democracies worldwide—to take measures that help to put out fires when they are small, yet the danger of conflagration is visible. If not extinguished, these fires may well lead to mass violence of one form or another. Early prevention of deadly violence, whether it is genocide or not, must become the highest priority of a world striving to be decent and civilized.

Part II of this book, on pillars of prevention, covers a wide span of activities. The most rapid possibilities are contained in Chapter 7, "Proactive Help in Preventing Mass Violence: Preventive Diplomacy and Beyond." They will require organizations such as the UN, the EU, and the community of established democracies to keep in close touch with all regions of the world so as to respond with empathy and concern in offering help promptly—early, ongoing action to prevent mass violence.

In most cases, these troubled countries will need respectful and sustained international help to build democratic socioeconomic development and to participate effectively in the world's institutions that can strengthen opportunity, build internal mechanisms of conflict resolution, and create reliable ways of meeting basic human needs and fostering decent intergroup relations. These are paths toward a decent world. For adult readers of this book, it is reasonable to expect that your children will gain some benefits from helping to build these pillars—and your grandchildren will benefit greatly.

Conclusion

What we are proposing now is deliberately ambitious. Although all the functions listed here are potentially of great value in meeting the dreadful challenge of human genocidal tendencies, they would have to be implemented step-by-step over a period of years. Moreover, they would in due course require the cooperation of several (or many) institutions and organizations striving for eventual global participation. All this is complicated and difficult. Yet there are special assets to be drawn upon. In the past decade, an international community has emerged in which much has been learned from research and practice about ways to prevent mass killing in intrastate wars and interstate wars. This growing body of knowledge and skill is largely applicable to genocide as well. These are, after all, variations on a theme of mass murder.

In this book, I summarize the main tools, strategies, and practices of preventing deadly conflict: the basic themes and some variations for intrastate and interstate warfare as well as genocide. Moreover, I describe the advantages and limitations of various international organizations for joining in this great enterprise, sorting out who can do what in the years ahead to prevent—or at least greatly reduce the risk of—mass killing. If there is a more crucial mission for humanity, I wonder what it could be.

CHAPTER 2

Paths to Genocide

Predisposing and Precipitating Factors and Their Relevance for Prevention

Forced Resettlement and Genocidal Behavior Before the Twentieth Century

The expulsion of an undesired population from a given territory carries with it forceful, injurious, often brutal treatment and extreme humiliation. It typically involves religious or ethnic discrimination, political or ideological animosities, or a combination of these. Such behavior has occurred throughout human history from antiquity to the present but greatly intensified in the late nineteenth and twentieth centuries. Recent events in the former Yugoslavia, Rwanda, and Darfur are a repetition of processes that nearly all other parts of the world have undergone in efforts to achieve ethnically distinct territories, group superiority, or control of highly valued resources. Children and adolescents are typically caught up in such horrors, and survivors are often left with permanent disabilities or psychological scars.

As early as the eighth century BC, Assyria made forced resettlement of conquered populations a state policy. In the European Middle Ages, population purges occurred primarily for religious reasons. Medieval Christianity used expulsion and massacre to rid itself of nonbelievers, targeting Jews in particular. Jews were expelled from England (1290), France (1306), Hungary (1349–1960), Austria (1491), Lithuania (1445), Poland (1494), and Spain (1492). In 1555 the Peace of Augsburg established conformity to the religious beliefs of the ruling prince as the basis of political order, and further expulsions occurred.

In the Western Hemisphere the white population applied its own brand of ethnic cleansing to the native American population. Extermination occurred at a slower pace and lower technological level, but in some cases the absolute number of dead approached modern levels. Four lethal results of the Spanish Conquest decreased the native population in Mexico from an estimated 12 million in 1519 to slightly more than one million in

1600: deliberate mass murder, forced labor, maltreatment, and epidemic disease. By any defensible definition of the word, this was a case of genocide. Historian Tzvetan Todorov considered it the logical outcome of colonial wars waged against alien peoples in a place far removed from the legal or ethical restraints of the invaders' homeland.[1]

The British and the French colonists of the time pursued policies similar to those of the Spanish, but they did not expand throughout the continent so quickly. Although it took a longer time, the ultimate fate of native Americans in much of North America was similarly grim. In 1492 they had an estimated population of more than 5 million; by 1892 it had dropped to 500,000.[2] From the seventeenth century through the nineteenth, continual mass deportations and a number of indiscriminate serial massacres occurred—many of them unabashedly celebrated. Bounties were given for Indian scalps, and even a crude form of germ warfare was practiced by infecting blankets with smallpox and distributing them to native Americans.[3] In the 1770s the Carolina delegation to the Continental Congress called it a Christian duty to extirpate the whole Cherokee "race."[4] Almost a hundred years later, Colonel John Chivington campaigned to kill and scalp all Indians, whatever their age or sex, since "nits make lice"—and in 1864 his troops butchered and scalped from 100 to 500 unarmed Indian women and children at Sand Creek in what is now Colorado. Up to the end of the nineteenth century, even nationally respected figures such as General William Tecumseh Sherman expressed implicit or even explicit endorsement of extermination.[5] Use of language suggesting demonization and dehumanization was common.

When the English first settled Australia in 1788 the aboriginal population numbered about 750,000. Some 600,000 died from diseases imported by the new settlers and another 20,000 in battle.[6] By 1911 only 31,000 Aborigines remained. Like their U.S. counterparts, European settlers in Australia held feelings toward indigenous peoples that were at the very least highly ambivalent. In 1867 a Queensland newspaper urged "a war of extermination" against aborigines. Even without totalitarianism and organized incitement by state authorities, ethnic extermination was a common theme in the nineteenth century.

The results of Belgian imperialism in the Congo mirrored those of Spanish imperialism in the New World. Natives who did not die from unfamiliar diseases or battle perished from overwork or abuse in mines and plantations. When native communities resisted or simply failed to deliver their quota of rubber, soldiers or rubber company "sentries" often responded with wholesale and indiscriminate slaughter. Between 1885 and 1920 the indigenous population of the Congo was halved, with a death toll of 10 million.[7]

The nineteenth century marked the first time that the complete destruction of an ethnic group became the goal of a state. The Ottoman government unleashed a war on Armenian villages in the late 1890s. This effort culminated in the devastation of 1915, when about 1.5 million Armenians were killed, following several decades of periodic violent outbursts.

The twentieth century began with what is arguably a fully developed modern genocide. In 1904 General Lothar von Trotha led German colonial forces against the rebel Hereros in South West Africa. He pledged to annihilate them and made good his word, first in a battle won by overwhelmingly superior western weaponry and then by ordering his forces to chase the entire Herero nation—men, women, and children—into the desert bordering their lands, poison the waterholes in the desert, and massacre any who could not escape them. His "extermination order" of October 1 declared that any Herero found in German territory—man, woman, or child, armed or unarmed—must be expelled or shot.[8]

The trademarks of modern genocide were therefore present well before the nineteenth century ended. For a number of reasons, genocidal behavior is deeply embedded in human history.

Evolution of Human Aggression, Attachment, and Intergroup Relations

In the 1960s and 1970s, I considered the evolution of human aggressiveness through the study of nonhuman primates, using a multidisciplinary approach to studying the social behavior of chimpanzees, both in their natural habitat and in a seminatural laboratory of behavioral biology at Stanford.[9] Chimpanzees are genetically closer to humans than any other species, and the study of these primates both illuminates their similarities to *homo sapiens* and allows consideration of who we are, including our predisposition to targeted violence against others.

Our most interesting and surprising discovery about chimpanzee aggression was that chimpanzee males organize into distinct communities that occupy chosen ranges and form border patrols to defend these ranges against males from other communities. During these routine forays, they actively seek opportunities for aggressive encounters. Violent fights between males from different communities frequently occur, and individuals are sometimes severely injured.

These systematic, brutal, and male-dominated attacks among chimpanzees are the closest phenomenon to human warfare observed in any nonhuman primate—though still a very long way from the manmade institutions of modern warfare and genocide. This evidence about chimpanzees, along with similar evidence of hostile responses to strangers of their own species in a variety of other nonhuman primates, suggests that the human tendency to react with fear and hostility toward strangers—and the related tendency to make negative in-group, out-group distinctions—has roots in our prehuman past.

Professor Richard Wrangham of Harvard University has studied the aggression of chimpanzees in their natural habitat for almost three decades. He summarized some relevant findings in a recent article.[10] In the 1970s, detailed observations of chimpanzee intergroup conflict inspired many comparisons between chimpanzee violence and human warfare. Subsequent long-term, carefully nonintrusive observations of chimpanzees in the wild have corroborated these comparisons. Data from five sites conclusively show the pervasiveness of chimpanzee intergroup aggression, and recent studies have clarified its motives and methods. Like their human counterparts, chimpanzee males organize to compete with males in neighboring groups to gain dominance over territory, food, and females; and in their decisions to attack strangers, they show a preference for low-risk battles. As these studies demonstrate, the behavioral biology approach offers valuable insights for understanding and addressing the roots of violence in our own species.

Wrangham further considered distinctive human behavior patterns in relation to a variety of other species, with primary attention to intraspecies killing—a pattern rare in other primates. He observed that most animals do not kill their own kind. Although many nonhuman primates form social groups and engage in combat over territory or resources with neighboring social groups of their own species, their combat typically involves threatening calls and gestures, chases, and skirmishes to convince the other side to retreat. It seldom results in death or even serious damage. Humans, on the other hand, regularly set out to kill. What makes our species different?

Examination of the human biological makeup may answer many questions about this tendency toward organized lethal violence against one's own species, but an environmental, social, and/or cultural context is required to explain the patterns of violence that actually occur. Within this total framework, biology is not the only determining factor. To accept that natural selection has preserved machinery of the body in humans and chimpanzees for conducting violent behavior does not mean that mass violence is inevitable. We need to understand both the nature of the machinery and the psychosocial factors that activate it.[11]

The Human Group in Evolutionary Perspective: Fostering Attachment and Avoiding Hatred in Our Children

Much aggressive behavior is undertaken in the service of attachment. Since developing and maintaining a network of close relationships has long been crucial to individual survival and reproductive success, it is likely that natural selection would have favored such aggressive responses over millions of years. Human survival depended on loyal membership in a group, including a readiness to defend it. Demagogues and tyrants have long utilized this tendency for their own purposes.

Moving beyond the ancient habits of blaming, dehumanizing, and attacking is very difficult but not impossible. For millennia we were utterly convinced that the earth was flat. So, too, we have believed in invidious in-group, out-group distinctions and harsh intergroup relations as an acceptable, even praiseworthy, way of life. But the earth is not flat, and we are all part of a single, worldwide, highly interdependent species. Understanding our aggressive tendencies will allow us to cope with them more successfully.

Child development can be viewed in the context of the human group and its ancient role in survival over many millennia. Though circumstances have changed drastically in modern times, the group is still vitally important and emotionally charged. How did belonging to a primary group get to be so important? Research on our closest biological relatives has clarified the heritage we amassed from our ancient ancestors during our long journey to full humanity.[12]

Monkeys and apes bear one offspring at a time and give that one a lot of attention. They have longer periods of immaturity than other mammals, including prolonged dependence on the mother—hence an intense mother-infant relationship. Safely in contact with the mother, the infant first learns about the wider social world by observation alone. Later learning often occurs in the context of play, not only with peers but also with older siblings and even with adults. Play in early life—often imitating the aggressive patterns of behavior we noted earlier—is not only enjoyable and instructive but necessary to full development. Thus, social learning flows naturally from the protective context of the mother-infant relationship into adaptation to the intimate primary group. The advantages of social organization include protection against predators and competitors; meeting nutritional requirements; protection against harsh climates; aid in dealing with injuries; facilitating reproduction; and preparing the young to meet the requirements and utilize the opportunities of a particular environment. All this highlights the heritage of positive group relationships and the powerful importance of group membership in the adaptation and survival of our ancient ancestors.[13]

These basic elements carried over into human adaptation. Fundamental attachments continue to be formed early in life through readily available social support networks, provided mostly by kin but also by others in the familiar proximity of a small society. This enduring property of strong, positive human relationships retains great importance in contemporary life.

But the links that tie individual survival and reproductive success to cooperative membership in a valued group are far richer and more complex among humans than in any nonhuman society. Human repertoires of learning and tradition evolved over many millennia, in a world of small, mainly stable, face-to-face groups of people united by enduring ties of kinship and mutual support.

A feeling of personal worth has long been predicated on one's sense of belonging to a valued group; a sense of belonging, in turn, depends on the ability to competently undertake the traditional tasks of one's society, to engage in mutually supportive social interactions, and to participate in the meaningful and emotionally significant shared experience of group rituals. The enduring group offers guidance, protection, and satisfaction—even life itself.

The family in one form or another has been the main source of education, economic activity, and social relationships throughout human history. The treatment of other groups figured prominently in the education it provided: whom to love, whom to hate, how to relate to others. Although other relationships are also important, none have quite the significance of those embedded in family and kin.

Today's world is very different from that of our ancestors, chiefly as a result of changes initiated in the Industrial Revolution. A key concern for the future of humankind is to extend the psychological concept of the human survival group to a much larger world community. In the entire span of human evolution, the period since the Industrial Revolution is a brief moment. But the technological, economic, and social changes in this instant of evolutionary history are probably more far-reaching than all the previous changes in human evolution put together. Not least, these transformations have affected the conditions of child and adolescent development. Today the ancient human organism grows up in a very new habitat.

Growing children and young adolescents now have increasingly less opportunity for participation in the adult world as industrialization has proceeded and the pace of technosocial change has accelerated. It is less clear to them how to be useful and earn respect. There is less continuity than ever before between the behavior of childhood and adolescence and that of adulthood. Other influences beyond family control now loom large in shaping youthful attitudes, beliefs, knowledge, and skills. And adults who attempt to guide their children's future cannot predict the environment they will face only decades in the future. These circumstances are conducive to high insecurity (psychological and economic) among youth—hence their susceptibility to charismatic leaders proclaiming hateful and/or utopian ideologies.

Throughout human evolution, kin-based group membership has been crucial to survival. We inherit through genes and customs a strong need for belonging in a primary group, but all too easily loyalty to our primary group may render us susceptible to hatred and violence toward other groups. Aggression toward other people has always been facilitated by the pervasive human tendency toward harsh dichotomizing between positively valued "us" and negatively valued "them."

Human attachments and group loyalty are intimately linked to intergroup conflict and war. We risk our lives and inflict great damage in the devoted service to a valued group, most recently the nation-state but also religious, ethnic, and political groups. These considerations apply to *genocide* too. Today human groups must also react to the massive and rapid changes of recent times. They are replete with novel opportunities but also with stressful experiences, notably the unprecedented scope and number of contacts—social, cultural, and economic—among people from many backgrounds, differing in every conceivable dimension. The new interdependence and globalization, made possible by such technological innovations as television, air transportation, and the Internet, are still evolving, and it is unclear how they will shape the new social order that is emerging.

Identity and Intergroup Relations

Since the world transformation in which we are now immersed creates much uncertainty, insecurity, and inequity, widespread frustrations result that may be transformed into virulent prejudices against minority populations, foreign populations, or infidels. Inflammatory ethnocentric and nationalistic politicians and religious fanatics have long understood the human tendency to seek someone to blame under circumstances of intensely felt frustration. This is a particularly significant point because of the contemporary world's heightened capacity for destruction. Part of this danger lies in the search for secure identity and clashes among identity groups. In dichotomous societies, the potential for intergroup conflict is greater than in societies with more complex, crosscutting identities.[14] Because individuals within a more complex social structure identify with a number of different groups, crosscutting intergroup linkages lessen the intensity of their dependence on any one group for meeting psychological needs for inclusion. Polarization is also reduced between groups, and tolerance tends to grow for out-groups in general, which helps to stabilize the society.

National identity is only one of many identities—occupational, religious, ethnic, linguistic, territorial, class, gender, and others. Throughout our history, as technology and organization have become more complex, new opportunities for conquest have emerged, old rivalries have intensified, the institution of war has been strengthened, and genocide has became a more feasible enterprise. Among these changes was the capacity for increased central control, mainly to support large military forces. Nation-states went beyond anything they could do before to create standardized educational systems, to impose uniform languages, and to promote, through propaganda and organized activities, citizen identification with the nation-state. These changes powerfully affected child rearing. Children were taught from infancy to accept these beliefs and emotions, including their hateful components. Some national, ethnic, and religious groups see their members virtually as a separate species. It follows that since foreigners are scarcely human, there is no moral imperative to treat them as such.

Most religions, including Islam, Judaism, Christianity, and Hinduism, contain zealous subgroups with harshly intolerant and angry orientations toward other groups. To proponents of these rigid religious factions, who frequently blame modern secular society for all their troubles, a universally imposed renewal of religion (their particular brand) is the answer. In extreme cases, infidels who resist are children of Satan or some other force of darkness and are fighting against the will of God. Any sort of punishment (even destruction) that will save true believers from the enticements of this evil, implicitly less-than-human brood is justifiable.

Any such "holy war" tends to provide a strong sense of community and mutually supportive solidarity within the group, but it also generates parochialism, hostile exclusion, and facile justification of mass violence. These are among the most difficult and dangerous problems facing the international community. Yet, nationalism and religion are not entirely closed to pluralistic tolerance. Some movements have shown openness to a diversity of members and might implement tolerant governance if given the opportunity.

Thus human nature includes some very dangerous inclinations, yet these are not insurmountable, nor do they lead inevitably to war or genocide. Relations between groups can become virulent when incited over time by leaders, yet intergroup relations, when shaped by positive influences, can become mutually beneficial and supportive. The factors that shape positive intergroup relations are profoundly significant for human well-being—and indeed, in the long run, for the survival of humanity.

Human beings readily learn in-group favoritism and bias. It is easy for them to form partisan distinctions between their own and other groups, to discriminate against other groups, to accept favorable evaluations of the products and performances of the in-group, and to accept unfavorable characterizations of other groups that go far beyond the objective evidence or the given situation. Experiments teach us how easily hostility forms and becomes deeply entrenched between groups and how unfairness exacerbates intergroup animosity. So, it is vital that schools and other child-rearing institutions provide a structure that encourages young people from different groups to reach valued common goals by transcending in-group bias in an atmosphere of collaboration, with a sense of belonging and a basis for hope in decent human relations.

Genocide-Prone Behavior in the Twentieth Century

What distinguished twentieth century genocides from genocides of the past? Have the newly labeled and increasingly frequent wars of "ethnic cleansing" set recent genocides apart from their predecessors? In a comparative analysis of ethnic cleansing in Europe during the twentieth century, Professor Norman Naimark of Stanford University addressed these and related questions.[15]

The term *ethnic cleansing* became part of our international consciousness when Serbians in Bosnia began the expulsion of Muslims in May 1992—as the first stage of their war. The Serbs first devised the term in the early 1980s to describe the Kosovar Albanian attack on the Serbs in neighboring Kosovo. Then it was applied to violence involving other peoples: against the Muslims by the Croats and against the Croats by the Serbs. The perpetrators were zealously determined to expel their victims from a territory they claimed as their own.

New terms are constantly being coined for old phenomena. At least since the beginning of recorded history, populations have been forcibly driven from their lands. *Ethnic cleansing,* the common name for this practice since 1992, is akin to *genocide,* a word Raphael Lemkin created during World War II to describe the Nazi Holocaust. The terms denote two related activities with a shared characteristic—intentionality to harm and remove a hated out-group. Whereas genocide is the intentional killing of an ethnic, religious, or national population in whole or in part, ethnic cleansing is the attempt to remove a people and every trace of their existence from a given territory. The goal of both is to dispose of the "alien" and claim their land and goods. The mildest form of ethnic cleansing is forced deportation; at the other extreme, it ripens into genocide, as killing becomes central to empty the land of a resistant people. So even if the initial intention of forced deportation is not murderous, the frequent result is genocide. In *The Wannsee Conference and the Final Solution,* Mark Roseman chronicled how the Nazis began with a policy of deportation of the Jews.[16] As this became more problematic, at Wannsee they proceeded to elaborate "the Final Solution." These phenomena are clearly related, and all too often, the first is seen years in advance as a pathway to the second. The definitions of how large a "part" of the group must be killed to qualify an act as genocide are necessarily fuzzy. In those atrocities, the intent is typically to drive out and/or destroy as large a part of the despised group as possible.

A characteristic of ethnic cleansing is the need to purge an "unclean" enemy from society, as witnessed in Russian, Serbo-Croatian, and German populations. Eugenics, a concept popularly embraced throughout Europe and the United States in the early twentieth century, was about racial cleansing. Use of the word *cleansing* has a double meaning: (1) purging the native community of its aliens, and (2) ridding one's own people of foreign elements. These beliefs support the personal acts of barbarism against neighbors and acquaintances.

Naimark placed twentieth-century ethnic cleansing in a distinct historical category influenced by certain characteristics of the state, the society, and the ideology of this period. The extreme nationalism that prevailed at the turn of the twentieth century fueled the brutal suppression of internal minority population groups and the potential for genocide. A tendency to homogenize the population was inherent in the increasingly concentrated power of twentieth-century states. Such power could provide distinctive popular benefits, including wide access to medical care, education, and general well-being. When this central power supported human dignity and human rights, citizens could use it to promote pragmatic problem solving and mutual tolerance. In less fortunate societies, state tyrants amplified popular fantasies of racial or ethnic degradation.

Ethnic cleansing, like genocide, requires wide use of broadcast media to promote the justification of deportation and to idealize the state through mass propaganda. World War I gave the modern nation-state an unprecedented opportunity to mobilize and engage the masses. It also made mass killing an acceptable routine.

Political leaders make ethnic cleansing possible by lighting the fires of resentment and hatred. But they do not act alone. They are supported by clients of the state and party—the police forces, the paramilitary and military, and supporting professionals such as lawyers, professors, doctors, and engineers. For example, Young Turk and Nazi doctors helped to develop ideologies of race. Radovan Karadzic, leader of the Bosnian Serbs and indicted war criminal, is a trained psychiatrist. Slobodan Milosevic had a law degree.

Comparative studies of ethnic cleansing also illuminate the slippery slope toward genocide and the formidable obstacles to preventing both horrors. State sovereignty makes it very difficult for international institutions to intervene, especially since their members are also sensitive to its claims and seldom define their own national interests in terms of promoting humanitarian values. Thus they feel disincentives to becoming involved in an effective and problem-solving way.

Naimark concluded that there are several elements common to twentieth-century ethnic cleansing: nationalistic violence, war, totality of displacement, destruction of monuments and memory, theft of property, and gender discrimination. Thus, there is no sharp borderline between ethnic cleansing, genocide, war, and other mass atrocities.

Ethnic cleansing always involves an armed perpetrator and a (mostly) unarmed victim. It is face to face, personal, and extremely vicious. Victims are seen as criminal and pay for their crime of being different.

Ethnic cleansings are closely linked to war. Like genocides, many happen during war or in the chaotic period between war and peace. War offers a convenient excuse for rulers to justify dealing with a "troublesome minority." At the start of World War I the Young Turks accused the Armenians of collaborating with their enemy, Russia. This provided the rationale for deporting them away from their homelands on the enemy's border. Nazis argued that the Jews supported both bolshevism and world capitalism, two mutually exclusive enemies of the Third Reich. Czechs and Poles after World War II claimed that rebuilding a stable east-central Europe hinged on the expulsion of their German minority populations. When Joseph Stalin and Lavrenty Beria deported the Chechens-Ingush and Crimean Tatars on charges of backing the Nazis, a strong unspoken incentive was the strategic geographic location and oil and gas riches of the lands from which the alleged sympathizers were expelled. Serbs carried out ethnic cleansing in the Bosnian war to win military security in the region and to protect their supply and communications lines.

Ethnic cleansing strives for total removal of every person belonging to a targeted group. Just as physical remnants are destroyed, so are language and culture, generally through the destruction of books, encyclopedias, and dictionaries. Names of towns and streets are changed, as are history books—and sometimes even gravestones and whole cemeteries.

Victims of ethnic cleansing are typically stereotyped as wealthy and eager to take advantage of their fellow citizens. This provides a fraudulent rationalization for the perpetrators to steal from their victims.

Women are special targets as breeders of the next generation of a despised people and as conduits to their children of their group's spiritual and cultural values. Furthermore, men who do not die in battle often emigrate first, hoping to send later for their wives and children, leaving their women exposed to attack. Harassment, humiliation, and rape are common crimes against women.

Naimark offered several reasons why he expected ethnic cleansing to continue in the foreseeable future. Rulers in some developing states continue to believe that modernization involves making the nation homogeneous by totally removing the "other" and seizing their property. Dictators frequently cling to the ideal of intense nationalism as a way to strengthen and maintain supremacy over their opposition, especially when that opposition belongs to an ethnic group other than their own and that of their supporters. They have powerful media at hand to mobilize populations. Countries with a weak civil society; a defective, disregarded, or absent constitution; and a poor economy can easily develop a harsh ideology and fall into the dangers of ethnic cleansing.

The twentieth century saw an international community impotent to stop or inhibit ethnic cleansing. One reason for this lack of international participation in the affairs of other nations was commitment to the putative "ideals" of Westphalian sovereignty, which allow tyrants freedom of action against their own people. The purpose of this book is to offer clear strategies, tools, and practices to prevent ethnic cleansing and above all, its first cousin, genocide.

How Can It Happen?

How is it possible that genocide and other mass violence should be so prevalent in a technically advanced world that calls itself civilized? Understanding the reasons must become a priority for research, education, and public policy.

Semantic ambiguity must not allow us to lose sight of our fundamental concern: the prevention of mass violence, especially mass murder, in its interrelated forms— especially genocide, war, and terrorism. This "family" of toxic human behavior patterns cries out for means of prevention. And yet the prevention of genocidal behavior is the great gap in this field of research. Even so, enough is known now to diminish greatly the occurrence of such behavior over the next few decades.

Professor James Waller, utilizing the work of many excellent behavioral scientists, has studied how ordinary people come to commit genocide and mass killing.[17] Since most societies do not commit genocide and most people do not become genocidal killers, Waller tried to explain how the elements of human nature and tendencies of individual human behavior as well as the mechanisms of social interaction within groups—and, especially, between in-groups and out-groups—come together in such a way that large numbers of ordinary people become perpetrators of genocide.

He effectively summarized the recent research findings of social psychologists and evolutionary scientists and organized them into a model that clarifies our understanding of how ordinary people come to participate in mass killing. His work agreed with the trajectory of this chapter and of our previous work on prevention of deadly conflict.

Under harsh, disappointing, frustrating, even humiliating conditions, the strong tendency in human behavior is to protect oneself and one's immediate family in survival terms; to protect the psychological self, the sense of worth as a person, the sense of still belonging to a valued group; to try to make frightening contemporary circumstances comprehensible or meaningful; and to find some framework in which to explain what is happening and how it might get better. It has always been too easy to look for scapegoats, readily available targets, to devalue certain specified out-groups perceived as dangerous or as responsible for the current difficulty—and in the process to join groups and adopt ideologies that justify harming those who are seen as the cause of the problems. Such frustrated and angry groups often stimulate the motivation to be aggressive toward out-groups and to harm the chosen scapegoats. These processes have been studied carefully by scholars in several disciplines, including, for example, distinguished social psychologist Professor Erwin Staub of Amherst.[18]

If a society has strongly depreciated and humiliated a particular group over a long period of time, and if that society places a strong value on obedience to authority; furthermore, if one or more of its mainstream in-groups hold beliefs about their own superiority, and yet they find themselves in distress, the conditions are ripe for violent assaults on a targeted victim group. Typically, this does not happen all at once. There is a gradual or stepwise progression of events until some fatal threshold can be passed, especially if there is no strong response from internal opponents or from outsiders who might be expected to object. A kind of habituation occurs in which small harmful acts come to seem familiar and acceptable. The larger harmful actions may then go forward, especially as justifications become more elaborate and familiar throughout the society. An ideology evolves that explains the whole problem and justifies the extensive harm being done to the target group. All too often, members of society who are not directly affected do very little to help the targets or uphold standards of common decency. Their passivity in the face of danger to others and the tacit acquiescence of outside groups—including nearby nations—make it easier for the damage to expand. On the other hand, active opposition by strong internal groups or by outside nations and international organizations can raise fears of retaliation or stir the moral values latent in the society. The considerations that apply to mass slaughter within a society also apply to the origins of war.

Under harsh conditions, it is very difficult to find a practical, positive course of action. A far simpler response is to turn against others, especially those already given a negative identity. It is easy to say "to survive, we must destroy those terrible people responsible for our situation; and when we do, we will enter a glorious new era."

Most societies have strong constraints against killing others, so potential genociders need to devise a process to overcome those inhibitions. Often leaders assume responsibility in the name of a higher good and find ways to diminish any sense of personal accountability among the public. Charismatic, inflammatory, and autocratic personalities qualify some individuals to take the role of leader. They select themselves and come forward. So do their principal followers: many early members of the Gestapo had long histories of violence, and the Nazi social code was entirely congenial to them.

Part of the process involves providing justification to bystanders for their passivity. This includes some denial of reality on the part of the public itself, as seen in the notoriously few people in Nazi Germany who allowed themselves to be aware of the slaughter going on in the concentration camps. They must also be made to devalue the targets still further. The genocidal propaganda is reframed in such a way that killing even comes to be seen as right, necessary, and praiseworthy.

Predisposing conditions to the Nazi Holocaust included an authoritarian culture, deeply embedded prejudices and ethnocentric orientation, and very difficult life conditions. Similar observations can be made about the Soviet Union right after World War I. There Stalin identified as the primary enemy those who had been wealthy and powerful under the tsarist regime rather than the Jews or other ethnic groups, who were secondary targets for abuse. His ideology justified violence in the name of social justice, to be achieved by the ruthless slaughter of those he accused of standing in its way. So, both in Germany and in the Soviet Union, millions perished in the name of a fancied higher good. Under both regimes, the ideology of violent out-group hatred was nurtured in childhood and strengthened in adolescence, especially in those selected by the ruling class as future leaders. The international community did little to oppose such growing hatred. This failure to intervene involved not only substantial denial of reality but also an underlying assumption that any killing would be restricted to other countries, mostly far away. That assumption turned out to be false, as must increasingly be the case in the highly interdependent, intimately connected world of the twenty-first century.

Leadership matters greatly in incitement to hatred and violence. Leaders with a wide variety of viewpoints and values competed for top positions in Germany and the Soviet Union during the 1920s, and the emergence of better leaders was conceivable. The ability of demagogic leaders to whip up and sustain widespread hatred and to implement genocidal programs is a crucial ingredient in the success of mass slaughter in the violence-drenched circumstances of war and revolution. The international community must find ways to recognize and strengthen the hand of moderate leaders and to thwart inflammatory leaders at an early stage.

The Preventive Orientation

Recently a variety of careful, multidisciplinary studies has enriched our understanding of genocides and "ethnic cleansing" throughout the twentieth century and into the twenty-first. These comparative, in-depth studies have significant implications for the prevention of genocide in the future.

In the 1960s and 1970s, genocide occurred in Indonesia, East Timor, Cambodia, Burundi, and Ethiopia. In the 1990s genocide came to Bosnia (1991–1995) and to Rwanda (culminating in 1994 with the slaughter of at least 10 percent of the population—about 800,000 people—in three months: see Chapter 5). Research on those atrocities has also contributed to our knowledge of the roots and processes of mass violence. Further understanding of genocide has also been provided by evidence from the archives of the former Soviet Union, illuminating the full scope of mass murders committed by the Soviets in the 1930s, during World War II, and in the postwar era.[19]

Research has placed a major focus on malevolent leadership. The more we can understand about how genocidal leaders made their ideologies and methods so compelling, the better our opportunity to foresee and prevent future genocidal episodes. Another focus of research is on the implementation of genocidal orders. Who does the killing and why?

Professor Eric D. Weitz made an important contribution to the understanding of genocide in *A Century of Genocide: Utopias of Race and Nation*.[20] By comparing four cases of genocide that took place in Nazi Germany, the Soviet Union under Vladimir Lenin and Joseph Stalin, the Khmer Rouge rule of Cambodia, and the former Yugoslavia, historian Weitz disentangled the common and unique qualities of each. The common features listed here suggest means of prevention that are potentially applicable worldwide:

1. The goal is to build a utopia in the near future, based on creating a homogeneous, superior ruling population. This overriding goal gives the regime the right or even

the duty to rid its country (or region or world) of any lesser beings that might serve as obstacles, threats, or contaminants.

2. Criteria are created to categorize the population rigidly and prejudicially by class, nationality, and race. (Other categories are also possible in this context, but whatever the category, the focus is on a harshly depreciated out-group.)

3. Genocide is gradually introduced and justified to the general public as circumstances permit. The chosen victim groups, already the objects of discrimination or exclusion, are vilified by propaganda. Repression and murder occur selectively at first as preparations are made for more extensive population purges.

4. There is a gradual movement from discrimination and isolated killings to more organized and systematic strategies of genocide. It takes time to create the logistics and machinery for large-scale implementation.

The years required to move these four categories into action offer possibilities for preventive actions by international organizations and democratic countries. All four genocides were extensive and highly organized policies of the state. The lethal reshaping of populations required cooperation among thousands of people over a period of years. Elaborate rituals were designed to rally large elements of the population. In all these cases of genocide, inflammatory use of radio, film, and print media, as well as roundups, deportations, and killings were obvious to the world. Thus, firm evidence of hatred and violence, influenced by hyperaggressive, hate-promoting leaders and mobilization for destruction gave highly significant warning long before it was too late for effective action.

Basing their ideologies in myths of race and/or nation, these genocidal regimes borrowed concepts from the Enlightenment, ideas of human progress, and nineteenth-century scientific advances to argue for improving the population. They maintained that certain segments of the population were incapable of improvement. These unredeemable groups varied with the genocidal regime in question but included the lower classes, the capitalist classes, Communists, the mentally ill, promiscuous women, homosexuals, the physically disabled, blacks, Jews, and criminals. Protecting society from those negative influences was the putative goal—purging a detested "racial" out-group. Once their differences were associated with race, it was easy to move from "race" to "underrace" and then to "subhuman."

The dominant group must come to see its potential victims as mortal threats (to make killing them an act of self-defense) or as subhuman, or both. Armenians, Jews, Bosnian Muslims, and Rwandan Tutsis were all portrayed as vermin: Julius Streicher, editor of the Nazi weekly *Der Stürmer*, called Jews "a germ and a pest, not a human being."[21]

Both the Nazi and Soviet regimes sprang from World War I. Its grand scale of killing inspired not only disgust but also fascination with, and lust for, power. Battlefield norms became the norms of politics[22]—complete with the use of brute force, violent conflict, and purging of populations—all putatively aimed at creating an improved social order, ethnocentric in character.

The regimes in Cambodia under the Khmer Rouge and in Serbia were also linked to recent wars. The Khmer Rouge was a radical example of a Communist movement that seized total power. It rid entire cities of their people and believed that efforts of will would double or even triple rice harvests. Yugoslavia, created as a result of World War I and

World War II, was an effort in the "postimperial national age" to form a multinational nation-state. Then Milosevic destroyed Yugoslavia's multinationality by using the brutal techniques employed by its old Communist rulers.

People were seduced into complicity for a variety of reasons: commitment to ideology and to new political regimes; the Nazi ideal of a pure society; the Communist ideal of an egalitarian society; or the Serbian perspective of the south Slav lands being controlled by a purely Serbian state. Psychological reasons included a desire for acceptance and belonging and the excitement and fulfillment of being associated with a winning group—at the dreadful expense of an out-group.

Phenomena such as roundups, deportations, and killings were similar in all four cases of genocide. These atrocities were possible because regimes granted complete powers to the extraordinarily inventive and ruthless perpetrators who acted as state agents. Perpetrators bonded together as a community with a kind of sacred cause (secular or religious) in the rituals of genocidal killings. Both men and women experienced such bonds. Women of the dominant group were rarely actively involved in brutality, but they often reveled as "complicit bystanders" in shows of violence as a manifestation of the strength of their valued group/beloved nation.

For genocide to emerge, there must be "historical junctures" that make it likely to occur. War and revolution are dehumanizing and destroy accepted norms of human interaction. Hence, there is a linkage between genocide and acute social crisis. Consider the Armenian genocide, which preceded but peaked during World War I; the Soviet expulsion of nationalities that began during the ten-year Great Transformation, whose huge disruptions created a social havoc that increased with the German invasion in World War II; Cambodia's purge of city people, minorities, and others labeled hostile to the new society, which occurred during U.S. bombings and new enthusiasms about revolutionary victory; and Bosnia and Kosovo, where Muslims were exposed to ethnic cleansing and systematic killing against the backdrop of the disintegration of Yugoslavia and violent wars of separation.

Incitement to Genocide

Susan Benesch's recent study of incitement to genocide in Rwanda is vividly informative.[23] In November 1991, she noted, the cover of *Kangura,* a Rwandan tabloid sympathetic to the Hutu, carried a picture of a machete. On its blade was written: "What weapons shall we use to conquer the *Inyenzi* once and for all?" *Inyenzi* (cockroaches), a slur used by Hutu leaders against rebel Tutsis in the 1960s, was being applied in the 1990s by hostile Hutus to all Tutsis.

In April 1994, after decades of continuing and escalating tensions between the Tutsis and Hutu that provided long-standing and ample warning of an impending crisis, the Rwandan armed forces, the presidential guard, and the ruling party's youth militia murdered about 800,000 Tutsis and moderate Hutus. Hassan Ngeze, the owner and editor of *Kangura,* had printed reams of anti-Tutsi vitriol, but he had not explicitly called for mass killing of Tutsi civilians. The International Criminal Tribunal for Rwanda indicted him in 1997 for incitement to genocide. Three judges had to decide whether he could be held responsible for the killings or whether his anti-Tutsi venom was simply an exercise in freedom of speech. Ngeze was tried along with the two founders of the radio station, Radio Télévision Libre des Mille Collines (RTLM), whose anti-Tutsi diatribes were even more inflammatory than Ngeze's: they had read out the names of people they thought should be killed, along with their automobile license plate numbers, so they could be spotted easily if they tried to escape. At the end of the three-year trial the judges—a Sri Lankan, a South African, and a Norwegian—issued a landmark ruling in international law in finding all three defendants guilty of the deaths of thousands of innocent civilians.

RTLM was so incendiary that the United States considered "jamming" its signal but never did. Indeed, the use of "jamming" devices to block incitements to genocide is an option that deserves serious consideration by the international community. In a speech over RTLM in 1994, Prime Minister Jean Kambanda called the station's continuing incitement to massacres "an indispensable weapon" against the "enemy."[24]

Incitement is a hallmark, and perhaps a prerequisite, of genocide. Every modern case of genocide has been preceded by a mass media propaganda campaign directed by political leaders. Days after the Nazis first gained power in 1933, Joseph Goebbels began to shut down anti-Nazi presses. Throughout the rest of the 1930s the Nazi-controlled media dispensed continuous anti-Semitic slurs, many taken from *Mein Kampf,* published years earlier in 1924. Numerous serious people foresaw the danger already in the 1920s: statesmen, diplomats, scholars, and journalists. Their warnings were drowned out for a variety of reasons that we shall consider in Chapter 4, on the Holocaust.

In the early 1990s, extremist Serbian forces gained control of so many television transmitters in Bosnia and Herzegovina that large areas received Serb-managed television only, which portrayed Croats and Muslims as a threat to the nation and urged the necessity of war for the sake of the people.[25]

As Benesch pointed out, recognizing the crucial importance of incitement in causing genocide does not ignore the role of long-standing prejudices. Incitement produces the fiercest results when the prejudices are already there and the listeners are receptive to hate speech. Nor does pleading incitement absolve people who participate in genocide from responsibility for their acts. In highlighting the influence of the media on people's actions, one is only recognizing that people do not spontaneously rise up en masse to kill. Incitement by leaders is a key step in the process. Because the act of genocide requires the participation of many, and not just an elite, a large number of people must come to condone killing.

Thus, incitement to violence against a particular group—clearly, vividly, intensely, and persistently expressed over extended time in various modalities—can have lethal effect. It is mentioned in the statutes of international tribunals and in the Genocide Convention as "direct and public incitement to genocide." Incitement also provides an important opportunity for preventive action before it is too late—for those who are *ready* to prevent. As we shall see, the best opportunities come long before incitement has put potential killers on the verge of explosion.

The international community stands warned. The years required to go from the initial jeopardy to full genocide offer an interval for the international community—if it is alert, well informed, morally committed, and organizationally prepared—to take preventive actions.

Further Observations on Predisposing Factors to Genocide-Prone Behavior

Many social and political elements can fuel mass murder—historical grievances and enmities; recent or bitterly rankling social traumas; arrogant elites prospering in the midst of widespread poverty; poor governance; poor education (including strong prejudice); rapid political, social, or economic dislocation; colonial occupation; war; and revolution.[26] These predisposing factors occur in various combinations, often reinforcing each other.

At the beginning of the twentieth century, the emergence of total wars that sucked in all noncombatants was facilitated by technological advances—mass production of light and heavy arms and other military matériel; development of weapons of mass destruction, including poison gas and biological weapons; rapid transportation by road and rail; and instant communication by means of radios, telegraphs, and telephones. National states, many with militarized bureaucracies and/or totalitarian tendencies, expected every citizen to be at the very least a patriot, often with strong chauvinistic connotation. Thus, whole populations became active aids to war or mass violence. Men who were old or otherwise unsuitable for conscription might serve the war effort in nonmilitary ways; women were viewed as industrial workers and mothers of future soldiers; and children, as future soldiers or future mothers/workers. The other side of this coin was dark indeed: whole populations were fair game for attack. In the case of state-sponsored genocides, incitement made them targets of mass murder.[27]

The Young Turks, Nazis, and Khmer Rouge all thrived in wartime conditions that allowed them to seize power, recruit followers, demand unquestioning support, inculcate fear and suspicion against groups they identified as dangers to the common welfare, censor reports of their own atrocities while they fabricated reports of their victims' crimes, and finally, to carry out mass deportations and slaughter. The social context of war and/or revolution erodes norms of restraint and codes of ethical behavior. Modern, technologically advanced methods of warfare have accelerated the slide to mass murder even as they conceal it. A related concern is the contemporary tendency of poor, developing countries worldwide to be sucked into unregulated civil conflict that traps and then trains teens—and even preteens—to be obedient and callous murderers.

From the long-term viewpoint, extensive poverty and drastic inequity, declining quality of life, rapid political or social change, and sharp economic downturns can create a sense of crisis that makes a population ready to scapegoat a vulnerable out-group and softens popular reluctance to kill others.

But even if these factors facilitate mass violence, they need not lead inevitably to genocide. Genocides are precipitated by leaders of extremist and violent political or religious sects or regimes who take advantage of predisposing elements and cultural myths, then skillfully work on them to incite their population to genocide. Of course, genocidal leaders do not have to be convinced fanatics (such as Adolf Hitler, Joseph Stalin, or Mao Zedong); they only need to be ruthless opportunists (such as Enver Pasha or Omar Hassan al-Bashir), who choose genocide as a convenient policy option that will allow them to seize or maintain power by quashing their opposition, solidifying their power base, and diverting attention from their own misrule. This readily happens in harshly autocratic or deteriorating governments. Thus, there is an intricate interplay of predisposing and precipitating factors.

In a comparative analysis of modern genocides, Professor Yehuda Bauer, a renowned historian and director of the International Institute for Holocaust Research at Jerusalem's Yad Vashem, described the Holocaust as an entirely explicable event that can be put into a historical perspective.[28] Bauer emphasized two conclusions: first, and most important, genocidal killing requires cooperation between the "leadership elite," the intelligentsia, and the masses; and second, efforts at preventing another Holocaust would benefit from an in-depth comparison of Germany during its societal crisis of the early 1930s with other societies suffering similar crises. Bauer pointed out that in the case of the Holocaust, the Nazis conceived a distinct plan for the complete physical annihilation of the Jews that was based on the creation of a totally new hierarchy made up of races, not on a reordering of social classes, religions, or nations. The "invented" master race would then be entitled to rule over everyone else and to enslave or murder all those who appeared to be different.[29]

The recurring and deeply plaguing question is how could the Germans—a highly cultured people—be convinced to become partners with their criminal leaders to engage in committing the worst crime in history? Ian Kershaw and Peter Merkl, distinguished scholars of the Nazi regime, have tried to answer this question.[30] In their view, the two main factors that led to mass killing were prejudiced consensus and propaganda. In the context of the failing Weimar Republic, the people voted "Nazi" because of the promise of a better Germany—one that could be economically revived and free from social crisis. There was a promise of utopia. Some of the elite were radical anti-Semites as a result of nineteenth-century influence, and many also subscribed to a "general racist ideology." This made it feasible for a Nazi layer of leaders to convert many German citizens into criminals. This horror was made possible because the masses would not meaningfully oppose such action owing to entrenched, traditional anti-Semitism as well as wishful thinking about Hitler's putative utopia.[31]

Bauer's emphatic conclusion is that when elites attain power with the goal of inflicting genocide on a targeted minority population, it is likely to occur if it meets no popular opposition and if there is a "psychological capture" of the intelligentsia.[32] Altogether, recent research illuminates variations on basic themes of predisposition to genocide.

Finding effective ways both to identify and to check violent, hate-mongering, extremist leaders and the conditions that nurture them before they take root demands interdisciplinary and comparative research to clarify basic issues of danger. It also requires international cooperation (over years, before the carnage) to use the knowledge for prevention, for meeting basic human needs, and for building decent intergroup relations.

CHAPTER 3

~ ~

An Illustrative Genocide

The Armenians

Precursor to Genocide: The Sick Man of Europe

From 1894 to 1896 the Ottoman sultan Abdul Hamid II was directly responsible for the massacre of perhaps as many as 100,000 of his Armenian subjects and indirectly responsible for an additional 100,000 deaths due to accompanying famine and disease.[1] U.S. and European attention was riveted first on the "Bloody Sultan's" atrocities during the 1890s and then on the culmination of these atrocities, beginning in 1915 in the *Armenian genocide* directed by the Young Turks. The two-decade prelude to the final genocide gave ample warning for prevention. Although most histories center largely or solely on the later period, popular concern about Armenian suffering was intense in the West from the 1890s through the 1920s.

Coexistence among the diverse peoples of the Ottoman Empire was based, as the Turkish historian Taner Akçam puts it, on "humiliation and toleration."[2] Non-Muslims were tolerated and allowed economic privileges, freedom from Islamic law (Sharia) and military service, and some self-rule on condition that they paid special taxes and accepted a visibly inferior position—expressed, for example, in restrictions against building new churches or synagogues, riding horses, living in houses taller than those of neighboring Muslims, testifying in court against Muslims, using arms to resist Muslim aggression, and even carrying arms. The clothing of non-Muslims was prescribed according to faith or ethnic affiliation and had to be distinct from that of Muslims.

Many Muslims viewed these restrictions and distinctions as part of a social pact reflecting a divine order and accordingly saw non-Muslim demands for equality as a violation of that pact. Muslims' hostility to egalitarian reform rose with their perception that many of the groups demanding it were at the same time reluctant to forgo their own traditional privileges, of which the most galling to Muslims were perhaps exemption from military duty and the protection of non-Muslims by Western states.

In the nineteenth century, as European ideals of nationalism and freedom spread, the empire's non-Muslim communities sought for themselves the basic rights and equality they saw respected in the West. Their repeated demands were met with repeated bloody repression from the sultan, and this gave European states, greedy for Ottoman lands, further opportunities to intervene in the name of humanitarianism. Wars with Europe that ended in humiliating defeats and loss of territory for the empire were followed by what were perceived as even more humiliating treaties that demanded reforms in the treatment of despised minorities. Muslims, whose strong ethnic and religious pride in their illustrious past was already raw and bruised by misrule, economic distress, military rout, and territorial loss, looked on the rising power and success of non-Muslims in the empire with a resentment not unlike that of southern whites in the United States toward blacks during Reconstruction and the civil rights struggle. Allowing a despised out-group to rise added personal social decline to their other humiliations.[3]

The feelings these rankling circumstances aroused, shrewdly exploited by Ottoman rulers to cover up their own disastrous misrule, help to explain the enthusiasm with which Muslims participated in atrocities, even though they surely do not justify or pardon them.

The sultan's massacres began in the spring of 1894, when Armenians in the area of Sasun protested extortionate taxation and resisted an abusive government official. Ottoman troops and their Kurdish contingents retaliated with an attack that left 3,000 Armenians dead.[4] A twenty-three-day slaughter resumed in August—regular Ottoman troops and the sultan's personal *hamidiye* regiments attacked Armenian peasants, alleging that they were rebelling against the Ottoman government. Containment of a revolt over taxes became an excuse to expand and continue the murders, as the world watched. A U.S. magazine reported that both insurgents and loyal taxpayers were treated alike.[5] When one village sent a priest and some elders, carrying tax receipts as proof of their payment, to meet the invading Ottoman troops, the village was surrounded and every inhabitant slaughtered.

These clear and vivid early warning signals of approaching genocide elicited European protests that forced the Ottoman government to conduct a formal inquiry into what it called "criminal proceedings of the Armenian brigands." The inquiry, which refused to hear Armenian evidence, was denounced internationally as a whitewash. England, France, and Russia sent consular representatives to Sasun to gather impartial evidence. C. M. Hallward, the British vice consul, estimated a death toll of 8,000 and rejected Istanbul's claim that the incident had been a rebellion rather than a massacre.[6] His published report demanded implementation of the human rights reforms in Armenia to which the sultan had already been compelled to agree in the treaties of San Stefano and Berlin in 1878 after defeat in the Russo-Turkish war.

A month before the time the sultan had promised those reforms would take effect, violence prevented their implementation. The sultan's calculated delays in producing reform led the Armenian nationalist Hunchak Party to hold a demonstration in Constantinople on October 1, 1895, to protest the Sasun massacres and gain European sympathy and support for Ottoman Armenians in their continuing plight. The demonstrators presented a petition with demands for fair taxation; guarantees of freedom of conscience and of public assembly; equality before the law; protection of life, person, and property; the right to bear arms for self-defense; and an end to persecution, mass political arrests, and torture. The demonstrators were attacked, and citywide slaughter continued for ten days despite repeated protests from foreign embassies. Massacres spread throughout the empire from October 1895 through January 1886—especially in those provinces (vilayets) where reforms had been promised.[7] These events were clear signals of worse to come.

The response from Europe and the United States was extensive humanitarian relief. By the end of 1895, broad coverage in magazines and newspapers caused Armenian relief organizations to spring up everywhere in the United States. A local New York City organization quickly grew into the National Armenian Relief Committee, led and supported by some of the most influential businessmen and church leaders in the United States. In 1896 the United States made Thanksgiving Day a national day of observance of the massacres.[8]

Perhaps the first use of the word *holocaust* to describe a human rights disaster appeared in a front-page headline of the *New York Times* on September 10, 1895.[9] An angry series on "The Armenian Troubles" running from 1895 to 1896 in *Harper's Weekly* gained wide readership with its vivid illustrations. The London *Graphic* outdid *Harper's* by printing actual photographs of slaughtered children and women.[10] In November 1895 historian James Bryce published an article in a U.S publication, *Century Magazine,* that called on the American people to save Armenia from extinction.[11]

In 1896, Senator Shelby Collum (R-IL) sponsored a resolution that urged Europe to ensure the just treatment of Armenians in accordance with Turkey's treaty obligations. The resolution passed both houses, but President Grover Cleveland refused to act on it, fearing that it would only cause the offended sultan to block humanitarian aid to the Armenians.[12] Then in August 1896 protesters from another Armenian political party occupied the Imperial Ottoman Bank in Constantinople to once again dramatize Armenian troubles to the world. A wholesale citywide massacre of Armenians followed that left an estimated 6,000 dead.[13] For two days after the demonstration Armenians were massacred in the streets of the capital by killers outfitted and encouraged by the sultan. Then he commanded the bloodshed to stop, and it stopped.

Abdul Hamid quickly began another round of massacres, purportedly to put down an Armenian rebellion that independent witnesses agreed never occurred. Johannes Lepsius, a German cleric who visited the Armenian provinces in 1896, estimated that 150,000 Armenians had been butchered and another 150,000 had died of the disease and famine that followed.[14] He explicitly placed responsibility for the Armenian massacres on the central government, calling the murders "nothing but an administrative measure" ordered in the name of the sultan and enthusiastically carried out by district officials. He attributed local Muslim participation to active encouragement by government authorities, the legitimation of violence in the name of the sultan and of Islam, and the opportunity for plunder without fear of resistance. A British vice consul sent to the Armenian provinces to investigate agreed in an 1896 report that the massacres—and incitement to commit them—had been centrally planned.[15]

Western outrage grew. In 1896, Americans Henry and William James decried English and U.S. passivity and called for united military intervention.[16] Stephen Crane rebuked the leaders of Europe for protesting rather than acting.[17] In 1903 Charlotte Perkins Gilman insisted presciently that crimes such as the Armenian massacres called for a system of international law "to restrain, prohibit, punish; best of all, to prevent."[18]

Estimates of the total number of massacre victims vary widely, from 50,000 to 300,000 dead or between 2 and 12 percent of the Armenian population.[19] (Probably around 10 percent is an accurate estimate.)

"Someone Has Got to Govern Turkey; Why Not We?"

In 1908 a coup allowed Sultan Abdul Hamid to remain in office but forced him to give up all political power.[20] The revolution that the coup set off brought to power the Committee of Union and Progress (CUP—best known as the Young Turks). At first they were not sure how to use their new authority. They tried reinstituting the liberal Ottoman constitution of 1876, but military defeat abroad and the demands of minorities at home turned them briefly to Pan-Islam.[21] They ultimately replaced those two ideas of state and society—both of which would have allowed Armenians to remain a part of the empire—with an extreme Turkish nationalism based on an exclusionary political myth of racial preeminence. Their new concept of "Turk" excluded all minorities but targeted especially the Armenians, increasingly seen as enemies who had to be destroyed.[22]

Professor Ronald Suny of the University of Michigan, a distinguished scholar of the Armenian experience, summarized the situation:[23]

> After centuries of governing the Armenians as a separate ethno-religious community, ... and conceiving of them as the "loyal millet," the Ottoman state authorities and Turkish political elites, including the Young Turks, began to see Armenians as an alien people, ... disloyal, subversive, "separatist," and a threat to the unity of the empire. This perception was compounded more broadly by anxiety about the relative economic success of Armenian businessmen and craftsmen, the competition for the limited economic resources, particularly land, between Kurds, Turks, and Armenians in eastern Anatolia, and a sense that Armenian progress was reversing the traditional imperial status hierarchy with Muslims above the *dhimmi.*

At first the Armenian political parties were delighted with the CUP-led victory in 1908. On August 4, 1908, the British ambassador reported that several thousand Armenians and Turks assembled to visit the graves of Armenian victims of the 1895 and 1896 massacres, and both Christian and Muslim clergy offered prayers over the dead.[24] Henry Morgenthau, an observant, humane, and resourceful public servant during his term as U.S. ambassador to Turkey from 1913 to 1917, painted the same picture of hope and cooperation:

> Armenian leaders had figured conspicuously in the Young Turk movement; these men apparently believed that a constitutional Turkey was possible. They were conscious of their own intellectual and industrial superiority to the Turks, and knew that they could prosper in the Ottoman Empire if left alone, whereas, under European control, they would have greater difficulty in meeting the competition of ... European colonists who might come in.[25]

When they first took power, the Young Turks' coalition included representatives of minority parties as well as Turkish moderates who planned to create a modern empire by introducing secular and Western values. Prince Sabaheddin supported liberal economic and political reforms and was sympathetic to some demands for greater minority autonomy. Rising young officers such as Enver Pasha and Talaat Pasha were pragmatists (or perhaps opportunists), inevitably focused, because of their background, on the empire's military status. They were open to any political ideas that could unite and strengthen the state—under their rule.

Events quickly deteriorated. In October 1912, after answering a number of uprisings with massacres, the Ottoman Empire declared war on Bulgaria and Serbia, and Greece responded by declaring war on the Ottoman Empire. Within a month the Ottomans suffered total defeat.

The Balkan wars lost the empire 70 percent of its European population and 85 percent of its European territory. After the Balkan wars, the only European land the Young Turks still held was a strip around the straits of Istanbul.[26] These losses, which removed a number of minority populations along with the European territory, inclined the CUP's leaders toward replacing pluralistic Ottomanism with a huge, exclusionary Pan-Turkish empire.[27] The Armenians became a rival nationality, the most dangerous in the empire, since their traditional Anatolian homeland was both the core of "Turkey," as newly invented by extreme nationalists, and was situated on the borders of enemy Russia. The Armenian aptitude for modernization, nurtured by their renaissance, seemed yet another threat to the dominance of nationalistic Turkish leaders.

Thus, territorial losses had crucial consequences both for the situation of the Armenians and for the evolution of the Young Turk ideology. Pan-Turkism preached that all Turkic-speaking peoples must unite in one political entity. Since Turkic-speaking peoples occupied an area as vast as the former Ottoman Empire, the theory of Pan-Turkism captivated nationalistic Young Turk leaders because it promised the old empire's territorial breadth without its minority problems. It also left minorities like the Armenians with very limited rights.

The Armenians had no desire to secede or join Russia. They knew that Russian control would not give them more freedom. But their continuing demands for more autonomy and for protection from the Kurds led England and other European powers—including Turkey's enemy Russia—to intervene. In February 1914, they pressured the CUP into appointing European inspectors to oversee relations between the vilayets. The mortified and increasingly rigid Young Turk leadership feared an imposition of reforms that would lead to a repeat of the Balkan humiliation and reacted by creating a sophisticated network of party branches in the provinces, dedicated to promoting extreme Turkish nationalism. It began indoctrination and paramilitary training for Turkish youth comparable to Hitler's later German youth programs. The Association for the Promotion of Turkish Strength, established in 1913, was intended to revive a mythic "warrior nation" through military training of Turkish youth. The War Ministry also sponsored paramilitary youth groups, supplying them with free rifles and ammunition to ready them for defense of the fatherland.

Like the Nazis, who called the Jew a "harmful bacillus," Pan-Turkish propagandists considered Armenians an invasive infection in Turkish society. Mehmed Reshid, a Turkish physician who became governor of Diyarbekir, compared Armenians to "dangerous microbes" that doctors had a duty to destroy. Nicknamed the "executioner governor," he was responsible for the death and deportation of many Armenians as well as for their torture by crucifixion and shoeing with horseshoes.[28]

Genocide-Prone Ideologies

Ben Kiernan found four ideological elements common to twentieth-century genocides, in different combinations—race, religion, territorial expansion, and attachment to the soil. Young Turk ideologues intertwined race and religion, looking toward a vast territorial expansion. Kiernan emphasized that prevention is enhanced if common features of the perpetrator's genocidal obsessions can be identified in advance.[29]

We have seen how territorial losses made expansionism an important part of the Young Turks' agenda. Turkish nationalists hoped to accomplish their dream of a vast "Pan-Turanian" empire in 1917–1918, when they invaded Russian Armenia after the collapse of the tsarist armies in the Caucasus and continued their massacre of Armenians, including some of the 300,000 Armenians who had fled massacres in the Ottoman Empire in 1915.

The exclusionary, intolerant, and ultimately lethal direction that Turkish nationalism took was not inevitable. The failure of the liberal nationalism of Prince Sabahaddin, and the liberals' fall from power, opened the way for the rise of Pan-Turkism and the Armenian genocide. "*Had the Great Powers,* even without Russia and Austria, *helped Turkish democracy* to establish itself, it is likely that even then the empire would have undergone grave tribulations, but the *Armenian Genocide possibly could have been averted.*"[30] (Emphasis added.)

CHAPTER 4

An Illustrative Supergenocide

The Holocaust

Nature and Scope of the Disaster

The Holocaust was an immense crime against humanity and is the quintessential genocide. It sought the annihilation of the entire Jewish population of Europe. It was the deliberate policy decision of a powerful state that mobilized all of its resources to destroy an entire people. They were killed not for what they had done but for the simple fact of their existence. Gypsies, Russians, Poles, and other eastern European peoples, and even ethnic Germans deemed physically or mentally defective were also victims of Nazi racial ideology. Nazi military, police officials, and guards practiced highly organized brutality on a previously unknown scale. Why were Jews worked to death on senseless, unproductive tasks when the Reich had an acute labor shortage? Why were skilled Jewish armament workers killed despite pressing military needs of the Wehrmacht? Why did the Nazis insist they were fighting an omnipotent Jewish power even as their mass murder of Jews revealed their enemy's powerlessness? Professor Robert Wistrich thoughtfully addressed these questions in 2001, drawing on decades of research on the Holocaust.[1]

The Nazis' millenarian worldview saw Jews as the source of all evils—especially internationalism, pacifism, democracy, and Marxism. They were declared responsible for Christianity, the Enlightenment, and Freemasonry. They were identified with urban civilization's fragmentation, rationalism, and moral laxity. They were said to stand behind the "rootless cosmopolitanism" of international capital and the threat of world revolution. Hitler's racist ideology and personal obsession insisted that the redemption of "Aryan" humanity depended on a Final Solution of the Jewish question. World War II was at once a war for territory and a battle against the Jewish minority throughout Europe.[2]

War made the Holocaust possible, though there were terrible prewar precursors. The grand scheme of degradation was published in 1924 in Hitler's *Mein Kampf*—years before he came to power—hence vivid warning.

The Holocaust required more than ideology to be implemented. It was also the product of the most technologically developed society in Europe, with a highly organized bureaucracy. The streamlined, industrialized mass killings carried out in death camps such as Auschwitz-Birkenau and Treblinka went beyond previous genocides in world history. But millions of Jews were also killed in more primitive ways in Russia, eastern Europe, and the Balkans. The Einsatzgruppen and police hunted down Jews and executed them in pit killings in forests, ravines, and trenches. Russian, Poles, Serbs, and Ukrainians also perished in the same manner. Three million Soviet prisoners of war died in German captivity.

Germany before 1933 was a state based on the rule of law, where despite long-standing prejudice, Jews had achieved remarkable economic success, were integrated into society, enjoyed intellectual and scientific accomplishment, and helped shape its modern culture. Hitler's rise to power would not have been possible without the humiliating German defeat in World War I, embodied in the Treaty of Versailles; the economic crises of the postwar Weimar Republic; and fear of Communist revolution. Anti-Semitism, even though central to Hitler and the Nazi leadership, was not the Nazi's main vote getter. But when Hitler came to power, racist anti-Semitism became the official state ideology of the Third Reich, reinforced by incessant, virulent propaganda and anti-Jewish laws.

The receptiveness of Germans and other Europeans to the demonization of Jews owed much to an older tradition of Christian anti-Judaism. Nazism, though it intended ultimately to uproot Christianity, built on age-old Christian prejudice against Jews.

Though Germans were the Holocaust's driving force, they found many willing collaborators among Lithuanians, Latvians, Ukrainians, Hungarians, Romanians, Croats, and others. Austrians (who had been annexed to the Reich in 1938) formed a disproportionate number of the Schutzstaffel (SS) killers, death camp commandants, and personnel involved in the Final Solution. Even official France collaborated, not in killing, but in deportation and in passing anti-Jewish legislation.

The Holocaust was a Europe-wide event that could not have happened unless millions of Europeans had wished to see an end to the age-old Jewish presence in their midst. This consensus was especially strong in the countries of east central Europe, where most Jews lived and kept their own cultural distinctiveness. But anti-Semitism was growing in western Europe and the United States, tied to hardships caused by the Great Depression, fear of immigrants, politically stimulated xenophobia, and the influence of fascist ideas.

This hostility is seen in the reluctance of British and U.S. policymakers to try to rescue European Jews from the Holocaust. Hitler inferred from these responses that he could continue his expansionism without risk and that the West would not interfere with his increasingly radical anti-Jewish measures. Plundering Jewish assets was an integral part of early Nazi policy and made Nazism attractive to many non-Jews. By 1939 it was clear that wartime conditions would greatly facilitate ethnic cleansing of Jews, Gypsies, and German "defectives."

All the resources of the modern German state were at the disposal of the SS in the death camps for the purpose of racial murder. Raul Hilberg observed that the machinery of destruction was German society organized as a whole.[3] Trains to the death camps would not have run without the indirect involvement of tens of thousands of Germans. Mass destruction utilized a highly bureaucratized, methodical society, modern in its systematic division of responsibilities and routinizing of operations.

Throughout his career Hitler pursued a policy of deliberate incitement against Jews while he left the execution of his policy to subordinates, depending on the long history of European anti-Semitism as a solid underpinning for mass murder. There is no reasonable way to blur the decisive role of Hitler and his close associates in initiating, centralizing, and unifying the multitude of regional actions.

The Holocaust was unprecedented in the hideous scale of the suffering inflicted on the victims and the depravity of their tormentors. Sadism and torture were common and were carried out with enthusiasm.[4] For the SS, to torture and destroy was a proof of maturity and superiority.

Primo Levi emphasized how the camp system sought to maximize the degradation of its victims by making them participate in their own victimization. Perhaps the most demonic of the Nazi crimes was giving their victims the filthiest part of their work: running the crematoriums, extracting corpses from the gas chambers, and pulling the gold teeth from the jaws of victims.[5]

Hitler admired Stalin. Before they started their own program of concentration camps, the Nazis studied closely how the Soviets had destroyed millions of people through forced labor in the gulags. The result was not total imitation; no industrialized killing process occurred in the Gulags. But Margerete Buber-Newmann, a survivor of both, observed that it was not easy to say which was less humane—immediate death in a gas chamber or a slow death from hunger.[6]

Stalin did not set out deliberately to murder the gulag population, because he needed them as slave labor to modernize Russia. He used Soviet camps to eliminate political enemies, and millions died there, but the camps were oriented to the production of wealth and the industrialization of a backward country. Mining of gold and other minerals and felling of timber for export were integral parts of the gulags. Thus, the two most destructive dictators of the twentieth century provided variations on the theme of mass murder.

Yehuda Bauer specified distinctive features of the Holocaust:

- People were killed merely for being born with grandparents of a certain lineage—Jewish.
- The killing was international in scope.
- The Nazi ideology bore no relation to reality.
- Although the Nazis did not invent the concentration camp, they used it to subject its inmates to a new level of humiliation.
- The Nazis left nothing positive behind them—only death camps and mass murder.[7]

How, then, can we explain the Nazis? There are many contributing factors. Bauer argued that a pseudointellectual elite took control in Germany, not because they had popular support for a murderous ideology but because they promised to lead the public out of the catastrophe in which Germany found itself after World War I into a "wonderful utopia." "The determining factor [of Nazi success] was that the layer of intellectuals—the academicians, the teachers, the students, the bureaucrats, the doctors, the lawyers, the churchmen, the engineers—joined the Nazi Party because it promised them a future and a status."[8] By identifying these intellectuals, professionals, and civil servants with the regime and publicizing their consensus for Nazi rule, the new government could convince the public that genocide was an unavoidable step toward achieving this utopia and enlist their services in carrying it out.

The churches, despite the gospel of love they preached and the Messiah they worshiped, remained silent about—if they did not collaborate in—the slaughter of his people by baptized murderers.

The Holocaust is remembered throughout the world as a universal symbol of evil because it represents the most extreme form of genocide, because it contains elements that are unprecedented, and because its victims, the Jews, had been significant contributors to modern civilization since the beginning of history.[9]

Missed Opportunities for Prevention

Ironically, the very fact that all of the democracies were sickened by the destruction caused by World War I and fearful of a recurrence made them ill-equipped to prevent it. Strong, popular pacifist movements arose that would later make vigorous diplomatic and military stances against aggression difficult. The European countries could not develop effective strategies of cooperation that might prevent genocidal behavior and war. And the League of Nations, which represented the first tentative effort in history to create a worldwide institution for international cooperation, was a much weaker body than today's UN even at its inception, before it became evident that the United States would not be a member. Nothing remotely comparable to the European Union existed. World War I may have chastened the nations of Europe and made them dread further armed conflict, but it had not taught them to stop viewing each other with reciprocal suspicion and feelings of rivalry (and, in the case of Germany, desire for revenge on all sides).

The bitter recollections of war and the greedy self-interested squabbles at the peace negotiations after it ended were two major reasons why the world's two leading democracies, Britain and the United States, returned to isolationism and disengagement from continental European affairs during the 1920s. Then came the devastating worldwide depression. Germany, already strapped with payment of reparations, was hit especially hard, but economic collapse also severely exacerbated existing internal class divisions throughout the West and turned the focus of almost all governments to domestic affairs during the early 1930s.

Western leaders were aware from the start of Hitler's worldview. *Mein Kampf,* published in 1924, vividly outlined Hitler's plan for a racially cleansed Europe under German domination. The dangers that German fascism and Hitler presented were quickly laid bare by a number of thoughtful statesmen and writers in the established democracies—notably, but not only, Winston Churchill. By and large these clear early warnings were dismissed in London, Paris, and Washington, where government leaders took it for granted that sober businessmen, the military, and other powerful interests in German society would eventually moderate Hitler's excesses. Throughout the West a lack of concern about what was happening in Germany pervaded governments, the media, and the general public.

In the beginning, Hitler's lawless rule even won a degree of sympathy. A number of foreign observers agreed with the majority of Germans that the weak and fractious Weimar Republic had met a predictable, even desirable end. Western conservatives were inclined to excuse—and in some instances, even admire—the style of fascism promoted by Hitler in Germany and Mussolini in Italy. Since the 1920s Western statesmen had been concerned that Germany might turn sharply toward the left (a concern that did not extend so far that they helped the weak Weimar Republic out of its dire economic situation). Hitler's Third Reich not only promised a stable Germany; his rabid antagonism to communism also made Nazi power seem a welcome bulwark against Marxist expansion in Eastern Europe.[10] Furthermore, throughout the West the targets of German aggression attracted painfully little sympathy—European Jews, long objects of widespread prejudice; Gypsies, universally vilified; Socialists and Communists, whom many feared far more than they feared the Nazis; and the vulnerable countries of eastern Europe, most of them unstable, fragile former territories of defunct empires, distant and politically insignificant. Even after Germany was finally acknowledged as a dangerous threat, many "leaders" still hoped that someone else, perhaps the USSR, perhaps decent and sensible Germans, would take the initiative and responsibility for checking Nazi ambitions.[11]

Today, historians such as R.A.C. Parker argue that had the West adopted the firm policies of deterrence advocated by Winston Churchill, World War II might well have been avoided.[12] But in the early 1930s, when determined, concerted preventive action could have had a real effect, other matters seemed more urgent than a ranting man with a comical moustache, who was, after all, restoring order and stability to his failing country. Serious political and economic action was not taken until the only response left was military action of unprecedented force—the catastrophe of World War II.

Narrow and short-term conceptions of national interest reinforced the West's failure to appreciate the true extent of the danger. The 1930s were a dangerous time. As on the eve of World War I, the distribution of international power and colonial wealth established in the nineteenth century was being challenged by ambitious nations. Germany, Italy, the USSR, and Japan—who had modernized or unified only after Britain and France had already built their colonial empires—all felt that as latecomers they were being unfairly denied their proper high status in the world order. Britain and France continued their efforts to preserve or improve their own global position. They did not recognize in Adolf Hitler a man who was more than willing to use massive violence not only to persecute his "internal enemies" but also to change forcefully the existing international order in his favor. What was needed was strong multilateral cooperation to mount a credible deterrence to his aggression. Just at that time, however, a retreat into isolation, in Europe but especially in the United States, had weakened international efforts at cooperation and opened the way for Hitler's bold, ruthless strokes. This isolationism further incapacitated the already feeble League of Nations, the one organization that might have been used to mobilize an effective, united opposition to Hitler.[13] No nation was willing to stand up to Hitler alone, and the West had abandoned its commitment to international cooperation and its avowed sense of responsibility for weaker nations. Nations large and small lacked the capacity and tools for effective preventive action.

Recent historians emphasize the powerful impact internal matters had on English and French policy in the 1930s (matters still important to this day in every country). The effects of the Great Depression and concerns about safeguarding their empires shaped the responses of those two nations to fascist aggression. Any benefit they imagined they might gain from checking Hitler, Mussolini, and Hirohito was balanced against fears of placing further burdens on their economy at home and their capacity to preserve their colonial possessions overseas.[14]

Most nations took it as a given truth that Britain's level of industrial development was based on its colonial dominions and that successful competition would require an empire of equal size.[15] And as victors of World War I, both England and France had considerably increased their already vast holdings (in large part at the expense of Germany). This was in fact a mixed blessing; reduced resources made this new property difficult to maintain. The great empires were further threatened by the growth of the Communist International (Comintern), which was eager, along with other leftist groups, to support colonial struggles for independence.[16] Nevertheless, the belief that a far-reaching empire was a requirement for lasting economic prosperity made its substantial cost acceptable.

World War I had created a general repugnance toward war. The victors of the war, however, saw no inconsistency in their peace-loving position and a very harsh interpretation of the Treaty of Versailles (1919), which imposed heavy economic reparations on Germany, stripped it of territory, and required it to accept primary responsibility for the war. The severe conditions and punitive implementation of this treaty undercut the authority of the fragile Weimar democracy and added to Germany's sense of grievance—a feeling that Hitler cultivated and manipulated by blaming others, especially Jews, for Germany's defeat.

Furthermore, the partnership of the former Allies did not remain solid. Each was suspicious of the other's imperial designs, particularly in the Middle East.[17] Support for international cooperation was declining outside Europe as well. The United States was not eager to continue its involvement in European affairs. Congress, with strong popular backing, defeated President Wilson in his struggle to make the United States a member of the League of Nations. Throughout the interwar period, many Americans felt they had been tricked into entering World War I by greedy Wall Street bankers, arms merchants, and wily Europeans. U.S. reluctance to maintain a positive involvement in continental affairs had a major influence on events in the 1930s.

In the east the Soviet Union's size and ideology made it a potential threat to western and central Europe. When Hitler's regime replaced the weak Weimar Republic, many in the West approved because of Nazism's clearly expressed opposition to communism and its promise to restore stability.

World War I had transformed the political map of eastern Europe. Austria-Hungary had disappeared, for the most part replaced by small, unstable states. A new, enlarged Poland was cobbled out of the former Hapsburg and Romanov empires. Most profound were the social effects of a war in which the human costs had been so terribly high. People spoke of a "lost generation" of young men. Displaced populations had been scattered across Europe. The global depression at the beginning of the 1930s was the finishing shock to the old international order.

Technological advances in communication, such as radio and film, allowed leaders to organize large-scale discontent and created genuine mass politics. Fascists and militaristic nationalists used the new technology to exploit popular dissatisfaction and gain tight control, as with Mussolini in Italy and the military junta in Japan.[18]

It was in Germany that these global changes had their most profound consequences. Soon after World War I, disenchantment and impatience with the powers of Europe led the United States to dun the British and French for prompt repayment of their war loans. This was a terrifying time of hyperinflation throughout Europe, and Germany was its greatest victim. The figures seem incredible today: at the height of the inflation, prices rose to 14,000 times their prewar level in Austria, to 23,000 times in Hungary, to 2,500,000 times in Poland, but to a billion times in Germany.[19] A German who sat down for an hour in a restaurant nursing a 5,000-marks cup of coffee would find it cost 8,000 marks when his check came.[20] Nevertheless, England and France responded to the U.S. demands by turning on Germany—already bitter, restive, and economically desperate—with their own demand for prompt payment of its reparations.

The great historian Gordon Craig has beautifully expressed the meaning of the demise of the Weimar Republic:

> While totalitarian regimes were consolidating their power in Russia and in Italy, an experiment was being conducted in Germany to determine whether a democratic republic could be made to work in that country. After 15 years of trial and crisis it failed, and the ultimate consequences of that failure were the Second World War and the death of millions of men, women and children. If some benevolent spirit had granted the peoples of Germany and neighboring European states even a fragmentary glimpse of what lay in store for them in the 1940s, it is impossible to believe that they would not have made every possible sacrifice to maintain the Weimar Republic against its enemies. But that kind of foresight is not given in this world, and the German Republic always lacked friends and supporters when it needed them most.[21]

The ill-designed parliamentary democracy of Weimar, based on a series of postwar compromises, was an object of scorn both at home and abroad and had gained few supporters by the beginning of the 1930s. Burdened with all of Germany's disastrous political and economic troubles following the war, the Weimar constitution became the target of nationalists bitter about Germany's diminished position in the world. To them Weimar symbolized all that was bad about Western liberal democracy, in a period when democracy was not nearly as widely accepted as it is today. The republic, dominated by the Social Democrats, was unable to reassert German strength in the world. Much of the German public had tired of its ineffective politics, exacerbated by the large number of constantly squabbling parties that made it impossible even to begin to deal effectively with such catastrophes as dizzying postwar inflation, and then depression, with epidemic unemployment. By the beginning of the 1930s, the government appeared unable even to maintain civil order, as paramilitary groups attached to parties from both the left and the right fought in the streets. To observers both in Germany and abroad, Communist revolution seemed imminent.[22]

In this context, as the eminent historian Fritz Stern noted, National Socialism promised prosperity after deprivation, strength after national humiliation, and stability after disorder. It attracted support from many elements of German society—workers, the middle class, aristocrats, students, members of the intelligentsia, adherents to a number of religious denominations, and many capitalists.

It was Germany's and the world's bad fortune that an adept and ruthless manipulator such as Adolf Hitler appeared to dramatize and exacerbate traditional racial and religious prejudices. His cynical identification with Christianity at the beginning of his career in piously Catholic Bavaria, an identification he also used to fuel anti-Semitism, is typical of his technique. In his early speeches Hitler often cited Christ's driving the Jewish "enemies of all mankind" from the temple. Like the Germans, he pointed out, Jesus had lived under a corrupt and incompetent government, contaminated by Jewish materialism. He portrayed Christ as a Siegfried-like warrior hero who preached an anti-Jewish and intensely nationalistic faith. From 1922 on, Hitler made impassioned speeches that claimed Jesus, when he drove the moneylenders out of the temple, was a trailblazer of the Nazi program against Jewish world domination, and Hitler promised that the Nazis would fulfill the task that Christ had begun—but could not accomplish—against his archenemy, the Jew.[23]

Hitler learned from the failure of Otto von Bismarck's Kulturkampf to avoid alienating the Catholic Church, even after his influence spread outside Bavaria. Protestants who tried to exclude Catholics from the Nazi Party were ousted or accused of national betrayal and working for Jewish interests. Hitler considered war between Christian denominations as a dangerous diversion from the "Jewish peril." This was a shrewd strategy in Catholic Bavaria, the cradle of the Nazi movement from 1919 to 1925, where he made use of long-standing anti-Jewish religious traditions as well as the popular equation of Jews and Communists. The fervent nationalism that many German Christians adopted after 1914 made a significant proportion of them enthusiastic supporters of Nazism.

The Catholic Church in Germany was less susceptible to the Nazis than Protestant denominations—as an institution it did not encourage strong nationalism. But negotiations with the Vatican had a successful result: like many Catholics in Europe, Pius XI found grounds for agreement with anti-Communist authoritarian regimes, and in July 1933 his concordat with the Third Reich gave international legitimacy to the Nazi regime and restricted the Church to its religious, educational, and pastoral functions. Civic institutions, from local choirs to women's groups to athletic clubs, were simply declared Nazi organizations and given Nazi leaders.

In the 1932 elections, the Nazis received 37 percent of all votes cast—a significant victory given Germany's divided politics.[24] The Nazis won power legally—but not absolute control.

Once in power, they fed German nationalism with pomp and spectacle that produced a superficial image of renewed national power.[25] They improved the economic circumstances of many people. They brought order to the streets, and the repressive means they used seemed acceptable at first, even welcome. An end to the fear of Communist revolution was an agreeable development for many both in Germany and in the international community.

The underside of the dictatorship soon appeared. In February 1933 a fire in the Reichstag became the excuse for an emergency decree that swept away the liberties guaranteed by the Weimar Constitution. Protections of speech and assembly and against unwarranted search and confiscation of property vanished.[26] Labor unions and opposing political parties were banned. The SS and the Sturmabteilung (SA) were given overriding police powers, and their offices became sites of state-sponsored torture and harsh intimidation. Concentration camps for dissidents were established. Jews became targets of an official program that aroused a virulent strain of traditional anti-Semitism.[27]

These activities were apparent to the German public and to any interested observer, but few chose to resist them. Some wishfully thought the regime would eventually be satisfied, that its latest power grab would become its last, and that it might be brought under control by other, more sober elements of German society. Others accepted to some extent the Nazi's specious justification that Germany's crisis situation made drastic action necessary, conveniently ignoring that the crisis had been deliberately and skillfully manipulated, exacerbated, and sustained by Nazi propaganda and brutality.

The excesses of the Nazi regime during its first years in power should have alerted leaders of the international community to action, but with few exceptions, they did not yet make the connection between lawless domestic violence and international aggression. Many in influential positions still believed that a revision of the Versailles Treaty would be enough to satisfy Hitler and continued to ignore striking evidence to the contrary, from *Mein Kampf* in 1924 to Hitler's increasingly aggressive, hateful public statements and actions over the years, before and during his accession to government leadership. Opportunities for prevention of war and genocide in these years were wasted.

An especially valuable issue in Hitler's search for popular support was the Versailles Treaty. His assaults on the settlement as grossly unfair to Germany found a sympathetic hearing. Many Germans, not only the nationalists, bitterly resented the slights of the treaty, and a number were willing to support an aggressive foreign policy to reverse them. And many outside observers in Europe and the United States considered the German objections legitimate and were willing to regard Hitler's violent rhetoric as pardonable political hyperbole. But Hitler's intentions went far beyond correcting the wrongs of an unjust treaty and restoring Germany's 1914 boundaries. In *Mein Kampf* he stated clearly that Germany must remove the Slavic threat by expanding eastward, bringing under German control a fertile land well situated to increase its security in Europe. For a short while after he took power, Hitler softened his talk about expansion so as not to awaken alarm while Germany was still weak, just as he later occasionally moderated his tone to lull his opponents into inaction and leave Germany unimpeded. Gordon Craig noted that although the Nazi regime occasionally assumed a more responsible public face, Hitler's foreign policy ambitions remained consistent and well known.[28] Hitler's vision, like the kaiser's before him, demanded massive violence on a global scale.[29] And this was apparent to anyone who cared to pay attention.

Hitler saw total control at home as essential to his preparation for war abroad. Directly after taking power he had banned all other political parties and organizations. He arranged with the Vatican to dissolve the powerful Catholic Center Party. He imprisoned Marxists and leftists. Hitler even turned on his own Sturmabteilung, the brown-shirted goons who had supported the party during its rise to power with bloody violence in the streets.

Hitler began to see Ernst Rohm, the leader of the SA, as a threat to his position. In June of 1934, in a spate of bloodletting that left 300 persons dead, Hitler liquidated the organization's leadership and took the opportunity to kill a number of other opponents of the Nazi regime. He quickly dissolved the SA in order to ensure the loyalty of the army, which had also felt threatened by the SA's strength. The Night of the Long Knives was a warning that even Hitler's longtime followers were not safe if they could threaten his authority.[30]

Once Hitler had consolidated power, he could begin to strengthen the German military, repudiate international commitments made by his Weimar predecessors, and test international resistance to his ambitions preparatory to pursuing them. Not all authoritarian governments plan expansionist wars; but as the Nazi experience illustrates, leaders who have brutally silenced public dissent in their own land have a free hand to carry out bloody policies in others; and those who conduct massive human rights abuse at home are likely to be harsh in their international relations.

Hitler and Europe, 1933–1936: Fatal Missed Opportunities for Prevention

In his classic monograph, *Germany, 1866–1945*, Gordon Craig clarified missed opportunities to prevent World War II. On the failure of the Allies to respond quickly and forcefully to Hitler's progress in the early 1930s, he wrote:

> The first *assessments by the Western governments* of Hitler's likely course in foreign policy were characterized by an *extraordinary amount of wishful thinking*. Despite the clear evidence provided by events inside Germany that the country's new rulers were contemptuous of law and morality and the standards of common decency in the treatment of those who disagreed with them, politicians in London and Paris showed no alarm about what this might portend for Germany's future behavior as a member of the international community.[31] (Emphasis added.)

Not everyone was fooled or indifferent. Already in 1933 the English and French ambassadors in Berlin had clearly and correctly assessed Hitler's threat to world peace in reports to their governments. The British ambassador mentioned the construction of concentration camps and cautioned that the aims of German policy were to "bring Germany to a point of preparation [for war], a jumping-off point from which she can reach solid ground before her adversaries can interfere." He added, "There is a mad dog abroad once more and we must resolutely combine either to ensure its destruction or at least its confinement until the disease has run its course."[32] Both the French and English diplomats urged their governments to refer to *Mein Kampf* for an understanding of Hitler's plans, and both recognized that the brutality occurring within Germany could expand its borders if Hitler were not stopped and stopped quickly.[33]

Some other influential members of the English government accurately identified Nazi intentions. In 1933, Sir Duncan Sandys predicted the remilitarization of the Rhineland. Sir Robert Vansittart, permanent undersecretary for foreign affairs for much of the 1930s, warned that only international cooperation would prevent Germany's speedy takeover of Austria and eventual move against Poland.[34] Their warnings were pushed aside.[35]

The failure of early awareness to generate an effective response is all the more tragic in light of the fact that Hitler, in his first years of power, was well aware of his real vulnerability. The purge of his SA leadership showed that he did not consider his control secure. Early that same year, plans for unification with Austria—which included the murder of its chancellor—created international protest and were eventually checked by Fascist Italy. Concerted international action at an early stage might well have restrained or even removed Hitler from power.[36]

The opposite occurred: a weak response emboldened him. As Ian Kershaw pointed out in his excellent biography, Hitler began a series of Saturday Surprises, boastful revelations that enhanced his menace. One week he disclosed that Germany had a new air force; the next that he was increasing his army fivefold, in defiance of the Versailles Treaty. This troubled his own military leadership, not because they disagreed with his objectives but because they thought (here as elsewhere) that the rashness of his methods might endanger Germany. Their concern, like that of the German public at large, turned into enthusiastic support when his risky actions met with no resistance.[37] This was a critical turning point. If a vanquished Germany could thumb its nose at the whole postwar network of treaties with impunity, Hitler's path to war and genocide was open in all its destructive potential.

The British were willing to give Germany wide latitude in areas that did not seem to conflict with essential British interests, and given their growing disengagement from the continent, they considered very few matters essential.[38] British leaders did not make a consistent and responsible attempt to educate the public about the extent of the emerging threat. Although two leading newspapers, the *London Times* and *Manchester Guardian*, both warned against permitting German repudiation of the Versailles Treaty, many British wishfully hoped that concessions would bring good relations with Germany.

The French felt betrayed and increasingly insecure. International cooperation was nowhere to be found, especially between the two most powerful democracies in Europe—despite the manifestly critical nature of the danger. The strength of the democracies was wasted. In 1935 the Western democracies had unchallenged strategic superiority over Germany on land, at sea, and in the air. German moves toward rearmament were not as significant a threat to peace as the West's reaction to them. It was timid diplomacy and the lack of international cooperation that encouraged Hitler to attempt the remilitarization of the Rhineland. He recognized that Germany was not yet strong enough to overcome military opposition, but he was convinced that a well-executed bluff could work. His assessment was correct. France, with by far the most powerful army in Europe, was nonetheless badly divided.[39] Nor was it confident about British support. In 1936 France found itself unsettled at home, without a sure ally abroad, and facing another war with Germany over the Rhineland.

Resolute military and diplomatic resistance would almost certainly have succeeded. Hitler's recklessness generated real anxiety and restiveness in his military leaders. If the French Army had resolutely resisted, the German forces would have had a humiliating defeat that might well have led to a military coup against Hitler. Hitler himself admitted later that the two days after German forces entered the Rhineland were the most anxious period of his life. He is reported to have remarked that if the French had defended the Rhineland, the Germans would have had to retreat with their tails between their legs.[40]

Even though a few French leaders contended that German boldness was a bluff, the French government and military succumbed to fear and indecision. A panicked French intelligence estimate inflated the 3,000 soldiers that Germany actually sent to the Rhineland into 295,000 men available for the operation. And France balanced these exaggerated estimates of Germany's strength against a serious underassessment of its own. Germany was just recovering from compulsory demilitarization, but French statesmen were very apprehensive, since they expected a Rhineland confrontation to expand into a larger war.

These inflated misgivings became excuses for inaction at a time when a single French division probably would have repelled the Germans.[41] French hesitation is considered a primary reason the Germans felt confident to move into the Rhineland. But poor judgment on the part of the international community deserves much blame. France had been left alone to oppose a resurgent Germany.

The Coming of War

World War II was a preventable war in the opinion of Winston Churchill, who made the theme of his history, *The Gathering Storm,* "How the English-speaking peoples through their unwisdom, carelessness, and good nature allowed the wicked to rearm." He held that German rearmament should have been forbidden from the start, that Britain and France should have joined against Germany when it moved into the Rhineland. He was right. After 1936, stopping Hitler became increasingly more difficult and costly. The relative military strength of the democratic powers declined as Germany relentlessly continued rearmament (a rearmament that involved developing state-of-the-art weaponry rather than relying on old military stock).

The period from 1935 to 1936 marks a decisive point on the road to cataclysmic war and genocide. With the move into the Rhineland, Hitler had abolished the constraints imposed on German military and industrial power after World War I. His foreign successes increased his support at home and German prestige abroad, convincing initially skeptical Italy and Japan to join the German camp, beginning in November 1936 with the Anti-Comintern Pact directed against the Soviet Union. At the same time, Hitler's successful disregard of Versailles led smaller nations to question the credibility of Britain and France, whose inaction planted seeds of doubt about their assurances of support to less powerful neighbors. In 1936, Belgium annulled a 1920 agreement for defense cooperation with France.

These triumphs emboldened Hitler to begin implementation of the vision he had elaborated in *Mein Kampf.* His plans began with the annexation of Austria and Czechoslovakia, followed by movement into eastern Europe to acquire an empire with the "living space" and natural resources necessary to make Germany a dominant world power.[42]

At the same time France and Britain remained almost exclusively concerned about preserving their own empires. The appeasement policy associated with Neville Chamberlain, who came to power in 1937, was really a continuation of the old national principle to prevent the rising powers, Germany and Japan, from encroaching on British imperial possessions.[43] What Germany did on the continent was not important unless its actions challenged what were seen as important British interests.

In 1938, Hitler solidified his power over German foreign and military policy. He took control of the German armed forces by replacing the old army high command with the Oberkommando der Wehrmacht, of which he became head.[44] Then he named as head of the Foreign Ministry an ambitious nonentity, Joachim von Ribbentrop, who was happy to approve any policy Hitler adopted.[45]

At this time, the democracies needed military strength and political determination, but both Britain and France were late to recognize the need to face a rearmed Germany. They were more worried that preparation for a confrontation in Europe would reduce resources available to defend their overseas possessions and weaken domestic economic recovery by increased military spending. Appeasement was an expression of *wishful thinking*.[46] British and French policy rested on a wishful appraisal of the Nazi threat and an unwillingness to face it. In principle, they might have avoided the draining expense of a military buildup by seeking an alliance with the United States, the Soviet Union—or both—to halt the growing Nazi danger.

The Soviet Union was a willing candidate for alliance. Its ideology, if not its leadership style, was totally antagonistic to Germany's, and Nazi rhetoric, rearmament, and ambitions for eastern expansion had made the USSR increasingly nervous. In 1935 it signed a mutual assistance pact with the French, who took care to stop short of a military alliance, and in 1936 it sponsored the Popular Front against fascism, acknowledging the need of temporary collaboration with capitalist regimes to oppose the greater danger posed by Hitler and his allies. But fear of communism was as powerful in Paris and London as fear of Nazism.[47]

Both Chamberlain and his predecessor, Stanley Baldwin, feared that Franco-Soviet cooperation might draw France into a war that would end by leaving much of Europe under Communist threat. And German expansion into eastern Europe might be valuable in containing the Soviets. Given these concerns, the British and French never seriously considered a close alliance with the Soviets.

The other major power that might have helped to constrain Hitler was the United States. President Franklin Delano Roosevelt had internationalist sympathies and considered Hitler a madman and a threat to world peace. But his urgent campaign for domestic reform left him little opportunity to promote an unpopular foreign policy in the face of entrenched isolationist interests.[48] His situation forced him into exploratory moves to discover what foreign policy actions the U.S. public would accept.[49]

In October 1937 in Chicago, a stronghold of isolationist sentiment, Roosevelt delivered his famous Quarantine Speech, which warned that treaty violations were creating "international anarchy" that would end in a conflict the United States could not escape and must act to prevent.

> An epidemic of world lawlessness is spreading.... When an epidemic of physical disease starts to spread, the community approves and joins in a quarantine of the patients in order to protect the health of the community against the spread of the disease.... War is a contagion, whether it be declared or undeclared. It can engulf states and peoples remote from the original scene of hostilities.[50]

But Roosevelt realized that the political climate would not allow him to follow his dramatic words with immediate action.[51] His politically essential delay had international consequences. It convinced Chamberlain that U.S. isolationism was so powerful that the United States could not be "depended upon for help if [Britain] should get into trouble." He concluded, "it is always best and safest to count on *nothing* from the Americans except words."[52] England became even more committed to a policy based on appeasement.

Hitler gobbled up Austria in March 1938 and was again gratified by the absence of opposition. Japan's expansion, which had led to armed conflict with Nationalist China in 1937, threatened British, French, and U.S. interests in Asia and made them reluctant to expend resources against Hitler that might leave their Pacific territories victims to the

Japanese, despite growing recognition that Hitler had to be stopped. Even Chamberlain was forced to note in the spring of 1938 that force was the only argument Germany understood.[53]

Upon digesting Austria—but just barely—the Nazi regime turned its eyes toward the Germans in Czechoslovakia's Sudetenland. Throughout the spring and summer, Czechoslovakia continued to reject German demands. Britain and France were both anxious that long-standing French agreements with the Czechs might drag France into a conflict, and both Britain and France began mobilization in September. War was only averted by Mussolini's call for a conference to resolve the dispute. Hitler actually wanted war but consented to a meeting in Munich. Only Germany, Italy, France, and Britain sat at the negotiation table. Czechoslovakia, Russia, and other interested eastern European countries in the region from Poland to Hungary were not invited to participate. Four major powers made globally momentous decisions on the basis of their own selfish interests and fears.[54] Fear of German military strength persuaded the British and French to accept the severing of the Sudetenland from Czechoslovakia.

Chamberlain's boast of "peace in our time" gave relief to people across Europe. Even Roosevelt sent him a two-word cable, "Good man."[55] In Britain, "God bless you, Mr. Chamberlain" was the title of a popular song. Appeasement appeared to have spared Europe another major conflict. But the Munich Agreement made war inevitable. In March, German forces devoured all that remained of Czechoslovakia, weakened by losing valuable factories and mines in the Sudetenland. Only then did the British begin full military discussions with the French general staff and offer guarantees to Poland.[56] But it was too late for Allied policies to have any effect other than inciting further German aggression. As for the United States, President Roosevelt could make only a few diplomatic efforts to check growing Nazi power. They were contemptuously dismissed by Hitler, who felt that the U.S. president's hands remained tied by U.S. isolationism.

In the summer of 1939, the British and French finally attempted to form an alliance with the Soviet Union against Germany. They were again too late. Anger at not being invited to participate in the Munich Conference, mistrust of the Western powers (which included fear of abandonment that would leave the USSR to battle Germany alone), and ambitions in eastern Europe led Stalin to sign a nonaggression pact with Nazi Germany on August 23.[57] This agreement made the German takeover of Poland possible.

But France and Britain had at last resolved to take firm action. When Germany invaded Poland on September 1, 1939, World War II began. The opportunity to halt German expansion by peaceful means had passed, and only total war could stop Nazi aggression. In the end, Hitler would be thoroughly defeated and discredited, but only at incredible cost, a cost that included the most extensive genocide the world has yet seen. As in other genocides, the context of war made it easier for the killers to implement their genocidal preferences.

The Allies missed their last opportunity for the peaceful prevention of World War II when they did not stop Hitler's Rhineland occupation in 1936. Joseph Goebbels, Hitler's close confidant and minister of propaganda, clearly realized that well-timed, early international preventive action would have stopped the Nazis. Goebbels sneered at Europe's indecisive response: if *he* had been the French premier in 1933, he would have seen that the strategy already spelled out in *Mein Kampf* clearly revealed Hitler as a danger—and would have marched against him. At that time, he admitted, the Allies could have won easily. Instead they let Germany become better armed than the rest of Europe—and only then did they start the war.[58]

Because of fearful hesitation, wishful thinking, faulty appraisal of danger, multiple prejudices, and lack of international cooperation during that crucial period, Europe—and the world—had to pay an inconceivable amount in lives, resources, and human suffering.

What Can the 1930s Tell the Twenty-first Century About Prevention of Genocide?

Do World War II and the Holocaust offer us clues on how to deal with ruthless, aggressively ambitious dictators and their power over obedient and enthusiastic followers? The second half of the twentieth century and the first decade of the twenty-first mainly indicate a tragic record of failure. But this book notes significant exceptions and learning processes.

The global context today is different from that of the 1930s. We have seen the end of colonialism and the fall of fascism and communism. International organizations such as the European Union, the United Nations, and the North Atlantic Treaty Organization (NATO) have been created that offer possibilities for cooperation far beyond anything available in the 1930s. Nevertheless the lessons of the 1930s are not limited to that period, and we must study them together with the lessons of the Cold War and the bloody 1990s. In a previous book I outlined some general principles that deserve serious consideration today.[59] These were foreshadowed in the introductory chapter of this book but deserve fuller consideration here, given their central relevance to the tragedy of the Holocaust and the crucial lessons to be learned from it.

1. Egregious human rights violations within a country are associated with a high risk of mass violence—they create internal polarization that may lead to civil war, and when they strengthen an ambitious despot's power over his subjects through control of the police and military, can serve as a precursor to external aggression.

2. Intolerance, prejudice, and ethnocentrism, especially when characterized by hypernationalistic or other fanatical orientations that insist on sharp dichotomies (us or them, for or against, true believer or infidel), can spread like infectious diseases throughout populations and across national boundaries. Once released, they are hard to contain.

3. Preventing deadly conflict—even genocide—hinges on the competence and the will of the international community to take early warnings seriously. Executing this task requires alert identification and a judiciously hardheaded case-by-case assessment of potentially spreading dangers—such as abuses of human rights, incitement to hatred and violence, or military build-up—in their first phases. Wishful thinking here can lead to catastrophic missteps. It encourages widespread denial, avoidance of serious problems, and delay in facing them. When necessity finally forces leaders to cope with such problems later, the costs and risks are inevitably much greater.

4. A major challenge is learning to make accurate appraisals of hyperaggressive leaders. When they offer reassurances, it is tempting to believe that the danger is under control. Since the means they use to seize and hold power tend to attract or create calculating, opportunistic, deceitful, intimidating, suspicious, and grandiose personalities, a realistic appraisal of such leaders must include consideration of their earlier behavior in a variety of situations and their most powerful associates.

5. Dictators and demagogues readily exploit the bitter frustrations and fears that their prospective followers experience during times of severe economic and social hardship and convert them to aggressive behavior. By fanning hatred they can consolidate support among their chosen in-group. Long-standing tensions among ethnic, religious, or other groups provide a fault line that ruthlessly opportunistic leaders may widen by identifying an out-group as a threat to the nation that must be eradicated and stirring up fears of in-group survival.

6. The human species is susceptible to genocide; the historical record makes this abundantly clear. The constraints against it are not powerful, especially when there is an autocrat or dictator in control and the culture has established prejudicial stereotypes to provide a convenient target. This is particularly dangerous since the international community is usually so reluctant to undertake concerted action.

7. Circumstances of extreme turbulence such as war, revolution, a failed state, or economic freefall are conducive to mass expulsion or genocide in the context of highly inflammatory leadership and authoritarian social structures.

8. The absence of clear opposition is conducive to the escalation of hatred and violence. Either internal or external opposition, preferably both, can be helpful. There can be a constructive interplay between opposition to a violent regime within a country and beyond its borders. For outsiders, it should be a powerful warning when the leadership is intransigent and uses terror against such opposition.

9. The best opportunity to prevent genocide is through international cooperative action to overthrow, or at least powerfully constrain, a genocidal regime—if possible, on the basis of strong warning information well before the genocide is under way.

10. Fear induced by a terroristic aggressor can readily lead to an overestimate of his strength or the difficulties in confronting the problem. This in turn is conducive to appeasement that whets the appetite of the aggressor.

11. Alternative approaches and policies beyond appeasement are almost always available. It is crucial to consider them seriously, not to avoid them on the basis of ideological preference, personal rigidity, or wishful thinking. There are usually more ways to block a genocide-prone leader than initially meet the eye, especially if the problem is recognized early and dealt with in a resolute way.

12. Careful preparation for serious danger is helpful, especially since it is so difficult to improvise under severe stress. Having institutionalized structures, criteria for intervention, problem-solving procedures, an array of tools and strategies—all this contributes to rational assessment, sound contingency planning, and effective responses.

13. Leadership is crucial. This involves the vision to recognize real dangers and the courage to address them, not impulsively, but thoughtfully. It requires the ability to transcend wishful thinking. It can be greatly enhanced by building genocide-relevant professional competence in the small advisory group and the institutional setting in which leaders make decisions—so that they can get the best available information, analyze it carefully, weigh their options, and reach conclusions for the general well-being. Moreover, authentic leaders must have the capacity to build constituencies for prevention through a base of public information and skill in forming political coalitions.

14. The multiple failures of cooperation in the face of grave danger during the 1930s, even among major democracies, point vividly to the need for international co-operation—pooling strengths, sharing burdens, dividing labor as necessary to cope with serious dangers.

15. Since dictatorial and/or failed states are so dangerous in their predispositions to mass violence, it is vitally important to build competent, democratic states. To do so, the international community will have to produce intellectual, technical, financial, and moral resources to aid democratically inclined leaders and peoples all over the world. Such aid, often multilateral in origin, may have to be sustained over many years as capacity is built within the country or region for coping with its own problems.

16. The painful lessons of U.S. isolationism and unilateralism in the 1920s and 1930s are even more salient now in the maximally interdependent and super-armed world that is emerging.

17. Many of these considerations apply not only to genocide but also to interstate war-fare and to intrastate violence, which have recently been so prevalent and intense.

In any event, preventing deadly conflict well before genocide occurs is essential.

Coda: What We Learn

Such conditions can occur again. The seductive justifications for hideous atrocities can be provided as they were by Hitler. Indeed, advanced communications can spread them more efficiently and vividly today than ever before, and the killing power of worldwide weaponry has moved beyond prior experience.

The events of the 1930s show that World War II was a conflict that was *preventable* even with the limited tools available at the time. This was strongly emphasized by Winston Churchill. Too often our view of history assumes that conflagrations are preordained. The purpose of this chapter has been to highlight those moments when preventive action could have been taken and to identify some of the factors that precluded action. One central obstacle to prevention was the narrow, shortsighted definitions of national interest, which undermined the high degree of international cooperation that was necessary to block Hitler's path to genocide and war.

As in the 1930s, we are today living through a period of profound change in our economic, social, cultural, and technological life. As in the 1930s, the international arena is not bounded by the global confrontation of two superpowers. Although the world does not now face a threat identical to that of Hitler's Germany, we have seen many incidents in recent decades of mass violence in various places and various forms. Today Islamic extremist leaders in the Middle East and the Persian Gulf are, in a sense, echoing Hitler's promise of a triumphant tomorrow—in their case an apocalyptic promise based more on resentment and perceived slight than on hope of a bright future for a populace in even more difficult circumstances than were the Germans of the Weimar Republic. The inadequacy of the response by the international community in these situations bears a disturbing similarity to the events of the 1930s. But, unlike the 1930s, we now have numerous international institutions, legal norms, economic measures, technological capabilities, and diplomatic practices that have been painstakingly built up since the catastrophe of World War II. If these resources are cultivated and exercised effectively, they can serve as *vital tools to prevent violent conflict and, above all, to prevent genocide.* This is the essential content of the present book.

One remarkable—indeed, almost incredible—aspect of the German story is what happened after World War II and the Holocaust. Today, Germany is a thriving democracy, a force for human rights, intergroup respect, and peaceful resolution of conflicts in Europe and elsewhere. This is not the place to describe the transformation, but it must be noted as an *authentic basis for hope.*

In the second half of the twentieth century, West Germany (to some extent under the tutelage of the United States) set about building democratic institutions, educating its children for peace, facing honestly up to its past, paying reparations to Israel, and giving real meaning to the term "never again." It is interesting that East Germany, under Soviet control, made none of these changes and moved slowly and ambivalently in this direction after German unification. It is a kind of experiment in nature: the democratic part of Germany overcoming its past and creating a far better future; the dictatorial part of Germany doing nothing of the sort until freedom came with the end of the Cold War. Altogether, the dramatic contrast of post-Holocaust with pre- and Holocaust Germany is a powerful testimonial to the influence of social conditions on human behavior. If in Germany, why not elsewhere?

CHAPTER 5

An Illustrative Genocide

Burundi-Rwanda

Burundi and Rwanda: Mirror-Image Disasters

The genocides and ongoing massacres that occurred over decades in Burundi and Rwanda illustrate once again that genocide is a deliberate political act, an act that does not happen without ample warning, an act that will almost inevitably recur in the absence of domestic and international restraints. Ongoing, increasing, and overlapping ethnic violence between Hutus and Tutsis in both countries was evident to the international community for decades before the infamous Rwanda genocide of 1994. The Burundi genocide in 1972, although not as widely publicized, shared similar historical circumstances with and influenced the Rwanda genocide in 1994. These preventable genocides were not prevented.[1]

Historical Background

Agriculturalists who spoke a Bantu language were living in the area that is now Burundi-Rwanda at least 2,000 years ago. An indigenous cattle-owning class that became known as Tutsi arose around 1000 AD, and a migrant pastoral people from the Nile region in the north later merged with them and eventually shared their name. By the fifteenth century, cattle owners were called Tutsi and farmers with no cattle were called Hutu, although *Tutsi* and *Hutu* had other meanings, usually connected with patronage or clientage. A third group, the Twa, made up less than 2 percent of the region's population. At the time European colonists arrived in the area, a Tutsi royal family ruled over Tutsis, Hutus, and Twas by means of complex, interrelated patronage systems and networks.

Germany claimed the area today called Rwanda and Burundi as a colony in 1885, but only began to occupy it ten years later. After World War I, the colony became a League of Nations mandate to be administered indirectly by Belgium. Belgian rule strengthened the dominance of the Tutsis (about 14 percent of the population) over the more numerous Hutus (about 85 percent). White colonial administrators regarded the Tutsis as descended from Ethiopians and possessed of "more Caucasian" physical characteristics than the Hutus and Twas. It followed that the Tutsis were the racial superiors and natural rulers of the Hutus and Twas.[2] The Belgians therefore entrusted Tutsis with governing their native subjects, all of whom were required to carry "tribal cards" that identified them as belonging to one of the three tribal groups, even though a long history of intermarriage had made clear-cut ethnic distinctions a matter of European fantasy. The use of tribal cards persisted until 1994, when perpetrators of the Rwanda genocide used them to detect Hutu victims.[3]

As an ominous precursor of 1994, in 1956, only three years before Rwanda's independence from Belgian rule, a failed Hutu uprising caused the death of about 50,000 Tutsis.[4] The main Hutu political party in Rwanda was the Mouvement Démocratique Républicain (MDR), led by Grégoire Kayibanda, who, with Belgian assistance, organized in 1959 the first of many Hutu pogroms against Tutsis. It produced thousands of corpses and an even greater number of refugees, who settled in camps in bordering Uganda, Zaire, and Burundi and planned revenge. In 1961, after three years of interethnic war, the MDR drove the Tutsi king into exile and a year later declared an independent republic of Rwanda, with Kayibanda its first president.

Kayibanda governed with the support of a small Hutu elite from the northern part of the country, and together they enriched themselves at public expense. To divert the attention of other less privileged Hutus from their corruption, they exploited long-standing Hutu-Tutsi antagonism. Their policy of gradually reducing the rights of the Tutsi minority was punctuated by massacres of Tutsis throughout Kayibanda's rule and afterward.[5] This increased both the population and the harsh animosity of the Tutsi refugee enclaves in neighboring countries, and massacres were often responses to attacks by Tutsi guerillas based outside the country.

Meanwhile, the influx of Tutsi refugees from Rwanda due to the Hutu repression generated feelings of insecurity among the ruling Tutsi minority in neighboring Burundi. Existing ethnic suspicion and tensions began to increase there—tensions between Hutus and Tutsis and also between two Tutsi groups, the Tutsi-Hima and Tutsi-Banyaruguru. They came to a head in May 1965, when, in Burundi's first postindependence election to the national assembly, Hutu candidates won twenty-three seats out of thirty-three. Disregarding the vote, the king appointed a Tutsi favorite as his new prime minister rather than a Hutu, as expected. In October 1965 angry Hutus attempted a coup that removed the old king but was severely repressed in a bloodbath. Hutus lost most of their leaders in the Tutsi backlash and became convinced that retaliatory violence was the only recourse that would gain them social equality and the political power they could see the Hutu majority exercising across the border in Rwanda. Hutus had been systematically denied access to all positions of responsibility in the Burundi government, civil service, and upper ranks of the armed forces, and this situation was particularly irksome to educated Hutus. In April 1972 university students, allied with the militant pro-Hutu Parti du Peuple, began an insurrection in the southern towns of Rumonge and Nyanza-Lac that claimed from 2,000 to 3,000 lives, mostly Tutsi.

The government of Burundi, then under the control of President Michel Micombero and a coterie of Tutsi-Hima, took advantage of the Hutu uprising to smother two sources of ethnic opposition at once. In the months just before the Hutu rebellion their government had reached a crisis of legitimacy when it imprisoned Tutsi-Banyaruguru political rivals on bogus charges. The Hutu rebels were an additional challenge to their authority but also a means of unifying Tutsi support against a common enemy that had demonstrated how dangerous it could be in the country next door. Within a week the government completely quashed the Hutu rebels. Despite his victory, Micombero declared martial law and enlisted military assistance from President (read dictator) Mobutu Sese Seko of Zaire. Paratroopers from Zaire secured the regional airport, allowing the Burundi army to move into the countryside, where Hutu civilians were butchered until August, resulting in a total death toll between 100,000 and 150,000. The government genocide also accomplished—by premeditated design—the destruction or exile of almost every educated Hutu in the country.

The planning of the genocide was largely the work of three Hima-Tutsi government officials. By inciting fear and hatred, they expected to unite disaffected Tutsis behind them, and by removing potential Hutu leaders, they hoped to eliminate the danger of future Hutu insurrection. Government radio urged Tutsis "to hunt down the python in the grass"—pythons that included primary schoolchildren, who were carried off in carloads and butchered after their classmates identified them. Hutu civil servants, university students, clergy, and even semiskilled workers shared their fate. At universities and technical schools, following an all-too-familiar genocidal pattern, groups of soldiers and members of a government-sponsored youth wing appeared in classrooms, called out a roll of Hutu students, and carted them away. Other Hutu students were assaulted and beaten by Tutsi students. And to tighten government control of the military and ensure its loyalty, soldiers with even one Hutu grandparent were removed from the armed forces and often executed.

Tutsis who tried to protect Hutus from destruction were also threatened with death, whereas those who were willing to participate in the slaughter received the victims' property as a reward. The army and the government youth group combined forces to carry out arrests and executions. If more hands were needed, they impressed local Tutsis into service, with the clear implication that it was the civic responsibility of every Tutsi male to defend his land against the Hutus. Tutsi refugees from Rwanda, settled in camps in the north of Burundi, eagerly accepted this responsibility, impelled by both hatred and fear of further Hutu attack. Still-bitter memories of what had occurred in Rwanda from 1959 to 1962 played a significant part in turning a repression into a genocide. Many Tutsis sincerely felt that they were waging a fight for their own survival.[6]

A government-issued white paper to the outside world protested that the Hutu insurrection was really an attempted genocide against Tutsis that had forced the government to protect itself and its imperiled citizens. The world received the explanation with courtesy. The head of the Organization for African Unity (OAU) expressed that body's "solidarity" with Burundi. Then UN Secretary-General Kurt Waldheim conveyed his "fervent hopes" for speedy attainment of peace, harmony, and stability in order for Burundi to achieve social progress, higher standards of living, and "other ideals and principles" expressed in the UN Charter.[7] A well-documented report that the U.S. mission in Bujumbura submitted to the U.S. secretary of state in refutation of Burundi's whitewash elicited no concern. In short, the response of the international community over these years of slaughter was essentially useless—or worse.

Thus Burundi became a mirror image of Rwanda, where minority Tutsis maintained their control of the army and the government and were able to massacre the subordinated Hutu population with impunity.

Meanwhile, Hutu leaders in Rwanda continued to share the same fascination with bloodletting-as-politics that their Tutsi counterparts displayed in Burundi. In 1973, Rwandan president Kayibanda lost power in a coup d'état led by his commander in chief, Juvénal Habyarimana. Government-orchestrated attacks on both the Tutsis and the former president's supporters followed, yielding an estimated death toll of 100,000.

Habyarimana, like Kayibanda, was from the north of Rwanda and continued to lavish patronage on Hutus of that region. He created a one-party state in 1975, making all Rwandans members of the Mouvement Révolutionnaire Nationale pour le Développement (MRND). Real power, of course, remained with the president, his guard, and the *akazu* (little house), a small group of cronies.

He continued the policy of restricting Tutsi rights. In 1973 Tutsis were purged from universities and other institutions. Habyarimana set ethnic quotas for public service employment, the largest sector of the economy after agriculture, and allowed Tutsis to hold only 9 percent of available jobs.[8] The 1990s would witness more small-scale massacres in Rwanda as a "Hutu power" movement grew, promoted by a powerful elite that hoped to remove the Tutsis completely. There was no secret about their aspirations.

Habyarimana's beleaguered government supported media propaganda that referred to Tutsis as cockroaches and incited violence to the point of total eradication (see Chapter 2, "Paths to Genocide"). Its reports highlighted and exaggerated Front Patriotique Rwandais (RPF) atrocities and warned that the returning Tutsis planned to reclaim property they had left when they fled the country. It repeated the European myth of Tutsis' Ethiopian descent and painted Tutsis as piratical outsiders who were once again descending from the north to pillage Rwanda's native inhabitants, the Hutus.[9] Weren't they supported by the president of Uganda, whom they had helped raise to power and whose Hima-Tutsi descent confirmed the existence of a foreign, ultimately Ethiopian conspiracy? It followed that *all* Tutsis were a threat that deserved violent repression—and the propaganda made it clear that anyone who tried to undermine plans for their extermination could also expect recrimination. A carefully designed use of images awakened powerful psychological elements of "devaluation, antagonism, and fear."[10] These inflammatory fantasies paved the way to genocide.

Many Hutus, still bitter about former humiliation and mistreatment as a subordinate group and fearful of invading Tutsi expatriates, were receptive to their leaders' propaganda. Acceptance of the government's tactics was also facilitated by Rwanda's hierarchical culture, which, reinforced by rigid child-rearing practices, highly valued obedience to authority. In addition, the Tutsis had attracted Hutu envy and resentment because they were a more educated group with better skills for jobs in the private sector, in large part owing to their favored status under colonial rule. Their position as a distrusted, well-educated group that had achieved success created a volatile situation similar to that of Armenians in the Ottoman Empire and Jews in Nazi Germany.[11]

Deteriorating economic conditions further aggravated the situation at the time of the 1994 genocide. In the late 1980s, overpopulation had become a serious problem. Rwanda, a landlocked central African state, is the most densely populated country in Africa (Burundi ranks second), with a predominantly agrarian economy and farming largely at subsistence level due to the overworked soil. An international drop in coffee prices in 1989 and in tin prices in the early 1990s added to Rwanda's troubles. Coffee was a main export of the country and tin its principal mineral wealth. Most employment other than farming was in the services sector, largely in the government,[12] and even in more prosperous times, corruption in the authoritarian government had siphoned profits to the rich while the general population remained in poverty.[13]

Thus difficult economic conditions, social injustice, political upheaval, power struggles and corruption within the Hutu leadership, fear of the Tutsis, and government propaganda, incitement, and coercion combined to encourage participation in genocide.[14]

In October 1993 a crisis occurred in Burundi that further destabilized the situation in Rwanda. An enforced stability of sixteen years had followed Micombero's slaughter of Hutus in Burundi. Then in August 1988 ethnic riots erupted in the north in Ntega and Marangara. The Parti de la Libération du Peuple Hutu (Palipehutu), an extremist Hutu party that refugee camps in Tanzania had produced in 1980, claimed responsibility for the murder of hundreds of Tutsi civilians. The Burundi army responded with a bloody assault that killed from 20,000 to 30,000 Hutus and sent 40,000 more across the border to Rwanda. This time the United States intervened and, by threatening a halt to economic assistance, pressured the Burundi government to carry out an investigation and punishment of the atrocities, to begin fundamental governmental reforms, and to allow Hutu refugees to return from Rwanda. Burundi president Pierre Buyoya was obliged to begin a policy of national reconciliation that led to adoption by popular referendum of a Charter of National Unity, promulgated in early 1991. Presidential elections in 1993 put Hutus in power with the landslide victory of Melchior Ndadaye and his Front pour la Démocratie du Burundi (Frodebu).

Burundi's electoral victory was short-lived. In October 1993, Tutsi extremists, unwilling to give up their entrenched privileges—not the least of which was control of the army—assassinated newly elected president Ndadaye. Until that time, Hutu hopes for peaceful advance through the moderate Frodebu party had limited the appeal of hardline Palipehetu calls to violence. Ndadaye's assassination set off armed rebellion, in which enraged Hutus massacred around 25,000 Tutsis, followed by Tutsi retaliation that killed at least as many Hutus.

These slaughters not only destroyed any hope of peace between Hutus and Tutsis in Burundi to this day; the complete break in trust was also felt in Rwanda. It directly fed the 1994 genocide there by reinforcing Rwandan Hutus' belief in the treachery and murderous inclinations of Tutsis. In addition, the violence drove at least 500,000 refugees from Burundi into Rwanda at a time of drought, reinforcing the government stereotype, widely disseminated by hate radio, of the Tutsis as bloodthirsty plunderers.

Neither the Burundi genocide of 1972 nor the Rwanda genocide of 1994 was a spontaneous outbreak of ethnic hatred. Both were designed and directed by the governments in power. But unlike the Burundi insurgents, a large proportion of the Rwanda rebels were refugees and children of refugees who had fled from Rwanda to Uganda after the 1959–1962 Hutu revolution and had formed the RPF in 1986. This allowed the Rwanda government to characterize them as bloodthirsty outsiders intent on pillaging and to unite resentful Hutus from south and central Rwanda behind the government in Kigali.

This was the situation when, on December 28, 1993, an RPF battalion entered Kigali to provide security for (Tutsi) opposition members of the new multiparty Rwanda government established under the Arusha peace agreement. But after President Habyarimana (the reelected Hutu incumbent) was sworn in on January 5, violent incidents, timed to obstruct peacemaking, erupted throughout Rwanda, providing an excuse to both rival parties to resist further cooperation, question their opponents' good faith, and gird themselves for continued armed struggle.

Then, on April 6, 1994, a plane en route to Rwanda's capital, Kigali, was shot down. Among the passengers killed were Presidents Juvénal Habyarimana of Rwanda and Cyprien Ntaryamira of Burundi. Government-organized violence erupted throughout the city and its surroundings. Perpetrators included members of the military, youths organized into paramilitary groups, and civilians they impressed into duty, such as neighbors and even members of mixed families.[15] The few Hutus who tried to protect Tutsis were killed in public. At first moderate Hutus were killed for political reasons. Later they were murdered for their property.[16]

Government army units, militia, and mobs set up roadblocks to massacre Tutsis and moderate Hutus. Local political leaders, police, and soldiers, carrying lists of the names and addresses of those chosen for slaughter, went from door to door to track down their victims. They murdered the prime minister of Rwanda and ten Belgians from the United Nations Assistance Mission in Rwanda (UNAMIR) troops sent to protect her. The Rwandan Patriotic Front and the Rwandan government forces resumed battle and rejected efforts at conciliation by UNAMIR commander Major General Roméo Dallaire and UN Secretary-General Special Representative Jacques-Roger Booh-Booh.[17]

UNAMIR's Belgian unit quickly withdrew, and efforts to control the genocide withered when the participating nations that remained in Rwanda prohibited their UNAMIR troops from engaging in combat unless they were attacked personally. (Only Ghana allowed its contingent to intervene to stop public slaughter.) Rwanda suffered more deaths in three months than the former Yugoslavia in more than four years of carnage: at least 800,000 Tutsis along with 50,000 Hutus who were not committed to the policies of the ruling elite or who belonged to the mistrusted southern population—at least one out of every ten citizens—were brutally killed; 500,000 were displaced within their country; and more than 2 million fled as refugees to other countries.[18]

Member nations of the Security Council, eager to avoid involvement, applied the term *tribal slaughter* to the carnage rather than the more accurate *genocide,* which would have compelled action under international law. The immediate response of the UN Security Council was to recall all but 250 of its 2,500 peacekeepers from Rwanda. UNAMIR's narrow mandate and reduced forces left it powerless to halt the genocide.[19] UNAMIR withdrew most of its personnel on UN Security Council orders soon after the genocide started and played little further role. Security Council members continued to deny that a genocide was occurring, disregarding intelligence that clearly identified the perpetrators and nature of the crimes. The U.S. government emphatically refused to support attempts to put together an African intervention force with Western logistical support. In effect, the U.S. and UN roles were not to prevent genocide but to permit it.

Yet while Rwanda's government troops were effective in slaughtering civilians, they could not repel the RPF, which resumed its military advance when the genocide began.

In June 1994 France dispatched troops to Rwanda (Operation Turquoise) to prevent the RPF from taking control of Rwanda and to end the genocide. But the French soon saw that the RPF was bound to win the war and withdrew.

The genocide stopped only after the RPF defeated the government army in July 1994 and took power, which it has held ever since. But armed violence did not end. The retreat of the Hutu government forces and the reprisal massacres perpetrated by the advancing RPF caused more than 2 million Hutus (among them the *akazu* and other Hutus who had directed the genocide) to flee into eastern Zaire (now Democratic Republic of Congo [DRC]), Tanzania, and Burundi. Very large refugee camps sprang up near the DRC-Rwanda border where thousands of refugees, in full view of the international media, died from infectious diseases before humanitarian agencies could bring relief. With the cooperation of Zaire's armed forces, armed former members of the Rwanda military and the notorious *interahamwe* ("those who stand/fight together") who had played an active part in the genocide and then fled with the other refugees, took control of the camps, seized supplies intended for humanitarian relief, and used the camps as a base for insurgency against the new Tutsi-led government in Rwanda. The UN disregarded the appeals of UN High Commissioner for Refugees Sadako Ogata to prevent further conflict, and violence escalated and spread, particularly into eastern Congo. After guerrillas made a number of raids into Rwanda in 1995, the newly established RPF-dominated Rwandan army invaded Zaire to close the camps in 1996, assisted by the also newly formed Alliance des Forces Démocratiques pour la Libération du Congo-Zaire (AFDL). Laurent Kabila, later the AFDL's leader, was already a prominent member. The combined operation sent 1.2 million Hutu refugees home to Rwanda and killed or drove the rest deeper into Zaire.

Again, former members of the *interahamwe* and government forces joined the fleeing Hutu refugees now returning to Rwanda, and in 1997 they joined in an uprising in the northwest, which was quelled in 1998 through a combination of military offensives, a controversial "villagization" program, and cooption of Hutu community leaders into the local government. Since then attacks in Rwanda have been infrequent. But violence involving a widening circle of African nations continues to the present day. The Rwanda conflicts helped spark a regional war that had taken 3 million lives by April 2001 and many more since.[20]

The Tutsi-dominated government has made attempts to promote unity and reconciliation.[21] It allows a multiparty government, but non-RPF cabinet ministers must retain approval of the ruling party.[22] From October 1999 to March 2000 a major reorganization in government removed from power the parliamentary speaker, the prime minister, three other cabinet ministers, and President Pasteur Bizimungu, who was succeeded by the vice president and minister of defense, Paul Kagame, and later tried and imprisoned for founding a political party that incited racial hatred.

In August 2003, Kagame was reelected president with 95 percent of the vote. EU observers of the election found instances of irregularity, fraud, and intimidation of the opposition. Kagame rejected the findings of the EU and accused them of partisanship.[23]

In Burundi the return to power of Pierre Buyoya in 1996, negotiations in Arusha that began in 1998, and the signature of the Arusha Peace Accord in 2000 have not ended war or begun a period of peace and economic revival in the country.[24]

Missed Opportunity

In 1997 the Carnegie Commission on Preventing Deadly Conflict, the Institute for the Study of Diplomacy at Georgetown University, and the U.S. army convened a panel of experienced military leaders to study General Dallaire's claim that military intervention in 1994 would have checked the Rwanda genocide. The panel concluded that a force of 5,000 adequately equipped, trained, and directed troops—sent to Rwanda two weeks after the plane crash—could have stopped the slaughter in and around the capital, blocked its spread to the countryside, and ended the civil war.[25]

Dallaire appraised the situation correctly. The killings—possibly even that of the president—were premeditated, directed by extremists in the dead president's own party in order to destroy the peace process.[26]

The intervening UN force General Dallaire proposed would have met strong resistance. Planned and systematic genocidal slaughter was intermingled with conventional warfare between the RPF and the Rwandan Government Forces (RGF). Military plans would have had to consider the role of the political parties, the refugee/displaced person crisis, security for humanitarian operations, and efforts to resume the Arusha peace process. And military action would be only one part of a comprehensive plan to achieve enduring peace in Rwanda. UN troops in Rwanda were in a position quite different from the intervention forces in Yugoslavia, which were integrated with diplomatic, humanitarian, and economic components in a comprehensive approach to resolving the conflict.[27]

Dallaire requested the following mandate, which the UN—pressured by leading Security Council members such as the United States—did *not* grant:

1. *First, stop the genocide*—if necessary, even by shooting to kill.
2. *Conduct a peace enforcement mission authorized to disarm* rear-area noncombatants and to collect information and protect witnesses for later prosecution of war criminals.
3. *Provide security at specific sites,* separated according to ethnic group.
4. *Ensure successful delivery of humanitarian aid.*
5. *Return the disputing parties to the Arusha peace accords* and establish a secure environment for a broad-based transitional government.

Dallaire's clearly formulated and carefully prepared plan might well have succeeded. Even a reduced UNAMIR force of 450 was able to protect displaced people in the capital area, and French troops sent into southwest Rwanda in June 1994 managed to save thousands without *any* French casualties.

Panelists of the Carnegie Commission suggested improvements to Dallaire's plan:

1. As it would often be impossible to distinguish genocidal violence from conventional violence that occurs in war, the intervening force should stop *all* violence and control the movement of all factions or groups.
2. Since most of the genocide was occurring in areas under RGF control, and most of its victims were perceived or actual supporters of the RPF, an intervening force that limited itself to stopping the genocide might seem to favor the RPF. At the very least

it would be accused by the government of assisting the rebels and by the rebels of assisting the government. In 1994 the government had protested it could not halt the genocide because it needed all its troops to oppose the RPF.

3. After the genocide had been halted, the RPF would need time to recognize the fact, and even then it might be unwilling to halt a successful military offensive. If the RPF were forced into negotiation before an almost assured victory, it would lose the chance to impose a conqueror's terms and a conqueror's justice on its opponents.[28]

4. Overall, the plan promised considerable risk for the intervening force and advantage to those who had disdained the peace process.

5. Large centrally directed forces would be less effective than small independent units that imposed specific behavior on belligerents. This would demand individual assessment and response as well as clear but comprehensive rules of engagement and training to apply the rules.

The panelists argued that the UN should have flown its whole force into the country at once with a mandate to halt all acts of violence, separate the two combatants, and stabilize the country by imposing rules of behavior on the entire population. One panelist who had witnessed the genocide argued that it did not become widespread until extremists saw that the world would not get involved and that UNAMIR's contingents would protect only themselves. Some senior officers on the panel stressed the value of swift and overwhelming force. They believed that the later the forces acted, the more men they would need and the more difficult the operation would become.[29]

The window of opportunity for successful intervention in Rwanda was small. Action after the last week in April 1994 would have required massive force because the violence had expanded to the countryside. Yet throughout the spring and summer of 1994 no consensus was reached about what to do.[30]

Several circumstances drained the will to act:

1. An effective peacekeeping force relies on sophisticated transportation and logistic capabilities that few nations have. The United States would have been the obvious candidate to lead. But Somalia had made the once-burned United States twice cautious, and other rich nations shared its reluctance to become involved.

2. The world was distracted by troubles in the former Yugoslavia.

3. The UN's role in international peacekeeping was in transition. For most of the twentieth century the principle of national sovereignty had been unquestioned, and deliberation was the UN's primary tool. But after the end of the Cold War, the UN has increasingly had to confront armed disputes within unstable countries prone to disintegration.[31]

Since Rwanda, serious efforts have been made to improve the UN's peacekeeping capabilities and procedures, but progress is slow, though significant. The potentially powerful Security Council seems more interested in avoiding responsibility than in preventing genocide. It was the powerful member states that prohibited the UN from acting—and then blamed Secretary-General Boutros Boutros-Ghali for failure.

The UN's inadequate response to the genocide was documented in 1999 in a candid independent report that Secretary-General Kofi Annan commissioned.[32] The report is blunt in its general assessment—for days after the plane crash, communications between UNAMIR and headquarters revealed a force in disarray, with no clear direction, little information about what was happening, and difficulty in maintaining contact with its own troops.[33]

The UNAMIR mission suffered from inadequate political analysis. The UN should have dispatched a knowledgeable and experienced political officer to support Dallaire and his team.

Communications between UN headquarters in New York, the mission, and other parts of the UN system were inadequate. Early indications of the risk of genocide mentioned in nongovernmental organization (NGO) and UN human rights reports of 1993 were not taken into account in planning for UNAMIR, resulting in a limited mandate and resources. The many warning signals were poorly reported to the Secretary-General and the Secretariat. Wishful thinking once again predominated.

The restricted mandate, inadequacy of peacekeeping staff, lack of resources, need for clarification of the rules of engagement, and a dire logistical situation facing the mission once the genocide started all had a devastating effect on the way the mission dealt with the crisis. In addition, UN member states exerted pressure on the Secretariat to limit the proposed number of troops, and—worse yet—UNAMIR was marginalized by France, Belgium, the United States, and Italy when they evacuated their nationals. The Security Council's delay in coming to a decision showed a tragic lack of unity in a situation where rapid action was essential. The international community should not have hesitated to acknowledge the gravity of the situation and should not have been afraid to call it genocide. A global publicity campaign might have put pressure on governments to act.

A major misstep was to allow Rwanda to remain on the Security Council. Its ambassador participated in council discussions and communicated them to his government. The council should have ousted Rwanda from the council and denounced its government's behavior forcefully. Were they sympathetic? Or just scared? Or just ignorant? Some may have been unwilling to set a precedent that might work against them in the future if they were caught in a similarly embarrassing situation.

The UN should have been provided with its own radio facility in Rwanda, and the inflammatory Radio Mille Collines should have been jammed. In the future, attention must also be paid to dissemination of genocidal messages over the Internet. This illustrates the growing dangers of intense and pervasive incitement to mass violence.

The tragedy of Rwanda did yield some lessons. The inquiry made the following recommendations:

- The UN—and in particular the Security Council and countries contributing troops—must prepare itself to act to prevent impending genocide or serious violations of human rights wherever they happen. The political will to act should not be subject to varying standards.
- The UN should enhance its early warning capacity through better cooperation both within the Secretariat and with outside actors, including NGOs and academic institutions.
- Protection of civilians in conflict situations must be improved.

- Security of UN and associate personnel, including local staff, must be enhanced. Existing rules to evacuate national staff from crisis areas should be changed, and cooperation between officials responsible for the security of different categories of staff in the field must be ensured. National evacuation operations must be coordinated with UN missions on the ground.
- An effective flow of information must be established within the UN system. Flow of information to the Security Council should improve, in particular on human rights issues.
- Suspending participation on the Security Council of a member state involved in circumstances such as the Rwanda crisis should be seriously considered.
- The international community should support postgenocide efforts to rebuild society in Rwanda, with particular attention to reconstruction, reconciliation, and respect for human rights, always considering the special needs of survivors, returning refugees, and other groups affected by the genocide.
- The UN should acknowledge its responsibility for not doing enough to prevent or end the Rwanda genocide. The Secretary-General should actively seek ways to build a new relationship between the UN and Rwanda.[34]

The first of the inquiry's recommendations was an action plan to prevent genocide that increases system-wide awareness and capacity to prevent and counteract genocide and other massive human rights violations, using lessons learned from Rwanda and the former Yugoslavia. Each part of the UN—as well as individual member states—should examine what actions they must take to avert such crimes. The plan should include a follow-up mechanism to ensure that the actions are performed effectively.

An essential part of the plan is the insistence that all programs to improve honest early warning and preventive capacity should include prevention of genocide as a required component. What response options and contingency plans are available? Specific training should be given to headquarters, agency, and program staff—and also to personnel in field missions—to identify warning signs of genocide, analyze them, and translate them into appropriate action.

This is the great weakness across efforts to deal with genocides: too little knowledge, too little skill, too little preparation to help the troubled country long before large-scale military action is required.

Conclusion

The consequences of the international failure to act during the Rwandan genocide show clearly that preventive intervention in situations of actual—or potential—mass violence or genocide is not only ethically imperative but also prudent. The cost of doing nothing is very high.[35] Aside from the massive toll in human lives, the destruction of Rwanda's institutional, social, and economic infrastructure will inhibit its development and democratization for years to come, and an entire generation—orphaned, maimed, and traumatized by violence—will need extensive and sustained outside assistance to repair postconflict conditions.[36] These conditions have led to continued violations of human rights, serious disease outbreaks, and the destruction of prospective markets and trading partners.

Nor is the damage confined to Rwanda. The killing there spread to neighboring countries. Some 1.7 million refugees exported violent conflict to Congo, which expanded to Zaire, Uganda, Zimbabwe, and beyond. The fighting still continues. It is self-deluding to call these conflicts "local" or even regional in their influence. As September 11, 2001, taught us, they can—and often do—create an environment that produces larger security threats by fostering international crime, arms proliferation, illegal traffic in weapons, political extremism, and terrorism. Millions have been killed in this region of Africa in the earliest years of the twenty-first century.

Nations and organizations that hesitate to intervene outside their own borders to prevent intergroup hostility and mass violence will face a far more costly cleanup and repair later—in addition to immense human suffering and loss of life. In Rwanda, international agencies, NGOs, and foreign governments have had to spend vast amounts of energy and money in humanitarian assistance and postconflict peace building.[37] Between 1994 and 1996 the United States *alone* spent $750 million on emergency work in Rwanda, a figure almost equal to the total annual U.S. aid program for all of Africa.[38] Developed countries pay in the form of humanitarian aid. But the poorer countries pay a greater price, since every conflict reduces the amount of international aid available for other vital needs—education, public health, environmental guardianship, and economic development.[39] Their avoidable and massive human suffering is an intolerable cost.

"Doing nothing" carries yet another devastating if unquantifiable cost. The inability to depend on the international community to act decisively in defense of human rights and the rule of law inspires cynicism and encourages the belief that aggression will go unpunished—or will even pay off handsomely. The various legal systems, treaties, and multilateral associations that cement and support the "international community" are voluntary in nature, without a sovereign authority to make and enforce decisions when consensus is lacking. In this case, legitimacy becomes the touchstone of international order. Multilateral cooperation provides individual states with frameworks for global transportation and communication, disease control, free movement of legal trade, cooperation to control illegal trade, nonproliferation of weapons, environmental protection, and many other benefits that contribute to shared well-being and prosperity.

The international community ignores unchecked violence at its own risk. Its failure to respond to mass slaughter teaches a lesson of lawlessness to disaffected groups who see no alternative to violence and also to ruthless dictators who are tempted to use violence to further their personal ambitions. This makes averting mass violence a matter of national, even global self-interest. It is striking to note the number of tyrants, small and large, who have openly admired Napoléon Bonaparte and even Hitler. Their heroes enjoyed success long enough to offer hope that mass violence and even genocide could be valuable policies, even though both tyrants were toppled at last—by international cooperation.[40] This norm of indifference requires changing, much like earlier toleration of slavery.

Preventing deadly conflict is neither inexpensive nor easy. But the costs of prevention are slight when compared to the costs of inaction or of doing too little, too late.[41]

CHAPTER 6

~ ~

Preventing Genocide

Leadership, Negotiation, Democracy, and International Help in the Vivid Example of South Africa

Nature and Scope of Oppression

As Cyrus Vance argued cogently, South Africa's experiences offer valuable insights about finding democratic ways to prevent civil wars and genocide and to reconcile a society with deep cultural, racial, and religious differences, compounded by a history of severe political oppression and extreme economic inequality.[1] What contributed to South Africa's transition to true democracy after many decades of harsh depreciation and mutual antagonism? Throughout these dangerous decades, how was genocide avoided?

Like many former colonies, South Africa has a history of bloodshed and violence. The Union of South Africa was formed when the South African Republic (the Transvaal) and the Orange Free State—both founded in the mid-nineteenth century by settlers of Dutch, German, and French ancestry, then occupied by the English during the Boer War in 1900—merged with two British colonies—the Cape Colony and Natal. In 1910 the new Union's constitution preserved the preexisting voting laws of each region, effectively disenfranchising colored and black South Africans and forbidding them a seat in the Union Parliament. South Africa's colonial ruler, Britain, approved the act establishing the Union over the protests of a primarily black group of prominent South Africans that traveled to London to argue against it.[2]

The 1910 constitution of the Union of South Africa, based on white supremacy, set the stage for apartheid when the Afrikaner-based National Party took control in 1948. From the very first—and in the face of opposition from the South African Native National Congress (later the African National Congress, or ANC)—whites enacted laws promoting ever greater discrimination and segregation. The Natives Land Act of 1913 set aside rural reserves covering 7.5 percent of the poorest agricultural land in the country for Africans (then 68 percent of the population) and barred them from buying or leasing land in the rest of the country, which was exclusively for whites. Coercive measures to enforce segregation and to route African workers to areas where whites needed their labor at prices they wanted to pay included the pass laws. To leave the reserves, later called "homelands," or to travel between urban townships, Africans were required to carry a pass book that identified them and authorized them to be in "white" areas. Thousands broke the laws to seek work or join their families. Between 1916 and 1981 around 250,000 people a year were arrested for infringements of the pass laws. Illegal shanty settlements sprang up everywhere.

In 1948, the hard-line Afrikaner National Party came to power in South Africa with a mandate to uphold white supremacy in perpetuity. Over the next fifteen years, it systematically enacted wide-ranging, harsh legislation to guarantee apartheid. Every human being was classified by race—white, African, Indian, or colored (of mixed origin). Interracial sex and marriage were outlawed, public facilities made separate, urban and workplace segregation strengthened, and multiracial trade unions prohibited.[3] The right of blacks to vote was totally abolished.

The Bantu Education Act of 1953 was a particularly galling example of the harsh legislation. At the time the act was passed, most black Africans were educated in churches and missions, and black secondary schools had much the same curriculum as white schools, even if their resources were fewer. As Nelson Mandela pointed out, the government spent six times as much for white education as for black; education was not compulsory for blacks and was free only in the elementary grades.[4] Few blacks graduated from high school. Mandela observed with justified bitterness:

> Even this amount of education proved distasteful to the [Nationalist Party].... The Afrikaner was traditionally hostile to Africans learning English, for English was a foreign tongue to the Afrikaner and the language of emancipation to us.... The Bantu Education Act transferred control of African education from the Department of Education to the much loathed Native Affairs Department.... African primary and secondary schools operated by the church and mission bodies were given the choice of turning over their schools to the government or receiving ... diminished subsidies; either the government took over education for Africans or there would be no education for Africans. African teachers were not permitted to criticize the government or any school authority. It was ... a way of institutionalizing inferiority.[5]

In 1953 and 1954 Hendrik Verwoerd, the minister in charge of black education, made the government's position clear in speeches to parliament: the only role of blacks in South Africa's "European" community was performing labor that did not extend above a certain level. Therefore existing schooling "misled" black children by allowing them to look through doorways they could never enter.[6] He concluded that education must match people's training with their opportunities in life. "In short," Mandela commented, "Africans should be trained ... to be in a position of perpetual subordination to the white man."[7] He added,

> The act and Verwoerd's crude exposition of it aroused widespread indignation from both black and white. With the exception of the Dutch Reform Church, which supported apartheid, and the Lutheran mission, all Christian churches opposed the new measure. But the unity of the opposition extended only to condemning the policy, not resisting it.... If all the other

churches had ... resisted, the government would have been confronted with a stalemate that might have forced a compromise. Instead, the state marched over us.[8]

Mandela and the ANC were forced to compromise. At first they argued that they should respond with an indefinite boycott of schools. Mandela, with his characteristic practical acumen, realized that people would lose confidence in the ANC if it promised more than it could perform. He recommended that the ANC limit its boycott to only a week, but his advice was overruled, and an indefinite boycott was declared. As Mandela assessed it, the campaign "clearly failed" to shut down the schools or do away with the Bantu Education Act. Alienation among blacks intensified. "For it was the Bantu Education Act that produced in the 1970s the angriest, most rebellious generation of black youth the country had ever seen."[9] Another consequence of the takeover of the educational system was that it led Desmond Tutu to give up his chosen career as a teacher in favor of the Anglican priesthood, thereby producing one of the world's most remarkable leaders.

The 1950s saw growing—for the most part nonviolent—protest against white minority rule, but when protest was repeatedly suppressed with ever harsher measures, popular resistance intensified in proportion. Despite international censure, the government punished the increasing opposition by further abridging civil liberties and implementing still harsher repression. After the police massacred sixty-nine unarmed Africans in 1960 at a demonstration against the pass laws in Sharpeville, south of Johannesburg, countrywide rioting and demonstrations occurred. The government declared a state of emergency, suspended habeas corpus, and placed the state under martial law. The two principal dissident movements, the ANC and the Pan Africanist Congress (PAC), were outlawed.[10] Members went underground or into exile and resorted to armed rebellion, and a number of their top leaders, including Nelson Mandela, were arrested. As Mandela described the situation,

> The countrywide police raid had led to the detention without trial of more than two thousand people [of] all races and all antiapartheid parties.... Units of the army had been mobilized and stationed in strategic areas around the country. On April 8, both the ANC and the PAC were declared illegal organizations, under the Suppression of Communism Act. Overnight, being a member of the ANC had become a felony.... Now even nonviolent law-abiding protests under the auspices of the ANC were illegal. The struggle had entered a new phase. We were now, all of us, outlaws.[11]

In 1961, partly in response to other African Commonwealth states' criticism of apartheid (supported by Canada and India), the South African government further isolated itself from the world community by leaving the British Commonwealth and declaring itself a republic. In South Africa the black consciousness movement was emerging as a political force during the late 1960s and 1970s, and a new, strong antiapartheid trade union movement was beginning, but open mass resistance to the government remained silenced.[12]

In 1975, when many antiapartheid political leaders were in jail, in exile, or banned from political activity, Desmond Tutu became the first black dean of St. Mary's Cathedral in Johannesburg. Instead of living in the exclusive white suburb where his deanery was situated, he moved to Johannesburg's black South Western Township (Soweto). On May

6, 1976, he wrote an open letter to then prime minister B. J. Vorster about the need for political change:[13]

> We [blacks] are aware that politics is the art of the possible. We cannot expect you to move so far in advance of your voters that you alienate their support. We are ready to accept some meaningful signs which would demonstrate that you and your government and all whites really mean business when you say you want peaceful change. First, accept the urban black as a permanent inhabitant of what is wrongly called white South Africa, with consequent freehold property rights. He will have a stake in the land and would not easily join those who wish to destroy his country. Indeed, he would be willing to die to defend his mother country and his birthright. Secondly, and also as a matter of urgency, repeal the pass laws which demonstrate to blacks more clearly than anything else that they are third-rate citizens in their beloved country. Thirdly, it is imperative, Sir, that you call a National Convention made up of the genuine leaders (i.e., leaders recognized as such by their section of the community) to try to work out an orderly evolution of South Africa into a nonracial, open and just society. I believe firmly that your leadership is quite unassailable, that you have been given virtually a blank check by the white electorate and that you have little to fear from a so-called right-wing backlash. For if the things which I suggest are not done soon and a rapidly deteriorating situation arrested, then there will be no right wing to fear—there will be nothing.[14]

In May 1976 black students went on strike to protest government attempts to impose Afrikaans, regarded as the language of the oppressor, in Soweto secondary school instruction along with English. Further boycotts followed, as well as isolated incidents of violence. On June 16, Soweto students organized a protest march. When armed white police used tear gas on them, the students answered with stones, and the police opened fire, killing thirteen-year-old Hector Peterson. Rioting spread to other areas, and by June 24 the official death toll was 140. The years of quiet resistance had ended.[15]

The black consciousness movement became a strong element in the protests. It had begun in South Africa in the 1960s, and in 1969 the South African Students' Convention (BPC) was created as its umbrella body. The government exerted harsh repression on the leaders of the movement, culminating in a two-year-long show trial in Pretoria that issued five- and six-year jail sentences for nine dissidents at the end of 1976.

Then Steve Biko, one of the movement's most effective advocates, was arrested on August 18, 1977, and delivered the next day into the custody of the Port Elizabeth Security Police. He was detained naked in a police cell for eighteen days without being questioned. His interrogation, accompanied by torture and beating, began on September 6, and by the next morning he had received a brain injury from blows to the head. When he fell into a coma and prompt medical attention became imperative, Biko, lying naked on the floor of a police van, was transported on September 11 to a hospital—in Pretoria, 750 miles away. He died on September 12, the tenth political prisoner known to die in custody that year. At first the government attributed his death to a hunger strike. Later, when the injuries he suffered demanded explanation, it was claimed he had resisted the police during interrogation. The minister of justice, Jimmy Kruger, told a party congress that Biko's death left him unmoved ("cold").[16]

The South African government, true to form, blamed black consciousness for the disturbance and outlawed twenty black consciousness organizations, along with their supporting groups. Most of the groups' leaders were arrested. The dissenting press also suffered: the *World,* a major black newspaper, was banned, and its editor and other journalists detained. White sympathizers such as C. F. Beyers Naude, a dissident Afrikaner church leader, and Donald Woods, a newspaper editor and friend of Steve Biko, were also banned. Woods left the country and published his story in a book, *I Found My Brother: Steve Biko.* It later became a movie that had a powerful effect in democratic countries.

More than 150,000 people attended Biko's funeral on September 25, including a large U.S. delegation and representatives of many other Western democracies. Thousands of mourners who crowded the streets outside increased their number. The Reverend Desmond Tutu, then Anglican bishop of Lesotho, was a speaker at the ceremony.[17]

When we heard the news "Steve Biko is dead" we were struck numb with disbelief.... It all seems such a senseless waste of a wonderfully gifted person.... What can be the purpose of such wanton destruction? ... What must we do which we have not done, what must we say which we have not said a thousand times over, oh, for so many years—that all we want is what belongs to all God's children, what belongs as an inalienable right: a place in the sun in our own beloved mother country.... Oh, God, how long can we go on ... appealing for a more just ordering of society where we all, black and white together, count not because of some accident of birth or a biological irrelevance, where all of us, black and white, count because we are human persons, human persons created in Your own image.[18]

The World Responds to Violent Oppression

Biko's death attracted international attention. In 1977 the UN Security Council imposed a mandatory arms embargo on South Africa, its first against a member state. How a sovereign state treats its populations has historically been considered solely the affair of the nation involved. But South Africa's system of apartheid had become recognized as an international concern. The UN Security Council labeled it a threat to international peace and security and in 1979 imposed economic sanctions on South Africa. How effective this would have been without the later decision of private banks to impose punitive measures on South Africa is unclear, but certainly the cumulative impact on the business community and on the government was powerful.[19] International economic sanctions were accompanied by grassroots campaigns in Europe and North America that urged corporations to discontinue investments in South Africa. They also had a major effect in encouraging peaceful change.

In 1983 the South African government tried disingenuously to answer the demand for equal rights by "broadening democracy" with a tricameral constitution that granted political participation to Indians and "coloreds" (people of mixed race) but totally excluded blacks—South Africa's largest and most heavily burdened group. In 1991 blacks represented 74.8 percent of the total South African population, whites 14.1 percent, Indians 2.6 percent, and coloreds 8.5 percent.[20] This exclusion fueled revolt in the 1980s, a period when political violence became a constant element of South African life. Between 1985 and 1989 political violence caused 5,387 deaths.[21]

Implementation of the new constitution in September 1984 led to widespread violence. School disturbances were followed by protests against the elections, in which only 18 percent of the coloreds and 16 percent of the ethnic Indians eligible to vote took part.[22] Violence broke out when white local councilors—who represented less than 10 percent of eligible voters—imposed rent increases in black townships south of Johannesburg. Protests widened on November 5 and 6 to become the biggest political strike in South Africa's history. Between September 3 and the end of 1984, at least 149 people were killed. To the world's horror, the very powerful and dangerous South African Defense Force was deployed in the townships in October. In the same month Desmond Tutu received the 1984 Nobel Peace Prize.[23] This was an important contribution of the international community to the democratic cause. His Nobel lecture, delivered in December, painted a heartrending picture of his homeland:

> I come from a beautiful land, richly endowed by God with wonderful natural resources.... There is enough of the good things that come from God's bounty ... for everyone, but apartheid has confirmed some in their selfishness, causing them to grasp greedily a disproportionate share.... They have taken 87% of the land, though being only about 20% of our population. The rest have had to make do with the remaining 13%. Apartheid has decreed the politics of exclusion: 73% of the population is excluded from any meaningful participation in the political decision-making processes of the land of their birth. The new constitution, making provision for three chambers, for whites, coloreds and Indians, mentions blacks only once and thereafter ignores them completely. Thus this new constitution, lauded in parts of the West as a step in the right direction, entrenches racism and ethnicity.... Blacks are expected to exercise their political ambitions in unviable, poverty-stricken, arid Bantustan homelands, ghettos of misery, inexhaustible reservoirs of cheap black labor, Bantustans into which South Africa is being balkanized. Blacks are systematically being stripped of their South African citizenship and being turned into aliens in the land of their birth. This is apartheid's final solution, just as Nazism had its final solution for the Jews in Hitler's Aryan madness. ...
>
> In pursuance of apartheid's ideological racist dream, over three million of God's children have been uprooted from their homes, which have been demolished, while they have been dumped in the Bantustan homeland resettlement camps. I say dumped advisedly: only rubbish or things are dumped, not human beings.... These dumping grounds are far from where work and food can be procured easily. Children starve, ... not accidentally but by deliberate government policy. They starve in a land that could be the bread basket of Africa, a land that normally is a net exporter of food. ...
>
> Apartheid has spawned discriminatory education, ... education for serfdom, ensuring that the government spends on a black child per annum for education only about one-tenth of what it spends on a white child. It is education that is decidedly separate and unequal. It is ... wantonly wasteful of human resources.... South Africa is paying a heavy price already for this iniquitous policy, because there is a desperate shortage of skilled manpower, a direct result of the shortsighted schemes of the racist regime. It is a moral universe that we inhabit, and good and right and equity matter in the universe of the God we worship. And so, in this matter, the South African government and its supporters are being properly hoisted with their own petard. ...
>
> Such an evil system ... relies on ... draconian laws such as the security legislation which is almost peculiar to South Africa. There are the laws which permit the indefinite detention of persons whom the Minister of Law and Order has decided are a threat to the security of the state. They are detained at his pleasure, in solitary confinement, without access to their family, their own doctor, or a lawyer. That is severe punishment when the evidence apparently

available to the minister has not been tested in an open court.... It is a far too convenient device for a repressive regime.... Many, too many, have died mysteriously in detention. ...

It is against this system that our people have sought to protest peacefully since 1912 at least, with the founding of the African National Congress. They have used the conventional methods of peaceful protest—petitions, demonstrations, deputations and even a passive resistance campaign.... The response of the authorities has been escalating intransigence and violence, the violence of police dogs, tear gas, detention without trial, exile, and even death....

There is no peace in Southern Africa. There is no peace because there is no justice. There can be no real peace and security until there be first justice enjoyed by all the inhabitants of that beautiful land.[24]

Thus, during the 1980s, genocide might well have occurred. The government possessed a powerful store of arms, including weapons of mass destruction. Its leaders were deeply prejudiced, self-righteous, and oriented to violence as a political solution. Moreover, millions of blacks were concentrated in remote, segregated areas, and the government could readily have added others in preparation for a "final solution." Yet there were also humane elements in both black and white populations that were oriented to pragmatic problem solving. As the decade came to an end, they gathered strength.

Unfair elections in South Africa became regular occasions for protest. On election day in 1989 more than 2 million workers throughout South Africa stayed home from work, and an exceptionally vicious police response to protests in Cape Town resulted in many deaths in black townships.[25] Archbishop Tutu, greatly shaken by the violence, called a protest march. Both black and white Capetonians were shocked by the brutality and supported his call. The mayor of Cape Town, Gordon Oliver, newly elected by white voters, unexpectedly came to the memorial service directly after his installation and stated to newsmen that he would join the march, illegal though it was. Tutu met with diplomats from twelve countries, including Britain, the United States, France, the Federal Republic of Germany, Australia, and Canada, and asked them to condemn police violence and to monitor the march.

Thus President F. W. de Klerk faced unrelenting domestic and international pressure in the opening days of his administration. The night before the march, two cabinet ministers told the archbishop by telephone that de Klerk would allow it. When Archbishop Tutu arrived at the cathedral, where the march was to begin, he found it jammed, with thousands spilling over into the streets. A crowd of 30,000 proceeded from the cathedral to City Hall, where Tutu's remarks were greeted with cheers and laughter.

There is nothing wrong with this beautiful country except for apartheid! There is nothing wrong with this beautiful country except for injustice! There is nothing wrong with this country except for the violence of apartheid!

And so we say to Mr. de Klerk, ... "You wanted us to show you that we can be dignified. You wanted us to show you that we are disciplined. You wanted us to show you that we are determined. You wanted us to show you that we are peaceful.... Mr. de Klerk, please come here! We are inviting you, Mr. de Klerk, ... Mr. Vlok, ... all the cabinet. We say, ... can you see the people of this country? Come and see what this country is going to become.

This country is a rainbow country! ... Mr. de Klerk, ... join us ... in this new South Africa.[26]

After the Cape Town march, other enormous marches occurred throughout the country, with broad church support. Political violence continued to flare up from time to time, sometimes very seriously. The most dramatic case was the murder of Chris Hani—but the seeds of conflict resolution were also being planted. On Easter Saturday, April 10, 1993, a right-wing Polish immigrant with links to the white Conservative Party gunned down the immensely popular black leader Chris Hani in his own driveway, leaving his corpse to be discovered by his young daughter. A neighbor who witnessed the crime, a white Afrikaner woman, informed the police of the fleeing assassin's automobile license, and he was promptly captured. All South Africa expected a bloody outburst of black anger.

Once again, leadership made a critical difference in determining that violence would no longer be used as a tool to halt South Africa's progress toward interracial reconciliation and democracy. Nelson Mandela immediately appeared on national television to ask for calm, reminding his audience— "*all* South Africans"—that it was a white woman who at her own peril had alerted the police and that violence would only serve those who wished to destroy the ideals of freedom and tolerance that "Chris Hani gave his life for."[27] This was in effect a presidential speech, even though Mandela had not yet been elected.

This pivotal crisis created an unofficial shift in the balance of power. De Klerk, unaware of its significance, merely issued a statement from his vacation home, whereas Mandela took control in using his enormous moral authority to promote peace. Black South Africans heeded Mandela's plea to forgo revenge, despite growing recognition of the danger of the white extreme right wing, which had a large constituency in the South African police and security forces. These militant elements might have triggered a genocide. Mandela and the ANC realized that they could not continue to expect unvarying restraint from an impatient constituency. They made the anger over Hani's murder an argument to press the National Party to fix a date for elections that would include all races, something negotiations had long deferred. When that date was set, another peaceful step toward democracy had been taken[28]—thus overcoming the danger of extreme violence.

Breakthrough: South Africa Seeks Conflict Resolution on All Levels

By 1989 a stalemate had developed between the government and the resisters of apartheid. The government had an overwhelming superiority in wealth, technological expertise, and powerful weapons, but the resistance had the strong advantage of popular support and moral standing, both inside and outside the country. Businesspeople were concerned about the economic consequences of international sanctions (especially financial) and boycotts.

A public breach in the impasse came in 1990 with President de Klerk's opening speech to parliament. In a dramatic political turnaround, he lifted the ban on rival political organizations, pardoned political prisoners, and promised free political expression for everyone. A few days later Mandela left prison after twenty-seven years, soon after to address a rally in Durban of about 100,000 supporters. Antiapartheid leaders rejoiced at de Klerk's measures but were justifiably wary. Nelson Mandela, who had been approached in prison as early as 1984 with "feelers" from the South African government, combined an astoundingly magnanimous absence of vindictiveness with clear-eyed awareness of his antagonists' motives:

> Despite his seemingly progressive actions, Mr. de Klerk was by no means the great emancipa-tor. He was a gradualist, a careful pragmatist. He did not make any of his reforms with the intention of putting himself out of power. He made them for precisely the opposite reason: to ensure power for the Afrikaner in a new dispensation. He was not yet prepared to negotiate the end of white rule. His goal was to create a system of power sharing based on group rights, which would preserve a modified form of minority power in South Africa. He was decidedly opposed to majority rule, or "simple majoritarianism" as he sometimes called it, because that would end white domination in a single stroke. We knew early on that the government was fiercely opposed to a winner-takes-all Westminster parliamentary system, and advocated instead a system of proportional representation with built-in structural guarantees for the white minority. Although he was prepared to allow the black majority to vote and create legislation, he wanted to retain a minority veto. From the start I would have no truck with this plan. I described it to Mr. de Klerk as apartheid in disguise, a "loser-takes-all" system. The Nationalists' long-term strategy to overcome our strength was to build an anti-ANC alliance with the Inkatha Freedom Party and to lure the Coloured Afrikaans-speaking voters of the Cape to a new National Party. From the moment of my release, they began wooing both Buthelezi [the leader of the primarily Zulu Inkatha Freedom Party (IFP)], and the Coloured voters of the Cape. The government attempted to scare the Coloured population into thinking the ANC was anti-Coloured. They supported Chief Buthelezi's desire to retain Zulu power and identity in a new South Africa by preaching to him the doctrine of group rights and federalism.[29]

Archbishop Tutu was also very generous, open to bargaining, and clear-eyed. Both Mandela and Tutu were aware that the government hoped Mandela would stumble after his release and lose his overwhelming popular support. Tutu wrote:

> I have to say [that de Klerk] has amazed me and in many ways I could not believe my ears.... I found it exhilarating, quite astounding that we seem to be at the dawn of the new South Africa for which so many people have striven.... It is not all that I hoped for but it is a very considerable part of it. Our people are not intransigent, crazy or anything of that kind. They are going to say, many of them, that we have made a very important breakthrough.... It is clear that [the government has] taken account of ... the pressures of international opinion, sanctions, and the pressures of our people. When I say "our people," I say black and white people who have been struggling for a new dispensation.... Extraordinary things can hap-pen once people sit down and look each other in the eyes and are no longer ogres to one another. I myself believe that given a measure of goodwill, and some trust ... we would see movement very rapidly.[30]

In a service of thanksgiving on March 6, 1990, Archbishop Tutu spoke at greater length about changes in South Africa.

> We have seen some extraordinary things, haven't we?
> Nelson is released, and they said, "[E]verything about him is really a myth. He ought to be kept in jail because if he comes out people are going to be disillusioned." Disillusioned! He truly is one of the greatest people around, his generosity of spirit. How, after twenty-seven

years, he can come out of jail and be so totally, totally unbitter, so ready to acknowledge the good that is in others, even others who made him suffer as much as he has suffered? It is not only he. You talk to people like Walter Sisulu and almost all of them.... We thank God, too, for our overseas partners and friends who have supported and continue to support our struggle with their prayers, with their pressure, with their sanctions. We say to them: Keep it up. Thank you, international community.... Let us also acknowledge that Mr. de Klerk has been courageous.[31]

On May 9, 1990, Archbishop Tutu explained to cadets at the U.S. Military Academy at West Point why he believed changes had occurred in South Africa.

Why now? Some of what is happening at home was due to the fact that the government tried repression. It thought that it would knock the stuffing out of our people, and our people said, "Not on your life.... No matter how long you succeed in oppressing a people ... ultimately you will come a cropper.... "The second reason ... is because the world has heeded our pleas and applied economic pressure on the South African government. Namibia is free and independent today because South Africa could no longer afford fighting in Angola and we want to say thank you to those who have responded to our appeal. Money or the lack of it helps to concentrate the mind pretty sharply. Third is the quite undoubted impact of the ending of the Cold War.... In South Africa the government used to talk about what they called the total Communist onslaught. Then when the Russians and this country began talking peace they could no longer ... speak about their fears of a Communism that was saying: We are no longer interested in expansion, we are interested in peace. ... I would want to add that we have been fortunate that at this present time in South Africa the State President is Mr. de Klerk rather than his predecessor, Mr. Botha.... But Nelson Mandela is also a key factor. Somehow a rapport has taken place between Mr. Mandela and Mr. de Klerk and you hear when they refer to each other the warmth, the respect that each has for the other. Those are the individuals who have a critical importance for what is taking place at home. ... There is no doubt at all in the end that we are going to be free ... because the cause which we uphold is a cause for justice. We are not seeking to dominate anybody. We are looking for a freedom that is going to be shared by all South Africans, black and white together. ... [32]

After the ANC had won a victory in the first democratically elected legislature in South African history, the National Assembly held its first meeting on May 9, 1994.[33] Archbishop Tutu acted as master of ceremonies at a celebration held that day. He first welcomed the new executive deputy president, F. W. de Klerk; then executive deputy president elect, Thabo Mbeki; and finally, the newly elected president, Nelson Mandela.

I can rightly call you fellow citizens, for on April 27 and 28 ... millions of us voted for the very first time. And a miracle happened. We discovered that we were South Africans and we have discovered that we are proud of that fact.... A new South Africa has come to birth.

We have said a resounding NO to racism ... to hatred ... to violence ... to alienation and division.... And we have said a loud and reverberating YES to freedom ... to reconciliation ... to forgiveness ... to peace [and to] unity.... We of many cultures, languages, and races are become one nation.[34]

President Mandela was inaugurated the following day, in front of what journalists called the largest gathering of heads of state and government since John F. Kennedy's funeral.

South Africa's transformation since 1990 has been called a "negotiated revolution."[35] Peter Gastrow, a lawyer and member of parliament who was involved in the establishment of the National Peace Accord (NPA) of 1991, observed that South Africa's transition was unprecedented but cautioned that it was neither inevitable nor irreversible.[36] Made necessary by the country's pervasive political violence, the National Peace Accord was a bold, even risky attempt at nationwide conflict resolution[37]

The need for transition to a better society became widely acknowledged, but this transition, morally and politically imperative as it was, in turn contributed to violence. The prospect of change generated unrealistic hopes and demands in blacks, fear and anxiety in whites, and increased competition among South Africa's political, socioeconomic, and ethnic groups—which will gradually diminish over decades to come.

The political instability that a pluralistic society can produce demands a political solution: institutional mechanisms that reduce intergroup conflict and maximize intergroup cooperation.[38] The conflict that modernization creates must be anticipated and resolved through political programs designed to involve deprived groups into political decision-making at all levels. These considerations guided the negotiations for a new constitution for South Africa that now accommodates the needs of a pluralistic society. After de Klerk's historic February 1990 speech, political leaders were faced with finding ways to minimize violence in the transition period before reforms had been put in place. The National Peace Accord came into being to meet this need. It deserves worldwide understanding.

The violence of the first years of transition must be seen in context. The coercive security measures practiced in the past had been justly rejected, and new measures, awaiting negotiation, had yet to emerge. At the same time, the competition inherent in negotiations for a new society intensified political rivalry and polarization. The difficulties of a complex situation were compounded by a severe economic recession, accompanied by widespread unemployment and poverty.[39]

This is the classic plight of fledgling democracies struggling to emerge from years of turbulence. When tensions and disturbances are intense, they can lead to civil war or revolution. The risk of genocide is then considerable.

The violence troubled South African leaders from every sector. Influential business-people expected sanctions would continue and negotiation efforts would stagnate unless bloodshed ended. The ANC felt violence was undermining its attempts to establish lasting local support and viable organizations. Powerlessness to end the armed strife embarrassed de Klerk and the National Party, weakened their negotiating strength, and played into the hands of white right-wing hard-liners. Chief Minister Mangosuthu Buthelezi aroused increasing local and international criticism for the serious commitment of their supporters to violence. By the end of 1990 it was clear that political violence was undermining progress toward constitutional negotiations and South Africa's long-term political stability.

The church was first to attempt a national intervention.[40] In March 1991, the South African Council of Churches (SACC) offered to convene a national meeting of all leaders of strife-torn communities. At this time South African churches were coming close to agreement. The Afrikaner churches were healing their deep historical divisions with the clerical critics of apartheid represented in the SACC, such as Methodists and Anglicans. Afrikaner churches had supported apartheid until 1986, when they finally rejected it; later, in 1990, they declared it a sin. Between 70 to 80 percent of South Africans profess to be Christians, so united church influence was powerful. In November 1990 a national church conference was held in Rustenburg. The 300 participants represented eighty denominations and forty religious organizations, all the churches and religious groups in South Africa except for two right-wing white churches. At that conference the major Afrikaner denomination, the Dutch Reformed Church, publicly confessed guilt for supporting apartheid, a confession that strengthened the mood of reconciliation expressed in the conference's Rustenburg Declaration. The declaration denounced apartheid, called for a democratic constitution in South Africa and a more equitable distribution of wealth, and urged churches to condemn all violence. The declaration also called on churches to coordinate their strategies and established a committee to arrange a peace conference to end the violence.

Buthelezi, who considered the SACC biased toward the ANC and its backers, answered with a denunciation of "naive" churchmen, who were nothing more than self-important busybodies eager to take control of the peace process in order to gain international attention.[41] This raised the question, if religious leaders were not acceptable facilitators, who could be?[42]

The Consultative Business Movement (CBM), an organization of progressive senior South African business leaders, recognized the need for both peace and a transformation of the country's political economy. CBM, with ninety corporate members, represented the largest mining, publishing, manufacturing, and chemical firms in the country, and it had a better relationship with the de Klerk government than did the SACC.[43]

CBM arranged three separate meetings with key sectors. The meetings produced no concrete results, but they made the CBM a recognized actor in negotiations for peace at a time when suspicions were elevated, alliances guardedly cautious, positions still unsettled, and violence unabated.[44]

Nelson Mandela was deeply concerned about the "war" that Inkatha had declared on ANC strongholds across the Natal Midlands, in which Zulu murdered Zulu, since partisans of both Inkatha and ANC were Zulus. Almost immediately after he gained his freedom, he addressed a mostly Zulu crowd of over 100,000 at King's Park, begging them to end the war immediately. His plea was rejected. He tried to arrange a meeting with Inkatha chief Buthelezi,[45] but his fellow ANC members vetoed that idea. He had also tried—in vain—to meet with the venerated Zulu king, hoping to gain his support against the more violent elements.

The breadth of the opposition to de Klerk's proposed peace summit was unexpected. South Africa's major labor organization, the Congress of South African Trade Unions (COSATU), refused to attend and demanded that an independent body convene the conference. Both they and the ANC declared at May Day rallies throughout the nation that a peace summit originating from such a partisan and violence-prone source had little legitimacy.

Organized commerce and industry, as represented by the conservative business group SACOB (South African Chamber of Business), countered with a formal statement and press advertisement calling for national support of the summit.[46] President de Klerk contended that it was the government's responsibility to call the summit because it held the ultimate authority for maintaining law and order. He asked the ANC to reconsider its ultimatum.

As May 9, the last day for the government to meet ANC demands, approached and it was clear that the government would not comply, church leaders shuttled between Mandela and de Klerk in an attempt to prevent a serious confrontation and to keep alive the hope of peace negotiations. A last-minute compromise between de Klerk and Buthelezi was reached just hours before the ultimatum was to expire, and when the day of the ultimatum passed none of the major political parties made it an issue. Shuttle diplomacy involving church, political, and business leaders appeared to have won the day.

Then key leaders decided to call a meeting that would bring all the political parties together and combine the forces of the churches, organized business, and other relatively less involved civil society groups. Although they could not induce the ANC to attend de Klerk's conference, they got its approval of de Klerk's acknowledgment that his meeting was only a beginning and that other meetings would be held with a more inclusive participation.[47]

The de Klerk peace summit of May 24–25, 1991, included representatives from the IFP, the Democratic Party, SACOB, CBM, and many government departments, self-governing states, and independent institutes. The ANC, the PAC, the Aznanian People's Organization (AZAPO), the Conservative Party, and the SACC abstained. This meant that the conference's decisions would not be binding on those essential actors who did not participate.

The conference, however, made some gains. Buthelezi publicly recognized that peace would require coexistence between the IFP and ANC. He proposed a peace secretariat that would create a network of regional and local "peace action groups" throughout the country—a recommendation later incorporated into the NPA.[48] The summit also chose the cochairman of the Rustenburg Church Conference committee, Louw Alberts, as facilitator for a second, more representative, all-party peace conference.

Alberts, a layman acceptable to de Klerk, the ANC, and most other groups that had shunned the first summit, collaborated with the Reverend Frank Chikane, another Rustenburg committee member and SACC leader, to select a racially and politically balanced facilitating body agreeable to all. Chikane looked for candidates acceptable to the ANC, the PAC, COSATU, AZAPO, the Communists, and others on the political left, and Alberts sought representatives acceptable to the government, business, and the IFP. They settled on thirteen figures from religion and business and agreed on a rotating chairmanship.[49] Most of the members knew each other.

To save face for all, Alberts arranged for lower-level leadership to do the negotiating and report the results to their superiors. The leaders would then advise them and send them back to further negotiation until a satisfactory agreement was finally achieved. The same approach was used with the National Peace Accord.[50]

Rotating the post of chairman kept any one party from being perceived as taking control. The delegates were asked to identify causes of political violence as well as ways of ending it. No debate was allowed as they stated their views and suggested solutions, all of which were recorded on flip charts. Permitting debate on certain inflammatory matters would have resulted in the meeting's collapse.[51] The main recommendations that emerged included a code of conduct for political organizations and for security forces as well as plans for socioeconomic development and implementation, such as a statutory standing commission and peace secretariats at national, regional, and community levels.

A respected committee created groups to work out a consensus document on (1) a code of conduct for political parties, (2) a code of conduct for security forces, (3) socioeconomic development, (4) implementation and monitoring, and (5) process, secretariat, and media.[52] Each working group had a balanced membership. The consensus reports were collated into the National Peace Accord, to be considered and agreed upon at a National Peace Convention in September 1991.

The September peace convention had an unprecedented attendance of leaders from all of South Africa's political, religious, business, and tribal groups (except for three white right-wing parties). Many of them had gained extensive mediating and negotiating skills in their work. Church leaders had mediated conflict between security forces and township dwellers during the political revolts of the 1980s. Business leaders had dealt with strikes and unions.[53] Their final product, the NPA, set out a vision for a new democracy, peace, and stability and provided for the establishment of a nationwide network of peace committees and other structures to realize these objectives. Universally accepted fundamental rights—freedom of conscience, speech, association, and assembly—and free participation in peaceful political activity were spelled out and endorsed.[54]

An important structure the accord established was the Commission of Inquiry Regarding the Prevention of Public Violence and Intimidation. The parliament created the commission, called the Goldstone Commission after its chairman, a few months before the accord that endorsed it was signed. Its function was to look into incidents of political violence, to explore their causes, and to identify who was responsible. It recommended steps to prevent public violence and intimidation and enjoyed some legal powers such as the power to subpoena witnesses and enter premises.[55] Overall, it earned worldwide respect that is to this day symbolized in its chairman, Judge Richard Goldstone.

At the grassroots level, breaches of the accord were dealt with by the parties themselves, through "mediation, arbitration, and adjudication." The National Peace Committee (NPC) was charged with handling breaches of the code of conduct for political parties. The National Peace Agreement was a far-reaching agreement.[56]

After the signing of the accord, structures for its implementation were set up. The NPC had at least one representative of each signatory to the accord, with a total of sixty members. Most were top-level, experienced politicians. Their leaders were highly regarded for promoting peace and reconciliation among all South Africans.[57]

The drafters of the NPA realized that to achieve peace the accord would have to address some of the underlying causes of the violence, such as poverty, lack of proper policing, and an unrepresentative and authoritarian system of government. In short, it would have to change South African society, a larger goal than one would ordinarily expect from a peace accord. The NPA expresses three objectives:

1. To create networks of peacemaking and peacebuilding mechanisms at the local level that would eliminate political violence
2. To promote democratization by creating a climate of greater tolerance that in turn would facilitate negotiations and cooperating multiparty government
3. To promote reconstruction and development, particularly in communities directly affected by the violence[58]

South Africa had never experienced democracy and had no tradition of political tolerance, as its continuing political violence made evident. Merely writing a new constitution could not solve this problem. Yet a strong, democratic, widely accepted constitution can help, and leading South Africans looked to it for guidance.

A 1993 evaluation by International Alert noted the South African Peace Accord structure's invaluable contribution in giving citizens, especially the most disadvantaged, channels to express their grievances with a justifiable hope of having them redressed and in bringing together former rivals through dialogue. The peace accord, despite its imperfections, served a crucial groundbreaking function during the transition to peace.[59]

Assistance from international observers was requested after a massacre at Boipatong in June 1992. Forty-eight people, most of them women and children, were killed when men from nearby hostels attacked their shack settlement, south of Johannesburg. At the appeal of Nelson Mandela to the UN to "find ways to normalize the deteriorating situation in South Africa," then Secretary-General Boutros Boutros-Ghali sent Cyrus Vance (U.S. secretary of state in the Carter administration) to South Africa on a fact-finding trip. Vance received unprecedented cooperation from all political groups, even the white right wing. He fostered and achieved broad support for allowing international observers into South Africa, something the government had opposed up to then.[60]

Following the fact-finding mission, UN resolution 772 of August 17, 1992, authorized the Secretary-General to deploy UN observers in South Africa. In 1994, the UN sent one of its most accomplished diplomats, Ambassador Lakhtar Brahimi, to help with the situation. The resolution further invited the Secretary-General to aid in strengthening NPA structures and called on international organizations such as the OAU, the Commonwealth, and the European Community (EC) to consider deploying their own observers in coordination with the UN and the NPA structures.[61]

The arrival of international observers from the UN, the EC, the Commonwealth, and the OAU also had a positive effect in making some no-go areas more accessible to non-dominant political groups. Their presence—along with peace committee members—at rallies and marches had a dampening influence on the enthusiasm of political rivals for violence. There was general consensus that the presence of international observers contributed greatly to the peaceful outcome. Political rivals—and security forces as well—put on their best behavior.[62] In large part, fear of appearing an aggressor before the rest of the world caused this restraint.

Changes in South Africa's political culture and attitudes were speeded up by effective programs that emphasized reconciliation, tolerance, shared respect, and democratic principles, beginning with the use of three-day seminars throughout the country for members of the peace structures. These seminars trained peace committee members in the content of the NPA and taught them how to run meetings and employ mediation, facilitation, negotiation, and other relevant skills.[63]

Building Democracy

In 1997, midway through Nelson Mandela's presidency, the Carnegie Commission on Preventing Deadly Conflict sponsored a two-day seminar in Cape Town, at which South

Africans who had participated in their country's transition to democracy were invited to reflect on past progress and future prospects and to examine how South Africa had succeeded in avoiding genocide or civil war.[64]

The seminar concentrated on three broad goals that every country struggling to build a sustainable democracy must meet: (1) a government generally recognized as accountable, competent, and fair; (2) broad-based economic well-being; and (3) social equity and opportunities. How and in what order each goal is achieved will depend on the country's history, culture, and resources as well as international cooperation to assist socioeconomic development.

The seminar began with South Africa's main challenge—the political transformation from apartheid to inclusive constitutional democracy—and stressed the role of leadership in opening the way for democracy and reconciliation; power sharing and the excellent constitution adopted on May 8, 1996; and the redefinition of South African national identity, a process that would include resolving past injustices by truth and reconciliation, not revenge. Next came the economic aspects of South Africa's transformation: in particular, dealing with unemployment and effectively implementing over the years the 1996 macroeconomic strategy. This is essential to South Africa's economic growth, increased equity, and sustainable self-government. Finally, the meeting addressed education, crime prevention, and free media. South Africa's long-term political success will depend not only on the government's capacity and willingness to meet the needs of the people but also on the people's capacity and willingness to assume their civic responsibilities and obligations. After the long history of repression, anguish, and intergroup hostility, the road ahead is necessarily a long and difficult one. The Mandela government started in a deep hole but frankly recognized serious socioeconomic problems and tried hard to be fair to all the people—and avoid a winner-take-all position.

Continued international support to strengthen South Africa's civil society is necessary. South Africa lacks the resources and administrative capacity to develop the social equity and citizen involvement needed to sustain democratic peace, yet movement in this direction continues. International investors should consider a successful South Africa as intrinsically valuable and a stimulus for the region, e.g., as a provider of advice and technical assistance in advancing democracy. All of this means that democracies progress only gradually, are always susceptible to backsliding, and need international help for at least a decade or two in order to achieve democratic consolidation.

In the political domain, three elements—extraordinary leadership, the new constitution, and the work of the Truth and Reconciliation Commission (TRC)—clarify how South Africa answered the threat of mass violence and built the foundations of sustainable democracy.

South Africa was fortunate in its leaders. De Klerk and his party might have refused to negotiate with the ANC and responded with even harsher repression. Mandela might have rejected sharing power with whites and intensified fighting. Both leaders were brave enough not to be swayed by those of their followers who demanded revenge. They were pragmatic problem solvers with moral authority. Moreover, they had a "depth on the bench" of potential democratic leaders, partly facilitated by international foundations and democratic governments beyond Africa.

In his essay on Nelson Mandela, prepared for the Carnegie Commission on Preventing Deadly Conflict in 1998, Archbishop Desmond Tutu offered invaluable insight into the sort of leadership South Africa was fortunate to have.

In 1988 Nelson Mandela was still in South Africa's apartheid prison system.... He would turn 70 that July, and his friend, the doughty president of the Anti-Apartheid Movement, Archbishop Trevor Huddleston, C.R., had suggested that the world should celebrate this birthday. Many young people ... from various parts of the United Kingdom ... converged on Hyde Park Corner in London on Nelson's birthday. The crowd that gathered ... was about a quarter million strong, mostly youngsters who had not even been born when Mandela went to prison. And yet here they were, gathered to honor this prisoner, as if he were a pop star. Why? ...[65]

Our modern-day world has often been described as hard-nosed and cynical, quite inhospitable to idealism and other noble ideas.... There was a contempt for weakness, and it didn't seem there was much room for goodness, gentleness, or caring. ...

The reaction of hundreds of people to [persons such as Nelson Mandela, Mother Teresa, and the Dalai Lama] is totally at variance with [that] conventional wisdom.... I contend that despite all appearances to the contrary, the world admires someone who is good, and the world recognizes goodness when it sees it. ...

And it seems that you establish your credibility by demonstrating that your involvement is not for personal aggrandizement.... People know the true leader is not in it for what he or she can get out of it. The ... acid test of this ... is whether one is ready to suffer.... There can be no question that Nelson has suffered. [H]e spent 27 years in jail and had declared at his trial that he was even ready to lay down his life for the cause to which he had committed himself. ...

[T]he authentic leader has a solidarity with those he or she is leading. This is particularly so when they are involved in a struggle for self-determination, for independence, and for freedom from an oppressive overlord. ...

The good leader is one who is affirming of others, ... coaxing them to become the best they are capable of becoming. This style of leadership is not coercive but plays to the strengths of others.... They are inspirational because ... they enable others to blossom and not to wilt. ...

I believe too that a good leader has intuition, ... the capacity to read the signs of the times, and ... this uncanny sixth sense of knowing when to go for it.... The real leader knows too when to make concessions, when to compromise, when to employ the art of losing the battle in order to win the war.

Many other factors supported remarkable leadership in South Africa's progress toward democracy and helped to avoid genocide:

- Both sides recognized that a sustained fight would be economically ruinous and would leave the victors few resources with which to consolidate their triumph and govern effectively. An all-out civil war or genocide would be utterly disastrous for *all* concerned.
- South Africa's economy, despite its huge disparities, still allowed reasonable prospects for all groups to earn respect and income. By the late 1980s a cross-racial consumer culture that prized pragmatism and negotiation for the sake of economic benefits was emerging. This orientation helped keep the society together.

- Black South Africans, increasingly determined to win their rights, could be kept down only by ever more costly repression. Continued white violence to defend the status quo would have been internationally condemned as genocide, and continued black violence against a white minority that had shown willingness to reform would have alienated powerful states outside Africa.
- The majority of both blacks and whites in South Africa held a common faith, Christianity, and Christian churchmen throughout the world joined with progressive South African religious leaders to challenge the moral status of apartheid. In 1987 all major Christian denominations united to issue a declaration condemning the apartheid regime. The declaration came at a critical moment in the debate within the South African white community about the future of minority rule. The extraordinary moral leadership of Archbishop Desmond Tutu and Nelson Mandela fostered nonviolent problem solving.
- The adoption in 1979 of labor legislation that allowed interracial collective bargaining, particularly in the mining sector, gave blacks real power and negotiating experience that contributed to the "bargaining culture" after 1990.
- During the 1970s and 1980s, domestic and international support of the anti-apartheid United Democratic Front grew as the apartheid government declined, economically and morally. It had become an international pariah, and its leaders were sensitive to this pressure. Yet the apartheid government remained very powerful in terms of its arms, which included nuclear, biological, and chemical weapons of mass destruction.[67] The capacity to implement genocidal policies was present.
- Whites, increasingly reluctant to make substantial sacrifices to preserve their political privileges, became resigned to what they perceived as an inevitable shift of political power to the black majority. Revelations of corruption in the National Party further weakened the government. Draft evasion, emigration, and capital flight increased, and polls recorded growing discontent with hard-line apartheid supporters.
- The South African government saw that its economy would not revive without international help—credit, investment, technology, and markets—help that was conditional on undertaking major political reforms.[66]

Independent international events also had an effect:

- The collapse of the Soviet Union removed a bogeyman that the National Party had used to maintain support at home and to quiet opposition abroad, especially in the West. It also dried up a source of encouragement for the more radical elements of the liberation forces, allowing Mandela to maintain his inherent preference for a moderate position, favoring the well-being of *all* the people rather than revenge. Gorbachev's peaceful policies were influential.
- International determination to resolve conflicts in Angola and Mozambique further isolated the South African government, which had helped to promote them. The wars also strained South African forces, which had to support the rebels in Angola and Mozambique while they put down disturbances at home.

- Finally, the foreign NGOs, private foundations, trade unions, universities, and other organizations that trained and advised democratic South Africans encouraged compromise and built the human and institutional capacity to bargain effectively and to implement agreements.

Mandela's genius was to reassure both sides by advocating a democratic government that would abolish white abuse of power but guarantee that revenge would not be taken against the white minority.

Stremlau and Zille warned that success in balancing individual and group rights would depend over the long term on an economy that remained strong enough not to disappoint the material hopes of the whites—hopes of keeping most of the wealth that entrenched economic privilege had given them—and of the overwhelmingly poor black majority, impatient to advance economically.[68]

A key element of Mandela's leadership is the development of civil society: his belief that neither government nor a particular leader can guarantee the development and well-being of a nation. During the apartheid period, international (mostly nongovernmental) organizations had worked to help South Africans build a civil society. These organizations taught people vigorous but nonviolent assertion of their needs, pragmatic problem solving, and mutual accommodation in improving conditions of life.

One significant example of a bold foreign initiative was the Carnegie Inquiry into Poverty and Development in Southern Africa, based at the University of Cape Town in the 1980s and directed by the distinguished labor economist Dr. Francis Wilson. (Later, when the government lifted the banishment of Dr. Mamphela Ramphele at Carnegie's urging, she joined Wilson as codirector and, in a dramatic turn of events, became the vice chancellor of the University of Cape Town in 1996.) Archbishop Desmond Tutu chaired the Task Force on Religion and Poverty, and other brilliant, courageous South Africans from all social backgrounds also contributed to the effort for equality of opportunity, the rule of law, and nonviolent conflict resolution.

The inquiry was unprecedented in its active inclusion of South Africans from all sectors and races. It drew upon the knowledge and research of a network of scholars and professionals in law, medicine, economics, religion, and business as well as community leaders, teachers, and social workers with firsthand knowledge of poverty at the local level. Twenty participating universities in the region trained black South Africans in research and leadership skills—a rare opportunity for them at that time. Poverty was studied in relationship to land use, law, food and nutrition, health care, education and training, transport, housing, social welfare, and other quality-of-life indicators. It was also studied for its effects upon families, migrant workers, women, children, and the elderly. Overshadowing it all was the impact of apartheid.

Professional publications, international meetings, media coverage—even a traveling art exhibit—disseminated the inquiry's findings and practical recommendations widely. They became influential in South Africa, Europe, and the United States, and their intent was fulfilled when Nelson Mandela was freed and democratic development ensued, involving broadly inclusive conflict resolution. In the 1980s, the Carnegie Corporation also convened a consortium of universities and foundations for South African development. Its members included foundation officers and university executives from a variety of institutions in a successful effort to foster cooperation in the interest of efficiency as well as broader participation. The Carnegie experience in South Africa shows the value of nongovernmental institutions in pursuit of peace and justice—and of disseminating throughout the world the lessons learned in that pursuit.

Another U.S. NGO, the Ford Foundation, became involved in South Africa as early as the 1950s, with support for human rights, legal assistance, education, and community development.[69] From 1952 to 1959, small grants mainly supported research on racial policies, practices, and attitudes; travel and fellowships for South African academics; and conferences of religious leaders on social and political issues. In 1959 Ford sought increased contact between Americans and South Africans, especially scholars and educational institutions. Communications between Afrikaans- and English-speaking South Africans were also promoted.[70] During the 1960s Ford grants supported exchanges, travel, and meetings for scholars, businesspeople, and government and religious leaders. Ford funding also improved educational opportunities for South African blacks[71] and enhanced the professional development of teachers in black South African universities. Also notable was Ford's generous funding to support the United States–South Africa Leadership Exchange Program, which continued through the 1980s. Together with the Carnegie inquiry, this program contributed significantly to the development of black South African leadership.

During the 1970s Ford widened its support to include legal defense for South African political detainees, to train black lawyers and bring test cases to question repressive or discriminatory laws.[72] At the same time, Carnegie support tested the extent to which the judicial system could treat blacks fairly and tried to widen that capacity.

Drafting a new constitution involved a careful examination of the experiences of other governments (primarily the Federal Republic of Germany) during a crucial period of confidence building. The new constitution, adopted in February 1997 after the addition of new amendments, attempted to balance the rights of individuals and groups, define the collective goals of the nation, and create a government that was truly democratic—representative, transparent, responsive, and accountable. A nation long managed by divide-and-rule policies sought "a formula that would guarantee rights for all *and* foster a greater sense of collective responsibility for the nation and its future."[73]

After the constitution was adopted it had to be approved by an eleven-member Constitutional Court—its members highly respected nationally and internationally. The court's recommendations to add a stronger bill of rights, guarantee the independence of "watchdog" agencies, and enhance the powers of provincial governments were accepted. The special significance of the court was its independence from the ruling powers. Indeed, the South African experience has been widely studied by emerging democracies elsewhere.

In December 1995, to encourage citizens to review—at a very personal level—what it meant to be South African, the government also established the TRC, a panel of seventeen with Archbishop Desmond Tutu as chair and Alex Boraine as vice chair (two highly respected persons). The commission's function was to forgive, not forget, the abuses of the apartheid era. Its main tasks were to decide on reparations for victims and amnesty for perpetrators who told the truth and to compile an official history of South Africa's transition to majority rule—a difficult and delicate balance to strike. Both truth and reconciliation were crucial.

The democratic process of selecting the TRC's members built confidence in its fairness. The extraordinary stature of Archbishop Desmond Tutu—unique in the world for his principles, ideals, and courage—gave singularly appropriate leadership to the TRC and ensured confidence within South Africa and beyond.

The TRC's hearings continued this democratic approach. They were conducted throughout the country and were open to the media and the public. Their openness provided an opportunity for public education and reconciliation and built public trust. Other features that contributed to the commission's success included powers of subpoena and of search and seizure, which gave its operations teeth, and a focus on the role of individuals. There was no blanket amnesty, which has proved ineffective in other countries because victims convinced themselves that general amnesty equaled impunity for all human rights violators.

The TRC's term was extended to avoid the charge that it granted only hasty and incomplete amnesty and reparations. Finally, more and more prominent individuals requested amnesty. Even de Klerk and deputy president Mbeki apologized before the TRC for former wrongs. Today, many countries are adopting the TRC model in various ways to handle transitions from tyranny to democracy.

Lessons of South Africa

The example of South Africa is important for several reasons. One is its status as a worldwide symbol of prejudice and ethnocentrism as well as of emotionally charged efforts at democratic reform and conflict resolution. The main purpose of this chapter is to show how people suffering from desperation, injustice, anger, and escalating violence were able to find their way out of an exceedingly dangerous predicament without falling into the hideous trap of genocide or other mass murder—despite political violence. It was a close call.

Many of the elements described in Chapter 2, "Paths to Genocide," existed in South Africa. We have emphasized throughout this chapter on South Africa counteracting elements that in the end prevented genocidal behavior from overwhelming the people. Especially important here was the emergence of extraordinary leadership characterized by commitment to democracy, with a concomitant commitment to nonviolent conflict resolution. The central point of overriding significance is that genocide was prevented.

Let us summarize the main factors that made possible this remarkable achievement, which has salutary implications for the entire world.

One important asset for South Africa in avoiding the ultimate catastrophe was the personality and character of Nelson Mandela. He was at all times restrained and careful in his judgment, not prone to revenge or any kind of violence. As South Africans and then the world got to know him over the years, people everywhere were profoundly impressed with his intellect, integrity, fundamental human decency, and dignity.

The same was true of Desmond Tutu. His deep dedication to religion in the service of common humanity has shone through all of his activities. In fact, he is in practice a great teacher as well as a great clergyman, informing us all about the ways in which we could honestly and constructively overcome the deepest problems of human relationships.

These leaders were influenced by the teachings and practice of Mohandas Gandhi, starting in 1907 and setting a vivid example of nonviolent assertion of universal human dignity and unceasing, courageous struggle for freedom from oppression.

Besides these two remarkable leaders, there were others, including the leaders of a strong antiapartheid trade union movement that emerged in the 1970s. These unions were able not only to gradually enhance the opportunities of their members but also to give practical experience of leadership in difficult situations. Like Mandela and Tutu, their primary orientation was toward pragmatic problem solving without violence. De Klerk, somewhat like Gorbachev, evolved into a democratically inclined pragmatist, mindful of world opinion and of European heritage.

Another helpful factor in the emergence of South Africa from decades of terrible repression was the support of the international community. For example, the UN Security Council, which rarely agrees on anything, imposed a mandatory arms embargo on South Africa, the first time it had ever taken such an action against a member state. It sent a distinguished, fair, and responsible representative, Cyrus Vance. So, too, many international organizations and institutions, governmental and nongovernmental, backed the aspirations of black South Africans in their quest for implementation of democratic values.

As the years of repression went by, black South Africans, with great courage, became increasingly outspoken in their responses in times of grief, oppression and violence—as occurred after the murder of the greatly admired young leader, Steve Biko.

As the government sought increasingly to hide severe oppression behind a facade of democratic-appearing institutions, the oppressed black South Africans more and more expressed their objections, deep concerns, and anguish. Yet for the most part they remained nonviolent in the face of the government's incendiary politics and relentless despotism.

One important landmark in the growing international cooperation for democracy occurred when Desmond Tutu was awarded the Nobel Peace Prize in 1984. In addition to giving well-earned recognition to a great person, this award provided an opportunity to acknowledge the singular value of nonviolent problem solving and the politics of inclusion. Tutu addressed this significant issue in his Nobel acceptance speech. Moreover, the occasion gave him the opportunity to explain to the world, perhaps more clearly and certainly more widely than ever before, the reason for the profound divisions and great danger in the South African situation. On this occasion, as on many others over the years, Tutu gave clear examples of universal human rights for the path to major political change that would be required for democracy in his beloved country. Thus, education of the public in many countries emerged as a significant factor.

Through discourse of this sort, now on a worldwide stage, lessons were learned about the similarity of apartheid to the repression of Hitler's Germany. The world learned about massive uprooting of peoples, forced relocations into marginal subsistence areas, and massive ethnic cleansing. With this awareness came increasing worldwide appreciation of the reasons for alarm and the extreme danger of such pervasive, harsh depreciation. To many observers, the situation in South Africa looked very much like a prelude to genocide. In effect, leaders such as Mandela and Tutu undertook a worldwide campaign of education to create attitudes and behavior that favored democracy without ever calling for violence. On the contrary, they did everything in their power to press for freedom and opportunity without undertaking any violent action. Over time the world came to see this remarkable combination of attributes as one of great potential value for any country, not only South Africa.

One remarkable aspect of this worldwide public education was the fact that the oppressed South African majority had carried on nonviolent problem solving and democratic advocacy from 1912 through Mandela's eventual freedom from prison decades later and, indeed, into the difficult transition period from harsh autocracy to democracy.

By the late 1980s, a hurting stalemate had developed. The government had overwhelming power and used it to maintain oppressive laws. Yet the oppressed opposition had growing moral and public support throughout the world.

President de Klerk, after exploring indirectly and then directly the possibilities of negotiating with Mandela, broke the impasse in 1990 with a speech to parliament of historic significance in which South Africa's harshest measures were abandoned and Mandela was allowed to leave prison after twenty-seven years. Among the factors that influenced this fateful decision was the desire of the ruling group in the apartheid government to avoid pariah status in the world, to find ways of restoring their economy, which had been damaged over decades—first by community boycotts, then by withdrawal of large international firms, and finally by international financial sanctions. Furthermore, they had an orientation toward democracy, at least within their own group, and came to see that expansion of democracy might be not only feasible but advantageous. Both de Klerk and Mandela had keen awareness of the consequences of all-out violence—which certainly could have ended in overt genocide—and concluded that this would be essentially mutual suicide. Therefore, negotiation, compromise, gradual change, and ultimate mutual accommodation would be a far better course. Both took major political and physical risks in this course of rapprochement, since very angry people in all South African groups were inclined toward violence. Mandela especially set a powerful example for his country and the world by combining a remarkably magnanimous attitude toward his oppressors with a clear awareness of the difficulties that would be encountered even after his freedom.

Another helpful factor during the years of apartheid and thereafter was the growing broad support for liberation and democracy on the part of South Africa's churches. The religious community gradually built national and even international momentum in the movement to end apartheid and enter a new, democratic, nonracial South Africa. The churches' opinion also facilitated extensive dialogue in many communities throughout the country and led to constructive negotiations on a larger scale.

The end of the Cold War had a significant effect on the resolution of the South African crisis. The government had long used the threat of a Communist takeover as a reason for maintaining its repression of blacks. With this threat removed, a major justification was also removed. In addition, Gorbachev set a superb example that was influential, both in his unwillingness to use force against the east central European countries and in his support of universal human rights and mutual respect among peoples—fundamental values that coincided with the doctrines being advanced by Tutu and Mandela. They sought an integration of peoples within South Africa with the benefits to be shared by all, black and white together. They emphasized the value of human diversity and the advantages this could have for a future democratic South Africa. Time and again, black South African leaders, and increasingly white South African leaders as well, emphasized that a better society could emerge through negotiations on the basis of mutual respect and sustained efforts toward equitable socioeconomic development.

Scholars who have studied democratic transitions over the past half century have emphasized the frequency with which political violence may flare in the early years of transition from a repressive to a democratic state. De Klerk, Mandela, Tutu, and others recognized that they must organize a systematic process to minimize violence during the transition. This was an exceedingly difficult task after decades of repression, violence, and retaliation. They organized efforts at all levels—local, regional, national, and even international—to deal with tensions that could lead to serious violence, especially as they saw growing, serious danger to their economy.

Once again, church leadership in national initiatives proved helpful, as did international support for nonviolent problem solving. The progressive elements of the business community, with their great influence, also gradually joined in these efforts to minimize political violence. There was much interaction among political leaders, church leaders, and business leaders in these negotiations. All concerned recognized that this conflict resolution was a process that would take years, not a single event, even one so dramatic as de Klerk's door-opening speech or Mandela's long walk to freedom after twenty-seven years in prison. The leaders of these efforts made it a principle to seek intergroup inclusion in the negotiating process. Throughout the transition, democratic values and procedures permeated the work of the various conflict resolution activities at all levels with a hopeful view that peace and development would in due course be achieved.

There was a systematic organization of conflict resolution processes during the transition to alleviate severe tensions. These included a code of conduct for political parties and organizations; a code of conduct for security forces; a national business committee, broadly composed; a national peace secretariat to help with implementation; national and local committees on conflict resolution; a distinguished commission of inquiry on the prevention of public violence and indeed intimidation; and an early start on socioeconomic development with an explicit emphasis on the contribution of equitable development to peace. Throughout these efforts, much attention was paid to conflict resolution at the grassroots level, strengthening the capacity of ordinary people to understand and work at mediation, negotiation, and adjudication.

In the midst of this turbulent though generally reasonable transition, the international community was helpful in a variety of ways. International observers, for example, from such important organizations as the UN, the European Union, the Commonwealth, and the Organization of African Unity were helpful, both in building a capacity for conducting conflict resolution activities and as an exemplar of respect for the emerging democratic South Africa. The many programs conducted by both national and international peace workers emphasized reconciliation, tolerance, shared respect, and democratic principles.

Overall, an extraordinary combination of personalities and circumstances helped greatly to avoid genocide in South Africa: compassionate, fair-minded, highly capable leaders among the oppressed; leaders of the repressive government who were able gradually (if all too slowly) to adopt a moderate, pragmatic leadership inclined toward negotiating; a pervasive democratic orientation within the black leadership and significant democratic elements in the white community; increasing opposition, both internal and external, to repressive practices and growing education of the public about the immense danger to all of a repressive approach that might lead to genocide; a basic orientation toward negotiation among adversaries at every level of society; and increasing skill in doing so, partly through the building of institutions of civil society with international help. The world's growing awareness of South Africa's courageous, intelligent, nonviolent problem solving has made it a valuable exemplar for many other countries around the globe, taking into account the many years that will be necessary to fulfill the aspirations of democratic South Africans.

PART II

PILLARS OF PREVENTION: STRATEGIES, TOOLS, AND PRACTICES

CHAPTER 7

Proactive Help in Preventing Mass Violence

Preventive Diplomacy and Beyond

Basic Orientation: Prevent Mass Violence by Early,
Ongoing Help to Countries in Trouble

A peaceful world, free from genocide, war, and terrorism, will depend on an international community, and especially the established democracies, ready and willing to be on the alert for sister countries in trouble and to apply skills, attitudes, and mechanisms in extending help to these countries to prevent bad outcomes. By countries in trouble we refer to such attributes as intergroup hostility, governmental repression of vulnerable groups subject to prejudicial stereotype, rising hate speech, systematic violation of human rights, and inclination to deal with problems by violence. The conundrum is that no favorable outcome can occur without substantial changes, and these are unlikely to happen without outside help. Yet those countries most in need, and especially those with repressive leaders, are most likely to be suspicious of and resistant to outside help. Most countries are likely to be responsive, however, seeing chances for a better way of life. The appropriate response for the established democracies is to maintain steady contact on a multilateral basis (as opposed to intervening late in a crisis situation) and with nonpatronizing attitudes and behavior that consistently reflect serious concern, sympathetic interest, empathy for suffering, respect for human potential, a vision of better opportunities, and the prospect of belonging in a valued group (such as the European Union). Such well-meaning outsiders can emphasize that they wish to make available the world's experience in dealing successfully with similar problems. They need not give highly specific prescriptions or threaten force (except in truly extreme circumstances, as evaluated by a group of democracies). They can illuminate options that would lead to a better life for the whole society that is in trouble. In essence, this is a mode of international relations that is practically helpful, constructive, and forward-looking. This concept is, in effect, a broad and strong version of preventive diplomacy. So let us now consider recent experience and knowledge of preventive diplomacy and see how it might be upgraded to avoid catastrophic human interactions.

Many Uses of Early Preventive Diplomacy

In an effort to improve the global capacity for violence prevention, Cyrus Vance (one of the great leaders in twentieth-century diplomacy) and I established the Carnegie Commission on Preventing Deadly Conflict in 1994. It comprised sixteen international leaders and scholars long experienced in conflict prevention and conflict resolution. The commission was greatly assisted by an excellent interdisciplinary staff and a distinguished global advisory council. It completed its extensive work in 1999, and follow-up efforts have continued since then toward setting precedents for use of these concepts.

Under the auspices of the Carnegie Commission and concomitantly with the Carnegie Corporation's regular grant-making activity, seventy-five books and reports related to prevention were published. In addition, the commission sponsored international meetings that brought together independent experts and policymakers from all over the world. The commission's main report, *Preventing Deadly Conflict,* has had an impact on the UN, the EU, and many democracies.[1] Taken together, this body of work constitutes a unique resource of practical tools and strategies for the prevention of war and genocide. This, in turn, has stimulated research and institutional innovation to strengthen tools, strategies, and practices for early, ongoing prevention of mass violence.

The commission urged that, as a practical necessity, governments, peoples, and international organizations set a high priority on building effective systems that can help troubled or divided societies move toward peaceful, mutually satisfactory ways of resolving conflicts and fostering democratic socioeconomic development. War and genocide are terribly grim subjects—yet we must have the courage to address them constructively before it is too late for all humanity.

We must strengthen an array of institutions and organizations that can use tools, strategies, and practices for preventing deadly conflict. This includes governments and intergovernmental organizations—not only the UN but also regional organizations (RO) such as the Organisation for Security and Cooperation in Europe (OSCE), the European Union, NATO, the African Union, the Organization of American States, and the Association of Southeast Asian Nations (ASEAN). There is also a highly significant array of institutions of civil society in democracies: the scientific and scholarly community, educational and religious institutions, as well as business, media, and NGOs that focus on preventing mass violence, such as the Carter Center. All these can help, but they must be strengthened for this purpose, especially by establishing systematic, explicit, ongoing mechanisms of cooperation.

An important example of NGO capability is the remarkable International Crisis Group (ICG). In less than a decade, under the inspiring leadership of Gareth Evans (former Australian foreign minister), the ICG has become one of the world's most respected and effective NGOs. The ICG describes itself as "an independent, nonprofit, nongovernmental organization" that deploys expert personnel on five continents to prevent and resolve deadly conflict through field-based analysis and targeted advocacy.[2]

The ICG stations teams of expert political analysts inside or near troubled countries and regions—hot spots or warm spots. They submit field assessments and recommendations for action in regular analytical reports directed at key international decisionmakers or governmental leaders in a position to implement policies that prevent or alleviate state crises and associated violence. The ICG supplements these reports with *CrisisWatch,* a monthly update of situations throughout the world that are on the threshold—or in the midst—of violent conflict.

Thus, ICG often helps significantly in preventive diplomacy, showing how constructive problem solving can avert mass violence. It clarifies genocide-prone situations and can lead the way to early, ongoing conflict resolution—partly by helping troubled governments and peoples understand latent opportunities and partly by stimulating the help of nearby governments and/or international organizations.

The most pervasive need is for the international community to be prepared and proactive in helping nations or groups in trouble rather than waiting for disaster to strike. In the short term, this makes it feasible to put out fires when they are small. In the long term, this essentially means help in acquiring attitudes, concepts, skills, and institutions for resolving internal and external conflicts. It means help in building political and economic institutions of democracy (see Chapters 8 and 9). There can be—and of necessity will be—many different international configurations through which such help can be provided. And it can be done in a way that is sensitive to cultural traditions and regional circumstances.

To offer such help especially involves relating to moderate, constructive, pragmatic leaders who are oriented to humane and democratic values. They exist all over the world, but their situation is often precarious. The international community can reach out to them and provide recognition in the context of an international support network—and in the long run help such leaders to build institutions capable of meeting basic human needs and coping with the conflicts that arise in the course of human interactions.

There is a considerable convergence of research and carefully considered experience in suggesting constructive modes of negotiating that offer real promise of meeting basic needs, addressing grievances seriously, and finding paths to mutual accommodation through joint problem solving. This approach to negotiation has much promise for preventive diplomacy, whether utilized by governments, intergovernmental organizations, or nongovernmental organizations.[3]

The experience of the OSCE, as well as that of the ICG, shows that the international community need not wait for a crisis. Instead, there can be ongoing programs of international help—offered by governments, intergovernmental organizations, and nongovernmental organizations—and points of entry that are well informed, empathic, and hopeful while firmly clarifying the need for third-party help. This builds the capacity of groups to address grievances effectively without violence and to establish permanent mechanisms for sorting out conflicts peacefully before they become explosive. As OSCE high commissioner on national minorities, Max van der Stoel functioned very effectively in this way for a decade at the end of the Cold War era—an inspiration for all who care about preventing violence. Scandinavian governments were very helpful. The distinguished Swedish diplomat, Rolf Ekéus, has since carried on this work. This experience is a splendid example of what is needed all over the world—quiet diplomacy and international cooperation for learning decent human relations and educating leaders in nonviolent problem solving and concrete steps toward democracy. I amplify this important example in Chapter 15 on the OSCE.

Problem solving involves a shared effort to find a mutually acceptable solution. The parties to a dispute talk freely to one another about their interests and priorities, work together to identify the core differences dividing them, open their minds creatively in search of alternatives that bridge their opposing interests, and jointly assess these alternatives in seeking circumstances of mutual benefit. The impact of problem solving on the outcome of conflict can be highly positive, especially the development of an integrative solution. There are several types of integrative solutions, along with the reformulating questions that make it possible to devise these solutions.

It is possible for a fully integrative solution to be reached, one that satisfies both parties' aspirations altogether. In reality, most integrative solutions are not that successful. They partially reconcile the parties' interests, allowing a reasonable settlement but one with some residual frustration that may be dealt with later. Usually, integrative solutions involve the development of novel alternatives and require much patience, creativity, and imagined futures. Integrative solutions are potentially so advantageous to the parties that they are worth pursuing with great vigor and determination.

The distinguished scholars Jeffrey Z. Rubin, Dean G. Pruitt, and Sung Hee Kim have effectively summarized problem solving in its key points for diplomacy.[4] Escalating conflict often reaches the point where both parties find the further use of confrontational tactics either unworkable or unwise. If yielding is also ruled out, as is so often the case to save face, the solution to stalemate must eventually be found in problem solving. Problem solving can be defined as any effort to develop a mutually acceptable solution to a conflict.[5]

1. If both sides make extravagant demands and are unwilling to yield, some way must be found to combine both parties' interests.
2. In general, the higher the joint benefits, the more stable the agreement will be.
3. The joint benefits of integrative solutions tend to strengthen relations between the parties. Strengthened relations are not only valuable in themselves; they also make it easier to find integrative solutions in later conflict-prone situations.
4. Integrative solutions usually contribute to the welfare of the two parties' broader community.

There is a dynamic interplay between scholarly research and diplomatic practice—this is already rewarding, e.g., in training of aspiring diplomats. It can become more valuable if a high priority is attached to such research and its interplay with practice in future years.

Varieties of Quiet Diplomacy: Tools for Prevention of Mass Violence

John Packer analyzed the nature of Max van der Stoel's "quiet diplomacy" for a UN related conference in 2005 that focused on this approach. Packer is a distinguished diplomat and scholar who worked in the extraordinary OSCE program for most of a decade.[6] Since their successful experience was with a regional organization, the OSCE, van der Stoel and Packer invited representatives of many other regional organizations in 2005, and there was a clear trend of growing exploration of early preventive diplomacy among these organizations. For example, ASEAN—which had earlier focused almost entirely on economic matters—was now protecting economic development from violence through methods similar to those of van der Stoel.

One form of diplomacy that may be brought to bear to prevent violent conflict or its recurrence is "quiet diplomacy." As its name implies, it is not "public," much less "megaphone" diplomacy. Neither is it secret; instead it is confidential and *discreet*. Unlike public diplomacy, clearly intended for domestic constituencies, and megaphone diplomacy, meant to call international attention (and, presumably, pressure) to address a given situation, the aim of quiet diplomacy is to create conditions in which parties feel comfortable to act, in particular allowing parties to evaluate positions and interests thoughtfully, to weigh options, and to consider independent and impartial advice. It does so by allowing dialogue to take place without the public scrutiny that risks parties' losing face or hardening their positions. It seeks to establish constructive relations at an early stage, thus creating a sort of "capital" of confidence, trust, and local knowledge—including personal contacts—all of which may be drawn upon, especially when tense situations arise. Through early and then long-term relationship building, the third-party actor is better able to draw attention to the enlightened self-interest of parties to a conflict, helping them to devise workable solutions to their problems. This requires credibility on the part of the third party, born of recognized status, experience, and skill for which commensurate resources are needed. It also requires the capacity to deliver expert assistance directly relevant to the conflict.

Quiet diplomatic engagement has optional strategies: notably *good offices, facilitation,* and *mediation.*

Good Offices

Perhaps the most prominent example of third-party engagement has been the good offices function of the heads of intergovernmental organizations, such as the UN Secretary-General. These are the important modalities for good offices engagement:

- *When:* most prominently at the outset of an effort to diminish conflict
- *How:* gaining entry at the good office provider's own initiative, with consent or by invitation of parties; guaranteeing a safe environment; formulating objectives for the process; access to information, expertise, and power to reward and coerce if necessary
- *Functions:* enquiries; fact finding; determination of legal rights and specific duties; intermediary, i.e., to transmit messages between parties; may then encourage exchange of information; may attempt to explain and interpret messages to receiving party; may propose procedures for continued exchanges and negotiations; may communicate with nongovernmental actors who are in a position to be helpful
- *Characteristics:* fair-minded outsider or highly respected insider; credibility, local knowledge, and sustainability over long term (mix of actors may be required to accomplish all three)

Facilitation

Facilitation describes third-party engagement, which provides a forum, space, and environment conducive to dispute settlement. Moreover, it actively seeks to solve the matters in dispute by bridging positions and advancing alternatives. These engagements work best at the earliest possible stage, when the sources of conflict are identified and addressed before high tension or violence emerges. Historically, it appears most effectively accomplished quietly—with quick, independent, and impartial action, promotion of a law-based approach, and reliance upon participating states for support and additional credibility.

- *When:* before underlying conflict erupts
- *How:* with consent and cooperation of states concerned; monitors potential problem areas; determines if involvement is needed and degree of positive impact; may address both predisposing and precipitating causes in hostility
- *Functions:* creates conditions for parties to initiate and maintain their own dialogue process; communicates and interprets international norms; makes recommendations of politically feasible solutions in line with those norms; explains advantages of adherence
- *Characteristics:* independence; cooperation; impartiality; confidentiality; trust and credibility; capable of gathering and analyzing information; inside contacts; persistence; may use media tactfully or even megaphone when other options are exhausted

Mediation

Mediation, a voluntary tool of peaceful conflict prevention and resolution, is related to but distinct from the parties' own negotiations. It is a noncoercive, nonviolent form of intervention of a third party to help resolve a conflict. In mediation, parties seek the assistance of or accept an offer of help from an outside actor to help them see constructive possibilities without resorting to the use of force or the authority of law. It may involve the commitment of the parties to respect the recommendations of the independent, resourceful, and impartial third-party mediator.

- *When:* An optimal range for the best moment: too early may make the intermediary unpopular with one or more parties; too late may mean the situation has deteriorated to the point where mediation is not possible.
- *How:* Communication—contact with parties; trust and confidence building; arranging for interactions; identifying underlying issues and interests; supplying missing information; transmitting messages between parties; allowing interests of all parties to be discussed; parties agree to involvement of outside mediator to facilitate process.
- *Formulation:* chooses meeting site; controls pace of meetings and physical environment; establishes protocol; ensures privacy; highlights common interests; controls timing; helps devise acceptable outcomes; helps parties save face and avoid humiliation; suggests compromises; shows there is no royal road to truth and happiness, but rather, diverse good options.
- *Characteristics:* Mediator is widely acceptable to all parties and their region, an open- and fair-minded third party who assists parties in reaching their own settlement; tends to be more appropriate than adjudication (binding third-party settlement) for politically hypersensitive disputes such as those involving national

honor, "vital" national interests, or the imminent use of force. There is an emerging movement to train a cadre of mediators at both high and medium levels of international organizations, especially the UN. This movement has much promise.

- *Gaining entry:* This is a crucial consideration in virtually all of preventive diplomacy. Techniques may include unsolicited offering, by making known the potential benefits—providing an authentic basis for hope. Respected fourth parties can recommend with legitimacy one or more suitable mediators.
- *Process:* The facilitator picks "low-hanging fruit," to develop confidence and sometimes to buy time or collect the fruit in a basket for a more comprehensive agreement or settlement. He or she has only one chance to make a good first impression, e.g., manifested by serious interest, knowledge of the situation, quiet conviction that the problem can be solved.
- *Addressing grievances:* In terms of problem-solving approaches and violence prevention, the third party almost invariably deals with grievances. Techniques to deal with these may involve a variety of paths out of the situation, e.g., reframing the arguments, floating trial balloons, and solving the problem by joint recognition of shared, common benefits, and the value of long-term relationships.

Shuttle Diplomacy

Shuttle diplomacy can be useful when direct communication between the parties involved may be impossible or counterproductive. The essence of the practice is the use of a trusted and discreet third party, skilled in problem solving, to transmit communications between the disputing groups and thus relieve them of the pressure to grandstand in face-to-face confrontations or in statements issued to the media. Through individual private meetings, the intermediary can relay questions and answers, clarify the opportunities, and suggest options for resolution of the conflict.

Multiparty Engagement

Multiparty engagement involves a range of actors—some combination of individuals, states, international organizations, and NGOs—working simultaneously or sequentially to address a given situation. It depends upon careful coordination and building upon the efforts of each actor in the process, with respect for all and no domination.

- *When:* to address an imminent or developing crisis situation
- *How:* in response to warning indicators or specific invitation by one or more parties
- *Functions:* bring significant and broad-based pressure to bear to resolve a situation viewed by the international community as urgent, unjust, and tractable (i.e., with apparent feasible solution). Pool resources to provide incentives for mutually beneficial conflict resolution. Any path toward genocide deserves prompt and special attention of highest capability.

Media Strategies

An accurately informed public can help in deescalation if aware of dangerous possibilities and safer options. To complement official diplomatic initiatives, media strategies can be used to raise awareness of the central issues or obstacles impeding positive progress and potentially to educate large segments of a population in a conflict situation of the beliefs, culture, and legitimate needs of differing national, religious, ethnic, or other groups with whom they are in conflict. Use of media may also provide impartial information to the local population. It is useful to provide information on how similar conflicts were resolved in other (preferably much admired) countries. Such positive and responsible use of media is all the more important to emphasize when, as we have already noted, there may also be hateful use of media to fan the flames of conflict, as, for example, in the notorious Milles Collines radio broadcasts in Rwanda. Independent, democratic sources of information can be so important that international organizations such as the European Union should establish their own media capacity for reaching conflict areas.

Some Lessons of Preventive Diplomacy

Preventive diplomacy can address both basic and proximate causes of tensions and hatred. In the process, it can contribute to the creation of mechanisms that enhance dialogue and cooperation among different groups and therefore encourage future management of disputes through peaceful means.

To build trust, quiet diplomacy adheres to the basic principles and norms of international law as well as respect for sovereignty. It must take into account the requirement that a regime protect *all* its people from abuse of human rights. Quiet diplomacy also requires timeliness—in addressing underlying issues before escalation occurs. Action is preventive rather than curative and therefore most effective at the earliest possible stage.

Such an approach may generate recommendations and can persuade governments and other actors to consider carefully the consequences of specific actions such as revengeful behavior toward ethnic Russian minorities in states of the former Soviet Union. This is a particularly telling example of quiet, preventive diplomacy, since the repercussions of discriminatory behavior may not be immediately obvious but may be destructive in the long term. The task can go far beyond encouraging dialogue or foreseeing consequences. As problem solver, the third party can facilitate contacts and processes between actors and bring expertise gained from comparable situations elsewhere. The problem solver helps to find or construct solutions, which can take the form of advice on policy and law in relation to political organization and participation, access to public goods (material resources, opportunities, positions, and prestige), elections, decentralization, constitutional reform, citizenship policies, maintenance of identities, the use of language(s), education, cultural policy, and bilateral relations including the conclusion and implementation of treaties.

Finally, preventive diplomacy may involve an advisory role that reflects back to the international community the lessons learned from particular situations and facilitates conflict prevention in the future. Successful preventive diplomacy is most likely to be achieved by well-informed, respected third parties supported by adequate resources.[7] Early, ongoing preventive diplomacy can move menacing groups or governments away from the illusory path toward mass violence by providing access to other paths that genuinely promise peace and prosperity in the long run.

Thus, the international community is learning to enhance its current capacities to prevent mass violence. Can we recognize serious dangers early enough? Can we help adversaries to understand the risks of violence before they have crossed the Rubicon? Can we help them strengthen their own capacities for conflict resolution? Can we mobilize internationally the intellectual, technical, financial, and moral resources to avert disaster and achieve just outcomes? Can preventive diplomacy lead to lasting improvements in the quality of life? These are profound worldwide challenges, because they may serve to prevent the onset of mass violence, which drastically transforms the nature of a conflict. Revenge motives severely complicate the situation; then resolution and even limitation of conflict are less likely to be effective. So early intervention in the form of preventive diplomacy is attractive, closely related to international cooperation in fostering democratic, equitable socioeconomic development. The latter involves other organizations and specialized skills with larger resources. But these long-term constructive efforts can effectively be stimulated by those conducting early preventive diplomacy.

Studies of Negotiation, Moving Toward Agreement, Solving Joint Problems for Mutual Benefit

Negotiation is at the heart of preventive diplomacy, whether face to face between adversaries or with the addition of a third party in mediation or arbitration. Therefore, we now examine conditions favorable to effective, fruitful negotiation. In the past several decades scholars have undertaken a wide range of inquiry having to do with real world negotiation in a variety of settings as well as experimental studies on simulated negotiation and links between the two.[8]

Shared interests often lie behind superficially opposing positions, and any interest may well be satisfied in a variety of ways. Each side typically has multiple interests. Altogether, a problem-solving orientation is useful rather than putting down the adversary or rigidly adhering to egocentric/ethnocentric positions.

To implement this approach, negotiators need extensive knowledge of the situation in conflict, including its social context, and creative thinking about different ways in which the parts might be fit together. Negotiators need to guard against premature closure, against commitment to a single royal road to virtue, against assuming that there is necessarily a fixed pie that must be carved up, and against leaving the solution of the adversaries' problem to the adversaries alone, even though they have the prime responsibility.

It is worth describing in some detail the accumulated consensus of recent work on factors likely to lead to successful negotiation and, moreover, likely to be useful in a fundamentally practical sense as skills that can be learned by negotiators. These include the following skills set.

1. The negotiation actively strives to address legitimate interests of both parties and to resolve them clearly, taking into account shared interests and the conditions required for maintenance of an agreement over extended time.
2. The procedures are efficient and task-oriented.
3. The negotiation seeks ways to improve the relationship between the parties over the long term, or at least to do no harm.
4. The negotiators adopt the outlook that both parties can win. Negotiation is not a harsh competition or a theatrical performance, though elements of these often enter in. Fundamentally, everyone concerned should gain something tangible by the time the process is completed. There must be ways to constitute a "victory" for adversaries if there are to be substantial and durable results.
5. Prepare for negotiation. Negotiations are likely to be more successful if the parties study the facts of the situation, including their social and political context; set reasonably clear goals; establish priorities among their goals; and draft a tentative course of action, especially with respect to initial steps and, importantly, including contingency plans. This involves serious efforts to understand the adversary, including background, attitudes, and probable expectations (e.g., Reagan and Gorbachev). Practice in situations similar to the actual negotiation can be helpful.
6. Keep in mind the needs of the negotiators and the constituencies they represent. These needs are necessarily varied, and therefore a wide range of factors must be taken into account in order to be responsive to them. An orientation of joint problem solving is useful in this context.
7. Consider sources of power and formulate tactics in light of such knowledge. The negotiators represent certain constituencies and indeed must usually keep in close touch with their constituencies. They cannot forget the sources of their power. Therefore, one is dealing not only with the individuals represented in the negotiating situation but also with a much larger number behind them. The capacity to influence each other's understanding and decisions is crucially dependent on the way these sources of power are perceived.
8. Foster effective communication. Communication between the negotiators must provide reasonably accurate information about needs and priorities, sometimes including the most basic human needs of the adversaries. Though calculated ambiguity is sometimes useful, clarity of communication is usually very important. Searching questions to clarify complex issues and to seek latent sources of potential agreement are essential. Sensitivity to nonverbal as well as verbal cues may help to understand where opportunities may exist as part of probing for underlying intentions and possible changes in outlook. Assumptions must be checked and understandings clarified in order to avoid the kind of misinterpretation that can badly undermine trust and even generate a sense of betrayal.
9. Monitor the behavior of other negotiators. The value of knowing your adversary is clear from experience. This means not only the individual directly involved, whose characteristics may indeed be of practical importance, but also the values, institutions, frustrations, and biases characteristic of his principal constituency.

10. Adapt to new conditions. Circumstances arise in which new information must be taken into account, the context of negotiations must be reappraised, or other insights assimilated. Such changes call for mid-course corrections. The ability to take account of new facts, to reformulate in light of wider horizons, and to create new proposals is part of adaptive behavior that favors effective outcomes.

11. Bring agreements to explicit conclusion. When mutually satisfactory solutions have been found to some major issues, and further negotiations have become counterproductive for the time being, there is a need to make explicit the agreements that have actually been reached. In most circumstances, there is long-term merit in achieving clarity and definiteness in such agreements. Even though a studied ambiguity may help to get an agreement by fuzzing over a difficult issue, it is perilous in the longer term because such ambiguity lends itself to wishful interpretations by both sides and then to charges of violation of agreement and even betrayal. Successful negotiators tend to minimize the potential for future misunderstanding by giving considerable explicit attention to the ways in which such misunderstandings might arise.[9]

One of the most interesting factors that emerge prominently in the research studies, including those that are experimental in nature, is the emphasis on status, respect, reputation, "face," and appearance of strength. This set of related needs for esteem may appear intangible and yet can have powerful effects on the progress of negotiations. Experimenters have varied status conditions deliberately in order to examine such effects. This research indicates that concern about appearance of strength or "face" motivates a great deal of negotiating behavior. It tends to be in sharper relief when the negotiators have an adversarial relationship. It is intensified when an adversary acts in a threatening way—often counterproductive.

Another interesting research finding has to do with the interdependence of the party's goals—e.g., nuclear war is mutual suicide. The adversaries depend on each other for survival. This is the widely useful concept of superordinate goals. Therefore nonviolent problem solving is for mutual benefit.

Four Important Studies Initiated by the Carnegie Commission on Preventing Deadly Conflict

Four important studies offer important insights into prevention of conflict: Bruce W. Jentleson, ed., *Opportunities Missed, Opportunities Seized: Preventive Diplomacy in the Post–Cold War Period* (1999); I. William Zartman, ed., *Preventive Negotiation: Avoiding Conflict Escalation* (2000); Melanie Greenberg, John H. Barton, and Margaret E. McGuinness, eds., *Words over War: Mediation and Arbitration to Prevent Deadly Conflict* (2000); and Connie Peck, *Sustainable Peace: The Role of the UN and Regional Organizations in Preventing Conflict* (1998).

These studies, which the Carnegie Commission on Preventing Deadly Conflict turned into books published by Rowman and Littlefield, looked carefully and systematically at different kinds of conflicts in different parts of the world, facing failure as well as successes to strengthen the capability of policy makers and practitioners in this crucial field.

The first three of these studies have a similar structure—an opening chapter by a leading scholar who lays out the problems, useful approaches, and an intellectual framework. This is followed by a series of meticulous case studies, each exemplifying a major facet of the problem, what was done, and what was not done. Finally, there is a substantial concluding chapter that draws together various strands of the evidence from the case studies, relates them to relevant research literature, and makes useful conclusions. Each study has a distinct perspective, and so they illuminate different facets of the problem. The fourth study, by Connie Peck, systematically considered a variety of regional organizations, their relations to the UN, and their potential for preventive diplomacy. It should be noted that the UN and regional organizations figured prominently in all these studies and offered genuine promise, especially on the basis of systematic cooperation led by the Secretary-General of each organization. The UN and the regional organizations now meet regularly for this purpose.

Research on the major conflicts of the 1990s shows clearly that early preventive engagement is better. At an early stage disputants are more likely to accept third-party mediation while the dispute is still local and limited. Preventive diplomacy undertaken before positions have hardened is more likely to achieve positive results. Also, disputes that are resolved early and peaceably are less likely to recur. Overall, the financial and human costs of this sort of early preventive action are likely to be much less than putting Humpty-Dumpty together again after he has been smashed.

Peck makes a very interesting proposal for the establishment of regionally focused "preventive diplomacy teams or units," linking UN headquarters and regional organizations as well as linking UN units around the globe with regional civil society. She formulates Regional Centers for Sustainable Peace—established under the auspices of either regional organizations or the UN or of both cooperatively. This would be a way to bring together the UN, regional organizations, nongovernmental organizations, and regional analytical centers. The proposed structure would integrate the most successful conflict prevention instruments, drawing widely on international experience while ensuring that they are tailored to local needs and circumstances. The horizontal transfer of knowledge and experience *within* each region is a distinctive feature of this proposal, in which regional actors who have developed successful models of good governance could assist their neighbors within the context of a regional effort aided, as necessary, by global support.

Regional centers would have two major foci. The first would be assistance in developing the structural processes for sustainable peace (with good governance at all levels of society). The second would be maintaining peace through assistance in dispute resolution and the development of institutional structures that would allow groups to become more effective at resolving their own problems over the long term.

Peck described ways in which regional programs for ongoing assistance in dispute settlement could offer expert help in reducing tension between groups, whether within or between states. These can be very briefly summarized as follows:

- Setting up regional programs for assistance in developing good governance— *before* mass violence has occurred. Thus preventive diplomacy can flow naturally

into structural prevention (long-term benefit), and the immediate conflict, once settled, can lead to measures that diminish the likelihood of other conflicts.
- Providing assistance in intrastate disputes (civil wars).
- Providing assistance in interstate disputes (international wars). It is interesting that there is similarity in inter- and intrastate conflict resolution, as also noted in the valuable study by Graham Allison and Hisashi Owada[10] on the potential contributions of the established democracies to preventing mass violence.

As the concepts and techniques of prevention are more widely understood, such UN–RO activities could become a potent force for peace—and a buffer against genocide.

Convergence of Evidence from All the Carnegie Commission Studies That Deal with Preventive Diplomacy

These recent studies converge on key points of success in preventive diplomacy. They send a to-whom-it-may-concern message to the international community: to governments, intergovernmental organizations (especially the UN and the EU), nongovernmental organizations of many kinds, and leaders in different sectors. Some recurrent elements of the preventive diplomacy message may be stated simply, and we reiterate them here because of their importance in preventing genocide.

1. Recognize dangers *early;* beware of wishful thinking.
2. Get the *facts straight* from multiple credible sources, including the history and culture of a particular latent or emerging conflict.
3. *Pool strengths*, share burdens, divide labor among entities with the capacity, salience, and motivation to be helpful.
4. Foster widespread *public understanding* of conflict resolution and violence prevention. This gives a basis for hope of *just settlement.*
5. Offer mediation early; *a fair-minded third party* with legitimacy can facilitate problem solving by adversaries.
6. Formulate *superordinate goals*—that is, goals highly desirable to both adversarial groups that they can only obtain by cooperation—i.e., mutual aid for mutual benefit.
7. Use *economic leverage:* carrots and sticks; identify what can be gained by peaceful settlement and lost by violence. Clarify incentives for conflict resolution.
8. *Support moderate, pragmatic local leaders*, including emerging leaders, especially democratic reformers. Buffer their precarious position.
9. Bear in mind the pervasive need of negotiators and their constituencies for *respect and dignity.* Help negotiators strengthen the cooperation among the constituencies within their own group. Maintain an attitude of shared humanity and possibilities for mutual accommodation.
10. *Upgrade preparation for preventive diplomacy* in relevant entities—for example, governments, the UN, regional organizations; established dedicated units for preventive diplomacy that combine knowledge and skill in early conflict resolution

and knowledge of the region; specific training for staff, updated in light of ongoing worldwide experience and research; roster of experts on call for leadership organizations such as the UN, the EU, and democratic governments.

Overall, if guidelines of this sort are incorporated into the thinking of governments, intergovernmental organizations, and peace-oriented nongovernmental organizations, it is likely that the risk of drifting into mass violence will be diminished. Ubiquitous human conflicts can be largely resolved high on the slippery slope that might otherwise lead to genocide.

A Look Back to Look Ahead

In early 1986, while the world was still deep in the Cold War, I formulated several guidelines and passed them directly to U.S. and Soviet leaders in both political and scientific spheres, bearing in mind that this was the most dangerous conflict in all of human history. These guidelines could have practical value for leaders of both countries in moving toward the end of the Cold War. They have continuing relevance in the post–Cold War era.

- No dehumanization; no harsh depreciation of the other. Criticize in civil discourse. Make carefully differentiated assessments rather than sweeping pronouncements.
- Make ongoing efforts to relate principles of decent human relations to specific actions of two countries (or two antagonistic groups within one country).
- Hold regular consultations at various levels—e.g., summits, minisummits, regional meetings. Thereby enhance mutual understanding of mutual benefit from diminishing the risk of nuclear war (or onslaught against a vulnerable group).
- Make agreements explicit. Build a cumulative series of crisis prevention agreements in this mode; i.e., practical safeguards despite adversarial position—no more Cuban missile crisis type of experiences; they are too hard to manage.
- Do not put the other in a humiliating position, either directly or in relation to allies.
- Resist the temptation to exploit local situations drastically—this can boomerang severely.
- Safeguard systematically and incessantly against inadvertent or accidental war.
- Do not sponsor terrorism against the other, directly or by client. View terrorism as a long-term danger to the relationship between the two countries and, indeed, to the world at large.
- Conduct ongoing serious negotiations of the major issues. Build a cumulative record of arms control agreements that enhance stability, are verifiable, have rigorous compliance, and greatly reduce the level of the stockpiles.
- Avoid grandiose interpretations of national interest. Learn to live in a multicentric world that respectfully accommodates many vigorous nations.
- Expand contacts widely in different spheres of activity and sectors of society; leading edges might include scientific and scholarly exchanges, cultural exchanges, and business transactions.
- Learn to treat minorities with respect.

Training for Preventive Diplomacy

To broaden and strengthen preventive diplomacy, to move toward early, ongoing capable help to countries in trouble, it is essential to build a solid infrastructure of training and research. A basic advantage of the current situation is that it has become feasible to build a worldwide cadre of experts in preventive diplomacy.

Connie Peck of UNITAR, based in Geneva, has been one of the leading persons in the entire UN system to develop training for violence prevention and conflict resolution.[11] Her work is oriented primarily to UN professionals and other diplomats. It draws heavily on the strongest research and best practices in the field. It is worth going into some detail because modern, research-based training—going beyond traditional diplomacy—is essential throughout institutions and organizations seeking to help in preventing mass violence, not least its most grotesque form, genocide. At the heart of such training is knowledge and skill in various forms of negotiation, especially mediation. Although the example of a training course here is in the UN, it might equally well be in the EU, the AU, democratic governments on every continent, or NGOs oriented to preventive diplomacy. In a 2004 paper, Peck discussed the need for training in violence prevention and conflict resolution and the development of the UN's first program in this area.[12]

The end of the Cold War saw the task of violence prevention increasingly imposed on the UN and regional organizations and complicated by the changing nature of conflict. During the last decade of the twentieth century and the first of the twenty-first, conflicts have most frequently occurred within states or arisen within a state and then spread to others. This has created a knotty problem for multilateral organizations, since their tools for the peaceful settlement of disputes have been traditionally intended for use in quarrels between states, not within them. The staff and diplomats of the UN and regional organizations have had to reassess the causes of contemporary conflict and their responses to it just at the time that cries for help came from all over the world over intrastate violence. In this context, as in others, little explicit attention is given to prevention of genocide, yet this work is highly pertinent.

The UN and the entire international diplomatic community need staff trained in knowledge and skills to prevent and resolve serious conflict—to diminish murderous inclinations, wherever they occur. Effective diplomats must be aware of the range and relative value of the options open to them. Staff charged with actually carrying out preventive diplomacy and peacemaking also need a solid understanding of the causes of conflict, the actions that lead to conflict escalation and deescalation, and the variety of strategies that have proved successful in resolving different sorts of conflicts and have diminished the contagion of hatred. They need training in negotiation and mediation that moves disputing parties toward a peaceful and mutually acceptable resolution of their problems.

Peck's program was the first to promote a system for preserving the lessons of good offices; an organized overview of the missions of good offices; a procedure for debriefing conflict resolution staff; accounts of the process of negotiation and the factors that hinder or facilitate its progress; analysis and evaluation of problems, lessons, and issues; and post hoc reviews of how to avoid similar problems in future.

To address these problems and bridge the gap between theory and practice,[13] Peck initiated training and research that evolved into the UNITAR Program in Peacemaking and Preventive Diplomacy. Other UN organizations have begun similar initiatives, but all these programs together represent only a fraction of what is needed.[14]

The program over the years has had two major goals: (1) to provide participants with the latest scholarly knowledge about conflict resolution, and (2) to collect and transmit the lessons practitioners of conflict resolution have learned through experience. Peck's sessions consider three approaches to dispute resolution—and their different outcomes—with emphasis on the need to strengthen interest-based mechanisms in the UN and its regional organizations:

1. The traditional *power-based approach* is the costliest of the three, not only in loss of lives and property but also in damaged relationships between the adversaries and the festering dissatisfaction on at least one side of the conflict that may lead to its renewal.
2. The *rights-based approach* is practiced by the UN International Court of Justice and the various human rights courts discussed in Chapter 11.
3. The UNITAR program emphasizes the *interest-based approach* as the least costly of the three. This approach analyzes the dispute, then considers how to address its causes. It explores both parties' interests (concerns, fears, aspirations, and needs) in order to sort out their motivations and devises an array of new options likely to satisfy at least some interests of both sides.[15]

Skills Training in the Practice of Interest-Based Problem Solving

This part of Peck's program offers hands-on practice in the skills required for preventive diplomacy and peacemaking. Exercises, simulations, role playing, and feedback teach how to listen and summarize, identify issues and interests, create and combine options, and search for objective criteria, principles, and precedents to solve problems, control emotions, and handle unfair negotiation tactics and difficult parties.

The negotiation segment starts with an exercise that illustrates Professor Morton Deutsch's "crude law of behavior": that cooperative and competitive behavior elicits responses in kind.[16] It also addresses the fact that traditional negotiation is commonly based on zero-sum assumptions and demonstrates that quality of communication substantially affects the negotiation process, as do efforts that build or destroy trust.

To give the training a specific and practical application, real situations are used as case studies. Trainees are given background material and a presentation by senior staff before they begin the exercise with an analysis of who should sit at the table, and in what capacity, during mediation. An experienced, deeply informed resource person discusses the difficulties and disputes that can occur in this initial process and the different kinds of negotiation that can take place at the table.

Each year the Fellowship Program examines more broadly how to improve the international system for violence prevention and conflict resolution. It draws on practitioners to consider the roles of the International Court of Justice, regional organizations, NGOs, track-two diplomacy, and the work of the OSCE high commissioner on national minorities, who, as we have noted, leads an outstanding example of consistent, ongoing preventive diplomacy. Long-term structural approaches to conflict prevention are emphasized, given the inextricable link between early diplomacy and, later, democracy, human rights, and peace. The program promotes the achievement of sustainable peace through the development of good governance, with emphasis on creating an environment of tolerance in intergroup relations.

Observing the success of the Fellowship Program, the Organization of African Unity (now the African Union) asked UNITAR to develop similar programs for Africa. In 2000 the annual UNITAR Regional Program to Enhance Conflict Prevention and Peacebuilding in Africa was established in Addis Ababa. It employs the methodology developed in the Fellowship Program, but its focus and personnel are African. It is strengthening collaboration among nations and institutions in Africa and developing a cadre of persons to assist peace processes there. The program was funded and encouraged by Canada, Germany, Norway, Sweden, and the United Kingdom. This illustrates the growing readiness of democratic governments to support research, training, and innovative practices in this field. These are efforts to meet the need for excellent training to strengthen preventive diplomacy and, in the process, to deepen understanding of the prevention of war and genocide. The utility of such training goes beyond the UN to other international organizations, public and private.

Strengthening the Capacity of International Leaders for Preventive Diplomacy

Cyrus Vance and I prepared a report for the UN Secretary-General, on behalf of the Carnegie Commission, on the role of personal envoys and special representatives of the Secretary-General.[17] Those who drafted the UN Charter gave the head of an international organization, for the first time, political-diplomatic prerogatives to conduct impartial third-party mediation on behalf of the international community. Secretary-General Kofi Annan gave strong leadership on strengthening the UN's preventive functions, including the use of personal envoys and special representatives in violence prevention and resolution.

The Carnegie report advocated a proactive approach for personal envoys and special representatives of the Secretary-General as a low-cost, low-risk instrument for enhancing the UN role in preventing and resolving deadly conflict. It suggested ways to expand the pool of candidates available to serve in these capacities and to increase the information available to them as well as the modest funding required to support their functions. Currently, the contributions of personal envoys and special representatives are undermined by the growing gap between the demand for more effective UN diplomacy on the one hand and limited financial resources on the other.

One function of special representatives is to provide the Secretary-General with firsthand authoritative information about what is going on in the field. In addition to fact-finding, these missions historically have been of value to conflict resolution in at least four ways:

1. Once the parties have accepted their involvement, special representatives and envoys have repeatedly demonstrated the importance of their persistence, patience,

and presence in order to keep the peace process alive when it might have collapsed.

2. As representatives or envoys become increasingly familiar with the substantive issues of the dispute, and if they maintain impartiality and credibility with both sides, they can reformulate the vision of a compromise package that otherwise would have eluded the antagonists.

3. International interests and norms are injected into the negotiating process. Typically, neither side in a dispute wishes to be isolated internationally and instead seeks political, economic, and security assistance. Thus, there are significant incentives for settlement.

4. Within the UN, especially the Security Council, the special representative can help to shape international consensus on what would actually be required to achieve a peaceful settlement.

The sooner the Secretary-General can begin to plan and undertake preventive action the better will be the chances for peace. Today's need for third-party mediation to prevent and resolve deadly regional conflicts is greater than ever, and the UN Secretary-General should be granted ample latitude for preventive diplomacy.

The world needs such programs badly in many governmental and international organizations. Picking up on the Vance-Hamburg observation that there was too little knowledge concerning the work of the special representatives of the Secretary-General (SRSG), Peck has carried out a program for briefing and debriefing SRSGs and envoys. The objective of the project is to preserve their experience and transmit their lessons to new personnel. Once again, major democracies have taken the lead: the United Kingdom, Sweden, Canada, and Switzerland. The work has led to a handbook for SRSGs and envoys. An annual SRSG seminar permits all special representatives to share their experiences and learn from one another. These innovations suggest ways in which research and training can strengthen the UN operations in preventive diplomacy—and similar gains are likely to be made by the EU and other international organizations.

Sweden, a pioneering country in early prevention of violence, has supported both the integration of conflict prevention elements into development programs and national and civic dialogues and mediation efforts as a way to resolve ongoing disputes before they become violent or lead to escalation. This work aims to build systematically the capacity of the UN, the EU, and national counterparts to implement development in a manner that leads to the amelioration of existing conflicts and prevention of violence.

Choosing "Entry Points" Carefully and Preparing for Entry— Overcoming Local and National Apprehensions

Extensive preparatory work is often necessary before the UN or other helpers can support emerging dialogue efforts in fragile situations. The best means of ensuring that violence prevention gains will survive political vicissitudes is to make intensive investments in providing a critical mass of individuals and institutions with the requisite skills and capacities. This is capacity building for early, ongoing resolution of conflict on a truly national basis.

The UN would not, could not, and should not attempt to monopolize preventive diplomacy. Regional and subregional organizations, national governments, and nongovernmental organizations may have comparative advantages in preventing certain intrastate or interstate conflicts. But in all cases, it helps for the Secretary-General to have a clear sense of current developments and assurance that an effective division of labor among the governments and organizations is accomplished.

The sort of training described here can be highly useful not only for the UN but also for strong international organizations such as the EU and for democratic governments everywhere. If we truly wish to break the historic mold of mass slaughter, we must train, prepare, and build the necessary skills throughout the world. In medicine and public health—concerned with saving lives and preventing human suffering, as we are with preventing mass killing—this is well established. The time has come to follow this example and develop such a professional cadre in this exceedingly dangerous field.

CHAPTER 8

Democracy and Prevention of Mass Violence

Basic Orientation

Democracies thrive by finding ways to deal fairly with conflicts and to resolve them below the threshold of mass violence. They develop ongoing mechanisms for settling disagreements.[1] People who live in pluralistic democracies become accustomed to diverse needs and learn the art of working out compromises that offer something to satisfy all groups involved. That is why the worldwide spread of democracies and the application of democratic principles to intergroup and internation conflicts are an essential part of preventing mass violence, especially genocide. Patiently constructing strong democracies everywhere strengthens an important tool for nonviolent conflict resolution worldwide. It is a difficult process, but the general tendency has been clear and strong over many years in many places. And much is being learned about how it can be done. A democracy cannot be imposed by force, nor will a single, premature election lead to peace and prosperity.

The attitudes, beliefs, procedures, and institutions essential to democracies are valuable in dealing with intergroup conflict at all levels, within or beyond state borders. Among them are using informal as well as official processes of negotiation and mediation; establishing norms of intergroup tolerance; and having respect for the viewpoints of other people and agreement on the value of mutual accommodation.

Democracies, even with periodic regressions, protect human rights better than nondemocratic societies, and their elected officials are less likely to engage in large-scale, egregious human rights violations that create intense fear, severe resentment, and a desire for revenge that leads to violence as the only way to redress grievances. Massive human rights abuses as a path to genocide are very unlikely in an established democracy.

The basic principles of democracy are attractive all over the world, even though entrenched autocratic powers resist them. Survey research in Africa and elsewhere shows a clear preference for democracy. Professor Robert Dahl, a leading scholar on democratic governance, pointed out some of its principal advantages, which are widely appreciated even if vaguely formulated in poor countries.[2]

Democracy offers a number of defenses against rule by cruel and vicious autocrats. It guarantees fundamental rights that other political systems do not allow. It ensures a broader range of personal freedom than any alternative. It provides ways for citizens to protect their fundamental interests. It provides extensive opportunities to choose the laws under which one lives. Similarly, it grants the freedom to exercise moral responsibility. It fosters individual human development more fully than any alternative. It encourages political equality and economic equality of opportunity. It has built-in checks that deter modern representative democracies from warring with each other, even though this may take one or two decades after the onset of democracy in a previously dictatorial country. It fosters an open economy that usually generates prosperity. Thus, the worldwide preference for democracy (with notable exceptions) is not a sentimental yearning for utopia, but rather a hardheaded, practical necessity to achieve the profound goals of human decency, peace, and prosperity in the long run.

All democracies need systematic, fair procedures of governance that are based on the consent of the governed. A system of representation is essential, but no single kind will work for every group. Around the world many different arrangements for democratic representation exist—parliamentary or presidential, centralized or federal, single-member districts or districts with proportional representation, the requirement of exceptional majorities for functions perceived as particularly vital, plebiscites for constitutional change, and special arrangements to protect the rights of vulnerable minorities. These variations share the common themes of fairness and widespread participation in decisions important to the lives of the population.[3]

These are fundamental and ambitious tasks. Many obstacles stand in the way of sustaining well-functioning democracies. Even with their fundamental advantages, democracies necessarily remain imperfect; they require constant vigilance and ongoing adjustments to avoid erosion of democratic values, practices, and institutions. The need to raise large sums of money in order to conduct modern, media-based campaigns is a serious threat to fairness and honesty. The persistence of prejudice in one form or another impedes democracy in every society—yet much less than in autocratic states that often have state-sponsored repression of minorities. Powerful special interest groups can damage the democratic process. The inability of some parliamentary systems to form governing coalitions can make pluralism unworkable. Even in the oldest and most powerful democracies the system must be constantly monitored, e.g., by universities, democracy-promoting NGOs, and governmental "watchdog" organizations. This emphasizes the continuing need to readjust the balance of power among the elements of the society, including the balance between majority rule and protection of minorities.

Democracy is structured to avoid massive concentration of political and economic power, in order to avoid painful inequity and even repressive control—yet public opposition to excessive concentration of wealth and power is essential. A highly centralized, command economy is not compatible with authentic democracy. Too much power is concentrated in a government that employs everyone, controls all resources, and can readily abuse human rights. Pluralism is at the heart of a lasting democracy: it permits and fosters the dynamic interplay of ideas and enterprises by parties and by a great variety of nongovernmental organizations on the basis of reasonably clear, agreed-upon rules—rules that reflect a fundamental attitude of tolerance, mutual respect, and sensitivity to human rights.

Democracies with strong market economies must guarantee safety nets for the seriously disadvantaged and make public arrangements for vital human requirements: e.g., education, health care, and the protection of public health as well as unemployment insurance. They must employ progressive taxation in the interest of public fairness and foster equality of opportunity. Indeed, all modern democracies make deliberate efforts, however imperfect, to balance market efficiency with social justice.

Civil society bolsters democracy by giving a practical demonstration of how democratic values evolve through nonviolent conflict. Nongovernmental groups compete with each other and with the state for the power to carry out specific agendas. Within the context of institutionalized competition, tolerance and acceptance of legally conducted opposition develop, thus fostering nonviolent solutions to social problems. These habits of understanding others and working out compromises are learned. Such skills are often necessary before the first election can be constructive. Civil society creates coalitions of individuals that initiate valuable political activities, e.g., in the service of equal opportunity or protection of human rights. Political parties are crucial components of civil society, since they are vital mediating institutions between the citizens and the government and give diverse peoples a genuine opportunity to join with like-minded others in a peaceful way.

Facilitating the Emergence of Democracy Through International Cooperation

The established democracies, strong now and getting stronger (e.g., the European Union), have learned a lesson from the hatred and violence of the twentieth century and are seeking to expand the opportunities for better human relations, internally and externally. This impulse to fulfill the promise of democracy with informed, proactive, sustained efforts to prevent deadly conflict through fair solutions and improved quality of life deserves strong encouragement. Indeed, this trend should become a worldwide trademark of established democracies. They can make the world's experience available to emerging, fragile democracies and offer tangible help. Democracy by military invasion is not a useful model.

Can the international community of democracies formulate a decent minimum of democratic facilitation for most, or eventually even all, countries? If so, that would mean a vigorous, sustained effort through the media and the formal educational systems to educate publics about the essential democratic experiences. What structures and functions are vital for the emergence of a viable democracy? How can the international community make them widely known and understood? Certainly a vaguely formulated aspiration has swept the world in recent decades and is reflected in survey research, even in very poor countries. The international community must translate this aspiration into the reality of emerging democracy by clarifying what it takes to make the system work and the basic benefits that can be foreseen. We will see in the next chapter how equitable socioeconomic development is a parallel requirement.

It is no coincidence that the international community of democracies includes the nations of the world that are strongest economically, politically, morally, militarily, scientifically, and technologically—not to mention most successful in protecting human rights and preserving decent human relations. These fortunate countries, with so much relevant experience in coping with the problems of modern societies, have a moral imperative to facilitate a systematic, deliberate, nonviolent, long-term democratization around the world. What can they do to foster a democratic atmosphere, democratic values, and democratic institutions worldwide? Their own differences make it apparent that they cannot adopt a rigid, one-size-fits-all approach, but one that considers historical circumstances, cultural traditions, and human ingenuity in each country, rich or poor. They must also recognize and correct their own flaws, such as flagrant abuse of power in the U.S. Watergate scandal.

The boost that transparency and the free flow of information always give to democracy suggests the extraordinary potential of new communications technologies to spread democratic ideals and aspirations. Several organizations in Europe and the United States are using new ways of enhancing technology for freedom of expression and democratic process. For example, the National Endowment for Democracy, ably led by Carl Gershman, is using new communications technologies to help build democracy.[4] Democracy flourishes in the free flow of information. Established low technology is useful too: books, newspapers, phones, faxes, television, posters, and flyers all are helpful. Still, the recent advances in the scope and interactivity of the Internet offer expanded opportunities. The Internet is playing an active role in the promotion of democracy in many ways, even in poor, remote areas that have been little associated with democracy. Yet it also lends itself to advocacy of hatred and techniques of terrorist violence—and ways must be found to buffer these influences.

Although governments certainly have a major role to play, efforts to spread democracy should not be thought of as purely governmental or as resting entirely on intergovernmental and international institutions. Nongovernmental organizations of many varieties have significant, even necessary, roles. And they too need international cooperation to be effective.

The World Movement for Democracy, led by an international steering committee and with headquarters in Washington, D.C., is an international network of NGOs working to build democracy. Initiated in 1999, the World Movement is inspired by the belief that the expansion of global communications and the emergence of an increasingly interdependent global economy have created new opportunities for opening closed societies and spreading information on ways to create and sustain democracy. It was created to enable grassroots democrats to assist each other by sharing information and experiences; devising local, regional, and global strategies; launching collaborative initiatives; and developing relationships of cross-border solidarity.

As a result of its first three global assemblies—in New Delhi, India, in 1999, São Paulo, Brazil, in 2000, and Durban, South Africa, in 2004—the World Movement encompasses a wide variety of regional and functional networks, such as the Africa Democracy Forum, the Transatlantic Democracy Network, the Network of Democracy Research Institutes, the Global Network on Local Governance, the International Movement of Parliamentarians for Democracy, the International Women's Democracy Network, and the Youth Movement for Democracy. In addition to facilitating the exchange of information and experiences, the networks conduct meetings and workshops, hold discussions online, and build the capacity of network participants. Links to these networks' Web sites are available on the World Movement's main site, www.wmd.org.

Democracy News, a monthly electronic newsletter, facilitates interaction among World Movement participants via e-mail exchange. It enables participants to call for collaboration on democracy projects, announce upcoming activities and events, report on the results of recent work, and call for action on behalf of World Movement participants who are facing danger as a result of their efforts to promote democracy. This movement is one promising example of helping to build a broadly inclusive network of vigorous democracies that can help achieve many of the goals set out in this book.

What are the most useful means for promoting democracy? In the case of new, emerging, and fragile democracies, it is valuable to strengthen the political and civic infrastructure of democracy—learning the give-and-take of free people seeking to accommodate each other's basic human needs. This involves technical assistance, long-term solidarity, and financial aid to build the requisite processes and institutions, including widespread education of publics about the actual working of democracy. It involves many kinds of help, adapted to each situation. Building the means to conduct elections at both the national and local level along with the establishment of legislative bodies at the national and local level is only one important element. It usually needs to be preceded by developing a modicum of civil society, so that people are ready to make good use of elections—not turning to fanatics who mislead and provoke hatred.

Aid must be directed at the prolonged task of establishing the democratic rule of law. This includes a broad-based and truly fair constitution, the creation of an independent judiciary with real capacity for implementing laws fairly, along with oversight institutions to provide for public accountability. Reforms must occur in the bureaucracy to ensure public administration of a professional (noncorrupt) nature. Civilian institutional capacities must be created to deal with security questions, both within and beyond the borders of the country, to temper the military and avoid murderous militias. Special measures to protect individual human rights, minority groups, and vulnerable sectors must evolve, especially nonviolent mechanisms to deal with conflict that are effective in solving practical problems and are accepted as fair to all.

These tasks are complex and usually prolonged, so it is highly desirable that the democratic community establish, singly and together, special funds for economic assistance that will be used to strengthen countries that show a serious effort to maintain democratic institutions tailored to be an enduring part of their societies. Both funding and technical assistance in many sectors must be sustained over a period of years to support the complex processes of building a democracy and coping with transient but strong tensions.[5] This is necessarily multilateral.

The international democratic community must also take the responsibility to intervene as best it can to protect fragile democracies when they are jeopardized by natural disasters, violent ethnic conflicts, or strong authoritarian currents within the society. It must develop a system of early warning that will alert fellow democracies that a new member of the community is slipping into crisis. Much more must be done to develop the use of international mediation at an early stage to prevent mass violence.[6] Building and sustaining new democracies require mechanisms to accommodate ethnic, religious, linguistic, and political diversity along with effective institutional arrangements to monitor sensitive issues likely to engender conflict.[7] The well-established democracies can use their embassies in emerging, fragile democracies as sites of technical and moral support, not only in building democratic institutions in relatively good times but also in detecting early signals that predict deadly conflict so that help can be mobilized.[8]

How can human rights be protected on a secure and enduring basis? Although it is useful for bilateral and multilateral diplomacy to pursue individual cases of human rights abuse, the democratic community should put its emphasis on systemic reforms. Other than the establishment of effective democratic institutions, there is no clear way to provide an enduring basis for treating human beings fairly and protecting human rights under a popularly accepted rule of law. The European experience in the second half of the twentieth century provides specific models for judicial means of protecting human rights.[9] These mechanisms are now being adapted to take account of the wider scope of emerging democracies in Europe. Its experience can usefully be considered in other parts of the world (see Chapter 11). This progress reflects learning from the bitter experience of Nazi and Communist repression.

A remarkable step that is largely a product of the 1990s is the international monitoring of election campaigns—their preparation, conduct, and aftermath—to guarantee that they are not an empty show. Democratic governments, the UN, regional organizations (especially the EU), and NGOs (notably the Carter Center) have all contributed here.

A unique NGO that provides inspiration for other NGOs, governments, and intergovernmental organizations is the Carter Center, based in Atlanta, Georgia, but functioning all over the world. The mission of the Carter Center is to strive for a world in which everyone has the opportunity to enjoy good health and live in peace.[10] Established in 1982 by former president Jimmy Carter and his wife Rosalynn, the center has worked in partnership with neighboring Emory University to improve the lives of people around the world.

Led by the Carters and supported by an independent board of trustees, the center's excellent staff "wage peace, fight disease," encourage civic development in sixty-five countries, and build hope by working both with those at the highest levels of government and also side by side with ordinary, often forgotten people.

The center has worked to strengthen democracies in Asia, Latin America, and Africa; to teach farmers in fifteen African countries how to double or triple grain production; to mediate or work to prevent civil and international conflicts; to set up conflict resolution workshops in strife-torn states; to combat preventable diseases in Latin America and Africa; and to help reduce the stigma of mental illness in the United States and abroad.

Successful elections require help before, during, and after an election—and the clear understanding that many elections will be necessary over space and time to build a truly representative democracy. The Carter Center was a pioneer in this work. Today, the EU and the UN play a large role.

Another good example of NGO democracy building is presented by the Project on Ethnic Relations (PER), founded in 1991 and superbly led by Allen H. Kassof and Livia B. Plaks.[11] PER began its work in Central Europe and the Balkans and remains deeply committed there. It seeks to make its special contribution by working with high-level leaders of opposing ethnic groups to encourage accountable, responsible, and inclusive government in multiethnic states. It has had substantial success in defusing the potential for ethnic violence by helping to forge concrete agreements and arrangements that offer practical patterns of good multiethnic governance.

Nongovernmental organizations have increasingly engaged in using democratic principles and mechanisms to help nations on the precipice deal with conflicts within their borders, particularly those arising from the resurgence of old, lingering prejudices and the political exploitation of ethnic nationalism.

Democratization was at the core of virtually all the comprehensive peace settlements in which the UN has participated in recent years—in El Salvador, Cambodia, Namibia, Mozambique, and Guatemala. Although each region has its own legacy of cultures, languages, and religions, fundamental democratic principles, applied in ways that fit local circumstances, are useful everywhere in resolving intergroup conflicts and preventing their escalation to violence. Significantly, the final major publication of UN Secretary-General Boutros Boutros-Ghali as he left office was "An Agenda for Democratization," a wise and farsighted document.[12]

It is particularly important for mediators to guide opponents toward developing a shared consensus about practical procedures to resolve difficult problems and from there toward creating institutions that give all citizens ready and reliable access to those procedures. Moreover, antagonists can be persuaded that cooperation will lead to greater benefits in the long run and that superordinate goals of compelling value to all concerned can be achieved only by cooperation. The successful examples of other countries and regions can provide emerging leaders—through site visits and other international forums—with a vivid sense of what is possible and how democratic processes work. The international cooperation necessary to achieve such change is measured in years of complicated joint efforts, often by strong organizations such as the European Union, the United Nations, or the community of established democracies.

A new organization emerged in June 2000. One hundred and seven states took part in the Community of Democracies ministerial meeting, convened in Warsaw, Poland, and adopted a Declaration Towards a Community of Democracies. They endorsed a wide-ranging set of democratic principles. The second meeting of this group, "Democracy: Investing for Peace and Prosperity," occurred two years later in Seoul, South Korea. The Community of Democracies affirmed that the essential elements of representative democracy in all its forms are:

- Respect for human rights—civil, political, economic, social, and cultural—including freedom of expression, freedom of the press, and freedom of religion and conscience
- Access to and free exercise of power in accordance with the rule of law
- The holding of periodic free and fair elections based on secret balloting and universal suffrage monitored by independent election authorities
- Freedom of association, including the right to form independent political parties
- Separation of powers, especially an independent judiciary
- Constitutional subordination of all state institutions, including the military, to the legally constituted civilian authority

The Seoul Plan of Action of 2002 provided various measures to promote regional democratic progress and education for democracy and good governance and to respond to threats to democracy. There was a third meeting in 2004 that seemed to some less action oriented than the earlier two. What comes next is unclear, but the concept is attractive. One interesting possibility would be for this group to form a democracy caucus at the United Nations, such as that recommended by a recent Council on Foreign Relations report as a "forum for building cooperation on issues of human rights and democracy."[13] Time and again the UN has helped to resolve disputes and reduce violence. But it can only realize its full potential for averting mass violence if it has superb leadership and the robust support of its member states—especially the established democracies.[14]

Thus, a democratic caucus would, first and foremost, attempt to block nondemocratic nations from membership on UN bodies that focus on democratic development. The caucus would also strongly support the UNDP, which works to strengthen legislatures, electoral systems, and other elements of the democratic governance. The UNDP also seeks to develop free and independent media while lending support and technical aid in establishing the preconditions of free, fair, and open electoral processes.[15]

Similar recommendations are made in a study prepared for the Carnegie Commission on Preventing Deadly Conflict by Professor Graham Allison of Harvard and Ambassador Hisashi Owada of Japan (now a judge on the International Court of Justice).[16] They show that the prevention of violent conflict is far better and more cost-effective than its cure and point out practical ways in which the community of established democracies could foster such prevention—acting partly through the UN and partly outside it— but always in the spirit of the UN Charter, which so strongly reflects the basic principles of democracy. One way or another, the established democracies (an expanding group of countries) will need to act in concert to build the pillars of prevention essential for blocking mass violence.[17]

Democratic Engineering and Power Sharing

As they establish democratic institutions, heterogeneous countries have many choices: confederation or federation, regional or functional autonomy, or institutionalized cultural pluralism within each nation and across national boundaries. Thus, the organizations offering help must be sensitive to local conditions and historical tensions.

One important option for conflict-riven societies is *democratic confederation,* a form of government that can foster tolerance and wide participation and can accommodate a variety of orientations and cultural preferences, even highly parochial ones. It is a de-centralized, loosely organized, inclusive, and accountable form of democracy that can effectively protect minorities, observe the rule of law, and give all its peoples fair representation. Local areas may have a high degree of autonomy, and distinct cultural groups may have extensive jurisdiction over their own affairs—yet they can draw upon the pooled resources of a larger economic and social entity. Confederations succeed best when they encourage a thriving civil society in which many nongovernmental organizations and voluntary associations pursue diverse interests and values in peaceful ways.

Some multiethnic societies can manage intergroup relations and maintain social cohesion by simple majority rule. But that form of democracy might not suffice in societies with deep ethnic divisions and little experience with popular self-government. In such cases, a combination of weak national identity and divisive political leaders easily leads to voting along strictly ethnic lines and a tyranny of the majority. This in turn creates deep resentment and erosion of trust in the democratic process. A better choice is often the adoption of mutually agreed upon power-sharing arrangements that encourage broad-based governing coalitions. This can result over time in an inclusive, well-integrated country.

Timothy Sisk explained in a Carnegie Commission–sponsored study that power-sharing arrangements are most likely to be succeed when a critical number of moderate political leaders, genuinely representative of the groups they claim to lead, agree to embrace pluralism and guarantee equitable distribution of resources by means of broadly accepted and flexible measures (preferably locally developed and region specific). The parties can gradually eliminate any extraordinary measures that power-sharing arrangements sometimes require and move toward a more integrative and liberal form of democracy.[18] They usually need outside help in envisioning the gains over time in such arrangements.

Assessing International Efforts to Foster Global Democracy

An important report, *Ten Years of Supporting Democracy Worldwide*, was published in 2005 by the International Institute for Democracy and Electoral Assistance (International IDEA), a respected prodemocracy institution based in Stockholm and worldwide in scope.[19] Here are the highlights of the IDEA report:

Democracy Building and Development

Democracy assistance and poverty alleviation strategies are two principal ways external financial aid has been used to support or strengthen self-government. Thomas Carothers (Carnegie Endowment for International Peace) regarded democracy assistance as aid expressly formulated to create or expand openings for democracy in nondemocratic countries.[20] Donors have increasingly tried to facilitate and support the transition to democracy in developing states through building capacity and institutions for good governance.

The Development Assistance Committee (DAC) of the Organization for Economic Cooperation and Development (OECD) has classified some of these many and varied activities under "participatory development and good governance," which covers everything from public sector management to peace building through such specific tasks as election management and creation or reform of a state's constitution, parliament, judiciary, democratic civil society, political parties, and civil-military relations.[21] A recent study estimated that about 10 percent of the overall volume of aid between 1990 and 2005 had been devoted to such activities in the area of democracy, human rights, and governance.[22] Though this is an increase, it is less than a powerful commitment.

Democracy, Poverty, and Political Change

The content and process of democracy building vary immensely. The challenges of democracy promotion and poverty reduction have spurred democratic donors to create development strategies that place basic norms such as human rights into a cultural and political setting that is relevant and credible to a specific society, whatever its idiosyncrasies.

The IDEA review of democracy building identified various approaches to democracy assistance that are essential contributors to democracies: civil society, elections, political parties, parliaments, civil-military relations, state reform, the rule of law, and good governance.[23] Established democracies have developed ingenious variations on these basic themes and have instituted new democracy-related funding, notably to promote prevention of deadly conflict, cultural cooperation, economic reform, and civic education. A number of donors have begun to reward recipient countries with additional aid if they demonstrate democratic progress and a willingness to undergo reform in the direction of equitable socioeconomic development.[24]

The most difficult problem is with intransigent, authoritarian states, which receive far less aid for democracy building than semiauthoritarian and posttransition countries. Burma, Zimbabwe, North Korea, Cuba, and Syria, for example, have provided hardly any openings for democracy-building aid, with the exception of funding to exiled prodemocracy groups and to nongovernmental organizations that monitor rights abuses in these states.

Russia is a special case. The remarkable democratic reforms begun under Gorbachev have eroded to a very worrisome extent—yet some democratic efforts persist. Russia's membership in the Council of Europe provides an opportunity to make that body a focal point for prodemocracy initiatives in Russia. Persistence in offering economic, political, social, and legal incentives will be worth pursuing to shore up that country's backsliding—along with honest critiques of authoritarian behavior. The Russian people have for so long lived under totalitarian or autocratic governments that they are not well prepared. It will take years of dedicated efforts to help their public benefit from democracy.

The largest share of funds to support civil society goes to NGOs, especially to the large human rights organizations. A typical arrangement involves a large international NGO working with a few important umbrella human rights NGOs in the target state. Much political aid is focused on basic human rights issues—opposition to such practices as torture, the death penalty, exclusionary hypernationalism, prejudice against minorities. Although their interests are inherently related, the human rights and democracy organizations have not been highly cooperative with each other. This is a shortsighted view that can become counterproductive.

There is a growing effort to strengthen high-initiative problem solving within each democratizing country, learning from the world's experience, yet adapting to particular opportunities in each country. Established democracies acting jointly can be especially helpful in these fundamental reform efforts.

Government-to-Government Institution-Building Aid

Donors are giving increased attention to helping recipients build a capable state that can meet the basic needs of its citizens. There has been a tendency to go beyond individual electoral campaigns toward longer-term capacity building in a variety of democratic processes and institutions. Parliamentary support is a dimension of democracy building that has been underrepresented; most funding has gone to strengthen the role of women in parliaments. Important as that is, the requirements of parliamentary institution building are broader.

The reform of civil-military relations has been seriously neglected and largely left to defense ministries. Where it has been incorporated into democracy assistance, it has typically been through the perspective of prevention of deadly conflict—a crucial contribution, but there is need for further useful investment, especially in civilian control of the military.

A central challenge for democracy assistance is to fashion a linkage between promotion of democracy, competent governance, and equitable socioeconomic development. This is an essentially new and exceedingly important field. There is much to be learned through research and careful observation of useful practices. An important aspect is the emergence of women from low status in health, education, economic opportunity, and political participation.

This careful, systematic work on democracy building around the world indicates the creative ferment in this field. It is only in the past decade that the world's established democracies have become energized to learn more about ways to help nondemocracies emerge from the darkness of repression, human rights violations, war, and genocide. A powerful movement is building to constrain the world's dictators and dehumanizers and to provide opportunities to fulfill the potential of their oppressed peoples. Still, there is a long way to go.

Prospects for Future Spread of Democracy

Professor Larry Diamond of Stanford University and the Hoover Institution, a leading scholar in the field of democracy, has argued persuasively that within fifty years it will be possible to achieve a world in which every government is a democracy.[25] He cited the "third wave" of democracy—the unprecedented growth and persistence of democracy around the world in the last quarter of the twentieth century. In a cross-cultural review of the regions of the world, Diamond noted that the Arab world is largely devoid of democracy, but he maintained that despite assumptions to the contrary, most Muslims, much like non-Muslims, support democracy. Democracy is becoming a universal value. There are elements of democracy in various Muslim countries (e.g., Indonesia) and now intellectual leadership toward democracy in Arab countries, albeit much of it conducted by expatriates.

Diamond examined the factors that encourage and sustain democracy—economic development and performance, international supports and pressures, and changing international norms and conventions. He gave international involvement and cooperation a crucial role.

It is possible—though it will not be easy—for the powerful established democracies to rid the world of authoritarian rule within the span of about two generations. The United States surpasses any potential adversary in military and economic terms and could play a strong role in the nonviolent promotion of democracy. It did so in the decades following World War II and could do so again in future decades. Despite serious governmental errors in the first decade of the new century, its civil society organizations and scientific community are very strong internationally. The EU, another powerful actor in the world, admits only committed liberal democracies to membership, though it helps others to achieve that sort of government. The majority of states throughout the world are now democracies of some kind. Democracy has become the only form of government broadly recognized as desirable and legitimate, even though the Iraq war has been a serious problem, reinforcing stereotypes about democracy promotion as a cover for military domination. Worldwide, that is certainly not the case. The belief that democratic government is a basic and universal human right has gained global momentum. Both individual nations and international organizations are more frequently and more vigorously promoting democracy and challenging the authoritarian regimes that perpetrate or permit systematic violations of human rights. A country's "responsibility to protect" the human rights of its population is key to the new concept of sovereignty.

In 1974, a rapid worldwide expansion of democracy began with the overthrow of the dictatorship in Portugal. By 1987 democracy had spread to nearly two-fifths of the world's states, although Eastern Europe, Africa, and the Middle East were still largely untouched. The fall of the Berlin Wall in 1989 and the collapse of the Soviet Union in 1991 changed the picture in Europe. Africa also began making a significant shift toward democracy with a 1990 "sovereign national conference" in Benin and the release of Nelson Mandela from prison in South Africa in 1994 and the subsequent building of South African democracy. By 1997, with strong pressure from external and internal donors, most African states allowed opposition parties, an open space for civil society, and free elections.

Today nearly three-fifths of the world's states are democratic. Of the 125 states that became democracies in the 1990s, only fourteen have returned to authoritarian rule—and democracy resurfaced in nine of them.[26] Professor Robert Dahl of Yale has noted a striking fact: if a modern democracy has lasted twenty years (one generation), it has an excellent chance of continued survival.[27] In principle, even the poorest of states has a chance to succeed in building a democracy. Even with periodic backsliding, this can be done. The fact that some of the world's most underdeveloped countries can achieve democracy flies in the face of autocratic, self-justifying ideologies of repression in the name of prosperity.

Amartya Sen, who won the 1998 Nobel Prize in economics in part by showing that democracies do not have famines, also demonstrated that impoverished peoples need to have a political voice and that democracy should not be thought of as a luxury only for the rich. Indeed, there is little evidence that poor people would reject democracy if given the choice.[28] Surveys across cultures show that ordinary citizens everywhere value democracy. Democracy was the preferred form of government for two-thirds of the Africans surveyed by the 2001 Afrobarometer poll in twelve (mostly poor) countries.[29] Latin Americans have had time to become dissatisfied with the way democratic rule works in their own countries, yet 57 percent still find it preferable to an authoritarian regime. Only 15 percent believe a caudillo would serve them better.[30]

In five countries of East Asia—Taiwan, South Korea, Hong Kong, the Philippines, and Thailand—more than two-thirds of the population agreed in 2001 that authoritarian rule should be replaced by democracy. The same is true for the twelve former Soviet bloc countries that successfully sought membership in the European Union.[31] They have made the requisite changes to build democratic institutions—all in a short time.

The 2001 Afrobarometer survey indicated that in Africa a large majority of both Muslims and non-Muslims support democracy. And deeper examination of the attitudes of African Muslims suggested that their negative responses to democracy were based on lack of information or on reasons other than religious.[32]

Moderate Muslims, including intellectual leaders, promote a more liberal interpretation of Islam that downplays hostile references in holy texts. They emphasize the moral teachings of Islam that are compatible with such democratic ideals as "accountability, freedom of expression, and the rule of law." Moderate Muslim religious leaders increasingly favor the separation of mosque and state.

The *Arab Human Development Report* of 2002, prepared by Arab scholars, noted with regret that Arab states have largely failed to participate in the "global wave of democratization" and acknowledged the damage to both human and political development as a result of this lack of freedom.[33] They insisted on the need for "comprehensive political representation in effective legislatures" to liberate human capabilities and make governance fully accountable. Their groundbreaking report was constructive and farsighted.

Amartya Sen believes that something is of universal value if people all over the world have a reason to see it as valuable, even if not everyone agrees to its value. According to this measure, democracy is becoming a universal value. A deep scholar and world citizen, Sen gave further basis for hope in a new book, *Identity and Violence*.[34]

Democracy Drivers

Diamond raised four questions to assess the chance that all countries will eventually become democratic:

1. What propelled the third wave of democratization?
2. Why have so few of the new democracies failed in the last quarter century?
3. What makes the remaining nondemocracies persist?
4. If we truly believe that countries not now democratic can become so, then how?[35]

Diamond began his answers to these questions with a sketch of some causes of democratization.

Economic development. Increasing national wealth brings pressure for democratization to the extent that it leads to such intervening effects as a better educated citizenry, a diverse middle class not directly connected to the government, and a more pluralistic and resourceful civil society—all leading to a less passive culture that is eager and ready to make its voice heard through democratic means.

South Korea and Taiwan offer the best examples of societies that became democracies when their economies flourished. Thailand, Brazil, Mexico, and South Africa follow, with less economic progress. But dictators have legitimized their power and resisted democracy in Malaysia and Singapore (the wealthiest authoritarian state) by identifying their rule with their societies' cultural values and beliefs. And some nations may be rich as measured by per capita income (e.g., states with large oil or mineral deposits), but they remain undeveloped in terms of education, civil society, rights of women, and state accountability to its citizens. Some, like Saudi Arabia, foster profound social and economic inequity.

Dictators frequently defend authoritarian rule (and their own in particular) as the only way to eliminate corruption, unite the country, or create economic growth. But these rationalizations are wearing thin in the twenty-first century. Self-serving dictators misdirect money and power to supporters, soldiers, and personal security forces intended to stifle disagreement. This may keep them in power for a while, but it usually cripples their country.

International actions and pressures. The third wave of democratization has been accompanied by a sea change in the outlook and policies of the wealthy democracies. It started in the United States, with Jimmy Carter's focus on human rights and Ronald Reagan's advocacy of democracy (at least in Communist countries). The National Endowment for Democracy was among the U.S. institutions created to give direction and support to movements, organizations, and institutions focused on the spread of democracy. Nearly a half billion dollars were spent by the end of the 1990s to encourage democracy development abroad.

The European Union joined the United States in this quest for democracy with great vigor and determination, working in postcommunist Europe with financial, organizational, technical, and moral incentives for democratization. All states who wanted to be a part of the EU and share in its peaceful prosperity were required to adopt "truly democratic practices and respect for fundamental rights and freedoms."[36] Over the past fifteen years the EU has provided political, technical, and economic assistance to help these candidate states achieve and maintain free political and economic conditions and to build democratic institutions and make them work well. The EU demonstrated a powerful magnet effect for democratic change. Someday other regional organizations may have similar achievements.

The Americas have begun to exert regional pressure to preserve democracy. The Organization of American States (OAS) adopted the Santiago Commitment to Democracy in June 1991. This document was to be consulted upon the overthrow of a democracy and has sometimes been useful, though it is uneven in application. Economic improvement for the rank and file is badly needed.

Changing international norms and conventions. The biggest transformation during the "third wave" has been the focus on human rights and on democracy itself as a right for all people. It has become a worldwide norm essential to elicit cooperation with other nations—in other words, "govern with the consent of the governed."[37]

At the very least, this progress has led to increased acceptance of help from a variety of actors: multilateral, national, and nongovernmental. It has also bolstered internal advocates of human rights and democracy. International normative and legal trends have helped this third wave of democratization. The aspiration for democracy is a sustaining factor for morale in many countries, despite ups and downs in their leadership and economic fluctuations.

Fewer Breakdowns

Three factors strengthen the likelihood that democracies of the third wave will not fail badly:

1. The wealthier a democracy gets, the more immune it becomes to backsliding, especially if the distribution of wealth is reasonably equitable.

2. Democracy has spread as people accept it for its intrinsic value. Citizens are in favor of democracy, despite its drawbacks, and see no legitimate alternative.
3. Reversing democracy comes at a high price. Leaders in both politics and the military know that in order to retain their regional political positions they must also retain their democratic system.

The international community must increase its commitment to full cooperation in supporting democracy and its consolidation over time. A united resolve will help to prevent regression in existing democracies and inspire more transitions to democracy, often in incremental but nevertheless significant steps. The European example—after all the disasters of the nineteenth and twentieth centuries—is dramatic. Cooperation among the EU, Council of Europe, OSCE, and NATO to foster democracy in the postcommunist countries of east central Europe and some others as well (notably Turkey) is a development of truly historic significance.

A worldwide culture of democracy requires continuing educational programs, along with political, economic, and social incentives—linked to clear and firm international norms. International actors must make loans and aid to authoritarian states conditional on humane, responsible, and increasingly democratic rule. These states are prone to massive human rights violations, even genocide, so the international community has a major responsibility to foster their movement toward democracy, with intensive efforts to avert genocide-prone behavior.

Can It Be Done?

Democratization of the whole world is possible only through international cooperation of governments and multilateral institutions. Participants will vary over time in their contributions of various resources and legitimacy, but the aggregate is powerful and can be exceedingly constructive. The U.S. government, formerly the preeminent leader, has lost prestige and moral standing in the eyes of the world. It must reestablish both if it is to help in the move toward democracy. Working closely with other nations is essential. Preemptive war is not a formula for promoting democracy or earning moral stature. More countries will adopt democracy and fewer resort to dictatorship if the established democracies are consistently supportive in a collaborative, problem-solving mode—relying primarily on political, economic, and social incentives.

Liberal democracy requires not only free and fair elections but also comprehensive fairness of political competition. The electoral arena is open, and the playing field is reasonably level. Money must not be the principal factor in elections—an important current problem in the United States. High-quality democracy requires some degree of public financing of parties and campaigns as well as full transparency in the reporting of all party and campaign contributions. This includes guaranteed access to the mass media for competing candidates, both presidential and parliamentary. These are high standards, not fully met in some of the affluent, established democracies. But they constitute a critical goal for which all legitimate democracies must strive.

A worldwide tendency is emerging toward inclusive development planning and participatory budgeting that directly involves communities in their own development. When they choose for themselves what portion of their taxes they want to use for roads, schools, clinics, or dams, communities gain a sense of ownership over the process and are encouraged to form alliances to ensure that the funds allocated on paper actually go to their intended uses.[38] The Carter Center, in cooperation with the World Bank, has helped several developing countries proceed in this way.

This requires developing civil society organizations that participate in decisionmaking along with governments and international institutions. No group can justifiably demand that all its interests be fully implemented, but every differing group should be heard, with full access and input to legislative committees and councils.[39] A difficult but important aspiration of a high-quality democracy is a modicum of political equality among citizens. To move in this direction, especially in poor countries, requires civic education to make participation meaningful—and incentives from established democracies.

People Power and Nonviolent Social Action for the Democratic Prevention of Mass Violence

Peaceful mass action can be a powerful force on behalf of democracy.[40] Recent decades have witnessed how it can defuse or prevent violent conflict, with profound political effects. In East Germany in 1989, street protests became common as citizens, heartened by Mikhail Gorbachev's policy of liberalization, demanded the right not only to move freely across borders but also to achieve democratic reform. The situation was dangerous: East Germany's leader, Erich Honecker, was a hard-liner who favored the traditional Soviet policy, violent repression of internal dissent. But Protestant clergy among the leaders of the popular movement used their status to ensure that the demonstrations remained peaceful, and their churches were used as sanctuaries to protect and assemble reform-minded activists—most notably the Nikolai Church in Leipzig, where on October 9 a crowd of nearly 70,000 people gathered in nonviolent protest. Organizers exerted strong social pressure to maintain order, and the security forces backed down from confrontation. Within days people from all walks of life joined the demonstration and swelled the number of protesters to more than 150,000.[41]

A number of cities throughout East Germany followed Leipzig's peaceful example. Their nonviolent behavior not only removed any plausible excuse for a government crackdown but also gave the protesters and their message considerable moral authority. The outwardly impervious East German regime tottered and then fell in November 1989. Here as elsewhere, leadership matters. For example, the revered conductor, Kurt Mazur, as well as several distinguished clergymen, not only sustained the demonstrations for liberty but also helped to keep them nonviolent. This is similar to the role of Archbishop Desmond Tutu in South Africa.

Other Soviet attempts to stifle reform were met by peaceful demonstrations. Czechoslovakia staged its Velvet Revolution with large peaceful demonstrations. In Mongolia hunger strikes and civil disobedience gained democratic concessions from the Communist regime (although Communists won the free elections that followed).[42]

Still other movements in the Philippines and elsewhere confirm the formidable strength of a united and resolute nonviolent population, even though some mass demonstrations, such as the one in Tiananmen Square in China, have been viciously repressed. Such protests build on the nonviolent movements of Mohandas Gandhi and Dr. Martin Luther King Jr., which can be forces not only for democratic change but also for the prevention of deadly conflict.[43] Challenging imperial power, racism, or authoritarianism is a dangerous proposition. It raises social issues difficult for the society at large to confront. Responding in kind to the brutal force that repressive systems use to maintain their power can begin a cycle of violence that leads to mass atrocities. In East Germany, Czechoslovakia, Mongolia, and more recently in Serbia, leaders and activists—and the people themselves—understood the true power of mass, nonviolent protest. They made sure that their well-prepared and disciplined demonstrations remained peaceful in the face of provocation. In this way they reduced the possibility of violent conflict and moved toward a just regime.

In his recent work, *Gandhi and Beyond: Nonviolence for an Age of Terrorism,* thirty-year peace activist and distinguished scholar David Cortright surveyed a history of social justice movements and emerged with relevant lessons for today's context.[44] Drawing on the work of Gandhi, Martin Luther King Jr., Dorothy Day, Cesar Chavez, and others, Cortright assessed the theories, actions, successes, and challenges of movements and their leaders and crystallized the ingredients for effective nonviolent action in the face of terrorism. Citing also the work of Gene Sharp, Peter Ackerman and Christopher Kruegler, and Saul Alinsky, Cortright explored several key elements for the success of nonviolent movements today: the awareness and manipulation of power dynamics; building and maintaining an institutional base; effective use of Internet-based organizing; clarity and creative articulation of modest immediate objectives and long-term vision; fundraising and financing; use of media; evaluation and intelligent use of potential tactics as well as the willingness to propose answers and alternatives; the understanding of what defines success; and perseverance to be "long-distance runners" for social justice.[45]

Movement of New or Restored Democracies

A 2005 report from the Helsinki Process, *Building Democracy from Manila to Doha: The Evolution of the Movement of New or Restored Democracies,* offered an additional illustration of how the worldwide movement can help build democracy on a sound and durable basis.[46] The New or Restored Democracies (NRD) movement includes more than 100 countries and is a UN function. Especially important is a paper, "An International Normative Framework for Democratization," by law professor Roy Lee.[47] It examined instruments of commitment and practice relevant to democracy and effective governance. Professor Lee listed all the important ingredients of democracy shared by the different entities that claim commitment to that form of government. These common ingredients are all directed at four principal goals: (1) to enhance citizens' participation in political activities and in social and economic development; (2) to advance justice, legal order and respect for human rights; (3) to improve accountability and transparency; and (4) to promote general agreement among diverse interest groups while respecting minority concerns.[48] His analysis highlighted the critical role democracy plays in mitigating global problems, from poverty to genocide.

Thus the commitment to democracy has grown in recent years—clear in principle and variable in practice but going forward. The remaining dictatorships and autocracies in both the General Assembly and the Security Council often betray the basic principles of the UN, but there is a reasonable chance that their influence will gradually diminish, especially if the United States returns to principles put forward by Franklin and Eleanor Roosevelt.

Since 1994, in the post–Cold War transformation, the General Assembly has adopted a series of resolutions to help new or restored democracies. These resolutions provide a legal basis for the United Nations to provide democracy assistance in response to requests from interested governments. They also encourage the established democracies to promote democratization and to lend their expert resources to the new or restored democracies. The net effect is a sharp increase in competence.

The many heads of state and government who gathered at UN headquarters in September 2000 to commemorate the millennium committed themselves to strengthening the capacity of all countries to implement the principles and practices of democracy and respect for human rights, including minority rights. They endorsed freedom, equality, solidarity, tolerance, respect for nature, and shared responsibility as fundamental values essential to peaceful international relations. Even though there is always a gap between initial rhetoric and implementing action, the trend is clear.

International Cooperation of Democracies to Prevent Mass Violence

There is clearly a need for coordinated action among established democracies, both to help build strong democracies out of weak ones and also to prevent deadly conflicts, above all genocide.[49] The capacity of established democracies for such action is profound. But it is not clear which of the several multilateral democracy organizations mentioned in this chapter will emerge as the leading actor—always open to cooperation with the others. It might function partly within the UN (as a democratic caucus) and partly outside (but always adhering to the high ideals of the UN Charter and the UN Declaration of Human Rights). Or it may turn out that these democracy-promoting and peace-promoting functions of the established democracies can best be carried out by a separate organization. In today's world, the best example is the European Union, exemplifying remarkable cooperation among twenty-seven democracies, some established and some new, and using this centralized strength to foster other democracies and to prevent war and genocide, reaching beyond Europe to help the African Union and others.

In any event, as new and fragile democracies emerge, such an organization, cooperating with the UN, could go a long way to establish core governance functions by

1. maintaining order with the least force necessary—none if feasible;
2. promoting physical security for all citizens to provide space for democratic institution building and ultimate consolidation; establishing a clear rule of law with wide public understanding and mechanisms for implementation; and
3. establishing civil discourse in the spirit of democracy, with respectful give-and-take, exposition of group interests, and learning fair compromises and mutual accommodation.

Moreover, such an organization could promote explicitly sustained antidotes to hatred and violence by

1. setting standards for fair, free elections and monitoring their conduct;
2. providing education at all levels—from children and youth to political and business leaders as well as scholars in institutions of higher learning—on specific paths to decent interpersonal and intergroup relations, conflict resolution, violence prevention, and enduring peace; and
3. mobilizing intellectual and moral leadership in the universities, religious institutions, and other powerful sectors to focus on these crucial issues—above all on prevention of war and genocide.

Building Democracy: The Hard and Hardest Cases

As we have seen, the world's democratic community has come to realize in the past decade that there is a strong desire almost everywhere to move in the direction of democracy. There is a general public sense worldwide that democracy means something like freedom, opportunity, and decent human relations. Moreover, we are learning that democratically inclined, moderate leaders have emerged in most countries. As a practical matter, it is often helpful to identify early in a conflict situation who these people are and what they are willing and able to do. They tend to be pragmatic, problem-solving people of talent and dedication, usually inclined toward tolerant, humane, and participatory values. But they are often in a difficult position, surrounded by autocrats or oppressors. They need all the help the international community can give them. The following list indicates the range of what can be done for them.

1. Recognition from respected individuals, groups, and nations—including praise, encouragement, solidarity, and consistent cooperation.
2. International contacts, preferably of an enduring character, that come to involve personal friendships and social support networks of like-minded people across national boundaries.
3. Technical assistance, especially opportunities to learn concepts, procedures, and institutions of democracy.
4. Financial assistance, which may involve facilitating trade, investment, and development aid, so that they have tangible ways of implementing democratic values and working toward equitable socioeconomic development.
5. More incentives for cooperation, for example, clarifying superordinate goals that they in turn can clarify for their peers in their own countries; showing that important economic, political, psychological, and technological gains for socioeconomic development can be accomplished if, and only if, there are intergroup and/or international cooperative efforts, especially including those that cross adversarial lines.
6. Mobilization of NGOs that are intrinsically worthwhile, e.g., that foster disease prevention or environmental protection and that are likely to help moderate leaders with

whom they often share important values. A few NGOs have been remarkably successful in this respect working on several fundamental lines: (1) conflict resolution; (2) cooperation of the scientific and scholarly community in addressing important problems, often international in scope and oriented to development; (3) humanitarian organizations, also frequently international, that take prompt and effective action to relieve human suffering; (4) NGOs concerned with the rule of law, e.g., helping in police training that protects society in a humane and fair-minded way.

To help in these ways, it is very desirable that pivotal international institutions do what they can to connect moderate leaders with sympathetic governments, the United Nations, the European Union, democratic international NGOs, and socially minded universities. Through such institutions, emerging democratic leaders may benefit from earned recognition, tangible aid, professional collaboration, and various modes of knowledge and skill. Altogether, such activities provide an authentic basis for hope in intergroup cooperation, regional cooperation, building capacity for internal conflict resolution, and, in the long run, building capacity through international cooperation for democratic socioeconomic development.

What can be done to shape the behavior of aggressive, hostile leaders in progressive directions? The international community, in one form or another, can provide incentives for cooperation. Economically, this can well mean superordinate goals: prosperity, international respect, technical aid such as building capacity in education and health as well as science and technology for development. That is the positive side: strong incentives for ameliorating hateful behavior and learning to work with others for the benefit of one's own national interest and earning personal respect. On the other hand, it is often necessary for the international community to provide constraints on aggression, for example, targeted sanctions against human rights abuses, such as freezing assets of abusive leaders, restricting their travel, and cutting off their access to lethal weapons. There are various deterrence strategies and thin blue lines, the crossing of which can lead to serious trouble. There are many modalities for constraints on aggression short of major military operations, although ready military strength in the background has considerable value in negotiating with such autocratic leaders. The international community is in the process of building a system of incentives and constraints to influence both moderates and extremists. Both exist in most countries. Clearly, whatever can be done to help the moderate leaders will tend to minimize violence and help in constructive nation-building.

Professor William Zartman of Johns Hopkins University has for decades been one of the leading scholars in conflict resolution, especially in Africa. Moreover, he has paid increasing attention to the application of his research in dangerous situations and has given his work a preventive orientation. He made famous the concept of "ripeness" for conflict resolution. In his recent research, he pointed out that "ripeness" is not absolute or a fixed property of conflicting parties, but rather that if there are friendly outside parties, especially respected international organizations, they can help to move a conflict toward "ripeness" for solution. By the same token, he found that effectiveness of conflict resolution was a function of consistent commitment. To succeed it is necessary for would-be helpers to invest the necessary resources, especially in time, capability, and sustained attention. He warned that the perfect must not be made the enemy of the good. He highlighted this point with reference to recent serious conflicts. When external parties finally recognized they did have a dog in the fights in Yugoslavia, Haiti, Liberia, Lebanon, Somalia, and Zaire, they were forced to do what they had not done earlier—but it took more effort and expense to accomplish less (or nothing at all) after the situations had deteriorated.[50] He urged, from the study of many such cases, the early offering of a wide range of diplomatic opportunities, from mediation to consultation and sometimes enforcement, if necessary. Mediation, like other forms of negotiation, requires an implication of the parties' legitimacy, the legitimacy of their interests to be protected, some understanding of the mutual stalemate in unilateral efforts to win, and recognition that none of the parties is seeking suicide. Indeed, it is often crucial for the parties to come to see that the violent path they are on can only lead to mutual suicide. Somehow, they must be helped to move past the wishful thinking of winner-take-all. Rather they must learn to give and take, compromise for the sake of all, and accommodate each other to foster peace and prosperity—and, indeed, to preserve their own lives.

Zartman pointed to the growing use of dialogue, which has been strongly and effectively advocated by such leaders in prevention as Sweden's ambassador Ragnar Ängeby. Dialogue opens informal talks between parties that focus on ordinary human experience and broad national issues rather than on the search for a definitive permanent conclusion to the central conflict. That is too much to expect all at once but may have long-term value. Dialogue is prenegotiation, seeking to dehorn the demons in each side's perception of the other and creating a positive atmosphere where substantive issues can be addressed. Even small, repeated steps can be helpful. Dialogue is necessarily informal, low-key, unpublicized, and yet often crucial to setting the stage for more focused mediation and negotiation.

Zartman's research also leads to three nonmilitary ways of deposing a seriously harmful ruler: (1) vote him out; (2) talk him out: (3) buy him out. These may be used alone or in combination and are preferable where possible to the violent option of taking him out. If the harmful leader can be impressed by an honest election supervised by international organizations, such as the European Union, and respected NGOs such as the Carter Center and Sweden's IDEA, then there is the strong advantage of providing a successor, thus limiting the dangers of a political vacuum that can be so easily filled with violent extremists. Usually the democratic removal of a harsh, autocratic leader needs active help from outside parties that are strong morally, economically, and militarily. In fact, some leaders cannot make such transitions quickly, but their "achievements" in graceful exit are appreciated elsewhere and thereby reduce the need for violent actions in subsequent cases. This is constructive "peer learning."

Understanding the autocrat-dictator can help considerably. What attracts him? What would be a good prospect for him once out of office? Thoughtful internal negotiation is often necessary—to persuade a bad leader to leave may involve appealing to his pride, his sense of accomplishment, his sense of belonging to a respected group of former leaders, and, of course, his personal safety. All of these provide points of dealing peacefully with some of the hardest cases. It should be emphasized that the successor, especially if elected democratically, should be helped as much as possible over years and in whatever ways make sense to the international community and the local population.

President Carter has observed from his rich experience that, when an autocrat or dictator agrees to an election under internal and international pressure, he always expects that he will win. But such leaders are typically unpopular and are likely to be defeated. Therefore people of stature, such as President Carter, are needed for follow up to help the defeated chieftain down from his pedestal without humiliation. Early retirement negotiations, like hostage negotiations, can begin when original demands give way to conditions for asylum.[51] Thoughtful diplomatic action can provide for the former leader a secure future, albeit much reduced in power, and this can make the transition more readily acceptable, though never easy.

Zartman observed that a dictator will consider conditions for retirement only if he is convinced that he cannot remain in power.[52] Mediators, always working in the context of the specific situation, can help in this respect by working with active policy leaders from various sectors of society to support the new leadership along democratic, nonviolent lines of development.[53]

Negotiation for early retirement of a rapacious head of state requires a powerful mediator, above all one who can exert the moral pressure in local terms that is necessary to reevaluate the present and provide the future security that is the basis of the bargain. In addition, it takes a mediator who is able to apply credible and painful sanctions tailored to perpetrators in the event of refusal. Such sanctions may include specific embargoes but also more general ostracism and a break in an important relationship. Finally, the mediator must not be susceptible to counterpressure from the target ruler and especially must not suffer more from the rupture of the relationship than does the perpetrator.

We have already seen a powerful transitional example in Chapter 6 on South Africa. In recent years, guidelines have emerged from research and assessment of best practices in transitions from nondemocratic to democratic governments. It turns out that similar principles apply across the spectrum of these transitions, but the problem is clearly more difficult if the country involved is in some state of disintegration, with harsh intergroup differences.

Key features help in such difficult democratic transitions:

1. Understand the local context in its historical, cultural, political, and social dimensions.
2. Mobilize and commit adequate military and financial resources.
3. Establish international legitimacy and active support for the predemocracy intervention.
4. Generate legitimacy and trust within the fragile democracy.
5. Hold local elections first and then gradually expand them to a larger scale. Provide the opportunity for people to learn the give and take, the necessary compromises, and mutual accommodation—a vital part of democratic process.
6. Help aspiring democrats to build political parties, to understand the value of free and fair elections, and to grasp the essence of resolving typical human conflicts below the threshold of mass violence. That, after all, is the fundamental reason for going to all this trouble of building democracy in the first place.

Ambassador Mark Palmer asserted that ridding the world of dictators should become a central focus of national security and foreign policy in democratic governments and organizations everywhere. It is morally wrong for democratic nations to watch passively while dictators torture and kill thousands of their own people or develop weapons of mass destruction that support worldwide terrorism. The world's democracies must combine economic, political, psychological, and—if necessary—military forces to oust the remaining dictators and create global democracy, which offers humanity its best chance for peace and prosperity.[54]

Conclusion

There is a growing ferment of desire for democracy in all regions of the world. Important commitments to democracy have been made, along with democratic policies, principles, and institutions. Norms and rules have emerged from the efforts of several intergovernmental organizations. Even though these overlap, a global concept of democracy and paths to implementation have emerged, and serious efforts are being made to bring this concept to fruition. When the entire world becomes essentially democratic, the terrible risks of war and genocide that have characterized human history will at last be greatly diminished.

CHAPTER 9

Fostering Equitable Socioeconomic Development

Democratic socioeconomic development on a worldwide basis offers humanity its best hope for producing conditions favorable to peaceful living, truly civilized relations, and mutual accommodation among rival groups—in short, for preventing war and genocide.

This is a much more practical goal today than it was a few decades ago, even though a long path still lies ahead. Investment in human and social capital is now generally accepted as a central part of development, especially in the form of promoting the health and education of girls and boys (and women and men) alike—to build a vigorous, dynamic population that is well informed, capable, fair-minded, intellectually curious, and mutually supportive in times of personal and social stress; it also takes the form of social support networks in communities that tackle their local problems constructively. The essential features of development—knowledge, skills, freedom, and health—can be achieved by sustained international cooperation—regional and global—that draws upon the unprecedented advances of modern science and technology.

Cumulative Evidence and Emerging Concepts of Democratic Development

Firmly grounding new democracies with fair market economies requires decades or even generations. Their older and more established counterparts, chiefly those in the affluent West, but also such rising democracies as Japan, India, and Brazil, must therefore be persistent and resourceful in working all over the world with democratic reformers to help them stay on the right track. The payoff is clear: the gradual increase of democratic and prosperous countries will reduce the likelihood of catastrophic wars and genocide. Thus, considerations of socioeconomic development strongly overlap with our preceding discussion of democracy.

We have learned important lessons from the successes and failures of socioeconomic development in Asia, Africa, and Latin America during the past half century. Yet much of the world's population still cannot rely upon ready access to food, water, shelter, and other necessities of life. Why are these obstacles to a decent existence still widely prevalent in a world where science and technology have made such powerful contributions to human well-being? How can we use these discoveries to reduce the kind of vulnerability that leads to desperation and violence? Research continues, and much is informative and useful.[1]

Development assistance, especially in the form of capacity building for meeting basic human needs through knowledge and skill, is crucial for very poor countries; their efforts to create decent living standards through development will fail without significant outside help that is not dominating but rather is in the mode of mutual problem solving. Fundamental, long-term solutions hinge on a state's own policies—attentive to its society's particular economic and social needs and to careful management of its natural and human resources—for developing the human assets to improve its quality of life, partly through international cooperation in adapting the world's knowledge and strengthening resources.

Many nations in the Southern Hemisphere or from the former Soviet bloc have had difficulty in taking advantage of opportunities available for economic and social development. They are seeking a strategy for development that is consistent with their own cultural traditions and distinctive situations and need help in finding out how to adapt for their own use valuable tools from the world's experience. It is surely in the interest of more fortunate countries, near and far away, to facilitate the expansion of knowledge, skills, freedom, and health in these countries so they can become contributing, responsible members of the international community rather than breeding grounds for social pathology, severe disease, and mass violence such as civil war and/or genocide. A serious obstacle in some countries is egocentric, ethnocentric, brutal, and corrupt dictators.

In this context, the Carnegie Commission on Preventing Deadly Conflict[2] emphasized that a country whose development does not include broad participation in the benefits of economic growth will not reduce its prospects for violent conflict. Indeed, the intense resentment and unrest that grossly unequal economic distribution provokes can easily create a seedbed for hatred, bloodshed, and terrorism. This reinforces the case for offering poor countries international cooperation in political as well as economic development, in the quest for new opportunities that meet basic human needs in a spirit of fairness and solidarity.

During the 1990s, substantial efforts to understand how development occurred in the second half of the twentieth century resulted in a broader view of the development process that recognized the crucial importance of human development and the firm link between social and economic advances. The human development reports of the UNDP have been one influential source of analysis. A series of these reports in the early 1990s (under the remarkable leadership of Mahbub ul Haq and with the eminent economist Amartya Sen as a major adviser) employed hard data and close, decades-long observation to make the case for the human factor in development.[3]

Amartya Sen carried this approach further in his book, *Development as Freedom*, in which he based development on the removal of major obstacles to freedom: poor economic opportunities due to systematic social deprivation, inadequate public services, social intolerance, tyranny, and state repression.[4] In his 2006 book, *Identity and Violence*, he clarified the importance of broad-based identities that overcome narrow, often hateful, identities based on a single attribute—e.g., ethnic or religious.[5]

Analyses issuing from the World Bank reflect considerable agreement with this outlook. A series of important papers by Joseph Stiglitz (another Nobel economist who in the 1990s was senior vice president of development economics and chief economist at the World Bank) examined the dramatic advances in much of the developing world during the last quarter century and provided unequivocal evidence that pessimistic remarks about never-to-be-developed countries are baseless.[6] But although remarkable gains in life expectancy and per capita annual incomes have occurred, significant regional differences exist, with sub-Saharan Africa lagging far behind. Stiglitz developed his analysis further in a new book on achieving fairness, hence broad prosperity, in better international trade.[7] He noted approvingly that the European Union's "everything but arms" initiative has already begun to put a "human face" on globalization of trade in striving to grant the poorest countries free export into Europe of all goods except arms.[8]

Good Governance

Good governance (a growing emphasis in development policy) has its own essential components. The state must have the capacity to serve the public good, with a sound understanding of what policies and rules best accomplish that mission. This requires trained and professional civil servants and state officials who follow established principles and work in structures designed to reward them for demonstrating commitment to the public good.[9]

This commitment must be strengthened by institutions that penalize betrayals of the public trust and linked to transparency in the conduct of state affairs, maintained through freedom of information about how the government makes its decisions, conducts its business, and spends public money.

Transparency is closely related to accountability, which enables society to monitor the responsibility of public officials. Thus, different institutions check and hold one another accountable, compelling them to justify their actions. Power is thus constrained, bound not only "by legal constraints but also by the logic of public reasoning."[10] High levels of secrecy in government are invariably linked to abuse of power—a deep concern in the United States.

Another hallmark of good governance is the rule of law. It provides a necessary basis for transparency and accountability. A well-governed state requires a constitution and laws that are widely understood and accepted by its citizens as just, clear, fairly and efficiently administered, and applicable to everyone. These legal institutions contribute to smooth functioning in all realms of life—economic, social, and political.[11]

To achieve all of these criteria of good governance is very hard, but they must represent a level of aspiration for which democrats consistently strive.

Good Governance and Conflict Resolution

From the viewpoint of this book, an exceedingly important dimension of good governance is conflict resolution—with multiple mechanisms. Broad participation of diverse groups (and both sexes) is important here. Democratic development is not only about choice at the individual level but also about difficult choices involving intergroup relations. What is in the public interest? A fair ongoing process of political participation and dialogue can help greatly to reconcile conflicting interests. Again, at least a decent minimum of opportunity for all—approximating equal opportunity to the extent possible—makes for cohesion without intimidation in a diverse society. Conflict resolution requires a general sense of fairness, justice, and transparency. Special attention must be given to ensure that all groups are distributed in ways that give each community or region some real influence over its own destiny. At the same time, a sense of national solidarity—without chauvinism—is essential.

In sum, when good governance of these dimensions takes place over years, it fosters social capital: networks and associations that draw people together in relations of trust, reciprocity, and voluntary cooperation for common aims and mutual benefits.

These conditions also stimulate the capacity to enforce the law, mediate disputes, keep order, collect taxes, promote trade, attract investment, and so foster equitable economic advancement.

> In defending human rights and property rights, in promoting equal access to opportunity based on talent and effort rather than power, and in providing a fair means for the resolution of disputes, the rule of law generates an enabling environment for economic growth. In incorporating groups that historically have been confined to the margins of society, good governance mitigates social conflict and harnesses the full range of talent and resources in the society.[12]

A major cause of widespread persistent poverty is bad governance—the inability or reluctance to direct public resources effectively to generate goods that benefit the whole community. If the state has the capacity and the will to provide its citizens with the fundamental communal necessities—the rule of nondiscriminatory law, the guarantee of basic rights for all, universal education and health care, clean water, roads, electricity, physical security, and an open, meritocratic bureaucracy—the poor will make their own way to economic well-being and remain there. Recognition of this fact should lead policymakers to plot their course accordingly, if they really care about their people and their nation.

Health and Development

Health has been curiously neglected until very recently in economic development efforts, as if it were a benefit to be achieved only in an advanced later stage of development. But a healthy, vigorous population is essential to build a dynamic, equitable, growing economy. The WHO Commission on Macroeconomics and Health, a distinguished worldwide group initiated by then director-general Gro Brundtland and chaired by Professor Jeffrey Sachs, made the case for greatly increased investment in health as a matter of economic development.[13] The benefits of globalization are potentially great, through increased exposure to new ideas, practical innovations, lifesaving technologies, and efficient production processes. Yet its benefits are not yet reaching hundreds of millions of the world's poor. Turmoil in one part of the world can spread rapidly to others, through terrorism, armed conflict, environmental degradation, or disease, as demonstrated by the dramatic spread of AIDS around the globe in a single generation.

Improving the health and longevity of the poor is a valuable end in itself, a fundamental goal of economic development. But it is also a *means* to achieving the other development goals. The links of health to poverty reduction and to long-term economic growth are powerful. A heavy burden of disease in low-income regions stands as a stark barrier to economic growth, and any comprehensive development strategy must therefore strive for its early, ongoing improvement. The AIDS epidemic could undermine Africa's development over the next generation and may cause tens of millions of deaths in India, China, and other developing countries unless checked. Opportunities for prevention and treatment are underutilized, but good examples exist.

The main causes of avoidable deaths in the low-income countries are HIV/AIDS, malaria, tuberculosis, childhood infectious diseases, maternal and perinatal problems, micronutrient deficiencies, and tobacco-related illnesses. Effective programs to control these conditions, in conjunction with enhanced programs of family planning, would allow families to have longer, healthier, and more productive lives. Secure in the knowledge that their children would survive, parents would choose to have fewer children and could therefore invest more in the education and health of each child. There is evidence of this in various countries, especially in the well-being of women. Improvements in health translate into higher incomes, higher economic growth, and reduction of overpopulation.

The key recommendation of the WHO commission was that the world's low- and middle-income countries should join in collaboration with high-income countries to expand the access of the world's poor to essential health services, with a focus on effective interventions specific to the targeted region. Low- and middle-income countries would commit increased domestic financial resources, principled political leadership, transparency, accountability, and mechanisms for broad community involvement to ensure that adequately financed health systems could operate effectively and would be dedicated to the most serious health problems, especially those that are amenable to prevention, such as cigarette-related cardiovascular diseases and cancers. Health-oriented behavior is a crucial responsibility of education for disease prevention. The affluent democracies would in turn commit substantial and sustained financial and technical assistance, especially to those countries that need help most urgently and are prepared to act constructively. The established democracies would make a great contribution to overcoming these deficiencies if, with the involvement of civil society, they helped build local capacity for honest, effective governance, science-based health care, and technical capability.

International scientific cooperation must facilitate basic and applied biomedical and public health research in low-income countries. Improved surveillance and reporting systems are urgently needed to enhance epidemiological knowledge by clarifying who suffers and dies of which diseases under what conditions. In public health, such knowledge is essential for disease prevention and control. In addition, there is a need for medical education and training of community health workers throughout the low-income countries, in such a way that lessons from the experience of one country can be utilized elsewhere, and new skills can be assimilated into practice. The World Health Organization, the World Bank, and international science academies such as the new InterAcademy Council have a great opportunity to diffuse sound knowledge and best practices rapidly, facilitated through the low-cost methods of the Internet.

The WHO commission recommended that each country specify a program of "essential interventions,"[14] using four main criteria for choosing them: (1) they should be technically effective and suitable for wide delivery; (2) they should target specific diseases that impose a heavy burden on a particular society; (3) the cost should not exceed their social benefits (such as life-years saved and spillovers such as fewer orphans or faster economic growth); and (4) the health of the poor should be emphasized. Such a program would yield economic and social benefits far greater than its costs.

A fundamental point the WHO commission made is that investments in people, particularly in terms of education and health, stimulate economic growth. This in turn provides resources that can be further invested in people, toward a higher level of development.

The 1990s taught us a stark, vivid lesson that we should have known before: countries with disintegrating, incompetent governments constitute a great danger, especially when they are poor and getting poorer, discriminatory and getting repressive. They create many kinds of suffering for their own people—and they tend to fall into the hands of harsh, indecent "leaders" with a proclivity for mass violence. The slide of such countries into degradation has led to mass expulsions, "ethnic cleansing," and refugee flows that destabilize the whole region; genocide; fostering of international terrorism; and the creation of breeding grounds for fatal and potentially pandemic infectious diseases. Tackling this problem is therefore not just a matter of altruism and generosity on the part of the more scientifically competent and affluent members of the international community but a matter of utmost significance to the achievement of a decent and secure world.

Links: Health, Development, and Peace

Good health is highly desired everywhere. The ability to prevent and treat disease is highly valued and largely transcends adversarial boundaries. How can we use this strong position to reduce human suffering and premature loss of life—not only by traditional means but by deliberately fostering development and peace throughout the world through the hopeful and unifying influence of effective health care?

In 2004, Dr. Margaret Hamburg, former commissioner of health of New York City and a high-level policy official in the Clinton administration, pointed out that health has a special role to play as an incentive for cooperation and a tool of diplomacy.[15] Initiatives that use health as a bridge to peace benefit from a convergence of potential assets.[16]

First, health is a universally acknowledged basis of well-being, prosperity, and productivity. A worldwide survey conducted by the Pew Research Center in 2002 found that respondents in a majority of countries—both developed and developing—considered health one of their two top concerns. They cited infectious diseases as the world's greatest danger, worse even than terrorism or war.[17]

Second, health interventions have both immediate and long-term impacts on people's lives. Even in countries decimated by AIDS, intensive, systematic, sustained efforts to reduce casualties mitigate fear, suffering, and death and inspire hope for national recovery and long-term development.

Third, health care initiatives can be readily acceptable even to adversarial parties, since they are largely nonideological and generally perceived as mainly free of the political, emotional, and ideological baggage that other programs carry.

Fourth, international collaborative health programs not only pool resources to offer increased hope and opportunity to suffering communities but also create trust and partnership among groups or nations formerly at odds.

Fifth, health programs can foster broader foreign policy and diplomatic goals in important ways by

1. Improving intergroup relations through mutually beneficial cooperative effort—often across adversarial tensions;
2. Promoting the economic progress that comes with a vigorous, healthy, and dynamic population;
3. Strengthening cooperation at the community level to achieve visible shared benefits;
4. Building firm working relationships between national governments through highly valued, shared health benefits;
5. Illustrating the mutual benefits hostile parties can achieve by peaceful cooperation in pursuit of a superordinate goal that can only be attained by such means;
6. Placing emphasis on the welfare of children, whose health and safety have a special meaning across cultural, religious, and national boundaries. Such efforts can create feedback loops to hostile parties: "If we can relate in this good way here, why not in other aspects of our lives?"

International health-related organizations, in cooperation with national entities and regional health organizations (especially the Pan American Health Organization [PAHO]), can create a critical mass of the knowledge and skills required for worldwide health and development, but they need leadership and resources to achieve collaboration in the service of preventing war and genocide.[18] Altogether, cooperative health initiatives can provide a bridge to mutually beneficial intergroup relations.

Sustained International, Multisectoral Cooperation Can Foster Equitable Development

Valuable help from outside partners fosters a constructive interplay of the governments of developing countries with internal and external business communities, provided there is vigilance to minimize corruption, inequity, and overwhelming concentration of wealth and power in the hands of an elite.

One of the fundamental underpinnings of successful socioeconomic development is comprehensive education, from preschool through graduate school. This must include women on an equal basis, not only as a matter of equity but also as a matter of economic stimulus.

Given the crucial role of science and technology in the economy of the twenty-first century, an important component of this effort must be education in mathematics, science, and technology. This should run the entire gamut of the sciences from physical to social and should include science-based professions, especially engineering, medicine, and public health.

To develop research capability, it is essential for each developing country to connect its emerging scientific community with the international scientific community. The role of an effective technical community in moving toward prosperity is clear—witness India. Moreover, the international ties that develop in this way can be helpful in other ways, especially in fostering democratic norms and helping to sort out interstate conflicts without violence, since cooperation among diverse scientists sets a good example and often generates creative ideas for dealing with intergroup or even international problems.

Economic Development to Prevent War and Genocide

UN Secretary-General Kofi Annan linked equitable economic development with conflict prevention in an address at the World Bank in 1999. He endorsed President James Wolfensohn's call for the bank and its partners to integrate a concern for conflict prevention into development operations. Annan said, "Democracy is, in essence, a form of nonviolent conflict management.... If war is the worst enemy of development, healthy and balanced development is the best form of conflict prevention."[19]

Several recurrent themes have emerged from world experience and scholarly examination of development cooperation and violence prevention.

Recognize the Importance of Preventing Deadly Conflict

In order to quench fires before they become unmanageable, an early warning system needs to be developed to alert policymakers to key areas of potential violence. Development strategies for a particular country or region must be based on an understanding of ways that aid can exacerbate or ameliorate ongoing tensions. Aid can be used in ways that foster mutual understanding and mutual benefit among adversaries and provide nonviolent means of addressing grievances by building capacity for ongoing conflict resolution (e.g., a fair justice system and public knowledge of conflict resolution and violence prevention).

Use Development Cooperation for Structural Prevention of Deadly Conflict

Aid providers must help to build capable states that can construct (with outside collaboration as needed) conditions of security, well-being, and justice for all citizens. Moving toward these vital desiderata greatly diminishes the risk of mass violence, both within developing countries and beyond. It is the intersection of these three conditions that is crucial for prevention of mass violence.

- Security is about safety from fear or threat of attack. But it is also about mutual accommodation so that different people can live together with a sense of fairness and mutual respect and of mutual benefit from cooperation.

- Well-being is about health and also about equal opportunity. This means opportunity for education, training, preventive health care, and constructive employment. Young men without skills or decent prospects are very susceptible to demagogic incitements to violence.
- Justice is about the right of each person to have a say in how one is governed and the right of each person to exercise that voice without fear of reprisals. Justice is also about accountability of those in power, bearing in mind that grave abuses of power manifested in widespread human rights violations can lead to war or genocide.

It is crucial for the international community not only to identify and support those elements of civil society, as well as governmental entities, that can reduce intergroup antagonisms and enhance attitudes of concern, social responsibility, and mutual aid within and between groups but also to provide the technical and financial resources they need to operate effectively. This is a special and critical kind of education for those so unlucky as to be born into very poor, unfair, repressive states.

Building National Capacities for Preventing Deadly Conflict

The UN and its partners do not usually have a mandate in situations of previolence prevention. That is a serious deficiency. A novel joint program of the UNDP and the United Nations Department of Political Affairs (DPA) opens entry points for UN help by focusing on the capacities, skills, and processes that national actors need in order to find common solutions to divisive national issues or critical policy questions through dialogue and negotiation. Given UNDP's central role in UN development activities, this work can foster nonviolent processes of development.

An experience-sharing program on conflict prevention and capacity-building initiatives has been developed among national counterparts across the southern African subregion, aided by UNDP country offices.

Sweden, a pioneering country in early violence prevention, has supported the integration of conflict prevention elements into development programs, especially civic dialogues and mediation efforts, to resolve ongoing disputes before they become violent.

Extensive preparatory work is often necessary before outsiders can initiate or support emerging dialogue efforts in fragile situations. The best means for ensuring that violence prevention gains survive political vicissitudes is to make strong investments in providing a critical mass of individuals and institutions with the requisite skills and capacities for peaceful problem solving.

What is necessary is for several UN agencies and other partners to build a standing framework that will provide support for internal violence prevention initiatives to be provided on a sustained basis. The same considerations apply to the EU, which has strong potential in this field.

Following a national conflict assessment conducted by the government of Nigeria with the support of the World Bank and UNDP in 2002, the office of President Olusegun Obassanjo established a national mechanism for the implementation of the results of this assessment. The longer-term objective of this mechanism is to build capacities at the national and local levels for the peaceful settlement of a host of potentially violent disputes over issues ranging from the distribution of oil wealth to the nexus of religion and law. In 2004, the Institute for Peace and Conflict Resolution in the office of the Nigerian president requested a UN agency to implement a training workshop for faculty of national training institutions in curricula for conflict resolution and management. Using this entry point, the UN is working to implement this opportunity.

Although these efforts are necessarily chancy in the face of all the tensions and difficulties in Nigeria, they do reflect a serious, constructive, systematic effort to create widely distributed, early, ongoing conflict resolution—from the highest national leaders to grassroots community organizations. This top-down and bottom-up combination has powerful long-run potential and is applicable to many countries.

When violent conflict undermines a country's economy, it creates chain reactions that perpetuate and increase economic loss by discouraging investment, both domestic and foreign, and precipitating capital flight. When violent conflict destroys a nation's physical capital—roads, bridges, and power systems—past investments are nullified and future recovery impeded. Years of economic development can be destroyed in a few months—or in a few days if weapons of mass destruction are used. When violent conflict subverts a state's educational infrastructure, it destroys a foundation for progress in other areas, such as health, nutrition, civic responsibility, and preparation for employment in a technological world.

When conflicts end, roads and bridges may be swiftly rebuilt with outside help. But broken institutions, loss of trust, intergroup hatreds, and desire for revenge can make renewed conflict more likely and renewed prosperity and growth more elusive. Violent conflict weakens states and can involve entire populations in a downward spiral of destruction that sucks in neighboring populations as well. Halting that spiral and redirecting it on a positive course is one of the most crucial tasks the international community has to confront.[20]

Why Democracies Excel in Socioeconomic Development

Joseph Siegle, Michael Weinstein, and Morton Halperin, distinguished policy analysts with extensive government experience, addressed the fundamental question, "Why Democracies Excel."[21] The assumption that states must first develop economically before they can sustain a democratic government is, in their view, unfortunate, both because data clearly contradict it and because it has led to damaging policies, including the implicit encouragement of state repression.

Recent evidence shows that economic growth is at least as strong in poor democracies as in poor autocracies. Furthermore, poor democracies tend to rank higher than their totalitarian counterparts on most indicators of social well-being and have far better success in avoiding catastrophes. Indeed, an autocratic political structure is often the decisive factor in keeping a nation poor.[22] By neglecting or denying this evidence—which the authors supported with many examples—policymakers often pursue a strategy of development before democracy that preserves the continuing cycle of destitution, violence, and tyranny.[23]

The indicators of well-being in the following list widen the lead of democratic poor states over their authoritarian equivalents.

- Life expectancy: Citizens of democracies have a life expectancy nine years longer on average than citizens of autocracies and an infant mortality rate 20 percent lower. Infant mortality reflects other elements of well-being, such as access to perinatal health care, adequate nutrition, clean water, and education for females.
- Education: Children in democracies have a 40 percent greater chance of attending secondary school than their fellows in autocracies.
- Agricultural productivity: Agricultural yields are 25 percent higher in democracies. Since at least 70 percent of the population of all poor countries is rural, higher productivity means more capital and food to invest in employment and trade as well as better nutrition.[24]

Periods of rapid economic growth in autocracies that development-first advocates use to support their claims seem "little more than spurts" of recovery from shrinking in hard times. Chile is an example. During its much vaunted thirteen-year economic growth under Augusto Pinochet, Chile in fact suffered two severe crises—a decline of 12 percent in gross domestic product (GDP) per capita in the mid-1970s and of 17 percent in the early 1980s. Not until the mid-1980s did Chile—by then democratic—sustain a per capita income level higher that that it had enjoyed in 1973, the year Pinochet's rule began.[25]

Poor democracies compare favorably with autocracies in several areas:

- Democracies invest more money in health and education than autocracies and generally use their resources more wisely in terms of human capital.
- Their scores range from 15 to 25 percent higher in the areas of observance of the rule of law and freedom from corruption.
- They endure fewer humanitarian crises. Amartya Sen observed in his classic research that no democracy with a free press has ever suffered widespread famine. The shortage of food is more political than biological. Authoritarian regimes are not much interested in the well-being of ordinary citizens, let alone the poorest.
- In sub-Saharan Africa, dictators have not been able to compete with democraticizing governments in controlling intrastate conflict: states committed to democratic reform there have experienced half the armed conflict typical of the region as a whole.[26]

There are good reasons why democratic institutions provide the most favorable environment for increasing economic, political, and social well-being in developing countries:

- They allow power to be widely shared.
- Democratic leaders, to win the popular support necessary to keep them in office, must work for the general well-being rather than gain support by favoring the interests of their clan, their clients, and other powerful groups.
- The checks and balances that characterize democratic governance are sometimes cumbersome, but they reduce the likelihood of "rash, narrowly conceived, or

radical policies that can have disastrous economic consequences."[27] Federated systems offer further protection against excessive concentration of power.

- They encourage openness and adaptability. A free and independent flow of information from many sources educates the public, suggests a broad array of policies for political leaders to choose from, and disseminates new ideas and beneficial practices in all fields—notably health, nutrition, agriculture, business, and environmental conservation. Openness provides the opportunity to identify and correct errors and reduces corruption, which can hamper economic growth by weakening efficiency and trust. Democracies also promote adaptability in their freedom to solve problems by trial and error and to profit from the lessons learned.
- In modern times, democracies create lasting political stability by defining clear mechanisms for political succession, with the advantage over authoritarian regimes in this regard—that the legitimacy of the succession is perceived as a result of both the rule of law and popular demand.

In contrast, authoritarian regimes tend to add economic monopoly to their political monopoly, permitting only groups and individuals they favor to gain the training, career opportunities, licenses, and other resources required for advancement.

Intensive Concentration on Ending Poverty

From the start of his career Professor Jeffrey Sachs, a gifted development economist, has worked on the ground in developing countries—Bolivia, Poland, the Soviet Union in the final phase of the Cold War, and, most recently, Africa. He has worked with scientists from many backgrounds—health, agriculture, geology—and he now heads the Earth Institute at Columbia University. In *The End of Poverty*, published in 2005, he boldly addressed "on-the-ground" solutions for ending poverty with a trenchant statement of fundamental issues.

Ending world poverty demands global cooperation, involving the agreement of a network of people who do not know and perhaps do not trust each other. Most people everywhere would admit that basic necessities for a life of dignity, health, and economic productivity include schools, clinics, roads, electricity, ports, soil nutrients, and clean drinking water. They might also agree that the poor need help to achieve those basic needs, but they might remain doubtful about finding practical ways to provide that help. Such doubts forget that most societies can avoid poverty if they are blessed with good harbors, commercial contacts, ample energy sources, hospitable climates, and protection against widespread disease. Providers of world aid must not blame the victims but focus on poverty-inducing situations such as geographic isolation, disease, and vulnerability to climate shocks by establishing effective new "systems of political responsibility."[28]

Sachs's strategy focuses on crucial investments in people and infrastructure that will give impoverished communities, both rural and urban, the tools and skills for sustainable development. Beyond plans, systems, mutual accountability, and financing mechanisms ("economic plumbing"), he relies on certain qualities of people in very poor countries—bravery, realism, and a sense of responsibility for themselves and for their children. They can make good use of strong opportunities for development. Providing education to all girls and boys, including education in science, technology, and conflict resolution, will be necessary.

Sachs emphasized five sorts of interventions crucial for development:

- *Agricultural improvements:* Access to appropriate modern farming techniques and requisite nutrients and other materials for increasing the fertility and productive life of both sown and fallow land, supplemented with small-scale irrigation systems and improved seeds, would all provide an enormous boost—augmented by storage facilities, large enough to protect the season's crop from rot and vermin in locally made, inexpensive bins.

- *Investments in basic health:* Sachs advocates village clinics that would support at least one doctor and one nurse for every 5,000 residents. These clinics could distribute and encourage the use of free antimalarial bed nets—a remarkably effective and inexpensive preventive measure—along with other essential health services, such as provision of antimalarial medicines; treatment for HIV/AIDS and for the opportunistic infections that accompany it; and training for village health workers, including birth attendants, who would provide sexual and reproductive health services and help reduce maternal mortality.

- *Investments in education:* Free meals for all primary-school children would improve the children's health, their ability to learn, and their attendance at school. Expanded vocational training could teach older children the techniques of modern farming, computer use, and basic infrastructure maintenance (such as skills in carpentry, electrical wiring, operation and care of diesel generators, water harvesting, and borewell construction and upkeep). Monthly village-wide classes could educate adults in basic hygienic practices (such as handwashing, a key element), HIV/AIDS prevention and malaria control, computer and mobile phone use, and other practical skills that are still widely unavailable in rural areas. Village experiments along these lines in sub-Saharan Africa have been encouraging. Their expansion is badly needed.

- *Power, transport, and communications services:* An electric power line or an independent generator would supply power to the villages for lights and computers in the school, for pumps to deliver safe well water, and for grain mills, refrigeration, and carpentry tools. Electric power could also be used to charge household batteries that would, for example, allow students to study after sundown.

- *Safe drinking water and sanitation:* Simple methods such as use of protected springs, borewells, and rainwater harvesting would ensure clean water.

Overall, we must help each low-income country to create a custom-tailored poverty reduction strategy that focuses on increased investments in areas (including democratic institutions) that both empower the poor and hold them accountable.[29]

The public sector should emphasize key investments for the common good: human capital (health, education, nutrition), infrastructure (roads, power, water and sanitation, environmental conservation), natural capital (conservation of biodiversity and ecosystems), public institutional capital (a well-run public administration, judicial system, police force), and knowledge capital (scientific research for health, energy, agriculture, climate, ecology).

The private sector should be mainly responsible for investments in business, including agriculture, industry, or services, and in knowledge capital (new products and technologies building on scientific advances) as well as for household contributions to health, education, and nutrition that complement the public investments in human capital. The general lesson of successful economies is that governments do best to concentrate on investments for the public good—schools, clinics, roads, basic research—and to leave highly specialized business investments to the private sector.

The Dangers of States Too Strong and States Too Weak

According to a UNDP report, governments that cannot or will not carry out their core functions are both a cause and a result of violent conflict.[30] The Commission on Weak States and U.S. National Security identified three common characteristics that increase the risk of violent conflict within a state's borders: the security gap, the capacity gap, and the legitimacy gap.[31]

- The security gap: Providing security is a basic function of a state. It includes protection from systematic human rights abuses, physical threats, violence, and widespread economic, social, and environmental dangers. In Sudan the government has deliberately destroyed the security of its black civilian population by encouraging Arab militias, as well as its own military, to attack them. This is the pathway that led to genocide in Darfur.
- The capacity gap: Governments unable or unwilling to supply and maintain basic services and infrastructure face resentment and loss of public confidence. Grievous neglect of disease prevention and health care has resulted in great human suffering and intense resentment.
- The legitimacy gap: Political, social, and economic rivalry can lead to growth or degenerate into violence. Governments unable or unwilling to develop broadly acceptable, unbiased, and accountable state institutions that articulate the interests and aspirations of different groups, arbitrate between them, and mediate disputes often see disputes descend into violent conflict over control of state resources, revenues, and power.

Vast inequality in income distribution and wealth is associated with serious social problems, such as pervasive resentment, rising crime, and a decline in personal safety. Inequality between regions and/or groups can enhance animosity and the belief that state power is being manipulated to give one group or region an advantage over another. Long-standing political and economic tensions can be dangerously exacerbated, and democracy undermined.

"Multistakeholder dialogue" is used widely in Latin American attempts to deal with conflicts between groups and regions by rebuilding political confidence. Its use is spreading in Africa. This approach starts from the principle that peaceful resolution of conflicts can be achieved and sustained only through trust and continued communication, but its success depends ultimately on effective government responses to the social and economic inequalities that originally produced the conflict.[32]

When a state has undeveloped political structures and a desperately poor population, but an enormous wealth of natural resources, it may become prey to what has been called the "resource curse." Ready cash from natural wealth allows political, military, and business leaders to accumulate vast resources while ignoring the needs of ordinary people and failing to develop healthy political and economic institutions. Control of the revenues from readily available resources often becomes a major cause of violent conflict among governments, rebels, and warlords. This is not inevitable. Botswana has avoided conflict by fair revenue sharing and used its diamond wealth to produce high growth and rapid human development. It is unfortunately a rare exception in circumstances of "resource curse," however.[33]

Whatever factors converge to fuel violent intrastate conflict, the consequences almost always become international in scope. Ethnic cleansing drove refugees from the Balkans into Western Europe and from Darfur into Chad, straining the resources of the host states. In addition, this sort of situation frequently arouses sympathy from citizens of the host state who share the refugees' ethnic affiliation and become very resentful of the adversary. In a host state that is divided, sympathizers may start their own civil war or at least encourage cross-border raids that in due course may lead to interstate war. Indeed, these situations approach the border of genocide—and sometimes cross over.

Failing states are an international concern because they become a home to warlords, criminal networks, and extremist groups that benefit from a power vacuum. They are conducive to all sorts of violence, including genocide.

The authors of this report affirmed that in violent conflict, as in public health, the first rule of success is "prevention is better than cure." And the most effective strategy for prevention is development.[34]

Science and Technology for Development

To participate in the global economy with reasonable prospects for prosperity, virtually every country in the world—and certainly every region—will need a modicum of technical competence. The opportunities provided by science and technology in the coming century will be vast, reaching far beyond all prior experience.[35] But how does this enormous potential become fulfilled equitably?

In an important editorial in *Science,* Mohamed Hassan, president of the African Academy of Sciences, observed that his continent's most serious problems—malnutrition, disease, and environmental deterioration—could be solved only by the efforts of a critical mass of African scientists, whose emergence and continuing existence depended on governments that provided them with both sufficient financial resources and unrestricted freedom of interaction with their colleagues at home and abroad.[36]

How is a poor developing country to succeed in diminishing the science gap? The scientific community is overwhelmingly located in and focused on affluent countries. Indeed, to say affluent is almost tantamount to saying technically advanced. Bruce Alberts, former president of the U.S. National Academies of Science, has brilliantly led a movement in the global scientific community to focus much more intellectual and technical strength on the problems of developing countries. One of the most encouraging enterprises is the new InterAcademy Council (IAC), a cooperative effort of eighteen major scientific academies, North and South, intended to provide the most penetrating, objective analysis of developing country problems—and global problems as well. Here leadership is vital on the basis of intellectual acuity, social responsibility, respect for the people of developing countries, and skillful diplomacy.

Many nations lack the scientific institutions and infrastructure to benefit from what is already known—much less to adapt new discoveries to their local needs. Insufficient cooperation exists among the world's scientific research institutions, especially with those in the developing nations. Moreover, linkages between social needs and long-term research agendas require much more scientific attention than they have so far received. Inadequate use is made of new communications networks that provide an opportunity for the world's scientific community to share its socially valuable knowledge and skill on an unprecedented scale.

The IAC is implementing an analytic program designed to improve access by all nations and peoples to the benefits of science and technology. Four major topics are being addressed—necessarily formulating specific foci within each one: (1) human resources; (2) research institutions; (3) scientific cooperation; and (4) global communications.

Emphasis is placed on institution strengthening of the scientific and engineering communities in developing countries, thereby facilitating their ability to formulate and implement wise and effective policies. This work will also strive to be helpful to international organizations. From the outset, there was an excellent working relationship with UN Secretary-General Kofi Annan, who gave strong encouragement. His successor is likely to continue this orientation. This new nongovernmental organization works on a project-by-project basis funded by international agencies and interested foundations. When it receives a project request, the IAC assembles an expert international panel to study the problem. Panel members serve on a voluntary basis. Each study panel prepares a report of its findings and recommendations. Following a peer review of the draft report, it is released to the sponsoring organizations and the public. Although primarily designed to respond to external requests, the IAC also undertakes self-initiated studies. Altogether, this remarkable social invention provides the opportunity to illuminate vital paths to development.

The first IAC report, *Inventing a Better Future: A Strategy for Building Worldwide Capacities in Science and Technology,*[37] was presented to Secretary-General Kofi Annan at the United Nations on February 6, 2004.[38] The IAC study panel that drafted this consensus report included experts from eleven different nations. On that occasion, Bruce Alberts praised the report for carrying out the commitment of member academies to apply sound scientific knowledge and evidence-based principles to the problems that affect all nations: poverty, hunger, disease, the effects of globalization, and economic change. Goverdhan Mehta, former president of the Indian National Science Academy, wisely emphasized that the culture and values of science, which both connect and transcend national cultures, were essential in creating a peaceful global community;

indeed, science benefits all societies, even those once torn by war and civil or economic conflict.[39]

The second report of the IAC, *Realizing the Promise and Potential of African Agriculture*,[40] was delivered to Kofi Annan at the United Nations headquarters on June 25, 2004,[41] and responded to his specific request for insight into ways to provide an adequate, sustainable food supply for Africa. After completing his ten-year tenure as UN Secretary-General, he has taken up the implementation of this report in cooperation with African scientific and political leaders as well as U.S. foundations.

Bruce Alberts has used the intellectual and technical power of the national academies to strengthen the capacity of numerous academies in developing countries. The IAC is one vehicle. The new African Science Academy Development Initiative is another. This new initiative directly engages African academies of science in building their capacity to provide independent, evidence-based advice to their governments and countries on health-related matters. Supported by a ten-year grant from the Bill and Melinda Gates Foundation, the U.S. national academies work especially closely with three science academies in Africa. The South African, Nigerian, and Ugandan science academies, competitively chosen on the basis of merit to participate in the program at the most intensive level, will receive support and collaboration in advisory activities. The aim is to strengthen each academy's capacity in infrastructure, experience, and personnel and also to encourage a relationship between each academy and its government so that the academy comes to be regarded as a trusted source of excellent scientific advice.

One illustrative activity might be to convene members of the academic community and representatives from government, industry, and others for ongoing discussions to illuminate critical health-related issues and potential solutions consistent with the society's priorities, values, and resources. Another activity might be to foster policy studies to explore in depth an issue of importance to the country and its government. The studies would offer evidence-based guidance to national decisionmakers concerned with improving the health of the people.

In addition to the three intensive partnerships, the project will involve a broader community of science academies from across the African continent in activities that will evolve over the life of the project. These will include annual symposia, collaborative workshops, and information resources generated through the program.

Several major health policy categories—fostering research and development, strengthening public health services, and linking clinical medicine and public health—will be informed by science-based analysis in light of Africa's crushing burden of illness.

The African Science Development Initiative is unfolding in the decade 2005–2015. Early activities include training each academy's staff as may be necessary and establishing contacts with appropriate government agencies and other organizations. Each country's program and the regional collaborations will move in an adaptive way in response to country experience and preferences. The objective is long-term sustainability, and the strategy will be modified as necessary to reach that target.

This is an ambitious venture, addressing some of the most difficult problems on earth, yet doing so with extraordinary intellectual, technical, organizational, and financial resources. What are the basic reasons for such extraordinary efforts to foster science and technology for development? The moral basis is our global shared humanity. Another basic reason is that if development fails, the result will be a breeding ground for infectious diseases, terrorism, civil war, mass migration of refugees, internally displaced persons, environmental degradation—even genocide. These are not in the national interest of affluent countries. Intimate, international interdependence makes faraway serious problems increasingly relevant to those of us who live in technically advanced, affluent countries. The rich and poor countries are more tightly bound together than ever before, for better in principle, but for worse in practice, unless we can make democratic socioeconomic development truly effective.

The immense power of science and technology can be brought to bear on development throughout the world. The technically advanced democracies can make a major contribution in fulfilling the promise of this approach, working in concert with many others—not dominating but stimulating and cooperating in international efforts.

The Scientific Community and the Avoidance of Catastrophic Destruction

We face the problem of intergroup violence in the twenty-first century in a world increasingly saturated with highly destructive weapons. We see in all parts of the world abundant prejudice, hatred, and threats of mass violence, including genocide. The historical record is full of every sort of slaughter based on perceived differences pertaining to religion, ethnicity, nationality, and other group characteristics. In this kind of world, the scientific community has a great responsibility to work in a reasonably unified way to address these profound and pervasive problems.

During the Cold War, the scientific community did much to cope with the nuclear danger. For example, leading scientists from the United States and the Soviet Union met regularly to seek ways to reduce the number of weapons and especially the likelihood of a first strike, to decrease the chance of accidental or inadvertent nuclear war, to find safeguards against unauthorized launch and against serious miscalculation, and to improve the relations between the superpowers through international cooperative efforts. The scientific community was also prescient in its exploration with the Soviets of biological terrorism. Moreover, it dealt effectively with behavioral and social aspects of reducing the nuclear danger.

These efforts brought together scientists, scholars, and expert practitioners to clarify the many facets of avoiding nuclear war. To generate options for decreasing the risk, they stimulated analytical work by people who knew various fields: e.g., advanced weaponry and its military uses, in-depth knowledge of the superpowers and other nuclear powers, geopolitical flash points, the broad context of international relations and policy formation and implementation (especially regarding the superpowers), human behavior under stress (especially leadership decisionmaking), and negotiation and conflict resolution. Collectively these efforts provided needed depth and new options for dealing with very dangerous issues. A dynamic interplay between the scientific community and the world of policy evolved and influenced leaders such as Gorbachev and Reagan.

The scientific community is the closest approximation we now have to a truly international community, sharing certain fundamental interests, values, standards, and curiosity about the nature of matter, life, behavior, and the universe. Its shared quest for understanding knows no national boundaries, has no inherent prejudices, no necessary ethnocentrism, and no requisite barriers to the free play of information and ideas. Recent advances in telecommunications draw the quest for global understanding closer than ever before.

The scientific community can provide a model for decent human relations and mutually beneficial cooperation that might transcend the biases, dogmas, and hatreds that have torn our species apart throughout history and have recently become so much more dangerous than ever before. Science can contribute to a better future by its ideals and its processes as well as by the specific content of its research. These examples show vividly the great promise of international scientific cooperation for equitable development and the benefit of all humanity.

Learning as We Go

We have earlier referred to the great value of the Marshall Plan and its evolution into the European Union. It was humanitarianism in the post–World War II shambles, it was a deeply cooperative plan for regional economic development leading to prosperity, and later it was a defense cooperation plan to deter dictatorial aggression. It was a serious, sustained effort that mobilized the creative energy of the smashed countries. It has demonstrated for more than half a century the profound value of deep cooperation for overcoming poverty and preventing war. Indeed, these are superordinate goals that can only be reached by mutually beneficial cooperation. That is the principle for rich and poor countries to apply in tackling these problems a half century later. It is not too late. Much has been learned worldwide that can be constructively applied on a sound base to today's hardest problems.

CHAPTER 10

Education for Human Survival

Basic Concepts

Fundamentally, modern humanity is a single, interdependent, crowded, worldwide, heavily armed species and, as such, must learn to live together with minimal hatred and violence. Today violence is more lethal and pervasive than ever before; for some, killing has become a way of life, and hatred is taught to young and old as the organizing principle for their society. Clearly, humans have a genetic base for ease of learning of aggression. It is equally true, however, that humans also have a genetic base for ease of learning of prosocial, empathic, and affiliative behaviors. Nonetheless, too little has been done to educate children and adults about constructive, humane, and peaceful ways to live together.

A well-documented body of research shows how culturally diverse groups of children, youth, and adults can be educated to live together harmoniously. The integrated knowledge provides the framework for significant change in educational priorities to cope with new imperatives of the diverse globalized world and for a shift to the learning and practice of prosocial behaviors across the entire lifespan. Therefore, education for peace should be one of the central pillars of modern education—not marginal or absent as it is now.

The basic concepts of education for peace and, ultimately, human survival have been poorly understood and little applied. In contrast, their opposites—education for hate and preparation for violence—have flourished in various epochs during past centuries. Large-scale education for hatred had a major revival in the latter part of the last century and continues to flourish to the present day in a growing number of hate-filled, extremist cultures. Often, the most destructive education has been sponsored by religious fanaticism and the ideological extremism associated with fantasies of racial or national superiority, as well as revenge for old grievances (as noted in Chapter 2). In the early years of the twenty-first century, the most vivid example of dangerous education has been the proliferation of a subset of radicalized madrassas: schools that are often operated by Islamic fundamentalists and, at times, sponsored by repressive regimes. Though it is difficult to get accurate information on these institutions, it will be useful to examine them carefully to better understand how modern, nonradicalized madrassas could once again become compatible with their prior historical cultural and religious values, which historically provided constructive and humane religious education.

This chapter focuses primarily on the new interdisciplinary knowledge and advances in educational practice that could be incorporated broadly to develop the genetic human heritage for prosocial behavior.

For new normative beliefs and actions to take hold, we must pay attention to the range of major influences that shape the attitudes, beliefs, and behaviors of children, adolescents, and adults toward other groups. From a life-span perspective, this spectrum involves developmentally appropriate prosocial education, starting with families, then schools, progressing from preschool through elementary and secondary schools into universities. In addition to schools, important roles are played by powerful community influences, including media and information technology, religious institutions, community nongovernmental organizations, and the public health system. All of these have underutilized potential for teaching prosocial behavior and attitudes essential to education for peace.

In *Learning to Live Together,* Beatrix Hamburg and I detailed the development of prosocial behavior through the years of growth and development into adulthood.[1] Significant knowledge continues to grow in many relevant fields—developmental and social psychology, child and adolescent psychiatry, public health, political science, and educational research. These resources can make it possible for people everywhere to learn to live together peacefully. The mainstream efforts to reform education curricula have largely neglected these topics. Yet an intellectual and moral ferment is stirring in the education field that gives a basis for educational innovations, tested strategies, new teaching tools, and substantial rather than exhortatory education for peace. There are also models for visionary leadership that promote education for peace in a range of democratic countries.

Fostering Prosocial Behavior from Infancy Through Young Adulthood

There are specific, constructive ways of fostering prosocial, cooperative, nonviolent problem solving in childhood and adolescence. Longitudinal field experimental research has studied methods to strengthen children's prosocial orientation and behavior. The results show that children in such intervention programs are more supportive of each other, more spontaneously helpful and cooperative, and more concerned about others than those in the conventional classes. In addition, the children in the prosocial activities are able to resolve conflicts in minimally aggressive ways, with more compromise, planning, and attention to the needs of the various individuals engaged in the conflict. They also manifest more democratic values. Effects clearly go beyond the classroom, and academic achievement is often enhanced.

Parents, teachers, and religious educators can be consistent models of sharing, helping, and comforting behaviors. This should be an explicit part of the educational climate. Prosocial classroom activities that are enjoyable to children, such as role-playing to promote feelings of sympathy, support their prosocial tendencies. Parents and teachers can also organize their community to press for responsible television programming that exposes children to more altruistic behavior rather than to severe violence.

Decades of research identify families and schools as the two most important institutions in democracies that influence children's predispositions to love and to hate.[2] Programs that teach conflict resolution take both into account and include the following:

- Social competence—listening skills, communication skills
- Tolerance and respect for others—awareness of biases, stereotypes
- Decisionmaking and interpersonal problem-solving skills
- Negotiation and mediation skills, with "win-win" goals, fairness, justice
- Nonviolent attitudes and conflict resolution strategies

Students need a serious curriculum with repeated opportunities to learn and practice cooperativeness and conflict resolution skills in joint problem solving. Here are a few examples of curricular concepts currently implemented in the developmental approach to prosocial learning and education for peace.

1. *Intergroup contact* has great potential to help overcome the deadly obstacles of the past. Friendly contact in the context of equal status has a strong positive effect of overcoming entrenched hostility and stereotypes, if such contact is supported by relevant authorities. It is effective when it is embedded in cooperative, mutually rewarding activity; is encouraged by a mutual aid ethic; and leads to tangible benefits for all. Such contact has been shown to increase positive attitudes and behaviors between previously suspicious or hostile groups as well as to promote cooperative, constructive patterns of interaction between them. Schools can be organized to facilitate favorable contacts and provide rewards for cooperation.
2. *Superordinate goals* have the potentially powerful effect of unifying disparate groups in the search for a vital benefit that can only be obtained by their mutual cooperation. We reiterate for emphasis that animosity tends to be reduced when there is equal status contact between groups in the pursuit of common goals and shared efficacy in reaching those goals.
3. *School conflict resolution programs* include (1) cooperative learning, (2) conflict resolution training, (3) constructive use of controversy in teaching, and (4) creation of dispute resolution centers.
4. *Peer mediation* has emerged as a valuable mode of learning conflict resolution skills and resolving school disputes. School mediation programs are spreading rapidly. Research suggests that school mediation programs have positive effects in reducing violence and enhancing self-esteem as well as social skills of the mediator. *Thus, students learn conflict resolution in practice as well as in theory.* Skills involved in active problem solving of this sort also encourage prosocial skills that can be used in other settings encountered over a lifetime.[3] School programs can actively encourage transfer of this learning to home and community.
5. *Assertiveness training* builds skill in taking advantage of opportunities without resorting to threats or violence. It illuminates constructive problem solving to meet basic human needs. Often it is carried out on a peer-mediated basis, supervised by teachers or counselors.

6. *Community service* draws together major strands of development: (1) the growth of prosocial behavior, (2) enhancement of empathy, (3) ability to learn in cooperative settings, (4) skill in resolving conflict without violence, (5) capacity to reach beyond the self in ways that overcome selfish, greedy orientations, and (6) creation of a sense of belonging in a valued group that is characterized by a sense of fairness and mutual aid.

7. *Learning prosocial behavior* occurs in widening circles through the years of early growth and development into adulthood. Such learning involves decent concern for others; readiness and ability to cooperate for mutual benefit; helping, sharing, and respecting others while maintaining integrity as an individual with basic self-respect and lifelong inclinations to expand horizons from the nuclear to the global family. Research in both experimental and naturalistic modes supports these opportunities. A fundamental challenge for education is to teach ways of enhancing prosocial behavior across traditional and even adversarial boundaries.

8. *Peace education* works toward giving children, adolescents, and young adults clear ideas about how to contribute to the creation of peaceful communities with standards of understanding, fairness, and justice in international relations. It clarifies the social conditions that are generally conducive to peaceful living.

9. *International cooperation* for democratic development, both political and economic, is central to the vision of world peace with justice. Pluralism is the heart of democracy. Here the attitudes of tolerance, mutual respect, and protection of human rights are valued and perpetuated. It is fundamentally important to educate specifically for democracy—ranging from the most basic principles to operational details and showing how the international community can nurture aspiring fragile democracies, taking into account cultural differences.

10. *Active worldwide cooperation of schools, universities, and international organizations* is long overdue. These groups need to provide war and peace content based on the world's best scholarship to replace the prevalent ethnocentrism in intergroup relations and hateful or ideologically dogmatic orientations. Such content that includes understanding of the culture, customs, and historical background of others can be adapted for different levels of child and adolescent development. It should include accurate information and analysis on genocide, with a strong emphasis on prevention as delineated in this book.

Education for Genocide Prevention

A prominent example of education for genocide prevention is Facing History and Ourselves (FHAO), a nonprofit organization founded by Margot Stern Strom and based in Brookline, Massachusetts. It offers an exemplary program to develop students' attitudes of understanding and compassion as well as their critical thinking skills. It encourages students to investigate devastating periods in history such as the Holocaust—in which violence, human degradation, and mass murder occurred—in ways that make them think about their own lives and how they might act personally to prevent hatred and violence between groups. It deepens their understanding of history and their ability to identify and explore root causes of atrocities that can lead to genocide. They study how to build and maintain democratic institutions and how to defuse conflict situations, individually and collectively, in which individuals or groups are at risk of demonization.

The quarter century of success Facing History and Ourselves has achieved is at least partly due to its treatment of teachers and students as partners in learning. Teachers are offered professional development activities, such as workshops and conferences, discussions with leading scholars on current and historical topics, and exploration of teaching techniques that employ visual arts, poetry, and community service.

FHAO has developed curricular materials for secondary school children that combine primary historical sources, fictional works, and other relevant readings. Their offices in several countries give teachers access to teaching methods and pertinent resources—including films, guest speakers, and opportunities to gain experience in leading discussions on difficult issues. The teachers then adapt the material to suit their own classroom situations. Affiliated programs have recently been developed in Eastern Europe and South Africa.

Its Web site, www.facinghistory.org, gives students and teachers access to historical information, audio and video clips, suggestions for teaching strategies, study guides, and discussion questions about genocide and about books concerning genocide (such as Elie Wiesel's classic work, *Night*[4]). For further information and study, it provides links to other valuable Internet sources that offer useful material for students and educators, such as the United States Holocaust Memorial Museum (http://www.ushmm.org) and Human Rights Watch (http://hrw.org). Students can also find links there to Web sites that give opportunities for extracurricular and volunteer activities, such as letter writing campaigns or essay competitions. In addition, a variety of educational and training opportunities is provided by the Holocaust Memorial, Yad Vashem in Jerusalem (www.yadvashem.org), the Armenian National Institute in Washington, D.C. (www.armenian_genocide.org), and other institutions supported by groups whose history has made them keenly sensitive to the horrors of genocide.

On a regular basis, FHAO undergoes both self-evaluation and external evaluation. External evaluations have found that students who have participated in the program have more knowledge of history than comparison groups, are better able to reason from a moral perspective, and exhibit more empathy and social interest. One study showed that they were more effective and more mature than the comparison group in their interpersonal and intergroup relationships and less likely to engage in fighting, racism, or ethnocentrism.

Creating cooperative learning environments is crucial. This does not mean that competition is eliminated from students' experience. In fact, healthy competition often inspires higher achievement, whether it is building a better instrument or developing gifted athletes or creative scientists. But excessive and harsh competition, especially in the classroom, creates a dichotomous atmosphere of winners and losers—a breeding ground for personal feelings of isolation, alienation, even humiliation; then, all too often, of hatred and violence toward the "winners."

Overall, there is much evidence to indicate that prejudice tends to be reduced with equal-status contact between groups in the pursuit of highly valued, challenging common goals and shared resources that create efficacy in reaching the common goals.

What about joint efforts to overcome the serious global problems of food, water, health, and the environment? Could these be viewed as superordinate goals? The world is one in which friendly personal contacts on an equal status basis and cooperative ventures can occur more readily than ever before, despite all the cultural barriers that have so long separated peoples. A great opportunity now is to identify superordinate goals in our global world, understand our shared necessity, and organize cooperative efforts to meet them.

Although there are many situations where in-group positive attitudes and out-group negativity are linked, there is clear evidence that this polarization is by no means inevitable. Gordon W. Allport clarified the possibility of building on the notion of "concentric loyalties"—where there is compatibility between loyalties of larger groups (for example, nations, humankind) and of subgroups (for example, family, profession, religion).[5] The needs of the in-group and out-group are seen as compatible if these groups are subsumed by the superordinate group. Out-groups can be perceived with indifference, sympathy, even admiration, as if to say, "We have our ways and they have their ways." Because the identity of individuals within a complex social structure includes attachments to multiple groups (such as religious, occupational, residential), they are apt to be fellow in-group members in one category and out-group members in another. Such crosscutting intergroup memberships lessen the intensity of the individual's dependence on any one group for meeting psychological needs for inclusion.

Universities: Opportunities for Learning to Live Together Peacefully

Considering education for peace, *Learning to Live Together* (mentioned earlier in the chapter) and *No More Killing Fields*[6] examined crucial substantive problems: causes and consequences of war; concepts and techniques of conflict resolution; conditions favorable to long-term peaceful relations. Universities, as premier intellectual leaders, must address these fundamental problems in their research and education, including newer concepts such as human security, operational and structural prevention, changing norms of national sovereignty with the responsibility to protect human rights, fostering democratic socioeconomic development through international cooperation, and renewing efforts to decrease and secure weapons of mass destruction on a universal basis. All of these are amplified in various chapters of this book.

Not only are universities able to provide undergraduate and graduate level courses for their own students, but they are uniquely positioned to "train the trainers" through teacher education and curriculum development for programs from kindergarten through high school. University scholars who have the most advanced knowledge have shown that they can work collaboratively with teachers, counselors, and others in precollegiate level public schools to stimulate students and enrich curricula in ways that meet their social responsibilities.

Guidelines have emerged for upgrading preventive capacities. There are specific ways in which the international community can strengthen its capability for promoting democratic governance, productive economic development, and nonviolent problem solving in dangerous situations by setting up mechanisms to address grievances promptly and fairly. There are helpful roles of national governments, intergovernmental organizations, nongovernmental organizations, and the pivotal institutions of civil society.

International cooperation for democratic development (both political and economic) is a basic pillar of prevention because it provides conditions conducive to peaceful living. The essential ingredients of such development center on knowledge, skill, freedom, and health. Knowledge is mainly generated by research and development; skills are mainly shaped by education and training; freedom is mainly made possible by democratic institutions; health is fostered by specific education and a vigorous public health system. These are vital subjects for curricula at all levels and in all countries, as well as for public understanding beyond the system of public education. Technologies (e.g., the Internet and compact disc read-only memory [CD-ROM]) can help universities cooperate in making valuable information readily available, especially in the educational systems of poor and troubled countries.

Despite its bloody historical record and current killing, the human species has shown that it is also capable of remarkable cooperation, mutual ties, loyalty, and compassion. Human groups must find ways to foster and maintain internal cohesion with a prosocial basis over long periods and without harsh depreciation of other groups. With the vast destructive capabilities of modern weaponry at the disposal of states, groups, and individuals, the current human propensity toward violence and intergroup conflict must be addressed in programs of education for peace that go far beyond previous experience.

The powerful sectors of society almost everywhere tend to show a resigned acceptance about these matters, often mistakenly viewing them as inevitable and a problem of someone else who is far away. Avoidance and denial can readily substitute for careful scrutiny, even in the face of oncoming genocide; pronouncement of authority often substitutes for evidence; rigid ideology substitutes for pragmatic problem solving in the service of conflict resolution. But this need not be so forever. It is essential to recognize the gravity of the dangers in order to mobilize the positive strengths necessary to overcome them.

The principles and practices of conflict resolution and violence prevention can readily be taught in all institutions of secondary and higher education.

In 2005, for example, Columbia University taught a course entitled "Preventive Diplomacy and Conflict Resolution in the United Nations: Integrating Theory and Practice."[7] The objective of the course was to draw together theories of conflict, negotiation, mediation, and conflict management with the practice of the United Nations and to underscore the capacity of international and governmental officials along with academics to understand ways in which preventive diplomacy and peacemaking can prevent or halt deadly conflict. Other innovative course offerings in prevention of deadly conflict can be found at the University of Victoria in Canada, Harvard, and Stanford. Many other good examples could also be given, including a strong program at the University of Bradford in England. A program at the University of Witswaterstrand in South Africa was organized over the past decade by Professor John Stremlau, now director of the peace program at the Carter Center.

Universities in developing countries should be a major focal point for the intellectual ferment now arising in the area of education in preventing deadly conflict. In the spring of 2001, a meeting of international experts was held at the United Nations, and opened by Kofi Annan, to discuss the possibility of University for Peace (UPEACE) having a renewed role in peace studies as part of a revitalization of the university to expand its programs worldwide. The United Nations University in Tokyo, part of the UN system, is another example of an institution that puts a significant focus on peace education and conflict resolution. The university makes use of research and capacity building to clarify and help resolve world problems of concern to the UN and member states.

Universities can actively foster peace education in secondary schools. The Stanford Program on International and Cross-Cultural Education (SPICE) is part of Stanford University's Institute for International Studies (IIS), an interdisciplinary research and education center. SPICE serves as a connection between Stanford and precollegiate public schools. It collaborates with researchers to clarify complex world issues that affect us all. The program's thoughtful, carefully reviewed, supplementary curricula, which weave proven, successful teaching strategies into each unit, are distributed to schools. The program also provides user-friendly guides to teachers and gives alternatives to the presentation of full units by offering individual lesson plans.

In close cooperation with the Stanford University faculty and other scholars, materials are prepared that reflect the best research worldwide. SPICE also makes it convenient to access its materials through dissemination centers throughout the United States. Its curricula are reasonably priced and easily obtained by telephone, facsimile, U.S. mail, and e-mail. In principle, they could come to have worldwide utility.

Preventing Deadly Conflict: Toward a World Without War is a prime example of a SPICE curriculum.[8] This ninety-six-page guide, complete with illustrative slides, was developed for students in secondary schools and community colleges. Its content is based to a considerable extent on the *Final Report* of the Carnegie Commission on Preventing Deadly Conflict, established in 1994 to "address the looming threats to world peace of intergroup violence and to advance new ideas for the prevention and resolution of deadly conflict."[9] The guide provides an excellent prototype for other universities seeking to develop similar curricula for schools on the subject of violence prevention.

We must find a basis for fundamental human identification across a diversity of cultures.[10] This shared quest for understanding, especially as already practiced by the scientific community, knows no national boundaries and no barriers to the free play of information and ideas. Many very productive and friendly international collaborations exist between individual scientists and scientific organizations. Freedom of scientific meetings, collaborative studies, and science student exchanges have greatly enhanced knowledge and led to great scientific advances. Education can help individuals to ask questions of practical importance bearing on fruitful cooperation and constructive lifestyles rather than prejudice, ethnocentrism, and hatred. Strong organizations covering wide sectors of science, technology, and education can take an increasingly active role in coping with this critical issue. Hostile attitudes, fanatical beliefs, and rigid ideologies from our past will often hinder such efforts, but human motivation for survival is strong, problem-solving capacities are great, and the time for adaptation is not yet too late.[11]

In the twenty-first century, it will be necessary in child and adolescent development to put deliberate, explicit emphasis on developing prosocial orientations and a sense of worth based not on the depreciation of others but rather on the constructive attributes of oneself and others. In counteracting our ancient tendencies toward ethnocentrism and prejudice, we will need to foster reliable human attachments, positive reciprocity, friendly intergroup relations, a mutual-aid ethic, and an awareness of superordinate goals requiring cooperation that include economic well-being, environmental protection, personal security—and indeed human survival. We must seek ways to expand favorable contact between people from different groups and nations. Educational, cultural, and scientific exchanges can be helpful. Joint projects involving sustained cooperation can provide the valuable experience of working together toward a superordinate goal.

In sum, education everywhere should convey an accurate concept of the contemporary human species—a vast, extended interdependent global family sharing fundamental human similarities and a fragile planet, yet saturated with weapons and hateful propaganda. All research-based knowledge of human conflict and the paths to mutual accommodation should be a part of education, conveying both the facts of human diversity and the common humanity we all share.

Fostering Harmony in Diversity

Earlier in this book we described the innovative and successful efforts over a difficult decade of Max van der Stoel, the first high commissioner on national minorities of the OSCE. The next OSCE high commissioner was Rolf Ekéus, a distinguished Swedish diplomat, who wrote:[12]

> I was delighted by the decision of the 2004 Bulgarian Chairmanship to assign priority to education on the OSCE agenda. As an "instrument of conflict prevention at the earliest possible stage," my job is to tackle the underlying causes of tension between minorities and majorities. Perhaps the most effective means of achieving this is by investing in educational policies and practices designed to meet the special needs and concerns of both.[13]

To help legislators and policymakers, as well as leaders of minority groups and NGOs, develop appropriate educational policies in line with international standards, van der Stoel issued the 1996 Hague Recommendations Regarding the Education Rights of National Minorities. These educational guidelines are designed to strengthen interethnic harmony and social cohesion in minority education across all school levels. Along with curriculum development, effective teaching methods are explained simply and succinctly. There is emphasis on achieving a prosocial school climate, equal opportunities for higher education at state universities, tolerance, mutual respect, and cooperation for mutual benefit.

The issue of language is important where hostile ethnic situations coexist. Language often defines a national minority and asserts the right of its members to maintain and develop their distinctive identity. The Hague Recommendations point out that this right can be pursued more readily if members of minorities gain knowledge of their mother tongue during the earliest period of their formal education. At the same time, to participate fully in the life of their nation, they have a responsibility to learn their state's majority language.[14]

"A typical destabilizing situation" arises when authorities try forcibly to spread the exclusive use of the state language to promote nationhood, and a strong minority sees this demand as an attempt to downgrade their group's language and culture. Drastic changes in language education can exacerbate ethnic tensions. When minority students continue to fail to qualify for entry into state institutions of higher education, the nation's qualified labor force will shrink—along with its international competitiveness and economic viability.

South East European University in Tetovo (northwestern Macedonia), an initiative of the high commissioner on national minorities, was founded in 1990 and is already a leader in the development of modern higher education in the Balkans. The university combines high academic standards with a focus on interethnic integration and cooperation. It supports Albanian language and culture but has an international European orientation, with a 25 percent non-Albanian student body and courses conducted in Albanian, Macedonian, and English. In 2005 its first graduating class began to address the shortage of Macedonian-Albanian graduates in the country's universities, and it has already increased the overall percentage of Albanians in the country's university student population from 5 to more than 12 percent.

Programs to meet the needs of minorities are more likely to be effective and accepted if the minorities involved participate in their design. Minority participation also demonstrates the sincerity and openness of the majority group that is promoting the programs. This is a movement only in its infancy that deserves serious attention

Language teaching must be combined with serious coverage of the history, culture, and traditions of *all* the nation's ethnic groups, majority as well as minority. Textbooks that ignore diversity—or, what is worse, treat it as a danger to the state—fuel intolerance and xenophobia.

The High Commissioner supports "interactive, student-centered methods. Teachers are encouraged to think of training as an opportunity for creativity, self-discovery, and further learning, an approach that stands in stark contrast to traditional methods."[15] A project in Moldova has ensured that nearly all the 1,200 middle school teachers of Moldovan as a second language have been trained in the latest teaching methods. The trainees, in turn, have produced a manual on teaching the state language.

To sum up the importance of education to the OSCE Secretariat, High Commissioner Ekéus cited a survey its Conflict Prevention Centre recently conducted of all OSCE education-related activities over five years. He believed this was a sign that the OSCE considered education an integral component of long-term security. The OSCE plans to continue, expand, and develop his work in education for the benefit of interethnic relations throughout its region.[16]

Can Media Help?

Public television has provided excellent models for promoting decent intergroup relations. Commercial television has greatly lagged in building on such models. In principle, television can portray human diversity while highlighting shared human experiences—including the common humanity of our adversaries, even in times of stress. But so far we have had only glimpses of its potential for reducing intergroup conflict.

Sesame Street was the first series to teach a curriculum to young children (especially those in low-income and minority families). The driving force was to build intellectual and social development in preschoolers and help them to become ready for school.[17] The close, ongoing collaboration of child development experts, television producers, and educational researchers made it a reality. *Sesame Street* also made possible systematic studies on the impact of educational television on children. Indicators are clear that *Sesame Street* exerts a positive influence on children's social behavior. Overall, significant effects in many countries have been found on children's academic skills and social behavior as a result of exposure to *Sesame Street*. As research on *Sesame Street* has demonstrated, entertaining and educational television programming can be developed in ways that reduce intergroup hostility across cultures, especially since the program now appears in more than 100 countries.

The research on television and children offers encouragement to find ways of diminishing exposure to violence in childhood and adolescence and to enhance media literacy as part of education. We can provide much more prosocial programming such as *Sesame Street,* not only for young children but for adolescents and indeed for adults.

Information Technology and Education for Peace

The past few decades have seen a profound revolution in our daily life through information technology.[18] In the 1990s some proponents of the World Wide Web made extravagant claims about its impact for good. Today we acknowledge the substantial benefits it has provided in improved communication and the spread of education and information across cultures, but we have also developed a sober recognition of its limitations. They often appear as the reverse side of its educational advantages: "Hate" Web sites, which range in intensity from verbal poison to explicit calls to violence, pose a real danger. They can use the Internet's potential for education and free individual expression to spread hate-filled arguments and specious justifications that push those who do not know better, or whose personalities or circumstances predispose them to hatred, toward derogatory distinctions against other groups—or even violence. These sources of miseducation must be countered with accurate information—every vicious lie must be answered with a hundred corroborated facts both on the World Wide Web and in other media. Happily, a number of relevant sites, most not specifically devoted to peace education, use the World Wide Web's global capacity to spread a positive view of the world's diversity and offer an unprecedented opportunity for children and youth to explore cultural differences and gain a constructive understanding of human similarities.

International Education: Seeing the Whole Wide World

The new technologies of communication and transportation have produced global interdependency and made billions of people our neighbors. They can no longer be strangers—they need us and we need them to create and sustain employment, provide safe travel, assure production and delivery of healthful food and clean water, and cooperate on problems without borders such as infectious disease, environmental pollution, terror, and national security. We must discard stereotypes and traditional antagonisms and find decent ways to interact with those former strangers, even with those who have been enemies.

What can be done to enhance the contributions of schools, colleges, and universities to achieving this necessary goal? First, broaden their curricula toward a substantial international and global perspective. Second, encourage and facilitate personal interactions among students from different cultures and countries. (Exchange programs and junior years abroad have broadened the outlooks and education of countless students.) Third, use technology to disseminate information about the rest of the world and to encourage long-distance contact with people abroad. Fourth, make teachers central to these efforts by preparing them and offering them in-service training with a global viewpoint. Finally, support and build international education policies that promote this essential goal of moving beyond the parochialism that too often prevails in the schools of many countries.[19]

Bullying

Bullying has been a highly prevalent and tolerated school experience throughout the world. Bullying involves severe humiliation of schoolmates who have been targeted by the perpetrators for repeated verbal and physical torment, owing to their difference, including identifiable ethnic or religious attributes, perceived physical weakness, or emotional vulnerability. Bullying behaviors at school occur most often at recess, in hallways, and in bathrooms. Bullying is not limited to school contexts, however; it occurs in neighborhoods as well. When bullying is allowed to flourish in schools, many children become afraid to go to school. Some even resort to suicide. Since 1990, a large and increasing percentage of its victims have had explosive violent responses. In the United States lethal school violence has become an increasing problem.[20] This disturbing trend was first reported in a study initiated by the U.S. Congress. In 1978 the "Safe School Study Report to Congress" (NIE-1978) shocked the nation with findings that 282,000 high school students and 5,200 teachers were physically assaulted every month in U.S. schools.[21] The violence of the school climate, plus increasing availability of firearms, paved the way for the subsequent lethal violence. A decade later, in the 1990s, there was a series of school shootings, highlighted by the Columbine school massacre. Careful review of these high-profile school tragedies revealed that most of them involved retaliation by students who were bullied and/or felt deeply humiliated by their classmates.

In Norway, there was no shocking firearm violence, but it became apparent that school bullying was commonly causing anxiety, anger, school refusals, depression, and suicide. Although the severity of the problem had gained wide recognition, a range of initial remedial efforts proved largely unsuccessful. Then in 1991 in Norway Dr. Dan Olweus published a comprehensive evaluation of programs that used a whole-school strategy instead of piecemeal programs to prevent bullying. This approach was found to be very effective. A key element was the adoption of a consensus resolve of all school personnel (including students, parents, and community) that bullying would not be tolerated. School norms were changed. Detailed information was gathered to guide helpful interventions. Students filled out anonymous questionnaires that cited the prevalence and conditions of bullying and responses of victims that they had experienced or witnessed. Based on all of the data from the comprehensive review of school programs and the extensive questionnaire data, actions were taken across all of Norway. Explicit rules about bullying were given to implement the "bullying will not be tolerated" environment. For example, children were given instructions to report bullying to an adult, to try to help the victim, and to keep the same rules outside of school. Booklets described the true severity of bullying and explained why it was not simply "child's play." The new school norms were detailed, and constructive actions to be taken by the parents were outlined. Teachers were provided videotapes on the subject and outlines for classroom discussions and role-playing exercises. Teachers were also encouraged to heighten their vigilance in hallways, staircases, and play areas during recess. Olweus reported in 1994 a 50 percent reduction in all bullying and a decrease in the severity of the residual bullying.[22]

This program was replicated and evaluated in Sheffield, England, by Peter K. Smith and Sonia Sharp, with similar results.[23] Both studies found that the maximal impact was among children and early adolescents. These studies of the whole-school approach to bullying have not led to extensive adoption of the program in many countries. It is an impressive model, however, which has a place in prosocial, nonviolent education, and the knowledge of it is spreading.

Education, Humiliation, and Mass Violence

Unfortunately, indeed tragically, in all parts of the world there are ample occasions for children and adolescents to experience humiliation in the course of their development. We are all familiar in one way or another with discrimination by age, class, gender, religion, ethnicity, nationalism, or other criteria that may readily cause some to become a depreciated out-group. The problem is ubiquitous. One great challenge is to organize educational institutions and experiences in such a way as to minimize lasting danger from humiliating episodes. In this way, the harsh reaction patterns, such as intense anger or even violence, may be minimized by buffering potential victims with resilience, self-esteem, and a web of mutually respectful human relationships. We need to be mindful of the danger of deep psychological scars conducive to hatred in the long term if we do not take prompt action to provide consistently constructive, supportive patterns in the educational experience.

To do so, schools at every level, from early childhood to young adulthood, must build in a strong sense of responsibility for their students. To address the humiliation problem adequately requires several systematic measures: (1) the social climate of the school; (2) the prosocial content of education; (3) creation of bases for earning self-esteem; (4) teaching of nonviolent, active coping strategies; and (5) learning from the terrible history of genocides as an essential educational experience that can provide both a moral and pragmatic basis for dealing with other dangers and other groups on the basis of understanding, fairness, and mutual benefit.

In developing conflict resolution curricula, schools can create environments that support the development of resilient characteristics in children in three ways:

1. Teaching conflict resolution strategies in principled ways that promote "win-win" outcomes and preserve or create positive relationships, thereby facilitating skills essential to the development of resilience. From the start of the conflict resolution encounter, the issue is put in the context of developing and sustaining a mutually rewarding relationship.

2. Conveying to youth that they have self-efficacy, the power to control their own behavior by making choices that satisfy their own needs while taking into account the needs of others. Mutual accommodation leads to mutual benefits.
3. Giving students the opportunity to resolve their conflicts peacefully by means of a conflict resolution education program that gives youth a powerful enabling sense of trust and problem-solving capability.[24]

In short, education has the capacity to minimize potentially humiliating experiences—if only we see this is a vital component of the education agenda and a contributor to healthy child development.

Overcoming Neglect of the Human Heritage in Education

It is curious and troubling that education has seriously neglected the fact that the destruction of human groups has a very long history—and neglected understanding of the conditions that favor such destruction. Often it is carried out in the name of one god or another—theological or secular religions will do—and religious wars were sometimes extremely brutal. Given the horrors of World War II and the associated Holocaust, it would have been plausible to suppose that a worldwide revulsion against mass violence would have occurred and that the second half of the twentieth century would have been free of such disasters. But that was not the case. Many millions of people were killed in their own countries. Prominent among these are Cambodia, Indonesia, Burundi, Nigeria, Paraguay, Sudan, Uganda, Yugoslavia, and Rwanda. Totalitarian governments have tended to follow Hitler's example as well as Stalin's and to kill not only individuals but also whole groups who are perceived as actual or potential enemies. How is it possible that such atrocious behavior should be so prevalent in a world that is in so many ways technically advanced and putatively civilized? Understanding such considerations can contribute to preventing such slaughter in the future and should become an integral part of education.

There is a spectrum of sporadic deaths, massacres, and, at times, genocide that is preceded by severe humiliation of the victims. Lethal humiliation of out-group members typically includes group depreciation as worthless and threatening as well as punitive social isolation, in ghettos or through forced migration, of the targeted persons or groups. These destructive, unrelenting humiliation practices are learned behaviors that often begin in early childhood and may continue throughout the life span. The humiliation is often sanctioned and fostered by influential members of the in-group and those in authority.

The genetic legacy of humans provides a biologic basis for ease of learning of in-group/out-group distinctions and for learning a repertoire of aggressive, hostile social and physical behaviors. This biology is not destiny, however. There is also a powerful genetic legacy that provides a biological basis for ease of learning prosocial and supportive behaviors. These behaviors are seen in the strong, affiliative bonds among family members and close circles of friends. These prosocial behaviors are also learned and can be nurtured over the lifespan, then taught, practiced, and rewarded by the social environment.

To say the least, education practices have been slow to adapt to dangerous circumstances, e.g., tensions of globalization, the presence and crowding of strangers, the hideous nature and scope of weaponry, the immense capacity for destructiveness, and the enhanced capacity for incitement to violence. There was a peace education movement through much of the twentieth century, spearheaded by a few great institutions such as Columbia University, but so far that type of activity has been marginal over most of the world. The need now is greater than ever before.

Overcoming Education for Hate

Religion, Hostility, and Education

Any kind of "holy war" (whatever the religion) tends to provide a strong sense of community with mutually supportive solidarity within the group, but concomitantly it generates parochialism, hostile exclusion, and facile justification of mass violence. This is one of the most difficult and dangerous problems facing the international community. We live in a time of violence driven by religious fanaticism and extremist ideological justification. Yet, religious nationalism is not entirely closed to pluralistic tolerance. This gives the international community an opening to reach out in friendship to moderate leaders and democratic reformers. With substantial help, they may over time change their societies. One crucial set of changes is the strengthening of education, fully including the education of women, teaching science and technology for the modern economy (looking toward broad prosperity), and practical understanding of nonviolent conflict resolution (looking toward peaceful coexistence). These efforts must overcome powerful historical traditions that are conducive to hatred and violence, especially in the hands of inflammatory leaders. So, education for peace must overcome both psychological and social obstacles—no easy task, yet surely not impossible—especially if there is strong social, economic, and psychological encouragement from the international community.

Madrassas and Other Sources of Education for Prejudice and Hate

Education for hate is an all too pervasive part of human experience. State-dominated media in prejudicial, repressive states often provide exceptional vividness and immediacy to hate messages. The fundamentally distorting nature of such education and its destructive effects deserve much more attention than they now receive. Education reform in many countries, even when excellent in other respects, is usually weak in the domain of preparing children for decent human relations and finding (or creating) nonviolent mechanisms for addressing serious grievances. This serious problem is most vividly highlighted in some of the madrassas that are very negative toward out-groups. Though they vary greatly, some even consider all humanity as an out-group—except for believers in their narrow version of fundamentalist Islam.

In 2005, William Dalrymple published an article on these schools.[25] We summarize his observations, bearing in mind that such emotionally charged institutions are difficult to study and to treat objectively.

The Haqqania, in the Northwest Frontier Province of Pakistan, is one of the most radical of the religious schools called madrassas. Many Taliban leaders, including Mullah

Omar, were trained there. The director of the madrassa, Maulana Sami ul-Haq, still boasts that whenever the Taliban issues a call for fighters, he closes his school and sends his pupils off to battle.

In his interview with Dalrymple, he expressed gratitude to President Bush for "waking" the Islamic world, thus facilitating his job of propagating Islamic ideology while offering free education, clothes, books, and lodging. As he pointed out, madrassas like his were the only sources of education for the poor.

U.S. actions aside, he added, Pakistanis were disgusted by their government's secularism, militarism, and corruption. They perceived Pervez Musharraf as a puppet of the West, antagonistic to faithful Muslims. Thus they turned to Islam as the only system that provided true justice.[26]

Sami ul-Haq's viewpoint is increasingly shared across Pakistan. An Interior Ministry report after September 11, 2001, counted twenty-seven times as many madrassas in Pakistan as there were in 1947: up from 245 to 6,870.[27] A report in July 2002 by the International Crisis Group (an organization of very high quality) estimated as many as 10,000 madrassas in Pakistan[28] with a total of more than 1.5 million students. A World Bank report of 2005, however, put the figure lower and reckoned that about 1 percent of all Pakistanis were educated in madrassas.[29] The true figure probably lies somewhere between the two estimates—not trivial in either case.

A good number of the madrassas are run by, or connected to, radical Islamist political parties in the umbrella group Muttahida Majlis-i-Amal (MMA). Their fundamentalist leaders have imposed a Taliban-like regime in Pakistan's Northwest Frontier Province that, among other strict and punitive rules, prohibits the public performance of music and representations of human figures.

Across Pakistan, religious belief has been radicalized: the tolerant Sufi-minded Barelvi form of Islam has lost ground to the more hard-line and politicized Deobandi, Wahhabi, and Salafi sects. The rapid growth of radical madrassas, financed mainly by the Saudis, began under General Mahammad Zia ul-Haq during the Afghan jihad of the 1980s. Some of the new madrassas were only one-room attachments to village mosques, but others became important institutions. The Dar ul-Uloom in Baluchistan now enrolls 1,500 boarders a year, along with 1,000 day students. Altogether, Pakistan's madrassas instruct an estimated 800,000 students and constitute a free Islamic education system running parallel to the inadequate state educational system.[30] Madrassas probably constitute a greater proportion of Pakistan's educational system than is the case in any other country, but they have increased throughout the Islamic world.[31]

To what extent do these madrassas prepare students to become terrorists? To what extent do they orient their students toward hatred and violence? There is significant variation.

About 15 percent of Pakistan's madrassas teach violence, and some provide military training. Madrassa students participated in the Afghan and Kashmir jihads and have been involved in sectarian violence, especially against the Shia minority in Karachi. Other religions support extremist schools, but they are fewer and less influential.

Recent studies have emphasized that madrassa graduates tend to be poor, pious villagers with little technical training, not the middle-class, politically sophisticated terrorists who plan Al-Qaeda operations around the world. Osama bin Laden and the men involved in the terrorist attacks on the United States and Europe were not trained in a madrassa or as clerics. They were secularly educated middle-class professionals. The French scholar Gilles Kepel considered them the privileged children of an odd marriage between Wahhabism and Silicon Valley, heirs not only to jihad but also to complex, globalized technology.[32]

Thus, there are several strands of education for Islamic extremism and hatred for infidels. The more violence-oriented madrassas constitute a significant source, but perhaps not the principal one, for recruiting violent extremists. There is all too little insight into the various sources for terrorism.

Additional insights are provided in an important new book by Professor Louise Richardson, executive dean of Radcliffe's Institute for Advanced Study at Harvard University.[33] Drawing on years of direct and indirect study of terrorists from a variety of countries, she concluded that virtually all terrorists aspire intensely to "three Rs": (1) revenge, (2) renown (in their own area and, if possible, in the world at large), and (3) reaction (from their enemies).

How does this cluster of dangerous three Rs evolve? She identified several risk factors that are common to this group: (1) a disaffected, alienated person, especially in youth; (2) a supportive (complicit) community; (3) an ideology for justification of killing; (4) intense loyalty to the terrorist in-group (a band of brothers).

Thus, there are clearly educational precursors to the fully formed terrorists: family and community influences; schools; religious institutions; recruitment by hateful adults; incitement by media and leaders. Thus, both formal and informal educational influences shape the ultimate disastrous outcome. The development of constructive counterinfluences at every level will be needed to diminish the now growing pool of emerging jihadists. Present policies of the democracies are largely ineffective, but a better range of options emerges from her study and similar ones that we have noted here.

Historical fluctuations in the nature of madrassa education illustrate how educational systems can vary over time—for worse or for better. For example, the rigid Deobandi madrassas spread throughout North India and Pakistan in the twentieth century and in the 1980s were supported by General Zia ul-Haq, the dictatorial ruler of Pakistan, and his Saudi allies. Ironically, the United States helped prepare madrassas for holy war as part of the Afghan jihad against the Soviet Union. The Central Intelligence Agency (CIA) financed the production of bloodthirsty madrassa textbooks "filled with violent images and militant Islamic teachings." When the Taliban took power, these textbooks were distributed for use in schools.[34]

Madrassas in India are quite different. They are peaceful and avoid politics. Several of modern India's greatest scholars are madrassa graduates. In a study of Indian madrassas, the Hindu scholar Yoginder Sikand described a chain of educational institutions in Kerala run by a group of professionals and businessmen who aim to reconcile current knowledge with Islam.[35] This group has promoted Muslim women's education in Kerala, and girls now outnumber boys in many of their madrassas. Thus the problem is not madrassas per se, but ultraradical establishments that teach students that jihadism is a legitimate and praiseworthy pursuit.

There are in fact promising directions toward a more humane and less violent development in childhood and adolescence. This in turn bears on the relations of human groups altogether. Education at all levels—from childhood to universities to political leaders—must illuminate the immense danger of contemporary weapons, find ways to greatly reduce the likelihood of their use, and foster intergroup relations of mutual accommodation.

There are opportunities for benign, compassionate religious education that can offset the hateful tendencies in so much religious education. Greatly respected world leaders such as Jimmy Carter and Desmond Tutu set an example that if followed by many others could, in time, set new prosocial, democratic standards of religious education on a worldwide basis.

Education for Political Leaders

At the adult level, education for political leaders in the prevention of war and genocide is a neglected and potentially valuable contribution to global security. During my fifteen-year presidency of the Carnegie foundation, educational innovations based on independent scholarship directly involved political and military leaders of the United States, Europe, Russia, and Africa. Independent experts illuminated knowledge and skill in preventing war and genocide. The dynamic interplay of these experts with distinguished governmental leaders was truly remarkable. Overall, it showed how research-based knowledge of human conflict and the paths to mutual accommodation can become a universal part of education, from childhood through adolescence to adult leaders of great stature, conveying both the facts of human diversity and our common humanity. All research-based knowledge about human conflict and the paths to mutual accommodation should be readily available to the highest levels of governments and of powerful institutions.

Preventing Youth Violence

One promising targeted strategy of wide applicability for preventing youth violence is the teaching of conflict resolution skills as part of health education or social studies in elementary and middle schools as well as high schools.[36] Research indicates that such programs can reduce violence; best results are achieved if this is embedded in a long-term, comprehensive program. Serious, in-depth conflict resolution training over extended periods is increasingly important in cultures saturated with violence—whether the origins are mainly political, religious, ethnic, or media-induced. The four main components of such programs are curriculum development, community-based prevention education, clinical treatment services, and media campaigns. Thus, they link the school with the community, drawing on diverse skills and resources that may be available.

High-risk youth in impoverished communities urgently need social support networks and life skills training, if they are to avoid alienation and hate. Both can be provided in schools and school-related health centers as well as in community organizations, including faith-based youth activities and sports programs. Communities must provide attractive, safe, growth-promoting settings for young adolescents during the out-of-school hours—times of high risk when parents are often not available to supervise their children. To the extent possible, it is useful to construct family-equivalent functions in poor, disadvantaged communities.

Overall, we can make substantial progress by deepening our understanding of human development, by increasing public understanding of our children's urgent needs and opportunities, and by strengthening our scientific and professional commitment to tackle these problems over a wide spectrum of constructive approaches. The success of such efforts would diminish not only the risk of school violence and community intergroup violence but also the susceptibility of youth to hate-promoting political demagogues and religious fanatics. Thus, the fundamental basis of violence prevention rests on substantial public understanding and support for basic ways of nurturing healthy child development while also providing specific antidotes to violence through targeted education and constructive social support systems that contrast with those of violence-oriented gangs and hateful ideologies.

Conclusion

The scientific and educational communities have a responsibility to conduct, analyze, and disseminate the results of solid interdisciplinary research on the causes of prejudice, intergroup hostility, hatred, and deadly conflict—and, even more important, the most constructive ways of dealing with those problems. These are subjects that demand pervasive inclusion at every level of education. Education for peaceful coexistence must begin with a reluctant, overdue acknowledgment of our ubiquitous human tendency toward violent intergroup conflict. We are all members of a potentially violent species with an inclination to form violent social organizations, and we must abandon the age-old practice of attributing malevolence primarily or solely to outside groups, however flattering that practice is to our self-esteem. Instead, we must recognize that the potentially violent species to which we all belong has equally strong benevolent and cooperative characteristics and has unused prosocial potential. The way we channel these contradictory traits at every level of education will make a critical difference in outcome. Entrenched in-group/out-group distinctions may once have served as an advantage in the survival of our species, but conditions have changed drastically since the era of the earliest humans. Modern technology has made us an interdependent, but jostling and heavily armed species, whose survival now depends on learning to live together as a single human in-group with a common identification in spite of diverse cultures and historical antagonisms. This must be one of the central pillars of modern education.

To diminish the likelihood of genocidal disasters, it is crucial to enhance orientations of caring, concern, empathy, social responsibility—ultimately, mutual aid within and between groups. To do so, we must prepare young people to live together in peaceful societies during their years of growth and development. Educating for the constructive resolution of life's ongoing conflicts through families, schools, universities, community and religious organizations, the public health system, and information technology is a fundamental challenge for the new century. Such education will have to transcend ethnic, religious, political, and national boundaries. It is time for people everywhere to seriously address prejudice and ethnocentrism as well as the greatly enhanced danger of these ancient orientations in the twenty-first century. Only by so doing can we nurture a common humanity that at last establishes decent, mutually beneficial human relations

Preventing Human Rights Abuses
Through International Justice

Basic Orientation

Successful conflict prevention strategies rest on three orientations, derived from a public health model that has saved countless lives. These orientations are (1) trained vigilance to detect and identify early signs of impending danger, (2) a comprehensive array of prepared and tested options to counteract it at its earliest stages of growth, and (3) the use of long-term, broad-based collaborative efforts to resolve its underlying causes. Prevention of deadly conflict starts with the recognition of the immense potential for danger of egregious, pervasive human rights violations, a common precursor of mass violence in various forms. Prevention is not simply smoothing over rough spots in intergroup or international relations—it requires creating a durable basis for peaceful conditions of living together.[1] Governments that abuse the rights of their own citizens are not likely to respect the rights of their weaker neighbors. In the long run, human rights abuses and the atrocities that typically follow them must be eliminated by promoting democracy, *equitable* market economies, and the strong civil institutions that protect human rights.

To this end, the Carnegie Commission on Preventing Deadly Conflict indicated steps the international community could take to prevent deadly conflict and thus protect human rights worldwide.[2] It called for strengthening international laws against deadly conflict and setting standards for deterring it, especially by integrating preventive reform efforts of international organizations and cooperating democracies and by establishing an early warning system that blocked human rights violations through the rule of law, democratization, and other human rights protection at the national level.

Democratic nations, working together, must monitor human rights both for their intrinsic value and for their value as early signals portending deadly conflict, up to and including genocide. Indeed, preventing human rights abuses consistently diminishes the risk that deadly conflicts will take place at all. With this in mind, President Clinton announced on December 10, 1998, the fiftieth anniversary of the signing of the Universal

Declaration of Human Rights (UDHR), that the United States would establish an early warning center on genocide to focus U.S. intelligence on uncovering potentially genocidal situations everywhere. Located appropriately in the intelligence and research division of the State Department, it was intended as part of a package aimed at strengthening the protection and promotion of human rights in general. Unfortunately, the fate of these promising efforts is now in doubt.

Recognition of early warning signals is futile without the preparation of a variety of policy options and contingency plans in response to them. Prominent among these responses is the development and implementation worldwide of clear concepts, orderly processes, and effective institutions to promote and protect human rights. No easy task! Yet it is too important to be neglected.

Establishing Human Rights After World War II and the Holocaust

Since genocide is the most appalling and egregious form of human rights abuse, and since the promotion and protection of human rights contribute substantially toward elimination of genocide, we have reason to be interested in the growth of the human rights movement, its progress, and its promise for the long term. Professor Louis Henkin of Columbia University, who has studied the human rights movement from its beginning more than fifty years ago, illustrated its remarkable growth, influence, and efficacy in a magisterial essay.[3]

International concern about the condition of human rights everywhere began early in World War II. Its normative and institutional foundations were established during the decades after the war and continue to the present day. These norms and institutions had furthered the human rights of billions of people by the end of the twentieth century. The universality of human rights became an ideology and is perhaps even the central ideology of the twenty-first century.

Owing to the remarkable leadership and perseverance of Eleanor Roosevelt, this principle received global recognition when the General Assembly of the United Nations approved the Universal Declaration of Human Rights on December 10, 1948, but it was prefigured in President Franklin Delano Roosevelt's "Four Freedoms" message to Congress on January 6, 1941. Speaking before the United States entered the war, President Roosevelt said: "In the future days, which we seek to make secure, we look forward to a world founded upon four essential human freedoms": freedom of speech, freedom of religion, freedom from want, and freedom from fear. Shortly thereafter Roosevelt and Churchill expressed, in the Atlantic Charter, their hope to see established "a peace that will afford assurance that all the men in all the lands may live out their lives in freedom free from fear and want." Thus they gave a prompt reinforcement to the core concept of universal human rights, that every human being has legitimate, recognized claims to specific freedoms and benefits by virtue of being human. They are not gifts owing to grace, love, charity, or compassion but rights that society has a moral, political, and legal obligation to respect and ensure.

The human rights concept grows out of earlier notions of "natural rights" in the writings of Enlightenment thinkers. An ideology of rights, crystallized in the Magna Carta, already existed in England through the common law. Eighteenth-century American and French revolutionaries articulated their own ideas and ideologies of human rights in the U.S. Declaration of Independence (as well as in earlier states' bills of rights) and in the French Declaration of the Rights of Man and of the Citizen. In the United States, the Constitution and Bill of Rights made an ideology of rights the heart of its "constitutionalism."[4]

This ideology suffered numerous vicissitudes and setbacks. In France, for example, the Reign of Terror swept it away; it was not restored until after World War II.

The United States essentially maintained the ideology of rights proclaimed in its Declaration of Independence—with the degrading exception of slavery. The U.S. Constitution guaranteed some individual rights, further elaborated in its first ten amendments, the Bill of Rights. Even so, slavery was maintained under the U.S. Constitution for three-quarters of a century, and racial equality and the equal protection of the laws were not established in writing until the Fourteenth Amendment was passed in 1868. Truly universal suffrage was only achieved through the Civil Rights Movement of the 1960s. And, of course, until 1954 the U.S. Constitution was interpreted to permit racial segregation. Thus, the United States, for all its democratic ideals, had to overcome many obstacles in reaching a comprehensive implementation of human rights. This is a lesson of worldwide significance: the achievement of human rights requires ceaseless vigilance and ongoing struggle.

In Europe, the most flagrant, widespread human rights abuses were perpetrated by Communists in the Soviet Union and by Fascists in Italy under Mussolini, in Spain under Franco, and, above all, in Nazi Germany.

From Constitutional Rights to International Human Rights

Henkin puts the post–World War II human rights movement in global perspective by observing that the "international human rights movement" is in reality a movement that affirms an international responsibility to promote, define, and safeguard national human rights, within national boundaries. It aims at setting acceptable and internationally accepted standards of human rights that all nations should meet and by which their rights records are judged—supported by legally binding commitments to respect those standards. The movement has generated international institutions that encourage and oversee the compliance of individual nations with these norms.[5]

In the foolish years before World War II, the concept of "sovereignty" permitted autocrats and tyrants to treat their own people as they wished without serious question from outside. In this myopic context, what Hitler did to Jews and other unwanted groups, including dissidents, was his own business. Movement from the perception of human rights as a purely domestic issue to a serious international concern began early in World War II. All of the nations at war with Germany adopted the Atlantic Charter as their statement of war aims. Even though cynics saw it only as a weapon in psychological warfare, many people in the midst of the war's anguish took it seriously, as "what we are fighting and dying for."

In 1944, representatives of the Allied powers met at Dumbarton Oaks in Washington, D.C., to plan the world order following their victory. The records of their conversations concerning the purpose of the UN, the new world organization they envisioned, include the phrase "to promote respect for human rights and fundamental freedoms." Henkin pointed out that the UN Charter specified promotion of respect for human rights as one of the purposes of the new organization and added that this was the first appearance of the phrase *human rights* in an important international treaty. Articles 55 and 56 committed all signatories to vigorous action in support of "universal respect for, and observance of, human rights and fundamental freedoms for all without distinction as to race, sex, language, or religion."[6]

The few words at Dumbarton Oaks led also to the Nuremberg trials and beyond, to the Convention on the Prevention and Punishment of the Crime of Genocide, the first international human rights treaty of the new world order. From Nuremberg one can see a direct line, with long delays and formidable obstacles (principally related to the Cold War), to the international tribunals established by the UN Security Council in the 1990s. The path from Dumbarton Oaks led to international commissions and committees and courts, to the UN High Commissioner for Human Rights, to a permanent International Criminal Court, and finally to the growing network of nongovernmental human rights organizations—such as Human Rights Watch and Amnesty International—all striving to induce compliance with international human rights standards throughout the world. Central to this history is the Universal Declaration of Human Rights.

The UN's Universal Declaration of Human Rights is widely considered one of the most important international instruments of the twentieth century, on a par with the United Nations Charter. Henkin pointed out its great accomplishments:

1. It helped transform the obsolete concept of "natural rights" into a prevailing political ideology, based on a universally attractive notion of *human dignity.*
2. It made the vague term *human rights* specific in a "triple decalogue" defining fundamental rights.
3. It "universalized" human rights by making their acceptance the heart of constitutionalism for all countries.
4. It "internationalized" human rights by redefining as an international concern matters that had once been the sole province of each sovereign nation. A "sturdy edifice of international norms and institutions" has been built on this new construction, and it has become a principal source of international law on human rights.[7]

Eighteen years of painstaking negotiation led to binding norms in two international covenants, the International Covenant on Civil and Political Rights (ICCPR) and the International Covenant on Economic, Social, and Cultural Rights (ICESCR). Many nations also adhered to conventions on further rights adopted and promoted by the United Nations, including the Genocide Convention, the Convention on the Elimination of All Forms of Racial Discrimination (CERD), the Convention on the Elimination of All Forms of Discrimination Against Women (CEDAW), the Convention Against Torture (CAT), and the Convention on the Rights of the Child (CRC).

The declaration contributed to historic developments in the second half of the twentieth century: the end of colonialism and the proliferation of independent states, the end of communism, and the establishment of democracy as the leading aspiration of the twenty-first century.

Some states have grouped into important regional systems for the protection of human rights. In Europe and in the Americas, regional organizations have developed strong human rights codes comparable to the Universal Declaration and the International Covenant on Civil and Political Rights, as well as institutions for enforcing them, such as national commissions and international courts that have enjoyed impressive success. Most notable is the experience of Europe, and so we now turn to its accomplishments.

The Growth of Human Rights in Europe

Shirley Williams, a great democratic leader in the UK and throughout Europe, has written a definitive account of European progress in human rights.[8] She pointed to the same Europe that contemptuously crushed human rights in the period of World War II as the architect less than a half-century later of the world's strongest institutional system for protecting them.[9]

The Nuremberg trials that began in February 1946 established the precedent that even rulers of sovereign states could be held responsible for acts condemned as criminal by international law. This was a preliminary step on the path to legally binding cooperation in enforcement.

In the immediate postwar years, Western Europe's dismal economic situation made it seem susceptible to communism, a looming threat to human rights. An economically strong Germany was an essential part of an economically strong Europe. But Germany's neighbors profoundly distrusted it. Alleviating their fears required continuing U.S. involvement in European security, first through the Marshall Plan and then the North Atlantic Treaty of 1949 that created NATO. All concerned were eager to move Germany toward democratic institutions and the rule of law within a closely integrated Europe. Williams reflected on the pleasant surprise of what came next. Germany's constitutional court not only became a stalwart protector of human rights; it also spurred the progress of human rights law throughout Europe by insisting that before the Federal Republic transferred its authority to the European Community, basic human rights had to be guaranteed under the protection of fully developed democratic institutions.

The Council of Europe was another essential actor in securing a democratic Western Europe. With the European Court of Human Rights at its heart, it enclosed all Western Europe in a community dedicated to maintaining human rights.[10]

Williams gave an institutional and historical overview of Europe's mechanisms for human rights promotion and protection, starting with efforts of the Council of Europe in maintaining and protecting human rights, as defined by the 1950 European Convention for the Protection of Human Rights and Fundamental Freedoms. She saw an evolution of human rights, from the 1957 Treaty of Rome, which established the European Economic Community, to the 1997 European Union Treaty of Amsterdam.[11]

The Council of Europe and the European Court of Human Rights

Thus, Europe has developed two independent legal entities that deal with human rights. The European Court of Human Rights in Strasbourg is attached to the Council of Europe, and the European Court of Justice (ECJ) in Luxembourg is associated with the European

Union. Although independent, these institutions influence each other. Taken together, they constitute a powerful bulwark for human rights.

The postwar years saw an outburst of creative thinking and institution building for human rights, democracy, economic cooperation, and nonviolent conflict resolution. Europe had learned bitter lessons. A key innovation was the European Convention on Human Rights (ECHR), still the core of the Council of Europe. It is a simple document, deeply influenced by the United Nations' 1948 UDHR but more binding—the ECHR is *enforceable* in the European Court of Human Rights. To become a member of the respected Council of Europe, a state must commit to upholding the ECHR. Each of the council's more than forty member states appoints one judge to the court and agrees to accept its judgments. The European Court of Human Rights and the Inter-American Court of Human Rights are the only international courts in the world that accept individual petitions against violations of human rights by the governments of member states. The foreign ministers of member states monitor compliance with the judgments of the European Court.

After the disintegration of the Soviet Union, the East and central European states asked to join the Council of Europe. The European Court of Human Rights became a full-time body in permanent session, with jurisdiction over the whole of Europe. Its institutions have substantially strengthened human rights and the promotion of democracy throughout Europe. This has been facilitated by educational programs for the countries of central and Eastern Europe in transition to pluralistic democracy. They include training of legal professionals and judicial institution building in more than twenty countries.

The Council of Europe was therefore in a favorable position to help the emerging democracies at the end of the Cold War. It had decades of experience in building democratic institutions with an independent judicial system and a deep commitment to norms and practices of human rights. Williams observed that it had no need for a radical change in its structure, which was originally designed to deal with new members. Membership in its community of established democracies has had a potent attraction that offers instant status and carries little negative baggage. Since decisions of its Court of Human Rights have equal authority over every member state, and every member state has the right to name one judge to the court, old and new members enjoy the same rank. Almost every state within the boundaries of Europe, from Turkey to Russia, has ratified the Convention for the Protection of Human Rights.[12]

The European Court of Justice, the highest court in the EC, is another bulwark of human rights. Its main responsibility is the interpretation of the treaties that established the EC and the EU. The court is part of the three "pillars" of the European Union delineated in the 1992 Maastricht Treaty. The first of these pillars is the European Community itself. The other two are intergovernmental: the second concerns foreign and security policy (sometimes referred to as CFSP, for "common foreign and security policy"), and the third is justice and home affairs (JHA).

The court quickly established two principles that have served as powerful weapons, allowed it to broaden its authority, and made a vital contribution to the continuing success of the European Community. The first, the principle of direct effect, makes EC law directly binding on member states, not indirectly through their national governments. The second, the principle of the supremacy of EC law, gives EC law precedence over national law, including national constitutional law, but this precedence is restricted to those areas over which the European Community has jurisdiction. The founders of the European Community could never have foreseen how much a fundamentally economic charter would contribute to advancing the human rights spelled out in other international agreements.[13]

Thus, the European Court of Justice has, along with political leaders, expanded the conception of the court's human rights responsibilities.

International human rights norms are now an integral part of European morality and policies. The EU learned from Bosnia, Rwanda, and Kosovo and is assuming a global role as a promoter of human rights and a significant source of financial aid for countries building democratic institutions. The Maastricht Treaty of 1992 linked EU external development policy to "developing and consolidating democracy and the rule of law, and to ... respecting human rights and fundamental freedoms." The EU, working closely with the OSCE and the Council of Europe, has supported programs of education about human and minority rights that extend far beyond the borders of Europe.

Europe has learned from a century or more of extensive human rights violations (colonial conquests, wars, genocides) that new norms, laws, and institutions must be firmly established, the benefits of international cooperation recognized, and a helping hand extended to peoples seeking freedom, human dignity, and nonviolent intergroup relations. The European experience offers an authentic basis for hope in all lands and provides a model for other regions to emulate, each in its own way, but consistent in adhering to basic human rights.

Other International Courts Pertinent to Genocide Prevention

Anne-Marie Slaughter, a distinguished professor of international law and dean of the Woodrow Wilson School of Princeton University, has studied ways in which courts cooperate internationally in vertical and horizontal networks to tackle practical problems.[14] An example of a vertical judicial network, operating globally, can be seen in the way the authority of the International Criminal Court is exerted. National courts have primary jurisdiction over cases involving genocide, war crimes, and crimes against humanity, but they are required to cede power to the ICC if they prove unable or unwilling to carry out a particular prosecution. Professor Slaughter argued that the international component of a vertical network can reinforce, support, and encourage improved performance in its corresponding domestic institutions. The purpose of the ICC is not to supplant, but to supplement national courts. One of its principal goals is prevention of a crisis by strengthening domestic officials and groups that support the rule of law. It wants national courts to try their own war criminals and perpetrators of crimes against humanity and genocide and offers inducements that range from supporting domestic groups that advocate trials to alerting recalcitrant domestic courts (and the criminal elites who intimidate them) that the international community is monitoring their actions.[15]

Richard Goldstone, a distinguished South African jurist, stated a strong preference for national trials, but he did recognize the importance of international tribunals in particular circumstances:

1. when the national government is unable or unwilling to prosecute
2. when there is a question of conflict of interest, because the national government is (or is perceived to be) in control of, complicit with, or sympathetic to the alleged criminals brought to trial
3. when the gravity of the crime gives the international or even the whole human community an interest in the case[16]

Goldstone cited the achievements of tribunals in the former Yugoslavia, Rwanda, and South Africa as evidence of the moral value of these international courts. The tribunals have widely publicized the norms of international humanitarian law. Their decisions represent the beginning of a new international jurisprudence that will have a beneficial influence on national law as well. They have brought into question many unfortunate lapses in humanitarian law, such as the distinction between international and intranational wars—a distinction so convenient to power-hungry dictators—and have started to move international humanitarian law from a state-centered approach toward a human rights–oriented approach. Their work, in Goldstone's opinion, takes "a positive step toward achieving international peace and justice."[17] The Security Council created the tribunals to disabuse would-be criminals of their illusions of impunity by alerting them that the international community will no longer simply stand by and wring their hands. The work of the international courts has given considerable strength to this message.

The state is not disappearing, but it is to some extent disaggregating. In today's increasingly globalized world, major problems tend to be no longer domestic but rather are domestic aspects of international problems. As national regulators, judges, and legislators encounter their foreign counterparts, they create horizontal networks that foster practical cooperation.

The Rome Statute that established an international criminal court foresaw direct working relationships between national and international tribunals. These relationships have already had significant unforeseen consequences, most notably when interactions between the European Court of Justice and domestic EU member-state courts triggered the establishment and operation of the EU legal system. More of such progress will certainly follow.[18]

When recommending the European Union's excellent work in this field as a stimulating model for other regions, one must take into account its distinctive advantages. EU member states have a shared history, area, and culture, as well as common political and economic beliefs, all of which have reinforced the EU's founders' original commitment to create "an ever closer union." An explicit mandate to cooperate, synchronize, and enforce EU and domestic laws encourages and justifies those activities in government networks within the EU. These networks also share a high degree of trust in each other, underpinned by the awareness that they will be partners for a long time.[19]

Other regional organizations will in due course be able to build similar strengths—but not quickly or easily. The importance of enduring relationships cannot be overemphasized—among nations as well as among individuals and families.

Following the Nuremberg trials, decades passed before national and international bodies began negotiations about establishing a permanent international court to punish war crimes, crimes against humanity, and genocide. One side in the negotiations, which included international law groups and NGOs—as well as Richard Goldstone and Louise Arbour, the ICC's original prosecutors—argued that an international court should be given primary jurisdiction over such crimes. The other side, which included the United States, some other states, and some national law groups, argued for "complementarity"—granting primary jurisdiction to national courts but giving the ICC "complementary" jurisdiction if the national courts were unwilling or unable to act.[20]

After much debate, the Rome Statute was adopted in 1999 and signed by 160 countries. It established a complementary jurisdictional structure, according to which the ICC may take jurisdiction of a case only after the ICC prosecutor judges a member state unable or unwilling to tackle it—and the prosecutor's decision is subject to review by an ICC panel. It will probably take years of litigation to establish precisely what "unable or unwilling" actually means in this context. Nonetheless, Slaughter argued, the ICC's relationship with national courts around the world is likely to make it a stronger and more effective institution. The relationship may well become a full partnership in which ICC decisions guide national courts in handling complex or newly emerging subjects in international criminal law.[21]

Slaughter envisioned a new model of states in which national government officials interact intensively with one another, adopt codes of best practices, and agree on cooperative solutions to shared problems.

Truth Commissions and the International Criminal Court

A valuable book by Priscilla Hayner of the International Center for Transitional Justice reviewed the experience of the many truth commissions that have sprung up in recent years as countries moved out of cruel regimes and sought better ones.[22] The inspiration for most of them is the South African Commission on Truth and Reconciliation, chaired by Archbishop Desmond Tutu. Hayner made a useful comparison between these commissions and the International Criminal Court. The agreement to create the International Criminal Court marks a major opportunity for international justice, even though its reach and its capacity for cases will be limited. The sort of crimes that fall under the ICC's jurisdiction make it likely that many of its cases will involve countries engaged in or emerging from civil wars or totalitarian rule—the same countries that are apt to have need of national truth commissions. This situation is bound to create sensitive legal and political issues about overlapping investigations, access to evidence, and the use and status of witnesses. Unfortunately, the long negotiations that established the International Court's jurisdiction produced little guidance on this matter. With the exception of national amnesties, its relationship to truth commissions was never directly addressed.[23]

The case of Bosnia illustrates the difficulties that can arise. The International Criminal Tribunal for the Former Yugoslavia, set up by the UN on an ad hoc basis to deal with extreme crimes in the former Yugoslavia, had been in progress for several years when in 1997 a truth commission was proposed for Bosnia. The international tribunal opposed it on the grounds that the truth commission's work would overlap with the tribunal's own investigations. Yet the tribunal in the distant Hague had received little attention from the press or public within Bosnia, and so had little educational or norm-setting effect. Supporters insisted that the truth commission was needed as a complementary body at the national level that would impartially explore and publicize the truth about severe human rights abuses. It would counteract the malicious, partisan, and conflicting versions of history taught within Bosnia by Serbs, Muslims, and Croats who wanted to perpetuate old animosities and incite renewal of violence. The truth commission would round out the work of the tribunal by helping to set the history of the conflict straight and seeking common ground for reconciliation of the three groups. It might even extend the tribunal's reach by expanding the information available to it.

The international tribunal's president and prosecutors objected that (1) a truth commission could subvert the tribunal's work by allowing individuals to ignore their obligations to the tribunal because they agreed to cooperate with the commission; (2) the public might make unreasonable demands for prosecutions because it could not distinguish the commission's findings of political responsibility from those of criminal responsibility; (3) the commission, with lower standards of evidence, might reach conclusions contrary to those of the tribunal; (4) the commission might "contaminate" evidence, especially through repeated interviewing of witnesses; and (5) the commission would be superfluous, since the tribunal was already providing historical truth.[24]

Although all of these are meaningful concerns, independent legal scholars have by and large concluded that there would be room for both an international criminal tribunal and a commission on truth and reconciliation in many situations. Taken together, they offer multiple opportunities for public understanding, for widespread efforts to learn from harsh experience, and even for hostile groups to work toward reconciliation. Attempts to coordinate such efforts might be complex and difficult, but so far, limited experience indicates that they have provided precedents of proven value and will offer further promise if carefully worked out in the decades to come. A valuable example of assistance in these matters is the International Center for Transitional Justice, a nongovernmental organization that makes the world's experiences in truth and reconciliation efforts available to many struggling countries and may in time be one source of help in building viable democracies.

Both truth commissions and courts have valuable educational functions. The presidentially appointed truth commission in Nigeria illustrates the formidable impact of public hearings. For a full year the Nigerian public was riveted to the commission's televised sessions. They were shown during the day, then repeated at night on several channels and played live on many radio stations. The appearance of many persons involved in past abuses provided a wide understanding of events that had taken place under military rule.

The exceedingly thoughtful, constructive work of the South African commission led by Archbishop Desmond Tutu was so compelling that it stimulated Peru, East Timor, and Sierra Leone to hold their own public hearings. A *New York Times* essay by Dennis Ross, former U.S. envoy to the Middle East in the Clinton administration, illustrated the commission's continuing importance as an example of an effective means not only toward national unification but also toward peace building.[25] Writing in 2005—just before Hamas's electoral victory—Ross maintained that the Palestinian leader, Mahmoud Abbas, should use South Africa's experience both to persuade his people that violence against Israel would not achieve an independent Palestinian state and to provide valuable inspiration for the culture of peace he was working for. Ross recognized that the African National Congress was not without shortcomings, but recommended it to the Palestinian leadership as an urgently needed, credible, and effective role model for assuming responsibility and rejecting violence in the pursuit of national liberation and a government based in decency.

There is a general point here—peer learning. Countries or groups in conflict can learn from others who have successfully come through similar experiences. Indeed, international organizations such as the EU and the UN can efficiently and clearly bring the world's experience to the attention of those caught up in a dangerous situation.

Priscilla Hayner, in a thoughtful afterword to the forthcoming Japanese edition of her book, noted the growing worldwide appeal of official truth commissions, which she admitted are "sometimes difficult but, overall, positive" in effect.[26] Since 2001, when *Unspeakable Truths* first appeared, at least thirteen new truth commissions—five of them large-scale endeavors—have been set up in Africa, Latin America, and Asia. Part of their appeal seems owing to the wide range of uses and forms to which a nonjudicial, nationwide, and broadly participatory investigation can be put, an investigation that is not limited to identifying criminals but also explores both the causes of the atrocities it was created to address and their implications for the future. The newer truth commissions are more likely than their predecessors to hold public hearings; this is vitally important in educating the public on the norms of government behavior and on their own (and others') rights. They tend to have stronger powers of investigation and use increasingly inventive approaches to investigation, such as community profiles, graveyard censuses, and more systematic and accurate surveys of crimes and their victims. Their investigations also tend to cover a longer period of time—Morocco's commission covered forty-four years. Their final reports might fill ten volumes, but their conclusions also appear in widely available (sometimes free) summaries, educational videos, and newspaper supplements—Sierra Leone issued a summarized report intended for children. Strong public involvement in these commissions is evident in the fact that political leaders have felt compelled to appear voluntarily before them, even when the commission had no power to force them to do so, and even when they themselves had been accused of abuses.

The growth of truth commissions shows an increased appreciation of the value of a holistic approach to reestablishing justice in a society after a history of atrocities or governmental repression and abuse.[27] Lack of resources alone would ensure that a policy limited to prosecution of crimes would leave many perpetrators unpunished and many victims unsatisfied. Both judicial and nonjudicial initiatives should be used to meet the many needs of a transitional society, and it is best to plan and design these multiple initiatives—truth-seeking programs, targeted prosecutions, reparations, legal reforms, and reconciliation programs—to complement and strengthen each other.

The most successful commissions observe and build on the experiences of others, tailoring them to meet the particular needs and history of their own country. One aspect of the truth commission in Timor-Leste (formerly East Timor) was purposely designed to reintegrate minor perpetrators into their communities through a process based on traditional local methods. Those guilty of crimes were required to make a formal apology, perform community service, or offer a symbolic payment in reparation before they were accepted once more as full members of the community. A public reconciliation ceremony followed. This might be seen as an improvement over the South African process, where offenders gained amnesty after no more than complete confession.

Human Rights: Pathway to International Cooperation for Preventing Genocide

There is a strong link between virulent human rights abuses and the instigation of deadly conflict—war or genocide or both. Conversely, reliable safeguards for human rights go a long way toward preventing mass violence.[28] When, in the post–World War II period, Eleanor Roosevelt and her valiant international collaborators set in motion the human rights movement, very few "sophisticated" observers expected a pervasive worldwide movement for human rights to follow. Yet that is what happened, in response to a deeply felt human need for decency. Human rights have increasingly transcended the boundaries of individual countries and become a legitimate domain of politics and human relations, not only for nation-states but also for international and regional organizations, both governmental and nongovernmental.

Human rights are a way to deal with a person's relation to public authority, with other persons, and, ultimately, with one's place in humanity.[29] They place a fundamental restraint on governments. The political struggle to implement these values continues, but we have gone a long way in half a century—indeed, beyond any previous historical achievement in human relations and international relationships. Human rights instruments provide guidance for good governance. When states use this guidance, as we have seen recently in Europe, they reduce grievances and, with them, the risk of violence. The Human Rights Covenants essentially promote well-functioning democracies. Recent increases in international communication and travel have graphically illuminated standards of decency and augmented human rights demands all over the world. It is no longer pardonable or easy for tyrants, petty or grand, to commit atrocities against their own people by hiding behind the shield of national sovereignty and domestic jurisdiction. It is still possible to do, as we see in Darfur, but most of the world is turning away from such atrocities.

The UN has been one vehicle for directing this movement, despite its many limitations. From 1945 to 1967 UN human rights activities consisted mainly of setting standards—i.e., producing the declarations and treaties that specified the human rights content of the UN Charter. Beyond 1967, the UN has consistently moved from promotion to protection of human rights, with investigation of states' human rights records, scrutiny of problems such as torture or disappeared persons, and a variety of technical assistance to states that want to improve their human rights behavior—e.g., help in incorporating standards into national constitutions, laws, and bills of rights; in setting up national human rights commissions; in training judges, lawyers, police officers, prison personnel, and armed forces; and in establishing parliamentary committees. Such constructive assistance builds national rules and mechanisms to protect and enforce human rights as well as national constituencies to press the case consistently, especially through vigorous nongovernmental organizations.

The UN's role has been difficult and variable, chiefly because so many of its members have been dictatorships. The UN has been successful on two fronts. It has been instrumental in educating the international community in human rights and in using human rights as an indicator for granting or withholding legitimacy to specific parties. Taken together, these accomplishments have had a significant long-term effect, despite the biases of many member states. The UN has raised aspirations and stimulated political groups, NGOs, and educators worldwide.

The growth and strength of human rights beliefs, norms, processes, and institutions have largely been a surprise throughout the world. One remarkable achievement of the human rights movement that occurred in a Cold War context has become known as the Helsinki Process. It began in 1973—at the instigation of the then Soviet Union—with the establishment of the Conference on Security and Cooperation in Europe (CSCE). The Soviet leadership wanted to secure an agreement that would in essence legitimize its hegemony in Eastern Europe. To get this, they had to agree to human rights provisions that ultimately contributed to the dissolution of the Soviet empire as well as its ideological rationalizations.

The first major agreement was the Helsinki Final Act, signed by CSCE heads of state in 1975. In this document, for the first time, respect for human rights and fundamental freedoms was recognized as a basic principle for regulating relations between states. As usual, there was much ambivalence about this step—on both sides of the Iron Curtain. But over time it had a contagious effect, especially as courageous dissidents fought for its implementation. Governmental leadership also became important as exemplified most vividly by Presidents Gerald Ford, Jimmy Carter, Ronald Reagan, and Mikhail Gorbachev.

The Helsinki Process fulfilled its promise as it moved beyond anti-Soviet rhetoric to principles and practices for the protection of human rights throughout Europe, east and west. A variety of vigorous, democratic, converging nongovernmental organizations arose in the post-Helsinki context. This movement has become a constructive part of the new European system for human rights and democracy, transformed that historically bloody continent, and proved a stimulating model for other continents as well. Thus, the Helsinki Process was a significant part of the worldwide movement toward an international regime for human rights and democracy that points in the direction of a regime for preventing genocide.

The Perspective of a Presidential Human Rights Leader

Jimmy Carter can be singled out as a presidential human rights leader.[30] He has pointed out that one of the sources of rising human rights awareness after World War II was the decolonization movement in Asia and Africa, accompanied by economic and political development.[31] These campaigns for independence and equal rights had a cross-pollinating character: Gandhi profoundly influenced Dr. King's thought, and he in turn inspired Nelson Mandela and Tibet's Dalai Lama.[32]

Technological advances accelerated the demand for fundamental rights: first radio and film, then television, and today the Internet give a clear picture of the advantages of a free life. Improvements in medicine and public health have provided better nutrition, sanitation, and basic health care and with this the energy and hope to strive for basic rights. NGOs, such as the Carter Center, have helped developing nations to take advantage of these opportunities.

Sadly, another traditional boost to the spread of human rights has been recently impaired: that is, U.S. leadership in promoting human rights around the world.[33] President Carter wrote that he was inspired by Harry Truman's and Lyndon Johnson's dedication to civil rights, and outlined the steps his own administration took to promote human rights (although he was too modest to point out that he was the first president to make that issue an explicit high priority in foreign policy). He argued against shortsightedly using U.S. support of human rights only as a propaganda weapon and stressed the importance of urging our sometimes autocratic allies to move toward higher standards.[34]

Because of the position of the United States as the greatest power on the globe and because of Carter's experience as president, his recommendations for future action are directed only to the United States, but they apply equally to other affluent developed nations (and we see them occurring in the EU). They include devoting resources to explore and develop what works in human rights promotion.[35] He gave specific mention to supporting institutions such as the ICC and covenants such as the Convention on the Rights of the Child, agreements to ban land mines, and the International Covenant on Social and Cultural Rights. About the last, he remarked that human rights include not only traditional political and civil rights but also the fundamental rights of access to food, shelter, medical care, and education, as well as physical security.[36]

The United States, and other influential nations as well, can exert strong pressure for constructive change and give hope to the oppressed when they back treaties and institutions that support the universal nature of human rights and encourage their enforcement. They must also take action, using their material and technical resources to reduce poverty and disproportionate economic inequity in less fortunate states. This will be done best by encouraging and cooperating with both governmental and nongovernmental organizations.

President Carter concluded with a fervent plea to "keep the faith in human action,"[37] reminding us that it is necessary, but not sufficient, to "think globally, act locally." Leaders of every kind—from teachers and community leaders to scientists and elected officials—must also "think globally" by helping to work out effective and responsible public action and policy. Activists everywhere can exemplify and encourage nonviolent resistance to oppression wherever it is found.

Can Institutions of International Justice Help to Prevent Genocide?

Why not? They make it less likely that mass murderers can act with impunity behind the shield of sovereignty. They have an important role in public education by developing and communicating compelling norms of decent human relations at all levels: intranational, intergroup, and international. They probably influence for the better those populations susceptible to hateful demagogues. Still, they are no panacea. Would a fanatic like Hitler be inhibited by the threat of an international criminal court at the end of his road? Probably not. But conditions would be less conducive to his virulent, destructive prejudices and actions, and the inhibiting influences on his supporters might well make a difference. Opposition to tyranny takes many paths—not least democratic rule of law, nationally and/or internationally. As in all genocide prevention, the necessary metric for efficacy is decades or generations. But surely the time has come to provide multiple obstacles to mass murder and to build a cumulative record of increasing knowledge and skill to prevent atrocity behavior in whatever ugly form it may take. People and societies have a decent, pragmatic, problem-solving aspect that may yet build concepts, processes, and institutions that help us make the best of our common humanity.

CHAPTER 12

Restraints on Weaponry

The Worst and Growing Dangers

Genocide is not like a tsunami that comes and goes, beyond our power to influence. The increasingly destructive capacities and hateful orientations of humanity are omnipresent, yet preventable. How we cope with this problem will have a profound bearing on humanity—indeed on human survival altogether.

"Small arms" and "light weapons" now cover the world wall to wall. This collective euphemism includes highly lethal machine-guns, mortars, automatic rifles, and rocket launchers. They killed millions in the 1990s, yet they are not classified as weapons of mass destruction (WMD). The ubiquitous presence and use of these weapons is enabled by their provision by "responsible" vendors. At most recent count, up to 80 percent of such arms were purchased from a handful of states, led by the United States, Russia, the UK, Germany, France, and China.[1] At the apex of the "food chain" of lethality, biological, chemical, and above all nuclear weapons have almost unimaginable killing power. These weapons have an intoxicating effect on political demagogues, religious fanatics, and ethnic haters, and the breakdown of Cold War restraints has led to a recent and exceedingly dangerous movement toward proliferation of nuclear weapons.

Global Restraints on Lethal Weapons:
Good Ideas and Mediocre Implementation

As we construct pillars of prevention of violence—the core message of this book—there is the urgent need to address squarely and strategically the unique risk posed by the most dangerous instruments of war—nuclear, chemical, and biological weapons. To this greatest threat from weapons of mass destruction great contemporary thinkers have, fortunately, applied themselves.

In 2006 an important international commission chaired by Hans Blix published a valuable report: "Weapons of Terror: Freeing the World of Nuclear, Biological and

Chemical Arms."[2] It largely coincides with the work of Perry, Nunn, Drell, and Allison, discussed below.

Professor William Perry of Stanford, former U.S. secretary of defense and a pioneer in restraining weapons of mass destruction, pointed out that some programs have been remarkably successful in reducing the risk of nuclear proliferation and terrorism.[3] Primary among these is the Nunn-Lugar initiative for cooperative threat reduction, which provided financial and technical assistance from 1991 onward.

When the Soviet Union collapsed, the security of its nuclear arsenal was at great risk. In a "unilateral-reciprocal initiative" in 1991, President George H. W. Bush declared that the United States intended to withdraw all its tactical nuclear weapons around the world and called on Russian president Gorbachev to do the same. Gorbachev agreed to meet the challenge, and before June 1992 all known Russian tactical nuclear weapons had been stored securely.[4] Before the two leaders could sign a treaty with binding verification they were both out of office. This has left serious problems in recent years.

The Nunn-Lugar initiative has already been responsible for the dismantling of more than 5,000 nuclear warheads and the complete elimination of nuclear weapons in the Ukraine, Kazakhstan, and Belarus. More than 6,500 Russian strategic nuclear warheads have been secured, the country's first chemical weapons disposal site is already at work, and three others are being built![5] Nunn-Lugar has flourished for a decade and a half despite obstacles in the United States and Russia. Programs to immobilize or commercialize leftover Soviet plutonium and weapons-grade uranium, material that was once intended for Soviet bombs, are now meeting the needs of peaceful power reactors producing energy. Perry proposed strengthening these proven programs, especially by extending the fruitful Nunn-Lugar efforts to tactical nuclear weapons (which are particularly dangerous in the context of terrorism because they are readily portable, more affordable, and more easily guided to specific, short-range targets) and by funding efforts to immobilize plutonium.

Former U.S. senator Sam Nunn, a great leader in minimizing the nuclear danger, has expressed deep concern over the likelihood that terrorists will acquire nuclear, biological, and chemical weapons.[6] Preventing this threat must become a central organizing principle of international security in the twenty-first century, because a truly global threat demands global cooperation. In particular, it is a threat that demands the collaborative leadership of both the world's nuclear superpowers, the United States and Russia, harnessing a coalition of influential nations to spearhead a global nonproliferation effort. They cannot rapidly reduce the hatred and ruthlessness of terrorists, but they can and must sharply reduce terrorists' access to weapons of mass destruction.

Since acquiring nuclear weapons and materials is the first, and by far the hardest, step terrorists must take in gaining nuclear capability—and every step that follows becomes progressively easier—the cheapest and most effective defense is to secure nuclear weapons and fissile materials against theft or sale everywhere they are stored. Russia and the United States must take the lead in forming a broad alliance of nations that will cooperate in identifying, accounting for, and rigorously safeguarding all these stocks.

Some important steps to accomplish this urgent responsibility include

1. Begin at home. Both the United States and Russia must identify, record, and secure the nuclear weapons and material in their own territories, with mutual guarantees

and reciprocal monitoring that is meaningful and credible to the rest of the world. This means prompt action to downgrade highly enriched nuclear materials for peaceful use and to consolidate dangerous materials in fewer, safer sites. Leaders in both countries should appoint a high-level official exclusively devoted to and responsible for this concern, able to integrate efforts across agencies in each government.

2. The United States and Russia must also obtain a precise reporting and inventory of the other's tactical nuclear weapons, supported by ample safeguards and reciprocal monitoring. Tactical nuclear weapons have smaller yields that vary from 0.1 kiloton to higher than the bombs that devastated Hiroshima and Nagasaki (10–15 kilotons), and even the low-yield weapons would cause far greater damage than the September 11, 2001, attack on the World Trade Center.[8] Arms control treaties do not include tactical nuclear weapons—a terrible error. The United States and Russia must overcome their traditional suspicion—in their own self-interest—and improve global security by putting all nuclear weapons under very close guard with the most effective protections.

3. The United States and Russia should create and lead a global coalition against catastrophic terrorism. It should as a first order of business include all the "declared" nuclear powers—certainly Russia and the United States. Then it should quickly expand to cover the globe, since no single nation (or pair of nations) can manage it alone—the pervasiveness and the very nature of the problem require a solution based on worldwide cooperation. The coalition's work would include

   • establishing accepted standards and cooperative programs for inventory, downgrading/dismantling, and secure storage of nuclear weapons and material;
   • strengthening border and export controls;
   • training and maintaining international response teams to prevent and deal with nuclear crises, including terrorism;
   • creating standards and protocols to control access to dangerous biological materials necessary for scientific research and to keep them out of terrorist (or other dangerous) hands;
   • restricting the spread of knowledge about how to construct biological weapons; and
   • preventing bioterrorism and, when prevention is impossible, mitigating its effects.[7]

U.S.-Russian cooperation and collaboration is, therefore, indispensable to success of nonproliferation. But for this to happen and prosper, there must be a greater mutual trust than has hitherto been the case. In a 2005 NATO report on weapons of mass destruction, rapporteur Pierre Claude Nolin chronicled the real progress made in reducing and protecting Russia's WMD arsenal but concluded that much still needed to be done in a sustained effort.[9] Russia's unwillingness to permit U.S. inspection of its nuclear and biological weapon storage sites seriously inhibits efforts to improve the security of weapons-grade nuclear material and biological pathogens from terrorists and rogue states. Nolin attributed some of that unwillingness to a continuing Cold War mind-set in which there is a reciprocal suspicion and reluctance on the part of the United States in affording Russian access.

U.S. inspection teams have not been allowed to evaluate the security at Russian military sites where plutonium and weapons-grade uranium are kept. Only half of the estimated 185 tons of plutonium and 1,100 tons of weapons-grade uranium stored in Russia have received upgraded security.[10] Defense analysts caution that terrorists and criminal groups could build a nuclear bomb out of as little as 17 pounds of plutonium or 55 pounds of weapons-grade uranium—and those groups are eager to get such material.

Nor have Russian authorities been willing to let U.S. inspectors assess security at many of the research laboratories used in the former Soviet Union's biological weapons program. At its peak, the program employed more than 60,000 workers at fifty-five sites and produced weapons that spread diseases such as anthrax, smallpox, brucellosis, and many others. The very lack of security at many of these sites makes Russians concerned that U.S. inspections could produce information leaks that might eventually alert terrorists to those locations, a security expert at a Moscow think tank reported—even as he added that Russian authorities had not done enough to secure biological sites.[11] Indeed, the Russian biological buildup during the Cold War was vast in scope, far beyond any conceivable military value and enough to do unimaginable damage. The United States, Russia, and other members of the Group of Eight (G8) have done a better job in getting rid of Russia's 40,000 metric tons of chemical weapons.

Vladimir Dvorkin, a nuclear security expert at the Russian Academy of Sciences' Center for International Security, recommended that both sides exchange data on the number and whereabouts of their tactical nuclear weapons.[12]

Altogether, the backsliding in recent years by Russia and the United States has made this problem harder. Pressure from the EU would be helpful in fostering more cooperative behavior. Other expert views may be cited in arguing the unique danger posed by weapons of mass destruction—and their unprecedented relevance to genocide as proliferation makes them available to hateful, fanatical leaders.

In 2005, former president Jimmy Carter made reasonable proposals for saving nonproliferation:

- NATO needs to deemphasize the role of its nuclear weapons and consider an end to their deployment in Western Europe. Despite its eastward expansion, NATO is keeping the same stockpiles and policies as when the Iron Curtain divided the continent.
- The comprehensive test ban treaty should be honored, but the United States is moving in the opposite direction.
- The United States should support a fissile materials treaty to prevent the creation and transport of highly enriched uranium and plutonium.
- Curtail U.S. development of the infeasible missile defense shield, which is wasting huge resources while breaking our commitment to the Anti-Ballistic Missile Treaty without a working substitute.
- Act on nuclear proliferation in the Middle East, an increasing source of danger in that region. Iran has repeatedly hidden its intentions to enrich uranium while claiming that its nuclear program is for peaceful purposes only. This explanation

has been given before, by India, Pakistan and North Korea, and has led to weapons programs in all three states.[13]

Professor Graham Allison of Harvard synthesized the evidence on risks of nuclear terrorism in an important recent book.[14] He gave a vividly accurate account of these problems, which can no longer be separated from genocide. Although Allison focused on the United States, the implications are worldwide.

Shortly after September 11, 2001, CIA officials startled the White House with an unconfirmed report that Al-Qaeda terrorists had stolen a 10-kiloton nuclear bomb from a Russian storage facility, shipped it into New York City, and were preparing to use it. This rumor was not true, but neither was it fanciful, given that:

- Russia's nuclear stockpiles hold large quantities of Cold War–era 10-kiloton weapons;
- Custody of the stockpiles is notoriously and alarmingly inadequate;
- Powerful nuclear weapons can be made small enough to carry easily and inconspicuously;
- U.S. borders are wide and porous—a White House humorist noted that terrorists might hide a small bomb in one of the packages of marijuana regularly shipped into major U.S. cities;[15]
- Deterrent threats of retaliation in kind would be next to impossible to execute, since an attack might originate in a failing state such as Afghanistan—or in a terrorist cell in England, France, Germany, or the Netherlands;
- Preventive negotiation would be equally impossible, even if agreement about terms was imaginable.

Compounding the peril is the fact that the aspiration to acquire weapons of mass destruction is not confined to states but is shared by nonstate actors. We know that Osama bin Laden has been seeking to buy nuclear weapons since at least 1992, when he approached South Africa, and that Al-Qaeda's success on September 11 leaves that group looking for an even more stunning follow-up to maintain its momentum in the public mind.

It is vital for the world to grasp the enormity of the damage. What would happen if a 10-kiloton bomb exploded in a metropolitan area? Within one-third of a mile of the blast, most structures would be totally destroyed, and the fatality rate would be 100 percent. Within three-quarters of a mile, serious damage to buildings would occur, along with the danger of a firestorm. Anyone directly exposed to the blast would suffer fatal radiation doses. Uncontrollable fires would consume a 1-mile area, and accompanying winds would spread radiation. The long-term damage to survivors of the radiation, as studies of Hiroshima victims illustrate, is substantial.

Nuclear theft has been documented both in the United States and in Russia: Allison asserted that more than twenty nuclear weapons could be built from the amount of nuclear material lost in Russia since the Soviet Union disintegrated.[16] In fact, admitted Russian losses probably represent only a small portion of the actual total; security about acknowledgment of theft might be stronger than the security of the weapons themselves. In 1997, for example, the well-respected Russian general Alexander Lebed let slip that eighty-four nuclear "suitcase" weapons had gone missing, then recanted and denied that Russia had ever produced such weapons, adding that if it had, all of them were completely secure, as was all of Russia's nuclear arsenal.[17] His belated denial flew in the face of many known facts and was very likely due to heavy pressure put on him by high Russian authorities.

Sources of nuclear materials exist outside the former Soviet countries. Pakistan today has about fifty ready-made nuclear weapons,[18] the materials and the skill to produce fifty more, a program that accelerated in 2006–2007, and, in the case of some of its knowledgeable citizens, sympathetic feelings toward the aspirations of radical coreligionists with violent orientations. North Korea, if less inclined to Muslim fundamentalism, has consistently been ready to sell its knowledge and materials for badly needed cash. And, to keep the United States from feeling too smug about the custody of its own stockpiles, Allison recounted security exercises in 1997 and 1998 in which members of U.S. Special Forces who simulated "terrorists" successfully outwitted guards and stole fissile materials from the Los Alamos National Laboratory in New Mexico and the Rocky Flats Nuclear Laboratory in Colorado.[19] Protection of America's 2 million pounds of highly enriched uranium and plutonium has improved little since then.

In 2003 U.S. intelligence agents inspected packages in a Malaysian cargo ship headed for Libya. The packages contained a large number of centrifuge parts for enriching uranium, sold by Pakistan's Dr. A. Q. Khan to Libya's Muammar el-Qaddafi.[20] What caused Qaddafi to shift direction and renounce the use of nuclear weapons at the end of 2003? Are there lessons for dealing with other dangerous states? Qaddafi was affected by the defeat and capture of Saddam Hussein, and he feared being next. But even in the 1990s Qaddafi had begun to distance himself from terrorism, owing in large part to the effects of two types of sanction: first, unilateral sanctions by the United States; then, after the Lockerbie bombing in 1998, worldwide sanctions by the UN. Foreign investment stopped, and Libya's economy waned, with oil production falling to less than half its peak and unemployment rising to 30 percent of the population, which had a high proportion of alienated, educated young men. When U.S. negotiators offered Qaddafi the opportunity for improved relations without demanding regime change, he agreed. Although the U.S. military threat was necessary to keep Qaddafi from backsliding—as was also the case with the 2003 shipment from Khan—the international sanctions helped greatly in making Libya a "success story."[21]

Allison concluded with three "nos": no loose nukes; no new nascent nukes; no new nuclear states.[22] Difficult as this may be to achieve, the putatively civilized world had better take these well-founded warnings seriously. The full strength of international diplomacy, including, if necessary, coercive diplomacy, should be brought to bear in an intensive, sustained effort. The stakes certainly involve mass destruction, genocide, and even human survival. If there were to be worldwide public concern over such immense stakes, international cooperation could become within reach. Ignorance, denial, and wishful thinking stand in the way.

Nuclear Arms Race in Asia: 2006

In a *New York Times* article of July 31, 2006, distinguished columnist Bob Herbert wrote about "A World Gone Mad."[23] He took note of the recent development in Pakistan, which he believed could become a much greater catastrophe than the war in Iraq and the war between Israel and its neighbors. He pointed out that Pakistan was making rapid progress on a powerful new plutonium reactor that would have the capacity to produce enough fuel for manufacturing forty to fifty nuclear weapons per year. This is happening at the same time that the Bush administration is making a large deal with India that will greatly enhance India's bomb-making capacity, probably to about fifty per year. This puts South Asia into a nuclear arms race that is reminiscent of the Cold War. Pakistan, for all its virtues, has a shaky government that harbors Al-Qaeda in at least one part of the country. Moreover, it is the home of the physicist A. Q. Khan, who is a master of nuclear proliferation, having been instrumental not only in designing Pakistan's nuclear weapons but also in providing crucial materials and expertise to Iran and North Korea, among others. Herbert compared the uncontrolled pursuit of ever more nuclear weapons by increasingly irresponsible owners to driving drunk at accelerating speeds and warned that China will certainly feel obliged to keep up with India and Pakistan.[24] In this context, he noted the wisdom of John F. Kennedy, who looked into the nuclear abyss during the Cuban missile crisis and came out of it with a powerful sense of our common humanity that far transcends our political or religious differences.

One dangerous possibility is that the military regime governing Pakistan will not be replaced by a democracy but by an Islamic militant regime. Such a regime, if controlled by a fanatical dictator, would be dangerous in many ways. It might decide to settle the Kashmir dispute "once and for all" by a nuclear attack on India. This might be called "politicide." By whatever name, it could have ramifications beyond our imagination. Such a regime might well provide nuclear weapons to terrorist groups who would undertake a more conventional genocide. In either case, the point is clear: the genocide problem must take into account the contemporary situation of weapons and their owners.

This problem of the nuclear arms race in Asia was addressed in October 2005 by Professor Ashton Carter of Harvard University, who is codirector with Professor William Perry of Stanford University of the Preventive Defense Program. He pointed out that, in order to make a nuclear weapon, it is necessary to have plutonium or highly enriched uranium. They do not occur in nature, and they are difficult to make. So far, it has required the resources of an established government to produce such materials, and, therefore, terrorists must get nuclear materials from a government. We have already considered this matter in relation to Russia and the United States.

Carter focuses on the singular problem of North Korea, with which he has been deeply involved diplomatically for some years along with Perry. Their efforts were put into a deep freeze during the first five years of this century, however. And so we have now reached a position in which it is likely that North Korea has made at least several nuclear weapons and is in the process of making more. One very dangerous aspect of this development is that North Korea has been happy to sell other advanced weaponry to anyone with the money to make the purchase. So far as we know, this would include terrorists. Another danger is that a North Korea heavily armed with nuclear weapons would likely stimulate other countries in the region to go the same route in order to protect themselves from a notoriously irresponsible regime. This might well mean that Japan, Taiwan, South Korea, and others in Asia would undertake a build-up of nuclear weapons.

The 2007 revival of serious negotiations with North Korea offers hope that this danger will diminish. A basic principle here, emphasized by the Carnegie Commission, is that direct negotiations with dangerous adversaries are essential—not cutting off communication, even with pariahs.

This grave situation of the arms race in Asia is related to other problems we have discussed. For example, if Iran does not make as rapid progress as it evidently desires for its nuclear arsenal, then it could probably buy weapons from North Korea or obtain them in some way from Pakistan through a derivative of the A. Q. Khan network. From time to time, Islamic radical militants have spoken about a "Muslim bomb" that would be sanctified in a religious way against Sunnis in Iraq or elsewhere, Hindus in Kashmir, Jews in Israel, or all manner of infidels in Europe and the United States. In fact, the growing Asian problem above all highlights the nature of the worldwide danger, including the possibilities of multiple genocides motivated by religious and/or political hatreds. If any danger could motivate the international community to come together in the most serious, sustained way to cooperate for survival, I wonder what it could be.

Rise of Terrorism: The Specter of WMD and Instant Genocide

"When the Shiites Rise," an important article by Professor Vali Nasr in the July–August 2006 issue of *Foreign Affairs*, is augmented by his book, *The Shia Revival*.[25] He delineated in detail the profound changes occurring in the Middle East around the growing influence and power of the Shiites, especially in relation to Iran. The fall of Saddam gave many Iraqis opportunities to redress past injustices, especially in what they perceived as serious maldistribution of power among the country's main communities. Thus, Iraq's Shiite majority now feels empowered and has become part of a broad Shiite revival that is likely to upset the sectarian balance of the region for years to come.

Shiites have much in common, especially a coherent religious view. Historically, they split off from the Sunnis in the seventh century over a fundamental difference about the prophet Muhammad's legitimate successors. Over the intervening centuries they have formulated a distinct view of Islamic laws and practices. Now, the great size of their population and Iran's technical sophistication give them much potential power. They constitute about 90 percent of Iranians and a large proportion in other countries in the Gulf region as well as in Pakistan. Altogether they amount to about 140 million people globally. Even though they are only 10 percent of the world's Muslims, they are an important minority, since most of the Shiites have long felt deprived and are now pressing hard for higher status and more political power.[26]

This Shiite emergence has produced a violent Sunni backlash that has spread far beyond Iraq's borders. There is a distinct possibility of a broad struggle for power between these two groups that could become so intense and violent as to threaten the stability of the entire region. The year 2006 was one of extreme violence between Sunnis and Shiites in Iraq. The depth of hatred is extraordinary.

King Abdullah of Jordan speaks of a new Shiite Crescent covering a very broad swath of the Middle East and cutting through traditionally Sunni-dominated areas. Thus a variety of governments and perhaps international organizations will seek ways to meet

Shiite demands insofar as feasible while easing Sunni anger and fear. This is likely to be one of the central issues of the Middle East for years to come.

If diplomatic tasks of that sort are undertaken, they will have to seriously engage Iran. It not only has the world's largest Shiite population, a huge network of influence among Shiites throughout the Middle East, and a determination to have its own nuclear weapons but its leadership also has a penchant for extremely radical, militant rhetoric. This leadership is most vividly exemplified by Iran's current president, Mahmoud Ahmadinejad, who has explicitly called on multiple occasions for the extermination of Israel.

So far, its genocidally inclined president has not been able to consolidate total power within Iran. He has tried to generate support in the region by escalating tensions with the United States and Israel. Iranian leaders have routinely blamed sectarian violence in Iraq, including the bombing of the Askariya shrine in February, on "agents of Zionism." Meanwhile, Tehran vigorously pursues nuclear power capable of bomb making. Ahmadinejad represents an apocalyptic element for whom the normal rules of fear of retaliation—using nuclear weapons—may not apply. Generally, is it possible to deter fanatical leaders who view retaliation as a path to martyrdom and paradise?

Nasr's account clarifies the intensity of intergroup hostility in a highly volatile part of the world in which prejudicial stereotypes are readily available, mass violence abounds, nuclear weapons are on the horizon, and therefore a kind of instant genocide is feasible—e.g., of Israel or of a concentrated Sunni population if Iran makes or buys nuclear weapons. For the world, this kind of instant genocide may become a major concern before long in various places. The problem deserves exceedingly high priority in the international community.

Containing the Gravest Danger Through Nuclear Diplomacy

Sidney Drell, a great physicist and arms control expert, collaborated with James Goodby, an eminent diplomat and also an arms control expert, in an important study that helps us to see a path toward diminishing the gravest danger.[27] Nuclear weapons can cause massive, almost unimaginable damage to civilian populations, damage that cannot be counteracted. Preventing nuclear proliferation is far preferable to restoring the face of the planet after nuclear devastation—if, indeed, that would be possible at all.

Given the universality, urgency, and catastrophic nature of nuclear danger, it is imperative that the United States ratify the Comprehensive Nuclear Test Ban Treaty to eliminate all nuclear tests and strongly encourage other states to follow suit.[28] All governments should make international consensus for enforcement of nonproliferation a top priority and strengthen the inspection authority of the International Atomic Energy Agency.

Sadly, some of the recent weakening of global resolve to confront nuclear disaster must be attributed to U.S. government actions and attitudes. It is imperative to mount cooperative efforts to manage, secure, and decrease nuclear weapons everywhere, regardless of their ownership.

The danger posed by terrorists and terrorist use of advanced technology tempts us to forget the major successes that patient, sometimes coercive diplomacy achieved throughout the 1950s and 1960s when first the Soviet Union and then China began to build up their nuclear arsenals. The West succeeded in containing the global nuclear threat without resorting to preemptive war—even though some policymakers enthusiastically supported that option. Skillful statecraft convinced most nations to cooperate in preventing nuclear weapons proliferation.

The limited extent of proliferation since Hiroshima and Nagasaki is even more remarkable given the number of nations (notably South Africa) that began planning and construction of nuclear weapons, only to give them up later. Other nations realized that global security—and their own with it—depended on cooperation in developing an international nonproliferation regime rather than on their own nuclear arsenal.

Those advances were reversed when India, Pakistan, and North Korea acquired and tested nuclear weapons, and Iraq and Iran sought to do so. Others may follow, as nonproliferation is losing its momentum, and the resulting arms race could soon make the use of nuclear weapons in national combat an internationally accepted possibility—probably mutual mass suicide. This spread of weapons technology increases the opportunities for nonstate terrorists to acquire nuclear arms and the skill to use them.

The landmark study of Drell and Goodby, who have received the highest awards for their work over many years in addressing the nuclear danger, focused on the urgent, critical need for formal arrangements involving key nations, especially the United States, Russia, and China, and for robust support of international organizations such as the International Atomic Energy agency in monitoring and inspecting and of the UN Security Council in enforcement. The study is invaluable in alerting us to the profound importance of an intensive, sustained, diplomatic effort by the international community to negotiate and monitor agreements that will avoid nuclear catastrophe, including instant genocides.

NGOs, Prevention, and Weapons Restraint

Gareth Evans has made a remarkable career as former foreign minister of Australia, co-chairing the commission that formulated the concept of the "responsibility to protect" and serving as a valuable member of the Carnegie Commission on Preventing Deadly Conflict and as president of the International Crisis Group. In 2005 he published a penetrating article on conflict prevention and NGOs.[29] Can NGOs help in the restraints on weaponry that are so badly needed?

NGOs have made an important contribution in pressuring national and international bodies to give their attention to conflict prevention and resolution. Since governments have made so little progress in restraining the proliferation and use of all kinds of highly lethal weapons, the peoples of the world must organize through NGOs to preserve their own survival.

NGOs have played an important role in pressuring governments to make systemic changes and in contributing their own input and skills into policy and implementation. Their roles have been as many and varied as their organizations—think tanks/research institutions/policy forums (such as Centres for Strategic Studies, Council on Foreign Relations, Institutes of International Affairs, and large foundations such as the Carnegie Corporation), watchdog operations (such as Amnesty International and Human Rights Watch), on-the-ground organizations that engage in mediation or confidence building (such as the Carter Center, the Open Society Institute, and the International Crisis Group), and humanitarian relief organizations (such as Médicins sans Frontières and CARE). Yet these organizations overall have not made an intense, sustained effort to constrain the most dangerous weaponry. They could do this in a worldwide cooperative effort.

A long presence in the region allows the International Crisis Group's experts to evaluate the dynamics of situations in target areas—currently Darfur, northern Uganda, and eastern Congo—and to produce monthly reports that not only update and analyze but also spell out concrete, informed recommendations for integrated action by policymakers, activists, and the public at large.

A systematic focus on conflict prevention since the early 1990s has not only increased our understanding of the causes of conflicts but also suggested a repertoire of measures to deal with them. These measures may be divided into two categories: long-term structural prevention and short-term direct operational prevention. These involve (1) political and diplomatic measures, (2) legal and constitutional measures, (3) economic and social measures, and (4) security and military measures.[30] An international consortium of NGOs is helping, and could help much more, in generating problem-solving ideas, educating publics, and pressing governments to take necessary and feasible actions—before it is too late.

Effective institutional structures are necessary at the global, regional, and national levels, and the role of international NGOs here is to keep pressuring governments and intergovernmental organizations to make the needed systemic changes.

In short, the NGOs could greatly influence publics, governments, and international institutions in many ways to increase consciousness on lethal weapons, deadly conflict, and genocide in the next one to two decades. It is a mission that should inspire people of high ideals everywhere. An example was provided by the strong NGO role in banning land mines. Now is the time to address a wider range of highly lethal weaponry.

A New Nuclear Prevention Initiative

In 2007, a group of well-known leaders in arms control and diplomacy—William Perry, Sam Nunn, George Shultz, and Henry Kissinger—issued an exceptional declaration on the essential requirement of the abolition of nuclear weapons for the human future.[31] Sidney Drell and Max Kampelman played a critical role in this initiative. They were all intimately involved with nuclear weapons during the Cold War and are aware that a full-scale nuclear war could well destroy most or all of humanity—what we might call "humanicide." In light of the highly dangerous developments sketched earlier in this chapter, e.g., the arms race in Asia, the possibility of humanicide has not disappeared with the end of the Cold War. From a practical standpoint, the abolition of nuclear weapons has now stimulated a ferment of activity on delineating the intermediate steps necessary to do this safely. These are technically complex and, above all, politically sensitive in the extreme. A series of analytical papers is being prepared in 2007 and will be followed by convening functions, so that the world can at least begin to understand what is necessary and feasible in the nuclear era. The work could have profound significance for prevention of instant genocide, nuclear war, and mass terrorism. It will be very difficult and will take years, probably decades, but it is not beyond human capacity. It is fundamentally in the vital self-interest of all humanity.

PART III

INSTITUTIONS AND ORGANIZATIONS: WHO CAN DO WHAT?

CHAPTER 13

Potential of the United Nations
for Preventing Mass Violence

Emerging Visions of UN Opportunities

On April 9, 2007, to commemorate the thirteenth anniversary of the Rwandan genocide, UN Secretary-General Ban Ki-moon affirmed the worldwide obligation to make prevention of genocide a priority. He emphasized that recent UN steps to meet that obligation—the appointment of a Special Adviser on the Prevention of Genocide and the creation of an Advisory Committee on Genocide Prevention—must be followed by "more—much more" and announced his intention to upgrade the post of Special Adviser to a full-time position at a higher level and to strengthen both the adviser and his Advisory Committee. He added that the world's governments have come to agreement on the responsibility of nations to protect their citizens and on its corollary, that if a nation ignores that responsibility, it is the duty of other nations to intervene on behalf of victim populations.

The challenge now, he concluded, was to "give real meaning to the concept" by putting it into operation: "Preventing genocide is a collective and individual responsibility. Everyone has a role to play: Governments, the media, civil society organizations, religious groups, and each and every one of us. Let us build a global partnership against genocide. Let us protect populations from genocide when their own Government cannot or will not."[1]

Secretary-General Ban recognizes that the UN alone cannot take on the tasks of prevention. In some situations, it must take the lead; in others, national, regional, or nongovernmental groups must be out in front.

How can the UN's vast experience be used to help extinguish conflicts at an early stage? How can the UN create paths to conflict resolution that are visible, attractive, and negotiable before conflicts become large and lethal?

Legitimacy and Moral Authority

The legitimacy of outside assistance is a critical determinant of its success. The UN, a universal organization whose Charter expresses the highest ideals (and explicitly specifies a mandate to prevent genocide), has considerable legitimacy throughout the world. It plays a vital role in establishing the terms of outside intervention and the broad consensus to support it. The strength of the UN lies both in its role as a legitimating forum that facilitates international collaboration and in its capacity to reflect the interests and intentions of member states, including their commitment to joint and cooperative action. With UN authorization, states, regional institutions, and nongovernmental actors can facilitate local solutions to local problems, using both private and public resources. Much has been accomplished and more can be done, especially with vigorous participation of the established democracies, now best exemplified by the EU.

After the Cold War, a pivotal change occurred in the international community's conception of national sovereignty.[2] As Ban Ki-moon observed, the conviction has grown that national sovereignty is not and cannot be a shield behind which governments are free to engage in atrocities; the international community is justified to intervene through the UN in "internal affairs" to prevent or resolve deadly conflict, render humanitarian assistance, aid transitions to more democratic systems of governance, and offer technical assistance to build the capacity for problem solving. Many countries—especially the autocratic and dictatorial ones—resist this change. Nevertheless, the reformulation of the concept of sovereignty to include as its fundamental element a nation's responsibility to protect its own people from human rights abuses has increasing promise as an effective check to tyranny.

The growing acceptance of the responsibility to protect and the changing nature of large-scale violent conflicts mean that more and more the United Nations has been called upon to take global norms, developed earlier to regulate peaceful relations *between* states, and apply them to conflicts *within* nation-states. The new interpretation of the doctrine of state sovereignty to include the responsibility to protect should not be construed to justify arbitrary intrusions into the internal affairs of states or the subjugation of the weaker by the stronger. To guard against the potential for abuse, the UN must lead the international community in developing a comprehensive and rigorous set of criteria for legitimate intervention as well as procedures for practical implementation. The UN can also use its moral authority to bring issues to the attention of the international community and put pressures on disputing parties to work toward resolution.

The United Nations: From Reaction to Prevention in the Twenty-first Century

Detlev Wolter, a distinguished German scholar and diplomat, has written a superb overview of the UN's transition from reaction toward prevention.[3] His comprehensive, visionary, and hopeful review of the UN's best opportunities for global prevention and for creating a durable peace covered fundamental problems and the best preventive ways in which the UN can deal with them. These include intellectual foundations for building an effective prevention regime that supports early, useful UN responses; new ways to achieve effective national, regional, and global prevention; overcoming fragmentation of UN efforts in security, violence prevention, disarmament, and development; making prevention operational; and the principle of sovereignty as responsibility.

UN Leadership in Prevention

The UN's universal legitimacy often elicits international cooperation. The Secretary-General (with the help of a strong Secretariat) must provide intellectual and moral leadership. The UN has traditionally had an important intermediary role in providing assistance in dispute resolution. Just as it helps states meet their human rights obligations or hold fair elections,[4] it can help with early, quiet diplomacy aimed at building a nation's own capacity for acquiring necessary skills and institutions. The UN Secretary-General's influence and diplomatic resources enable him to bring disputing parties together in a constructive atmosphere.

The Adventure of Peace: Dag Hammarskjold and the Future of the United Nations, a collection of articles by eminent scholars and high-level UN officers, highlighted Dag Hammarskjold's pioneering work in preventive diplomacy.[5] Hammarskjold not only coined the term; he also achieved surprising successes by putting it into practice in the face of powerful constraints and paved the way for its much broader implementation, both by future Secretaries-General and also by a wide range of leaders associated with the UN. He emphasized the potential of diplomacy by third parties, leaders in international affairs who have no axe to grind in a specific conflict, but seek only to foster peaceful solutions in the interest of the international community—before the outbreak of mass violence. Since the end of the Cold War, his concepts of preventive diplomacy have expanded and now hold a growing role in the policies of democratic governments and international organizations everywhere.

Hammarskjold's approach always involved an effort to find common ground between the adversaries. In an illuminating essay, the brilliant diplomat Jan Eliasson and distinguished scholar Peter Wallensteen summed up Hammarskjold's approach as prevention by bringing opposing sides together. His remarkable skill at personal diplomacy and his willingness to travel extensively when flight was far less convenient than today made him a welcome and respected source of help.[6] Eliasson and Wallensteen highlighted his concern with the early phases of conflict and the formulation of timely proposals for resolution before a huge conflagration broke out. Hammarskjold recognized that small, dangerous situations tend to grow if they are ignored and become a threat to international peace and security. Such situations are, therefore, within the legitimate scope of the UN's mandate. The authors paid tribute to his leadership in early preventive diplomacy: "Many of the regional organizations that have now become important UN partners were only created in recent years. This is a testimony to the continuous development of international alternatives in the promotion of preventive diplomacy. There are now many options available."[7] As an example of the expanded use of his methods, the authors noted how Sweden and the European Union addressed the emerging crisis in Macedonia in 2000. Anna Lindh, then foreign minister of Sweden and a pioneer of prevention, worked closely with Javier

Solana and Christopher Patten of the EU to apply Hammarskjold's concepts, and together they prevented what might have become a disaster.

Hammarskjold's successors continued to use their position of Secretary-General to promote prevention. After the Cold War and near the end of his term of office, Secretary-General Boutros Boutros-Ghali issued three major studies on the UN's historical core values that could guide the UN in the first decades of the twenty-first century: "Agenda for Peace," "Agenda for Development," and "Agenda for Democratization.[8] Secretary-General Kofi Annan continued groundbreaking work with a number of studies that offered suggestions for improving the UN, including self-criticism. Among them were Brahimi's report on peacekeeping; a report on preventing armed conflict at the outset of the twenty-first century; a series of major speeches by Kofi Annan on human rights, democracy, and creating a culture of prevention (published by the Carnegie Commission on Preventing Deadly Conflict); detailed analyses of the genocidal tragedies of Rwanda and Srebenica in the former Yugoslavia; and reports on the responsibility to protect and on putting human security on a par with national security as well as the report of the Secretary-General's high-level panel in 2004 and his own follow-up report in 2005. Finally, his 2006 report on prevention of armed conflict updated the landmark report on this subject in 2001.[9]

These excellent publications and many associated international meetings stimulated a change of international norms and provided a stronger intellectual and moral basis for the UN, for member states, and for the international community as a whole. The translation of such civilized norms into accepted practice and implementing institutions will no doubt take many years to complete—but the process is under way.

In the Carnegie Commission publication of his speeches and reports, Secretary-General Annan considered how an international culture of prevention can be built over time and underscored the vital role the UN has to play in its formation.[10] For the long term, he emphasized human security as an essential ingredient of national security. This sort of security requires a society based on fairness, with good government that is transparent, impartial, and just, allowing equal access to economic opportunity. With his integrative mind, Secretary-General Annan linked security policy with development, poverty eradication, protection of our common environment, and the spread of human rights and democracy.

The UN can, directly or indirectly, employ respectful engagement with states to resolve impending violent conflict and build equitable development through democratic institutions. Annan advocated not only early preventive diplomacy in "hot spots" but also fostering democratic socioeconomic development as the best infrastructure for enduring peace. Virtually all of the comprehensive peace settlements in which the UN has participated in recent years involved democratization as a crucial element (e.g., El Salvador, Cambodia, Mozambique, Guatemala, East Timor).[11]

The UN has a network of well-trained, professional, dedicated staff and representatives in almost every country in the world. This adds on-the-ground knowledge to a commitment to help. Gareth Evans has suggested placing an international early warning system in the UN Secretariat, based in the Secretariat's Department of Political Affairs, with added staff to monitor the world's six major geographic regions and teams of well-trained mediators for deployment to troubled areas.[12] Some movement in this direction has occurred in the first decade of the twenty-first century.

The Secretary-General has available the information to clarify opportunities and approaches for preventive action and should be free to alert the Security Council to take appropriate action. A number of circumstances call for the Secretary-General to do this: the possibility that a regional dispute might employ weapons of mass destruction, evidence of movement toward genocide, large flows of refugees threatening to destabilize neighboring countries, evidence of systematic and widespread human rights violations, forcible overthrow of democratically elected governments, serious damage to the environment, and rapid arms build-up in tense situations. Thus, the Secretary-General can stimulate the UN system to bring serious problems to the attention of the international community and to use its moral and extensive tool kit to help disputing parties work toward resolution.

Special Representatives

One proven way in which the UN can employ the resources of experienced diplomats is in the capacity of special representatives of the Secretary-General (SRSGs). The Secretary-General needs an international panel of conflict resolution experts—as exemplified by Lakhtar Brahimi and the late Cyrus Vance—with the extensive experience, intellect, integrity, and distinction that would give them world recognition as suitable envoys for violence prevention missions. These experts, in turn, need support staff with thorough knowledge of different regions of the world—something the UN is in a good position to supply. The SRSGs and senior staff collaborators should combine expertise in both the principles and techniques of conflict resolution with in-depth knowledge of a particular region, including the main historical and cultural factors bearing on a specific conflict. Peck's studies on strengthening the knowledge base for preventive diplomacy and the practical leadership of the Secretary-General in this vital field are illuminating here.[13]

The SRSG's job requires constant negotiation with a wide range of actors. Supported by his group of experts, he must develop the mission's objectives and strategy after careful study of the situation. He must develop a solid working relationship with the conflicting parties, with all those involved in the decisionmaking process, and also with the local population in order to create agreement through constant persuasion, problem solving, and the skillful use of economic, political, and psychological leverage. The SRSG's team must aim for collaboration with UN specialized agencies, funds, and programs; coordinate regional and subregional organizations as well as appropriate NGOs; and relate to the media to raise international understanding. They must also work with UN member states through ambassadors on the ground and at UN headquarters to gain political support and find resources to sustain the mission effectively.

Finally, he must keep the Security Council informed. The SRSG should report directly to the Council, and Council members should visit the mission area to observe the situation firsthand. The UN has extensive relevant experience, but concerted international efforts are still in their adolescence.

Ethnopolitical conflicts are often amenable to resolution, through strategies of accommodation that start with preventive diplomacy and go on to guaranteed full civil and political rights, economic development focused on reducing poverty, political institutions and practices that recognize cultural diversity and cherish human rights, and political arrangements that protect vulnerable groups. Ethnic conflict and violence—precursors to genocide—usually decline in states that adopt these policies.

In a study for the Carnegie Commission, Connie Peck developed a highly promising practical model, growing out of UN experience and research: regional centers for sustainable peace, established under the auspices of the UN, or regional organizations, or both.[14] This UN regional approach emphasizes regional promotion of capable democratic government, coupled with preventive diplomacy—early, and then ongoing as may be necessary. The structure she proposed would draw on broad international expertise to determine the most successful conflict prevention instruments and adapt them to local needs and circumstances. These centers represent a promising way to pool the strengths of the UN, intergovernmental regional organizations (such as the EU), nongovernmental organizations, and regional analytical centers in a comprehensive preventive system.

Educational Role of the United Nations in Violence Prevention

As the world becomes more interdependent, tension, suspicion, and hostility are bound to grow—especially in times of drastic transition. The UN can be a powerful force in public education aimed at countering intergroup violence. Since the UN has worldwide responsibility for helping in conflict resolution, it must work to create a world constituency for prevention. The policy community in much of the world is not familiar with the principles and techniques of conflict resolution. The UN must lead in the education of both policymakers and general publics.

It can support and reward leaders committed to conflict resolution, build educational opportunities worldwide, and provide useful early information about growing dangers. Contending parties throughout the world must be educated about the nature and consequences of ethnocentric hostility: the action-reaction cycles of violence, the build-up of revenge motives, and the proliferation, escalation, and addiction to hatred and killing that emerge from intergroup conflict.

In cooperation with universities and research institutes, the UN could sponsor world leadership seminars that include new heads of state, foreign ministers, defense ministers, and development ministers. These seminars could clarify how the UN and other organizations can help states avoid violent conflict and, most important, deal nonviolently with problems of intense nationalism, ethnocentrism, prejudice, hatred, and violence. Through leadership seminars and wide use of the whole array of dissemination media, the UN can make available to the world information about both conflicts in general and particular conflicts; the responsible handling of weapons by governmental leaders and policymakers; the adverse consequences of weapons build-up, especially of weapons of mass destruction; the skills, knowledge, and prestige properly associated with successful conflict resolution; equitable socioeconomic development, including the new uses of science and technology for development; and cooperative behavior in the world community. Prevention of genocide should be included as an aspect of every topic.

Tools for Violence Prevention Available
to the UN Security Council

Elizabeth Cousens of the International Peace Academy outlined some resources available for preventing violence to the UN Security Council.[15] Since the UN Charter gave the Security Council a central role, and since its performance in that role has often been disappointing, the focus must be on what it can do better than in the past.

Agenda-setting and fact-finding missions, diplomatic initiatives, economic sanctions, peace operations, and peace enforcement are instruments the Council can deploy to prevent outbreak or escalation of mass violence.

Normative and symbolic tools: The Council can publicize a potential conflict to attract diplomatic and public attention and to mobilize resources. Throughout the 1990s the Council increasingly engaged in highly visible diplomacy, through greater interaction with the media, encounters with key NGOs, and frequent field missions. The Council can also use presidential statements, press releases, and resolutions to alert conflicting parties about the boundaries of legitimate behavior—especially when they reflect diplomatic unity within the Council, hard as that is to achieve.

Diplomatic and noncoercive tools: The Council has three valuable diplomatic tools. First, it can mobilize broad support for diplomatic efforts of the UN or others, as when it authorizes fact-finding missions and investigations to support mediation efforts through special representatives, the Secretary General himself, or regional organizations. Second, the Council can send its own members on fact-finding missions to improve its deliberations by reporting the situation on the ground and can also raise the visibility of the problem by taking a problem-solving interest and communicating directly with conflicting parties. The Council's third option is to engage in direct negotiations to prevent violence. East Timor is a clear example: a mission in 1999 galvanized regional and Council action, leading to authorization of a multinational force and a broad transitional peace operation. The recurrence of violence in 2006 elicited a quick UN response.

Semicoercive tools: The Council can send troops or observers to a potential conflict zone to prevent conflict. This may (rarely) involve preventive deployment to separate adversaries and otherwise buffer aggression.

Coercive tools: Tools at the disposal of the Security Council include arms embargoes, disarmament efforts, targeted or broader sanctions, and international criminal justice mechanisms.

Arms embargoes: Embargoes can have a deescalating effect in ongoing conflicts. Imposed at the end of a conflict, they can form part of a stabilization strategy to prevent recurrent conflict. *Economic and other sanctions,* though primarily used to contain an existing conflict, can also be part of a preventive effort. Studies that examine sanctions and their efficacy stress the importance of carefully targeting these instruments on perpetrators to avoid both collateral and perverse effects. In general, coercive tools have been very difficult to organize, chiefly because of disagreement among Council members and reluctance of member states to provide necessary resources. The UN is able to do only what its member states permit, and many of them—unabashedly self-interested or outright dictatorships—consistently block constructive action.

The Role of UN Agencies in Prevention,
Both Structural and Operational

A common misunderstanding about the UN is that it consists essentially of the Secretary-General, the Security Council (hobbled by the absolute veto power given to the five powers left standing at the end of World War II), and the unruly General Assembly. Both the Council and the Assembly have constructive capacities, but they are hampered by authoritarian, dictatorial, and hegemonic member states. Yet the UN has many agencies that clearly do much good in the world, not least in the area of prevention, both operational and structural. Among them, the World Health Organization has acted rapidly and effectively to stave off a catastrophic worldwide epidemic of severe acute respiratory syndrome (SARS) and earlier (in 1980) to eradicate smallpox. UNICEF probably does more for the education, health, and well-being of children in poor countries than any other entity in the world. The World Food Program has been highly effective in providing sustenance to victims of disaster. The UN High Commissioner for Refugees has vast experience in coping with refugee problems: in the 1990s Sadako Ogata set valuable precedents and provided immense humanitarian services. The UN High Commissioner for Human Rights has nearly worldwide staff and excellent leadership. (In its first year, the new Human Rights Council was not successful.) The World Bank and the United Nations Development Programme have done valuable work in socioeconomic development, so important in building competent, democratic, and ultimately prosperous nations. In the past decade they have become more democratically oriented, they focus more on people and less on monuments, they foster cooperation of public and private sectors in building market economies, they cooperate more with each other, they have major resources, they cover the world, and they pay serious attention to preventing deadly conflict. All this provides powerful incentives, skills, and hope to move poor countries away from poverty, tyranny, repression, epidemic diseases, and breeding grounds for terrorism.

The United Nations Environment Programme (UNEF) deserves strong support. Environmental resource issues often lie at the heart of conflicts that hold the potential for mass violence.[16] Existing tensions can be deepened by deliberate manipulation of resource shortages for hostile purposes (for example, using food or water as a weapon). Competition between or within nations for natural resources such as water increases the potential for conflict. Climate change is beginning (sooner than expected) to have serious effects that could precipitate violence. Environmental degradation and resource depletion have a role in promoting conflict that is bound to continue and increase in areas characterized by political instability, rapid population growth, poverty, and societal stress.

Finally, UNITAR, a small gem in the crown of the UN, conducts excellent training and research all over the world on subjects of great practical importance for the international community, such as climate change. Connie Peck's work there has made outstanding contributions to the understanding and practice of preventive diplomacy.

These few examples of valuable and effective UN agencies illustrate that it is not just a windy debating society, but a global network of competence, skills, and dedicated people making the world better than it was before. To work effectively, it needs farsighted, constructive participation of the international community, in particular the established democracies. Its assets can be helpful in the prevention of deadly conflict generally and of genocide specifically. It is a vital challenge to consider how effective components of the United Nations might be extended (e.g., the World Health Organization, UNICEF, the UN Development Programme, and the Department of Political Affairs) in order to strengthen its role in preventing genocide-prone violence, reaching just settlements, and fostering healthy development throughout the world. Richard Haass, president of the Council on Foreign Relations (CFR), pointed out the valuable antiterrorist role the UN Security Council has played since September 11, 2001, by fostering international cooperation in intelligence and police work. He also mentioned the importance of the World Trade Organization in resolving trade disputes fairly.[17]

The Role of the International Community

Throughout his tenure at the UN, Kofi Annan emphasized the crucial role of the international community (especially democracies) in fostering prevention. Among other things, the international community can

1. encourage people-centered security in troubled areas, which means advocating and helping to build democracy;
2. ensure that development assistance policies do not exacerbate risks of conflict—for example, access to loans and grants should be fair to all rather than limited to privileged groups;
3. in the case of global corporations, whose power has been increasing relative to that of states, advocate and act as exemplars of good governance through constructive interaction with the UN, as exemplified in the Global Compact, which protects human rights and diminishes conflict;
4. build a well-functioning collective regime that is prepared for strong political—and, if necessary, military—engagement to contain and resolve conflict.

Strengthening the United Nations for Prevention of Mass Violence

International Pooling of Strengths

The tasks of prevention require international pooling of strengths, sharing of burdens, and division of labor. Without a commonly accepted international system of violence prevention, many different efforts toward prevention are made in a groping, uncoordinated way. More widely accepted and regularized arrangements are necessary, and the UN can surely be helpful in working them out. For example, the UN Department of Political Affairs might well become a focal point for facilitating UN prevention activities all over the world, especially in collaboration with the new Undersecretary for Prevention of Genocide and Mass Atrocities (located in the Executive Office of the Secretary-General).

Cooperation Between the United Nations and an International "Democratic Caucus"

In a study prepared for the Carnegie Commission on Preventing Deadly Conflict, Professor Graham Allison of Harvard and Hisashi Owada (formerly Japan's ambassador to the UN, now on the International Court of Justice) pointed out practical ways in which the community of established democracies could foster effective and cost-effective prevention—acting partly through the UN and partly outside it—but always in the spirit of the UN Charter, which so strongly reflects the basic principles of democracy.[18]

A CFR task force, in exploring ways the United States could be effective at the UN, came to a similar conclusion.[19] It recommended that the United States strengthen its relationship with the European Union. The two bodies, representing the world's leading democracies, could make a powerful team, and they should support each other to the maximum extent—both within the UN and outside it. The EU has been receptive to this approach. For its part, the United States should avoid behavior that weakens its influence both at the UN and in the world, alienates other nations, and costs respect that matters when the United States needs cooperation, as is increasingly the case out of practical necessity. The world is interdependent, and international cooperation is essential.

In representing virtually all of the world's nations, the UN gives a voice to repressive governments guilty of serious human rights violations. Since democracies and nondemocracies tend to be segregated geographically (though this is changing as democracy spreads through the world), some of the regional subdivisions of the UN are strongly influenced by nondemocratic regimes. These regimes cooperate to block some of the democratic nations' humane initiatives. The Council on Foreign Relations suggested that the established democracies institutionalize a *democracy caucus* at the UN "as a forum for building cooperation on issues of human rights and democracy."[20] It could also unite to block nondemocratic nations from membership on UN bodies that focus on democratic development and firmly support the work of the UNDP in strengthening legislatures, fair electoral processes, and other elements of democratic governance as well as in developing free and independent media.

The CFR report suggested that the United States and the UN should spell out explicitly how essential the promotion of human rights, democracy, development, and poverty eradication is to a long-term strategy to overcome terrorism.

Implementing Prevention with Democratic Socioeconomic Development

Nothing is more conducive to structural, long-term prevention of mass violence than democratic socioeconomic development. Although other elements of structural prevention are important, democratic development tends to pull them along. The social and economic elements of democratic development combine in ways that foster security, well-being, and justice. Still, transition to an open democratic society can be turbulent, and outside help is often crucial. The legitimacy and capability of the UN in providing this help has been demonstrated on almost every continent.

The UN is learning from the European experience: OSCE, Council of Europe, and especially the economically powerful European Union, for which democracy, protection of human rights, the rule of law, and a market economy are the basic requirements for membership. These cooperative European institutions have had a strong influence on Eastern European countries emerging from authoritarian regimes—and, in the process, moving toward peaceful conflict resolution as well as economic benefits. Their examples suggest what might be done on other continents. In practice, the European countries are generally constructive members of the UN and provide much of its strength. There is a good chance for more explicit linkages of the UN with organizations of this kind in the years ahead.

Working Together to Maximize Leverage for Prevention

A Group of Friends of the Secretary-General (seriously interested and fair-minded member states) could be formed to provide a useful source of influence. The presence of a preventive mission itself is a source of influence on political leaders, their constituents, and the population at large. The better their training, the deeper their commitment, and the more substantial their experience, the more likely they are to be effective. All too often, these favorable conditions are not met. Yet there is a trend toward learning from these experiences to become institutionally more effective.

Two main carrots are economic support and legitimacy.[21] A study of actual attempts at conflict resolution confirms that positive incentives offering the parties a promising future are more likely to be effective than negative pressures.[22]

Cooperation between the UN and regional organizations (ROs) can help struggling nations achieve such reforms. An important report on UN-RO relations for violence prevention was prepared in 2006 under the excellent leadership of Finland's Tapio Kanninen and strongly endorsed by the Secretary-General. Such cooperation offers real promise for strengthening international efforts for prevention.

UN and Regional Organizations: Partners in Violence Prevention

The first decade of the twenty-first century saw an unprecedented intellectual ferment in and around the United Nations to find ways to strengthen its efforts to prevent mass violence. In April 2006, international experts assembled in Vienna to explore partnerships between the United Nations and regional organizations for crisis prevention and early conflict resolution. Dr. Catherine Guicherd of the International Peace Academy prepared an incisive report of the meeting.[23]

The participants were in agreement that the UN has an important role in making international preventive actions legitimate and can be very helpful to regional organizations. In most cases of impending serious conflict, the UN is not the best candidate to implement proposed solutions. The lead is often taken by strong member states, regional organizations, or sometimes even international financial institutions. A sort of "grand coalition" is needed to put all the pieces of the operation together, especially the three factors considered crucial for success: (1) sufficient power (political, economic, and, if necessary, military); (2) enough money, soon enough, to implement constructive actions; and (3) wide agreement among the adversaries about the legitimacy of those who are trying to help in a preventive role.

To put together this kind of combination, international actors also need a "tool box" from which to select those tools most appropriate for the situation, as well as a clear process to guide their choices. All concerned are helped by clear, well-documented practical information about best practices in all forms of violence prevention, including worldwide mediation capacity and substantial economic incentives for peace. The UN is becoming increasingly helpful in making that useful "tool box" available to many players in the international community. The UN, working with regional organizations, can also be helpful in connecting political institutions that provide moral authority and social legitimacy with those that contribute to the economic development process.

Special attention is now paid to mediation, especially in early preventive diplomacy. Indeed, almost every regional organization is now engaged in such activity. So, there is an eagerness to learn from the world's experience, particularly since some of the regional organizations are quite new to this field. UN-RO cooperation can be very helpful in spreading the lessons learned from successful experience throughout the world.

Establishing universally accepted norms is important. Both the UN and its partner ROs can help in a bad situation by clarifying how a particular universal norm is applicable to the situation being mediated. The new Mediation Support Unit of the UN Department of Political Affairs is compiling the UN's experience in a variety of conflicts all over the world. One of the most encouraging developments in preventing deadly conflict long before it verges on genocide is the prospect of a worldwide cadre of mediation professionals acting under the auspices of the UN and/or regional organizations.

Military Functions

The UN has historically been ill-prepared for military functions. Yet it cannot be credible and effective in fostering global peace unless it has competent military capability, not for fighting wars, but for separating adversaries to make space for mediation and for protecting groups at high risk while settlement efforts proceed.

Member states with strong military forces might designate military units for UN actions and give them special training and joint exercises. This would make a rapid deployment force available in agreed upon situations. Other member states could augment these forces with standby agreements. Permanent members of the Security Council have the ability to veto a particular operation; temporary members and nonmembers of the Council might be given the right to refuse to take part.

Sir Brian Urquhart suggested an additional option: a highly trained UN volunteer military force of approximately 5,000 soldiers that the Security Council could use for rapid deployment to trouble spots.[24] This force, unlike peacekeeping forces, would be trained both in combat and in negotiation, with the mandate to use force if necessary to stabilize circumstances at an early stage in low-level but dangerous conflicts, especially those involving irregular militias and similar groups. Such a force could be deployed in the early days of an impending crisis to get the situation quickly under control and to prepare the way for preventive diplomacy that would address the immediate precipitating causes of the conflict. Then a longer-term process could begin to resolve the fundamental causes.

Deployment of the Standby High Readiness Brigade (SHIRBRIG) to the Ethiopia-Eritrea conflict in 2001 represents one modest step toward building UN capacity for rapid deployment. The SHIRBRIG units arranged for their own deployment to the UN

Ethiopia-Eritrea Mission. This allowed the UN to concentrate on assembling vessels to carry non-SHIRBRIG forces. Despite self-deployment, however, SHIRBRIG arrived nearly ninety days after Security Council authorization, due to its reliance on slow commercial transport. SHIRBRIG units were extremely well equipped and well prepared when they did arrive, however; they sustained themselves completely and raised the standard against which other troop contributors from less developed nations might be measured. Although this higher standard could have a positive impact, it could also create polarization in the mission between have and have-not contingents. In sum, SHIRBRIG's deployment sets a precedent for member-state commitment to undertake action in a crisis. It has a real but modest potential for increasing UN capacity for rapid deployment.

UN Limitations and Security Council Constraints

The limitations of the United Nations are well known and widely discussed. During his tenure, UN Secretary-General Kofi Annan addressed some disadvantages the UN faces in developing a preventive system:

1. With limited resources and a massive agenda, the Secretary-General and the Security Council are overburdened and are forced to focus on crisis situations rather than preventive strategies.
2. Although its Charter allows the UN to respond to threats or breaches of peace within or among states, it often has trouble dealing with conflicts involving nonofficial bodies and internal disputes, and so far has had problems with very early prevention.
3. The UN is hindered in its security efforts by the threat of a veto in the Security Council. The Permanent Five (the members with veto power) have been slow to grasp the significance of prevention.
4. The high stakes surrounding the UN's involvement in a conflict sometimes make states apprehensive about bringing their conflict to it. The Security Council may be inflexible or partisan or may pass resolutions that cannot be implemented, as it did in the former Yugoslavia.
5. The UN struggles to be organizationally efficient but has the image of being wasteful and is hampered in administrative reform by a variety of member states, especially autocratic ones.

There are many other constraints on Security Council action.

Normative limitations: Past debates over violence prevention and especially humanitarian intervention have noticeably shifted the UN's violence prevention agenda toward encouraging member states to engage in their own preventive efforts, thereby limiting the Council's responsibility and also its contributions.

Strategic uncertainty: It is often difficult to assess what kinds of engagement might be effective. (This situation provokes fear of failure.)

Operational capacity: The Council lacks rapid deployment forces or any similar capacity for swift action. This constraint is due in part to the Global North's suspicions of the UN and unwillingness to entrust such capacities to a collective body and also to the South's suspicions of UN intervention as a threat to national sovereignty. This is a critical gap, given the brief chance for Council action when conflict has erupted but not yet escalated into mass violence.

Political limitations: The limits of the Council's preventive ability are ultimately set by the political interests of the Permanent Five and other powerful states. This applies both to placing a troubling situation on the Council agenda and to determining how it is handled, once there. Another important limit is set by the unwillingness of key states to deploy troops in cases where they do not perceive their vital interests are involved or fear adverse effects on domestic affairs. Furthermore, when powerful member states are directly involved, conflicting interests and loyalties can make the Council reluctant to act.

Still, the desirability of violence prevention in both internal and external conflicts has become broadly accepted. Moreover, there have been important though rare innovations, such as preventive deployments, and increasing sophistication in the use of established techniques such as special representatives and direct diplomacy through Security Council missions. The Council needs to be better informed about the necessity and feasibility of prevention. It needs continuing education on prevention to soften the rigidity of the Permanent Five and to inform nonpermanent rotating Council members. The most amenable cases for constructive Council action are those where there is a shared strategic interest and where the instruments required allow for mobilizing resources gradually—for example, Macedonia—or where a strong regional power takes an interest in a manageable conflict—for example, Australia in East Timor.

Working Together to Provide Appropriate Mandates and Adequate Resources

The difficulty of obtaining general agreement at the UN is notorious. General Roméo Dallaire, the very capable commander of UNAMIR, remarked—after his forces were tragically reduced while the genocide in Rwanda was raging—"As long as these states procrastinated, bickered, and cynically pursued their own selfish foreign politics, the UN and UNAMIR could do little to stop the killing."[25]

A strong case can be made for instituting into a mission the flexibility that would allow it to change mandates quickly to keep pace with changing conditions on the ground. This would require keeping the Security Council well informed and deeply committed—no easy demand in view of the Council's checkered history. NGOs concerned with human rights, democracy, and peace need to monitor and put public pressure on the Security Council.

Promise and Obstacles: The 2005 UN Summit

Jeffrey Laurenti, a senior fellow in international affairs at the Century Foundation in New York, published an insightful recapitulation of the September 2005 UN summit meeting—a highly visible meeting intended to strengthen the UN.[26] He noted that it was soon apparent that there would be no "radical changes," given the obstacles imposed not only by the autocratic and dictatorial regimes in the General Assembly but also by right-wing factions in the United States. Many developing countries were critical of both the U.S. and the Secretary-General's reform proposals. In the absence of strong, cohesive leadership by the world's democracies, little could be accomplished.

One of the great divisions among member states has been whether the UN should be the center of an international system or simply an occasionally useful auxiliary to powerful national bodies and regional coalitions. Although survey research for many years has shown majority support in the United States for the UN, hard-line conservatives want to diminish its status to an adjunct of Washington's policies rather than an institution that is beneficial to the whole world, as the Roosevelts had envisioned. Most agree on the UN's value in technical areas of global significance, such as civil aviation, weather forecasting, public health, and food safety standards. Even most conservatives now agree that UN agencies should take the lead in international responses to humanitarian emergencies. Capable technical agencies can still become suspect, however, when they make choices that offend powerful private constituencies. Although the World Health Organization earned global respect for its campaigns against smallpox, polio, HIV/AIDS, the Ebola virus, and SARS, its opposition to tobacco use and unaffordable drug prices has stirred criticism.

The UN is whipsawed between different kinds of opposition, e.g., from large military powers such as the United States, Russia, and China and from autocratic leaders of poor countries. This strongly undermines UN efficacy, and the blame is then heaped on the UN Secretary-General and the Secretariat, as if the member states had no power.

The peaceful resolution of political issues was the UN's original reason for being, and its effectiveness in maintaining peace is the criterion most Americans use to rate its performance. Laurenti detailed how the UN's role in peace, politics, and security has greatly expanded since the end of the Cold War. Formerly its role on the ground was limited to sending lightly armed peacekeepers to monitor hostile parties—trying to keep peace where there was no peace to keep, and then being blamed by the perennial cynics. Today UN peacekeeping troops enforce peace settlements and hold war-riven societies together until the rival parties learn to live together. Once the Secretary-General only offered "good offices" as an impartial mediator between belligerents. Today UN special representatives might construct a transitional government in a war-torn country or even act as head of an interim international administration.

Today, the UN monitors elections and sets the standard for electoral fairness and legitimacy. UN weapons inspectors earned respect for their effectiveness in Iraq, thus strengthening the global authority of impartial UN arms verification.[27] The award of the 2005 Nobel Peace Prize to the UN's International Atomic Energy Agency and its current head, Mohamed El Baredei, signifies the value of another technical agency with important bearing on nuclear weapons.

Until the end of the Cold War the Security Council's authority to order "complete or partial interruption of economic relations" was used only once, for an arms embargo against South Africa's apartheid government. In 1990 the Security Council imposed harsh sanctions against Iraq to force it out of Kuwait, and even after U.S.-led military action accomplished that goal, the Council left the sanctions in place until Iraq's disarmament was verified, later mitigating them with its "oil for food" program.

Extensive UN sanctions helped persuade Libya to hand over airline bombers, Serbia to agree to a peace settlement in Bosnia, and Sudan to expel Osama bin Laden.

The ineffectiveness of the United Nations Protection Force in Bosnia in protecting civilians confirmed the skepticism that many felt about the UN in the area of security and strengthened U.S. reluctance to place U.S. troops under UN command. This bias spread to Britain and France, who insisted that their troops serve with, but not under the command of, UN peacekeeping forces in Sierra Leone and Congo, just as the Americans did in Somalia. In the 1990s, reliance on NATO instead of the UN for peacekeeping and peace enforcement became established Washington policy everywhere except in Africa.

Nevertheless, the United States firmly supported excellent proposals made in 2000 by an international panel led by Lakhtar Brahimi to improve UN capacities for effective peacekeeping. The UN's department of peacekeeping operations used these new capabilities well in such difficult areas as Sierra Leone, Liberia, Congo, and southern Sudan. The United States also welcomed the one new institution that Secretary-General Annan proposed to the 2005 summit—a peace-building commission designed to give continuing international reinforcement to fragile political settlements *after* peacekeeping troops have left. This gap in preconflict prevention is a serious omission.

The incessant threat of a veto by Russia, China, or the United States hangs over the Security Council, and efforts for a more broadly representative Security Council have been repeatedly rejected over the past decade. For example, the Bush administration opposed a proposal by Japan and Germany for six new permanent (and ultimately perhaps veto-holding) members and at least four new elected members. Council reform is a source of tension both between the Global North and South and between the United States and its traditional allies. Thus it is unlikely to occur in the foreseeable future.

Secretary-General Annan considered the lack of progress in reforming the Security Council one of the 2005 summit's two biggest failures, the other being the lack of progress on nuclear nonproliferation and disarmament. This most dangerous of all problems was completely neglected in the 2005 summit outcome document.

Hopeful Signs for the Long Term

Decline in Some Forms of Political Violence: Influence of the United Nations

Supported by five governments, the *Human Security Report* is the most comprehensive annual survey of trends in mass violence. Its 2005 report indicated that several forms of political violence had declined worldwide since the early 1990s.[28] After nearly five decades of inexorable increase, the number of genocides declined somewhat after the Cold War (here the time interval is so short that the result is ambiguous). Data also suggest that wars are not only becoming less frequent but also less deadly.[29] Analyzing the causes of the improvement in global security since the early 1990s, the *Report* argued that the UN played a critically important role in spearheading an upsurge of international conflict prevention, peacekeeping, and peace-building activities.[30]

The report identified three major political changes that have made a significant difference in diminishing political violence.

1. The end of colonialism meant the end of colonial wars. From the early 1950s to the early 1980s, colonial wars made up between 60 and 100 percent of all international conflicts, depending on the year.
2. The Cold War, which had driven approximately one-third of all conflicts in the post–World War II era, ended. This removed the main threat of war between the superpowers (except for accidental or inadvertent launch of nuclear weapons) as well as the end of proxy wars they promoted.
3. An unprecedented upsurge of international activities designed to stop ongoing wars and prevent new ones took place in the wake of the Cold War. These activities included (1) a sixfold increase in UN preventive diplomacy missions (to keep wars from starting), (2) a fourfold increase in UN peacemaking missions (to end ongoing conflicts), (3) a fourfold increase in UN peace operations (to reduce the risk of wars recurring), and (4) an elevenfold increase in the number of states subject to UN sanctions (which can help pressure warring parties into peace negotiations).[31]

The UN stimulated much cooperation in these and related efforts. The World Bank, donor states, regional organizations (especially the European Union), and NGOs worked closely with UN agencies—and played independent roles as well. But the UN, the only international organization with a global security mandate, has been the leading player. A variety of commissions and independent research has highlighted innovative practices, synthesized research, and given guidance in this field.

This study confirmed other research. A RAND Corporation study, for example, found that two-thirds of the UN's peace-building missions had succeeded. In addition, the sharp increase in peacemaking efforts led to a significant increase in the number of conflicts that ended in negotiated settlements.[32] The long-term research of Professor Ted Robert Gurr of Maryland showed similar results.[33]

The *Human Security Report* pointed out that in the long run, equitable economic development, increased state capacity, and the spread of inclusive democracy play a vital role in reducing the risk of political violence. The UN and the EU, among others, are fostering such beneficial changes. Still, the *Report* warned against complacency. Although wars and war deaths are down, it reported some sixty armed conflicts in progress as of 2005. Gross abuses of human rights, widespread war crimes, and ever deadlier acts of terrorism are still widely prevalent. The spread of nuclear weapons is terrifying. Since the underlying causes of conflict are rarely addressed, the risk of new wars breaking out and old ones reappearing remains very real; ditto for genocide. Consolidating democratic socioeconomic development is a slow process. UN security efforts could be strengthened if member states were willing. Still, the genocide in Darfur highlights the continuation of atrocities, and the explosion of one nuclear weapon could drastically change the picture. Despite these cautions, there is some evidence that the world is beginning to learn how to cope with destructive human tendencies. Serious, sustained efforts, informed by research, can do much to prevent the worst disasters.

Reforms of the UN to Enhance Its Efficacy

In *The Parliament of Man*, the distinguished historian Paul Kennedy gave a magisterial overview of the UN's roots and functions and a careful analysis of recent proposals for reform.[34] He recognized the widening contributions of the UN to democracy building, equitable development, the status of women and children, and the protection and health of the environment as well as human rights. It is interesting, however, that the word *genocide* is not listed in his book's index. The word did occur in a few places in the text, but only briefly, and with no suggestion that the UN had a significant contribution to make in this field. He noted that Rwanda was the worst episode in the history of the UN but did not suggest how it might prevent future Rwanda-like genocides. Phrases such as "prevention of deadly conflict" or "prevention of mass violence" do not appear in the index, nor do the concepts they represent have a prominent role in the text. Kennedy's scholarship concerning the UN is both long-term and very much up to date because of his prominent role in drafting official reports on how to improve UN performance for its fiftieth anniversary. His coverage of the UN system is comprehensive, yet he was evidently not impressed with the UN's future outlook with respect to preventing war and genocide, unless structural reforms are made.

He believed that the enormous changes in world conditions between 1945 and 2006, including major new problems such as global warming, have made most of the UN structures obsolete. He considered, for example, measures for making the Security Council more representative and for developing significant functional links between the Security Council and the General Assembly. But he was not optimistic that such improvements would occur. Some middle-of-the-road reforms that he did suggest might be feasible with great effort and political struggle but are hardly momentous in their promise.

Those countries who got special advantages at the start, such as the five permanent members of the Security Council with their veto power, are seen as very unlikely ever to give up their privileges. The newer rising powers, locked out of what they consider their rightful high status, are inclined to block new initiatives, often out of envious resentment. Kennedy may be right that little more can be done in restructuring the organization beyond what Kofi Annan achieved. Yet the temple need not be torn down and rebuilt to make it useful to its constituents. Indeed, Kennedy implicitly identified the singular opportunity of the UN in the next generation: to find ways to address serious problems without making fundamental reforms in its structure. Some valuable functions have already emerged within the UN's existing structure, or with only slight modifications to it. The UN's development of preventive diplomacy is a good example. Even more central is its increasing focus on the prevention of genocide.

The United Nations in Prevention of Genocide

On April 7, 2004, in an address to the Commission on Human Rights in Geneva, Kofi Annan expressed his fervent desire to leave as his legacy a UN better equipped to prevent genocide and to act decisively to end it when prevention fails.[35] He therefore announced that in memory of the victims of Rwanda, he would launch an Action Plan to Prevent Genocide that involved the whole UN system, thus setting a unique precedent:

1. *Prevent Armed Conflict.* Genocide usually occurs during war, which suspends the taboo against taking human—even civilian—life.

- Strengthen the capacity of countries to prevent conflict, at both local and national levels.
- Act at the regional level to prevent conflict from spilling over from one country to another.
- Be alert to environmental problems and the competition for natural resources they generate.
- Work with international financial institutions, civil society, and the private sector to ensure that young people receive education and employment to give them a stake in society and discourage gang and militia membership.
- Protect the rights of minorities, the most frequent targets of genocide.

2. *Make the Highest Priority Protecting Civilians When Armed Conflict Occurs.*
   - Remind all parties to the conflict of their responsibility under international law to protect civilians from violence.
   - Strengthen UN peacekeepers by empowering them to use force in defense of their mandate, which explicitly includes protection of local civilians, common targets of violence and rape.
   - Put the mandates and resources of all peacekeeping forces under constant review by both the Secretariat and the Security Council, with the threat of genocide in mind, and be ready to strengthen those forces rapidly.

3. *End Impunity.*
   - Hold to account everyone responsible for genocide.
   - Build and maintain robust judicial systems, both national and international, to prosecute genocidal crimes.

4. *Give Early and Clear Warning.* Be vigilant to detect the signs of approaching genocide in time to avert it.
   - Listen to reports of civil society groups.
   - Listen to the UN High Commissioner on Human Rights, who is well informed by special rapporteurs, independent experts, groups, and treaty bodies.
   - Gather all information in a focused manner and analyze it in a way that allows suggestions for appropriate action.
   - Create a new post, Special Adviser on the Prevention of Genocide, who will report through the Secretary General to the Security Council, the General Assembly, and the Commission on Human Rights.
     1. His mandate will cover not only genocide but also mass murder and other large-scale human rights violations.
     2. He will work closely with the High Commissioner to collect information on threats of genocide and their links to international peace and security.
     3. He will deliver early warning to the Security Council and UN as a whole.
     4. He will recommend appropriate actions to the Security Council.
     5. *Take Swift and Decisive Action.* Genocide is a crime against humanity, and humanity must respond decisively in self-defense. Its instrument should be the UN, specifically the Security Council.

Special Adviser to the Secretary-General on the Prevention of Genocide

In July 2004, Secretary-General Kofi Annan announced that he had chosen Juan E. Méndez as his first Special Adviser on the Prevention of Genocide.[36] As outlined by the Secretary-General in a letter to the Security Council President, the adviser's mandate is to *give early warning* to the Secretary-General and the Security Council about situations that could develop into genocide and to make recommendations to the Council about how the UN can prevent the threatened genocide. The source of the Special Adviser's mandate is Security Council Resolution 1366 (2001), in particular the paragraphs below:

- p. 18 "acknowledging the lessons to be learned ... from the failure of preventive efforts that preceded such tragedies as the genocide in Rwanda ... and resolving to take appropriate action within its competence ... to prevent the recurrence of such tragedies."
- p. 5 "Expresses its willingness to give prompt consideration to early warning or prevention cases brought to his attention by the Secretary General."
- p. 10 "Invites the Secretary General to refer to the Council information and analyses from the United Nations system on cases of serious violations of international law, including international humanitarian law and human rights law; and on potential conflict situations arising ... from ethnic, religious, and territorial disputes, poverty, and lack of development and expresses its determination to give serious consideration to such information and analyses."[37]

The Special Adviser has these tasks:

1. Collect existing information, in particular from within the UN system, on massive and serious violations of human rights and international humanitarian law based on religious, ethnic, or racial hatred that, if not prevented or halted, might lead to genocide.
2. Give early warning to the Secretary General, and through him to the Security Council, of situations that could lead to genocide.
3. Recommend actions to prevent or halt genocide to the Security Council through the Secretary General.
4. Act as liaison with the UN system on activities for prevention of genocide and work to enhance the UN capacity to analyze and manage information on genocide or related crimes.

His central task is to help the Secretary-General define steps to prevent the deterioration of situations into genocide. The Special Adviser will not determine whether the situation is a genocide as defined by the Convention on the Prevention and Punishment of the Crime of Genocide. His activities, intended to allow the UN to act quickly,[38] will focus on spotting genocide-prone or genocide-susceptible situations, without waiting for genocide to occur.

As discussed earlier, the world's heads of state met in an extraordinary summit at the UN Headquarters in New York in 2005. Their outcome document of September 15, 2005, endorsed the UN's efforts to prevent genocide. Although the terms of the endorsement were general, they showed noteworthy progress in an institution that has been sluggish in its commitment to this problem during the past half century. The summit declaration stated that

> 138. Each ... state has the responsibility to protect its populations from genocide, war crimes, ethnic cleansing and crimes against humanity. This responsibility entails the prevention of such crimes, including their incitement.... We accept that responsibility and will act in accordance with it. The international community should, as appropriate, encourage and help states to exercise this responsibility and should support the United Nations to establish an early warning capability.
>
> I. The international community, through the United Nations, also has the responsibility to use appropriate diplomatic, humanitarian and other peaceful means, in accordance with ... the Charter, to help protect populations from genocide, war crimes, ethnic cleansing, and crimes against humanity. In this context, we are prepared to take collective action, in a timely and decisive manner, through the Security Council, in accordance with the UN Charter, including Chapter VII, on a case-by-case basis and in cooperation with relevant regional organizations as appropriate, should peaceful means be inadequate and national authorities manifestly failing to protect their populations from genocide, war crimes, ethnic cleansing and crimes against humanity. We stress the need for the General Assembly to continue consideration of the responsibility to protect populations from genocide, war crimes, ethnic cleansing, and crimes against humanity and its implications.... We also intend to commit ourselves, as necessary and appropriate, to help states build capacity to protect their populations from genocide, war crimes, ethnic cleansing and crimes against humanity and to assist those which are under stress before crises and conflicts break out.
>
> II. We fully support the mission of the UN's Special Adviser for the Prevention of Genocide.[39]

Secretary-General Annan's successor, Ban Ki-moon, has given strong support to implement these concepts. A vital international norm has been globally endorsed and may gradually evolve into patterns of effective action. The new director of this effort is a distinguished world leader, Francis Deng.

The Secretary-General set two important precedents at once by appointing a Special Adviser on the Prevention of Genocide. It was the first time any prevention professional had been appointed at such a high level, reporting directly to the Secretary-General. Moreover, it was the first time that a unit focusing specifically on genocide prevention had ever been created at the UN. In 2006, he strengthened this effort by appointing a distinguished worldwide committee to advise him on ways of strengthening genocide prevention in the future, with particular attention to the Special Adviser on the Prevention of Genocide. It is my privilege to chair this committee, and I offer my perspective on the UN's potential here.

The UN's growing preventive orientation has begun to emphasize primary prevention—that is, prior to any killing, an approach that considers major risk factors for the entire population and ways to buffer them before serious damage occurs. The UN can survey the world's experience, seek to extract the most promising actions, and make them available to groups in distress, nation-states, regional organizations, and nongovernmental organizations. Over time, the UN can develop a comprehensive program of prevention, a set of principles and practices for long-term prevention of genocide and war, with mechanisms for ongoing conflict resolution below the threshold of mass violence, capacity for helping to solve intergroup problems, and models for assisting democratic socioeconomic development that meets basic human needs. A number of practical steps can be taken to identify areas at serious risk of genocide and other mass violence and to offer help to the troubled country or region from the international community.

1. Establish an ongoing process, drawing on readily available information from all sources, to identify targets, scapegoats, and out-groups.
2. Monitor trends of hatred and dehumanization of groups that are identified in a vulnerable position.
3. Offer help in conflict resolution and prevention of mass violence in situations of this kind—e.g., by early strong mediation.
4. Help to build internal capacity of member states (with their agreement) for early, ongoing conflict resolution, including essential concepts, techniques (e.g., negotiation), and institutions (e.g., an independent judiciary).
5. Help leaders and the public understand the merits of these enterprises, showing how a country afflicted with deep divisions will find that such measures serve its own interests, and offer the prospect of belonging to a valued group (such as a regional organization for economic cooperation) and earning respect and economic and political benefits in the international community.
6. Identify predisposing factors—for example, economic deterioration, social disorganization, an alienated position with prospects of war and/or revolution in the background. The earlier such problems are identified and the better they are understood, the greater the opportunity for international organizations to help.
7. Enlist the help of key member states who are strongly interested in the genocide problem and how to overcome it. Persuade them to commit intellectual, technical, financial, and moral resources.

The Secretary-General's Special Adviser on the Prevention of Genocide cannot lead in all of these fundamental, long-term activities. But he can stimulate and encourage those in the UN system who have such responsibilities, and he can help the Secretary-General strengthen them by identifying opportunities for cooperation among worldwide departments and agencies, as well as other international organizations.

Conclusion

There are powerful constraints imposed on the UN's own efficacy in matters of peace and security. These constraints are chiefly imposed, in different ways, by the member states themselves. The root cause of these constraints is an egocentric, ethnocentric, shortsighted preoccupation with outmoded conceptions of sovereignty.

The central body for peace and security—including prevention of genocide—is the Security Council, where most power lies with the Permanent Five, each of which has veto power. What kind of strength do its members exhibit for preventing war and genocide? In 2007, the answer is, not much. The United States, the originator of the UN and still its most powerful member, is extremely ambivalent. It often blocks humane, forward-looking measures. It often treats the Secretary-General shabbily. It has faded far from its stellar performance of the post–World War II period in leading or even strongly supporting democratic socioeconomic development. Russia and China, though their leaders have improved since the days of Stalin and Mao, are still a long way from becoming democracies and protecting human rights. France is France: sometimes brilliant, often haughty, often obstructionist, erratic at best (despite its great culture and cuisine). The UK's efforts to maintain the "special relationship" with the United States sometimes carry it astray. Altogether, this is not an inspiring leadership group.

The Security Council's revolving-door membership (including the Permanent Five) makes it difficult to build a body of knowledge, skill, and shared values that would be essential to prevent mass violence. Further, it is all too easy for them to shift blame to the Secretary-General. (Perhaps the initials, SG, really stand for "scapegoat.") In fairness, communication between the Security Council and the Secretary-General has grown, along with increased awareness of the practical necessity to help the poorest countries climb out of their morass and serious efforts to master the tools and strategies of prevention.

What about the General Assembly? Consisting of nearly 200 countries, north-south/east-west/rich-poor, it provides a unique worldwide forum for mutual education and for building intergroup friendships. Yet it is an unwieldy body for arriving at agreements, resolving disputes, or providing effective administration. Many of its member states are autocracies or outright dictatorships. It has a long-term undercurrent of envious resentment on the part of the poor countries toward the rich countries, especially the United States. It was ambivalent about Kofi Annan's championing of human rights and democracy and vigorous efforts for the prevention of armed conflict during his entire term of office. It shows little promise so far in efforts to prevent genocide—witness Darfur.

In the long run the Security Council and the General Assembly might contribute to the prevention of war and genocide, especially if leaders of high caliber emerge. But in the near term, these two major UN bodies cannot be counted on to take major steps in that direction. The Secretary-General and several UN agencies offer greater promise, but they are constrained by the Security Council, the General Assembly, and recalcitrant member states.[40]

The primary base for efforts to prevent genocide may well emerge elsewhere, but the UN must play a significant part in genocide prevention, in ways that build on its distinctive strengths. The appointment of Francis Deng, a superb Undersecretary for the Prevention of Genocide and Mass Atrocities, in 2007 offers an authentic basis for hope that the UN may move gradually toward fulfillment of its potential.

CHAPTER 14

The Promise of the European Union
for Prevention of Genocide

How Can the Established Democracies Lead in Prevention?

The formidable resources of the established democracies give them great potential to form groupings that can recognize early warnings of imminent conflict and respond promptly with preventive actions. Yet their track record in prevention is not inspiring. Recently a focus on prevention has emerged, however, and its impact on policy has been especially impressive in the European Union since 2001, when that body announced its Göteborg Programme on conflict prevention, a cooperative approach to solving disputes peacefully and to dealing with their root causes. It is now an important element of the external relations of the European Union. The rotating Presidency of the EU meant that Sweden, a pioneer in prevention of violent conflict, was able to take the lead in creating this program.

Individual states have some advantages over international bodies or coalitions in undertaking preventive action. But unilateral preventive actions by individual states can also have significant drawbacks. States wisely reluctant to act alone can establish a "friends group," "contact group," or other ad hoc cooperative international coalition. Even a few countries working together can substantially increase their sources of information, their range of policy options, and the checks and balances of multiple inputs. They are unlikely to rush prematurely into military action and more likely to use other instruments effectively.

Particularly significant in this context is the growing community of established democracies. By and large, they are stable and sturdy, technically advanced, relatively affluent, and demonstrably able to work together effectively in many situations. Some excellent examples of their successful cooperation are the European Union and its ultimate parent, the Marshall Plan; NATO; the G8; the OECD; and the OSCE. Of course, on occasion the established democracies have failed badly, as indicated by their apathy in the early years of Yugoslavia's ruin, especially their inaction during the early years of the conflict in Bosnia; their total failure in dealing with the Rwandan genocide; and now their prolonged dithering over catastrophe in the Sudan in the face of Chinese recalcitrance. How can they become more effective on a consistent basis in dealing with violence-prone states or groups, and in particular, how can they develop regular and clear-cut mechanisms of prevention?

There is much promise in an ever closer cooperation among established democracies— the enlarging group of nations that share humane values, effective mechanisms for coping with conflict, and formidable resources for preventing mass violence. In the face of a foreseeable path toward atrocity behavior, even genocide, they can act effectively in appropriate groupings all over the world, whether or not the UN is able to act—functioning within the spirit of the UN Charter but not limited by its political and procedural constraints in the face of great danger. This would provide a flexible system of action for peace and justice. It would amount to an extensive voluntary coalition, arranged in different configurations for different situations, according to the requirements and opportunities of a particular conflict.[1] In 2007, more than ever before, democratic governments gave explicit attention to preventing mass violence (mainly through their foreign ministries) and cooperated as an informal consortium as well as in structured organizations. The European Union is the clearest example of a set of established democracies sharing basic humane and peaceful values, able to act effectively, and morally committed to prevent genocide.

In the decades ahead more and more countries will emerge as full-fledged democracies and concomitantly develop technical, economic, and moral strength. This expanding fellowship of democracies, representing a growing international culture of fairness, will provide a larger pool of strength to address emerging problems by establishing and drawing on accepted standards and procedures. Sometimes these democracies might act entirely within the UN system; sometimes outside it; and sometimes both at once. This set of nations has the opportunity within sight to upgrade and regularize their cooperation in preventing violence.

Increasingly, the established democracies are destined to take the lead in formulating norms of decent behavior for all humanity. In so doing, they should strive to reach beyond themselves and at least include emerging democracies; to the extent possible, they should include the entire international community. It is likely in this era of pervasive communication that democratic norms of decent behavior will continue to spread throughout the world and appeal to the majority of people in most countries, even if they offend tyrannical administrations.[2] In any event, they can provide a focal point for coalescence on a particular problem of exceptional gravity.

The European Union and the Prevention of Genocide

The work of the EU in preventing mass violence is characterized by international cooperation and reaching out to poor countries. The role of the UN is underlined as well as EU assistance in the development of regional organizations such as the African Union. Measures are being taken to improve the EU's capability to counter threats of genocide. Work is under way to improve the European Commission's ability to respond to identified root causes and early warning signs of genocide, other mass murder, and ethnic cleansing. One concrete result is the inclusion of the search for impending genocide as an important indicator for the EU's early warning bodies assessing potential conflicts.

As stated in the EU Programme for the Prevention of Violent Conflicts (the Göteborg Programme),

The international community has a political and moral responsibility to act to avoid the human suffering and the destruction of resources caused by violent conflicts. The European Union is a successful example of conflict prevention, based on democratic values and respect for human rights, justice and solidarity, economic prosperity, and sustainable development. The process of enlargement will extend this community of peace and progress to a wider circle of European states.

In line with the fundamental values of the EU, the highest political priority will be given to improving the effectiveness and coherence of its external action in the field of conflict prevention, thereby also enhancing the preventive capabilities of the international community at large.

Conflict prevention calls for a cooperative approach to facilitate peaceful solutions to disputes and implies addressing the root causes of conflicts. It is an important element of all aspects of the external relations of the European Union. The development of the European Security and Defence Policy (ESDP) has, since the outset, also been intended to strengthen the EU's capacity for action in the crucial field of conflict prevention.

In keeping with the primary role of the UN in conflict prevention, EU actions will be undertaken in accordance with the principles and purposes of the UN Charter. Recalling that the main responsibility for conflict prevention rests with the parties concerned, assistance to local and regional capacity building [for conflict resolution], according to principles of local ownership, is of particular importance.

The European Union, through this programme, underlines its political commitment to pursue conflict prevention as one of the main objectives of the EU's external relations. It resolves to continue to improve its capacity to prevent violent conflicts and to contribute to a global culture of prevention. ...

Political priorities for preventive actions

Successful conflict prevention relies on preparedness to take action before a situation deteriorates into violence. Development of policy options must start with clear political priorities and direction, set out through regular reviews of potential conflict areas.

In order to set clear political priorities for preventive actions:

- the Council will schedule a broad consideration of potential conflict issues at the outset of each Presidency,[4] including at the time of the yearly orientation debate, prepared with assistance from the High Representative, relevant Council bodies, including the Political and Security Committee (PSC),[5] and the Commission, to identify priority areas and regions for EU preventive actions,
- the implementation of preventive strategies will be monitored by the Council, drawing on contributions from the Secretary General/High Representative (SG/HR) and the Commission. ...

Early warning, action, and policy coherence

Successful prevention must be based on accurate information and analysis as well as clear options for action for both long- and short-term prevention. It requires enhanced field cooperation. Coherence must be ensured in early warning, analysis, planning, decision making, implementation, and evaluation. ...

[F]ull use will be made of information from field-based personnel of the UN and the OSCE, as well as other international organizations and civil society.[3]

The mutual support and concentration of expertise in prevention of mass violence provided by an EU center for prevention of genocide could make a crucial difference. The center could elicit cooperation to pool strengths, share burdens, and divide labor in the tasks of genocide prevention. It could affiliate with other institutions for particular tasks, e.g., an EU core linked to the UN, NATO, and OSCE. It could stimulate the international community in many ways to understand genocide, to recognize early signs of trouble in genocide-prone societies, and to provide response options/contingency plans for preventive action. This concept is developed in Chapter 18.

The remarkable, ongoing progress of the EU in preventing deadly conflict during the past decade shows that, for all the difficulties, opportunities can rapidly arise in this field.

Nature of the European Union

The European Union is a remarkable, indeed unprecedented, family of democratic European states, working together for peace and prosperity.[6] It arose in reaction to the horrors of World War II and the Holocaust. European statesmen had the vision to see the beauty of cooperation—first at the economic, and then at the political level, but now at the level of human relations in the broadest sense. The EU includes five institutions, each with a specific role:

- European Parliament (elected by citizens of the member states)
- Council of the European Union (representing the member state governments)
- European Commission (the EU's executive body)
- Court of Justice (ensuring compliance with the law)
- Court of Auditors (controlling management of the EU budget)

They are flanked by five other important bodies:

- European Economic and Social Committee (expresses the views of organized civil society on economic and social issues)
- Committee of the Regions (expresses the views of regional and local authorities)
- European Central Bank (responsible for monetary policy and managing the euro)
- European Ombudsman (deals with citizens' complaints of maladministration by any EU institution or body)
- European Investment Bank (helps achieve EU objectives by financing investment projects)

Thus, the comprehensive nature of the EU is clear. Initially, six countries made up the EU: Belgium, Germany, France, Italy, Luxembourg, and the Netherlands. Denmark, Ireland, and the United Kingdom joined in 1973, Greece in 1981, Spain and Portugal in 1986, and Austria, Finland, and Sweden in 1995. In 2004 its greatest enlargement took place when ten new countries joined: Cyprus, the Czech Republic, Estonia, Hungary, Latvia, Lithuania, Malta, Poland, Slovakia, and Slovenia. And on January 1, 2007, Bulgaria and Rumania entered the EU. To become eligible for membership, these countries had to develop democratic institutions—a novel experience for many of them and certainly a beneficial one.

In its early years, cooperation among EU countries focused on trade, but now the EU also deals with such subjects as citizens' rights; ensuring freedom, security, and justice; job creation; regional development; environmental protection; and making globalization work equitably.

The economically powerful European Union is a strikingly successful example of how close cooperation and understanding among nations that had waged massive wars against one another within living memory was able to lead to reconciliation that is the basis for peace and prosperity. As the most prominent representative body in one of the wealthiest and most influential areas of the globe, the EU is well placed to play a major role in preventing violent conflict. The EU has an extensive set of instruments for structural long-term and direct short-term preventive actions. The long-term instruments include development cooperation, trade, arms control, human rights, and environmental policies as well as political dialogue. The union also has a broad range of diplomatic and humanitarian instruments for short-term prevention. It uses its instruments to address root causes of conflict, such as poverty, lack of good governance and lack of respect for human rights, and competition for scarce natural resources. It can use not only its civilian and military crisis management capabilities but also the diplomatic instruments of its members. It can also wield trade policy instruments, cooperation agreements, development assistance, economic cooperation, and social and environmental policies as mechanisms and incentives to assure peace.

What the EU is currently seeking to achieve is an extensive coordination of these different capabilities with an explicit focus on prevention. This is an innovative approach to international affairs. Only a few years after prevention was established as a priority in the European Union, there is much evidence of progress and long-term commitment.

All major EU components are striving to mainstream conflict prevention within their areas of competence. EU's political dialogue is used in a systematic way to address potential conflicts and promote violence prevention. There are specific actions in support of democracy; particular attention is paid to support electoral processes, including electoral observers; administration of justice; improving police services; and human rights training for the whole security sector—all as a means of contributing to the prevention of deadly conflict.

In order to increase cooperation and build effective partnerships:

- The EU has intensified practical cooperation with the UN system, the OSCE, the Council of Europe, other regional and subregional organizations, and the international financial institutions.
- In accordance with agreed-upon principles, the EU and NATO, in developing their cooperation in crisis management, notably in the western Balkans, are contributing to conflict prevention.
- Exchange of information, dialogue, and practical cooperation with humanitarian actors such as the International Committee for the Red Cross (ICRC), relevant NGOs, and academic organizations are being strengthened.

- Joint training programs for EU, UN, and OSCE field and headquarters personnel are under way.

The European Union's dedication to a vigorous, proactive, and coherent program to prevent deadly conflict makes it a very strong candidate to sponsor a center for the prevention of the ugliest form of violence, genocide. Genocide may represent only a fraction of armed violence, but it has a powerful damaging effect—not only in terrible suffering and the loss of life but also in breeding and nurturing hatreds that make likely the continuing recurrence of bloodshed in the country of origin and the spillover of refugees and dangerous situations into neighboring countries. The hope that the world can eradicate genocide must not be dismissed as a chimera. The moral outrage it creates strengthens the hope that it can be eliminated. The European experience puts it into sharp focus.

The Centrality of Europe in Fostering International Cooperation for Democratic Development and Prevention of Mass Violence

Timothy Garton Ash, a distinguished observer of Europe, made the case for strong cooperation among the established democracies, especially the Transatlantic Alliance, in coping constructively with global problems and minimizing the risk of mass violence.[7] He contrasted the "rich north" and "poor south." About 1 billion of the world's 6 billion population are rich, with an average daily income of seventy dollars. At the other end of the spectrum, more than 1 billion people, largely in the "poor south," subsist on less than one dollar a day.[8] In the developing countries of the Southern Hemisphere, the grim picture of severe malnutrition, disease, and weakness associated with this poverty is becoming more widely understood. The gap between rich and poor is greater than ever. This is a global problem of profound significance, with moral, political, economic, and health dimensions that are all conducive to violence.

The governments of developing countries must themselves take the first responsibility for development. As Amartya Sen has observed, causal links between freedom and development operate in both directions.[9] More and more, donor countries and organizations are requiring good governance from the countries to which they provide aid, so that their money does not end up in the pockets of corrupt leaders and their friends. Yet help from outside, especially help oriented toward building knowledge, skill, and constructive institutions, is almost always essential. Ash advocated international democratic cooperation to meet these desperately important needs. He saw more evidence of promise in Europe than the United States in this regard. He strongly emphasized development aid, removal of trade barriers, and relief of oppressive debt accumulated by past autocrats and dictators.

Ash made the case that, despite burgeoning world population, there is enough food to feed the world. The central problem with both food and water is equitable distribution, and this in turn rests on substantial democratic cooperation. Indeed, these problems, as well as the impending global energy crisis and the consequences of global warming, all require an unprecedented level of technical, intellectual, and international cooperation on a solid moral basis of our common humanity. These points are entirely consistent with Chapters 8 and 9 in this book.

To meet these challenges, Europe and the United States must ally with democracies outside the traditional free West (such as Japan, India, and South Africa)—and also with groups struggling for freedom in nations still not free.[10]

Europe has a great role to play in global transformation for survival. As Ash reminded us, Europe's story is the story of how a vast continent with only four free countries in 1942 became a continent with only one *un*free country (Belarus) in 2002.

Ash observed that the EU draws nations in by both "magnetic" and formal induction. Because Europeans not in the EU have been so strongly attracted to joining it, they have accepted its intrusive yet highly desirable demands for membership, as stated in the Copenhagen criteria: free elections, the rule of law, free markets, and respect for individual and minority rights.

Ash argued that Europeans, taught by their own barbaric experiences during the last century, have an obligation to intervene to help prevent imminent genocide everywhere. They must also foresee and forestall the harsh lesson that this century threatens, by finding ways to ensure that dictators and fanatics will not get their hands on weapons of mass destruction. If they justly reject a Bush-style unilateral preemption, they must jointly work out and agree upon feasible and effective methods of multilateral prevention. Military action must always remain the last resort in these plans, for both moral and practical reasons.[11]

He recommended a constant dialogue to coordinate (1) removal of barriers to free transatlantic commerce, (2) activities of NATO with whatever sort of military capacity the EU develops, (3) aid and development for poor countries, and (4) environmental protection. Together with other democracies and the UN, Europe should agree upon rules for "just wars" and "just interventions" into the internal affairs of other states.

Franklin Delano Roosevelt enumerated four basic freedoms: freedom from want, freedom from fear, freedom of speech, and freedom of religion. Ash reinforced these basic concepts and suggested ways of implementing them in the twenty-first century. These issues are largely political, economic, scientific, and technological. He emphasized that force should be the last resort and considered military interventions justifiable only if a genocide is actually in progress or if a terrorist group or rogue regime is clearly on the verge of obtaining weapons of mass destruction with the unmistakable intention of using them on someone (including its own people). Except in the most urgent circumstances, interventions should get explicit UN approval or at least approval of what Ash called a "double majority" of established democracies and of the countries in the region involved.

He listed ways to extend freedom:

- Urge our governments and companies to link trade and investment to respect for human rights and democratic political and legal conditions.
- Urge our parliaments to give money to foundations that work for democracy in unfree countries.
- Give our own money and time to nongovernmental organizations that work for freedom in other countries.
- See that the Internet, international broadcasting, and scholarships for foreign students expose unfree peoples to the benefits of a free society.
- Ensure that Europe provides fledgling democracies with a comprehensive "toolbox" of practical lessons from its own experiences on such topics as how to draft a

constitution, reconcile a bitter past, dispose of nuclear silos, and construct a system of economic security.[12]

In another recent study of Europe's centrality in the quest for a better world, Mark Leonard highlighted the EU's ability to attract potential enemies into a profitable association, conditional upon acceptance of its liberal set of values—and, in so doing, to strongly influence the rest of the world.[13] Originally intended as an economic union of limited European extent, the EU has within only a half century converted a warring continent into a region of peace. It has evolved, both by plan and by chance, into what Leonard considered the most revolutionary structure in international politics since the nation-state, and it uses its novel "transformative power" (a combination of economic weight, compelling ideals, and skillful diplomacy) to create binding networks of association through a common market, institutions, and laws that comprise a structure very different from the traditional nation-state's hierarchical organization. In the twenty-first century the "old Europe" that U.S. politicians have derided will become a major influence on global political, social, and economic development and institutions.[14]

Leonard noted the many obstacles the EU has experienced, such as the recent rejection of its proposed constitution, and observed that every setback has led to a stronger union. Europe has used the process of integration to overcome the challenges it had to face after World War II. An explicit commitment to democracy and an impressive body of humane and equitable international law give added worth to its appeal as an example to the rest of the world.[15]

The end of World War II saw a Europe devastated by charismatic leaders with extravagant visions and reluctant to trust in them again. The creators of the new Europe tended to be obscure yet capable technocrats whose vision was to prevent a recurrence of armed violence on the continent. When ex-Soviet applicants to the EU agreed to abide by their "80,000 pages of laws," monitors were sent to work with them and see they actually obeyed them. This meant reconstructing these countries from the ground up, thus changing them forever.[16] The key to success of the European model is that surveillance is voluntary and common to all. This means that it can be exercised without a huge and expensive enforcement apparatus. Europe has a vital interest in strengthening international law because the very basis of the EU is an international treaty. In encouraging other common markets in Africa, Asia, and Latin America, the EU seeks to create similar communities of interest.

Regional associations are springing up all over the world: The African Union in Africa; ASEAN, the Shanghai Cooperation Organization, and the South Asian Association for Regional Cooperation (SAARC) in Asia; Asia-Pacific Economic Cooperation (APEC) in the Pacific rim; and the Mercado Común del Sur (MERCOSUR), the North American Free Trade Agreement (NAFTA), and the Free Trade Area in the Americas. As the members of these regional organizations realize benefits from working together, Leonard predicted, they will gradually follow the European model of pooled sovereignty.[17] The new regionalism does not mean military alliances; it means peaceful associations that support global development, regional security and stability, and open markets. Its growth can have a snowball effect on world order.[18]

Working with Others

The European Security Strategy makes effective multilateral engagement a strategic objective of the EU. Close partnerships with a variety of international, regional, and local actors have underpinned all EU conflict prevention activities. One major thrust is toward collaboration with the UN, African regional organizations, and civil society.

- The EU/UN Joint Declaration of September 24, 2003, agrees to closer cooperation in crisis management, with emphasis on planning, training, communication, and sharing best practices.
- On matters of peace and security, the EC Communication on EU/UN relations aims to consolidate international support of UN objectives and to facilitate joint planning, development of strategic partnerships with specialized agencies, and direct and pragmatic cooperation and coordination.[19]
- A strategic partnership with the UNDP on conflict prevention has been negotiated.
- In January 2003 the UN Secretary-General met with the EU Presidency, with Secretary-General/High Representative (SG/HR) Solana, and with the European Commission.
- The Secretary-General's visits were followed by the establishment of contacts both at senior levels and between steering committees to coordinate crisis management.
- The Commission has a desk-to-desk dialogue with UN teams about five countries, including an agreement to share early warning information about them.

All of this points toward the feasibility of UN-EU collaboration in prevention of genocide.

A number of activities furthered EU cooperation with regional and subregional African organizations to foster peace and security in Africa:

- The AU commissioner for peace and security met with Javier Solana and was invited to the Commission on Peace and Security.
- A joint Global Control System (GCS)/Commission mission went to Addis Ababa to develop political dialogue between the EU and the AU and to explore how the EU could help the AU set up workable institutions in a sustained effort for capacity building.
- The UN and the EU undertook a study of how the international community can strengthen the capacity of the Economic Community of West African States (ECOWAS) in peace and security action and how to develop synergy between UN and EU activities in the region.
- EU commitment to building capacity for conflict prevention, management, and resolution within regional organizations includes a 16-million-euro Conflict Prevention, Management, and Resolution program in Eastern and Southern Africa within the overall context of the AU.
- Cooperation with African regional organizations is being reinforced by creation of a Peace Facility for Africa, by work on European Security and Defence Policy (ESDP) in Africa, and by European Development Fund (EDF)[20] disbursements.

The Irish rotating Presidency stressed increasing effective cooperation between the EU and civil society organizations in conflict prevention. This was a central theme at a Dublin meeting in 2003, involving representatives from civil society organizations, EU member states, partner governments, and the UN. The conference found much agreement among governments, EU/UN institutions, and their NGO/civil society counterparts in their approaches to conflict prevention. The meeting made concrete recommendations in its Dublin Action Agenda on the Prevention of Violent Conflict for closer cooperation through more structured dialogue, regular liaisons, and joint work in addressing security challenges. Thus, since the inception of its conflict prevention program in 2001, the EU has been making year-by-year progress.

Toward More Coherent Action

A long-term challenge for the EU is effective coordination of its many instruments for conflict prevention—in crisis management, politics, trade, and development—and linking them with member state activities to attack the root causes of conflict and state vulnerability. It has seen some progress in this area.

Substantial movement toward a more coherent, structured, and long-term instrument to promote African peacekeeping operations, based on the principles of African ownership and solidarity, has been made by support of the Peace Facility for Africa with 250 million euros from the European Development Fund as a transitional mechanism. In addition to deployment of peacekeeping troops and related capacity building, it will support conflict prevention by reinforcing early warning systems, conflict mediation, and ceasefire observation and by seeking to create conditions in which longer-term development assistance can resume.

A coherent approach to placing trade in the framework of violence prevention is also necessary. An example of progress here is the incorporation of mutual conditionality clauses into trade and cooperation agreements with partner countries. Trade in natural resources that fuel conflict is of particular concern. The Kimberley Process Certification Scheme (KPCS), in operation since 2003, links trade policies to violence prevention by preventing diamonds that support conflict from entering the legitimate diamond trade. The scheme now covers almost all international production of and trade in rough diamonds. The EC chairs the Working Group on Monitoring in the Kimberley Process and has introduced a comprehensive system of "peer review." The KPCS is widely seen as an innovative model for multilateral instruments of conflict prevention. The UN General Assembly reaffirmed its strong support for the KPCS in an April 2004 resolution.

Enhancing Capability for Prevention of Mass Violence

The EU is committed to using a wide range of instruments—in accordance with the UN Charter and international law—to prevent violent conflict. "This requires early upstream application of all instruments at the EU's disposal"[21] and the ability to respond rapidly to incipient conflict.

The Irish Presidency explored EU civilian capabilities in the field of crisis management with particular attention to preventive action and to a smooth transition from intervention in the conflict to longer-term development and institution building during postconflict reconstruction. The EU common training policy within the ESDP will help to build a common European security culture with conflict prevention at its center. The EC training project on civilian crisis management included two specialized courses on conflict transformation in spring 2004. An academic postgraduate fellowship has been established in Ireland to focus on the role of the EU in conflict prevention and resolution.[22]

With respect to rapid response, member states are asked to achieve complete capability in 2007. Particular attention will be given to standards, training, and assessment of rapid response capabilities, to ensure their interoperability and effective use.

The EU has continued to reinforce early warning capability and to strengthen the link between early warning and early action through the integration of an enhanced range of resources from member states and the refinement of early warning methodology. An important task is to link early warning capabilities with the new planning capabilities in the service of preventing genocide and state failure.

The EU emphasizes that broad economic and social development, along with poverty reduction, is essential in alleviation of the conditions of extreme inequality and exclusion that fuel grievances and conflict. Research must increasingly provide the basis for the development of conflict prevention capabilities. Research cooperation is fostered to gain better understanding of what triggers conflict and what measures can be developed to prevent or mitigate it.[23]

A More Active European Union

The European Security Strategy (ESS) recommends a more active application of the full spectrum of instruments for crisis management and conflict prevention, including political, diplomatic, military and civilian, trade, and development tools. The commitment of the EU to violence prevention in the face of great difficulty is shown by its sustained and evolving engagement in Africa.

The EU has not shied away from genocide-related missions. It supported the African Union in convening the parties involved in the Darfur crisis to seek an agreement on conditions for establishing a Ceasefire Commission and deploying monitors. The EU and AU collaborate in the Darfur monitoring mission, with financial support through the Africa Peace Facility and with participation of EU observers. The EU is trying to help in one of the world's worst situations.

In the western Balkans the EU Police Mission in Bosnia Herzegovina (EUPM) strengthened local institutions in preparation for the EU-led ESDP mission in Bosnia Herzegovina that has replaced NATO's Stabilization Force. This is a noteworthy transition. In the Former Yugoslavian Republic of Macedonia (FYRM), a new EU police mission is monitoring, mentoring, and advising the country's police, helping to fight organized crime, and promoting European policing standards.

The new EU special representative in the southern Caucasus is supporting mechanisms for settling the conflicts over Abkhazia, South Ossetia, and Nagorno-Karabakh.

Immediate assistance was provided in creating transparency, credibility, and legitimacy in the Georgian presidential and parliamentary elections in early 2004. Fundamentally, the EU's assistance strategy is dedicated to the prevention of conflict.

> Conflict prevention and conflict resolution are essential elements of the EU's overall policy of promoting human rights and democratization around the world. The European Initiative for Democracy and Human Rights provides support for the development of early warning, mediation, reconciliation, and confidence building measures implemented by grass-roots and international NGOs, the promotion of common training modules for civilian staff to be deployed in international crisis management missions, and the strengthening of the capacity of international, regional or local organizations involved in conflict prevention.[24]

The Stockholm International Forum met in January 2004 to commit Europe's leaders to the prevention of genocide. At the conference, Javier Solana emphasized the EU's commitment to prevention and effective multilateralism. I have quoted some of his powerful remarks in Chapter 1.

Further Observations on EU Potential

A newly published volume dedicated to the late Anna Lindh, former foreign minister of Sweden and a pioneer in violence prevention, contained several contributions that were exceptionally well informed and covered different (though related) facets of EU work for prevention of mass violence.[25] It is important to emphasize that the world is only beginning to realize the depth and breadth of the EU's commitment to prevention of mass violence—which foreshadows an increasing role in genocide prevention.

Conflict Prevention as an Instrument in the EU's Security Toolbox

Included in the 2005 Anna Lindh volume is a chapter by Jim Cloos, who serves at the General Secretariat of the EU Council of Ministers as Director in charge of Transatlantic Relations, Latin America, United Nations, Human Rights, and Counter-Terrorism. The chapter's title, "Conflict Prevention as an Instrument in the EU's Security Toolbox," indicates how important—and how practical—prevention has become as an ingredient of EU foreign policy. At the head of Cloos's article is the motto: "Speak softly, but carry a big carrot."[26] Cloos reminded us that conflict prevention is much cheaper than its overused alternative, military intervention-*cum*-postconflict reconstruction. The annual budget of the OSCE high commissioner on national minorities adds up to less than the purchase price of one fighter plane. Reducing the risk of civil war in developing countries to the level developed countries currently enjoy would produce gains three times greater than the total global aid budget in 2004. In short, "preventing a conflict is a win-win situation for everyone involved."[27] Since this is so, why does the international community react so slowly to emerging crises—in those cases when it generates the political will to react at all? In the first place, neither prospects for prevention nor activities involving prevention attract headlines. And the ever-present multitude of acute and urgent problems leaves little opportunity to deal with chronic troubles that threaten, but have not yet erupted into, murderous situations—even when they can be identified in advance. But conflict prevention is vital to our own security and the best way to prevent the intense suffering of millions.

Anna Lindh knew this. Her influence is clearly seen in the EU's Göteborg Programme—which represents the EU's first conceptualization of prevention efforts.[28] Two years later the ESS endorsed both structural conflict prevention and short-term preventive actions: "We need to develop a strategic culture that fosters early, rapid, and, when necessary, robust intervention.... We need to be able to act before countries around us deteriorate, when signs of proliferation are detected, and before humanitarian emergencies arise. Preventive engagement can avoid more serious problems in the future."[29]

The EU is itself an effective conflict prevention project. The purpose of its creation was to build a zone of peace by voluntarily pooling sovereignty and institutions, and it has worked so well that later generations have forgotten the reason it was established. Enlargement allowed the EU to expand its special kind of structural conflict prevention: "The carrot of membership is the EU's greatest asset."[30] Conflicts involving national minorities had to be resolved before accession, in many cases with the joint assistance of the EU and the OSCE high commissioner on national minorities. Entry into the EU was the incentive for applicant states to agree to international help, and this encouraged cooperation with the high commissioner, whose recommendations had to be met before accession was approved. In making use of OSCE standards, the EU reinforced OSCE efforts rather than duplicating them.

Using the prospect of membership as an incentive to reform has its limits. But making external assistance, trade, and other benefits conditional on progress in the areas of democratic reform, the rule of law, human rights, and acceptance of a market economy is a valuable approach that is likely to have similar value in other parts of the world, especially if the EU offers its tutelage, technical assistance, and sustained, sympathetic encouragement. The European Neighbourhood Policy (ENP) offers the same approach to states bordering the EU—without, however, extending the prospect of EU membership.

> Building on its own experience with a rules-based approach, the EU is an active proponent of what is called effective multilateralism. The ESS states, "the best ... security is a world of well-governed democratic states. Spreading good governance, supporting social and political reform, dealing with corruption and abuse of power, establishing the rule of law and protecting human rights are the best means of strengthening the international order." The basic idea here is that by locking countries firmly into the international system, they will eventually be transformed.... That is why it is a European priority to strengthen the UN, equipping it to fulfill its responsibilities and to act effectively.[31]

Kofi Annan's proposed UN reform is based on a comprehensive concept of security that stresses the link between development, security, and human rights, with violence prevention at its core. The EU wants to pursue this effort: it is becoming the biggest contributor of development aid in the world and is increasing its monitoring of countries at risk. EU cooperation with the UN is remarkable.

The new EU intelligence capacity, the Situation Centre (SITCEN), has access to information and intelligence from all member states. Every enlargement has brought the EU new expertise, and this is especially important for prevention of mass violence. The Mediterranean countries brought focus on neighbors to the South, and the new member states brought attention to the East. In the enlarged EU, it is likely that at least one of its twenty-seven members will take an interest in a given conflict and convince others of its importance, so that helpful action can be taken before disaster occurs.

High Representative Javier Solana plays an important role in preventive diplomacy, especially mediation and facilitation. As we have seen repeatedly in this book, leadership matters, and his leadership is extraordinary. He can work on an ad hoc basis with member states, as he did in Ukraine with the Polish and Lithuanian presidents. Representing an EU of twenty-seven states, he has far more leverage than a representative of a single state, provided the twenty-seven have coherence. Special representatives (SR) are also an important conflict prevention tool. The EU has appointed them for the Great Lakes, the Middle East peace process, Moldova, and the south Caucasus.

Successful EU preventive diplomacy must involve not only government actors but also civil society. In Ukraine at the end of 2004, the high representative's mediation would not have been successful without the solid and resolute support of civil society, which refused to be deprived of an electoral victory. Several EU programs encourage, train, and support civil society and democratic political parties in various countries over the long term.

Using its own experience as a model, the EU promotes and assists regional integration all over the world, helping regional associations such as the AU build their own capacity.

EU deployment in 2003 of a military force (Operation Concordia) in the FYRM was a valuable addition to NATO efforts; it contributed to preventing a civil war and to building an environment favorable to political settlements. In Bosnia and Herzegovina the replacement of the NATO Stabilization Force (SFOR) by Operation EUFOR (European Union Force) Althea means that the EU is now assuming a major role in maintaining a secure environment.

Three developments will reinforce EU crisis management and prevention of mass violence:

1. The creation in 2005 of a civilian and military cell in Brussels for crisis management planning and coordination of civilian and military operational instruments and structures. The cell, under the SG/HR (Javier Solana), will help coordinate civilian operations and build capacity to plan and run an autonomous EU military operation.

2. The planned creation of fifteen battle groups by 2010 will allow the EU to engage in autonomous rapid response operations, both stand-alone missions and starting points for larger operations. A battle group may be formed by a framework nation or by a coalition of member states. The objectives of the EU are to make the decision to launch an operation within 5 days after its approval by the Council, and in response to a crisis or at the urgent request of the UN, to undertake simultaneously two battle-group size operations for a period up to 120 days. Forces should be on the ground no later than 10 days after the EU decision to launch the operation. This sort of operation may separate adversaries, protect vulnerable people, and foster early conflict resolution.

3. Since adoption of the Joint Declaration on EU-UN Cooperation in Crisis Management in 2003, EU-UN cooperation has progressed in the areas of planning, training, communication, and best practices. A high-level staff-to-staff steering group

to monitor developments has been created. EU-UN cooperation has also increased in the area of helping regional organizations such as the AU build their own crisis management capacity.

The EU has traditionally emphasized the more structural long-term aspects of conflict prevention, but it is now complementing this approach by developing a strong capacity for crisis management and early prevention. The need to link the two is now generally recognized. These are essentially the same categories formulated by the Carnegie Commission on Preventing Deadly Conflict (1994) and also adopted by the UN: "structural prevention" (long-term) and "operational prevention" (near-term impending crisis).

In line with its belief in multilateralism, the EU wants to work with other partners to promote this combined approach. It has increased cooperation with the UN and the African Union. It has sought synergistic collaboration with NATO. Both conflict prevention—which is far cheaper than dealing with conflict after it erupts—and continued engagement in reconstruction to prevent recurrence of violence are necessary tasks for joint multilateral action. The moral basis for this approach is clear and compelling.

Development Cooperation as a European Tool of Conflict Prevention

Louis Michel, the European Commissioner for Development and Humanitarian Assistance, has studied development carefully. In "Development Cooperation as a European Tool of Conflict Prevention," the chapter he contributed to the 2005 Anna Lindh volume, he pointed out that development and security are "complementary agendas."[32] Sustainable development cannot occur in highly insecure areas, and development is an essential condition for lasting security. EU development cooperation, with its long-term presence on the ground and array of policy tools, is very well suited both to the prevention of state fragility and conflict and to the support of dialogue, reconciliation, and other peacebuilding efforts.

Severe poverty is one root cause of state fragility. Michel estimated that fragile states contain 14 percent of the world's population but that nearly 30 percent of that population lives on less than one dollar a day. Better development cooperation, including effective delivery of more financial aid, will give a major boost to these countries, but it is not enough. Corruption, human rights abuse, natural resources profiteering, and absence of rule of law are common signs of fragile or nonfunctioning state institutions and bad governance.[33]

Development cooperation can play an important preventive role by not waiting for a crisis, but becoming involved in the security systems of developing countries through stable and effective partnerships. This cooperation should encourage a security system governed by the same rules as the rest of the public sector and military forces firmly under the political control of civilian authority. Involvement in security is fundamental for conflict resolution and reconciliation as well as for prevention of new conflicts.

Europe can best contribute to conflict prevention by providing adequate and effective development assistance that takes state fragility and conflict into account. The EU is working to mainstream prevention into its development packages. Europe must search out every appropriate entry point to strengthen a fragile state's good governance, institutional capacity, and ability to deliver basic services. Donors must stay involved no matter how difficult the situation, to maintain the trust and cooperation of needy populations, the long-term success of aid programs, and international security.[34]

In not yet acute but still difficult cases the main priorities for EU support are to continue regular dialogue, support institutional capacity building, recognize human rights, and make efforts to meet the basic needs of all, especially the most vulnerable. The EU and its partners agree that respect for three important principles—fundamental human rights, democratic principles, and the rule of law—constitutes an essential element of partnership agreements.

Scarcity and/or very unequal sharing of natural resources can cause, exacerbate, and perpetuate violent conflict in developing countries. In conflict-riven countries, fair handling of land tenure issues must form an essential part of governance, both to maintain peace and to create conditions that foster economic growth. Recognition of the importance of land issues has led the EU to develop common guidelines to support land policy reforms in developing countries. Strategies for poverty reduction must take into account the basic need of access to clean water. This also leads to interstate conflicts over sharing water from common sources "unless a mechanism is in place to deal with sharing of water resources, utilization and management, and distribution of benefits."[35] Timber and mining revenues have financed violent conflict in a number of developing states. The EU is trying to address this problem.

To promote peace, security, and good governance in Africa, the EU cooperates closely with the UN to support the AU in its efforts to take responsibility and leadership in promoting African development. The Peace Facility, designed to finance peace operations led, operated, and staffed by Africans, is funded entirely from the European Development Fund. The AU urgently needs to strengthen its capacity in conflict prevention and postconflict reconstruction to make long-term development possible. This difficult task will require long-term cooperation among the EU, AU, and UN.

The Africa Peer Review Mechanism (APRM) was established in 2004 to improve governance through mutual learning and sharing of best practices among African countries. Twenty-three states have joined.

Many political and operational steps have been taken to strengthen the EU-UN partnership. For example, steps have been taken to synchronize UN and EU conflict prevention activities at the level of country assistance: The Commission and the UN Secretariat agreed in 2003 to start a desk-to-desk continuous dialogue on conflict prevention and risk prevention in certain countries. In 2008, there is a strong possibility of explicit links between new units of the EU and the UN in genocide prevention (see Chapter 18).

The EU's Göteborg Programme: A Sharp Focus on Preventing Violent Conflict and Determined Implementation

There is no case in the field of preventing deadly conflict where an institution has come so far so fast as the European Union. In the 1990s, the Carnegie Commission on Preventing Deadly Conflict had a stimulating effect on the UN leadership and also the government of Sweden; the two worked together well and still do. Sweden developed an action plan with the inspiration of the then foreign minister, Anna Lindh, and the vision of the recent (2006) foreign minister, Jan Eliasson, as well as the insights of Ragnar Ängeby and, especially in relation to the EU, of Anders Bjurner. This Swedish brain trust, among its many leadership functions in prevention, took its plan for preventing violent conflict to the EU during the Swedish Presidency in 2001. When this was well received, Anders Bjurner (a highly respected Swedish diplomat) was assigned to the EU, where he had a very creative three-year stint in which he did much to build the EU's prevention program conceptually, organizationally, and functionally. A variety of EU political leaders and an excellent secretariat took up this mission with dedication. Thus the 2001–2006 period yielded some highlights that will be broadly summarized here.

In May 2006, a very important report on EU activities in the implementation of the EU Programme for the Prevention of Violent Conflicts was prepared by a technical committee for the European Council. It was formulated in the context of the fundamental values of the EU, in which the highest political priority is given to improving the effectiveness and coherence of its international work in the prevention of violent conflict. This also enhances the preventive capabilities of the international community altogether.

The EU has created innovative tools and mechanisms, has assessed their practical value, and is steadily seeking ways to combine existing EU mechanisms for an even stronger impact on achieving and maintaining peace. The plan now is to strengthen EU coordination of preventive action in situations of submerged or rising tension and to develop further appropriate cooperation with international organizations, e.g., the UN, the OSCE, the Council of Europe, the African Union, and NATO, as well as other regional and subregional actors to improve dialogue and long-term joint ventures. This requires training in relevant areas of conflict prevention; enhancement of cooperation with non-state actors, prevention-oriented NGOs, academic institutions, and the private sector in the area of conflict prevention; strengthening EU early-warning mechanisms through coordinated information sharing between member states, with the EU institutions, and with like-minded international partners, and by making functional use of the EU watch list; and strengthening the capacity of regional organizations and civil society in early warning, addressing root causes, promoting dialogue, and reconciliation.

Conflict prevention and conflict resolution are essential elements of the European Union's overall policy on promoting human rights and democratization around the world. This includes the special needs of women, including the role of professional women in conflict prevention and participation of women at all levels in peace processes. The EU also has a strong commitment to the promotion and protection of the rights of children and in particular those affected by armed conflict.

The EU has shown its ability to build and sustain mutually reinforcing partnerships for prevention with the UN, the OSCE, and other international and regional organizations as well as with civil society. EU action is guided by principles of value-added and comparative advantage. It cooperates with the OSCE, with an emphasis on learning from best practices in recruitment, training, and procurement. Especially through the Africa Peace Facility, the EU works with the African Union and subregional African organizations.

The EU has in recent years established working relations with many countries in different parts of the world pertinent to preventing deadly conflict. Even though these are essentially new, they offer considerable promise based on earlier experience and increasing commitment. These relations include a variety of African countries, the United States,

Canada, Russia, Indonesia, China, India, Japan, Latin America, and of course a variety of European countries and nearby neighbors. Thus, the EU is emerging as a broadly international—almost global—organization that is deeply committed to prevention of war and genocide, technically capable, increasingly sophisticated in respect to both operational and structural prevention, and highly cooperative with a variety of constructive entities.

Conclusion

Overall, the EU has made remarkable progress in a few years in developing an effective approach to preventing violent conflict through building partnerships for prevention with other actors as well as strengthening its own capabilities. It is integrating instruments effectively and taking a very active, informed approach to conflict-related issues. The European Security Strategy placed prevention at the center of EU efforts to address violent conflict and other security threats. This provides an exceptionally suitable basis for leadership in the prevention of genocide in the years ahead.

CHAPTER 15

Organisation for Security and Cooperation in Europe

Its Potential for Preventing Genocide

As we have seen, European regional organizations offer promise for prevention of mass violence not only in Europe but throughout the world—at least by the examples they provide. They sustain norms of democratic national behavior and facilitate the transition of countries toward democracy, respect for human rights, the rule of law, and an equitable market economy, all of which are essential features of decent societies. They have been directly helpful in worldwide institution building for peace and democracy.

The OSCE is a worthy addition to their number, and its membership extends beyond Europe. Its work has gained much respect and credit because of its keen interest and deep involvement in early conflict prevention as well as its skillful use of the many mechanisms it has at its disposal.[1]

The OSCE, as the Conference on Security and Cooperation in Europe (CSCE) was renamed at the start of 1995, is the largest regional security organization in the world, with its headquarters in Vienna and offices and institutions in Copenhagen, Geneva, The Hague, Prague, and Warsaw. Its fifty-six participating states in Europe, Central Asia, and North America give it a reach that extends from "Vancouver to Vladivostok" in conflict prevention, crisis management, and postconflict rehabilitation.[2]

The OSCE approach to security is comprehensive in its coverage of security-related issues and cooperative in its requirement that all OSCE participating states have equal status and all major decisions be based on consensus.

OSCE Structures and Institutions

Through its structures and institutions, the OSCE provides a forum for consultation and negotiation among its participating states.[3] Its decisions are made at three levels. The summits represent the highest level of decisionmaking. Between summits, the Ministerial Council's decisions ensure that OSCE activities maintain its central political goals. The chief decisionmaking body of the OSCE, the Permanent Council, meets weekly to decide the Organisation's daily business. Decisions are made by consensus.

The process is coordinated by member states currently holding the chairmanship of the Organisation.

The Forum for Security Cooperation (FSC) meets weekly to clarify military aspects of security in the OSCE area.[4] It aims to create openness and transparency in military issues and to reduce the risk of armed conflict, with an emphasis on implementation of OSCE confidence- and security-building measures, which allow exchange and verification of defense information—no nasty surprises.[5]

The FSC does reviews of small arms and light weapons that comprise seven information exchanges: (1) national marking systems; (2) manufacture control procedures; (3) export policy, procedures and documentation, and control over brokering; (4) destruction techniques and procedures; (5) national procedures for stockpile management and security; (6) annual information exchanges on numbers of small arms seized and destroyed; and, the most significant, (7) annual information exchanges on small arms imports to, and exports from, other participating states. Difficult as it is to achieve arms control in this area, the OSCE has at least made a serious, systematic effort that could in due course build worldwide momentum.

Under the Conventional Arms Transfers exchange, participating states share information each year on their exports and imports of conventional weapons, as defined in the UN Register of Conventional Arms: battle tanks, air-cushion vehicles (ACVs), artillery systems, combat aircraft, attack helicopters, warships and missiles, and missile launchers. They also complete a questionnaire on their policy, practices, and procedures for the export of conventional arms and related technology. This too is a pioneering effort in a dangerous and badly neglected area of arms control.

The Economic and Environmental Forum meets once a year in Prague to discuss economic and environmental factors that affect security in the OSCE area.[6] Seminars before each Economic and Environmental Forum prepare those attending. The EU and NATO have begun to engage in these functions. Between summits, decisionmaking and governing power lies with the Ministerial Council, whose members are the foreign ministers of OSCE participating states.[7]

At their Maastricht meeting in 2003, the OSCE Ministerial Council endorsed a politically binding document to create mechanisms that reduce risks posed by the huge stockpiles of conventional weapons and ammunition in the OSCE area, the residue of conflicts and earlier disarmament processes. A particular concern is the risk of diversion to terrorists and criminal groups.[8] This agreement is similar in principle to the Nunn-Lugar Cooperative Threat Reduction Initiative between the United States and Russia.

To support member states in dealing with such problems on their own, the document provides practical procedures for the destruction of surplus weapons stockpiles, including indicators of surplus and risk, and specific security measures that are voluntary, transparent, complementary, and sustainable. It opens the door to financial and/or technical assistance from the international community. Although this is a good model, participation is uneven. As noted in Chapter 12, there is an urgent need for an international NGO movement to put pressure on recalcitrant governments in the quest for restraints on weaponry.

The Parliamentary Assembly convenes member-state parliamentarians to promote parliamentary involvement in the OSCE and establish norms on critical issues of war and peace. Its Edinburgh Declaration of 2004 on coping with new security threats

- condemns terrorism in all forms and urges the international community to conduct a "war against terrorism" that combats its underlying causes and is waged according to the principles of the UN Charter and international law, including human rights and refugee protection law;
- calls upon the OSCE to help countries in its orbit achieve sustainable development and take advantage of globalization;
- urges that resources of the OSCE high commissioner on national minorities be increased to protect minorities new to the OSCE area as a result of recent migration;
- urges member states to honor the obligation that no circumstance of any kind may be invoked to justify torture; nor may orders from a superior officer or a public authority be so used;
- recommends designation of an envoy to guarantee OSCE commitments to battle racism, anti-Semitism, and xenophobia; and
- strongly encourages the appointment of women to OSCE posts.[9]

The secretary-general (who acts as the OSCE chief administrative officer) heads the Secretariat, which supports OSCE field activities and maintains contacts with international and nongovernmental organizations. It also coordinates OSCE economic and environmental activities; politico-military activities; administrative, financial, and personnel services; conference and language services; information technology; and press and public information.[10]

The secretary-general and the Secretariat provide the operational support to carry out the OSCE's tasks of early warning, conflict prevention, crisis management, and postconflict rehabilitation throughout its area.

The Office of the Representative on Freedom of the Media monitors media in OSCE states and gives early warning of violations of freedom of expression, a basic human right vital to the development of civil society.[11] The representative provides a rapid response to serious noncompliance with OSCE principles and commitments by seeking direct contacts with the state and other parties involved, assessing the facts, and offering help to resolve the issue.

The Office for Democratic Institutions and Human Rights (ODIHR) is responsible for the promotion of human rights and democracy in the OSCE area.[12] Based in Warsaw, it has more than 100 staff members active throughout the OSCE area. The 1992 Helsinki Document charged the ODIHR with helping member states to "ensure full respect for human rights and fundamental freedoms, to abide by the rule of law, to promote principles of democracy and ... to build, strengthen and protect democratic institutions, as well as promote tolerance throughout society." In accordance with its mandate, the ODIHR

- observes and assists national and local elections;
- provides practical support in consolidating democratic institutions through both long-term institutional and capacity-building programs and shorter-term projects to strengthen civil society and democratic governance;
- provides OSCE field missions with training, exchange of experiences, and regional coordination;

- contributes to early warning and conflict prevention by monitoring how participating states meet human rights commitments; and
- provides regular human rights training for government authorities, civil society, and OSCE staff.

In all its activities, the ODIHR uses a network of partners in related areas, such as international and local nongovernmental human rights organizations and international governmental organizations. Especially prominent among the latter are the UN Office of the High Commissioner for Human Rights, the Council of Europe, and the EU, which has become increasingly important in most of these issues.

The Office of the High Commissioner on National Minorities was established in 1992 to resolve ethnic tensions that might threaten peace or friendly relations between or within participating states. A government's mistreatment of its minority groups can be a precursor of genocide or can turn those groups to violent insurgency—or both. The OSCE's comprehensive approach treats peace and security as dependent upon the realization of justice and respect for human rights.

The high commissioner's work in conflict prevention and resolution has attracted worldwide interest and admiration. His mandate permits rapid and independent action: he is authorized to use his personal judgment to identify and decide what problems to address, without first obtaining approval from the Permanent Council or the state(s) involved. For a decade this independence and flexibility enabled Max van der Stoel, the OSCE's first high commissioner on national minorities,[13] to create his own constructive model of early, ongoing, and resourceful preventive diplomacy to defuse dangerous situations in Eastern Europe.[14] His successor, the distinguished Swedish diplomat Rolf Ekéus, has explicitly continued and built upon van der Stoel's approach. I have highlighted some of its valuable concepts, procedures, and accomplishments in Chapter 7, "Proactive Help in Preventing Mass Violence," and Chapter 10, "Education for Human Survival."

The purview of the high commissioner is conflict that involves national minorities and threatens international peace or security. His charge is to provide early warning and to reduce tensions before violent conflict begins. The basic theme of his work is that early intervention conducted in a cooperative context can keep disagreements and conflicts from developing into mass violence.

The commissioner's view of minority rights is based on the OSCE's Copenhagen Document of 1990, which guarantees to national minorities full equality before the law as well as such basic rights and freedoms as the use of their own language in private and public life; the freedom to establish their own educational, cultural, and religious institutions; and the right to unhindered contact with other minority group members. These protections, binding on all OSCE participating states, are spreading "from Vladivostok to Vancouver," but countries still vary greatly in their implementation.

Van der Stoel made two major points about ensuring participation of national minorities in public life, with the overall goal of "integrating diversity."[15] First, minorities should have an effective voice in their state's central government, guaranteed through special arrangements if necessary. The aim is to strike a balance between the needs of the state and the minority groups. Members of minorities should be able to maintain and develop their distinct identities while, at the same time, respecting state authority and participating in and contributing to the wider society. Second, in accordance with the principle that governing institutions should be committed to "good governance"—acting for the welfare of their total population, creating and maintaining conditions of equality and opportunities for all to pursue their own aspirations—the state should guarantee minority groups some degree of self-governance. The Office of the High Commissioner helps to resolve disputes by assembling experts and representatives of both the government in question and its dissatisfied minorities, using venues such as round tables. Attention is sometimes given to nonterritorial autonomy for minorities, that is, a devolution of powers that allows minority groups some authority over key matters affecting them. A major theme of all this work is the creation of civil societies that protect human rights, including minority rights.

The high commissioner's job requires him to protect human rights by addressing good governance within a democratic society. His mandated authority to collect information directly from any source and his right to freedom of movement within any member state give him the opportunity for significant involvement in state affairs—always exercised with sensitivity to local history, culture, and leaders. The high commissioner often sends visitors to trouble spots to make accurate assessments of troubling situations and uncover ways to facilitate solutions. The high commissioner's aim is to help opposing parties find accommodation in a problem-solving atmosphere that avoids further inflaming an already smoldering situation.

Interethnic conflict prevention often requires the friendly cooperation of a community of nations and other groups whose norms and values center on human rights. In such cases the commissioner advocates the intervention of neutral third parties (OSCE, EU, or Council of Europe) to appeal to moderate elements in society. Both his informal, low-key diplomacy and his public education programs have been oriented to prevent polarization.

The collaboration of other international organizations (such as the EU, which may withhold valued membership to uncooperative states) is vital in giving parties a strong incentive to resolve their problems. International help in developing their own institutions, legislation, and other mechanisms to assure minority rights shows the parties how to minimize violence and earn international respect and new opportunities.

The high commissioner's independence does not mean that he works alone. He cannot operate without the political support of OSCE member states. He is accountable to member states through the chairman-in-office of the Permanent Council, to whom he reports confidentially on his findings and overall progress in particular situations. The commissioner's mandate balances a privileged access to information with the explicit requirement that he act confidentially to maintain trust and cooperation from all parties and to avoid the intransigent positions that public attention sometimes provokes.

The commissioner may issue occasional public statements that support particular legislation or offer his views on a specific event. Thus, quiet diplomacy is backed by transparency and accountability. He has increased his effectiveness through ties with other international organizations, including the UN High Commissioner for Refugees (UNHCR), the UNDP, and other parts of the UN as well as the European Commission and the Council of Europe. This cooperation also helps to ensure that consistent messages are sent, particularly regarding treatment of minorities.

The high commissioner's effectiveness depends upon his perceived fairness. But impartiality does not mean neutrality. He may support positions held by disputing parties if he believes they are just and advance the resolution of the conflict, but he uses international standards and OSCE values (to which all member states have agreed) to assess competing claims and find a solution likely to be accepted by all parties.

Overall, the high commissioner contributes greatly by making informed recommendations to governments of participating states regarding the treatment of their national minorities. This office has done much to educate new and fragile democracies about decent intergroup relations. The primary work in preventive diplomacy of the OSCE high commissioner on national minorities is clearly having a constructive influence worldwide.

An Illuminating Experience: Baltics in the 1990s

An example of the Organisation's groundbreaking work is its preventive diplomacy in the Baltic states during the early 1990s.[16] After the independence of Latvia, Lithuania, and Estonia from the Soviet Union in 1991, long-unresolved ethnic tensions surfaced—a legacy of bitter resentment toward the Russians who had ruled there for decades as agents of Soviet domination. Issues about language, education, voting rights, and citizenship emerged after independence that created serious tension between the Baltic peoples and the substantial ethnic-Russian population that remained in each state. The tension was exacerbated by the presence of Russian troops, based there during the Soviet occupation and not recalled after the collapse of the USSR.

This situation affected larger European security issues as well: the strategic location of the three countries made them a substantial economic and military concern not only to Russia but also to the other countries on the Baltic littoral, which were concerned about the continued presence there of Russian forces.

In the early 1990s Latvia, Lithuania, and Estonia threatened to pass laws that seriously restricted the rights of their ethnic Russian minorities. Their actions made the withdrawal of Russian troops uncertain and portended dangerous ethnic conflict. The United States joined with the Nordic nations neighboring the three Balkan states in multilateral negotiations that raised the hope of membership in valued international organizations such as the OSCE, the Council of Europe, the European Union, and the United Nations as incentives to encourage abandonment of discriminatory policies. The high commissioner on national minorities clearly stated that such policies would only lead to trouble and were not compatible with membership in the OSCE or other European bodies. Criticism such as this, backed up by incentives on the part of the United States and European states—particularly Sweden—had a persuasive effect on the Baltic governments. Eager to get the benefits that membership in international institutions bestows, they moderated their policies and came to provide minority rights in accordance with broader European standards.

Diplomacy was coupled with international financial support to ease the withdrawal of Russian troops, whose removal had been a contentious issue throughout. The United States provided much of the money for loans to help with the cost of dismantling Russian bases and housing Russian troops when they returned home. International organizations, especially the OSCE, played a significant role by providing oversight and mediation at critical points. The process was not smooth, but it was bloodless, and the last Russian troops left the Baltic states in late 1994.

The events in the Baltic states show how early warning, if heeded, can greatly facilitate the success of preventive diplomacy, especially when it is multilateral and coordinated. International organizations played an important role by stepping in when individual states could not or would not undertake certain activities that prevent violence. They had the credibility to serve as monitors that individual states did not have in the eyes of the disputing parties. Tackling serious problems with foresight from a variety of angles provided opportunities for successful outcomes.[17]

The high commissioner has been increasingly involved in projects on the ground that directly address interethnic problems likely to become sources of conflict—sometimes simply by providing frameworks to mitigate the problems, such as educational projects that range from producing new school textbooks to establishing a new university. To deal with recurrent concerns, he has convened internationally respected experts to work out general recommendations on such topics as education and linguistic rights of national minorities and their effective participation in elections and public life.[18] The commissioner also explored issues of national minorities and the electronic media in cooperation with the representative on freedom of the media and independent experts, trying to set in motion long-term consideration of fairness and decency in these sensitive matters.

Can Others Use This Approach?

The value of the Office of the High Commissioner's work has gained wide recognition. The UN Secretary-General has recommended that Europe make extensive use of the high commissioner and that other continents create a similar office. An international seminar was held in Lund, Sweden, in 1999[19] to consider what elements of the high commissioner's approach could be successfully transferred to other multilateral bodies, and a similar meeting was held at the UN in 2006.

The high commissioner's still-evolving approach has valuable elements that may be applicable in many contexts:

- its flexibility, dynamism, and confidentiality, which have enhanced its effectiveness in quiet diplomacy and capacity building
- its discreet, proactive, value-based problem solving
- its ability to act as an insider in working closely with all factions and as a third party in maintaining such characteristics as the authority to exert pressure toward democratic values
- its function as a "normative intermediary" that assists states to meet their international obligations with a view to maintaining international peace

Integrating Diversity

As OSCE high commissioner on national minorities, van der Stoel considered one of his principal tasks the integration of ethnic or cultural diversity in the states whose tensions he was asked to help resolve.[20] Unlike forced assimilation, which totally absorbs a minority into the state's majority and may destroy its identity as a group, integration maintains the distinctive identity of the minority while at the same time incorporating it as part of the general society.

Even predominantly homogeneous states contain minorities with whom the majority population must learn to live justly and peacefully. Therefore, integrating diversity is a basic element of both conflict prevention and respect for minority rights. It is a purpose of both international law and good governance.[21]

An important part of encouraging integration, van der Stoel believed, is recognizing, protecting, and promoting the identity of minorities. This means creating and fostering opportunities for interaction between minority and majority communities under favorable conditions and allowing members of minority groups full participation in public life while showing sensitivity and responsiveness to different linguistic and educational needs. To resolve the conflicting demands of minority self-determination and the integrity of the state, van der Stoel advocated a modicum of self-governance and "internal self-determination"—nongeographic autonomy. He stressed that "such autonomies should not be confused with separatism, since they rely upon common understandings and shared institutions of rule of law, respect for human rights, common security and destiny."[22] He pointed out that a variety of rarely explored arrangements could satisfy the needs of minorities for partial self-government without risking state fragmentation. This is an area in which democratic experimentation—even democratic engineering—offers a variety of problem-solving approaches.

Van der Stoel's position taught him that citizenship can be a central issue in such states as Estonia and Latvia, for example, where "stateless" persons make up a high percentage of the population. In such cases, citizenship is the basis for evenhanded intercultural integration. Van der Stoel considered it one of his principal duties to encourage governments, by means of information, ideas, and technical assistance, to grant all ethnic and religious groups in their population full rights of citizenship, thus integrating diversity by creating a balance between the rights of the individual and the obligations of the citizen. This, in turn, promotes peace and positive intergroup relations by reducing resentment about inferior status and offering everyone a stake in society.

Attributes such as language, history, symbols, and culture contribute to the sense of identity by which individuals, groups, and nations define themselves and create a collective bond. Individually and collectively, people wish to protect and promote their identity and to discourage threats to its continuance. Ethnic or religious differences within a state, when perceived by its majority population as threats to the identity of "the nation," generate interethnic tensions. Van der Stoel made it a point to be sensitive to these questions of identity and stressed the need for governments to respect the dignity and differences of all their citizens.

In his negotiations, van der Stoel tried to get the disputing parties to focus on concrete proposals to resolve issues intrinsically related to identity (such as language, education, culture). By turning the debate to specific policies, legislation, matters of human rights, and government practice, the parties could put the views of both sides into perspective and find cooperative, pragmatic solutions.

It is essential to maintain adequate structures for thoughtful dialogue between a government and its minority populations in order to resolve problems through cooperation and to build shared understanding, trust, and expectation of progress. Since the problems that call for dialogue are seldom easily resolved on a permanent basis, it is often advisable to establish ongoing, periodic councils or round tables or even an independent governmental body such as an ombudsman or a special ministry to receive and respond to minority complaints. The development of these institutions and processes signals the state's willingness to take seriously minorities' concerns and the minorities' willingness to participate in the political life of their country. Van der Stoel consistently encouraged participation in civic affairs, acceptance of pluralism, and an inclusive response to diversity. Thus, he encouraged open and peaceful processes of social integration that accommodate differences.

Van der Stoel believed that "because of the centrality of language to ethnic identity, the process of ensuring the linguistic rights of minorities is critical to the advancement of minority rights overall and human rights generally."[23] Most of the language disputes in which he was involved dealt with the use of minority languages in the public sphere.

In 1996 he asked the Foundation on Inter-Ethnic Relations to assemble internationally recognized experts to prepare recommendations on the linguistic rights of national minorities as "a useful reference for the development of State policies and laws."[24] The resulting Oslo Recommendations Regarding the Linguistic Rights of National Minorities, issued in 1998, deal with linguistic rights concerning names, religion, community life and nongovernmental organizations, the media, economic life, administrative authorities and public services, independent national institutions, the judicial authorities, and the denial of liberty. This provides a variety of paths to mutual accommodation in intergroup relations.

Education, particularly in the areas of language, history, and culture, is indispensable to preserve, enrich, and transmit both ethnic and national identity. Most of the educational issues that van der Stoel helped resolve dealt with curriculum, language, control over minority education, and tertiary education. His general rule in resolving the problem of control of education was to encourage "local solutions to local problems," and he tried to persuade states to decentralize educational authority. In any event, universities can be an important locus for helping diverse peoples to learn to live together amicably.

The current high commissioner on national minorities, Rolf Ekéus, underscores the activities of his office in fostering interethnic harmony through education and puts them in the context of prevention of mass violence,[25] as we discussed in Chapter 10, on education.

From our perspective, this orientation, which van der Stoel and Ekéus have put into effective practice, is both necessary and feasible in all intergroup relations, provided that the community of democratic nations makes an effort to sustain it. Books such as *Learning to Live Together*[26] can help students, teachers, and policymakers. We have seen the national high commissioner as both an effective diplomat and now also a leader in education.

OSCE Conflict Prevention Centre

The Conflict Prevention Centre (CPC) became an independent OSCE office in 1991. Today, it is one of the main departments of the Secretariat of the OSCE.

The CPC supports OSCE activities in the field by coordinating the activities of the missions and assisting the implementation of their mandates. Among its day-to-day responsibilities are continuous liaison and follow-up of OSCE missions in regard to the execution of OSCE political decisions. It is also the focal point in the Secretariat for the OSCE's politico-military role, giving prevention of hatred and violence an address where a troubled group can turn for help in time of need. The Centre is responsible for supporting the OSCE chairman-in-office and secretary-general in the areas of early warning, conflict prevention, crisis management, and postconflict rehabilitation. Thus, it contributes to a coherent approach in a range of activities undertaken by the missions themselves or in conjunction with the various OSCE institutions.

Under the guidance of the secretary-general, the CPC also assists the relevant OSCE negotiating and decisionmaking bodies, such as the Permanent Council and the Forum for Security Cooperation. In particular, the CPC provides support for the implementation of confidence- and security-bulding measures. This involves maintaining databases on information exchanged as well as maintaining a computer network designed to facilitate direct communicaion between capitals (the OSCE Communications Network). It organizes seminars and workshops and, at the request of participating states, assists with the implementation of politico-military documents and other commitments entered into by participating states.

The turning point for the OSCE was the opening of the first large mission in the former Yugoslavia, the mission to Bosnia and Herzegovina in December 1995. This dramatic expansion of OSCE activities in the field led to changes within the OSCE Secretariat. The next major phase in the CPC's development came in the aftermath of the Kosovo crisis and the experiences gathered from the rapid establishment of the largest OSCE field activity to date, the Kosovo Verification Mission in 1998–1999. These experiences led to recognition of the need to drastically enhance the Secretariat's operational capabilities. We call attention to the Conflict Prevention Centre because it illustrates how a focal point for prevention can have far-reaching effects.

Terrence Hopmann's study of the OSCE gave a comprehensive assessment of its potential.[27] He emphasized that preventive missions need clear goals, with complementary strategies to achieve them. In planning and implementing interventions, missions must coordinate closely with interested NGOs. They are most effective when they attend closely to issues such as human rights, minority rights, democratization, freedom of the media, and the rule of law. Finally, missions are only as strong as their members—successes are directly related to personnel. Training in negotiation, mediation, conflict resolution, cultural sensitivity, and gender balance on the team is valuable.

The OSCE continues its momentum in the new century as an innovative and effective regional organization. It has the flexibility to adapt to a new international atmosphere and the agility to intercede in a variety of situations. Its failures to prevent violence in Chechnya and Kosovo were balanced by its contributions to prevention of violence in Macedonia, the Crimea, and the Baltics. It should be further strengthened in its own region, and its experience should be used in other areas of the globe. For example, peer learning in collaboration with the African Union could have mutual benefit.

Overall, the OSCE has moved from a modest start to a dynamic, multifaceted, valuable organization in a "moment" of human history. Its special merit is a sharp focus on prevention of hatred and mass violence with a well-organized cadre of professionals to implement this orientation. It has established precedents that are proving helpful all over the world—as if "Vancouver to Vladivostok" were not enough.

Because it is impeded by a requirement for consensus among its members—which, in international terms, means total unanimity—the OSCE is not well positioned to become the leader in prevention of genocide. But it is an enthusiastic and capable partner and collaborator in this enterprise, with many skills to contribute. The OSCE has much to contribute to prevention of genocide. Yet it has limited resources—far fewer than the European Union—and major actions require the agreement of all its many members. That is likely to present delay and even obstruction in dangerous situations. Still, it has provided valuable lessons for those interested in preventing genocide.

CHAPTER 16

The North Atlantic Treaty Organization

An Instrument to Help in Preventing Genocide

Origins and Evolution of NATO's Capacities in Cooperative Efforts

The North Atlantic Treaty Organization was created in the aftermath of World War II as the Soviet Union became alienated from its former allies, occupied most of Eastern and central Europe, and, under the brutal leadership of Joseph Stalin, defiantly faced Western Europe as well as the United States.

In response, the Western allies formed a close alliance that became an exceedingly powerful military force, bridging the North Atlantic between Western Europe and North America. As the decades passed, its functions broadened somewhat to include a modicum of diplomatic, educational, and scientific functions. With the end of the Cold War, at the outset of the 1990s, NATO broadened its activities considerably, creating relationships with additional countries, expanding diplomatic and civil-military functions, and considering "out of area" tasks.

In 1994, to enhance security and stability throughout Europe and to strengthen ties with countries emerging from the former Soviet Union, the member countries of the North Atlantic Alliance invited the emerging democratic states in Eastern Europe to join them by creating the Partnership for Peace.[1] This Partnership for Peace program expanded and intensified political and military cooperation throughout Europe, thereby diminishing threats to peace and promoting the commitment to democratic principles that are essential to the alliance. In joining the partnership, these states subscribed to the preservation of democratic societies, freedom from coercion and intimidation, maintenance of the principles of international law, and civilian control of the military.[2] In emphasizing these values, they were emphasizing their desire for NATO membership—which most of them have now achieved.

The states reaffirmed their commitment to fulfill in good faith the obligations of the Charter of the United Nations and the principles of the Universal Declaration on Human Rights; specifically, to refrain from the threat or use of force against the territorial integrity or political independence of any state, to respect existing borders, and to settle disputes by peaceful means. They also reaffirmed their commitment to the Helsinki Final Act (human rights) and all subsequent OSCE documents—to the fulfillment of the commitments they have undertaken in human rights and arms control. These were years of remarkable transformation in East-West relations and, indeed, in European history.

The Euro-Atlantic Partnership Council (EAPC) was formed in 1997 to enhance the efforts of the Partnership for Peace in both an expanded political dimension of partnership and practical cooperation. It observed carefully and complemented the activities of the OSCE, the European Union, and the Council of Europe[3]—again valuable interinstitutional cooperation. EAPC maintained important principles for the success of cooperation between allies and partners: inclusiveness, providing opportunities for political consultation and practical cooperation to all allies and partners equally, and distinctive roles, so that partners could decide for themselves the level and areas of their cooperation with NATO.

In late 2002, NATO undertook a comprehensive review of all of these newer activities.[4] It reaffirmed its strategic concept of outreach and openness, preserving peace, promoting democracy, contributing to prosperity, and fostering genuine partnership among all democratic Euro-Atlantic countries. The commitment aimed to enhance the security of all, to exclude none, and to overcome disagreements that could lead to violent conflict. These ties proved very attractive to the countries of east central Europe and served a "magnet" function similar to that of the European Union.

A Broader Approach to Security in the NATO "Family"

Allies have welcomed requests by partners for political consultations with the alliance, individually or in smaller groups, on issues of special political and security importance to them. Consultations led to more systematic political relationships. Allies consulted with partners to develop further cooperation in civil emergency planning to protect the civilian population from weapons of mass destruction, terrorist attacks, technological accidents, and natural disasters. This included work on ways to promote interoperability between relevant national capabilities. In years ahead, this is likely to include ways of coping with impending genocide.

Thus, allies and partners developed a broader approach to security in their political consultations and other discussions. They sought complementarity with other international organizations in their response to security challenges, such as weapons of mass destruction and terrorism. Thus, cooperation with the EU and the UN became feasible and desirable.

Recognizing that the struggle against terrorism requires collaborative efforts of the international community, member states of the Euro-Atlantic Partnership Council endorsed a Partnership Action Plan Against Terrorism.[5] To this end, they explored ways to facilitate the exchange of operational information about terrorists and their networks. The plan emphasized increased cooperation at national, subregional, regional, and international levels to strengthen the global response to terrorism. This is a plan that could extend to prevention of genocidal tendencies as well. NATO can intensify consultations and information sharing on terrorism and also on threats of genocide as a matter of vital priority in light of democratic principles, international law, and sheer human decency.

Building Peace in Crisis Regions: The Role of NATO

The alliance has led three complex, peace-support operations—in Afghanistan, Bosnia and Herzegovina, and Kosovo.[6] It handed responsibility for a fourth—in the Former Yugoslav Republic of Macedonia—to the European Union in April 2003 after the alliance had successfully stabilized the situation there. The capabilities and expertise to manage such complex operations have been dramatically enhanced during the past decade, primarily in response to the wars of Yugoslavia's dissolution. Lessons learned in Bosnia and Herzegovina, Kosovo, and the Former Yugoslav Republic of Macedonia are extremely relevant elsewhere and, indeed, have been adapted to Afghanistan.

The wars of Yugoslavia's dissolution, and especially the Bosnian war, caught the international community largely unprepared. Initially, the United Nations was the principal institution attempting to broker an end to hostilities, keep the peace in regions where a cease-fire had been agreed upon, and alleviate the suffering of noncombatants. Over the years, NATO became involved in support of the United Nations through various air- and sea-based support operations—enforcing economic sanctions, an arms embargo, and a no-flight zone—and by providing the United Nations with detailed military contingency planning of safe areas and the implementation of a peace plan.

These measures helped to contain the conflict and save lives but in the end proved inadequate to bring an end to the war. The turning point in the Bosnian war came, significantly, when NATO took the lead, launching a two-week air campaign against Bosnian Serb forces in the summer of 1995. This paved the way for the Dayton Agreement, the peace accord ending the Bosnian war that came into force on December 20, 1995, under which a 60,000-strong NATO-led Implementation Force (IFOR) took military responsibility for the peace process.

The deployment of IFOR, which included soldiers from both NATO and non-NATO countries, was the alliance's first military engagement on land and has contributed greatly to reshaping its post–Cold War identity. NATO became an increasingly effective instrument for military and political crisis management. There could be no military success in isolation. This helped forge closer links between the peacekeeping force and its civilian counterparts, including, for example, developing a doctrine for civil-military cooperation.

NATO deployed in Kosovo after a seventy-eight-day air campaign launched to halt a humanitarian catastrophe. The decision to intervene—probably the most controversial in the alliance's history—followed more than a year of fighting within Kosovo, the failure of international efforts to resolve the conflict by diplomatic means, and a strong determination on the part of NATO allies to prevent the kind of ethnic-cleansing campaigns seen earlier in Bosnia and Croatia.

Yugoslavia was NATO's first venture into genocide-prone territory. Although the prevention of genocide prior to the necessity for military action is certainly preferable, there are times when military strength is essential—either in the background to strengthen diplomatic efforts or in the foreground, as in Yugoslavia.

Military victory was the first step on a long road to building a durable, multiethnic society free from the threat of renewed conflict. In addition to helping to preserve a secure environment, both the Kosovo Force (KFOR) and SFOR have been actively involved in helping refugees and displaced persons return to their homes, seeking out and arresting individuals indicted for war crimes, and helping to reform the domestic military structures in such a way as to prevent a return to violence—all tasks that require a long-term commitment.

Whereas it took close to three-and-a-half years of bloodshed in Bosnia and a year of fighting in Kosovo before NATO intervened to bring these conflicts to an end, the alliance became engaged in spring 2001, at the request of the Skopje authorities, in an effort to prevent an escalating conflict in the Former Yugoslav Republic of Macedonia from degenerating into full-scale civil war. Together with other international organizations, the alliance helped to head off a greater conflict and launch a process of reconstruction and reconciliation.

NATO's first three peace-support operations took place in Europe, yet the need for long-term peacebuilding is global. NATO foreign ministers recognized this at a meeting in Reykjavik, Iceland, in May 2002, agreeing that "to carry out the full range of its missions, NATO must be able to field forces that can move quickly to wherever they are needed, sustain operations over distance and time, and achieve their objectives."[7] This decision effectively paved the way for NATO to deploy for the first time outside the Euro-Atlantic area, in Afghanistan.

Starting in August 2003, NATO has led the International Security Assistance Force (ISAF), a UN-mandated force tasked with helping provide security in and around Kabul, the capital of Afghanistan, in support of the Afghan Transitional Authority and the United Nations Assistance Mission in Afghanistan. ISAF has helped to develop reliable security structures, identify reconstruction needs, and train Afghan security forces. This remains a difficult situation.

In order to be effective when deploying far from alliance territory, NATO militaries must invest in power-projection capabilities. To meet this challenge, the alliance adopted a series of measures at its November 2002 Prague summit aimed at ensuring that NATO is equipped for the full spectrum of modern military missions. It involves the creation of a NATO Response Force, which will give the alliance the capacity to move a robust force quickly, to deter or respond to attack. Such a force could be very helpful in a genocide-prone situation by keeping the would-be perpetrators away from their likely victims and providing space for coercive diplomacy to prevent mass killing.

EU-NATO Cooperation

An effective working relationship between the European Union and NATO is critical to successful crisis management, and in some cases might well prevent genocide. A breakthrough came on December 16, 2002, with the adoption of the EU-NATO Declaration on ESDP. Since then, the European Union and NATO have negotiated a series of documents on cooperation in crisis management, known by insiders as the "Berlin-plus" package, which made it possible for the European Union to take over from NATO responsibility for peacekeeping in the Former Yugoslav Republic of Macedonia on April 1, 2003.

The Berlin-plus arrangements seek to avoid unnecessary duplication of resources and comprise four elements. These are (1) assured EU access to NATO operational planning; (2) the presumption of availability to the European Union of NATO capabilities and common assets; (3) NATO European command options for EU-led operations, including developing the European role of NATO's deputy supreme allied commander, Europe (SACEUR); and (4) adaptation of the NATO defense planning system to incorporate the availability of forces for EU operations.

The Berlin-plus arrangements were put into practice in Operation *Concordia*, the European Union's first military deployment in the Former Yugoslav Republic of Macedonia. At the time, the survival of the Former Yugoslav Republic of Macedonia was at stake. Implementing a key lesson learned from the experience of KFOR and SFOR, NATO worked closely with the European Union and the Organisation for Security and Cooperation in Europe from the political level to the field level, and the three organizations presented a unified international stance to both sides of the conflict. In April 2003, NATO handed responsibility for this operation to the European Union.

Cooperation of NATO and the EU in Genocide-Prone Situations

A ceremony in Sarajevo marked the historic conclusion of the NATO-led SFOR in Bosnia and Herzegovina and the launch of the European Union's follow-on EUFOR.[8] SFOR was brought to a successful end nine years after NATO deployed forces in Bosnia and Herzegovina in 1995 in its first peacekeeping operation. The transition reflected the improved security situation in the country.

The progress the country had made by 2004 would have been unimaginable in the early 1990s. People no longer lived in fear, state institutions had been created, there was growing respect for human rights, and intergroup relations were much improved.

Even though the European Union assumed responsibility for peacekeeping operations, NATO maintained a headquarters in Sarajevo to assist the country with defense reform. It also carried out some operational tasks in coordination with the European Union, including counterterrorism and help in apprehending persons indicted for war crimes.

All this demonstrated growing cooperation between NATO and the European Union. The whole experience highlights the value of both organizations—separately and together. The potential of the cooperation, not only in military matters but also in economic, political, and civil affairs, is impressive in dealing with genocide-prone situations. Thus, the EU and NATO agreed on mutual crisis consultation arrangements that provide for efficient and rapid decisionmaking in both organizations, with their sharing of improvisation and consideration of strategies in the face of a looming crisis.

In many current conflicts, the basic nature of the state is at the heart of the problem. Thus, the international community finds itself called upon to reform dysfunctional institutions, including the state administration, the legal system, and even the media (especially if they are promoting hatred). In addition to the military aspect, many other activities have become necessary for an effective peace-building operation. Only a careful, well-planned, and coordinated combination of civilian and military measures can create the conditions for long-term peace, based on good governance and democratic socioeconomic development.

These examples show how a cooperative, democratic, broadened NATO can help in the prevention of genocide. Although this book clearly emphasizes ways of preventing genocide that are not military in nature, and although the EU itself has developed military capacity adequate for most early genocide prevention tasks, the availability of powerful, diversified NATO forces would often be helpful in a background capacity and might sometimes be crucial if strong force is needed (most likely owing to international delay in addressing signs of emerging, serious trouble). Thus, cooperative arrangements with NATO, especially involving the EU, could be a formidable asset in preventing genocide.

Prospects for NATO's Future

Without formal declaration, NATO has recently been exploring a new and global reason for existence—preserving peace in dangerous areas throughout the world. In this new century it has acted as a peacekeeper in Afghanistan, given training to Iraqi security forces and logistical assistance to the AU mission in Darfur, and contributed to humanitarian relief of tsunami victims in Indonesia, to hurricane Katrina victims in the United States, and to earthquake victims in Pakistan.

When the collapse of the USSR occurred, uncertainty arose about how best to use the alliance's strength. The United States considered taking advantage of the "peace dividend" by focusing the role of Western military forces on peace building, support to humanitarian relief efforts, and prevention of ethnic conflict and genocide.[9] After the September 11 terrorist attacks, NATO allies for the first time volunteered to deploy their forces outside allied territories, under the treaty provision that an attack on one member state was an attack on all of them. The United States, reluctant at first, but overextended in Iraq, accepted NATO's offer to deploy peacekeeping forces in Afghanistan, and those forces have grown from 5,000 troops to about 15,000 in 2007.

NATO's evolving and expanding role is in large part due to increased international awareness of the twenty-first century's global interconnectedness, which allows instability in one part of the world to exert a catastrophic effect in far distant regions and enables terrorist cells to communicate, organize, and plan across all borders.

Coping with global problems at their sources requires a global reach. NATO activities outside Europe, although imperative, are inhibited in principle by Article 10 of its charter, which restricts membership to Europe and North America, and by Article 6, which essentially limits NATO to defending member countries, their territories, and their forces within those territories.

NATO leaders are discussing these problems carefully. High on their agenda is how to strengthen relations with friendly democracies outside the transatlantic area, such as Japan, Australia, and New Zealand. The United States and the UK have proposed "global partnerships" to create a network with established democracies outside Europe. Ivo Daalder and James Goldgeier considered this proposal an excellent start but believed it should go further.[10] The foreign policy concerns of both the United States and Western Europe are increasingly focused on the Middle East, Asia, and Africa. If the stated purpose of the NATO founding treaty is to "safeguard the freedom, common heritage and civilisation of [the member states'] peoples, founded on the principles of democracy, individual liberty and the rule of law,"[11] it makes sense in a tightly interconnected world to choose new members according to their democratic values rather than their regional location. As Daalder and Goldgeier pointed out, politically appropriate Australia would be a member more sympathetic to NATO's objectives (and, incidentally, possessed of more resources) than geographically correct but dictatorial Belarus.[12] And a membership encompassing a larger territorial spread might make it easier for NATO forces to obtain use of regional bases and overflight privileges. NATO has already cooperated with friendly nations in ad hoc coalitions beyond Europe or North America.

Daalder and Goldgeier argued that these "global partnerships" should be seen as a possible first step toward formal membership. NATO should use the model it developed in the 1990s with its Partnership for Peace, which began by allowing the forces of former Warsaw Pact countries to join with NATO in training exercises and peacekeeping efforts. Later, those who qualified were admitted into NATO as full members.

A wider membership would be more effective than ad hoc coalitions, since it would create reliable forces that had trained, planned, and exercised together, resulting in the "interoperability" that has hitherto allowed NATO to react quickly and competently to crises. A broader membership would not necessitate a change in NATO's basic operating and command structures.

Some have objected that an expanded NATO would find it hard to reach consensus about action when a crisis occurred. But doubling its original membership did not cause NATO a problem, in part because no member has a power of veto. Dissenting members state their objections or, if in strong disagreement, can abstain from the operation in question. Others fear that widened membership might weaken the unity and commitment expressed in the founding treaty. But the "all for one, one for all" unity that Article V calls for was based not so much on love and brotherhood as on a common strategic interest in security and preservation of democratic values, then perceived as threatened by a formidable foe. In 1990 we saw how common interest could create a large coalition, including all of NATO's members, to oppose the invasion of Kuwait. And terrorists—especially if they can get a nuclear bomb—are an alarming common threat to virtually all nations.

NATO should evolve with the times to represent not just the transatlantic community but a global community of democracies. A regional organization is not adequate to help substantially with global security. NATO must extend its alliance to democracies worldwide on the basis of their commitment to NATO's founding principles. In so doing, it could—if needed—help to prevent the most antidemocratic crime of all, genocide.

PART IV

CONCLUSION

CHAPTER 17

Summing Up

Essential Points for Preventing Genocide

Most of us have seen a documentary or old newsreel portraying the incredible brutality of genocides ranging from the Holocaust to Darfur. If you cast your mind back to such pictures, you can grasp a little of the horror; but not the smells, the cries of anguish, and much else that reflects the mass slaughter of a people just because they were exactly that—a people cast in the role of inhuman scum, scapegoats, utterly vulnerable targets, putatively guilty of all sorts of crimes against the perpetrators, but in fact guilty of nothing except being alive—but not alive for long.

It is exceedingly hard to comprehend how supposedly decent human beings could commit such atrocities—over and over again from decade to decade, generation to generation, century to century. The spectacle has been so despicable that all sorts of efforts have been made to deny the existence of genocides, or to claim exaggeration, or to say it is simply a natural disaster like a tsunami, about which nothing can be done in the way of prevention. It is so hard to face these dreadful events, so hard to understand how they could happen, so hard to know what could possibly be done to prevent them. Hence, the scholarly and practitioner literature on genocide has very little to say about prevention.

There are deeply moving accounts of the victims' sufferings, heartrending expressions of their anguish and courage in the face of horrendous circumstances. Profoundly sensitive and thoughtful observers such as Elie Wiesel have done a great service by helping us to remember—not only the Holocaust but other genocides as well—and to draw the world's attention to impending dangers of genocides to come. Such work gives a powerful stimulus to explore how such ultimate cruelty and brutality could in fact be prevented. In-depth efforts to do so have been very rare, because of the complexity of the problem and the exceedingly grim nature of the experiences. But we must try. This chapter draws together the highlights of the entire book and hence the essence of preventing genocide.

My work draws on a great deal of research, field observations, and careful descriptions of the paths to genocide. It relates this most poignant body of information to the growing research literature on prevention of mass violence by building what I call pillars of prevention. These are structures of human relations, good governance, constraints on aggressive behavior, the movement toward worldwide protection of human rights and individual dignity through democratic institutions, construction of equitable socioeconomic development, widespread application of conflict resolution concepts and techniques, wise but politically fragile efforts to restrain the availability and use of highly lethal weapons—and, perhaps must fundamentally, development of a global movement to use such knowledge to educate children, youth, political leaders, and, indeed, all humanity to learn to live together in peace through mutual benefit from informed cooperation.

These pillars of prevention are mostly long-term measures that are useful for prevention of all sorts of mass violence: war, genocide, and crimes against humanity. They depend largely on international organizations, especially the democratic member states.

These pillars are multipurpose in preventing human suffering related to hatred and violence. War and genocide have important shared properties—often virulent prejudice predisposes to civil war, revolution, or interstate war. Under those conditions, the door is opened to genocide as the norms and institutions that restrain genocidal behavior are badly eroded. Killing becomes the order of the day, and established targets become exceedingly vulnerable. So it is highly desirable and increasingly feasible for the international community—especially the established democracies worldwide—to take measures that help to put out fires when they are small, yet the danger of conflagration is visible. If not extinguished, these fires may well lead to mass violence of one form or another. Early prevention of mass violence—whether genocide or not—must become the highest priority of a world striving to be decent and civilized.

The international community must make every effort to help countries or regions in trouble—manifested in growing hatred and emerging violence. Many countries will benefit, some quickly, some slowly, some not at all—yet over decades or generations, virtually all can benefit from building these pillars of prevention.

These pillars cover a wide span of preventive activities. The most rapid are the ones covered in the section, "Proactive Help, Especially Preventive Diplomacy." They will require organizations such as the UN, the EU, and the community of established democracies to keep in close touch with all regions of the world so as to respond with empathy and concern in offering help promptly—early, ongoing action to prevent mass violence—e.g., mediation of conflict and helping to build internal capacity for nonviolent problem solving.

But this is not the end of the matter. In most cases, these troubled countries will need respectful and sustained international help to build democratic socioeconomic development and to participate effectively in the world's institutions that strengthen opportunity, build internal mechanisms of conflict resolution, find reliable ways of meeting basic human needs, and foster constructive intergroup relations. These are paths toward a decent world.

Horrible as genocide is, we need to recall other dreadful experiences that have been successfully brought to resolution. In my lifetime, we have seen the end of colonialism and imperialism; unprecedented advances in science and technology making possible great advances in health and the foreseeable end of abject poverty; the worldwide spread of human rights since Eleanor Roosevelt's Declaration of Human Rights in 1948 and the successful U.S. civil rights movement of the 1960s, one century after Abraham Lincoln ended slavery; the end of Fascist and Communist totalitarianism; the end of the Cold

War—the most dangerous conflict in history; the end of apartheid and the emergence of democracy in South Africa—and indeed, the spread of democracy throughout most of the world. All of these have limitations and periodic setbacks, but they represent great advances bearing upon the worst problems of humanity.

The example of South Africa is important for several reasons. It was a worldwide symbol of prejudice and ethnocentrism as well as emotionally charged efforts at democratic reform and conflict resolution. The South African experience in overcoming apartheid shows how people suffering from terrible injustice, anger, and escalating violence were able to find their way out of an exceedingly dangerous predicament without falling into the hideous trap of genocide. Especially important here was the emergence of extraordinary leadership characterized by commitment to democracy, with a concomitant commitment to nonviolent conflict resolution.

Indeed, leadership matters greatly in overcoming all of these severe problems, and humanity must learn to recognize and cultivate leaders of vision, courage, and humane and democratic policies and to reinforce their commitment to nonviolent problem solving. How to do this should become a substantial part of the international agenda, including formal education, the media, the Internet, and discourse of international organizations.

A major focus of research has been on malevolent leadership. The more we can understand about the ideologies and actions of such leaders, the better our opportunity to foresee and prevent future genocidal episodes. Another focus of research is on the implementation of genocidal orders. Who does the killing and why?

Political leaders make genocide possible by lighting the fires of hatred, but they do not act alone. They are supported by machinery of the state, the dominant political party, the police forces, and paramilitary and military forces as well as professionals such as lawyers, professors, doctors, and engineers. This time interval to build the machinery of genocide can be utilized for prevention. Effective prevention is facilitated by ample warning time. Warning time is typically not weeks or even months, but actually years. Genocide is not like a tsunami that bursts upon humanity with hardly any warning.

Incitement is a hallmark, and probably a prerequisite, of genocide. Every modern case of genocide has been preceded by a mass media propaganda campaign directed by political leaders.

Altogether, the international community no longer has a viable excuse for inaction. The years required to go from the initial jeopardy to full genocide offer an interval for the international community—if it is alert, well informed, morally committed, and organizationally prepared—to take preventive actions—the earlier and more cooperative the better.

For about fifteen years the international community, stimulated in part by the Carnegie Commission on Preventing Deadly Conflict, has turned its attention to learning from research and innovative practices about ways to prevent mass brutality and atrocity in their various forms. Now at last it is paying serious attention to the most grotesque of all such behaviors, genocide.

In opening the General Assembly of the UN in September 2006, Secretary-General Kofi Annan generously expressed his appreciation for the Carnegie Commission and his hopes for the implementation of their concepts and practices—not least in the United Nations.

I very much regret that I cannot be with you today. I was looking forward to this occasion, and I am particularly grateful to President Eliasson for organizing today's debate. As you know, one of my consistent objectives as Secretary-General has been to move the United Nations from a culture of reaction to one of prevention. This, after all, is what is implied by the very first words that our founders used to express their purpose in founding the Organization—"to save succeeding generations from the scourge of war."

In the first year of my tenure the Carnegie Commission on Preventing Deadly Conflict, chaired by my dear friend David Hamburg and the late, much lamented Cyrus Vance, inspired us all with its ground-breaking report. Since then, encouraged by the General Assembly and the Security Council, we in the Secretariat have sought to build on the Commission's work. I submitted my first report on the subject in 2001, an interim one in 2003, and now I am pleased to submit the latest progress report, a main finding of which is that "a culture of prevention is indeed beginning to take hold at the United Nations." Indeed, in many parts of the world we are working to resolve disputes peacefully; and we are seeking more and more to build a preventive approach into other aspects of our work, notably those concerned with economic and social development.[1]

Pillars of Prevention

Proactive Help, Especially Preventive Diplomacy

The international community cannot afford to wait for a crisis. Governments, intergovernmental organizations, and nongovernmental organizations must establish permanent mechanisms for settling conflicts peacefully before they become explosive and must collaborate in offering ongoing programs of international help that build the capacity of groups to resolve grievances without violence. Fortunately, momentum has grown toward using techniques of active, nonviolent problem solving and sharing of experience across national boundaries to profit from the world's experience in different local conflicts. Tackling serious grievances as early as possible denies political demagogues and hateful fanatics the long-rankling discontent that makes incitement to violence easier.

Important recent studies (sponsored by the Carnegie Commission on Preventing Deadly Conflict) converge on key points of preventive diplomacy. Some recurrent elements of their message to the international community may be stated simply in guidelines that will diminish the risk of drifting into disasters:

1. Do not be lulled by wishful thinking: recognize dangers early.
2. Get the facts straight, directly from multiple credible sources, and be sure to include in their evaluation the history of the particular latent or emerging conflict and the culture of the parties involved.
3. Pool strengths, share burdens, and divide labor among national and multilateral entities according to their capacity, salience, and motivation to assist in achieving peaceful relations and meeting basic human needs.
4. Foster widespread public understanding of conflict resolution and violence prevention. This gives a basis for hope of a just settlement.
5. Offer mediation early; a fair-minded and trusted third party can facilitate problem solving before adversaries harden their attitudes and positions.

6. Formulate and promote superordinate goals—that is, goals highly desirable to both opposing groups, which they can obtain only by cooperation.

7. Use economic leverage—both carrots and sticks—to indicate what can be gained by peaceful settlement and lost by violence. Propose incentives for conflict resolution that can be used to heal serious wounds.

8. Support moderate, pragmatic local leaders, whether established or emerging, in particular democratic reformers. Bolster their precarious position and integrate them into like-minded international networks.

9. Bear in mind the pervasive need that negotiators and their constituencies have for respect and dignity. Help negotiators strengthen the cooperation among the factions within their own group and guard against "spoilers." Maintain an atmosphere of shared humanity and hope for mutual accommodation.

10. Upgrade training for preventive diplomacy in relevant entities—for example, national governments, the UN, regional organizations—notably the EU. Establish dedicated units for preventive diplomacy that maintain knowledge and skill in early conflict resolution and knowledge of the particular region. Provide specific instruction for staff, updated in light of ongoing worldwide experience. Keep a roster of experts on call for leadership organizations such as the UN and democratic governments.

Fostering Worldwide Democracy

Democracies thrive by finding ways to deal fairly with conflicts and resolve them below the threshold of mass violence. They develop ongoing mechanisms for settling disagreements. That is why they are so important in preventing mass violence, especially genocide. But these very ambitious goals require the worldwide spread of democracies and the application of democratic principles to intergroup and internation conflicts. People who live in pluralistic democracies become accustomed to diverse needs and learn the art of working out compromises that are satisfactory to all groups. This does not mean democracy imposed by force, nor does it mean that a single, premature election will lead to peace and prosperity. But it does mean that patiently constructed democracies, based on fair processes of mutual accommodation, offer the best chance for nonviolent conflict resolution.

Democracies, even with periodic regressions, protect human rights better than nondemocratic societies, and their elected officials are less likely to engage in large-scale, egregious human rights violations that create intense fear and severe resentment. Massive human rights abuses as a path to genocide are very unlikely in an established democracy.

The basic principles of democracy are attractive all over the world, even though entrenched autocratic powers resist them. Survey research shows that the majority in most developing countries would prefer democracy.

All democracies need systematic, fair procedures of governance that are based on the consent of the governed. A system of representation is essential, but no single kind will work for every group. These variations share the common themes of fairness and widespread participation in decisions important to the lives of the population.

Pluralism is at the heart of a lasting democracy; it permits and fosters the dynamic interplay of ideas and enterprises by parties and by a great variety of nongovernmental organizations on the basis of reasonably clear, agreed-upon rules—rules that reflect a fundamental attitude of tolerance, mutual respect, and sensitivity to human rights. These habits of understanding others and working out compromises are learned. The established democracies can make the world's experience available to emerging, fragile democracies and offer tangible help. Other than democratic institutions, there is no clear way to provide an enduring basis for treating human beings fairly and protecting human rights under a popularly accepted rule of law.

The international cooperation necessary to achieve such change is measured in years of complicated joint efforts. That is why cooperative efforts through strong organizations are so often necessary—especially the European Union, United Nations, and the worldwide community of established democracies. One way or another, the established democracies (an expanding group of countries) will need to act in concert to build the pillars of prevention essential for blocking mass violence.

There is clearly a need for coordinated action among established democracies both to help build strong democracies out of weak ones and to act jointly to prevent deadly conflicts, above all genocide. Their capacity for such action is profound. But it is not clear which of the several multilateral democracy organizations will emerge to promote effective action on these crucial problems. It might function partly within the UN (as a democratic caucus) and partly outside (but always adhering to the high ideals of the UN Charter and the UN Declaration of Human Rights). Or it may turn out that these democracy-promoting and peace-promoting functions of the established democracies can best be carried out by a separate organization. In the world of 2006, the best example is the European Union, exemplifying remarkable cooperation among twenty-seven democracies, some established and some new, and using this centralized strength to foster other democracies and to prevent war and genocide, reaching beyond Europe to help the African Union and others. We might call this EU-plus.

A global organization of democracies can promote explicitly sustained antidotes to hatred and violence by

1. setting standards for fair, free elections and monitoring their conduct, fostering civil society through which people learn mutual accommodation;
2. providing guidance for education at all levels—from children and youth to political and business leaders as well as scholars in institutions of higher learning—on specific paths to decent interpersonal and intergroup relations, conflict resolution, violence prevention, and paths to enduring peace; and
3. mobilizing intellectual and moral leadership in the universities, religious institutions, political parties, business community, and other powerful sectors to focus on these crucial issues—above all on prevention of war and genocide.

Dictatorships are naturally destructive. They are prone to genocide. Using any means at their disposal, dictators are likely to serve themselves at the expense of their people. Therefore, the community of democracies must move from a general wish for democracy to a concrete, practical plan for achieving it.

Fostering Equitable Socioeconomic Development

Democratic socioeconomic development on a worldwide basis offers humanity its best hope for producing conditions favorable to preventing war and genocide.

This is a much more practical goal today than it was a few decades ago, even though a long rugged path still lies ahead. Investment in human and social capital is now generally accepted as a central part of development, especially in the form of promoting the health and education of girls and boys (and women and men) alike—to build a vigorous, dynamic population that is well informed, capable, fair-minded, open-minded, and mutually supportive in times of personal and social stress and that also has social support networks that enable communities to tackle their local problems constructively. The essential features of development—knowledge, skills, freedom, and health—can be achieved by sustained international cooperation that draws upon the unprecedented advances of modern science and technology.

Firmly grounding new democracies with equitable development requires decades or even generations, so their older and more established counterparts, chiefly those in the affluent West but also such rising democracies as Japan, India, Brazil, and South Africa, must be persistent and resourceful in working all over the world with democratic reformers. Socioeconomic development links with democracy as crucial ingredients for genocide prevention.

Development assistance, especially in the form of capacity building, for knowledge and skill and especially for nonviolent problem solving is crucial for very poor countries. Such countries must generate internal motivation, ingenuity, and dedication to foster their own distinctive development. Yet their efforts to create decent living standards and fair-minded human relations will usually fail without significant help from established democracies, international organizations, NGOs, and multinational firms. In terms of crucially constructive developments that must take place within poor countries, but have often been neglected, two stand paramount—health and education.

Health has been curiously neglected in economic development efforts, as if it were a benefit to be achieved only in an advanced later stage of development. But a healthy, vigorous population is essential to build a dynamic, equitable, growing economy.

Improving the health and longevity of the poor is a valuable end in itself, a fundamental goal of economic development. But it is also a *means* to achieving the other development goals. The links of health to poverty reduction and to long-term economic growth are powerful. The burden of disease in some low-income regions, especially sub-Saharan Africa, stands as a stark barrier to economic growth, and any comprehensive development strategy must therefore strive for its prompt, substantial improvement.

The established democracies can make a great contribution to overcoming these deficiencies if, with the involvement of civil society, they help build local capacity for honest, effective governance, science-based health care, technical capability, and public health infrastructure. At a time of unprecedented advances in biomedical sciences and public health, it is urgent that research and development redirect efforts to pursue the treatment and prevention of the world's most devastating diseases—concentrated in developing countries.

Education for Human Survival

One of the fundamental underpinnings of successful socioeconomic development is comprehensive education, from preschool through graduate school. This must include women on an equal basis, not only as a matter of equity but also as a matter of economic stimulus. A crucial and badly neglected function is education for violence prevention, conflict resolution, and mutual accommodation. There is a substantial body of research to support such education.[2]

Given the crucial role of science and technology in the economy of the twenty-first century, an important component of this effort must be education in mathematics, science, and technology. This should run the entire gamut of the sciences from physical to social and should include science-based professions: engineering, medicine, public health, and social work. It must include education for learning to live together—preventing hatred and violence in the development of children and youth.

To develop research capability, it is essential for each developing country to connect its emerging scientific community with the international scientific community. The role of an effective technical community in moving toward prosperity is clear. Moreover, the international ties that develop in this way can be helpful in other ways, especially in fostering democratic norms and helping to sort out interstate conflicts without violence, since cooperation among diverse scientists sets a good example and often generates creative ideas for dealing with intergroup or even international problems. Education must include conflict resolution—as happened notably during the Cold War in higher education and political/diplomatic leadership.

The scientific community can provide a model for decent human relations and mutually beneficial cooperation that might transcend the biases, dogmas, and hatreds that have torn our species apart throughout history and have recently become so much more dangerous than ever before. Science can contribute to a better future by its ideals and its processes as well as by the specific content of its research. Recent examples show vividly the great promise of international scientific cooperation for the benefit of all humanity.

Use of International Justice to Reduce Human Rights Abuse and Mass Violence

Prevention of deadly conflict starts with the recognition of the immense dangers of egregious, pervasive human rights violations, typically enforced by and in repressive states—human rights violations so crucial for genocide and ethnic, religious, and international wars. Sooner or later, these atrocities must be prevented, and bad outcomes averted, by promoting democracy, equitable market economies, and the creation of strong civil institutions that protect human rights. Prevention is not simply smoothing over a rough spot in intergroup or international relations—it requires creating a durable basis for peaceful conditions of living together, especially by protecting the human rights of all the people.[3]

This calls for integrating efforts of international organizations and cooperating democracies to provide an early warning system for blocking serious human rights violations through the rule of law, democratization, and other national human rights protections. Prominent among the steps toward prevention of genocide is the worldwide promotion and protection of human rights by clear concepts, orderly processes, and effective institutions.

Genocide is the most appalling form of egregious and pervasive violation of human rights, the ultimate degradation of human dignity. Conversely, promotion and protection of human rights represent a compelling avenue toward elimination of genocide. Therefore, we have reason to be interested in the growth of the human rights movement, its progress, and its promise for the long term. They are inherent rights by virtue of being human—not given by grace, love, charity, or compassion—in other words, claims that society is morally, politically, indeed legally obligated to respect and ensure. The achievement of human rights requires ceaseless vigilance and ongoing struggle.

Some groups of states have developed important regional systems for the protection of human rights. In Europe and in the Americas, regional organizations have developed strong human rights codes comparable to the Universal Declaration and the International Covenant on Civil and Political Rights as well as institutions for enforcing them, such as national commissions and international courts that have enjoyed impressive success. Most notable is the experience of Europe, where a dramatic turnaround has occurred in a few decades. This includes the democratizing magnet effect of the EU.

Europe has developed multiple legal entities that deal with human rights. Taken together, they constitute a powerful bulwark for human rights. Thus, Europe has learned from more than a century of extensive human rights violations (colonial conquests, wars, genocides) that new norms, laws, and institutions must be firmly established, the benefits of international cooperation recognized, and a helping hand extended to peoples seeking a new birth of freedom, human dignity, and nonviolent intergroup relations. The European experience is intrinsically important but also offers specific guidance and an authentic basis for hope in all lands.

There is a strong link between virulent human rights abuses and the instigation of deadly conflict—war or genocide or both. Conversely, reliable safeguards for human rights go a long way to prevent mass violence.[4] Human rights have increasingly transcended the boundaries of individual countries and become a legitimate domain of politics and human relations, not only for nation-states but also for international and regional organizations, both governmental and nongovernmental.

Human rights instruments provide guidance for good governance. When states use this guidance, they reduce grievances and, with them, the risk of violence. The growth and strength of human rights beliefs, norms, processes, and institutions have largely been a surprise throughout the world—and a powerful stimulus to further progress.

Restraints on Highly Lethal Weapons

"Small arms" and "light weapons" now cover the world wall to wall. This collective euphemism includes highly lethal machine-guns, mortars, automatic rifles, and rocket launchers. They killed millions in the 1990s. They are not classified as weapons of mass destruction, and only modest efforts have been made to get a handle on this problem. The ubiquitous presence and use of these weapons is enabled by their provision by major nations. At the extreme of lethality, biological, chemical, and above all nuclear weapons have almost unimaginable killing power. Highly lethal weapons have an intoxicating effect on political demagogues, religious fanatics, and ethnic haters. There is a recent and exceedingly dangerous movement toward proliferation of nuclear weapons in the context of fanatical leadership.

We have reached a point in human history in which all populations, states, and regions are vulnerable to large-scale casualties from well-organized, fanatical haters, religious and political ideologues, repressive states, or deeply troubled young men. The threat is one that already involves many countries, and, in principle, could involve all. This should stimulate the building of internationally cooperative efforts to overcome the very dangerous terrorism problem. As a practical matter, the problem simply cannot be overcome without a high degree of international cooperation. Since acquiring nuclear weapons and materials is the first, and by far the hardest, step terrorists must take in gaining nuclear capability—and every step that follows becomes progressively easier—the cheapest and most effective defense against them is to secure nuclear weapons and fissile materials everywhere they are stored. Some progress has been made, but much more is needed.

In point of fact, the growing Asian and Middle East problems above all highlight the nature of the worldwide danger, including the possibilities of multiple genocides motivated by religious and/or political hatreds. It is difficult to contemplate any stronger stimulus for the international community to come together in common cause and in urgent cooperation for survival.

Some programs have been remarkably successful in reducing the risk of nuclear proliferation and terrorism. For example, the Nunn-Lugar initiative for cooperative threat reduction, in concert with other measures, has already been responsible for the dismantling of well over 5,000 nuclear warheads and the complete elimination of nuclear weapons in Ukraine, Kazakhstan, and Belarus. We must strengthen these proven programs, especially by extending the fruitful Nunn-Lugar efforts to include tactical nuclear weapons (which are particularly dangerous in the context of terrorism because they are readily portable, more affordable, and more easily guided to specific, short-range targets) and by funding efforts to immobilize plutonium.

Since the whole world is in jeopardy, global cooperation should become feasible. There must be a broad alliance of nations that will cooperate in identifying, accounting for, and rigorously safeguarding all the nuclear stocks in the world. The strongest countries (and many others) should offer security assurances to nations that voluntarily forgo nuclear weapons and join a common effort to build a robust international antiproliferation system. Strong countries can offer economic and trade benefits, especially in the area of energy supplies. They can supplement economic incentives with measures that enhance security in various ways—far more so than the possession of nuclear weapons.

There is no doubt these utterly crucial tasks in avoiding nuclear catastrophe (including instant genocide) require deeply international, long-term efforts, including diplomatic, political, economic, moral, and psychological responses. The NGOs worldwide could greatly influence publics, governments, and international institutions in many ways to increase concern about lethal weapons, deadly conflict, and genocide in the next one to two decades.

Who Can Do What?

Having now considered the circumstances in which genocide may occur, both its aggravating and mitigating factors, and the need for early constructive responses, it is logical to reflect on those international bodies that are uniquely positioned to play the most constructive roles in preventing mass violence, including genocide. These are the United Nations, the European Union, NATO, and the Organisation for Cooperation and Security in Europe. Others will emerge in the years ahead.

Potential of the UN for Preventing Mass Violence

The legitimacy of outside assistance is a critical determinant of its success. As a universal organization with high ideals, the UN has considerable legitimacy throughout the world. It plays a vital role in establishing the terms of outside intervention if necessary and the broad consensus to support it. The UN can, directly or indirectly, foster respectful engagement with states for resolution of impending violent conflict and building equitable development through democratic institutions. Moreover, it is playing an important and growing role in preventive diplomacy.

Prevention of mass violence cannot be the responsibility of the UN alone but demands the stalwart participation of a wide array of institutions in the international community. In some situations, the UN may take the lead; in others, individual governments or regional or nongovernmental organizations may be called upon to do so. This work of addressing and treating the root causes of violence is unglamorous, laborious, and difficult—entailing, as we have described in detail, a long process of sustainable socioeconomic development, grounded in respect for human rights and legitimate government. This blend of ingredients is indispensable for preventing deadly conflict on an enduring basis. To do so requires deep international engagement in cooperative development, sustained over many years.

Obstacles and Assets of the UN

The UN has many strengths but also serious limitations:

1. With modest resources and a massive agenda, the Secretary-General and Security Council are overburdened and are forced to focus on crisis situations more than preventive strategies.
2. Although its Charter allows the UN to respond to threats or breaches of peace within or among states, it often has trouble dealing with conflicts involving nonofficial parties and internal disputes, and so far has had problems with very early prevention.
3. The UN is hindered in its security efforts by the threat of a veto in the Security Council. Though the Council varies in composition over time, it is generally not deeply committed to democratic, humane, compassionate values.
4. The high stakes surrounding the UN's involvement in a conflict sometimes make states apprehensive about bringing their conflict to it. The Security Council may be inflexible or partisan or may pass resolutions that cannot be implemented, as it did in the former Yugoslavia.
5. The UN struggles to be organizationally efficient, but has the image of being wasteful, and is hampered in administrative reform by a variety of member states, especially autocratic ones.

Despite its shortcomings, the UN's considerable resources and opportunities make it an indispensable part of any regime of preventing genocide and war:

1. It has a worldwide organizational network, composed, to a large extent, of capable, dedicated professional people.
2. The Secretary-General's diplomatic resources, strengthened by his moral authority, enable him to bring disputing parties together in a constructive atmosphere.
3. The UN can bring issues to the attention of the international community and put moral and other pressure on disputing parties to work toward resolution.
4. It can assemble the political and economic power of problem-solving governments to create a package of preventive action.
5. It can make available to any troubled country or region the entire world's experience, knowledge, and skills pertinent to building durable mechanisms for conflict resolution and peaceful intergroup relations.

The UN can be strengthened in ways that would permit it to use its unique scope and legitimacy to foster political, social, and economic conditions in which a civil and just international society might evolve.[5] Enhancing the UN's ability to respond rapidly to prevent large-scale violence should receive high priority.

The Secretary-General needs high-level special representatives available either in his own Secretariat or through a collaborative relationship with nongovernmental organizations. In either case, the special representatives of the Secretary-General and the senior staff collaborators should combine expertise in two bodies of knowledge: the principles and techniques of conflict resolution and in-depth knowledge of a particular region, including the main historical and cultural factors bearing on a specific conflict.

There are ways in which regional programs for assistance in dispute settlement can reduce tension between groups, whether within or between states, both in near-term and long-term accomplishments. As the concepts and techniques of violence prevention are more widely understood, such UN-RO-NGO activities could become a potent force for preventive diplomacy in the short run and also for democratic socioeconomic development in the long term.

In the area of education, the UN should sponsor world leadership seminars, in cooperation with universities and research institutes. These leadership seminars might include new heads of state, new foreign ministers, new defense ministers, and new development ministers. Ongoing leadership seminars could clarify how the UN and other institutions and organizations can help states avoid violent conflict and, most important, deal with problems of nationalism, ethnocentrism, prejudice, hatred, and violence. Through leadership seminars, a wide array of publications, and the Internet, the UN can make available to the world experience bearing on conflicts in general and on particular conflicts; the responsible handling of weapons by governmental leaders and policy makers; the likely consequences of weapons build-up, especially weapons of mass destruction; the skills, knowledge base, and prestige properly associated with successful conflict resolution; economic development, including the new uses of science and technology for development; and cooperative behavior in the world community, including the handling of grievances. Prevention of genocide should be high on this agenda.

International policymakers must make sustained efforts to identify and promote those factors that foster the emergence of viable political processes in violence-prone societies. Negotiated settlements based on short-term compromises are more likely to endure if they include strategies and actions that move toward the gradual elimination of the prejudices, misperceptions, insecurity, exclusion, and animosity that poisoned intergroup relations in the first place. Agreements should be followed up with systematic problem solving and monitoring to facilitate improved intergroup relations over the long term and to strengthen the capacity for building fair, resilient, problem-solving political processes.

Secretary-General Annan identified six categories of core prevention activities in a detailed review of the United Nations system: (1) early warning, information, and analysis; (2) good offices and mediation; (3) democracy, good governance, and a culture of prevention; (4) disarmament and arms control; (5) equitable socioeconomic development; and (6) human rights, humanitarian law, and international justice. If future leaders of the UN carry this agenda forward, the UN's contributions could become very important globally. These considerations apply to genocide as well as to other mass violence.

In 2004, in a landmark speech in Stockholm, then UN Secretary General Kofi Annan made an impressive commitment to genocide prevention:

> There can be no more important issue, and no more binding obligation, than the prevention of genocide. Indeed, this may be considered one of the original purposes of the United Nations.... We must attack the roots of violence and genocide: ... intolerance, racism, tyranny, and the dehumanizing public discourse that denies whole groups of people their dignity and rights. We must protect especially the rights of minorities, ... genocide's most frequent targets.[6]

He therefore announced that in memory of the victims of Rwanda he would launch an Action Plan to Prevent Genocide that would involve the whole UN system.

Most of the world's heads of state and government met in an extraordinary summit at the UN headquarters in New York in September 2005. Their Outcome Document of September 15, 2005, endorsed the UN's efforts to prevent genocide. Although the terms of the endorsement were general, they nevertheless were noteworthy in an institution that had not made appreciable strides on this problem during the preceding half century.[7]

This high-level, worldwide endorsement of prevention aspirations now needs stronger implementation. The Secretary-General set two important precedents at once by appointing a Special Adviser for the Prevention of Genocide in 2004. It was the first time any prevention professional had been appointed at such a high level, reporting directly to the Secretary-General. Moreover, it was the first time that a unit focusing specifically on genocide prevention had ever been created at the UN. In 2006, the Secretary-General strengthened this effort by appointing a strong, worldwide committee to advise him on ways of strengthening genocide prevention in the future.

The Special Adviser for the Prevention of Genocide cannot provide detailed leadership on all of the fundamental, long-term activities inherent in the pillars of prevention. But he can give stimulation and encouragement to those in the UN system who have such responsibilities, and he can help the Secretary-General to strengthen them by identifying opportunities for cooperation among various departments and agencies throughout the world as well as other international organizations, such as the EU.

These are not easy tasks, and rapid transformation of the problem of genocide is unlikely. Yet the stakes are so high, the human suffering so great, the promise of better human relations so valuable, that the UN must do everything in its power to prevent genocide and other crimes against humanity. The same considerations apply in large part to other international organizations.

The UN must be a significant part of serious genocide prevention. This book notes various ways in which necessary preventive functions could be strengthened within the UN's worldwide system and in its links with other organizations.

Leadership for Prevention of Genocide and War: The Promise of the European Union

The formidable resources of the established democracies give them great potential to form groupings that can recognize early warnings of imminent conflict and respond promptly with preventive actions. Yet their track record has not yet matched this potential. Recently a focus on prevention has emerged, however, and its impact on policy has been especially impressive in the European Union since 2001, when that body announced its Göteborg Programme on conflict prevention, which involves a cooperative approach to peaceful solutions of disputes and to attacking their root causes. It is now considered an important element of the external relations of the European Union. The rotating presidency of the EU meant that Sweden, a pioneer in prevention of violent conflict, was able to take the lead in creating this program in 2001.

Thus, an inherent advantage of the EU is a set of cooperating democracies. The European Union is a remarkable, indeed unprecedented, family of democratic European countries, working together for peace and prosperity. It arose in reaction to the horrors of World War II and the Holocaust. European statesmen had the vision to see the beauty of cooperation, both at the economic and at the political level, and now at the level of human relations in the broadest sense. The EU includes five institutions, each with a specific role, and the superb leadership of Javier Solana in mediating international conflict.[8]

There is much promise in an ever closer cooperation among established democracies—the enlarging group of nations that share humane values, effective mechanisms for coping with conflict, and formidable resources for preventing mass violence. In the face of foreseeable genocide, they can act effectively in different groupings all over the world, whether or not the UN is able to act—functioning within the spirit of the UN Charter but not limited by its political and procedural constraints in the face of great danger. This can provide a flexible system of action for peace and justice. The European Union is the clearest example of a set of established democracies sharing basic humane and peaceful values, able to act effectively, and morally committed to preventing genocide—and working on ways to translate this into action. EU-plus could provide a worldwide stimulus for an organization of democracies focused on preventing war and genocide.

The economically powerful EU is a strikingly successful example of how close cooperation and understanding between nations that waged massive wars against one another within living memory can lead to reconciliation that is the basis for peace and prosperity. As the most prominent representative body in one of the wealthiest and most influential areas of the globe, the EU is well placed to play a major role in preventing violent conflict. It can use not only its civilian and military crisis management capabilities but also the diplomatic instruments of its members, political and economic. It can also wield trade policy instruments, cooperation agreements, development assistance, economic cooperation, and social and environmental policies as mechanisms and incentives to assure peace.

Using the prospect of membership as an incentive to reform is valuable (the magnet effect) but has limits. But making external assistance, trade, and other benefits conditional on progress in the areas of democratic reform, the rule of law, human rights, and acceptance of a market economy is a valid approach that may well come to have similar value in other parts of the world, especially if the EU offers its tutelage, technical assistance, and sustained, sympathetic encouragement. It is not difficult to imagine a network of regional organizations around the globe, all functioning on EU principles, each in its own way. Such a network would have unprecedented promise for preventing mass violence.

High Representative Javier Solana plays an important role in preventive diplomacy, especially mediation and facilitation. Leadership matters, and his leadership is extraordinary. Representing an EU of twenty-seven states, he has far more leverage than a representative of a single state, provided the twenty-seven have coherence. SRs are also an important conflict prevention tool for the EU—as they are for the UN.

Since adoption of the Joint Declaration on EU-UN Cooperation in Crisis Management in 2003, EU-UN cooperation has progressed in the areas of planning, training, communication, and best practices. A high-level staff-to-staff steering group to monitor developments has been created. EU-UN cooperation has also increased in the area of helping regional organizations such as the AU build their own crisis management capacity. Such EU-UN cooperation in preventing genocide would have great potential.

The EU has in recent years established working relations with many countries in different parts of the world pertinent to preventing deadly conflict. Although these are essentially new, they offer considerable promise based on earlier experience and increasing commitment. These relations include a variety of African countries, the United States, Canada, Russia, Indonesia, China, India, Japan, Latin America, and of course a variety of European countries and nearby neighbors. Thus, the EU is emerging as a broadly international—almost global—organization that is deeply committed to prevention of war and genocide, technically capable, increasingly sophisticated in respect to both operational and structural prevention, and highly cooperative with a variety of constructive entities, not least the UN. Explicit functional linkage between these two vast international organizations in genocide prevention would have historic significance.

Organisation for Security and Cooperation in Europe:
Its Potential for Preventing Genocide

The OSCE is the largest regional security organization in the world, with a reach that stretches from "Vancouver to Vladivostok": fifty-six participating states in Europe, Central Asia, and North America. It is active in early warning, conflict prevention, crisis management, and postconflict rehabilitation.[9] Its work has gained much attention and credit.[10]

The OSCE is a worthy paradigm because of its focus on early conflict prevention, its willingness to become deeply involved, and the many mechanisms it has available. It can start a process of early and ongoing conflict resolution through politics, legislation, education of leaders, and roundtable discussions involving diverse sectors of society.

In planning and implementing interventions, preventive diplomacy missions coordinate closely with interested NGOs. They are most effective when they attend closely to issues such as human rights, minority rights, democratization, freedom of the media, and the rule of law. Finally, missions are only as strong as their members. Successes are directly related to personnel. Training in many aspects—negotiation, mediation, conflict resolution, cultural sensitivity, and gender balance on the team—is valuable.

In accordance with its mandate for promoting democracy, the OSCE

- observes national and local elections and offers election assistance;
- provides practical support in consolidating democratic institutions through both long-term, multiyear, institutional, and capacity-building programs and short-er-term, high-impact projects to strengthen civil society and democratic governance;
- helps OSCE field missions implement human dimension activities through training, exchange of experiences, and regional coordination;
- contributes to early warning and conflict prevention by monitoring how participating states meet human dimension commitments; provides regular human rights training for government authorities, civil society, and OSCE staff; and
- helps participating states use human rights principles to meet their international legal obligations and OSCE commitments on terrorism.

The OSCE Office of the High Commissioner on National Minorities, established in 1992, seeks early resolution of ethnic tensions that might endanger peace or friendly relations between participating states. At the end of the Cold War, tension between groups was severe and threatened civil war, possibly even war with Russia, or genocidal fury. The high commissioner's work has elicited worldwide interest and admiration.

In the 1990s the OSCE high commissioner on national minorities, Max van der Stoel,[11] set a constructive, ingenious example of early, ongoing preventive diplomacy in dangerous situations in Eastern Europe[12]—an example that now has worldwide influence. The source of his view of minority rights is the OSCE's Copenhagen Document of 1990, which guarantees to national minorities their human rights and fundamental freedoms with full equality before the law. These include the use of their mother tongue in private and public life; the establishment of their own educational, cultural, and religious institutions; religious freedom; and the right to unimpeded contact with other minority group members. These protections are binding on all OSCE participating states.

The Office of the High Commissioner is constantly receiving and analyzing information and visiting trouble spots. This allows early accurate assessment of troubling situations and ways to facilitate solutions. Nationalist issues that threaten to boil over can be broken down into core elements that can be dealt with in practical terms. In cases ranging from minority language rights in Slovakia through legislative policy on minorities in Croatia to minority education in Romania, the high commissioner's goal is to avoid inflaming a situation and to help opposing parties find accommodation in a problem-solving atmosphere.

Overall, the high commissioner contributes greatly by making informed recommendations to governments of participating states regarding the treatment of their national minorities. This office has done much to educate new and fragile democracies about decent intergroup relations.

It is clear that OSCE has much potential to contribute to prevention of genocide. Yet it has limited resources—many fewer than the European Union —and its many members must agree on major actions. That is likely to present delay and even obstruction in dangerous situations. Still, it has provided valuable lessons for those interested in preventing genocide.

NATO: The Potential for Preventing Genocide

The highly respected NATO was created in the aftermath of World War II as the Soviet Union became alienated from its former allies, occupied most of Eastern and central Europe, and, under the brutal leadership of Joseph Stalin, defiantly faced Western Europe as well as the United States.

In response, the Western allies formed a close alliance that became an exceedingly powerful military force, bridging the North Atlantic between Western Europe and North America. As the decades passed, its functions broadened somewhat to include a modicum of diplomatic, educational, and scientific functions. With the end of the Cold War, at the outset of the 1990s, it broadened its activities considerably, creating relationships with additional countries, expanding diplomatic and civil-military functions, emphasizing democracy, and considering "out of area" tasks.

In late 2002, NATO undertook a comprehensive review of the Euro-Atlantic Partnership Council and Partnership for Peace.[13] It reaffirmed its strategic concept of outreach and openness, preserving peace, promoting democracy, contributing to prosperity, and fostering genuine partnership among all democratic Euro-Atlantic countries. The commitment aimed to enhance the security of all, to exclude none, and to overcome disagreements that could lead to violent conflict. These ties proved very attractive to the countries of east central Europe and served a "magnet" function similar to that of the European Union. Both fostered the transition to democracy and, in due course, their entry into NATO. Cooperation with the EU and the UN has become feasible and desirable.

The opportunities for achieving alliance objectives through political means are greater than ever before. Although the defense dimension remains indispensable, more prominence is now given to economic, social, and environmental issues as a means of promoting security and democratic transformation in the Euro-Atlantic area as a whole.

Joint activities aimed at finding common solutions to common security challenges have led to important achievements in overcoming past prejudices and in establishing a clear vision of the mutual benefits to be gained from cooperation.

Yugoslavia was NATO's first venture into genocide-prone territory. Although the prevention of genocide prior to the necessity for military action is certainly preferable, there are times when military strength is essential—either in the background, to strengthen diplomatic efforts, or in the foreground, as in Yugoslavia. This book emphasizes early preventive action that does not require major military efforts, but sometimes in genocide-prone situations these are necessary for massive lifesaving protection.

In the very hard cases of genocide-prone behavior, preventive diplomacy may require coercive measures that are not overtly military but benefit from military participation in contingency planning and conduct of some pressures on the perpetrating country—for example, targeted sanctions such as freezing the assets and prohibiting out-of-country travel of the perpetrators and their families; economic disinvestments, especially through sanctions imposed by international banks; establishment of no-fly zones; indictment by the International Criminal Court. Coercive diplomacy involves more options than military ones, yet some are military (e.g., imposition of no-fly zones); others have more credibility to oppressive leaders if they know that a formidable military presence is readily available. Here NATO could be helpful as it becomes more flexible in its modes of operation.

NATO's first three peace support operations took place in Europe, yet the need for long-term peace building is global. NATO foreign ministers recognized this at a meeting in Reykjavik, Iceland, in May 2002, agreeing that "[t]o carry out the full range of its missions, NATO must be able to field forces that can move quickly to wherever they are needed, sustain operations over distance and time, and achieve their objectives."[14] This decision effectively paved the way for NATO to deploy for the first time outside the Euro-Atlantic area, in Afghanistan. The African Union urgently needs its help, e.g., to develop an AU rapid deployment force.

In order to be effective when deploying far from alliance territory, NATO militaries must invest in power projection capabilities. It involves the creation of a NATO response force, which can give the alliance the capacity to move a robust force quickly, to deter or respond to attack. Such a force could be very helpful in a genocide-prone situation by keeping the would-be perpetrators away from their likely victims and providing space for coercive diplomacy to prevent mass killing.

An effective working relationship between the European Union and NATO is critical to successful crisis management and in some cases might well prevent genocide. The European Union and NATO have negotiated a series of documents on cooperation in crisis management, known by insiders as the "Berlin-plus" package, which made it possible for the European Union to take over from NATO responsibility for peacekeeping in the Former Yugoslav Republic of Macedonia in 2003. NATO worked closely with the European Union and the Organisation for Security and Cooperation in Europe from the political level down to the field, and the three organizations presented a unified international stance to both sides of the conflict.

Thus, a cooperative, democratic, broadened NATO can help in the prevention of genocide. Even though this book clearly emphasizes ways of preventing genocide that are *not* military in nature, and even though the EU itself has developed military capacity adequate for most early genocide prevention tasks, the availability of powerful, diversified NATO forces would often be helpful in a background capacity and might sometimes be crucial if strong force is needed (most likely due to international delay in addressing signs of emerging, serious trouble). Thus, cooperative arrangements with NATO, especially involving the EU and AU, could be a formidable asset in preventing genocide. In our ever more interconnected world, it now behooves us to think of NATO as a truly global arrangement and to admit new members according to their democratic values rather than their regional placement, with special attention to peace-building alliances.

A wider membership makes more operational sense than ad hoc coalitions, since it can create reliable forces that have trained, planned, and exercised together, resulting in the "interoperability" that has hitherto allowed NATO to react quickly and competently to crises. There is both a strategic and a moral imperative to employ the uniquely valuable instrument of NATO as a force for global peace and orderly, peaceful democratic development—to represent not just the transatlantic community but a global community of democracies. NATO must extend its alliance to democracies worldwide on the basis of their commitment to NATO's basic principles. In so doing, it could if needed help to prevent the most antidemocratic crime of all, genocide.

＊＊ ＊＊

CHAPTER 18

International Centers for the Prevention of Genocide

Unprecedented Historic Opportunities

Much promising work on prevention has been widely scattered over the world's landscape in recent years. Two focal points, each in a great international organization, could provide an extremely valuable reservoir of knowledge, skills, and best practices as well as a home base for mobilization of many different institutions and organizations that could make good use of such information. This applies both to operational (short-term) and structural (long-term) means of prevention. Such focal points could stimulate worldwide cooperative efforts in the next few decades to bring an end to genocide. Such an ongoing service would stimulate new ideas, new research, new education, and new modes of cooperation among diverse entities that can contribute to prevention of genocide. In so doing, the centers could keep the world's focus on this dreadful problem and provide authentic hope for effective action.

An essential part of genocide prevention in a new era would be to establish international centers for the prevention of genocide—probably two, with complementary functions, one in the United Nations and one in the European Union. I had the privilege over the past two years of chairing an advisory committee to the UN (Kofi Annan and then Ban Ki-moon) and another to the EU (Javier Solana) to consider such centers. The UN Center is now up and running under the vigorous leadership of Francis Deng, and the EU Center is emerging in 2008.

These centers, taken together, can perform a number of valuable activities that would help to build pillars of prevention of mass violence, focusing on genocide and other forms of mass violence in terms of early measures that would stop the slide toward mass atrocities long before genocide occurs. Some useful measures are stated here:

1. Assemble a long-term, core professional staff with a critical mass of knowledge and skill drawn from scientists, scholars, diplomats, lawyers, political and military leaders, and specialists in the fields of conflict resolution and violence prevention.

The centers would particularly formulate preventive measures at various levels of danger and feasible contingency plans. They would diminish the terrible difficulty of improvising under severe stress.

2. Systematically monitor the world's conflict situations, not only where violence is under way but also in "hot spots" (or "warm spots") where danger of hatred and violence is developing over the longer term.

3. Establish an integrated warning response system that focuses on the possibility of genocide, ethnic cleansing, and related extensive human rights violations, including war. This system would allow prompt acquisition of warning indicators, their analytic evaluation by experts, and the ready availability of this information to policymakers who are dedicated to implementing effective responses taking into account the full array of options.

4. Develop over years a network of cooperating organizations: the UN, EU, OSCE, NATO, African Union, Organization of American States, and ASEAN—perhaps others. These bodies can perform different tasks of prevention with help from a center's intellectual resources, stimulation, coordination, support, and moral authority. Some are well suited to operational prevention (preventive diplomacy in foreseeable crises) and others to structural prevention (democratic socioeconomic development).

5. In development aid, trade agreements, and investment transactions, attach a high priority to education for resolving conflict, overcoming prejudice, and preventing mass violence—i.e., relate education to economic progress and peaceful relations. Change norms away from violent pseudosolutions.

6. Encourage supporting nations to use their appropriate ministries to disseminate information about hateful situations prone to genocide. The educational system, the media, the Internet, religious institutions, and NGOs are important for this purpose. Urge relevant authorities to neutralize or block media incitement to genocide.

7. Foster cooperative networks of like-minded institutions of civil society—especially scientific and scholarly communities, educational and religious organizations, businesses, the media, and high-quality NGOs oriented to democracy, human rights, and decent human relations—that can employ their particular tools and strategies for preventing atrocities and work together to heighten public understanding, clarify effective actions, and build constituencies for prevention that, in turn, will support leaders when they address genocide-prone situations.

8. Offer training to people already engaged in, or preparing to enter, professional positions in national or international bodies likely to be involved in prevention of genocide-prone situations, with the goal of building a worldwide cadre of professionals who will make the prevention of deadly conflict an integral part of their work. This should include systematic, high-level, ongoing training of diplomats, military officers, development professionals, conflict resolution experts, and leaders in education, religion, business, and the sciences. They should understand that the task is to catch dangerous situations with constructive alternatives before reaching the brink of genocide.

9. Offer grants and technical assistance to strengthen education at every level in the prevention of deadly conflict. This would include development and distribution

of research-based textbooks and curricula and collaboration with educators throughout the world to build their capacity for long-term implementation of these curricula. It would include the creation of faculty positions and advanced fellowships linking universities in developing and developed countries.

10. Stimulate grants to universities and research institutes to support research on factors that cause, exacerbate, mitigate, and, most important of all, prevent genocide.

11. On a regular basis, convene from all over the world scholars, diplomats, military experts, and leaders in business, religion, and media who are interested in the prevention of genocide. Disseminate their findings and recommendations to policymakers and policy advisers and, indeed, to the general public to build public and political support for the prevention of mass violence.

Overall, the two centers should elicit cooperation to pool strengths, share burdens, and divide labor. In so doing, they would keep the world's focus on prevention of genocide and constitute a great repository of knowledge and skill on the prevention of mass violence altogether. They could stimulate a variety of departments, agencies, and functional units in the UN, the EU, democratic governments, or other constructive entities.

The UN established in 2004 an unprecedented unit on prevention of genocide at a high level (in the office of the Secretary-General) and strengthened this unit in 2007, appointing as its leader the distinguished international leader Francis Deng. Links between the European Union and the United Nations explicitly focusing on prevention would have the potential for strong synergy. The functions listed here could be divided between the two centers, relying on comparative advantage, and some could be performed jointly.

With its wealth of human capital, huge economy, and firmly established democratic principles and practices, the EU has recently emerged as a strong candidate for an international center for the prevention of genocide. Several of its member states have a deep moral commitment to the prevention of genocide. It already has an excellent program of preventing deadly conflict, on which further genocide-relevant prevention can be built. Moreover, it has excellent cooperation with the UN, OSCE, NATO, and the African Union. Yet it could not in the near future carry out all the functions listed here for such centers. They would have to be developed over several years and shared with the UN center in complementary functions.

There is a widely accepted (though vaguely formulated) belief among political leaders that one cannot know about the occurrence of genocide until the last minute and that the only recourse then must be a large-scale military response that no one wants to undertake. Thus, there is hardly any useful action that can be done. This is the tsunami shibboleth. But research shows there is always ample warning time of great danger—headed toward mass violence—whether or not it fits the classic definition of genocide. This provides time to prepare constructive response options and contingency plans, provided there is a critical mass of knowledge and skill to do so. This is where genocide prevention centers could be crucially helpful. They can recognize in advance trends in hatred and incipient violence, atrocity outbreaks, growing human rights abuses—i.e., genocide-prone or genocide-susceptible behavior. The issue is preventing deadly conflict as early as possible and not waiting for full-blown genocide.

The UN's worldwide departments, agencies, and programs—in cooperation with regional organizations, especially the European Union, and with excellent NGOs such as the International Crisis Group and the Carter Center—can contribute not only to early warning but also to response options, contingency plans, and ongoing help to countries in trouble.

There are a number of practical steps that can identify areas at serious risk of genocide-related mass violence and offer help to the troubled country or region from the international community. The two centers could be very helpful in mobilizing the necessary skills to implement these practical steps:

1. Establish an ongoing process, drawing on readily available information from all sources, to identify vulnerable targets, scapegoats, and depreciated out-groups.
2. Monitor trends of hatred and dehumanization toward the groups that are identified in such a vulnerable position.
3. Offer help in conflict resolution and prevention of mass violence in situations of this kind. What kind of help?
   - Early, strong mediation;
   - Help in building internal capacity of member states for early ongoing conflict resolution, including essential concepts, techniques (e.g., negotiation), and institutions (e.g., an independent judiciary); and
   - Help in guiding leaders and the public to understand the merits of these enterprises, showing how a country caught up in deep antagonism will find such measures to serve its own interests, as well as earning respect and economic as well as political benefits in the international community.
4. Identify strong predisposing factors, for example, severe economic deterioration and inequity, social disorganization with failing governance, repression by elites, and alienated passions with prospects of war and/or revolution in the background. The earlier such problems are identified and the better they are understood, the greater the opportunity for international help.
5. Enlist the help of key member states of international organizations who are strongly interested in the genocide problem and how to overcome it. Persuade them to commit intellectual, technical, financial, and moral resources.

Close cooperation between the EU and the UN has much potential for carrying out this mission for the first time in history. Over the years, if the EU and the UN were to provide favorable examples, relevant information, and tangible help, it is entirely possible that a network of cooperating organizations covering the world could be built for the purpose of preventing mass violence.

There is a wealth of information available to these two international centers for the prevention of genocide. In addition to the worldwide UN units, there are regional organizations, universities, human rights groups, humanitarian relief agencies, and academic, faith-based, and other civil society organizations that can provide valuable input. They can provide field resources, relying on dedicated people who have much knowledge and can provide early warnings of genocide-prone behavior so that help can be given long before the catastrophe.

The essential functions over the long term would include preventive diplomacy, building of democratic institutions, fostering equitable socioeconomic development, protecting human rights, constraining the availability and use of deadly weapons, and promoting education for peace with justice and positive intergroup relations—i.e., building the pillars of prevention. They are the heart of the matter for the world of the future.

Sooner or later, preferably sooner, an active role should be played by an organization acting on behalf of the community of established democracies. At present, the closest approximation is the European Union. It could serve as a focal point for involving established democracies all over the world in a systematic way. Those democracies that are not members of the European Union could have a clearly defined and well functioning affiliation with it (EU-plus). This might be a transitional arrangement for a decade or so—and become the precursor of a fully developed global democratic organization of great strength.

One of the early efforts of international organizations aspiring to prevent genocide would be to offer substantial training to people already engaged in or preparing to enter positions relevant to prevention of mass violence in national or international bodies. In this way, a cadre of professionals in this field could be developed within a decade—to assume on a global basis the same essential task of saving lives and diminishing human suffering that public health professionals already perform in their area of competence. Public health is a very good model for prevention of massive human suffering and unnecessary deaths.

I have earlier referred to a set of remarkable improvements in the human condition during my lifetime. These suggest that prevention of genocide is also within human capacity. It is fitting to close with a comment on slavery. This was a plague through much of history. Now at last it has essentially come to an end in most of the world, though nasty pockets still exist. In this context, the distinguished scholar, Professor David Brion Davis of Yale University, whose lifelong work has illuminated the rise and fall of slavery in the Western hemisphere, made a hopeful observation. In 1770 a growing slave trade was spreading black slavery—then protected almost without opposition by law and religion—throughout the New World. But in 1888, only 118 years later, the practice became outlawed everywhere in the West when Brazil finally freed its slaves. Davis acknowledged slavery's lingering harsh legacy of racism and its contribution to the devastation of Africa but concluded that this unprecedented "positive note of willed ... moral achievement" should inspire hope in other movements for immense social change and a reluctance to accept the world as we find it.[1]

Thus we see in the history of slavery—as well as the decline of colonialism, fascism, and communism—great changes that are strong expressions of emerging human decency, despite great travail, and yet also expressions of a need for constant vigilance to mobilize human capacities for fully learning to live together in personal dignity and shared humanity at last. In the progress cited earlier (e.g., the transformation of post-Holocaust Europe), there is an authentic basis for hope. Now, for the first time in human history, after centuries of genocides, humanity is on the verge of a serious, informed, sustained effort to prevent recurrence.

CHAPTER 19

⟐ ～   ⟐

Recent Advances in Prevention
of Mass Violence

Since the time of the original publication of this book, several developments have continued the progress noted at the conclusion of the previous chapter.

Preventive Diplomacy:
Kofi Annan's Inspiring Example in Kenya, 2008

Kofi Annan's forty-one-day mediation marathon in Kenya in early 2008 rescued both the country and its surrounding region from catastrophe, and it vividly demonstrated the need to employ preventive diplomacy at an early stage of conflict.[1] Annan not only created peace out of violence, he also turned a crisis into an opportunity to get a troubled nation to deal in depth with problems that had been festering beneath a seemingly placid surface.

Kenya, though recognized as a troubled state by experts, had been widely praised as a model of political and economic stability in Africa and a magnet for international tourists and investors. Then it suddenly erupted into ethnic warfare. Results of an irregular presidential election in December 2007, which returned the incumbent president to power, produced riots throughout the country; these were followed by bloody reprisals from all hostile parties, abetted by police who chose sides according to their ethnic affiliations. When Kenya's postelection violence in 2007 finally ceased, well over 1,000 were dead, more than 300,000 were displaced, and the ominous possibility of larger-scale violence was looming on the horizon.

The flare-ups in Kenya should not have been a total surprise. A number of the country's postindependence campaigns—Kofi Annan recalled five since independence[2]—had been followed by ethnic discontent and riots that grew more brutal and rancorous with each election. As happened in Rwanda, elected leaders in Kenya had used their power to enrich themselves, as well as trusted members of their families and tribes, with land and offices at the expense of other tribes, which were condemned to live as part of the 60 percent of Kenya's population subsisting on less than $1 a day.

The two rival presidential candidates—incumbent Mwai Kibaki, leader of the Party of National Unity (PNU) and a member of the favored Kikuyu tribe, and Raila Odinga, leader of the Orange Democratic Movement (ODM) and a member of the marginalized Luo tribe—obstinately refused to meet and negotiate a resolution to the conflict. Neither was without guilt: evidence of electoral irregularities on the part of Kibaki's PNU was indisputable, and the ODM had taken part in organizing violence following the elections: the PNU accused it of "ethnic cleansing."

Archbishop Desmond Tutu quickly arrived in Kenya to plead with the two leaders to find a peaceful resolution to the dispute. But even such a universally revered figure could not persuade the two rivals to meet. Other attempts, from four former presidents of African countries and members of the African Leaders Forum,[3] were similarly rebuffed. Genocide became a real concern as Kenya began to look like Rwanda in 1994. But this time, things were different. If these early efforts at peacemaking produced no results, they at least alerted the antagonists that the world was watching and gave future mediators a sense of the problems to be faced. They would promptly suggest to a master diplomat elements of a successful strategy.

Recognizing that little time remained to avert total disaster, on January 8, 2008, John Kufuor, Ghana's president and the newly elected head of the African Union (AU), asked his fellow national Kofi Annan to go to Kenya as head of a prestigious mediation team of three, which he named the Panel of Eminent African Personalities. The very name implied the importance of the crisis to the whole region. The other members of the panel were Graça Machel (Mrs. Nelson Mandela) and Benjamin Mkapa, former president of Tanzania. The AU panel was tasked to find a peaceful resolution. Technical assistance from the UN Department of Political Affairs (DPA) was helpful; so, too, was the Centre for Humanitarian Dialogue, a Geneva-based foundation. There was also diplomatic support from much of the international community.

Annan arrived in Kenya on January 22, 2008. He had prepared carefully. Just before the Kenya negotiations started, he placed call after call to U.S., European, and African leaders and emphasized the importance of having a single mediation process. Lack of international unity would encourage the two opposing parties to stall, to resist a fixed agreement so they could play one power against another and find the best bargain. Throughout the negotiations, Annan discouraged "high-profile visitors" unless they had a very specific objective that would coordinate fully with his agenda.[4] The United States received Annan's special attention, with gratifying success. Secretary of State Condaleezza Rice regularly submitted U.S. draft statements on Kenya to him for approval before she issued them. During the negotiations, Rice—and, after initial hesitation, President George W. Bush—also gave full support to Annan's demands for a coalition government, support that included threats of isolation and undesirable economic and legal consequences for Kibaki and his government if they refused to cooperate.[5]

Immediately upon arrival in Kenya, Annan met with civil society groups, religious and women's groups, and the business community. He found them well organized but uncertain about how—or even whether—to use their influence constructively. After pointing out to a group of businessmen that they represented 85 percent of the gross domestic product (GDP) in Kenya, he remarked, "This is power. How did you try to influence events, talk to the politicians and the governments before the explosion?" No one answered.[6] To keep these groups engaged, Annan used the media and other means to maintain their support throughout the negotiations by making progress transparent and open. He purposely portrayed even ambiguous or disappointing situations in the most positive light possible to encourage his followers, keep them demanding more in the way of constructive compromise, and lead them to perceive foot-dragging as obstruction.

On January 24, within two days of his arrival, Annan succeeded in arranging a closed meeting between Kibaki and Odinga, a breakthrough that symbolized public acknowledgment from each side of his opponent's legitimacy. Still, neither side was fully committed to the negotiations. Kibaki regularly objected—both personally and through his followers—that as president of a sovereign state, he was offended by international "meddling." Odinga objected that Kibaki had stolen the presidency.

On January 29, the first of eighteen often turbulent negotiation sessions began, with each presidential candidate represented by a team of four trusted backers from the Kenyan government or the legal profession. The decision not to have the two principals in the dispute engage personally in the negotiations had a clear advantage: if their representatives succeeded in hammering out an agreement on the most contentious issues and in the process secured public approval and backing, there would be less danger that the principal leaders would lose face, become implacable, or withdraw.

Annan's next tasks as mediator were to set protocols, firmly establish the pace and timing of the negotiations, and get agreement on an appropriate agenda—a "road map." All this was to be fully reported in the media.

In order to win momentum for the negotiations with a positive beginning—and to convince the antagonists that agreement did not mean weakness—he put at the top of the agenda "low-hanging fruit": two urgent matters that were promptly resolvable because of the alarm they created among those on both sides of the conflict. The first was to stop the violence immediately and restore civil rights and liberties; the second was to deal with humanitarian needs and promote reconciliation and recovery. Achieving these goals would provide a secure environment and a good foundation on which to build agreement for the third and more difficult item on the agenda—a political solution to the crisis. That, in turn, would facilitate the accomplishment of item four—agreement about how to address the country's long-term needs, such as land reform; reduction in poverty, inequality, and joblessness (especially among youth); and promotion of national cohesion and governmental transparency and accountability. The public time line set for resolving these goals called for a week to halt the violence, four weeks to resolve the other short-term issues, and a year for getting a grasp on the long-term root problems.

Annan managed to get significant agreement on the first two points of his agenda by February 4. The inclusion of outside experts continued throughout the negotiations and was valuable both in keeping the negotiators focused and in advising them of how similar problems had been settled in the past.

Agreement on political arrangements proved more difficult. At first, discussions amounted to bickering about the disputed election. Kofi Annan firmly rejected calls for a recount or reelection; he recognized that following such a path would only lead to more killings.[7] Instead, recognizing the importance of the issue to the Kenyan population, he set up an independent committee to investigate the election and make recommendations for reform. He also arranged for a truth and reconciliation commission with civil society input.[8]

Only in mid-February, after the ninth negotiating session, was the crucial question raised about governmental reform that would allow a system of "power sharing" by the two rival leaders. With the expressed agreement of the Kenyans, Annan used his ability to enlist outside help. To explain the workings of a coalition government, he invited in a high German official who had helped form Angela Merkel's Grand Coalition when she narrowly won the chancellorship. Annan explained that Kenya was in a crisis that no one party could deal with alone; only by working together would they be able to pass reforms. He then related how Germany had worked out a similar problem, and he helped to formulate a proposal that tailored Germany's experience to Kenya's situation and needs.

Kibaki would remain president, but his strong unitary authority would be balanced by that of his new prime minister, Odinga, whose responsibilities in that office would be redefined and substantially strengthened. Consistent with Annan's faith in transparency, public opinion on this proposal was tested by media exposure, and it met wide approval. Negotiators representing President Kibaki, however, responded by raising objections that this was an attempt to weaken him, and they expressed horror at the idea of tampering with Kenya's "holy" constitution. They sought to gain popular support by referring to the united international pressure for a final agreement in Kenya as "meddling" by Western powers that wished to continue their domination of Africa. Odinga's supporters answered by accusing Kibaki's party of arrogance, bad faith, and obstruction. Vague threats of mass action circulated.

Annan was aware that a genuine redistribution of presidential power would create legal and constitutional issues. Working from the principle that political differences are often worked out best with technical solutions, he had Hans Corell, a former UN legal counsel, work with legal experts from both negotiating teams. They soon developed a provision for creating the post of prime minister in a coalition government. The draft proposed formation of a coalition government and made suggestions about its form and the powers of its officers. The new role of the prime minister was a serious point of contention. To what extent (if at all) should he be given executive powers that might restrain those of the president? Should the president have the authority to dismiss him at will? Did granting the prime minister these new powers require a constitutional amendment?

Annan ingeniously smoothed over semantic quibbling and tried to rally the negotiators by pointing to the positive goals already achieved. He called on the two rival leaders to do their work, as his panel of three had done theirs, and give clear instructions to their followers about ways of coming to an agreement. But the impasse persisted, and the talks seemed to be losing momentum. Nevertheless, with Annan's steady encouragement and insights, both sides gradually returned to serious negotiations.

Since the appointed negotiating teams could not fully agree, it was incumbent on their leaders, Kibaki and Odinga, to accomplish what their representatives could not. The clear implication was that blame for the failure to make peace in Kenya would ultimately fall on its two leaders; success, however, would gain them international credit for statesmanship. Public reaction was on Annan's side, and his persistent leadership brought the leaders together.

On February 28, Kibaki and Odinga were closeted together to engage in direct negotiations. A draft outline of the matters under negotiation had been prepared, with disputed points or language bracketed, and the two were expected to reach a final accord on all the issues still in contention. Present as facilitators were Kofi Annan, President Mkapa, and President Jakaya Mrisho Kikwete of Tanzania, the new chair of the AU. Annan had invited Kikwete to sit in on the discussions because, as leader of the AU, he symbolized African solidarity and concern about Kenya. But that was not the only reason. He also had experience in sharing power with a prime minister who possessed even more authority than was proposed for Kenya's prime minister. Thus, he could argue from personal knowledge that power sharing could work without weakening the president's office. The only other participants in these direct negotiations were legal experts, who examined (as was Annan's consistent preference) all points of negotiation from a technical standpoint—in this case, whether they required a constitutional amendment.

After five and a half grueling hours, the Agreement on the Principles of Partnership of the Coalition Government was finally formulated, and it was immediately signed in a public ceremony, with full media coverage. No opportunity was allowed for second thoughts. The Draft National Accord and Reconciliation Act was quickly sent to Parliament to be included in the constitution, and the transitional government was given a five-year term, after which elections would occur in accordance with the findings of the Electoral Review Committee. All the measures proposed to Parliament were passed on March 6 without change.

A compromise had been reached without either side suffering a loss of face or being perceived as yielding to any external coercion aside from the opinions of their own public. The peace was seen as the choice of the Kenyan leaders and the Kenyan people.

Of course, matters do not end there. The spirit of peace, coexistence, and compromise must be maintained through the efforts of both the Kenyan people and the international community. When the agreement was signed, Kofi Annan once again brought together representatives of civil society, the churches, and the business community and told them the new agreements had great promise but must not be left to the politicians alone. He emphasized that Kenya was their society, too, and that they had to be active and vigilant to ensure the agreements were honored. He reminded them that when the negotiations began, he had promised to make them transparent and public because the people had to monitor them. He urged members of civil society to become involved in setting up regular mechanisms for monitoring their government.[9]

There is also hope that the Kenyan government and the world at large are becoming aware of the value of their investment in peace. Right after the agreement, in March 2008, a Kenyan delegation led by Vice President Kalonzo Musyoka visited the International Tourism Bourse in Berlin.[10] At a "Kenya Event" dinner for "tourism stakeholders," the vice president proudly characterized his diverse delegation as the "face of the upcoming grand coalition." Aware of the problems tour operators faced in attracting tourists to Kenya after the violence in 2007, he assured visitors to the Kenya booth that his country would take "aggressive" action to dispel the nation's image as a dangerous destination for tourists.

At the same tourism conference, the vice president held a meeting, followed by a joint press conference, with Frank-Walter Steinmeier, German foreign affairs minister, and

Heidemarie Wieczoreck-Zeul, German minister for economic cooperation. The meeting included an appeal from the vice president for continued assistance in reconstruction, financial aid to farmers, and long-term assistance in education and infrastructure. Wieczoreck-Zeul responded with a rather pointed expression of regret for the troubles of 2007 and emphasized her desire for Kenyan leaders to do everything possible to prevent its recurrence, ending with the assurance that Germany and the European Union (EU) would remain friends of Kenya.

There is no guarantee that Kenya's peace will be lasting. But it is clear that the negotiations saved the country from ruin in the short run, at least, and the long-term measures built into the agreement offer promise of a good outcome. At the international level, the political will created and the lesson of how effective multilateral, united pressure can be in preventing violent conflict make the Kenya negotiations an encouraging model of successful, nonmilitary implementation of the principle of early conflict resolution.

Kofi Annan was a masterful mediator and enlisted skilled negotiators who knew each other and had a basis for cooperation. In turn, they (and especially Annan) enlisted the support of the people of Kenya for a peaceful settlement and plans for a better future. There are lessons for the world in this experience, even though there is inevitably a long way to go, as reflected in a meeting convened by Annan on the Kenya dialogue and reconciliation one year later. This meeting involved well-informed people with extensive knowledge of conflict resolution in general and Kenya in particular. They considered ways of reducing the risk of recurrence in the run-up to the 2012 elections.

Training and Support in Preventive Diplomacy

International organizations and democratic governments need staff with the knowledge and skills required to prevent serious conflict—to diminish violent inclinations, wherever they occur.[11] To be effective, diplomats must be aware of the range and relative value of the options open to them. To carry out preventive diplomacy, they also need a solid understanding of major causes of conflict, actions likely to lead to conflict escalation or deescalation, and a variety of strategies that have proved successful in resolving conflicts and diminishing the contagion of hatred. Thus, they need training in negotiation and mediation that moves disputing parties toward a mutually acceptable resolution of their problems. To address these problems and bridge the gap between theory and practice, Connie Peck, a leading scholar in this field, initiated training and research that evolved into the United Nations Institute for Training and Research (UNITAR) Program in Peacemaking and Preventive Diplomacy. This program has become increasingly influential in recent years. It has been expanded to teach and learn worldwide by sharing experiences of high-level Special Representatives of the Secretary-General (RSGs) in Conflict Prevention. The use of special representatives by UN secretaries-general has greatly increased in the field of preventive diplomacy, where their potential effect is greatest.

The growing numbers of representatives working in conflict prevention can benefit substantially from the experiences of those who have worked in peacebuilding.[12] Peck's UNITAR Programme for Briefing and Debriefing Special and Personal Representatives and Envoys of the Secretary-General has held exhaustive interviews with current and past RSGs about their experiences. These interviews have now become highly salient in the work of the UN; some have been published and made available to those who work in the field. Peck has convened the RSGs so that they can directly share experiences and learn from each other—another form of peer learning that is especially useful in conflict resolution.

Peck finds that preventive diplomacy works best when it begins early. RSGs should not wait for a situation to become "ripe"; they should be ready, on the spot, from the beginning and prepared to develop the ripening process in a direction that turns away from violent conflict. Even if parties to potential conflict are unwilling to accept mediation from RSGs, these representatives should persuade the parties to admit them in small roles (for instance, as observers) so they can be there when needed and help opposing parties to take immediate advantage of a favorable opportunity. RSGs can start with nonsensitive dialogue, such as understanding history and culture.

RSGs concur about the importance of deciding on only one "lead actor" as mediator in a peace process, in order to eliminate mixed messages and minimize opportunities for hostile parties to play one mediator against another. The significance of this approach was clear with Kofi Annan in Kenya.

Another matter pertinent to preventive diplomacy is determining which of the opposing parties should be included in a peace process. Although making room for extremists at the table presents a danger that they will act as spoilers, forbidding powerful extremists to participate can lead to a fragile agreement that could be spoiled from the outside by an excluded group with broad support or lots of weaponry; moreover, such a group might even use its exclusion from the talks as further justification for its opposition. If, instead, groups of this type are allowed to participate, a skillful diplomat has the chance to insist that their demands and methods remain consistent with the principles of the UN Charter—a world statement of decency. As a means of counteracting and diluting the influence of spoilers, other RSGs recommend the broad inclusion in talks of highly regarded representatives of positive positions, such as respected religious leaders or elder statespeople. Women must be included as an important part of the decisionmaking, since they bring talent and often bear the brunt of the decisions that are made.

One RSG conclusion is that it is valuable to begin negotiations with a framework agreement that commits the parties to participation and denies them the choice to withdraw unilaterally, that defines the structure and format of the negotiations as well as the representatives and mediator involved in them, and that sets rules about dealing with the media.

A successful diplomat has to begin work with serious research on the specific conflict being mediated. The agenda of the negotiations must include the central grievances and positions of all sides; these grievances and positions must be expressed in neutral terms. Diplomats must also assume a problem-solving manner that recognizes the interests—concerns, fears, and aspirations—that lurk behind the outward manifestations of conflict. Identifying interests is a means to finding a solution to the conflict, since grievances are often the result of exclusionary policies based on unfair institutions.

One of the mediator's jobs is to alert the stronger party to the long-term negative consequences of continuing the conflict, both in the domestic destruction of lives, resources, and infrastructure and in the loss of status in the region and the larger world community.

Most RSGs recommend gathering up all the results of long negotiations into one draft, a comprehensive negotiating text that can be passed from one party to the other(s) for discussion and then, after rewording and amendment by the mediator, returned for another review, with the expectation that each revision will draw the negotiation nearer to a conclusion acceptable to all. Keeping the revisions in the hands of the mediators maintains their control over the process and guarantees that the interests of each party will be considered. Parties must be made to understand that no one side will get everything it wants or requests. All RSGs emphasized the need for persistence and optimism. Speed and setting arbitrary deadlines can be self-defeating in formulating a lasting agreement; in fact, such approaches may actually backfire and discredit the mediator. Peck's research provides an informative basis for hope in preventive diplomacy.

Mediation Support Unit: A Promising Innovation

In a new plan for reorganization in 2008, UN Secretary-General Ban Ki-moon aimed to transform the Department of Political Affairs into "a more proactive and effective platform for preventive diplomacy, including mediation, at the service of Member States."[13] This effort represents DPA's first major restructuring since its inception in 1992.

In a report to the General Assembly, Ban emphasized that "now focus must be put on the Organization's capacity to prevent and resolve conflict—a better investment than dealing with the costly aftermath of war and a critical investment to ensure the billions of dollars spent on development by Member States, the international financial institutions and the United Nations itself are not wasted when armed conflict or war erupts."[14] This closely follows the outlook of the Carnegie Commission on Preventing Deadly Conflict.

Lynn Pascoe, a veteran career diplomat, heads DPA and has moved consistently to implement the Secretary-General's approach in 2008 and 2009. By the same token, Francis Deng, the distinguished Undersecretary-General for Prevention of Genocide and Mass Atrocities, has emerged as a world leader in the prevention of mass violence; his unit has made substantial progress in the field and works closely with DPA.

DPA, especially in its regional divisions, represents the UN's primary resource for preventive diplomacy, often in the form of the Secretary-General's "good offices."[15] DPA gives support to envoys and missions everywhere in the world, aids the Secretary-General in day-to-day diplomacy, and overall provides strategic leadership in conflict prevention to the entire UN system. A crucial part of this opportunity is third-party mediation, among the UN's best tools to prevent and resolve dangerous conflicts everywhere—providing it builds on its present momentum in this direction.

In October 2006, a continually upgraded Peacemaker data bank (www.un.org/peacemaker) for professional mediators was established as a reference. Its intended users are not only professional negotiators and staff from the UN but also those from UN member states, regional organizations, other international bodies, and nongovernmental organizations (NGOs). By late 2007, the data bank had registered more than 5,000 users, and its value increased in 2008.[16]

This data bank received a UN-wide award in 2008 because it offered access to peace agreements, peace agreement summaries, literature on peacemaking issues, a substantial legal library applicable to peacemaking, and links to other useful Web sites. Peacemaker also provides lessons, case briefs, guidance notes, and comments on peace processes and agreements, gathered from actual UN experience and chiefly in the form of interviews with the peacemakers themselves. Even the most talented and persuasive mediators cannot get far without resources that include a practical and professional support staff with knowledge specific to the occasion. Military means may be useful in the short term for checking a particular conflict, but only political solutions achieved through negotiations offer hope of putting a definitive end to a conflict—and doing so without an intervening disaster.

The Mediation Support Unit (MSU) in the United Nations Department of Political Affairs was created in 2006 due to the need for professional support to "good offices" activities, including preventive diplomacy in various forms and especially official mediation of disputes. This need was expressed by Special Representatives and Special Envoys of the Secretary-General, as well as the General Assembly.

The MSU is designed to be a locus of expertise, best practice, and knowledge management on mediation-related activities worldwide. It serves the United Nations as a whole, regional and subregional organizations, and other peacemaking bodies. It works through existing chains of command so that its primary clients are the regional divisions of DPA, the United Nations Department for Peacekeeping Operations (DPKO), and, through them, the UN senior officials in the field and partners such as the African Union. It draws on the experience of the United Nations to develop guidelines, operational tools, and training opportunities, and it manages the Peacemaker online data bank. In close cooperation with the regional divisions in DPA and DPKO, it supports ongoing mediation efforts in two main ways: (1) by offering country- or region-specific operational support, and (2) by offering institutional and capacity-building support.

The support takes a variety of forms, including:

- Researching and advising on substantive and technical issues, such as border demarcation, structuring cessation of hostilities agreements, civil society participation, amnesty provisions, minority rights, confidence-building measures, natural resource sharing, and implementation of peace agreements and other matters;
- Participating in peace talks in an advisory capacity, on a short-notice standby basis if necessary;
- Organizing dialogue, workshops, and training for parties in conflict;
- Funding and participating in fact-finding and mediation missions; and
- Identifying, deploying, and funding external experts

MSU is now strengthening several mechanisms that will enhance the UN expertise on mediation over the medium-to-long term. These mechanisms fall into four main categories:

1. *Channeling expertise.* One of the most common requests fielded by MSU is to identify and assist with deploying experts or making arrangements for experts to provide long-distance advice to mediators and UN missions in the field. For this purpose, one important initiative is the Standby Team, a joint venture of the Norwegian Refugee Council (NRC) and the DPA. The NRC is responsible for logistics and

administration, and the DPA manages political and policy elements of the team's mission. During the team's first year, the Norwegian government generously assumed most of its costs, including expenses for recruitment, start-up funds, and travel to the field. The Norwegian government has long been an innovative supporter of the UN prevention activities under the leadership of such distinguished international figures as Gro Brundtland and Jan Egeland. A roster of prescreened experts can be called upon regularly, and this is a growing enterprise, linking with skillful external entities. The MSU is also creating a network of former expert mediators who agree to provide advice on an ad hoc basis, even if only for a short time.

2. *Guidance, best practices, and lessons learned.* The lack of applicable institutional memory on peacemaking and mediation was one of the primary gaps identified by Kofi Annan's High-Level Panel on Threats, Challenges and Change, whose recommendation for a mediation support capacity in DPA led to the eventual establishment of MSU. This problem is well on the way to being resolved, first and foremost through the online data bank Peacemaker (www.un.org/peacemaker).

3. *Building regional capacity.* MSU support is available to partners in regional organizations. The unit is helping to establish a secretariat for the African Union's Panel of the Wise. To deepen the partnership with regional and subregional organizations, MSU is holding consultations in each region of the world.

4. *Training.* MSU has mobilized donors and created partnerships with training institutions to deliver training on general mediation techniques, as well as more specialized aspects of mediation. All the training courses are open to the UN system and to partners in regional and subregional organizations. A leadership example is provided by the Folke Bernadotte Academy of Sweden, especially through Ambassador Ragnar Ängeby, a pioneer in modern prevention. The MSU is also building ways for the United Nations to assemble, organize, and share the lessons of its mediation around the world. It has designed standardized templates for UN envoys to use when they report completed assignments, and it is drawing up standard programs for educating envoys setting off on a new mission and debriefing them on their return. Much of this information will be posted on the UN Peacemaker Web site. MSU also provides mediation training to midlevel staff from a number of UN departments. This effort is a good example of the worldwide spread of mediation skills and resources, now becoming available at different levels of government and nongovernmental organizations. A less well known but highly significant contribution to this field is a 2009 paper by Priscilla Hayner on guidance for mediators in negotiating justice,[17] with special attention given to truth and reconciliation commissions. Hayner is one of the world's experts on such commissions. She is cofounder of the International Center for Transitional Justice in New York and head of its Program on Peace and Justice. She helped Kofi Annan in his Kenya diplomacy. Her paper deals with key topics: justice and peace agreements, including recent trends and implementation; process and public participation in peace talks; understanding amnesties; the implications for mediators of the new International Criminal Court; and emerging lessons and best practices for achieving justice in peace negotiations. This publication has practical value in the training of mediators and illustrates the wide range of their involvement in the prevention of mass violence.

The UN Secretary-General Speaks Out for Mediation

In an unprecedented event, the Secretary-General of the United Nations submitted a special report to the Security Council in April 2009 on enhancing mediation and its support activities.

Summary. The present report examines the challenges faced by the United Nations and its partners in providing professional mediation assistance to parties in conflict. It describes the need for experienced and knowledgeable mediators and support teams, with women adequately represented, and sufficient resources to provide assistance at an early stage to help parties design and pursue processes that will address the root causes of their conflicts, overcome obstacles that block progress, and achieve agreements that lead to sustainable peace. It discusses the importance of building local, national and regional capacity for mediation and the need for coherent partnership between the United Nations, regional and subregional organizations, States and non-governmental organizations. The cost-effectiveness of mediation in the constructive resolution of disputes is highlighted.[18]

The report covers the experience of the United Nations and regional organizations in mediation. It deals with such crucial topics as resolving disputes in a timely manner, establishing a lead actor, selecting the most appropriate mediator/mediation team, engaging the parties early, structuring mediation to address the root causes of conflict, managing spoilers, accommodating peace and justice, mediating throughout implementation, providing mediation support, strengthening regional capacity for mediation, and strengthening national/local capacity for conflict prevention/resolution.

Although the Security Council does not have a distinguished record in conflict resolution, there was exceptional interest in this report. Indeed, thirty-seven countries, members of the Security Council and others, endorsed the concept of building professional strengths for the UN in mediation.

Connie Peck, drawing on her extensive research and training, played an important role in the preparation of this unusual report, in cooperation with prominent members of the Department of Political Affairs—a vital unit of the UN Secretariat for carrying forward this work over the long term. Altogether, mediation is an area in which the UN is able to take more initiatives than in many other spheres. Mediation is also highly pertinent to the new unit on the prevention of genocide, headed by Francis Deng.

Building Violence Prevention into Development

The United Nations Development Programme (UNDP) has offices with professional staff in 166 countries[19]—offices that make available to developing countries the world's knowledge, experience, and resources to help them work out their own best answers for equitable socioeconomic development and achieve their own definition of a better life.[20] For this purpose, UNDP can call upon its worldwide staff and its many partner organizations.

The UN has increasingly recognized that violent conflict can readily destroy socioeconomic development; therefore, it is vital to build conflict resolution mechanisms into development projects. Such dynamic leaders in UNDP as Gay Rosenblum-Kumar, Chetan Kumar, Kathleen Cravero, and Sakiko Fukuda-Parr have done much in recent years to link prevention with development. They have provided a growing body of evidence that unless conflict is managed early and well in the process of development, it can lead to violence in ways that prohibit or destroy the innovations for prosperity that development is intended to achieve. Indeed, even successful development tends to stir latent conflict, since resources are reallocated, even if inadvertently. This, in turn, can readily lead to tensions between class, ethnic, or religious groups. Thus, helping developing countries to build their own national capacities for early, ongoing conflict resolution and indeed violence prevention constitutes a crucial and growing part of development. So, initiatives have been taken to build social cohesion in various countries, involving some combination of government, political parties, and institutions of civil society. The media and the military can play a constructive role in these efforts.

The UNDP's Bureau for Crisis Prevention and Recovery (BCPR) is becoming a storehouse of experience, methods, and tools for the prevention of crises, for reducing the risk of natural disaster, and for recovery after crises. BCPR advises UNDP senior management on those issues, and it works in the field with UNDP country offices and, through them, with their host governments, providing technical help, expertise in best practices, and financial resources. BCPR incorporates opportunities for violence prevention into UNDP long-term development policies and programs. It promotes links between UN peace, security, and development objectives, and it helps governments build their capacities to manage crisis situations.[21]

Rapid response is a priority in effective crisis prevention. In 2006, UNDP created an immediate crisis response initiative, nicknamed the SURGE Project. It dispatches trained and specialized UNDP staff to country offices within days of an emerging crisis. UNDP's international network of experts also contributes to drafting regular procedures for effective immediate response. These experts have placed online (and regularly update) valuable tools such as checklists for prompt response and templates for planning as well as resource mobilization.[22]

The essential role of women in development has received increasing recognition—for reasons of equity, family solidarity, and economic advancement. BCPR now plans all its programs with a strong commitment to promoting women's equality, and it trains its professionals to promote women's inclusion. Special emphasis is given to (1) stopping violence against women; (2) providing justice and security for women; (3) involving women as decisionmakers, especially in peace processes; (4) encouraging men and women to work as equals in efforts to build and transform their society; and (5) including women's issues on national agendas—for instance, opportunities for education.[23]

Closely related to the establishment of stability and security is the expansion of the rule of law, a step-by-step process that demands long-range commitment. Observance of the rule of law strengthens national institutions and stakeholders in their ability to prevent or halt human rights violations. This, in turn, fosters a favorable environment in which democratic governance can grow. It is best begun before a serious conflict erupts or very soon after its onset.

In early 2007, BCPR created the Conflict Prevention and Recovery Team, with knowledge and expertise in conflict prevention; rule of law; armed violence reduction; small arms, mines action, and cluster munitions; and disarmament, demobilization, and reintegration (DDR) of ex-combatants. In 2009, it added to its practical skills in each of these areas.[24]

UN peace and development advisers, including conflict prevention specialists, are increasingly involved in UNDP operations, especially in constructing a framework for crucial cooperation between UNDP and DPA on the deployment of advisers and a methodology for country-specific collaboration at UN headquarters to support violence prevention efforts anywhere in the world.

There are several recent examples of successful UNDP efforts in such prevention. UNDP worked with Bolivia to build a comprehensive dialogue about equitable distribution of its oil and mineral wealth. UNDP helped Ghana set up its National Peace Council, which, at the request of Ghana's president, mediated internal conflicts and advised the major political parties on methods of choosing presidential candidates. In early 2009, Ghana completed a successful presidential election (including a runoff) with international monitoring and without violence.

The growing commitment to including conflict resolution mechanisms in development initiatives has stimulated the recruitment and training of specialists in planning effective conflict prevention initiatives; assisting aspiring democracies in building internal mediation capacities; and disseminating specific, practical strategies for engaging reluctant national actors and dealing with the complex historical, economic, ethnic, or cultural issues involved in emerging conflicts.

Another significant initiative is the emerging cooperation of UNDP and the large Japan International Cooperation Agency headed by a great leader, Sadako Ogata. Its basic elements consist of: (1) addressing structural conditions oriented to the root causes of conflict, (2) reconsidering development cooperation priorities to avoid unwittingly contributing to social tensions and instead promoting peacebuilding incentives, and (3) filling a global policy gap by striving to meet the Millennium Development Goals. The initiative takes into account the important human security perspective, in which Ogata has been a pioneer; this includes the root causes of conflict and the strengthening of fragile states.[25]

The Genocide Prevention Task Force in the United States

For the first time in American history, a group of high-ranking former government officials have recommended institutional initiatives to the U.S. government to engage in genocide prevention.[26] The report of the Genocide Prevention Task Force, *Preventing Genocide: A Blueprint for U.S. Policymakers,* was published late in 2008 as a set of recommendations to the new administration.[27] It should be noted that this report could, if implemented, become a remarkable advance in U.S. policy, including international cooperation for the prevention of mass violence.

The report emphasizes that mass killings and atrocities have continued despite repeated calls of "never again," constituting a direct assault on universal human values, above all the right to life. The report highlights the fact that if the United States does not engage in *early* prevention, the spillover effect of violent conflict in fragile states will entail large costs in terms of coping with human suffering, feeding refugees, and managing long-lasting regional crises. Despite popular belief, the prevention of genocide is an achievable goal. It is possible to recognize warning signs and prevent genocide "with the right organizational structures, strategies and partnerships."

The case for preventing genocide and mass atrocities must begin with the president, ideally early in the new administration. Action has been inhibited by the absence of an overarching policy framework or a standing interagency process, together with a vague, uninformed sense of futility among policymakers. The Genocide Prevention Task Force urges the new president to make this a national priority: "We recommend a new standing interagency mechanism for analysis of threats and coordination of appropriate preventive action as part of a comprehensive policy framework for genocide prevention."[28] This entity might well be analogous to the centers for prevention at the United Nations and the European Union, proposed by the author of this book and now under way.

The means and ends of genocide prevention dovetail with other U.S. priorities, such as the promotion of democracy and equitable socioeconomic development, and provide a crucial opportunity for progress, quite possibly of global significance.[29]

Assigning resources to match priorities. The task force recommends increased and flexible funding directed toward preventing genocide and mass atrocities: Congress should invest $250 million in new funds for crisis prevention and early response.

A comprehensive strategy. In order to prevent genocide, the government should draw on a wide range of analytic, diplomatic, economic, legal, and military instruments and engage a variety of partners. The United States has a range of tools and options available "between the extremes of doing nothing and sending in the Marines."

Early warning: assessing risks and triggering action. Assessing risks and generating an early warning of potential atrocities are the first steps toward prevention. The task force recommends that the director of national intelligence begin the preparation of a national intelligence estimate on worldwide risks of genocide and mass atrocities. This estimate would be included in annual testimony to Congress. "Acute warning of potential genocide or mass atrocities must be made an 'automatic trigger' of policy analysis" and formulation of constructive early response options in keeping with the proposals made previously in this book.

Early prevention: engaging before the crisis. "With international partners, we must engage leaders, develop institutions and strengthen civil society within high-risk countries. Doing so will reduce capacities and motivations for mass violence." Funding should be expanded for crisis prevention in countries at risk "through a new genocide prevention initiative funded through existing foreign assistance mechanisms."

Preventive diplomacy: halting and reversing escalation. The Genocide Prevention Task Force recommends the creation of a new, high-level interagency body, "an Atrocities Prevention Committee," dedicated to responding to signs of preparation for genocide. The body would improve U.S. crisis response and provide better, more coherent, and more timely strategies for preventive diplomacy. "This new committee should prepare interagency genocide prevention and response plans for high-risk situations." These recommendations, though not highly developed, are entirely consistent with those of this book, both in chapter 7 and in the present chapter.

Employing military options. Military options can play an important role in deterring and suppressing violence (though waging war after a genocide is under way is neither an attractive nor a feasible course). The report recommends that genocide prevention and response be incorporated into national policy guidance for the military and defense. Presumably, the authors had in mind rapid deployment to separate or otherwise inhibit adversaries in order to make space for third-party mediation and subsequent direct negotiations between adversaries. The United States should strengthen its support for and cooperation with international partners, including the UN and the African Union, to build their capacities for effective military response to mass atrocities if that should become necessary.

International action: strengthening norms and institutions. These tasks cannot be accomplished alone; the United States must build on existing strengths such as those of the UN, EU, and AU. According to the report, international and regional institutions must be helped in their efforts to become effective vehicles for prevention: "We recommend that the United States launch a diplomatic initiative to create an international network for information sharing and coordinated action to prevent genocide."

The report encompasses the following key themes:

- Genocide and mass atrocities threaten core American values and national interests. With presidential leadership, preventing genocide must become a national priority.
- Preventing genocide is an achievable goal. Working with international partners, the United States can take practical steps to prevent mass atrocities at every stage, including early tensions. The choice is *not* between doing nothing and large-scale military intervention.
- The administration should develop and implement a government-wide policy to prevent genocide and mass atrocities, including the creation of standing institutional mechanisms to ensure that the U.S. government takes timely and effective action.

Key recommendations in the report include:

- Creating an interagency atrocities prevention committee in the National Security Council to analyze trends toward mass atrocities and even genocide—considering appropriate preventive action at every stage, especially early on the path to danger
- Making the warning of mass impending or genocide an "automatic trigger" of policy review
- Developing military guidance on genocide prevention and early response and incorporating this guidance into doctrine and training
- Preparing interagency, multifaceted plans for high-risk situations that are susceptible to genocide

- Investing $250 million—less than $1 for every American each year—in new funds for crisis prevention and early response
- Making $50 million of this amount available for urgent off-cycle activities to prevent or halt emerging genocidal crises
- Launching a major diplomatic initiative to create an international network for information sharing and coordinated action to prevent mass atrocities and impending genocide
- Providing assistance to build the capacity of international partners—including the UN and regional organizations—to prevent genocide and related mass atrocities

EU-Related Activities in Genocide Prevention: New Developments

In the fall of 2008 and throughout 2009, the Republic of Hungary played a very thoughtful and dynamic role in relation to the activities of the European Union in protecting human rights and preventing genocide.[30] The Hungarians undertook well-informed, construc-

---

Box 19.1 Genocide Prevention Task Force

Task Force Members

Madeleine Albright, Cochair
William Cohen, Cochair
John Danforth
Thomas Daschle
Stuart Eizenstat
Michael Gerson
Dan Glickman
Jack Kemp
Gabrielle Kirk McDonald
Thomas R. Pickering
Julia Taft (1942–2008)
Vin Weber
Anthony Zinni

Key Staff

The Genocide Prevention Task Force was convened by the United States Holocaust Memorial Museum, the American Academy of Diplomacy, and the United States Institute of Peace (USIP)

Brandon Grove, Executive Director
Ann-Louise Colgan, Project Manager
Lawrence Woocher, USIP
John Hefferman, Holocaust Museum
Abiodun Williams, USIP

---

tive planning, announced by the minister of foreign affairs, Dr. Kinga Göncz. Authority was delegated to a capable diplomat, Ambassador István Lakatos. With his leadership, an international group formulated a concept paper for establishing an international center on the prevention of genocide,[31] building on the earlier work done for the prominent EU leader Javier Solana, in collaboration with his superb chief of staff, Enrique Mora.[32]

Upon the commission of the High Representative/Secretary-General of the European Union Javier Solana, the Madariaga Foundation, then headed by Raymond Georis, initiated a feasibility study on establishing what would become the International Centre for the Prevention of Genocide and Crimes against Humanity within the European Union, which was completed by a steering group in 2006. The Hungarian planning effort in 2009 relies heavily on this feasibility study and on the building blocks established by the UN that are useful to the EU.

- The five-point action plan of the UN Secretary-General (UNSG) to prevent genocide, presented in April 2004
- The appointment of Juan Méndez by the UNSG as a special adviser on the prevention of genocide in 2004
- The establishment by the UNSG of the Advisory Committee on the Prevention of Genocide, chaired by David Hamburg
- The appointment of Undersecretary-General Francis Deng as full-time successor to Juan Méndez in 2007

Thus, there is a cumulative quality to the EU-related work in this field and growing cooperation between the EU and the UN.

The Hungarians emphasize, as we have in this book, that the progression of events toward genocide is gradual and that the years between an initial threat and full genocide offer ample warning time for the international community to take preventive action. They set out a series of proposals regarding what is needed.

- One of the major problems is the *lack of institutional capacity*. Genocide prevention, like conflict prevention in other fields, needs to be further *institutionalized*. There is need for *focal points* in each region of the world, for knowledge and skills for the prevention of mass violence. These entities should collect information; monitor, recognize, and assess the situations by using specific tools; and trigger preventive steps.
- To be effective, the *focal points* should be strongly *connected to a well-prepared international organization (the EU), with special links to UN institutions and agencies.* They should also be connected to any other relevant institutions or regional organizations (such as the African Union, the Organisation for Security and Cooperation in Europe, the Organization of American States (OAS), and the Association of Southeast Asian Nations) that offer complementary strengths and cooperative opportunities, and should include strong NGOs such as the International Crisis Group and the Carter Center.
- *International cooperation and the establishment of a solid network* is needed to regularly and systematically share information, avoid duplication, share burdens, pool

strengths, divide labor, and create the necessary synergies to trigger timely action by mobilizing appropriate cooperative efforts.

- A focal point associated with a great international organization (such as the EU) could provide an extremely valuable reservoir of knowledge and skills, as well as a homesite for the mobilization of many different organizations and institutions that could make good use of such information. Such an enduring focal point could stimulate worldwide cooperative efforts in the next few decades to bring an end to genocide.
- Security, peace, development, and human rights are mutually interlinked and require *comprehensive actions, capabilities, and application of a broadly integrative approach.*
- Genocide and mass atrocities ought to be recognized as the ultimate level of violent conflicts, even human degradation. The prevention of deadly conflict is a crucial organizing principle for international and intergroup relations. Therefore, the most urgent necessities in the contemporary international agenda include *raising awareness of, educating about, and disseminating information on* the concept of prevention, with a special focus on the prevention of genocide.

The Hungarians seek to clarify tools that will help the international community in working with a troubled country. The Centre could be very helpful in mobilizing the necessary knowledge and skills to use these tools effectively by:

1. Establishing an ongoing process, drawing on readily available information from all sources, to identify vulnerable targets, scapegoats, and depreciated out-groups.
2. Monitoring trends of hatred and dehumanization toward the groups that are identified in such a vulnerable position.
3. Offering help in conflict resolution and prevention of mass violence in situations of this kind. Such help could involve:
   a. Offering early, strong mediation—as led by Kofi Annan for the African Union in Kenya in 2008, an excellent example of preventive diplomacy with strong short-term benefits and positive implications for long-term measures as well.
   b. Building the internal capacity of member states for early and ongoing conflict resolution, including essential concepts, techniques (e.g., negotiation), and institutions (e.g., an independent judiciary).
   c. Helping leaders and the public understand the merits of early, ongoing conflict resolution with international cooperation as appropriate, as well as helping to find ways of improving intergroup relations, especially through superordinate goals that are mutually beneficial for a country under stress. Such actions can bring together adversarial groups because the groups learn to perceive what they have to gain through cooperation or at least through tolerance of other groups.
4. Identifying strong predisposing factors, such as economic deterioration, social disorganization, and alienated populations with prospects of war and/or revolution in the background. The earlier such problems are identified and the better they are understood, the greater the opportunity for international help. The most effective

approach to providing international help for countries inclined toward intergroup violence involves empathy and pragmatic problem solving, not coercion.

5. Enlisting the help of key member states that are strongly interested in the genocide problem and how to prevent it, as well as persuading them to commit intellectual, technical, financial, and moral resources.

Thus, the emerging Hungarian initiative in the EU effort is highly consistent with similar work of the UN and with the themes of this book. A series of international meetings starting successfully in June 2009 in Budapest is under way to advance implementation.

Nongovernmental Organizations Strengthening Their Efforts in Prevention: The Carter Center

The Carter Center illustrates the ways in which nongovernmental organizations engaged in advancing human rights and democracy can help to prevent deadly conflict, even including genocide.[33] The prevention of mass violence has been a central preoccupation of President Jimmy Carter throughout his career. Now, under the inspired leadership of John Stremlau, the Peace Program shows how NGOs can become effective players in the struggle to rid the world of deadly conflict and genocide by helping to entrench human rights and democratic values.

Developing Democratic Election Standards

The Carter Center played a pivotal role in developing democratic election standards, which are rooted in core principles of international human rights, notably the Universal Declaration and the related covenants. The Carter Center continually seeks to build international consensus about what constitutes a credible election, and in the process, it makes it increasingly difficult for one side or the other to revert to extraconstitutional mass violence. This form of preventive action is rooted in international human rights law.

The Carter Center has been working with the community of election observation practitioners to develop a strong basis of international human rights norms and standards to guide election observation assessments. Several institutions constitute the community of election observers, most prominently including the European Union, which has recently released the second edition of the *Compendium of International Standards for Elections*. Standards developed by the EU and other institutions provide valuable criteria that share many basic principles. In recent years, observer groups have recognized the importance of developing common definitions, guiding principles, and a code of conduct for their missions, helping to ensure that all organizations are working under the highest professional standards of impartiality, integrity, and transparency.

Several examples illustrate the Carter Center's important monitoring projects. For instance, the center's efforts to defend the integrity of the Electoral Commission in Ghana as the only authoritative and legitimate arbiter in vote counting were definitely preventive: the 2009 elections were successful, even though escalating tensions during the final round might have led to extraconstitutional action by the government, which could have triggered mass violence along ethnic lines.

Human Rights Defenders Initiative

The Carter Center has always focused on human rights concerns during transitions to democracy, and its recent Human Rights Defenders Initiative provides an impetus for policymakers to give sustained attention to human rights in long-term, complicated transitions to democracy. Distinctive among human rights organizations, the Carter Center's initiative has been successful in influencing high-level international policymakers and developing a grassroots knowledge of the human rights conditions in targeted countries. The initiative provides an opportunity for human rights defenders to raise their individual and collective voices about the most pressing human rights problems throughout the world, with the aim of spreading awareness and initiating public action, as well as proposing solutions to policymakers.

Each year, an international meeting—the Human Rights Defenders Policy Forum—identifies major human rights challenges. At the forum, prominent defenders alert the international community to the most serious human rights problems in their societies. They propose specific solutions, often creative in nature. Utilizing its special relationship with U.S. policymakers and UN human rights officials, the Carter Center follows up on these recommendations. The program responds to the need for a systematic approach for informing policymakers of human rights on the ground and for shaping more effective human rights policies in the United States and the United Nations, as well as the EU, OAS, and AU. One vital result has been the increased willingness of such policymakers to address human rights issues *before* they escalate into atrocities.

The Importance of Ongoing Carter Center Engagement

The Carter Center has a special ability to play a convening role with U.S. policymakers and their United Nations counterparts, thereby deepening information on human rights problems and options for solution. The convening of policymakers with human rights defenders represents an alternative to the common confrontational relationship, which is all too often unproductive. Bringing policymakers who are concerned with promoting and protecting human rights together with those on the front lines creates a dialogue that can result in creative solutions, serving the interests of all concerned.

The near future is likely to witness:

- Expanding dialogue with policymakers
- Network building for defenders' human rights organizations
- Strengthening of UN human rights mechanisms
- Institutionalizing year-round follow-up
- Developing cutting-edge multimedia outreach and monitoring tools
- Strengthening partnerships with intergovernmental organizations as well as international human rights nongovernmental organizations

NGOs such as the Carter Center can help emerging, fragile democracies to *prepare* for elections well in advance by providing settings in which different groups can learn the arts of compromise, respect, and mutual accommodation.

Ghana: Success in Democracy and Development

A recent success story in this domain can be found in the pair of excellent elections coordinated in Ghana. Supporters of democracy around the world celebrated the January 2009 inauguration of Ghana's new president, Professor John Evans Atta Mills, who defeated the leader of the incumbent party in a very close runoff election. After surviving a postcolonial period of turbulence and military rule, Ghana has had five successful national democratic elections since 1992.[34] Political strength has helped sustain a rate of annual growth in excess of 6 percent, attracting foreign investment with exports of raw materials and agriculture, light industry, an emerging service sector, and the prospect of large offshore oil revenues beginning in 2010.[35] Nevertheless, inequity is a serious problem in Ghana.

The latest election moves Ghana toward equitable socioeconomic development with access to education, health care, economic opportunity, and diminished corruption. An important lesson of Ghana's democratic progress is the power of a constitution rooted in a popular rejection of past abuses. The constitution has established executive term limits; a minimum 50 percent plus 1 requirement for electing a president, which forges national coalitions; and a strong and independent Electoral Commission empowered to determine election results and subject only to judicial review.[36] Two broad-based political parties have emerged as a result.

Strengthening the integrity of the process, several hundred international election observers, along with 4,000 local observers, were deployed throughout the country, operating according to a set of principles developed jointly by the Carter Center, the United Nations Electoral Assistance Division, and the National Democratic Institute. The observers were unanimous in concluding that the Electoral Commission had conducted the election in a credible manner that was peaceful, transparent, and generally free of intimidation.[37]

Commonwealth: A Significant International Organization Clarifies Civil Paths to Peace

Understanding and respect are valuable in themselves, as necessary elements of human coexistence.[38] Equally important, their active promotion works to counteract mass violence and terrorism, whose success is based on deliberate encouragement of their opposites—disrespect and intolerance.

Following a resolution at the Commonwealth Heads of Government (CHOG) Meeting—an influential international organization—"to explore initiatives to promote mutual understanding and respect among all faiths and communities in the Commonwealth,"[39] the Commonwealth secretary-general invited Amartya Sen, the distinguished Nobel economist, to head a commission that would investigate and report on "civil paths to peace," to be submitted at a 2007 CHOG meeting in Uganda. Sen and the other members of the blue-ribbon committee—John Alderdice, Kwame Anthony Appiah, Adrienne Clarkson, Noeleen Heyzer, Kamal Hossain, Elaine Sihoatani Howard, Wangari Muta Maathai, Ralston Nettleford, Joan Rwabyomere, and Lucy Turnbull—presented in the final report policies that would promote understanding and respect, as well as practical ways to apply those policies to the real world. The Commonwealth secretary-general, after consulting with Commonwealth governments, is preparing specific plans for a program of action.

Composing a third of the world's population and with a fifty-three-state membership that spans all regions of the world, all levels of development and wealth, and almost all faiths, the Commonwealth champions the spread of transparent and accountable democratic government, the rule of law, human rights, gender equality, and economic development.

Commonwealth members take advantage of their historical ties to exchange administrative, educational, and legal ideas and best practices in giving aid to the most vulnerable members of society in the poorest countries. The commission reminds us that "the Commonwealth is not just a family of nations; it is also a family of peoples,"[40] and as such, it offers a cultural and intellectual marketplace where representatives of its fifty-three governments and eighty-five professional and civil society organizations can form affiliations, create consensus, and work together as equals. This "Commonwealth approach," which relies on shared respect and understanding of others' viewpoints, was what Nelson Mandela meant when he declared in 1994, "The Commonwealth makes the world safe for diversity."[41]

September 11, 2001, created intense international anxiety about terrorism, religious extremism, and violent conflict—and at the same time, it gave a tremendous boost to defining world conflict in cosmic, overarching terms, expressed most famously in Samuel Huntington's declarations about an inescapable "clash of civilizations," Muslim and non-Muslim. The commission believes that such a narrow analysis, which disregards how broadly members of *all* faiths differ in terms of defining their religious beliefs and in the priority they attach to their religious identity, may do more to promote fear, divisions, and terrorism than it does to "defeat" them. Their report is in part an effort to depart "from old ways of thinking about the centrality and the alleged inviolability of cultural confrontations" and consider evidence-based analyses that identify the multiple causes of conflict, define the limited role of culture in arousing conflict, and explore successful ways to deal with conflict at all stages.

Cultural misunderstanding and biases—religious and otherwise—contribute to disrespect and hatred that can lead to violence, but they are not the only or primary causes, nor do they lead inevitably to violence. Attention should turn from supposedly irreconcilable cultural differences and concentrate instead on examining the ways those differences are exploited by power-seeking groups or hate-mongering leaders who take advantage of traditional inequalities or grievances in order to gain followers through preaching violence. This approach can lead to recommendations of effective and specific policies to prevent violent clashes that seem grounded in cultural differences.

To investigate the many ways in which violence emerges and sometimes is provoked, the commission starts with the links between respect, understanding, and peaceful coexistence and then moves to the reverse side of this analysis, the connections between unrest, disaffection, and violence.

First, regarding the importance of poverty and inequality in creating unrest, hatred, and violence, one should note that although the relationships are not automatic or fixed, they do exist. In attending to inequality and poverty per se, one must also carefully consider their psychological effects. Feelings of humiliation and resentment, for example, often extend far back into the history of relations between unequal groups, and they must be understood when they erupt into confrontation. When perceptions of inequity and disrespect are justified, they must be remedied. The commission points to the 1982 Scarman report, a response to riots in the Brixton area of London that protested police unaccountability and racial discrimination. Its "detailed diagnoses" substantially lessened racial tensions.[42] Even if misunderstanding—sometimes provoked by extremists for personal ends—turns already hostile perceptions into near paranoia, perceived grievances and reports of injustice must be respectfully heard in an open and fair civil process. In addition, the stubborn persistence of traditional prejudice demands the systematic and regular evaluation of any remedial policies that are adopted.

The commission recommends the "Commonwealth approach" to achieve world coexistence, in giving inclusive political participation—with all groups eligible and welcome to express themselves—a principal role in its "multilateral" strategy.

A state's promotion of a strong national identity is not at all incompatible with an enthusiastic acceptance of pluralism in culture, faith, and language. In fact, if a nation encourages all its citizens—whatever their class, race, faith, or origin—to share a strong national identity, it makes citizens of every persuasion equal in their right to national political participation, even those who have just become citizens. A nation's tolerance of diversity, essential to defusing intergroup violence and discrimination, can also be strengthened by supporting the development of a great variety of civil society organizations and encouraging wide-ranging participation in them. Belonging to a broad mixture of associations dilutes an individual's unquestioning allegiance to a primary or even a single identity, and the existence of a variety of civil associations keeps members of the public alert to matters they might otherwise ignore. Anger about not being heard can lead to violence; civil groups provide their members a voice in peaceful political participation and can educate both members and policymakers in arriving at decisions that affect them. Women's participation, too often inadequately guaranteed, is essential here. Commonwealth member countries can share each other's many and varied experiences in promoting such associations.

The commission points out the vital role of strong, free, and diverse media in furthering political participation and awareness, in educating for tolerance, and in giving the public a vigorous forum for publicizing incidents of injustice (as well as proposing their solutions). Given the media's power to distort and inflame a divisive situation, the commission stresses the need to encourage the media to train their staff both in journalistic skills and in professional responsibility.

Making a broad and liberal (nonsectarian) education available to all should be an absolute priority, both to oppose narrow-minded exclusion and disrespect of the "other" and to create equal social and career opportunities for children of every background. (This neglected mission is exactly consistent with Chapter 10 in this book.) The instruction of young people must include training in the use of logic and reason to make judgments, not only for their intrinsic value in a liberal education but also as preparation to become good citizens. A special place should be given to a curriculum at all levels that promotes tolerance of diversity and recognizes the constructive role that each element of the nation has played in its history. Discussion about the meaning and value of citizenship in a diverse society of equals must be included, and it would be valuable in helping recent immigrants adapt to their new nation.

Public education should not omit sports, an essential ingredient in youthful development. Sports should be as available to all as classroom learning, without discrimination on grounds of sex or social, racial, economic, or religious status and also without discrimination on grounds of mediocre athletic performance. Even people with disabilities should have a chance to participate. For a superior athlete, excelling in sports can add glory to one's nation *and* one's identity group, as well as publicizing the contribution that members of all groups can make by working as a team and representing their nation. The Commonwealth Games and the Commonwealth Youth Games are examples of international sports events that promote respect and understanding through the participation of athletes from all groups and nationalities.

Both within a nation and within a community of nations, efforts to unilaterally impose solutions to conflict have had very mixed results. In contrast, multilateral cooperation and consultations have contributed enormously to arriving at enduring strategies for achieving and preserving peace and security. An approach based on discussions that attempt to gain common understanding and build consensus offers benefits for everyone. Multilateralism is also valuable in battling international injustice in cases where poor countries or regions have been excluded from the benefits of global economic restructuring and from the power to influence the direction this restructuring should take. The injustice that rankles these marginalized nations is not economic alone. It extends to perceptions that the larger nations exploit the weaker ones as pawns in service of their global political, economic, and military interests.

The commission recommends that the Commonwealth secretary-general increase his use of good offices to defuse and resolve international grievances and that the Commonwealth increase its cooperation with the UN and other international organizations to settle disputes and confrontations multilaterally.

Commonwealth dialogues and discussions should avoid limiting the definition of an individual's identity to religion or ethnic affiliation and emphasize the wide diversity of identities that coexist in every human. Neglecting this diversity diminishes both the individual and the ability to find areas of shared interest that would allow more points of entry to promote tolerance, respect, peaceful coexistence, and a global outlook. A people's cosmopolitan identity also deserves attention.

In international matters, civil paths must become an integral part of multilateral approaches across borders. Within nations, efforts to reduce intersectarian tensions are essential elements of the civil approach to peace. Here, the encouragement of an inclusive national political identity should be enthusiastically pursued. The secretary-general is consulting with leaders of the Commonwealth nations about expanding initiatives in this area, which could build on the Commonwealth's existing programs or work alongside those of other organizations, such as the United Nations. These civil paths to peace, which emphasize respect and tolerance for all peoples, apply to the world, not just the Commonwealth.

Greatly Diminishing the Nuclear Danger

As the years since the end of the Cold War have passed, much less has been done about diminishing the nuclear danger than most people assume.[43] This has been especially true since the overthrow of President Mikhail Gorbachev. Indeed, he and President Ronald Reagan, at their Reykjavik summit in 1986, had proposed steps toward the elimination of nuclear weapons altogether. Their words were not political palaver. Rather, they reflected a deep commitment on the part of both men to rid the world of incomparably deadly weapons that could serve no useful purpose, military or otherwise. But these men were inhibited by some of their hardline advisers and by constraints of domestic politics in each country, and so their dream was not fulfilled.

Twenty years later, honoring the memory of that historic summit and their extraordinary vision, a group of scientists, scholars, and political leaders decided to revive the concept and begin a serious effort—necessarily extending over some years—to reduce nuclear weapons to zero. In order to do so, they recognized that it would be essential to formulate a step-by-step process in which deep analytic work would address the *technical* and *political* obstacles standing in the way of such progress. Among the leaders of this effort were Professors Sidney Drell, George Shultz, and William Perry of Stanford University and Senator Sam Nunn of the Nuclear Threat Initiative. Others active in the enterprise were Henry Kissinger, Graham Allison, Matthew Bunn, Ashton Carter, James Goodby, Rose Gottemoeller, David Hamburg, Siegfried Hecker, David Holloway, Max Kampelman, Richard Lugar, Jack Matlock, Michael McFaul, William Potter, Scott Sagan, Roald Sagdeev, and Richard Solomon.

The rationale for this very formidable venture is the recognition that steps being taken now are inadequate given that we are at a nuclear tipping point. The prospect of nuclear weapons falling into utterly irresponsible hands is a very real possibility. Deterrence is decreasingly effective and increasingly hazardous. The spread of weapons continues. Many are on hair-trigger alert.

In January 2007, following their first conference, Shultz, Perry, Kissinger, and Nunn—former high officials of the U.S. government, two Republicans and two Democrats—issued a statement in the *Wall Street Journal* calling for a global effort to reduce reliance on nuclear weapons, prevent their spread, and ultimately put an end to them.[44] This call stimulated latent interest and deep concern—and opened up serious consideration of constructive options, including a statement by Gorbachev that nuclear weapons were most precarious for security and no longer served that aim. Various high government officials in different countries asserted the need for steps toward achieving a world free of nuclear weapons.

In October 2007, inspired by these reactions, Shultz and Drell, working with Perry, Kissinger, and Nunn, convened veterans of the past six administrations along with a number of other experts on nuclear issues for a conference at Stanford University's Hoover Institution. The analytic papers prepared for this conference surpassed any previous work in clarifying what obstacles would have to be overcome and how this exceedingly hard feat could be accomplished. The group identified near-term steps that could be taken by the United States and Russia, both of which have a special obligation to demonstrate leadership because the majority of nuclear weapons are still in these two countries.

The group recommended that this dialogue must be broadened on an international scale, reaching far beyond the United States and Russia and including nonnuclear and nuclear nations. An international consensus on priorities should be achieved, since *people everywhere are at great risk.*

The group also recommended the creation of an international system to manage the risks of the nuclear fuel cycle and agreement for further reductions in U.S. and Russian nuclear forces. The ultimate vision must focus on moving toward zero, and a clear statement was made to that effect.

In February 2008, to mobilize a broad international consensus on these critical issues, a meeting was held under the auspices of the Norwegian Foreign Ministry. Sidney Drell, an eminent physicist and arms control expert who has provided a powerful impetus and intellectual leadership in this bold nukes-toward-zero initiative, augmented the summary of this meeting that he helped to prepare, and I draw heavily on it here.[45] He summarized steps that must be taken as soon as possible and four longer-term ones, requiring the leadership of the United States and Russia, which together possess more than 90 percent of the world's nuclear warheads. The intent is to greatly reduce nuclear danger in the short term and start on the path to a world free of nuclear weapons.

1. *Extend key provisions of the Strategic Arms Reduction Treaty of 1991.* This treaty has clarified the vital task of verification, but it is scheduled to expire in December 2009. The United States and Russia must extend the essential verification provisions of this treaty. They should also urgently implement the reductions agreed upon in the 2002 Moscow Treaty on Strategic Offensive Reductions, limiting each of these countries to between 1,700 and 2,200 operationally deployed strategic nuclear warheads by the end of 2012 but putting no limits on nondeployed ones. There are no longer credible targets for so many nuclear weapons.

2. *Take steps to increase the warning and decision times for the launch of all nuclear-armed ballistic missiles, thereby reducing risks of accidental or unauthorized attacks—more dangerous now than deliberate attacks by either the United States or Russia.* Reliance on launch procedures that deny command authorities ample time to make extremely careful decisions is dangerous and wildly inappropriate. Developments in cyberwarfare pose new threats that could have disastrous consequences if the command-and-control systems of any nuclear weapons state were compromised by hostile hackers during a crisis. Yet procedural modifications in the launch process could reduce the risk of a catastrophic nuclear accident to near zero. Further steps could be implemented in time by introducing mutually agreed and verified physical barriers in the command-and-control sequence. Such actions have worldwide significance in decreasing the reliance on nuclear weapons.

3. *Discard any existing operational plans for massive attacks that still remain from the Cold War days.* This obsolete policy is an exceedingly dangerous relic of the Cold War.

4. *Undertake negotiations directed toward exploring cooperative multilateral ballistic missile defense and early warning systems, as proposed by Presidents G. W. Bush and Vladimir Putin at their 2002 Moscow summit meeting.* This step might well include agreement on plans for countering missile threats to Europe, Russia, and the United

States from the Middle East. In addition, efforts to establish the Joint Data Exchange Center in Moscow, which was agreed to at that 2002 summit, should be completed. The feasibility of missile defense remains doubtful, and reducing tensions in this area could foster progress on other issues.

5. *Intensively accelerate work to provide the highest possible standards of security for nuclear weapons, as well as for nuclear materials everywhere in the world, in order to prevent terrorists from acquiring a nuclear bomb.* Nuclear terrorism is a real and urgent threat. There are nuclear weapons materials in more than forty countries around the world, and there have been attempts to smuggle nuclear material in Eastern Europe and the Caucasus. If a terrorist group were able to obtain highly enriched uranium (HEU), it is plausible that it could make a nuclear explosive such as the one that obliterated Hiroshima. The most effective tool for reducing this risk is to strengthen security for all nuclear weapons and weapons-usable materials worldwide. Preventing the theft of nuclear weapons and materials would also block a major shortcut for states seeking nuclear weapons. The United States, Russia, and other nations have worked together in the Nunn-Lugar cooperative threat reduction programs, discussed earlier in this book; and more can be done with new leadership. The International Atomic Energy Agency (IAEA) should play a key role in future efforts to reduce the nuclear danger.

6. *Start a dialogue within the North American Treaty Organization (NATO) and with Russia on enhancing the security of nuclear weapons designed for forward deployment and moving steadily toward a careful accounting for them and, in due course, their elimination.* These small and portable nuclear weapons are most likely the devices terrorist groups would choose to acquire, and they deserve much more attention than they have received. NATO should decide to achieve a new strategic concept with the goal of having zero deployed nuclear weapons in Europe. This step would require resolving disagreements over conventional force deployments.

7. *Strengthen the means of monitoring compliance with the nuclear Non-proliferation Treaty (NPT) as a counter to the global spread of advanced technologies.* Progress in this direction is urgent in view of the global spread of advanced technology, especially for uranium enrichment. This effort should require the application of monitoring provisions designed by the IAEA to all signatories of the NPT. This added capacity would allow challenges, on-site, timely inspections of suspect activities. Such steps will require incentives for participating nations—some mix of political, economic, psychological, and security measures.

8. *Adopt a process for bringing the Comprehensive Test Ban Treaty (CTBT) into effect, which would strengthen the NPT and aid international monitoring of nuclear activities.* The CTBT has been signed by 178 states and ratified by 144. To enter into force, it must be ratified by all 44 states deemed nuclear capable. To date, 35 have done so, but 9 are still holding out. China, Egypt, Indonesia, Iran, Israel, the United States, North Korea, India, and Pakistan have yet to sign the treaty. The United States was the treaty's first signatory in 1996 and should now initiate a serious bipartisan congressional review. Since Washington failed to ratify it in 1999, there have been major improvements of the international monitoring system for identifying and locating treaty violations. The system now has 90 percent of its 321 facilities in

place, and it impressively displayed its sensitivity in rapidly locating, identifying, and measuring the yield of a recent North Korean test. Technical progress now permits high confidence in the reliability, safety, and effectiveness of the U.S. nuclear arsenal under a test ban. The Comprehensive Test Ban Treaty Organization is deploying new monitoring stations to detect nuclear tests. The United States and all reasonable nations should urgently support this work even before ratification of the treaty.

9. *For fundamental progress on a longer timescale, it is necessary to achieve major reductions in U.S. and Russian nuclear forces beyond those recorded in the U.S.-Russia Strategic Offensive Reductions Treaty. As the reductions proceed, other nuclear nations must become involved. There must be worldwide awareness of the necessity to reduce the nuclear danger.* A scenario for further reductions discussed in those conferences could lower the number of operationally deployed strategic nuclear warheads from the roughly 2,000 permitted under the Moscow Treaty to 1,000, followed by a second stage of reductions down to 500 deployed with perhaps another 500 in a responsive force. A critical third stage would limit the two countries to a strategic nuclear force with a total of 500 warheads, all in a responsive force and none operationally deployed. As such progress is made, commitments will be required from other nuclear powers to limit their own nuclear forces, which will necessitate transparency with their inclusion in a regime of monitoring and verification.

10. *Develop an international system of controls to manage the risks of the nuclear fuel cycle.* The growing global demand for energy to meet civilian aspirations has led to a renewal of desires to build nuclear reactors for this purpose. But this expansion inevitably will lead to an increase in the spread of sensitive nuclear fuel cycle technologies through enrichment of uranium at the front end and reprocessing spent fuel at the back end of the cycle. This situation would put prevention of nuclear proliferation in jeopardy. International mechanisms will have to be devised to guarantee that low-enriched uranium required for power reactors is available if necessary, that the fuel will remain under stringent multilateral controls, and that the spent fuel will be removed to internationally operated facilities. There should be no discrimination between nuclear and nonnuclear nations.

11. *Complete a verifiable treaty that prevents nations from producing nuclear materials for weapons (Fissile Materials Cut-off Treaty [FMCT]) and controls existing materials (Fissile Materials Control Initiative [FMCI]).* This vital challenge will require acceleration of negotiating efforts that have long been stalled. It will require developing mechanisms to verify and enforce the cutoff in production and the controls over existing material. It will also be necessary to develop and implement technical alternatives to using highly enriched uranium in many research and commercial installations around the world. Drell emphasizes that these three ambitious but crucial tasks will create daunting new demands on intelligence for monitoring full compliance with their provisions. This monitoring can occur when nuclear forces are reduced to much smaller numbers than we now have—preferably with all in a nondeployed responsive force. International control of the entire fuel cycle for civilian nuclear power will have to be established, and fissile material controls as well as production cutoffs will need to be negotiated. The United Kingdom and

Norway are taking the lead in improving the verification of nuclear disarmament. They can do much to determine requirements for the verifiable elimination of nuclear weapons.

12. *Turn the goal of a world without nuclear weapons into a practical enterprise among nations, by applying the necessary political will to build an international consensus on priorities.* This step is the most difficult challenge and is both politically stressful and emotionally charged.

The preceding steps are basic building blocks for creating a safer world. These technical steps must confront political conditions of growing complexity and difficulty. They call for political cooperation on a global scale, beyond friends and allies. The Gorbachev-Reagan vision of Reykjavik is essential to progress. But the vision must be implemented by *political* as well as *technical* measures, requiring deep and persistent analysis. Thus, an incisive and far-sighted formulation has emerged from these conferences. It has received strong support from the new American administration and the same is expected from the Australian-Japanese Commission on Disarmament in 2010.

On April 1, 2009, a joint statement was issued by President Dmitry Medvedev of Russia and President Barack Obama of the United States:

> Reaffirming that the era when our countries viewed each other as enemies is long over, and recognizing our many common interests, we today established a substantive agenda for Russia and the United States to be developed over the coming months and years. We are resolved to work together to strengthen strategic stability, international security, and jointly meet contemporary global challenges, while also addressing disagreements openly and honestly in a spirit of mutual respect and acknowledgement of each other's perspective.[46]

The two leaders affirmed their joint commitment to move toward a nuclear-free world, recognizing the particular need for U.S. and Russian leadership in this area. They discussed the achievement of arms control and reduction through a step-by-step process, fulfilling their obligations under the Treaty on Non-proliferation of Nuclear Weapons and through the pursuit of "new and verifiable reductions in our strategic offensive arsenals." They identified the first step to be replacement of the Strategic Arms Reduction Treaty with a new, legally binding treaty that negotiators would begin to work on immediately. They did so and the results were reported at the meeting of the two presidents in July 2009.

Later in April 2009, President Obama made a major speech in Europe amplifying these concepts, endorsing the vision of a world free of nuclear weapons, and outlining intermediate steps to be taken toward that goal, entirely consistent with the work of the leaders mentioned earlier in this section.

This mission may well be the most important and the most difficult one in the entire field of preventing mass violence. It is heartening, despite all the obstacles, that so many distinguished leaders in so many fields and so many countries are facing up to the dangers and applying their formidable abilities with great dedication. Together with the other initiatives outlined in this book, significant progress toward violence prevention is being made. No one ever thought it would be easy. But neither is it beyond human capacities.

CHAPTER 20

"Pioneers in the Prevention
of Mass Violence"

Filmed Interviews Organized by
David Hamburg for Insight into
the Evolution of the Prevention Movement

Since positive movement on the vital agenda of this book requires educating the general public of democratic countries as well as the scientific community and the policy community, we have undertaken additional ventures. One is a unique set of twenty-eight filmed interviews with leaders of the prevention movement, some of whose careers in that field began early in the Cold War. Their views are central to the content of this book. The unique compilation of interviews will be freely distributed throughout the world so that students, scholars, and policymakers and their advisers can take advantage of the rich experience and wisdom reflected in the work of these leaders, the "pioneers in the prevention of mass violence." The interviews, conducted by David Hamburg, were filmed in 2008 by Rick English, under the direction of Eric Hamburg.

From late 2007 through 2008, we elicited the generous cooperation of leading figures in preventing mass violence, representing a wide range of valuable perspectives on this crucial topic. Featuring eminent scholars and world leaders, the interviews constitute an archive of historical significance and include such transformative figures as Desmond Tutu, Kofi Annan, and Amartya Sen (the complete list of interviewees follows). It is important to understand how this movement was initiated and/or revived—probably for the first time since the momentous events in the first few years following World War II and the Holocaust. The people interviewed, though not constituting the entire list of major contributors to the movement, give a vivid sense of their personal experiences, the transformation of their thinking, the initiation of innovative practices, and the formulation of preventive policies. They also convey a sense of momentum, with which their advance may well continue.

Filmed Interviews:
Pioneers in the Prevention of Mass Violence

1. Allison, Graham
   Douglas Dillon Professor of Government and Director of the Belfer Center for Science and International Affairs, John F. Kennedy School of Government, Harvard University
2. Annan, His Excellency Kofi
   Former Secretary-General of the United Nations, Nobel Peace Laureate
3. Bartoli, Andrea
   Founding Director, Center for International Conflict Resolution, Columbia University
4. Dallaire, Senator Roméo
   Senator and Retired Lieutenant General, Canada, and Force Commander of United Nations Peacekeeping Force in Rwanda, 1993–1994
5. Dement, William
   Professor of Psychiatry and Behavioral Sciences, Emeritus, and Founder of the Sleep Disorders Center, Stanford University
6. Deng, Francis
   Undersecretary-General for Prevention of Genocide and Mass Atrocities and Special Advisor of the Secretary-General, United Nations
7. Diamond, Larry
   Senior Fellow, Hoover Institution, and Professor by Courtesy of Political Science and Sociology, Stanford University; Coeditor, Journal of Democracy
8. Drell, Sidney
   Senior Fellow, Hoover Institution, and Professor Emeritus of Theoretical Physics, Stanford Linear Accelerator Center (SLAC), Stanford University
9. Evans, The Honorable Gareth
   President Emeritus, International Crisis Group, Former Foreign Minister and Attorney General of Australia, and Cochair, International Commmission on Nuclear Non-Proliferation and Disarmament
10. Farquhar, John
    Professor of Medicine and of Health Research and Policy, Emeritus, Stanford University
11. Hamburg, Beatrix
    DeWitt Wallace Distinguished Scholar and Cochair, Social Medicine and Public Policy, Weill Cornell Medical College, and President Emeritus, William T. Grant Foundation
12. Hamburg, David
    DeWitt Wallace Distinguished Scholar and Cochair, Social Medicine and Public Policy, Weill Cornell Medical College, and President Emeritus, Carnegie Corporation of New York
13. Hamilton, The Honorable Lee
    President and Director of the Woodrow Wilson International Center for Scholars and Former Chair, Foreign Affairs Committee, U.S. House of Representatives

14. Jentleson, Bruce
    Professor of Public Policy and Political Science, Terry Sanford Institute of Public Policy, Duke University
15. Katchadourian, Herant
    Professor Emeritus of Psychiatry and Human Biology, Stanford University, and Former President, Flora Family Foundation
16. Lute, Jane Holl
    Assistant Secretary-General for Peacekeeping Operations, United Nations, and Former Executive Director, Carnegie Commission on Preventing Deadly Conflict, now Deputy Secretary, Department of Homeland Security
17. Méndez, Juan
    President, International Center for Transitional Justice, and Former UN Special Advisor to the Secretary-General on Prevention of Genocide
18. Nunn, The Honorable Sam
    Chief Executive Officer, Nuclear Threat Initiative, and Former Chair, Armed Service Committee, U.S. Senate
19. Otunnu, Olara
    President, LBL Foundation for Children, Former Undersecretary-General and Special Representative for Children of Armed Conflict, and Former President, International Peace Academy
20. Perry, The Honorable William
    Professor of Management Science and Engineering, Stanford University, and Former U.S. Secretary of Defense
21. Rubin, Barnett
    Director of Studies and Senior Fellow, Center on International Cooperation, New York University, and Former Director, Center for Preventive Action, Council on Foreign Relations
22. Sachs, Jeffrey
    Economist; Professor and Director, Earth Institute, Columbia University; and Special Advisor to the Secretary-General, United Nations
23. Sen, Amartya
    Development Economist; University Professor; Senior Fellow of the Society of Fellows, Harvard University; and Nobel Laureate in Economics
24. Solana, His Excellency Javier
    Secretary-General, Council of the European Union
25. Speedie, David
    Senior Fellow, John F. Kennedy School of Government, Harvard University, and Former Chair of International Peace and Security Program, Carnegie Corporation of New York
26. Tutu, Archbishop Desmond
    Archbishop Emeritus of South Africa, and Nobel Peace Laureate
27. Urquhart, Sir Brian
    Former Undersecretary-General for Special Political Affairs, United Nations, and Adviser to every Secretary-General of the United Nations since the UN founding

28. Williams, Baroness Shirley
    *Adviser on Nuclear Proliferation to Prime Minister Gordon Brown and Former Leader
    of the Liberal Democrats, House of Lords*

Both the documentary and the filmed interviews are available online from the Stanford
University Library at http://lib.stanford.edu/pg.

Notes

Note to Introduction

1. "Let us resolve to confront genocide and work to prevent mass atrocities, beginning with greater action to stop the killing in Darfur," from "Statement of Barack Obama on Holocaust Remembrance Day" (Chicago, May 2, 2008), available at the Organizing for America Web site, http://www.barackobama.com/2008/05/02/statement_of_barack_obama_on_h.php.

Notes to Chapter 1

1. Kofi Annan, "Keynote Address" (speech delivered at Stockholm International Forum, Conference Four, "Preventing Genocide: Threats and Responsibilities," January 26, 2004). Published in *Stockholm International Forum, Conference Four, Preventing Genocide: Threats and Responsibilities* (Stockholm: Regeringskanzliet, 2004), 18–20. Available at http://www.manskligarattigheter.gov.se/stockholmforum/2004/conference_2004.html and at http://www.un.org/News/ossg/sg/stories/statments_search_full.asp?statID=51.

2. Javier Solana, "Preventing Genocide: Threats and Responsibilities" (speech delivered at Stockholm Conference on Genocide, January 28, 2004). Available at http://europa-eu-un.org/articles/en/article_3176_en.htm (accessed February 12, 2005).

3. Alexander N. Yakovlev, *A Century of Violence in Soviet Russia* (New Haven, CT: Yale University Press, 2002).

4. Kofi A. Annan and Elie Wiesel, *Confronting Anti-Semitism* (New York: Ruder Finn Press, 2006).

5. Ibid., 13–17. Available at http://www.un.org/News/Press/docs/2004/sgsm9375.doc.htm.

6. Ibid., 51.

7. Ibid., 56.

8. See also Harold H. Saunders, "Interactive Conflict Resolution: A View for Policy Makers on Making and Building Peace," in *International Conflict Resolution After the Cold War*, ed. Paul C. Stern and Daniel Druckman, 251–293 (Washington, DC: National Academy Press, 2000).

9. David A. Hamburg, "Growing Up in a Time of Violence: Multiple Perspectives on Prevention," in *No More Killing Fields: Preventing Deadly Conflict* (Lanham, MD: Rowman and Littlefield, 2002), 1–16.

10. See R. J. Fisher, "Conclusion: Paths Toward a Peaceful World," in *The Social Psychology of Intergroup and International Conflict Resolution*, ed. R. J. Fisher, 236–250 (New York: Springer-Verlag, 1990).

11. David A. Hamburg, "Preventing Deadly Conflict" (Plenary Lecture at the fiftieth Pugwash Conference on Science and World Affairs, Cambridge, England, August 6, 2000).

12. Ibid.

13. David A. Hamburg, "International Cooperation for Prevention: Emerging from the Shadows," in *No More Killing Fields: Preventing Deadly Conflict* (Lanham, MD: Rowman and Littlefield, 2002), 219–250.

14. The EU Programme for the Prevention of Deadly Conflict, known as the Göteborg Programme, is available at www.eu2001.se/static/eng/pdf/violent.PDF.

Notes to Chapter 2

1. Tzvetan Todorov, *The Conquest of America,* trans. R. Howard (New York: Harper and Row, 1985), cited in *The Specter of Genocide: Mass Murder in Historical Perspective,* ed. Robert Gellately and Ben Kiernan, 22 (New York: Cambridge University Press, 2003).

2. Gellately and Kiernan, *The Specter of Genocide,* 22.

3. Ibid., 23.

4. Ibid., 378.

5. Ibid., 24.

6. Ibid.

7. Ibid., 25.

8. Ibid., 26.

9. See David A. Hamburg and Jane van Lawick-Goodall, "Factors Facilitating Development of Aggressive Behavior in Chimpanzees and Humans," in *Determinants and Origins of Aggressive Behavior,* ed. W. W. Hartup and J. DeWit, 59–85 (The Hague: Mouton, 1974); and Jane Goodall and David A. Hamburg, "Chimpanzee Behavior as a Model for the Behavior of Early Man: New Evidence on Possible Origins of Human Behavior," in *American Handbook of Psychiatry,* ed. David A. Hamburg and H. Brodie, vol. 6 (New York: Basic Books, 1975).

10. Michael L. Wilson and Richard W. Wrangham, "Intergroup Relations in Chimpanzees," *Annual Review of Anthropology* 32 (2003): 363.

11. Richard Wrangham, "Why Apes and Humans Kill," in *Conflict: The 2005 Darwin College Lecture Series,* ed. Martin Jones and Andy Fabian, 43–62 (Cambridge: Cambridge University Press, 2006).

12. See B. B. Smuts et al., eds., *Primate Societies* (Chicago: University of Chicago Press, 1986); W. C. McGrew, L. F. Marchant, and T. Nishida, eds., *Great Ape Societies* (Cambridge: Cambridge University Press, 1996); and D. A. Hamburg and E. R. McCown, eds., *The Great Apes* (Menlo Park, CA: Benjamin/Cummings Publishing Company, 1997).

13. Smuts et al., *Primate Societies;* McGrew, Marchant, and Nishida, *Great Ape Societies.*

14. M. B. Brewer, "The Psychology of Prejudice: Ingroup Love or Outgroup Hate," *Journal of Social Issues* 55, no. 3 (1999): 429–444.

15. Norman M. Naimark, *Fires of Hatred: Ethnic Cleansing in Twentieth-Century Europe* (London: Harvard University Press, 2001), 1–16, 185–199.

16. Mark Roseman, *The Wannsee Conference and the Final Solution* (New York: Picador, 2002).

17. James Waller, *Becoming Evil: How Ordinary People Commit Genocide and Mass Killing* (New York: Oxford University Press, 2005).

18. Erwin Staub, *The Roots of Evil* (New York: Cambridge University Press, 1989).

19. Terry Martin, "The Soviet Union" (presentation for the Committee on Conscience, U.S. Holocaust Memorial Museum Conference, "Stepping Back from the Brink: Studies in the De-escalation of Group Targeted Violence," Washington, DC, January 14–16, 2004).

20. Eric D. Weitz, *A Century of Genocide: Utopias of Race and Nation* (Princeton, NJ: Princeton University Press, 2003).

21. Quoted in Susan Benesch, "Inciting Genocide, Pleading Free Speech," *World Policy Journal*, 21, no. 2 (Summer 2004): 65.

22. Isabel V. Hull offered a related viewpoint in "Military Culture and the Production of 'Final Solutions' in the Colonies," in *The Specter of Genocide: Mass Murder in Historical Perspective*, ed. Robert Gellately and Ben Kiernan, 141–162 (New York: Cambridge University Press, 2003). She saw the dominance of military culture in colonial government as linked to later adoption of military norms by political leaders.

23. Benesch, "Inciting Genocide, Pleading Free Speech," 62–69.

24. Ibid.

25. Ibid.

26. Gellately and Kiernan, *The Specter of Genocide*, 374–375.

27. Ibid., 21.

28. Yehuda Bauer, "Holocaust and Genocide: Some Comparisons," in *Lessons and Legacies: The Meaning of the Holocaust in a Changing World*, ed. Peter Hayes, 36–46 (Evanston, IL: Northwestern University Press, 1991).

29. Yehuda Bauer, *Rethinking the Holocaust* (New Haven, CT: Yale University Press, 2001), 267.

30. Ian Kershaw, *Hitler, 1889–1936: Hubris* (New York: Norton, 1998); and Peter H. Merkl, *The Making of a Stormtrooper* (Princeton, NJ: Princeton University Press, 1980).

31. Bauer, *Rethinking the Holocaust*, 268–269.

32. Bauer, "Holocaust and Genocide," 46.

Notes to Chapter 3

1. Peter Balakian, *The Burning Tigris: The Armenian Genocide and America's Response* (New York: HarperCollins, 2003), 5.

2. Taner Akçam, *A Shameful Act: The Armenian Genocide and the Question of Turkish Responsibility* (New York: Metropolitan Books, 2007), 23.

3. See ibid., 24–35.

4. Balakian, *The Burning Tigris*, 55–56.

5. Ibid., 56.

6. Robert Melson, *Revolution and Genocide: On the Origins of the Armenian Genocide and the Holocaust* (Chicago: University of Chicago Press, 1996), 45.

7. Ibid., 46; Balakian, *The Burning Tigris*, 58.

8. Balakian, *The Burning Tigris*, 68–70.

9. Ibid., 11.

10. Ibid., 126.

11. Ibid., 118.

12. Ibid., 71.

13. Melson, *Revolution and Genocide*, 46.

14. Balakian, *The Burning Tigris*, 110.

15. Melson, *Revolution and Genocide*, 47–48.

16. Balakian, *The Burning Tigris*, 123–124.

17. Ibid., 130–131.

18. Ibid., xiv, xv.

19. Melson, *Revolution and Genocide,* 47.

20. Balakian, *The Burning Tigris,* 144.

21. Melson, *Revolution and Genocide,* 139.

22. Ibid., 143.

23. Ronald Grigor Suny, "Why the Armenian Genocide? How We Can Understand the Deportations and Massacres of the Ottoman Armenians" (public lecture for the Bay Area Armenian Professor Society and the Stanford University Armenian Students' Association, Stanford, California, March 18, 2006). Reproduced with permission of the author. See also Suny, "Rethinking the Unthinkable: Toward an Understanding of the Armenian Genocide," in *Looking Toward Ararat: Armenia in Modern History* (Bloomington: Indiana University Press, 1983), 94–115; and Suny, "Religion, Ethnicity, and Nationalism: Armenians, Turks, and the End of the Ottoman Empire," in *In God's Name: Genocide and Religion in the Twentieth Century,* ed. Omer Bartov and Phyllis Mack, 23–61 (New York: Berghahn Books, 2001).

24. Melson, *Revolution and Genocide,* 156.

25. Henry Morgenthau, *Ambassador Morgenthau's Story,* ed. Ara Serafian (Reading, PA: Taderon Press, by arrangement with Gomidas Institute Books [Ann Arbor, 2000]), 189, quoted by permission of the Gomidas Institute.

26. Melson, *Revolution and Genocide,* 160–161.

27. Balakian, *The Burning Tigris,* 159–160.

28. Ibid., 163–164.

29. Ben Kiernan, "Twentieth-Century Genocides: Underlying Ideological Themes from Armenia to East Timor," in *The Specter of Genocide: Mass Murder in Historical Perspective,* ed. Robert Gellately and Ben Kiernan, 29–51 (New York: Cambridge University Press, 2003). See also Ben Kiernan, *Blood and Soil: A World History of Genocide and Extermination from Sparta to Darfur* (New Haven, CT: Yale University Press, 2007).

30. Melson, *Revolution and Genocide,* 165.

Notes to Chapter 4

1. Robert S. Wistrich, *Hitler and the Holocaust* (New York: The Modern Library, 2001).

2. Saul Friedlander, *The Years of Extermination: Nazi Germany and the Jews, 1939–1945* (New York: HarperCollins), 2007; and Saul Friedlander, *Nazi Germany and the Jews,* vol. 1, *The Years of Persecution 1933–1939* (New York: Harper Perennial), 1998.

3. Raul Hilberg, *The Destruction of the European Jews,* vol. 3 (New York: Holmes and Meier, 1985), 994; quoted in Wistrich, *Hitler and the Holocaust,* 219.

4. See, for example, Wistrich, *Hitler and the Holocaust,* 217–236.

5. Primo Levi, *The Drowned and the Saved* (*I Sommersi e i salvati*), trans. Raymond Rosenthal (New York: Summit Books, 1988), 30ff., cited in Wistrich, *Hitler and the Holocaust,* 232.

6. Margerete Buber-Neumann, *Déportée à Ravensbrück* (Paris: Seuil, 1988), 53.

7. Yehuda Bauer, *Rethinking the Holocaust* (New Haven, CT: Yale University Press, 2001), 267ff.

8. Ibid., 268.

9. Ibid., 270.

10. Michael Jabara Carley, *1939: The Alliance That Never Was and the Coming of World War II* (New York: Ivan Dee, 1999), 5–6; see also Gordon Craig, *Germany, 1866–1945* (New York: Oxford University Press, 1978), 521.

11. Carley, *1939: The Alliance That Never Was,* 30.

12. R.A.C. Parker, *Churchill and Appeasement* (London: Macmillan, 2000).

13. Richard Overy, *The Origins of the Second World War,* 2d ed. (New York: Longman, 1998), 96–100.

14. Ibid., 16–17.

15. Gordon Craig, *Europe Since 1815* (New York: Holt, Reinhart, and Winston, 1961), 442–443.

16. Sheila Fitzpatrick, "Socialism and Communism," in *Columbia History of the Twentieth Century,* ed. Richard Bullet, 214 (New York: Columbia University Press, 1998).

17. Overy, *The Origins of the Second World War,* 16.

18. Walter Laqueur, *Fascism: Past, Present, Future* (New York: Oxford University Press, 1996).

19. Richard J. Evans, *The Coming of the Third Reich* (New York: Penguin Books, 2003), 109.

20. Ibid., 106.

21. Craig, *Europe Since 1815,* 600. Reprinted with permission of Wadsworth, a division of Thomson Learning: www.thomsonrights.com.

22. Fritz Stern, *Dreams and Delusions: National Socialism in the Drama of the German Past* (New York: Vintage, 1987), chaps. 5 and 6; and Detlev J. K. Peukert, *The Weimar Republic: The Crisis of Classical Modernity,* trans. Richard Deveson (New York: Hill and Wang, 1989).

23. Wistrich, *Hitler and the Holocaust,* 122–123.

24. Stern, *Dreams and Delusions,* 124.

25. Ibid., 172–173.

26. J. Kenneth Brody, *The Avoidable War: Lord Cecil and the Policy of Principle, 1933–1935,* vol. 1 (New Brunswick, NJ: Transaction, 1999), 102.

27. Lucy S. Dawidowicz, *The War Against the Jews* (New York: Bantam, 1976); Bernard Lewis, *Semites and Anti-Semites: An Inquiry into Conflict and Prejudice* (New York: Norton, 1999); Gotz Aly, *"Final Solution": Nazi Population Policy and the Murder of the European Jews* (New York: Oxford University Press, 1999); and James M. Glass, *"Life Unworthy of Life": Racial Phobia and Mass Murder in Hitler's Germany* (New York: Basic Books, 1997).

28. Craig, *Germany, 1866–1945,* 676–678.

29. Ibid., 678.

30. Fritz Redlich, *Hitler: Diagnosis of a Destructive Prophet* (New York: Oxford University Press, 1999), 97–99.

31. Craig, *Germany, 1866–1945,* 673.

32. Brody, *The Avoidable War,* 43–145.

33. Craig, *Germany, 1866–1945,* 674–675.

34. Brody, *The Avoidable War,* 146.

35. Roy Denman, *Missed Chances: Britain and Europe in the Twentieth Century* (l, 1996).

36. Ruth Henig, *The Origins of the Second World War, 1933–1939* (New York: Routledge, 1991).

37. Ian Kershaw, *Hitler, 1889–1936* (New York: Norton, 1998), 550–552.

38. Overy, *The Origins of the Second World War,* 20–21.

39. Craig, *Germany, 1866–1945,* 675–677.

40. Kershaw, *Hitler,* 588.

41. Ibid. French apprehension about Germany's strength evokes the West's current view of Iran, whose self-proclaimed might and readiness with regard to troop numbers and equipment have been taken at face value. Such fears have been described as the "Mussolini syndrome," referring to the way the British and French grossly overestimated Italy's will and capacity in the early 1930s.

42. Richard Overy, "Misjudging Hitler: A.J.P. Taylor and the Third Reich," in *The Origins of the Second World War Reconsidered: A.J.P. Taylor and the Historians,* 2d ed., ed. Gordon Martel, 103–104 (New York: Routledge, 1999).

43. Overy, *The Origins of the Second World War,* 18–19.

44. Overy, "Misjudging Hitler," 101–102; and Klaus P. Fischer, *Nazi Germany: A New History* (New York: Continuum, 1995), 413–414.

45. Fischer, *Nazi Germany,* 402.

46. Overy, *The Origins of the Second World War,* 21.

47. Carley, *1939: The Alliance That Never Was,* chap. 1.

48. David Kennedy, *Freedom from Fear: The American People in Depression and War* (New York: Oxford University Press, 1999), 404.

49. Barbara Farnham, *Roosevelt and the Munich Crisis: A Study of Political Decision Making* (Princeton, NJ: Princeton University Press, 1997), 79–80.

50. Franklin D. Roosevelt, "Quarantine the Aggressors," October 5, 1937. Available at http://tucnak.fsv.cuni.cz/~calda/Documents/1930s/FDR_Quarantine_1937.html (accessed March 16, 2006).

51. Kennedy, *Freedom from Fear,* 406.

52. Sidney Aster, "'Guilty Men': The Case of Neville Chamberlain," in *The Origins of the Second World War,* ed. Patrick Finney, 64 (New York: Arnold, 1997); and Kennedy, *Freedom from Fear,* 407–408.

53. Overy, *The Origins of the Second World War,* 27.

54. Andrew Crozier, *The Causes of the Second World War* (Malden, MA: Blackwell, 1997), 143–144.

55. Farnham, *Roosevelt and the Munich Crisis,* 119.

56. Overy, *The Origins of the Second World War,* 63.

57. Carley, *1939: The Alliance That Never Was,* chap. 6.

58. See Fischer, *Nazi Germany,* 402–403.

59. David Hamburg, *No More Killing Fields: Preventing Deadly Conflict* (Lanham, MD: Rowman and Littlefield, 2002), 43–45.

Notes to Chapter 5

1. David A. Hamburg, *No More Killing Fields: Preventing Deadly Conflict* (Lanham, MD: Rowman and Littlefield, 2002), 51.

2. See Robert Melson, "Rwanda," in *The Specter of Genocide: Mass Murder in Historical Perspective,* ed. Robert Gellately and Ben Kiernan, 326ff. (Cambridge: Cambridge University Press, 2003).

3. René Lemarchand, "The Rwanda Genocide," in *Century of Genocide, Second Edition: Critical Essays and Eyewitness Accounts,* ed. Samuel Totten, William S. Parsons, and Israel Charny, 397 (New York: Routledge, 2004).

4. Ervin Staub, "The Origins of Genocide, Rwanda" and "Bystanders as Evil, The Example of Rwanda," in *The Psychology of Good and Evil: Why Children, Adults, and Groups Help and Harm Others* (Cambridge UK: Cambridge University Press, 2003), 341–350.

5. Scott R. Feil, *Preventing Genocide: How the Early Use of Force Might Have Succeeded in Rwanda* (New York: Carnegie Corporation, 1998), 1ff.

6. Lemarchand, "The Rwanda Genocide," 324–328.

7. Ibid., 329.

8. Feil, *Preventing Genocide,* 44.

9. Lemarchand, "The Rwanda Genocide," 398.

10. Staub, "The Origins of Genocide, Rwanda," 342.

11. Ibid.

12. Feil, *Preventing Genocide,* 36.

13. Staub, "The Origins of Genocide, Rwanda."

14. Ibid.

15. Ervin Staub et al., "Healing, Reconciliation, Forgiving and the Prevention of Violence After Genocide or Mass Killing: An Intervention and Its Experimental Evaluation in Rwanda," *Journal of Social and Clinical Psychology* 24, no. 3 (2005): 299ff., citing A. Des Forges, *Leave None to Tell the Story: Genocide in Rwanda* (New York: Human Rights Watch, 1999); Mahmoud Mamdani, *When Victims Become Killers: Colonialism, Nativism and the Genocide in Rwanda* (Princeton, NJ: Princeton University Press, 2001); and Gerard Prunier, *The Rwanda Crisis* (New York: Columbia University Press, 1995).

16. Des Forges, *Leave None to Tell the Story,* quoted in Staub, "Bystanders as Evil."

17. Feil, *Preventing Genocide,* 1.

18. Ibid., 2.

19. Ibid., 3.

20. Karl Vick, "Death Toll in Congo War May Approach 3 Million," *Washington Post,* April 30, 2001.

21. Staub et al., "Healing, Reconciliation, Forgiving and the Prevention of Violence After Genocide or Mass Killing," 299ff.

22. From the Web site of the Institute for Security Studies, http://www.issafrica.org/AF/profiles/rwanda/Politics.html (accessed June 21, 2005).

23. Ibid.

24. Lemarchand, "The Rwanda Genocide," 332.

25. Feil, *Preventing Genocide,* 3.

26. Ibid., 6.

27. See Alan J. Kuperman, "The Other Lesson of Rwanda: Mediators Sometimes Do More Harm than Good," *SAIS Review* 16, no. 1 (Winter/Spring 1996): 221–240.

28. Feil, *Preventing Genocide,* 16.

29. Ibid.

30. Ibid., 22.

31. Ibid.

32. *Report of the Independent Inquiry into the Actions of the United Nations During the 1994 Genocide in Rwanda* (UN Doc. S/1999/1257, December 1999).

33. Ibid., 30, 35.

34. Ibid.

35. Michael Brown and Richard N. Rosecrance, *The Costs of Conflict: Prevention and Cure in the Global Arena* (Lanham, MD: Rowman and Littlefield, 1999).

36. Staub et al., "Healing, Reconciliation, Forgiving and the Prevention of Violence After Genocide or Mass Killing."

37. Carnegie Commission on Preventing Deadly Conflict, *Preventing Deadly Conflict, Final Report* (Washington, DC: Carnegie Commission on Preventing Deadly Conflict, 1997), 20–21.

38. John Stremlau, *People in Peril: Human Rights, Humanitarian Action, and Preventing Deadly Conflict,* Report to the Carnegie Commission on Preventing Deadly Conflict (New York: Carnegie Commission on Preventing Deadly Conflict, 1998), 12.

39. Carnegie Commission on Preventing Deadly Conflict, *Preventing Deadly Conflict,* 21.

40. Hamburg, *No More Killing Fields,* 57.

41. Brown and Rosecrance, *The Costs of Conflict.*

Notes to Chapter 6

1. Cyrus Vance, "Foreword," in John Stremlau and Helen Zille, *A House No Longer Divided: Progress and Prospects for Democratic Peace in South Africa,* Report to the Carnegie Commission on Preventing Deadly Conflict (New York: Carnegie Corporation of New York, 1997), v.

2. See John Allen in Desmond Tutu, *The Rainbow People of God: The Making of a Peaceful Revolution,* ed. John Allen (New York: Doubleday, 1994), 3.

3. Ibid., 4.

4. Nelson Mandela, *Long Walk to Freedom: The Autobiography of Nelson Mandela* (Boston: Little, Brown and Company, 1994), 144–146.

5. Ibid., 145.

6. Allen in Tutu, *The Rainbow People of God,* 5.

7. Mandela, *Long Walk to Freedom,* 145.

8. Ibid., 145–146.

9. Ibid., 148.

10. Allen in Tutu, *The Rainbow People of God,* 6; Mandela, *Long Walk to Freedom,* 206–208.

11. Mandela, *Long Walk to Freedom,* 211.

12. Allen in Tutu, *The Rainbow People of God,* 6.

13. Ibid., 11–12.

14. Ibid.

15. Ibid., 13–14.

16. Ibid., 15.

17. Ibid., 15–16.

18. Tutu, *The Rainbow People of God,* 16–17.

19. Stremlau and Zille, *A House No Longer Divided,* 4.

20. Peter Gastrow, *Bargaining for Peace: South Africa and the National Peace Accord* (Washington, DC: United States Institute of Peace Press, 1995), 9.

21. Ibid.

22. Ibid.

23. Allen in Tutu, *The Rainbow People of God,* 85ff.

24. Tutu, *The Rainbow People of God,* 86ff.

25. Allen in Tutu, *The Rainbow People of God,* 185ff.

26. Ibid., 187–188.

27. Nelson Mandela, "Address to the Nation by ANC President, Nelson Rolihlahla Mandela, on the Assassination of Martin Thembisile (Chris) Hani," April 10, 1993. Available on the ANC Web site, http://www.anc.org.za/ancdocs/history/mandela/1993/sp930410.html.

28. See Patti Waldmeir, *Anatomy of a Miracle: The End of Apartheid and the Birth of the New South Africa* (New York: W. W. Norton, 1997), 223 ff.

29. Mandela, *Long Walk to Freedom,* 502–504.

30. Tutu, *The Rainbow People of God,* 192.

31. Ibid., 196ff.

32. Ibid., 199–202.

33. Allen, in Tutu, *The Rainbow People of God,* 266.

34. Ibid., 267.

35. Heribert Adam and Kogila Moodley, *The Negotiated Revolution* (Johannesburg: Jonathan Ball Press, 1993).

36. Gastrow, *Bargaining for Peace*, vii.

37. Ibid.

38. See Anthony S. Mathews, *Freedom, State Security and the Rule of Law: Dilemmas of the Apartheid Society* (Cape Town: Juta, 1986), 284, cited in Gastrow, *Bargaining for Peace*, 8.

39. Gastrow, *Bargaining for Peace*, 9.

40. Ibid., 15.

41. Ibid., 17.

42. Ibid.

43. Nelson Mandela believed that de Klerk's—and the South African government's—friendship with the IFP was an attempt to undercut ANC strength by building an anti-ANC alliance with the IFP and attracting the colored Afrikaans-speaking voters of the Cape to a new National Party. Mandela, *Long Walk to Freedom*, 503–504.

44. Gastrow, *Bargaining for Peace*, 18.

45. Mandela, *Long Walk to Freedom*, 502.

46. Gastrow, *Bargaining for Peace*, 20.

47. Ibid., 22–24.

48. Ibid., 24.

49. Ibid., 26.

50. Ibid., 26–27.

51. Ibid., 30.

52. Ibid., 32.

53. Ibid., 35–37.

54. Ibid., 43.

55. Ibid., 46.

56. Ibid., 47.

57. Ibid., 48–49.

58. Ibid., 58.

59. International Alert, *Mission to Evaluate the National Peace Accord and Its Peace Structures Report,* chap. 3 (London: 1993), 7. Cited in Gastrow, *Bargaining for Peace*, 72.

60. Gastrow, *Bargaining for Peace*, 72.

61. Ibid., 73.

62. Ibid., 73–74.

63. Ibid., 76–77.

64. Stremlau and Zille, *A House No Longer Divided.*

65. Desmond Tutu, "Leadership," in *Essays on Leadership* (New York: Carnegie Corporation of New York, 1998), 67–70. Reprinted with permission.

66. Stremlau and Zille, *A House No Longer Divided*, 10–11.

67. See Helen E. Purkitt and Stephen F. Burgess, *South Africa's Weapons of Mass Destruction* (Bloomington: Indiana University Press, 2005).

68. Stremlau and Zille, *A House No Longer Divided*, 13.

69. See http://www.fordfound.org/publications/ff_report/view_ff_report_detail.cfm?report_index=23.

70. Melvin J. Fox, "Trip to the Union of South Africa—December 1959," Ford Foundation Report no. 0020765, January 4, 1960.

71. See http://www.fordfound.org/publications/ff_report/view_ff_report_detail.cfm?report_index=295.

72. See http://www.fordfound.org/publications/ff_report/view_ff_report_detail.cfm?report_index=237.

73. Stremlau and Zille, *A House No Longer Divided*, 15.

Notes to Chapter 7

1. Carnegie Commission on Preventing Deadly Conflict, *Preventing Deadly Conflict, Final Report* (New York: Carnegie Commission on Preventing Deadly Conflict, 1997).

2. "About Crisis Group." Available at www.icg.org (accessed July 25, 2006).

3. Warren Christopher, "The Negotiator" (Jackson H. Ralston Lecture, Stanford Law School, Palo Alto, California, October 9, 1998).

4. Jeffery Z. Rubin, Dean G. Pruitt, and Sung Hee Kim, *Social Conflict: Escalation, Stalemate, and Settlement*, 2nd ed. (New York: McGraw-Hill, 1994).

5. Ibid., 172; material reproduced with the permission of the McGraw-Hill companies.

6. John Packer and Craig Collins, "Options and Techniques for Quiet Diplomacy" (discussion paper prepared for a UN-related conference in New York, July 24, 2005).

7. Ibid.

8. Stephen Weiss-Wik, "Enhancing Negotiators' Successfulness: Self-Help Books and Related Empirical Research," *Journal of Conflict Resolution* 27 (December 1983): 706-735; and William Ury, *Getting to Peace* (New York: Penguin, 1999).

9. Roger Fisher and William Ury, *Getting to Yes: Negotiating Agreement Without Giving In* (New York: Penguin, 1983).

10. Graham Allison and Hisashi Owada, "The Responsibilities of Democracies in Preventing Deadly Conflict: Reflections and Recommendations," Carnegie Commission on Preventing Deadly Conflict Discussion Paper, July 1999.

11. Connie Peck, "Training as a Means to Build Capacity in Conflict Prevention: The UNITAR Approach," in *Conflict Prevention: From Rhetoric to Reality*, vol. 2, *Opportunities and Innovations*, ed. David Carment and Albrecht Schnabel, 227–249 (Lanham, MD: Lexington Books, 2004).

12. Ibid.

13. See Alexander George, *Bridging the Gap: Theory and Practice in Foreign Policy* (Washington, DC: United States Institute of Peace Press, 1993).

14. Peck, "Training as a Means to Build Capacity in Conflict Prevention," 229.

15. See William Ury, *Getting Disputes Resolved: Developing Systems to Cut the Costs of Conflict* (San Francisco: Jossey-Bass Publishers, 1988).

16. Morton Deutsch, *The Resolution of Conflict: Constructive and Destructive Processes* (New Haven, CT: Yale University Press, 1973).

17. Cyrus R. Vance and David A. Hamburg, *Pathfinders for Peace: A Report to the UN Secretary-General on the Role of Special Representatives and Personal Envoys* (New York: Carnegie Commission on Preventing Deadly Conflict, 1997).

Notes to Chapter 8

1. See David A. Hamburg, *No More Killing Fields: Preventing Deadly Conflict* (Lanham, MD: Rowman and Littlefield, 2002), 151–170.

2. Robert A. Dahl, *On Democracy* (New Haven, CT: Yale University Press, 1998).

3. Ibid., 38, 44–61, 113–114, 145–147.

4. Carl Gershman, "The Internet and Democracy-Building: The NED Experience" (paper presented at an International Workshop organized by Great Britain's Foreign and Commonwealth Office, Wilton Park, UK, April 27–28, 2001). Available at http://www.ned.org/about/carl/apr2701 .html. Carl Gershman is the president of the National Endowment for Democracy.

5. Thomas Carothers, *Aiding Democracy Abroad: The Learning Curve* (Washington, DC: Carnegie Endowment for International Peace, 1999).

6. Melanie C. Greenberg, John H. Barton, and Margaret E. McGuinness, *Words over War: Mediation and Arbitration to Prevent Deadly Conflict*, Carnegie Commission Series (Lanham, MD: Rowman and Littlefield, 2000).

7. Timothy D. Sisk, *Power Sharing and International Mediation in Ethnic Conflicts* (Washington, DC: U.S. Institute of Peace, 1996).

8. Arturo Valenzuela, *The Collective Defense of Democracy: Lessons from the Paraguayan Crisis of 1996* (New York: Carnegie Commission on Preventing Deadly Conflict, 1999).

9. Connie Peck, *Sustainable Peace: The Role of the UN and Regional Organizations in Preventing Conflict* (Lanham, MD: Rowman and Littlefield, 1998), 106–113.

10. Information is available at http://www.cartercenter.org/aboutus/aboutus.htm (accessed July 20, 2006).

11. See PER's Web site, www.per-usa.org.

12. Boutros Boutros-Ghali, *An Agenda for Democratization* (New York: United Nations, 1996), available at http://www.nidg.org/towards-a-global-civil-society/NRD/an-agenda-for-democratization.pdf.

13. Council on Foreign Relations and Freedom House, *Enhancing U.S. Leadership at the United Nations: Report of an Independent Task Force*, David Dreier and Lee H. Hamilton, Co-Chairs; Lee Feinstein and Adrian Karatnycky, Project Co-Directors (New York: Council on Foreign Relations, 2002). Available at http://www.cfr.org/content/publications/attachments/ UN_TaskForce.pdf.

14. See Hamburg, *No More Killing Fields,* 311–312.

15. Council on Foreign Relations and Freedom House, *Enhancing U.S. Leadership at the United Nations,* 3.

16. Graham T. Allison and Hisashi Owada, *The Responsibilities of Democracies in Preventing Deadly Conflict: Reflections and Recommendations,* Carnegie Commission on Preventing Deadly Conflict Discussion Paper, July 1999.

17. See the Web site of the National Endowment for Democracy, www.ned.org.

18. Sisk, *Power Sharing.*

19. International Institute for Democracy and Electoral Assistance [International IDEA], *Ten Years of Supporting Democracy Worldwide* (Stockholm: International IDEA, 2005).

20. Carothers, *Aiding Democracy Abroad.*

21. International IDEA, *Ten Years of Supporting Democracy Worldwide.*

22. Ibid., 30.

23. Ibid.

24. Ibid.

25. Larry Diamond, "Universal Democracy?" *Policy Review* (June and July 2003): 3–25. Diamond is a senior fellow at the Hoover Institution and coordinator of the Democracy Program of the Center for Democracy, Development, and the Rule of Law at Stanford University's Institute for International Studies. He is coeditor of *The Journal of Democracy.*

26. Ibid., 5.

27. Dahl, *On Democracy,* 38.

28. Amartya Sen, "Democracy as a Universal Value," in *The Global Divergence of Democracies*, ed. Larry Diamond and Marc F. Plattner (Baltimore, MD: Johns Hopkins University Press, 2001). Cited in Diamond, "Universal Democracy?" 11.

29. Diamond, "Universal Democracy?" 11.

30. Ibid.

31. Ibid.

32. Ibid., 12.

33. *Arab Human Development Report 2002: Creating Opportunities for Future Generations* (New York: United Nations Development Programme/Regional Bureau for Arab States, 2002), 2, 105–120.

34. Amartya Sen, *Identity and Violence: The Illusion of Destiny* (New York: W. W. Norton, 2006).

35. Diamond, "Universal Democracy?" 13.

36. Ibid., 15.

37. Ibid., 16.

38. Ibid.

39. Larry Diamond, "Democracy, Development, and Good Governance: The Inseparable Links" (Annual Democracy and Governance Lecture, Center for Democratic Development, Accra, Ghana, March 1, 2005).

40. Hamburg, *No More Killing Fields*, 170–172.

41. Mary King, *Mahatma Gandhi and Martin Luther King, Jr.: The Power of Nonviolent Action* (Paris: UNESCO, 1999), 419–420.

42. Peter Ackerman and Jack Duvall, *A Force More Powerful: A Century of Nonviolent Action* (New York: St. Martin's, 2000), 421–454.

43. Stanford Program on International and Cross-Cultural Education, *Preventing Deadly Conflict: Toward a World Without War* (Stanford, CA: Stanford University Freeman Spogli Institute for International Studies, 2000), 125–127.

44. David Cortright, *Gandhi and Beyond: Nonviolence for an Age of Terrorism* (Boulder, CO: Paradigm Publishers, 2006).

45. Erkki Tuomioja, "Foreword," in *Building Democracy from Manila to Doha: The Evolution of the Movement of New or Restored Democracies*, ed. Tapio Kanninen and Katarina Sehm Patomäki, 10 (Helsinki: Ulkoasiainministeriön Julkaisuja, Helsinki Process Publication Series, 2005). Tuomioja is the minister of foreign affairs of Finland.

46. Kanninen and Patomäki, *Building Democracy from Manila to Doha*.

47. Roy Lee, "An International Normative Framework for Democratization," in *Building Democracy from Manila to Doha*, ed. Kanninen and Patomäki, 16–132. Professor Lee, now professor of law at Columbia University, is a former director in the UN Office of Legal Affairs. He published an earlier version of this groundbreaking paper in 2003 for the UN Department of Political Affairs and later submitted it to the Fifth Conference of New or Restored Democracies in Mongolia.

48. Ibid., 82.

49. See Allison and Owada, *The Responsibilities of Democracies in Preventing Deadly Conflict*, Carnegie Commission on Preventing Deadly Conflict Discussion Paper, July 1999. See also John Shattuck, *Freedom on Fire: Human Rights Wars and America's Response* (Cambridge, MA: Harvard University Press, 2003).

50. I. William Zartman, *Cowardly Lions: Missed Opportunities to Prevent Deadly Conflict and State Collapse* (Boulder, CO: Lynne Rienner Publishers, 2005), 213.

51. Ibid., 222.

52. Ibid., 223.

53. Ibid., 224.

54. Mark Palmer, *Breaking the Real Axis of Evil: How to Oust the World's Last Dictators by 2025* (Lanham, MD: Rowman and Littlefield, 2003), 316–321.

Notes to Chapter 9

1. Paul Collier, *The Bottom Billion: Why the Poorest Countries Are Failing and What Can Be Done About It* (New York: Oxford University Press), 2007.

2. Carnegie Commission on Preventing Deadly Conflict, *Preventing Deadly Conflict, Final Report* (New York: Carnegie Corporation of New York, 1997).

3. Mahbub ul Haq, *Reflections on Human Development* (New York: Oxford University Press, 1995).

4. Amartya Sen, *Development as Freedom* (New York: Knopf, 1999).

5. Amartya Sen, *Identity and Violence: The Illusion of Destiny* (New York: Norton, 2006).

6. Joseph E. Stiglitz and Lyn Squire. "International Development: Is It Possible?" *Foreign Policy*, no. 110 (Spring 1998): 138–151.

7. Joseph Stiglitz and Andrew Charlton, *Fair Trade for All: How Trade Can Promote Development*, Initiative for Policy Dialogue Series C (New York: Oxford University Press, 2006). See also Stiglitz, *Making Globalization Work* (New York: W. W. Norton, 2006).

8. Joseph Stiglitz, *Globalization and Its Discontents* (New York: W. W. Norton, 2002), 246.

9. Larry Diamond, "Democracy, Development, and Good Governance: The Inseparable Links" (Annual Democracy and Governance Lecture, Center for Democratic Development, Accra, Ghana, March 1, 2005).

10. Ibid. See also Andreas Schedler, "Conceptualizing Accountability," in *The Self-Restraining State: Power and Accountability in New Democracies*, ed. Andreas Schedler, Larry Diamond, and Marc F. Plattner, 15 (Boulder, CO: Lynne Rienner Publishers, 1999).

11. Diamond, "Democracy, Development, and Good Governance."

12. Ibid.

13. WHO Commission on Macroeconomics and Health, *Macroeconomics and Health: Economic Development*, Report of the Commission on Macroeconomics and Health, Jeffrey D. Sachs, chair (Geneva, Switzerland: World Health Organization, 2001). Available at http://www.cid.harvard .edu/archive/cmh/cmhreport.pdf.

14. Ibid., 10.

15. Personal communication.

16. David A. Hamburg, "Conflict Prevention and Health: An Array of Opportunities," in *Anna Lindh Programme on Conflict Prevention, 2006 Edition*, ed. Anders Mellbourne, 33–44 (Hedemora, Sweden: Gidlunds förlag, 2006).

17. The Pew Research Center for the People and the Press, the Pew Global Project, *What the World Thinks In 2002: How Global Publics View: Their Lives, Their Countries, The World, America* (Washington, DC: Pew Research Center, 2002), 8, 18, 25, 48, 50. Available at http://people-press .org/reports/pdf/165.pdf.

18. David A. Hamburg, "Health as a Bridge to Peace" (paper delivered to the World Health Organization, New York City, February 10, 2005).

19. Kofi Annan, *Towards a Culture of Prevention: Statements by the Secretary-General of the United Nations* (New York: Carnegie Commission on Preventing Deadly Conflict, 1999), 28–29.

20. UN Development Programme, *Human Development Report 2005, International Coopera-tion at a Crossroads: Aid, Trade and Security in an Unequal World* (Washington, DC: UNDP, 2005), 161.

21. Joseph T. Siegle, Michael M. Weinstein, and Morton H. Halperin, "Why Democracies Excel," *Foreign Affairs* 83, no. 5 (September/October 2004): 57–71.

22. Ibid., 57.

23. Ibid.

24. Ibid., 59

25. Ibid., 61.

26. Ibid., 62–71.

27. Ibid.

28. Jeffrey D. Sachs, "On-the-Ground Solutions for Ending Poverty," in *The End of Poverty: Economic Possibilities for Our Time* (New York: Penguin Press, 2005), 226.

29. Ibid., 243.

30. UN Development Programme, *Human Development Report 2005,* 162.

31. Ibid., 162–163.

32. Ibid., 164.

33. Ibid., 166.

34. Ibid., 168.

35. Rodney W. Nichols, "Linking Science and Technology with Global Economic Development: A US Perspective," COSTED Occasional Paper no. 5, Committee on Science and Technology in Developing Countries, 1999.

36. Mohamed H. A. Hassan, "Can Science Save Africa," *Science* 292 (June 2001): 1609.

37. Inter Academy Council Report, Study Panel on Promoting Worldwide Science and Technology, Jacob Palis and Ismail Serageldin, co-chairs, *Inventing a Better Future: A Strategy for Building Worldwide Capacities in Science and Technology* (Amsterdam: Inter Academy Council, 2004). Available at http://www.interacademycouncil.net/CMS/Reports.aspx.

38. Inter Academy Council, "Science and Technology Research Found Critical to National Development," press release, February 6, 2004. Available at http://usinfo.state.gov/xarchives/display.html?p=washfile-english&y=2004&m=February&x=20040206162944XCretroP0.1297876.

39. Ibid.

40. Inter Academy Council Report, Study Panel on Agricultural Productivity in Africa, Speciosa Kazibwe, Rudy Rabbinge, and M. S. Swaminathan, co-chairs, *Realizing the Promise and Potential of African Agriculture* (Amsterdam: Inter Academy Council, June 2004). Available at http://www.interacademycouncil.net/CMS/Reports.aspx.

41. United Nations, "Study of African Agriculture to Be Presented to Secretary-General Kofi Annan at United Nations on 25 June," press release note no. 5873, June 21, 2004. Available at http://www.un.org/News/Press/docs/2004/note5873.doc.htm.

Notes to Chapter 10

1. David A. Hamburg and Beatrix A. Hamburg, *Learning to Live Together: Preventing Hatred and Violence in Child and Adolescent Development* (New York: Oxford University Press, 2004).

2. Morton Deutsch, *Resolution of Conflict: Constructive and Destructive Processes* (New Haven, CT: Yale University Press, 1973).

3. M. Van Slyck, M. Stern, and J. Zak-Place, "Promoting Optimal Adolescent Development Through Conflict Resolution Education, Training, and Practice: An Innovative Approach for Counseling Psychologists," *The Counseling Psychologist* 24 (1996): 433–461.

4. Elie Wiesel, *Night*, trans. Marion Wiesel (New York: Hill and Wang, 2006).

5. G. W. Allport, *The Nature of Prejudice* (Cambridge, MA: Addison-Wesley, 1954); cited in M. B. Brewer, "The Psychology of Prejudice: Ingroup Love or Outgroup Hate," *Journal of Social Issues* 55, no. 3 (1999): 429–444.

6. David A. Hamburg, *No More Killing Fields: Preventing Deadly Conflict* (Lanham, MD: Rowman and Littlefield, 2002).

7. School of International and Public Affairs, Columbia University, International Affairs, Course U8556, "Preventive Diplomacy and Conflict Resolution in the United Nations: Integrating Theory and Practice." Available at http://www.columbia.edu/cu/sipa/COURSES/2000-2001/u8556.html.

8. Stanford Program on International and Cross-Cultural Education, *Preventing Deadly Conflict: Toward a World Without War* (Stanford, CA: Stanford University Freeman Spogli Institute for International Studies, 2000). The grade range of this curriculum is secondary to community college.

9. Carnegie Commission on Preventing Deadly Conflict, *Preventing Deadly Conflict: Final Report* of the Carnegie Commission on Preventing Deadly Conflict (New York: Carnegie Corporation, 1997).

10. Amartya Sen, *Identity and Violence: The Illusion of Destiny* (New York: Norton, 2006).

11. David A. Hamburg, "Prejudice, Ethnocentrism, and Violence in an Age of High Technology," in *Carnegie Corporation of New York Annual Report* (New York: Carnegie Corporation of New York, 1984), 3–15.

12. Rolf Ekéus, "The Education Solution: Fostering Harmony in Diversity," *OSCE Magazine* (December 2004): 20–24. Available at www.osce.org.publications.

13. Ibid., 20.

14. Ibid., 21.

15. Ibid.

16. Ibid., 24.

17. Joan Ganz Cooney, *The Potential Uses of Television in Preschool Education: A Report to the Carnegie Corporation of New York* (New York: Carnegie Corporation of New York, 1996).

18. Hamburg and Hamburg, *Learning to Live Together*, 353–354.

19. See ibid. for a more detailed discussion.

20. Beatrix A. Hamburg, Delbert Elliott, and Kirk R. Williams, eds., *Violence in American Schools: A New Perspective* (New York: Cambridge University Press, 1998).

21. National Institute of Education, *Violent Schools—Safe Schools: The Safe School Study Report to Congress* (Washington, DC: U.S. Government Printing Office, 1978). See also Hamburg, Elliott, and Williams, *Violence in American Schools*.

22. Dan Olweus, "Bullying at School: Long-Term Outcomes for the Victims and an Effective School-Based Intervention Program," in *Aggressive Behavior: Current Perspectives,* ed. L. Rowell Huesmann, 116ff (New York: Plenum Press, 1994).

23. Peter K. Smith and Sonia Smart, eds., *School Bullying: Insights and Perspectives* (London: Routledge, 1994).

24. E. M. Hetherington and R. D. Parke, *Child Psychology: A Contemporary Viewpoint*, 5th ed. (New York: McGraw-Hill, 1999), 537.

25. William Dalrymple, "Inside the Madrasas," *New York Review of Books* 52, no. 19 (December 1, 2005): 16–20.

26. Ibid., 16.

27. Ibid.

28. A more recent report estimates their number as high as 20,000. See International Crisis Group, *Pakistan: Karachi's Madrasas and Violent Extremism,* Asia Report no. 130 (Brussels: International Crisis Group, 2007), 5. See also International Crisis Group, *Pakistan: Madrasas, Extremism and the Military,* Asia Report no. 36 (Brussels: International Crisis Group, 2002), i. This figure was amended July 15, 2005.

29. Tahir Andrabi, Jishnu Das, Asim Ijaz Khwaja, and Tristan Zajonc, "Religious School Enrollment in Pakistan: A Look at the Data," World Bank Policy Research working paper series no. WPS 3521, 2005, 4ff. Available at http://www-wds.worldbank.org/external/default/WDSContentServer/IW3P/IB/2005/02/28/000112742_20050228152509/Rendered/PDF/wps3521.pdf.

30. Dalrymple, "Inside the Madrasas," 17.

31. Olivier Roy, *Globalized Islam: The Search for a New Ummah,* CERI Series in Comparative Politics and International Studies (New York: Columbia University Press, 2006), 93; see the review by Max Rodenbeck, "The Truth About Jihad," *New York Review of Books,* August 11, 2005, cited in Dalrymple. "Inside the Madrasas."

32. Gilles Kepel, *The War for Muslim Minds: Islam and the West* (Cambridge, MA: Belknap Press, 2006), 112.

33. Louise Richardson, *What Terrorists Want: Understanding the Enemy, Containing the Threat* (New York: Random House, 2006).

34. The *Washington Post* Web site has a full report on these textbooks: see Joe Stephens and David B. Ottaway, "From US, the ABC's of Jihad," March 23, 2002. Available at http://www.washingtonpost.com/ac2/wp-dyn/A5339-2002Mar22?language=printer.

35. Yoginder Sikand, *Bastions of the Believers: Madrasas and Islamic Education in India* (New Delhi: Penguin India, 2004).

36. Hamburg and Hamburg, *Learning to Live Together,* 348ff.

Notes to Chapter 11

1. David A. Hamburg, "Human Rights and Warfare: An Ounce of Prevention Is Worth a Pound of Cure," in *Realizing Human Rights: Moving from Inspiration to Impact,* ed. Samantha Power and Graham Allison, 322 (New York: St. Martin's Press, 2000).

2. Carnegie Commission on Preventing Deadly Conflict, *Preventing Deadly Conflict, Final Report* (New York: Carnegie Corporation, 1997).

3. Louis Henkin, "Human Rights: Ideology and Aspiration, Reality and Prospect," in *Realizing Human Rights: Moving from Inspiration to Impact,* ed. Samantha Power and Graham Allison, 3–37 (New York: St. Martin's Press, 2000).

4. Ibid., 5.

5. Ibid., 8

6. Ibid., 9.

7. Ibid., 11.

8. Shirley Williams, "Human Rights in Europe," in *Realizing Human Rights: Moving from Inspiration to Impact,* ed. Samantha Power and Graham Allison, 77–110 (New York: St. Martin's Press, 2000).

9. Ibid., 77.

10. Ibid., 81–82.

11. Ibid., 78.

12. Ibid., 86.

13. Ibid., 88–89.

14. Anne-Marie Slaughter, *A New World Order* (Princeton, NJ: Princeton University Press, 2004).

15. Ibid., 26–27.

16. Richard J. Goldstone, "Advancing the Cause of Human Rights: The Need for Justice and Accountability," in *Realizing Human Rights: Moving from Inspiration to Impact*, ed. Samantha Power and Graham Allison, 206–207 (New York: St. Martin's Press, 2000).

17. Ibid., 208–210.

18. Slaughter, *A New World Order*, 67.

19. Ibid., 134.

20. Ibid., 148–149.

21. Ibid., 149–150.

22. Priscilla B. Hayner, *Unspeakable Truths: Facing the Challenge of Truth Commissions* (New York: Routledge, 2001).

23. Ibid., 206

24. Ibid., 207.

25. Dennis Ross, "Pretoria Calling," *New York Times*, October 20, 2005, A27.

26. Priscilla Hayner, *Unspeakable Truths: Facing the Challenge of Truth Commission*, Japanese ed. (forthcoming).

27. Martha Minow, *Between Vengeance and Forgiveness: Facing History after Genocide and Mass Violence* (Boston: Beacon Press, 1999).

28. David A. Hamburg, "Human Rights and Warfare: An Ounce of Prevention Is Worth a Pound of Cure," in *Realizing Human Rights: Moving from Inspiration to Impact*, ed. Samantha Power and Graham Allison, 321–336 (New York: St. Martin's Press, 2000).

29. See also David P. Forsythe, *The Internationalization of Human Rights* (Lexington, MA: Lexington Books, 1991).

30. Jimmy Carter, "The American Road to a Foreign Rights Policy," in *Realizing Human Rights: Moving from Inspiration to Impact*, ed. Samantha Power and Graham Allison, 49–61 (New York: St. Martin's Press, 2000).

31. Ibid., 50.

32. Ibid., 51.

33. Ibid., 52.

34. Ibid., 55.

35. Ibid., 56.

36. Ibid., 57.

37. Ibid., 60.

Notes to Chapter 12

1. Richard F. Grimmett, *Conventional Arms Transfers to Developing Nations, 1999–2006*, CRS Report for Congress (Washington, DC: Congressional Research Service, 2007), 4, 22ff. Available at http://www.fas.org/asmp/resources/110th/RL34187.pdf.

2. The Weapons of Mass Destruction Commission, "Weapons of Terror: Freeing the World of Nuclear, Biological and Chemical Arms," final report, Stockholm, Sweden, June 1, 2006.

3. William J. Perry, "Preparing for the Next Attack," *Foreign Affairs* 80, no. 3 (November/December 2001): 31–45.

4. See Graham T. Allison, *Nuclear Terrorism: The Ultimate Preventable Catastrophe* (New York: Henry Holt and Company, Times Books, 2004), 69.

5. Pierre Claude Nolin, *The Security of WMD Related Material in Russia*, NATO report 178 STC 05 E, December 2005, Sections II:B 13ff and IV:61ff. Available at www.naa.be.default.asp?SGIRTCYT=695 (accessed June 1, 2006).

6. Sam Nunn, "Our New Security Framework," *Washington Post*, October 8, 2001. Available at http://www.nti.org/c_press/c3_opeds.html.

7. See Sam Nunn and Michele Flournoy, "A Test of Leadership on Sea Island," *Washington Post*, June 8, 2004. Available at http://www.nti.org/c_press/c3_opeds.html. See also Sam Nunn, William Perry, and Eugene Habiger, "Still Missing: A Nuclear Strategy," *Washington Post*, May 21, 2002. Available at http://www.nti.org/c_press/c3_opeds.html.

8. Nolin, *The Security of WMD Related Material in Russia*.

9. Ibid. See also Alex Rodriguez, "NATO: Russia Resisting Efforts to Secure WMD," *Chicago Tribune*, December 22, 2005. Excerpted at the Metropolitan Medical System segment on the Federal Emergency Management Agency Web site: http://mmrs.fema.gov/news/terrorism/2005/dec/nter2005-12-22.aspx (accessed June 1, 2006).

10. Nolin, *The Security of WMD Related Material in Russia*, Section II:E.39.

11. Ibid., Section III:44–58.

12. Rodriguez, "NATO: Russia Resisting Efforts to Secure WMD."

13. Jimmy Carter, "Saving Nonproliferation," *Washington Post*, March 28, 2005, A17.

14. Allison, *Nuclear Terrorism*.

15. Ibid., 2.

16. Ibid., 10.

17. Ibid.

18. The Weapons of Mass Destruction Commission, "Weapons of Terror: Freeing the World of Nuclear, Biological and Chemical Arms," 37. See also Allison, *Nuclear Terrorism*, 75.

19. Allison, *Nuclear Terrorism*, 83.

20. Ibid., 61.

21. Ibid., 170–175.

22. Ibid., 140–175.

23. Bob Herbert, "A World Gone Mad," *New York Times*, July 31, 2006, A17.

24. Ibid.

25. Vali Nasr, "When the Shiites Rise," *Foreign Affairs* 85, no. 4 (July/August 2006): 57–74; Nasr, *The Shia Revival* (New York: W. W. Norton, 2006).

26. Nasr, "When the Shiites Rise," 59.

27. Sidney D. Drell and James Goodby, *The Gravest Danger: Nuclear Weapons* (Stanford, CA: Hoover Institution Press, 2003).

28. In September 1996, 71 states signed the Comprehensive Test Ban Treaty, including five of the eight states then holding nuclear arms. By 2006, 176 states had signed, and 132 had ratified the treaty. (These did not include India, Pakistan, and North Korea. Both India and Pakistan conducted nuclear tests in 1998, and North Korea withdrew from the 1968 Nuclear Non-Proliferation Treaty [NPT] in 2003.) To enter into force, the Comprehensive Test Ban Treaty must be ratified by the 44 Annex 2 states. China, Colombia, Egypt, Indonesia, Iran, Israel, and the United States have signed but have not ratified it. The earlier NPT of 1968 attempted to limit the spread of nuclear weapons. One hundred eighty-eight states are signatories, and in 1995 the treaty was extended indefinitely.

But two (India and Pakistan) of the seven states that have openly tested nuclear weapons and one possible nuclear power (Israel) have not ratified it, and North Korea left it.

29. Gareth Evans, "Conflict Prevention and NGOs," in *Anna Lindh Programme on Conflict Prevention, 2005 Edition: Development, Security and Conflict Prevention,* ed. Anders Mellbourn, 121–136 (Hedemora, Sweden: Gidlunds förlag, 2005).

30. Ibid., 128.

31. See George P. Shultz et al., "A World Free of Nuclear Weapons," *Wall Street Journal,* January 4, 2007, A15.

Notes to Chapter 13

1. "On Anniversary of Rwanda Genocide, Secretary-General Says Current Challenge Is to Make Responsibility to Protect Operational," UN Department of Public Information, Secretary-General SG/SM/10934 AFR/1519, April 5, 2007. Available at http://www.un.org/news/press/docs/2007/sgsm10934.doc.htm (accessed April 17, 2007).

2. Milton J. Esman and Shibley Telhami, eds., *International Organizations and Ethnic Conflict* (Ithaca, NY: Cornell University Press, 1995).

3. Detlev Wolter, *A United Nations for the 21st Century: From Reaction to Prevention* (Baden-Baden, Germany: Nomos-Verlag, 2007).

4. Connie Peck, *Sustainable Peace: The Role of the UN and Regional Organizations in Preventing Deadly Conflict* (Lanham, MD: Rowman and Littlefield, 1998).

5. Anna Mark-Jungkvist and Sten Ask, eds., *The Adventure of Peace: Dag Hammarskjold and the Future of the United Nations* (New York: Palgrave Macmillan, 2006).

6. Jan Eliasson and Peter Wallensteen, "Preventive Diplomacy," in *The Adventure of Peace: Dag Hammarskjold and the Future of the United Nations,* ed. Anna Mark-Jungkvist and Sten Ask, 292 (New York: Palgrave Macmillan, 2006).

7. Ibid., 296.

8. Boutros Boutros-Ghali, "An Agenda for Peace: Preventive Diplomacy, Peace Making and Peace Keeping: Report of the Secretary-General Pursuant to the Statement Adopted by the Summit Meeting of the Security Council on 31 January 1992, A/47/277-S/24111 (17 June 1992)," available at www.un.org/Docs/SG/agpeace.html; Boutros-Ghali, "An Agenda for Development: Report of the Secretary-General Boutros Boutros-Ghali, A/48/935 (6 May 1994)," available at www.un.org/Docs/SG/agdev.html; Boutros-Ghali, "An Agenda for Democratization: Supplement to Reports A/50/332 and A/51/512 on Democratization (17 December 1996)," available at www.library.yale.edu/un/un3d3.htm.

9. Kofi Annan, *Progress Report of the Secretary-General on the Prevention of Armed Conflict* (sixtieth session, agenda item 12, 06-39322 [E], September 2006).

10. Kofi Annan, *Towards a Culture of Prevention: Statements by the Secretary-General of the United Nations* (New York: Carnegie Commission on Preventing Deadly Conflict, 1999).

11. Melanie C. Greenberg, John H. Barton, and Margaret E. McGuinness, *Words Over War: Mediation and Arbitration to Prevent Deadly Conflict,* Carnegie Commission series (Lanham, MD: Rowman and Littlefield, 2000).

12. Gareth Evans, *Cooperating for Peace: The Global Agenda for the 1990s and Beyond* (St. Leonard's, Australia: Allen and Unwin, 1993).

13. See Connie Peck, "Special Representatives of the Secretary-General," in *The UN Security Council: From the Cold War to the 21st Century,* ed. David M. Malone, 325–339 (Boulder, CO: Lynne Rienner Publishers, 2004).

14. Connie Peck, *Sustainable Peace: The Role of the UN and Regional Organizations in Preventing Conflict,* Carnegie Commission Series (Lanham, MD: Rowman and Littlefield, 1998).

15. Elizabeth M. Cousens, "Conflict Prevention," in *The UN Security Council from the Cold War to the 21st Century,* ed. David M. Malone, 108–115 (Boulder, CO: Lynne Rienner Publishers, 2004).

16. A 1998 study on the subject, more pertinent than ever, is Donald Kennedy et al., *Environmental Quality and Regional Conflict, A Report to the Carnegie Commission on Preventing Deadly Conflict* (New York: Carnegie Corporation of New York, 1998). Available at http://wwics.si.edu/subsites/ccpdc/pubs/ken/ken.htm.

17. See Richard N. Haass, *The Opportunity: America's Moment to Alter History's Course* (Cambridge, MA: Perseus Publishing, 2005).

18. Graham T. Allison and Hisashi Owada, "The Responsibilities of Democracies in Preventing Deadly Conflict: Reflections and Recommendations," Carnegie Commission on Preventing Deadly Conflict Discussion Paper, July 1999.

19. Council on Foreign Relations and Freedom House, *Enhancing U.S. Leadership at the United Nations: Report of an Independent Task Force,* David Dreier and Lee H. Hamilton, Co-Chairs; Lee Feinstein and Adrian Karatnycky, Project Co-Directors (New York: Council on Foreign Relations, 2001). Available at http://www.cfr.org/contents/publications/attachments/UN_TaskForce.pdf.

20. Ibid., 3.

21. Interview with Jean Arnault, Geneva, November 2001. Arnault is the SRSG in Afghanistan, head of UNAMA (the UN Assistance Mission in Afghanistan). He succeeded Lakhtar Brahimi.

22. Greenberg, Barton, and McGuiness, *Words over War,* 366.

23. Catherine Guicherd, "Building Partnerships for Crisis Prevention, Conflict Resolution and Peacebuilding Between the United Nations and Regional Organizations," *International Peace Academy (IPA) Meeting News,* April 4–5, 2006. Available at the International Peace Academy Web site, http://www.ipacademy.org/Publications/Publications.htm. See also an outstanding earlier study: Elizabeth M. Cousens, Chetan Kumar, and Karin Wermister, eds., *Peacebuilding as Politics: Cultivating Peace in Fragile Societies* (Boulder, CO: Lynne Rienner Publishers, 2001).

24. Brian Urquhart, "The Outlaw World," *New York Review of Books* (May 11, 2006): 25–28.

25. Roméo Dallaire, "The End of Innocence," in *Hard Choices: Moral Dilemmas in Humanitarian Intervention,* ed. Jonathan Moore, 78–79 (Lanham, MD: Rowman and Littlefield, 1998).

26. Jeffrey Laurenti, "Grand Goals, Modest Results: The UN in Search of Reform," *Current History* 104, no. 686 (December 2005): 431–437.

27. Ibid., 433.

28. Andrew Mack, ed., *Human Security Report 2005: War and Peace in the 21st Century,* University of British Columbia Human Security Centre (New York: Oxford University Press, 2005), 1–2. Available at http://www.humansecurityreport.info.

29. Ibid., 34f.

30. Ibid., 155ff.

31. Ibid., 148ff.

32. James Dobbins et al., *The UN's Role in Nation Building: From the Congo to Iraq* (Santa Monica, CA: RAND Corporation, 2005).

33. Monty G. Marshall and Ted Robert Gurr, *Peace and Conflict 2005,* Center for International Development and Conflict Management (College Park: University of Maryland Press, 2005).

34. Paul Kennedy, *The Parliament of Man: The Past, Present, and Future of the United Nations* (New York: Random House, 2006).

35. United Nations, "Kofi Annan, Address of the UN Secretary-General to the Commission on Human Rights in Geneva 7 April 2004," published in United Nations, "'Risk of Genocide Remains Frighteningly Real,' Secretary-General Tells Human Rights Commission as He Launches Action Plan to Prevent Genocide," press release SG/SM/9245 AFR/891 HR/CN/1077 (New York, April 8, 2004). Available at UN Information Service Vienna, http://www.unis.unvienna.org/unis/pressrels/2004/sgsm9245.html.

36. July 12, 2004, news report on www.un.org/apps/news/story.asp?NewsID=11313&Cr=genocide&Cr=genocide&Cr1= (accessed July 13, 2004).

37. UN Security Council Resolution 1366 (2001), adopted August 30, 2001, pp. 2 and 3. Available online at www.un.org/docs/scres/2001/sc2001.htm.

38. Kofi Annan, "Outline of the Mandate for the Special Adviser on the Prevention of Genocide," annex to "Letter dated 12 July 2004 from the Secretary-General addressed to the President of the Security Council," UN Security Council document S/2004/567.

39. "Outcome Report of UN Summit of September 14–16, 2005, UN General Assembly, Resolution 60/1, Adopted by the General Assembly on the 2005 World Summit Outcome, October 24, 2005, agenda items 46 and 120," 30. Available at http://www.un.org/summit2005/documents.html.

40. See Adam LeBor, *"Complicity with Evil": The United Nations in the Age of Modern Genocide* (New Haven, CT: Yale University Press, 2006).

Notes to Chapter 14

1. Harlan Cleveland, *Birth of a New World: An Open Moment for International Leadership* (San Francisco: Jossey-Bass, 1993).

2. John Baylis and Steve Smith, eds., *The Globalization of World Politics* (New York: Oxford University Press, 1997).

3. The statement is available at www.eu2001.se/static/eng/pdf/violent.PDF.

4. Every six months, the Presidency of the European Union passes from one member state to another. The country holding the Presidency chairs formal and informal meetings of the EU Council in Brussels, in Luxembourg, and in its own cities. The head of that country chairs meetings of the European Council. The Presidency of the Council has an essential role in its legislative and political decisionmaking. It also chairs working groups that prepare the ministerial meetings of the Council. The Presidency represents the Council in its dealings with the other EU institutions, such as the European Parliament and the European Commission. The member state holding the Presidency also represents the EU internationally, in close cooperation with the EU's high representative for the common foreign and security policy, Javier Solana, and the European Commission. Finally, the Presidency acts on behalf of the EU in international organizations, conferences, and fora.

5. The PSC, also known from the French as COPS (Comité politique et de securité), observes the international situation to help shape EU foreign policy and its implementation. Comprising member state representatives with the rank of ambassador, as well as representatives of the Commission and of the secretary-general of the Council, the PSC is invaluable for EU crisis management activities. See www.eu2004.nl/default.asp?CMS_ITEM=8D74BD1EDC2840A1AF8B536CD4FCEE91X1X59462X24.

6. "The European Union at a Glance." Available at www.europa.eu.int (accessed July 26, 2004).

7. Timothy Garton Ash, *Free World: America, Europe, and the Surprising Future of the West* (New York: Random House, 2004).

8. Ibid., 149.

9. Amartya Sen, *Development as Freedom* (New York: Knopf, 1999), cited in Ash, *Free World*, 151.

10. Ash, *Free World*, 169.

11. Ibid., 199.

12. Ibid., 226.

13. Mark Leonard, *Why Europe Will Run the 21st Century* (New York: Public Affairs, 2005).

14. Ibid., xi.

15. See John Gillingham, *European Integration 1950–2003: Superstate or New Market Economy?* (New York: Cambridge University Press, 2003), 502.

16. Leonard, *Why Europe Will Run the 21st Century*, 9, 45.

17. Ibid., 138.

18. Ibid., 139.

19. European Commission Communication COM(2003) 526 final, September 10, 2003.

20. The EDF, established in the 1957 Treaty of Rome to give technical and financial assistance to African countries with colonial and historical links to Europe, has become the main instrument for EC aid for development cooperation in the African Caribbean Pacific (ACP) countries and the Overseas Countries and Territories (OCT). Information available at http://europa.eu.int/scadplus/leg/en/lvb/r12102.htm.

21. Committee for Civilian Aspects of Crisis Management, "Draft Report to the European Council on EU Activities in the Framework of Prevention, Including Implementation of the EU Programme for the Prevention of Violent Conflicts," 10051/04, Brussels, June 2, 2004.

22. Ibid.

23. European Union, "Research for a Secure Europe," March 15, 2004. The report proposed an annual minimum of 1 billion euros to fund the development of security systems, including those necessary for the success of EU conflict prevention missions.

24. "Draft Report to the European Council on EU Activities in the Framework of Prevention, Including Implementation of the EU Programme for the Prevention of Violent Conflicts, 10022/1/04 REV1," Brussels, Council of the European Union, June 2, 2004, 16. Available at http://register.consilium.eu.int/pdf/en/04/st10/st10022-re01.en04.pdf.

25. Anders Mellbourn, *Development, Security and Conflict Prevention, Anna Lindh Programme on Conflict Prevention, 2005 Edition* (Hedemora, Sweden: Gidlunds förlag, 2005).

26. Jim Cloos, "Conflict Prevention as an Instrument in the EU's Security Toolbox," in *Development, Security and Conflict Prevention, Anna Lindh Programme on Conflict Prevention, 2005 Edition*, ed. Anders Mellbourn, 14–23 (Hedemora, Sweden: Gidlunds förlag, 2005).

27. Ibid., 14.

28. Ibid., 14–15.

29. European Security Strategy, quoted in Cloos, "Conflict Prevention as an Instrument in the EU's Security Toolbox," 15.

30. Cloos, "Conflict Prevention as an Instrument in the EU's Security Toolbox," 15.

31. Ibid., 16-17.

32. Louis Michel, "Development Cooperation as a European Tool of Conflict Prevention," in *Development, Security and Conflict Prevention, Anna Lindh Programme on Conflict Prevention, 2005 Edition*, ed. Anders Mellbourn, 59 (Hedemora, Sweden: Gidlunds förlag, 2005).

33. Ibid., 60.

34. Ibid., 62.
35. Ibid., 66.

Notes to Chapter 15

1. David A. Hamburg, *No More Killing Fields: Preventing Deadly Conflict* (Lanham, MD: Rowman and Littlefield, 2002), 287–288.
2. Information from OSCE factsheet. Available at http://www.osce.org/item/13554 .html?ch=53 (accessed March 22, 2007).
3. Ibid.
4. Ibid.
5. Ibid.
6. OSCE information is available at www.osce.org/eea/13052.html (accessed March 22, 2007).
7. Information from OSCE factsheet. Available at http://www.osce.org/item/13554 .html?ch=53 (accessed March 22, 2007).
8. "Countering the Threat of Excess Small Arms and Ammunition in Tajikistan." Available at http://www.osce.org/item/23257.html (accessed March 22, 1007).
9. The Edinburgh Declaration of the OSCE Parliamentary Assembly is available at http://www.oscepa.org/admin/getbinary.asp?FileID=531 (accessed March 22, 2007).
10. OSCE information is available at www.osce.org/secretariat/13076.html (accessed March 22, 2007).
11. Information from OSCE factsheet. Available at http://www.osce.org/item/13554 .html?ch=53 (accessed March 22, 2007).
12. Information from ODIHR Factsheet. Available at http://www.osce.org/odihr/13421.html (accessed March 22, 2007).
13. Hamburg, *No More Killing Fields,* 122–124.
14. Max van der Stoel, "Democracy and Human Rights. On the Work of the High Commissioner on National Minorities of the OSCE," "Early Warning and Early Action: Preventing Inter-Ethnic Conflict," and "The Involvement of the High Commissioner Is No Stigma, but an Act of Solidarity," in *Peace and Stability Through Human and Minority Rights,* ed. Wolfgang Zellner and Falk Lange (Baden-Baden, Germany: Nomos Verlag, 1999). A cogent summary of this experience by van der Stoel's excellent deputy, John Packer, is included in Chapter 7 on preventive diplomacy; for an additional discussion see John Packer, "The Role and Work of the OSCE High Commissioner on National Minorities as an Instrument of Conflict Prevention," in *Sharing Best Practices on Conflict Prevention: Strengthening UN Capacities for the Prevention of Violent Conflict—The UN, Regional and Subregional Organizations, National and Local Actors—IPA Policy Report* (New York: International Peace Academy, 2002), 10–14.
15. Walter A. Kemp, ed., *Quiet Diplomacy in Action: The OSCE High Commissioner on National Minorities* (The Hague: Kluwer Law International, 2005), 121–122.
16. Hamburg, *No More Killing Fields,* 128–129.
17. Heather F. Hurlburt, "Preventive Diplomacy: Success in the Baltics," in *Opportunities Missed, Opportunities Seized: Preventive Diplomacy in the Post–Cold War World,* Carnegie Commission on Preventing Deadly Conflict Series, ed. Bruce W. Jentleson, 91–107 (Lanham, MD: Rowman and Littlefield, 1999).
18. The Hague Recommendations Regarding the Education Rights of National Minorities (1996); the Oslo Recommendations Regarding the Linguistic Rights of National Minorities (1998); Lund Recommendations on the Effective Participation of National Minorities in Public Life (1999);

and Guidelines to Assist National Minority Participation in the Electoral Process (2001), a collaboration with other organizations.

19. Foundation on Inter-Ethnic Relations, *The Lund Recommendations on the Effective Participation of National Minorities in Public Life* (The Hague: Foundation on Inter-Ethnic Relations, 1999). Available at http://www.osce.org/documents/hcnm/1999/09/2698_en.pdf.

20. See Kemp, *Quiet Diplomacy in Action.*

21. "Recurrent Themes and Issues," Kemp, *Quiet Diplomacy in Action,* 105–136.

22. Ibid., 109.

23. Ibid., 123.

24. Ibid.

25. Rolf Ekéus, "The Education Solution: Fostering Harmony in Diversity," *OSCE Magazine,* December 2004, 20.

26. David A. Hamburg and Beatrix A. Hamburg, *Learning to Live Together: Preventing Hatred and Violence in Child and Adolescent Development* (New York: Oxford University Press, 2004).

27. P. Terrence Hopmann, "The Organization for Security and Cooperation in Europe: Its Contribution to Conflict Prevention and Resolution," in *International Conflict Resolution After the Cold War,* ed. Paul C. Stern and Daniel Druckman, 569–616 (Washington, DC: National Academy Press, 2000), and "Scholar Searches for Long-lasting Security in Postcommunist Regions," *Briefings,* the Watson Institute for International Studies at Brown University (Winter/Spring 2000).

Notes to Chapter 16

1. "Partnership for Peace: Invitation Document Issued by the Heads of State and Government Participating in the Meeting of the North Atlantic Council, Brussels, January 10, 1994." Available at www.nato.int/docu/basictxt/b940110a.htm.

2. "Partnership for Peace: Framework Document Issued by the Heads of State and Government Participating in the Meeting of the North Atlantic Council in Brussels, January 10, 1994." Available at www.nato.int/docu/basictxt/b940110b.htm.

3. "Basic Document of the Euro-Atlantic Partnership Council," Sintra, Portugal, May 30, 1997. Available at www.nato.int/docu/basictxt/b021121a.htm.

4. "Report on the Comprehensive Review of the Euro-Atlantic Partnership Council and Partnership for Peace," Prague summit, November 21, 2002. Available at http://www.nato.int/docu/basictxt/b021122e.htm.

5. "Partnership Action Plan Against Terrorism," Prague summit, November 22, 2002. Available at http://www.nato.int/basictxt/b021122e.htm.

6. "NATO Crisis Management," NATO Public Diplomacy Division, NATO Briefing, October 2003 (accessed December 28, 2004).

7. "Final Communiqué, Ministerial Meeting of the North Atlantic Council Held in Reykjavik on 14 May 2002 (Reykjavik, Iceland: May 14, 2002)," NATO Public Data Service, Paragraph 5. Available at NATO press archives, http://ls.kuleuven.be/cgi-bin/wa?A2=ind0205&L=natopres&T=0&F=&S=&P=1022.

8. Information available at http://www.nato.int/docu/update/2004/12-december/e1202a.htm (accessed December 28, 2004).

9. Ivo Daalder and James Goldgeier, "Global NATO," *Foreign Affairs* 85, no. 5 (September/October 2006): 108.

10. Ibid.

11. "Preamble," The North Atlantic Treaty, April 4, 1949. Available at http://www.nato.int/docu/basictxt/treaty.htm.

12. Daalder and Goldgeier, "Global NATO," 111.

Notes to Chapter 17

1. Kofi Annan, "Message of the UN Secretary-General to the Open Debate of the General Assembly on His Report on the Prevention of Armed Conflict," New York, September 7, 2006.

2. See David A. Hamburg and Beatrix A. Hamburg, *Learning to Live Together: Preventing Hatred and Violence in Child and Adolescent Development* (New York: Oxford University Press, 2004).

3. David A. Hamburg, "Human Rights and Warfare: An Ounce of Prevention Is Worth a Pound of Cure," in *Realizing Human Rights: Moving from Inspiration to Impact,* ed. Samantha Power and Graham Allison, 322 (New York: St. Martin's Press, 2000).

4. Ibid.

5. Kofi Annan, *We the Peoples: The Role of the United Nations in the Twenty-first Century* (New York: United Nations, 2000).

6. Kofi Annan, "Keynote Address" (Speech delivered at Stockholm International Forum, Conference Four, "Preventing Genocide: Threats and Responsibilities," January 26, 2004). Published in *Stockholm International Forum, Conference Four, Preventing Genocide: Threats and Responsibilities* (Stockholm: Regeringskanzliet, 2004), 18–20. Available at http://www.manskligarattigheter.gov.se/stockholmforum/2004/conference_2004.html and at http://www.un.org/News/ossg/sg/stories/statements_search_full.asp?statID=51.

7. "Outcome Report of UN Summit of September 14–16, 2005, UN General Assembly, Resolution 60/1, Adopted by the General Assembly on the 2005 World Summit Outcome, October 24, 2005, agenda items 46 and 120," 30. Available at http://www.un.org/summit2005/documents.html.

8. "The European Union at a Glance." Available at www.europa.eu.int (accessed July 26, 2004).

9. OSCE information available at www.osce.org/general/ (accessed July 28, 2004).

10. David A. Hamburg, *No More Killing Fields: Preventing Deadly Conflict* (Lanham, MD: Rowman and Littlefield, 2002), 287–288.

11. Ibid., 122–124.

12. Max van der Stoel, "Democracy and Human Rights. On the Work of the High Commissioner on National Minorities of the OSCE," "Early Warning and Early Action: Preventing Inter-Ethnic Conflict," and "The Involvement of the High Commissioner Is No Stigma, but an Act of Solidarity," in *Peace and Stability Through Human and Minority Rights,* ed. Wolfgang Zellner and Falk Lange (Baden-Baden, Germany: Nomos Verlag, 1999).

13. "Report on the Comprehensive Review of the Euro-Atlantic Partnership Council and Partnership for Peace," Prague Summit, November 21, 2002. Available at www.nato.int/docu/basictxt/b021122e.htm.

14. "Final Communiqué, Ministerial Meeting of the North Atlantic Council Held in Reykjavik on 14 May 2002 (Reykjavik, Iceland: May 14, 2002)," NATO Public Data Service, Paragraph 5. Available at NATO press archives, http://ls.kuleuven.be/cgi-bin/wa?A2=ind0205&L=natopres&T=0&F=&S=&P=1022.

Note to Chapter 18

1. David Brion Davis, *Inhuman Bondage: The Rise and Fall of Slavery in the New World* (New York: Oxford University Press, 2006), 1, 331.

Notes to Chapter 19

1. For their generous cooperation in making this information available, I am deeply grateful to Kofi Annan; Elisabeth Lindenmayer, senior Columbia University researcher and longtime UN collaborator with Kofi Annan; Ruth McCoy, chief of staff to Kofi Annan; and Priscilla Hayner, director of the Peace and Justice Program at the International Center for Transitional Justice.

2. K. Annan, interview conducted on March 20, 2008, with David Hamburg.

3. Ibid.

4. Ibid.

5. Roger Cohen, "How Kofi Annan Rescued Kenya," *New York Review of Books,* August 14, 2008, 51–53.

6. K. Annan, interview.

7. Ibid.

8. Ibid.

9. Ibid.

10. Web page of the Kenyan Ministry of Foreign Affairs, www.mfa.go.ke/mfacms/index .php?option=com_content&task=view&id=191&Itemid=62.

11. This information was generously provided by the following individuals, to whom I am most grateful: Connie Peck, principal coordinator for the Program in Peacemaking at UNITAR; Nita Yawanarajah, political affairs officer at the UN Department of Political Affairs Mediation Support Unit; Ambassador Ragnar Ängeby of Folke Bernadotte Academy in Sweden; Priscilla Hayner, director of the Peace and Justice Program of ICTJ; and Kelvin Ong, senior political affairs officer of the UN Department of Political Affairs Mediation Support Unit.

12. Connie Peck, "The Role of Special Representatives of the Secretary-General in Conflict Prevention," in *Third Parties and Conflict Prevention: Anna Lindh Programme on Conflict Prevention, 2008 Edition,* ed. Anders Mellbourn and Peter Wallensteen (Stockholm: Gidlungs Förlag, 2008), 223–232.

13. "DPA Strengthened," *Politically Speaking: Bulletin of the United Nations Department of Political Affairs* (Spring 2009): 5, available at http://www.un.org/Depts/dpa/newsletters/DPA% 20bulletin_spring09.pdf.

14. Ban Ki-moon, "Report to the 62nd Session of the UN General Assembly," United Nations A/62/521, November 2, 2007.

15. "Strengthening the Department of Political Affairs: A 'Critical Investment' in Preventing and Resolving Conflicts," *Politically Speaking: Bulletin of the United Nations Department of Political Affairs* (Winter 2007–2008): 1–3, available at http://www.un.org/Depts/dpa/newsletters/DPA% 20Bulletin%20Winter%202007–2008.pdf.

16. "Mediation Support Unit in Motion," *Politically Speaking: Bulletin of the United Nations Department of Political Affairs* (Winter–Spring 2007–2008): 4, 15, 23.

17. Priscilla Hayner, *Negotiating Justice: Guidance for Mediators* (New York: Center for Humanitarian Dialogue and the International Center for Transitional Justice, February 2009).

18. UN Security Council, Report of the Secretary-General on enhancing mediation and its support activities, 8 April 2009, S/2009/189, available at www.unhcr.org/refworld/docid/49e6f2880 .html (accessed July 2, 2009).

19. This information was made available by Gay Rosenblum-Kumar, public administration officer at the UN Department of Economic and Social Affairs; Chetan Kumar, interagency liaison specialist at the Bureau for Crisis Prevention and Recovery, UNDP; and development economist Sakiko Fukuda-Parr, professor of international affairs at the New School. I am deeply grateful for their generous help.

20. Bureau for Crisis Prevention and Recovery Web site, http://www.undp.org/cpr/we_are/we_are.shtml.

21. BCPR OVERVIEW, June 19, 2008, available at http://www.undp.org/cpr/documents/BCPROverview_Jun08.pdf; "About BCPR," *CPR Newsletter* 1, no. 1 (Winter 2005): 1–2.

22. *Bureau for Crisis Prevention and Recovery 2007 Annual Report* (New York: UNDP, July 2008), available at http://www.undp.org/cpr/AnnualReports/2007/AnnualReport2007_Full_LoRes.pdf.

23. Ibid.

24. Ibid.

25. Sakiko Fukuda-Parr and Robert Picciotto, "Conflict Prevention and Development Cooperation" (paper prepared for the JICA/UNDP-sponsored project for policy dialogue on conflict prevention and violent conflict, background paper 1 for the project, May 28, 2007).

26. I am most grateful to Lawrence Woocher, senior program officer, USIP Center for Conflict Analysis and Prevention, for his generous cooperation in making this information available.

27. Genocide Prevention Task Force, *Preventing Genocide: A Blueprint for U.S. Policymakers* (Washington, DC: United States Holocaust Memorial Museum, the American Academy of Diplomacy, and the Endowment of the United States Institute of Peace, 2008).

28. Ibid., xvi.

29. Ibid., xvii–xviii.

30. For generously providing this information, I am deeply indebted to Javier Solana; his chief of staff, Enrique Mora; and Ambassador István Lakatos, Foreign Ministry of Hungary.

31. "Concept Paper for the Establishment of an International Centre for the Prevention of Genocide and Mass Atrocities," October 2008, prepared by the Foreign Ministry of Hungary primarily for its government.

32. Here is a quotation from the concept paper that reflects both the cumulative effort and the determination of the Hungarian government to make a major contribution: "The Concept Paper is based upon the excellent work initiated by the Madariaga Foundation and conducted by a Steering Committee chaired by Dr. David Hamburg. The Government of Hungary would like to take this opportunity to express its gratitude for all those dedicated experts, diplomats, and international civil servants who do their utmost in the interest of the establishment of the Centre."

33. I am deeply grateful to John Stremlau, vice president for peace programs at the Carter Center, for his generous cooperation in making this information available.

34. John Stremlau, "Commentary: A Victory for Democracy in Africa," *CNN.com* (January 12, 2009), available at http://www.cnn.com/2009/WORLD/africa/01/12/stremlau.ghana/index.html.

35. Ibid.

36. Ibid.

37. Ibid.

38. I deeply grateful to Amartya Sen, professor of economics and philosophy at Harvard University, for his generous cooperation in making this information available.

39. Commonwealth Commission on Respect and Understanding, *Civil Paths to Peace: Report of the Commonwealth Commission on Respect and Understanding* (London: Commonwealth Secretariat, August 2007), 9.

40. Ibid.

41. Ibid., p. 10.

42. Ibid., p. 11.

43. I thank arms control expert Sidney Drell, professor emeritus of the Stanford Linear Accelerator Center, for his generous cooperation in making this information available.

44. George P. Shultz, William J. Perry, Henry A. Kissinger, and Sam Nunn, "A World Free of Nuclear Weapons," *Wall Street Journal*, January 4, 2007, A15.

45. Sidney D. Drell, "Report from Hoover/Nuclear Threat Initiative Conference: Reykjavik Revisited—Steps Toward a World Free of Nuclear Weapons: Stanford University" (presented at the International Conference on Achieving the Vision of a World Free of Nuclear Weapons, Oslo, February 26–27, 2008).

46. Office of the Press Secretary, the White House, "Joint Statement by President Dmitriy Medvedev of the Russian Federation and President Barack Obama of the United States of America," April 1, 2009.

Bibliography

Adam, Heribert, and Kogila Moodley. *The Negotiated Revolution.* Johannesburg: Jonathan Ball Press, 1993.

African Union. http://www.africa-union.org.

Akçam, Taner. *A Shameful Act: The Armenian Genocide and the Question of Turkish Responsibility.* Translated by Paul Bessemer. New York: Henry Holt/Metropolitan Books, 2006.

Allison, Graham T. *Nuclear Terrorism: The Ultimate Preventable Catastrophe.* New York: Henry Holt and Company, Times Books, 2004.

Allison, Graham T., and Hisashi Owada. "The Responsibilities of Democracies in Preventing Deadly Conflict: Reflections and Recommendations." Carnegie Commission on Preventing Deadly Conflict Discussion Paper, July 1999.

Allison, Graham T., and William L. Ury, with Bruce J. Allyn. *Windows of Opportunity: From Cold War to Peaceful Competition in U.S. Soviet Relations.* Cambridge, MA: Ballinger Publishing, 1989.

Allport, Gordon W. *The Nature of Prejudice.* Cambridge, MA: Addison-Wesley, 1954.

Aly, Gotz. *"Final Solution": Nazi Population Policy and the Murder of the European Jews.* New York: Oxford University Press, 1999.

Annan, Kofi. "Progress Report of the Secretary-General on the Prevention of Armed Conflict." Sixtieth session, agenda item 12, 06-39322 (E), September 2006.

———. *Towards a Culture of Prevention: Statements by the Secretary-General of the United Nations.* New York: Carnegie Commission on Preventing Deadly Conflict, 1999.

———. *We the Peoples: The Role of the United Nations in the Twenty-First Century.* New York: United Nations, 2000.

Ash, Timothy Garton. *Free World: America, Europe, and the Surprising Future of the West.* New York: Random House, 2004.

Balakian, Peter. *The Burning Tigris: The Armenian Genocide and America's Response.* New York: HarperCollins, 2003.

Bandura, Albert. *Aggression: A Social Learning Analysis.* Englewood Cliffs, NJ: Prentice Hall, 1973.

———. "Moral Disengagement in the Perpetration of Inhumanities." *Personality and Social Psychology Review* 3 (1999): 193–209.

Bartov, Omer, and Phyllis Mack, eds. *In God's Name: Genocide and Religion in the Twentieth Century.* New York: Berghahn Books, 2001.

Bauer, Yehuda. "Holocaust and Genocide: Some Comparisons." In *Lessons and Legacies: The Meaning of the Holocaust in a Changing World,* edited by Peter Hayes, 36–46. Evanston, IL: Northwestern University Press, 1991.

———. *Rethinking the Holocaust.* New Haven, CT: Yale University Press, 2001.

Baylis, John, and Steve Smith, eds. *The Globalization of World Politics.* New York: Oxford University Press, 1997.

Benesch, Susan. "Inciting Genocide, Pleading Free Speech." *World Policy Journal* 21, no. 2 (Summer 2004): 62–69.

Boutros-Ghali, Boutros. "An Agenda for Democratization: Supplement to Reports A/50/332 and A/51/512 on Democratization (17 December 1996)." Available at www.library.yale.edu/un/un3d3.htm.

———. "An Agenda for Development: Report of the Secretary-General Boutros Boutros-Ghali, A/48/935 (6 May 1994)." Available at www.un.org/Docs/SG/agdev.html.

———. "An Agenda for Peace: Preventive Diplomacy, Peacemaking and Peace-keeping: Report of the Secretary-General Pursuant to the Statement Adopted by the Summit Meeting of the Security Council on 31 January 1992, A/47/277–S/24111 (17 June 1992)." Available at www.un.org/Docs/SG/agpeace.html.

Brewer, M. B. "The Psychology of Prejudice: Ingroup Love or Outgroup Hate." *Journal of Social Issues* 55, no 3 (1999): 429–444.

Brody, J. Kenneth. *The Avoidable War: Lord Cecil and the Policy of Principle, 1933–1935.* Vol. 1. New Brunswick, NJ: Transaction, 1999.

Brown, Michael, and Richard N. Rosecrance. *The Costs of Conflict: Prevention and Cure in the Global Arena.* Lanham, MD: Rowman and Littlefield, 1999.

Bundy, McGeorge, William J. Crowe, and Sidney D. Drell. *Reducing Nuclear Danger: The Road Away from the Brink.* New York: Council on Foreign Relations Press, 1993.

Bunn, Matthew. *Securing the Bomb 2007.* Cambridge, MA: Belfer Center, Harvard University, 2007. Available at www.nti.org/securingthebomb.

Carley, Michael Jabara. *1939: The Alliance That Never Was and the Coming of World War II.* New York: Ivan Dee, 1999.

Carment, David, and Albrecht Schnabel, eds. *Conflict Prevention from Rhetoric to Reality.* Vol. 2, *Opportunities and Innovations.* Lanham, MD: Lexington Books, 2004.

Carnegie Commission on Preventing Deadly Conflict. *Perspectives on Prevention: Preventive Diplomacy, Preventive Defense, and Conflict Resolution: A Report of Two Conferences at Stanford University and the Ditchley Foundation.* New York: Carnegie Corporation of New York, 1999.

———. *Preventing Deadly Conflict, Final Report.* Washington, DC: Carnegie Commission on Preventing Deadly Conflict, 1997.

Carnegie Council on Adolescent Development. *Great Transitions: Preparing Adolescents for a New Century.* Concluding Report. New York: Carnegie Corporation of New York, 1995.

Carnegie Council for Ethics in International Affairs. http://www.cceia.org/index.html.

Carothers, Thomas. *Aiding Democracy Abroad: The Learning Curve.* Washington, DC: Carnegie Endowment for International Peace, 1999.

Carter, Jimmy. "The American Road to a Foreign Rights Policy." In *Realizing Human Rights: Moving from Inspiration to Impact.* Edited by Samantha Power and Graham Allison, 49–61. New York: St. Martin's Press, 2000.

———. *Our Endangered Values: America's Moral Crisis.* New York: Simon and Schuster, 2006.

Carter Center. http://www.cartercenter.org/homepage.html.

Chartock, Roselle, and Jack Spencer, eds. *Can It Happen Again? Chronicles of the Holocaust.* New York: Black Dog and Leventhal, 1995.

Cheadle, Don, and John Prendergast. *Not on Our Watch: The Mission to End Genocide in Darfur and Beyond.* New York: Hyperion, 2007.

Chesterman, Simon. *You the People: The United Nations, Transitional Administration, and State-Building.* New York: Oxford University Press, 2004.

Chirot, Daniel, and Clark McCauley. *Why Not Kill Them All? The Logic and Prevention of Mass Political Murder.* Princeton, NJ: Princeton University Press, 2006.

Cirincione, Joseph. *Bomb Scare: The History and Future of Nuclear Weapons.* New York: Columbia University Press, 2007.

Cleveland, Harlan. *Birth of a New World: An Open Moment for International Leadership.* San Francisco: Jossey-Bass, 1993.

Cloos, Jim. "Conflict Prevention as an Instrument in the EU's Security Toolbox." In *Development, Security and Conflict Prevention, Anna Lindh Programme on Conflict Prevention, 2005 Edition.* Edited by Anders Mellbourn, 14–23. Hedemora, Sweden: Gidlunds förlag, 2005.

Cohen, Roger. "How Kofi Annan Rescued Kenya." *New York Review of Books,* August 14, 2008, 51–53.

Collier, Paul. *The Bottom Billion: Why the Poorest Countries Are Failing and What Can Be Done About It.* New York: Oxford University Press, 2007.

Collins, Craig, and John Packer. *Options and Techniques for Quiet Diplomacy.* Conflict Prevention Handbook Series, 1. Stockholm: Folke Bernadotte Academy, 2006.

Commonwealth Commission on Respect and Understanding. *Civil Paths to Peace: Report of the Commonwealth Commission on Respect and Understanding.* London: Commonwealth Secretariat, August 2007.

Cooney, Joan Ganz. *The Potential Uses of Television in Preschool Education: A Report to the Carnegie Corporation of New York.* New York: Carnegie Corporation of New York, 1996.

Cordesman, Anthony H., and Khalid R. Al-Rodhan. *Iran's Weapons of Mass Destruction: The Real and Potential Threat.* Washington, DC: Center for Strategic and International Studies/CSIS Press, 2006.

Cortright, David. *Gandhi and Beyond: Nonviolence for an Age of Terrorism.* Boulder, CO: Paradigm Publishers, 2006.

Council of Europe. http://www.coe.int.

Council on Foreign Relations (including the Center for Preventive Action). http://www.cfr.org.

Cousens, Elizabeth M. "Conflict Prevention." In *The UN Security Council from the Cold War to the 21st Century.* Edited by David M. Malone, 108–115. Boulder, CO: Lynne Rienner Publishers, 2004.

Cousens, Elizabeth M., and Chetan Kumar, with Karin Wermester, eds. *Peacebuilding as Politics: Cultivating Peace in Fragile Societies.* Boulder, CO: Lynne Rienner Publishers, 2001.

Craig, Gordon. *Europe Since 1815.* New York: Holt, Rinehart and Winston, 1961.

———. *Germany, 1866–1945.* New York: Oxford University Press, 1978.

Crozier, Andrew. *The Causes of the Second World War.* Malden, MA: Blackwell, 1997.

Daalder, Ivo, and James Goldgeier. "Global NATO." *Foreign Affairs* 85, no. 5 (September/October 2006): 105–113.

Dadrian, Vahakn N. *The History of the Armenian Genocide.* Rev. ed. New York: Oxford University Press, 1997.

Dahl, Robert A. *On Democracy.* New Haven, CT: Yale University Press, 1998.

Dallaire, Roméo. *Shake Hands with the Devil: The Failure of Humanity in Rwanda.* New York: Carrol and Graf Publishers, 2004.

Dalrymple, William. "Inside the Madrasas." *New York Review of Books* 52, no. 19 (December 1, 2005): 16–20.

Davis, David Brion. *Inhuman Bondage: The Rise and Fall of Slavery in the New World.* New York: Oxford University Press, 2006.

Dawidowicz, Lucy S. *The War Against the Jews.* New York: Bantam, 1976.

Deák, István. "The Crime of the Century." *New York Review of Books* (September 26, 2002): 48–51.

———. "Improvising the Holocaust." *New York Review of Books,* September 23, 2004, 78–81.

Denman, Roy. *Missed Chances: Britain and Europe in the Twentieth Century.* London: Cassell, 1996.

Des Forges, Alison. *Leave None to Tell the Story: Genocide in Rwanda.* New York: Human Rights Watch Report, 1999. Available at Human Rights Watch Web site, http://www.hrw.org/reports/1999/rwanda/index.htm.

Deutsch, Morton. *The Resolution of Conflict: Constructive and Destructive Processes.* New Haven, CT: Yale University Press, 1973.

Devji, Faisal. *Landscapes of the Jihad: Militancy, Morality and Modernity.* Ithaca, NY: Cornell University Press, 2005.

Diamond, Larry. *Developing Democracy: Toward Consolidation.* Baltimore, MD: Johns Hopkins University Press, 1999.

———. "Universal Democracy?" *Policy Review* (June and July 2003): 3–25.

Dobbins, James, Seth G. Jones, Keith Crane, Andrew Rathmell, Brett Steele, Richard Teltschik, and Anga Timilsina. *The UN's Role in Nation Building: From the Congo to Iraq.* Santa Monica, CA: RAND Corporation, 2005.

Dreier, David, and Lee H. Hamilton, Co-Chairs; Lee Feinstein and Adrian Karatnycky, Project Co-Directors, Council on Foreign Relations and Freedom House. *Enhancing U.S. Leadership at the United Nations: Report of an Independent Task Force.* New York: Council on Foreign Relations, 2002. Available at http://www.cfr.org/content/publications/attachments/UN_TaskForce.pdf.

Drell, Sidney D., and James Goodby. *The Gravest Danger: Nuclear Weapons.* Stanford, CA: Hoover Institution Press, 2003.

du Toit, André. *Understanding South African Political Violence: A New Problematic?* Geneva: UN Research Institute for Social Research, 1993.

Ekéus, Rolf. "The Education Solution: Fostering Harmony in Diversity." *OSCE Magazine,* December 2004. Available at www.osce.org.publications.

Eliasson, Jan, and Peter Wallensteen. "Preventive Diplomacy." In *The Adventure of Peace: Dag Hammarskjold and the Future of the United Nations.* Edited by Anna Mark-Jungkvist and Sten Ask. New York: Palgrave Macmillan, 2006.

Esman, Milton J., and Shibley Telhami, eds. *International Organizations and Ethnic Conflict.* Ithaca, NY: Cornell University Press, 1995.

European Union. http://europa.eu.

Evans, Gareth. "Conflict Prevention and NGOs." In *Development, Security and Conflict Prevention, Anna Lindh Programme on Conflict Prevention, 2005 Edition.* Edited by Anders Mellbourn, 121–136. Hedemora, Sweden: Gidlunds förlag, 2005.

———. *Cooperating for Peace: The Global Agenda for the 1990s and Beyond.* St. Leonard's, Australia: Allen and Unwin, 1993.

Evans, Richard J. *The Coming of the Third Reich.* New York: Penguin Books, 2003.

———. *The Third Reich in Power.* New York: Penguin Books, 2005.

Feil, Scott R. *Preventing Genocide: How the Early Use of Force Might Have Succeeded in Rwanda.* New York: Carnegie Commission on Preventing Deadly Conflict, 1998.

Feinstein, L. *Darfur and Beyond: What Is Needed to Prevent Mass Atrocities.* Council Special Report no. 22. New York: Council on Foreign Relations, 2007.

Finney, Patrick, ed. *The Origins of the Second World War.* New York: Arnold, 1997.

Fisher, R. J., ed. *The Social Psychology of Intergroup and International Conflict Resolution.* New York: Springer-Verlag, 1990.

Fisher, Roger, and William Ury. *Getting to Yes: Negotiating Agreement Without Giving In.* New York: Penguin, 1983.

Forsythe, David P. *The Internationalization of Human Rights.* Lexington, MA: Lexington Books, 1991.

Friedlander, Saul. *Nazi Germany and the Jews.* Vol. 1, *The Years of Persecution, 1933–1939.* New York: Harper Perennial, 1998.

———. *The Years of Extermination: Nazi Germany and the Jews, 1939–1945.* New York: Harper-Collins, 2007.

Gastrow, Peter. *Bargaining for Peace: South Africa and the National Peace Accord.* Washington, DC: United States Institute of Peace Press, 1995.

Gellately, Robert. *Lenin, Stalin, and Hitler: The Age of Social Catastrophe.* New York: Alfred A. Knopf, 2007.

Gellately, Robert, and Ben Kiernan, eds. *The Specter of Genocide: Mass Murder in Historical Perspective.* New York: Cambridge University Press, 2003.

Genocide Prevention Task Force. *Preventing Genocide: A Blueprint for U.S. Policymakers.* Washington, DC: United States Holocaust Memorial Museum, the American Academy of Diplomacy, and the Endowment of the United States Institute of Peace, 2008.

George, Alexander, and David A. Hamburg. "Toward an International Center for Prevention of Genocide." *Foreign Policy Forum* 15/16 (2005): 85–95.

George, Alexander L. *Bridging the Gap: Theory and Practice in Foreign Policy.* Washington, DC: United States Institute of Peace Press, 1993.

———. "Crisis Prevention Reexamined." In *Managing U.S.-Soviet Rivalry: Problems of Crisis Prevention,* 365–398. Boulder, CO: Westview Press, 1983.

George, Alexander L., Philip J. Farley, and Alexander Dallin, eds. *U.S.-Soviet Security Cooperation: Achievements, Failures, Lessons.* New York: Oxford University Press, 1988.

Gillingham, John. *European Integration 1950–2003: Superstate or New Market Economy?* Cambridge: Cambridge University Press, 2003.

Glass, James M. *"Life Unworthy of Life": Racial Phobia and Mass Murder in Hitler's Germany.* New York: Basic Books, 1997.

Glover, Jonathan. *Humanity: A Moral History of the Twentieth Century.* New Haven, CT: Yale University Press, 2000.

Goldstein, Joshua S. *The Real Price of War: How You Pay for the War on Terror.* New York: New York University Press, 2004.

Goldstone, Richard J. "Advancing the Cause of Human Rights: The Need for Justice and Accountability." In *Realizing Human Rights: Moving from Inspiration to Impact.* Edited by Samantha Power and Graham Allison, 206–207. New York: St. Martin's Press, 2000.

Goodall, Jane, and David A. Hamburg. "Chimpanzee Behavior as a Model for the Behavior of Early Man: New Evidence on Possible Origins of Human Behavior." In *American Handbook of Psychiatry,* vol. 6. Edited by David A. Hamburg and H. Brodie. New York: Basic Books, 1975.

Gorbachev, Mikhail. "On Nonviolent Leadership." In *Essays on Leadership,* 67–70. New York: Carnegie Commission on Preventing Deadly Conflict, 1998.

Gourevitch, Philip. *We Wish to Inform You That Tomorrow We Will Be Killed with Our Families: Stories from Rwanda.* New York: Farrar, Straus and Giroux, 1998.

Greenberg, Melanie C., John H. Barton, and Margaret E. McGuinness. *Words over War: Mediation and Arbitration to Prevent Deadly Conflict.* Carnegie Commission Series. Lanham, MD: Rowman and Littlefield, 2000.

Grimmett, Richard F. *Conventional Arms Transfers to Developing Nations, 1999–2006.* CRS Report for Congress. Washington, DC: Congressional Research Service, 2007. Available at http://www.fas.org/asmp/resources/110th/RL34187.pdf.

Gurr, Ted Robert. *Minorities at Risk: A Global View of Ethnopolitical Conflicts.* Washington, DC: United States Institute of Peace Press, 1993.

Haass, Richard N. *The Opportunity: America's Moment to Alter History's Course.* Cambridge, MA: Perseus Publishing, 2005.

Hamburg, Beatrix A., Delbert Elliott, and Kirk R. Williams, eds. *Violence in American Schools: A New Perspective.* New York: Cambridge University Press, 1998.

Hamburg, David A. "Conflict Prevention and Health: An Array of Opportunities." In *Anna Lindh Programme on Conflict Prevention, 2006 Edition.* Edited by Anders Mellbourne, 33–44. Hedemora, Sweden: Gidlunds förlag, 2006.

———. "Human Rights and Warfare: An Ounce of Prevention Is Worth a Pound of Cure." In *Realizing Human Rights: Moving from Inspiration to Impact.* Edited by Samantha Power and Graham Allison, 321–336. New York: St. Martin's Press, 2000.

———. *No More Killing Fields: Preventing Deadly Conflict.* Lanham, MD: Rowman and Littlefield, 2002.

———. *Preventing Contemporary Intergroup Violence and Education for Conflict Resolution.* New York: Carnegie Commission on Preventing Deadly Conflict, 1999.

Hamburg, David A., and Beatrix A. Hamburg. *Learning to Live Together: Preventing Hatred and Violence in Child and Adolescent Development.* New York: Oxford University Press, 2004.

Hamburg, David A., and E. R. McCown, eds. *The Great Apes.* Menlo Park, CA: Benjamin/Cummings, 1997.

Hamburg, David A., and Michelle B. Trudeau. *Biobehavioral Aspects of Aggression.* New York: Alan R. Liss, 1981.

Hamburg, David A., and Jane van Lawick-Goodall. "Factors Facilitating Development of Aggressive Behavior in Chimpanzees and Humans." In *Determinants and Origins of Aggressive Behavior.* Edited by W. W. Hartup and J. DeWit, 59–85. The Hague: Mouton, 1974.

Haq, Mahbub ul. *Reflections on Human Development.* New York: Oxford University Press, 1995.

Harvard University, JFK School of Government, Belfer Center for Science and International Affairs. http://belfercenter.ksg.harvard.edu.

Hassan, Mohamed H.A. "Can Science Save Africa?" *Science* 292 (June 2001): 1609.

Hayner, Priscilla B. *Unspeakable Truths: Facing the Challenge of Truth Commissions.* New York: Routledge, 2001.

———. *Negotiating Justice: Guidance for Mediators.* New York: Center for Humanitarian Dialogue and the International Center for Transitional Justice, February 2009.

Henig, Ruth. *The Origins of the Second World War, 1933–1939.* New York: Routledge, 1991.

Henkin, Louis. "Human Rights: Ideology and Aspiration, Reality and Prospect." In *Realizing Human Rights: Moving from Inspiration to Impact.* Edited by Samantha Power and Graham Allison, 3–37. New York: St. Martin's Press, 2000.

Hetherington, E. M., and R. D. Parke. *Child Psychology: A Contemporary Viewpoint.* 5th ed. New York: McGraw-Hill, 1999.

Hewitt, J. Joseph, Jonathan Wilkenfeld, and Ted Robert Gurr. *Peace and Conflict 2008.* Boulder: Paradigm Publishers, 2007.

Hitler, Adolf. *Mein Kampf.* Translated by Ralph Manheim. New York: Houghton Mifflin, 1943.

Hochschild, Adam. *King Leopold's Ghost: A Story of Greed, Terror and Heroism in Colonial Africa.* Boston: Houghton Mifflin, 1998.

Homer-Dixon, Thomas F. *Environment, Scarcity, and Violence.* Princeton, NJ: Princeton University Press, 1999.

Hopmann, P. Terrence. *Building Security in Post–Cold War Eurasia.* Peaceworks no. 31. Washington, DC: United States Institute of Peace Press, 1999.

———. "The Organization for Security and Cooperation in Europe: Its Contribution to Conflict Prevention and Resolution." In *International Conflict Resolution After the Cold War.* Edited by Paul C. Stern and Daniel Druckman, 569–616. Washington, DC: National Academy Press, 2000.

Huddleston, Trevor. *Naught for Your Comfort*. New York: Collins, 1977.

Hull, Isabel V. "Military Culture and the Production of 'Final Solutions' in the Colonies." In *The Specter of Genocide: Mass Murder in Historical Perspective*. Edited by Robert Gellately and Ben Kiernan, 141–162. New York: Cambridge University Press, 2003.

Hurlburt, Heather F. "Preventive Diplomacy: Success in the Baltics." In *Opportunities Missed, Opportunities Seized: Preventive Diplomacy in the Post–Cold War World*. Edited by Bruce W. Jentleson, 91–107. New York: Carnegie Commission on Preventing Deadly Conflict, 1999.

Inter-Academy Council Report, Study Panel on Agricultural Productivity in Africa, Speciosa Kazibwe, Rudy Rabbinge, and M. S. Swaminathan, co-chairs. *Realizing the Promise and Potential of African Agriculture*. Amsterdam: Inter Academy Council, 2004. Available at http://www.interacademycouncil.net/CMS/Reports.aspx.

Inter-Academy Council Report, Study Panel on Promoting Worldwide Science and Technology, Jacob Palis and Ismail Serageldin, co-chairs. *Inventing a Better Future: A Strategy for Building Worldwide Capacities in Science and Technology*. Amsterdam: Inter Academy Council, 2004. Available at http://www.interacademycouncil.net/CMS/Reports.aspx.

International Center for Transitional Justice. http://www.ictj.org.

International Criminal Court. http://www.icc-cpi.int/Menus/ICC?lan=en-GB.

International Crisis Group. http://www.crisisgroup.org.

International IDEA. *Ten Years of Supporting Democracy Worldwide*. Stockholm, Sweden: International Institute for Democracy and Electoral Assistance, 2005. Available at http://www.idea.int/publications/anniversary/upload/Inlay_senttoprint_30May05.pdf.

International Peace Institute. http://www.ipacademy.org.

Jentleson, Bruce W., ed. *Opportunities Missed, Opportunities Seized: Preventive Diplomacy in the Post–Cold War World*. Carnegie Commission on Preventing Deadly Conflict Series. Lanham, MD: Rowman and Littlefield, 1999.

Jones, Bruce W. *Peacemaking in Rwanda: The Dynamics of Failure*. Boulder, CO: Lynne Rienner Publishers, 2001.

Kanninen, Tapio, and Katarina Sehm Patomäki, eds. *Building Democracy from Manila to Doha: The Evolution of the Movement of New or Restored Democracies*. Helsinki Process Publication Series. Helsinki: Ulkoasiainministeriön Julkaisuja, 2005.

Kennedy, Donald, et al. *Environmental Quality and Regional Conflict, a Report to the Carnegie Commission on Preventing Deadly Conflict*. New York: Carnegie Corporation of New York, 1998. Available at http://wwics.si.edu/subsites/ccpdc/pubs/ken/ken.htm.

Kennedy, Paul. *The Parliament of Man: The Past, Present, and Future of the United Nations*. New York: Random House, 2006.

Kemp, Walter A., ed. *Quiet Diplomacy in Action: The OSCE High Commissioner on National Minorities*. The Hague: Kluwer Law International, 2005.

Kepel, Gilles. *The War for Muslim Minds: Islam and the West*. Translated By Pascale Ghazaleh. Cambridge, MA: Belknap Press, 2006.

Kershaw, Ian. *Hitler, 1889–1936: Hubris*. New York: Norton, 1998.

Kiernan, Ben. *Blood and Soil: A World History of Genocide and Extermination from Sparta to Darfur*. New Haven, CT: Yale University Press, 2007.

Ki-moon, Ban. "Report to the 62nd Session of the UN General Assembly." United Nations A/62/521, November 2, 2007.

King, Mary. *Mahatma Gandhi and Martin Luther King, Jr: The Power of Nonviolent Action*. Paris: UNESCO, 1999.

Kuper, Leo. *The Prevention of Genocide.* New Haven, CT: Yale University Press, 1985.

Kuperman, Alan J. "The Other Lesson of Rwanda: Mediators Sometimes Do More Harm Than Good." *SAIS Review* 16, no. 1 (Winter/Spring 1996): 221–240.

Lancaster, Carol. *Foreign Aid: Diplomacy, Development, Domestic Politics.* Chicago: University of Chicago Press, 2007.

Laqueur, Walter. *Fascism: Past, Present, Future.* New York: Oxford University Press, 1996.

Laurenti, Jeffrey. "Grand Goals, Modest Results: The UN in Search of Reform." *Current History* 104, no. 686 (December 2005): 431–437.

Lemarchand, René. "The Burundi Genocide" and "The Rwanda Genocide." In *Century of Genocide, Second Edition: Critical Essays and Eyewitness Accounts,* edited by Samuel Totten, William S. Parsons, and Israel Charny, 321–338 and 395–414. New York: Routledge, 2004.

Leonard, David K., and Scott Straus. *Africa's Stalled Development: International Causes and Cures.* Boulder, CO: Lynne Rienner Publishers, 2003.

Leonard, Mark. *Why Europe Will Run the 21st Century.* New York: Public Affairs, 2005.

Lewis, Bernard. *The Emergence of Modern Turkey.* New York: Oxford University Press, 1961.

———. *Semites and Anti-Semites: An Inquiry into Conflict and Prejudice.* New York: Norton, 1999.

Lund, Michael. *Preventing Violent Conflicts: A Strategy for Preventive Diplomacy.* Washington, DC: United States Institute of Peace Press, 1996.

Lyman, Princeton N. "South Africa in Retrospect." In *Beyond Humanitarianism: What You Need to Know About Africa and Why It Matters.* Edited by Princeton N. Lyman and Patricia Dorff, 45–68. New York: Council on Foreign Relations/Foreign Affairs, 2007.

Lyman, Princeton N., and Patricia Dorff, eds. *Beyond Humanitarianism: What You Need to Know About Africa and Why It Matters.* New York: Council on Foreign Relations/Foreign Affairs, 2007.

Mack, Andrew, ed. *Human Security Report 2005: War and Peace in the 21st Century.* University of British Columbia Human Security Centre. New York: Oxford University Press, 2005. Available at http://www.humansecurityreport.info.

Mamdani, Mahmoud. *When Victims Become Killers: Colonialism, Nativism and the Genocide in Rwanda.* Princeton, NJ: Princeton University Press, 2001.

Mandela, Nelson. *Long Walk to Freedom: The Autobiography of Nelson Mandela.* Boston: Little, Brown, 1994.

Marks, Susan Collins. *Watching the Wind: Conflict Resolution During South Africa's Transition to Democracy.* Washington, DC: United States Institute of Peace Press, 2000.

Marshall, Monty G., and Ted Robert Gurr. *Peace and Conflict 2005.* Center for International Development and Conflict Management. College Park, MD: University of Maryland, 2005.

Mathews, Anthony S. *Freedom, State Security and the Rule of Law: Dilemmas of the Apartheid Society.* Cape Town, South Africa: Juta, 1986,

McCormick, John. *The European Superpower.* New York: Palgrave Macmillan, 2007.

McGrew, W. C., L. F. Marchant, and T. Nishida, eds. *Great Ape Societies.* Cambridge: Cambridge University Press, 1996.

Meier, Deborah W. "Undermining Democracy: 'Compassionate Conservatism' and Democratic Education." *Dissent* (Fall 2006): 71–75.

Mellbourn, Anders, ed. *Development, Security and Conflict Prevention, Anna Lindh Programme on Conflict Prevention, 2005 Edition.* Hedemora, Sweden: Gidlunds förlag, 2005.

———. *Development, Health and Conflict Prevention, Anna Lindh Programme on Conflict Prevention, 2006 Edition.* Hedemora, Sweden: Gidlunds förlag, 2006.

Melson, Robert. *Revolution and Genocide: On the Origins of the Armenian Genocide and the Holocaust.* Chicago: University of Chicago Press, 1996.

Mendelson, Sara E., and John K. Glenn. "Democracy Assistance and NGO Strategies in Post-Communist Societies." Working paper of the Carnegie Endowment for International Peace, 2000.

Merkl, Peter H. *The Making of a Stormtrooper.* Princeton, NJ: Princeton University Press, 1980.

Michel, Louis. "Development Cooperation as a European Tool of Conflict Prevention." In *Development, Security and Conflict Prevention, Anna Lindh Programme on Conflict Prevention, 2005 Edition.* Edited by Anders Mellbourn, 59–75. Hedemora, Sweden: Gidlunds förlag, 2005.

Milgram, Stanley. "Behavioral Study of Obedience." *Journal of Abnormal and Social Psychology* 67 (1963): 371–378.

———. "The Compulsion to Do Evil: Obedience to Criminal Orders." *Patterns of Prejudice* 1 (1967).

———. *Obedience to Authority: An Experimental View.* New York: Harper and Row, 1974.

Minow, Martha. *Between Vengeance and Forgiveness: Facing History After Genocide and Mass Violence.* Boston: Beacon Press, 1999.

Morgenthau, Henry. *Ambassador Morgenthau's Story.* Edited by Ara Serafian. Reading, PA: Taderon Press, 2000. Ann Arbor, MI: Gomidas Institute Books.

Muscat, Robert J. *Investing in Peace: How Development Aid Can Prevent or Promote Conflict.* Armonk, NY: M. E. Sharpe, 2002.

Myers, David G. *Social Psychology.* 3rd ed. New York: McGraw-Hill, 1990.

Naimark, Norman M. *Fires of Hatred: Ethnic Cleansing in Twentieth-Century Europe.* London: Harvard University Press, 2001.

Nasr, Vali. "When the Shiites Rise." *Foreign Affairs* 85, no. 4 (July/August 2006): 57–74.

Newman, Leonard S., and Ralph Erber. *Understanding Genocide: The Social Psychology of the Holocaust.* New York: Oxford University Press, 2002.

Nichols, Rodney W. "Linking Science and Technology with Global Economic Development: A U.S. Perspective." COSTED Occasional Paper no. 5. Committee on Science and Technology in Developing Countries, September 1999.

Nolin, Pierre Claude. "The Security of WMD Related Material in Russia." NATO report 178 STC 05 E, December 2005. Available at www.naa.be.default.asp?SGIRTCYT=695.

North Atlantic Treaty Organization (NATO). http://www.nato.int/cps/en/natolive/index.htm.

Ogata, Sadako. *The Turbulent Decade: Confronting the Refugee Crises of the 1990s.* New York: W. W. Norton, 2005.

Olweus, Dan. "Bullying at School: Long-Term Outcomes for the Victims and an Effective School-Based Intervention Program." In *Aggressive Behavior: Current Perspectives,* edited by L. Rowell Huesmann, 97–130. New York: Plenum Press, 1994.

Organisation for Security and Cooperation in Europe. http://www.osce.org.

Overy, Richard. "Misjudging Hitler: A.J.P. Taylor and the Third Reich." In *The Origins of the Second World War Reconsidered: A.J.P. Taylor and the Historians,* 2d ed. Edited by Gordon Martel, 103–104. New York: Routledge, 1999.

———. *The Origins of the Second World War.* 2nd ed. New York: Longman, 1998.

Packer, John. "The Role and Work of the OSCE High Commissioner on National Minorities as an Instrument of Conflict Prevention." In *Sharing Best Practices on Conflict Prevention: Strengthening UN Capacities for the Prevention of Violent Conflict—The UN, Regional and Subregional Organizations, National and Local Actors—IPA Policy Report,* 10–14. New York: International Peace Academy, 2002.

Palmer, Mark. *Breaking the Real Axis of Evil: How to Oust the World's Last Dictators by 2025.* Lanham, MD: Rowman and Littlefield, 2003.

Parker, R.A.C. *Churchill and Appeasement.* London: Macmillan, 2000.

Peck, Connie. "Special Representatives of the Secretary-General." In *The UN Security Council: From the Cold War to the 21st Century*. Edited by David M. Malone, 325–339. Boulder, CO: Lynne Rienner Publishers, 2004.

———. *Sustainable Peace: The Role of the UN and Regional Organizations in Preventing Conflict*. Carnegie Commission Series. Lanham, MD: Rowman and Littlefield, 1998.

———. "Training as a Means to Build Capacity in Conflict Prevention: The UNITAR Approach." In *Conflict Prevention: From Rhetoric to Reality*. Edited by David Carment and Albrecht Schnabel. Vol. 2, *Opportunities and Innovations*, 227–249. Lanham, MD: Lexington Books, 2004.

———. "The Role of Special Representatives of the Secretary-General in Conflict Prevention." In *Third Parties and Conflict Prevention: Anna Lindh Programme on Conflict Prevention, 2008 Edition*, ed. Anders Mellbourn and Peter Wallensteen. Stockholm: Gidlungs Förlag, 2008, 223–232.

Perry, William J. "Preparing for the Next Attack." *Foreign Affairs* 8, no. 6 (November/December 2001): 31–45.

Peukert, Detlev J. K. *The Weimar Republic: The Crisis of Classical Modernity*. Translated by Richard Deveson. New York: Hill and Wang, 1989.

Pond, Elizabeth. *The Rebirth of Europe*. Rev. ed. Washington, DC: Brookings Institution Press, 1999.

Power, Samantha. *A Problem from Hell: America and the Age of Genocide*. New York: Basic Books, 2002.

Power, Samantha, and Graham T. Allison, eds. *Realizing Human Rights: Moving from Inspiration to Impact*. New York: St. Martin's Press, 2000.

Project on Ethnic Relations. http://www.per-usa.org.

Prunier, Gerard. *The Rwanda Crisis: History of a Genocide*. New York: Columbia University Press, 1995.

Purkitt, Helen E., and Stephen F. Burgess. *South Africa's Weapons of Mass Destruction*. Bloomington: Indiana University Press, 2005.

Redlich, Fritz. *Hitler: Diagnosis of a Destructive Prophet*. New York: Oxford, 1999.

Reeves, Eric. "Watching Genocide, Doing Nothing: The Final Betrayal of Darfur." *Dissent*, Fall 2006, 5–9.

Richardson, Louise. *What Terrorists Want: Understanding the Enemy, Containing the Threat*. New York: Random House, 2006.

Rose, Richard. "How Muslims View Democracy: Evidence from Central Asia." *Journal of Democracy*, 13, no. 4 (October 2002): 102–111.

Roseman, Mark. *The Wannsee Conference and the Final Solution*. New York: Picador, 2002.

Roy, Olivier. *Globalized Islam: The Search for a New Ummah*. CERI Series in Comparative Politics and International Studies. New York: Columbia University Press, 2006.

Rubin, Barnett L. *Blood on the Doorstep: The Politics of Preventive Action*. New York: Century Foundation Press, 2002.

Rubin, Jeffery Z., Dean G. Pruitt, and Sung Hee Kim. *Social Conflict: Escalation, Stalemate, and Settlement*. 2nd ed. New York: McGraw-Hill, 1994.

Sachs, Jeffrey D. *The End of Poverty: Economic Possibilities for Our Time*. New York: Penguin Press, 2005.

Sageman, Marc. *Understanding Terror Networks*. Philadelphia: University of Pennsylvania Press, 2004.

Sale, Kirkpatrick. *The Conquest of Paradise*. New York: Plume, 1992.

Saunders, Harold H. "Interactive Conflict Resolution: A View for Policy Makers on Making and Building Peace." In *International Conflict Resolution After the Cold War*. Edited by Paul C. Stern and Daniel Druckman, 251–293. Washington, DC: National Academy Press, 2000.

Schedler, Andreas, Larry Diamond, and Marc F. Plattner. *The Self-Restraining State: Power and Accountability in New Democracies.* Boulder, CO: Lynne Rienner Publishers, 1999.

Schnabel, Albrecht, ed. *Conflict Prevention from Rhetoric to Reality: Organizations and Institutions.* Lanham, MD: Lexington Books, 2004.

Schofield, J. W. "Promoting Positive Intergroup Relations in School Settings." In *Toward a Common Destiny: Improving Race and Ethnic Relations in America.* Edited by W. D. Hawley and A. W. Jackson, 257–289. San Francisco: Jossey-Bass, 1995.

Sen, Amartya. "Democracy as a Universal Value." In *The Global Divergence of Democracies.* Edited by Larry Diamond and Marc F. Plattner, 3–18. Baltimore, MD: Johns Hopkins University Press, 2001.

———. *Development as Freedom.* New York: Knopf, 1999.

———. *Identity and Violence: The Illusion of Destiny.* New York: Norton, 2006.

Sherif, Muzafer, and Carolyn Sherif. *Groups in Harmony and Tension: An Integration of Studies on Intergroup Relations.* New York: Octagon, 1966.

Shultz, George P., William J. Perry, Henry A. Kissinger, and Sam Nunn. "A World Free of Nuclear Weapons." *Wall Street Journal,* January 4, 2007, A15.

Siegle, Joseph T., Michael M. Weinstein, and Morton H. Halperin. "Why Democracies Excel." *Foreign Affairs* 83, no. 5 (September/October 2004): 57–71.

Sisk, Timothy D. *Power Sharing and International Mediation in Ethnic Conflicts.* Washington, DC: United States Institute of Peace Press, 1996.

Slaughter, Anne-Marie. *The Idea That Is America: Keeping Faith with Our Values in a Dangerous World.* New York: Basic Books, 2007.

Slaughter, Anne-Marie. *A New World Order.* Princeton, NJ: Princeton University Press, 2004.

Smith, Peter K., and Sonia Smart, eds. *School Bullying: Insights and Perspectives.* London: Routledge, 1994.

Smuts, B. B., D. L. Cheney, R. M. Seyfarth, R. W. Wrangham, and T. T. Struhsaker, eds. *Primate Societies.* Chicago: University of Chicago Press, 1986.

Solana, Javier. "The Health Dimension to Security." In *Anna Lindh Programme on Conflict Prevention, 2006 Edition.* Edited by Anders Mellbourne, 9–14. Hedemora Sweden: Gidlunds förlag, 2006.

Soros, George. *The Age of Fallibility.* New York: Public Affairs, 2006.

Stanford University (including the Center for Democracy, Development and Rule of Law and the Freeman Spogli Institute for International Studies). http://www.stanford.edu.

Stannard, David. *American Holocaust: The Conquest of the New World.* New York: Oxford University Press, 1992.

Starr, Paul. *Freedom's Power: The True Force of Liberalism.* New York: Basic Books, 2007.

Staub, Ervin. "The Origins of Genocide: Rwanda" and "Bystanders as Evil: The Example of Rwanda." In *The Psychology of Good and Evil: Why Children, Adults, and Groups Help and Harm Others,* 341–346 and 346–350. Cambridge: Cambridge University Press, 2003.

———. *The Roots of Evil: The Origins of Violence and Other Group Violence.* New York: Cambridge University Press, 1989.

Staub, Ervin, Laurie Anne Pearlman, Alexandra Gubin, and Athanase Hagengimana. "Healing, Reconciliation, Forgiving and the Prevention of Violence After Genocide or Mass Killing: An Intervention and Its Experimental Evaluation in Rwanda." *Journal of Social and Clinical Psychology* 24, no. 3 (2005): 299ff.

Stern, Fritz. *Dreams and Delusions: National Socialism in the Drama of the German Past.* New York: Vintage, 1987.

Stiglitz, Joseph. *Globalization and Its Discontents.* New York: W. W. Norton, 2002.

———. *Making Globalization Work.* New York: W. W. Norton, 2006.

Stiglitz, Joseph, and Andrew Charlton. *Fair Trade for All: How Trade Can Promote Development.* Initiative for Policy Dialogue Series C. New York: Oxford University Press, 2006.

Stiglitz, Joseph E., and Lyn Squire. "International Development: Is It possible?" *Foreign Policy,* Spring 1998, 138–151.

Stockholm International Forum, *Conference Four, Preventing Genocide: Threats and Responsibilities.* Stockholm, Sweden, January 26–January 28, 2004, sponsored by the Swedish government. Available at http://www.manskligarattigheter.gov.se/stockholmforum/2004/conference_2004 .html.

Straus, Scott. *The Order of Genocide: Race, Power, and War in Rwanda.* Ithaca, NY: Cornell University Press, 2006.

Stremlau, John. *People in Peril: Human Rights, Humanitarian Action, and Preventing Deadly Conflict.* New York: Carnegie Commission on Preventing Deadly Conflict, 1998.

Stremlau, John, and Helen Zille. *A House No Longer Divided: Progress and Prospects for Democratic Peace in South Africa.* New York: Carnegie Commission on Preventing Deadly Conflict, 1997.

Suny, Ronald Grigor. *Looking Toward Ararat: Armenia in Modern History.* Bloomington: Indiana University Press, 1983.

Tessler, Mark. "Islam and Democracy in the Middle East: The Impact of Religious Orientations on Attitudes toward Democracy in Four Arab Countries." *Comparative Politics* 34 (April 2002): 337–254.

Tilly, Charles. *Democracy.* New York: Cambridge University Press, 2007.

Totten, Samuel, William S. Parsons, and Israel W. Charny, eds. *Century of Genocide. Critical Essays and Eyewitness Accounts.* 2nd ed. New York: Routledge, 2004.

Tutu, Desmond. "Leadership." In *Essays on Leadership,* 39-65. New York: Carnegie Commission on Preventing Deadly Conflict, 1998.

———. *The Rainbow People of God: The Making of a Peaceful Revolution.* Edited by John Allen. New York: Doubleday, 1994.

UN Development Programme. *Human Development Report 2005, International Cooperation at a Crossroads: Aid, Trade and Security in an Unequal World.* Washington, DC: UNDP, 2005.

United Nations. *A More Secure World: Our Shared Responsibility.* Report of the Secretary-General's High-Level Panel on Threats, Challenges, and Change. New York: United Nations, 2004.

———. "Report of the Independent Inquiry into the Actions of the United Nations During the 1994 Genocide in Rwanda." UN Doc. S/1999/1257, December 1999.

———. *The Responsibility to Protect.* Report of the International Commission on Intervention and State Sovereignty. New York: United Nations, 2001.

———. http://www.un.org.

United Nations Department of Political Affairs. http://www.un.org/Depts/dpa.

United Nations Development Programme, Bureau for Crisis Prevention and Recovery (also contains Mediation Support Unit). http://www.undp.org/cpr.

UN Security Council. *Report of the Secretary-General on Enhancing Mediation and Its Support Activities (S/2009/189).* April 8, 2009, S/2009/189, available at www.unhcr.org/refworld/ docid/49e6f2880.html (accessed July 2, 2009).

United States Institute of Peace. http://www.usip.org.

Urquhart, Brian. "The Outlaw World." *New York Review of Books* (May 11, 2006): 25–28.

Ury, William L. *Getting Disputes Resolved: Developing Systems to Cut the Costs of Conflict.* San Francisco: Jossey-Bass, 1988.

———. *Getting to Peace.* New York: Penguin, 1999.

Ury, William L., and Richard Smoke. *Beyond the Hotline: Controlling a Nuclear Crisis, a Report to the United States Arms Control and Disarmament Agency.* Cambridge, MA: Harvard Law School Nuclear Negotiation Project, 1984.

Valenzuela, Arturo. *The Collective Defense of Democracy: Lessons from the Paraguayan Crisis of 1996.* New York: Carnegie Commission on Preventing Deadly Conflict, 1999.

Vance, Cyrus R., and David A. Hamburg. *Pathfinders for Peace: A Report to the UN Secretary-General on the Role of Special Representatives and Personal Envoys.* New York: Carnegie Commission on Preventing Deadly Conflict, 1997.

van der Stoel, Max. "Democracy and Human Rights. On the Work of the High Commissioner on National Minorities of the OSCE," "Early Warning and Early Action: Preventing Inter-Ethnic Conflict," and "The Involvement of the High Commissioner Is No Stigma, but an Act of Solidarity." In *Peace and Stability Through Human and Minority Rights.* Edited by Wolfgang Zellner and Falk Lange, 132–138, 162–170, 144–147. Baden-Baden, Germany: Nomos Verlag, 1999.

Van Slyck, M., M. Stern, and J. Zak-Place. "Promoting Optimal Adolescent Development Through Conflict Resolution Education, Training, and Practice: An Innovative Approach for Counseling Psychologists." *Counseling Psychologist* 24 (1996): 433–461.

Waldmeier, Patti. *Anatomy of a Miracle: The End of Apartheid and the Birth of the New South Africa.* New York: W. W. Norton, 1997.

Wallensteen, Peter. *Conflict Resolution: War, Peace, and the Global System.* Thousand Oaks, CA: Sage Publications, 2002.

Waller, James. *Becoming Evil: How Ordinary People Commit Genocide and Mass Killing.* New York: Oxford University Press, 2002.

Wallimann, Isidor, and Michael Dobkowski, eds. *Genocide and the Modern Age: Etiology and Case Studies of Mass Death.* Syracuse, NY: Syracuse University Press, 2001.

Weapons of Mass Destruction Commission Final Report. "Weapons of Terror: Freeing the World of Nuclear, Biological, and Chemical Arms." Stockholm, 2006. Available at www.wmdcommission.org.

Weiss-Wik, Stephen. "Enhancing Negotiator's Successfulness: Self-Help Books and Related Empirical Research." *Journal of Conflict Resolution* 27 (December 1983): 706–735.

Weitz, Eric D. *A Century of Genocide: Utopias of Race and Nation.* Princeton, NJ: Princeton University Press, 2003.

WHO Commission on Macroeconomics and Health. *Macroeconomics and Health: Economic Development.* Report of the Commission on Macroeconomics and Health, Jeffrey D. Sachs, chair. Geneva, Switzerland: World Health Organization, 2001. Available at http://www.cid.harvard.edu/archive/cmh/cmhreport.pdf.

Wiesel, Elie. *Night.* Translated by Marion Wiesel. New York: Hill and Wang, 2006.

Williams, Shirley. "Human Rights in Europe." In *Realizing Human Rights: Moving from Inspiration to Impact.* Edited by Samantha Power and Graham Allison, 77–110. New York: St. Martin's Press, 2000.

Wilson, Michael L., and Richard W. Wrangham. "Intergroup Relations in Chimpanzees." *Annual Review of Anthropology* 32 (October 2003): 363–392.

Wistrich, Robert S. *Hitler and the Holocaust.* New York: Modern Library, 2001.

Wolter, Detlev. *A United Nations for the 21st Century: From Reaction to Prevention.* Baden-Baden, Germany: Nomos-Verlag, 2007.

World Bank. *Development and the Next Generation.* Washington, DC: World Bank, 2006.

———. *Sustainable Development in a Dynamic World: Transforming Institutions, Growth, and Quality of Life.* Washington, DC: World Bank/Oxford University Press, 2003.

Wrangham, Richard. "Killer Species." *Daedalus* 133, no. 4 (Fall 2004): 25–35.

———. "Why Apes and Humans Kill." In *Conflict: The 2005 Darwin College Lecture Series.* Edited by Martin Jones and Andy Fabian, 43–62. Cambridge: Cambridge University Press, 2006.

Wrangham, Richard, and Dale Peterson. *Demonic Males: Apes and the Origin of Human Violence.* Boston: Houghton Mifflin, 1996.

Wrangham, Richard W., and Michael L. Wilson. "Collective Violence: Comparisons Between Youths and Chimpanzees." In John Devine, James Gilligan, Klaus A. Miczeck et al., eds., *Annals of the New York Academy of Science* 1036 (March 2005): 233–256.

Yahil, Leni. *The Holocaust: The Fate of European Jewry, 1932–1945.* Translated by Ina Friedman and Haya Galai. New York: Oxford University Press, 1990.

Yakovlev, Alexander N. *A Century of Violence in Soviet Russia.* New Haven, CT: Yale University Press, 2002.

Zartman, I. William. *Cowardly Lions: Missed Opportunities to Prevent Deadly Conflict and State Collapse.* Boulder, CO: Lynne Rienner Publishers, 2005.

———. "The Strategy of Preventive Diplomacy in Third World Conflicts." In *Managing U.S.-Soviet Rivalry: Problems of Crisis Prevention.* Edited by Alexander L. George, 341–363. Boulder, CO: Westview Press, 1983.

Zartman, I. William, ed. *Preventive Negotiation: Avoiding Conflict Escalation.* Carnegie Commission on Preventing Deadly Conflict Series. Lanham, MD: Rowman and Littlefield, 2000.

Index

Abbas, Mahmoud, 187
Abdullah, King, 199
Accountability, 290; police, 310
Ackerman, Peter, 133
Advisory Committee on the Prevention of
    Genocide, 304
African Leaders Forum, 289
African National Congress (ANC), 72, 74, 78, 79,
    81–84, 87
African Union (AU), 3–4, 17, 99, 114, 234, 243,
    254, 269, 281, 284, 285, 289, 292, 296, 297,
    304, 305; crisis management and, 241, 242;
    in Darfur, 261; human rights issues and,
    307; military response and, 302; preventive
    diplomacy and, 112
Agreement on the Principles of Partnership of
    the Coalition Government, 292
Ahmadinejad, Mahmoud, 200
Akçam, Taner, 36
Al-Bashir, Omar Hassan, 3, 34
Alberts, Bruce, 155, 156
Alberts, Louw, 84
Albright, Madeleine, 303
Alderdice, John, 309
Alinsky, Saul, 133
Allison, Graham, 8, 110, 124, 193, 196, 197, 213,
    312; filmed interview of, 318
Allport, Gordon W., 164
Al-Qaeda, 174, 196, 198
American Academy of Diplomacy, 303
Ängeby, Ragnar, 137, 243, 297
Annan, Kofi, 69, 155, 219, 221, 224, 226, 239, 294,
    305, 317; anti-Semitism and, 11; Carnegie
    Commission and, 266–267; cooperation and,
    13; Darfur and, 4; on democracy, 147; filmed
    interview of, 318; genocide prevention and,
    5, 9, 147, 216, 276, 283; High-Level Panel and,
    297; IAC and, 155, 156; leadership of, 114,
    212; negotiations and, 283, 290–291, 293;
    peace and, 165–166; preventive diplomacy

by, 288–293; security policy and, 207; special
    advisers to, 223
Anti-Semitism, 33, 35, 43, 44, 49, 247; lessons of,
    11–12
Apartheid, 73, 74, 77–78, 79, 82, 83; end of, 87,
    89, 93, 94, 266; impact of, 90
Appiah, Kwame Anthony, 309
Armenians, genocide of, 12, 20, 32, 36, 37, 39, 41
Ash, Timothy Garton, 232, 233
Atrocities Prevention Committee, 301
AU. See African Union
Australian-Japanese Commission on
    Disarmament, 316

Baldwin, Stanley, 54
Ban Ki-moon, 4, 5, 204, 224, 283, 295
Bartoli, Andrea: filmed interview of, 318
Barton, John H., 108
Bauer, Yehuda, 35, 44
BCPR. See Bureau for Crisis Prevention and
    Recovery
Benesch, Susan, 32, 33
Beria, Lavrenty, 27
Beyers Naude, C. F., 76
Biko, Steve, 75, 76, 93
Bin Laden, Osama, 174, 219
Bizimungu, Pasteur, 66
Bjurner, Anders, 243
Blix, Hans, 192–193
Bonaparte, Napoléon, 71
Booh-Booh, Jacques-Roger, 65
Boraine, Alex, 91
Bosnia, 32, 184, 186, 219, 227, 240, 258; genocide
    and, 10, 30; NATO and, 259
Botha, P. W., 81
Boutros-Ghali, Boutros, 68, 86, 123, 207
Brahimi, Lakhtar, 86, 207, 208, 219
Brixton riots, 310
Brundtland, Gro, 143, 297
Bryce, James, 38

About the Author

David A. Hamburg, M.D., is DeWitt Wallace Distinguished Scholar at Weill Cornell Medical College. He is President Emeritus of the Carnegie Corporation of New York, where he served as President from 1982 to 1997. Hamburg has a long history of leadership in the research, medical, and psychiatric fields. He has been Professor at Stanford University and Harvard University as well as President of the Institute of Medicine, National Academy of Sciences and President of the American Association for the Advancement of Science.

He was a member of the U.S. Defense Policy Board with Secretary of Defense William Perry and Cochair with former Secretary of State Cyrus Vance of the Carnegie Commission on Preventing Deadly Conflict. The commission published many books and monographs in its five-year life (1994–1999), covering diplomatic, political, economic, and military aspects of prevention. Distinguished scholars and practitioners contributed on a worldwide basis.

He was a member of President Clinton's Committee of Advisors on Science and Technology and the founder of the Carnegie Commission on Science, Technology, and Government. Dr. Hamburg is currently chairing two distinguished parallel committees at the United Nations and European Union on the prevention of genocide—one reporting directly to the UN Secretary-General, first Kofi Annan and now Ban Ki-moon—and the other to Javier Solana, Secretary-General of the Council of the European Union.

Dr. Hamburg also serves on the Advisory Board of the Center for Preventive Action of the Council on Foreign Relations, the Advisory Council of Stanford's Freeman Spogli Institute of International Studies, and the Harvard International Advisory Council. He is Distinguished Presidential Adviser on International Affairs, National Academy of Sciences. He is the author of *Today's Children* (1992); *No More Killing Fields* (2002); and *Learning to Live Together* (2004).

Dr. Hamburg received the Foreign Policy Association's Medal; the 25th Anniversary Medal of the International Peace Academy; the Sarnat International Mental Health Award of the Institute of Medicine, National Academy of Sciences; the National Academy of Sciences Public Welfare Medal (its highest award); and the Presidential Medal of Freedom (the highest civilian award of the United States).